CONCEPTUAL AND HISTORICAL ISSUES IN PSYCHOLOGY

This unique textbook offers an inspirational and engaging guide to psychology's past and present, told through fascinating stories about the discipline's charismatic personalities and the controversies they generated. Geoff Bunn introduces students to an array of conceptual and analytical tools for critical thinking and demonstrates how to apply these tools to understand a variety of historical controversies, psychological theories, and individual personalities.

Each chapter focuses on a core area of psychological study and integrates both conceptual and historical issues in a 'guide on the side' approach, encouraging students to form their own opinions of what they have read. The book takes an inclusive approach, integrating equality, diversity, human rights, and intersectionality issues throughout, and introduces students to often overlooked figures and areas of study.

The text is supported by an extensive tutor guide featuring lesson plans, resources, key sources, recommended readings, and tried-and-tested classroom exercises that utilise tools for critical thinking. This is the ideal undergraduate textbook for conceptual and historical issues in psychology, whether taught as a stand-alone course or integrated into other psychology modules.

Geoff Bunn is Reader in Psychology at Manchester Metropolitan University, UK, and an internationally-recognised researcher in the history of psychology and education.

BPS Core Textbooks Series

Series editor: Simon Goodson

Routledge in partnership with British Psychological Society are pleased to present their flagship textbook program, the BPS Core Textbooks Series. Aimed at a global undergraduate readership, these volumes are designed to be core texts for course adoption, covering all key subject areas in Psychology.

Diversity, equity and inclusion is at the heart of the series. Each book includes a strong focus on all aspects of diversity, including decolonising the curriculum and an understanding of the value of multiple perspectives. There is also a spotlight on employability, to explain why a grounding in basic theoretical areas is necessary for careers in Psychology. There is also a focus on real-world applications and life skills, to help students explore the use of psychological theory to answer real-world questions. These full colour books include a range of pedagogical features, illustrations and figures, with content to emphasise critical thinking and study skills and the unpicking of pseudoscience.

Books are available in traditional print format, as well as our innovative enhanced eBook format. This includes integrative features such as pop-up keyword definitions, hypertext links to web-based resources, short-answer/open-ended questions, multiple-choice and true/false quizzes and video clips. There is a series website hosting additional digital resources for both students and instructors to tie in with learning objectives.

The books in the BPS Core Textbooks Series are essential reading in the core areas in any Psychology honours degree or conversion-level course. They are also relevant as secondary reading in related disciplines.

Titles in the series:

Cognitive Psychology in a Changing World
Linden Ball, Laurie Butler, Sue Sherman, Helen St Clair-Thompson

An Introduction to Cyberpsychology, 2nd edition
Edited by Gráinne Kirwan, Irene Connolly, Hannah Barton, Marion Palmer

For more information about this series, please visit: www.routledge.com/our-products/book-series/BPSCT

CONCEPTUAL AND HISTORICAL ISSUES IN PSYCHOLOGY

An Inclusive, Innovative, and Critical Approach

GEOFF BUNN

Routledge
Taylor & Francis Group
LONDON AND NEW YORK

Designed cover image: Getty © andresr

First published 2026
by Routledge
4 Park Square, Milton Park, Abingdon, Oxon OX14 4RN

and by Routledge
605 Third Avenue, New York, NY 10158

Routledge is an imprint of the Taylor & Francis Group, an informa business

British Library Cataloguing-in-Publication Data
A catalogue record for this book is available from the British Library

ISBN: 978-1-032-93346-7 (hbk)
ISBN: 978-1-032-93345-0 (pbk)
ISBN: 978-1-003-56548-2 (ebk)

DOI: 10.4324/9781003565482

Typeset in Stone Serif
by Apex CoVantage, LLC

Access the Instructor and Student Resources: routledgelearning.com/bpscoretextbooks

Contents

Preface

Psychology has some of the best stories in all of science. That is why every chapter in this textbook begins with one. Many of these stories are intriguing. Some are mysterious or enigmatic. A few are admittedly disturbing. But all of them are inspiring, one way or another. Each one offers a glimpse into how psychology has been shaped, not only by new ideas and innovative studies but by conflicts, hidden agendas, social movements, political pressures, and the messiness of human life. The 36 stories collected here reveal how psychology has operated in the past, how it works today, and how it might be imagined differently in the future.

The aim of this book is to inspire you to engage with the fascinating, sometimes surprising, but always vibrant field of *Conceptual and Historical Issues in Psychology*, or CHIP. Whatever area of psychology you are drawn to—understanding minds, measuring behaviour, exploring identity, or improving lives—CHIP matters. It is the one area of psychology that connects to all the other areas, because it asks questions that are relevant to every area of psychology: what is psychology? Where did it come from? What impact has it had?

To help you answer these questions, every chapter pairs a compelling historical case study with a critical thinking tool, a practical way of examining the assumptions, concepts, techniques, and power relations embedded in psychological theory and practice. The critical thinking tools are crucial because doing psychology is always an act of choice: choosing how to describe people, deciding what counts as knowledge, and determining how that knowledge is applied. Understanding psychology's history means understanding those choices, past and present, and being equipped to make better ones in the future.

At the end of every chapter you'll find a short list of suggested reading, curated signposts to help you explore further. And if this work excites you, you will be glad to know that CHIP has a vibrant, welcoming community: an international network of researchers, students, books, journals, and conferences dedicated to asking these questions and keeping these conversations alive. You are warmly invited to become part of it. This book offers simple but powerful encouragement: absorb the history, grasp the critical tools, and then ask yourself the most important question of all–what kind of psychology do you want to help create?

Acknowledgements

The completion of this book owes an immense debt to the scholarly community engaged in *Conceptual and Historical Issues in Psychology*. I am profoundly grateful to my colleagues and fellow researchers and educators whose friendship, rigorous scholarship, thoughtful critiques, and enduring commitment to this field have shaped and inspired my own contribution.

I would like to extend my sincere thanks to my family for their extraordinary patience and understanding throughout the writing of this book. I am indebted to Ann King for her meticulous attention to detail in copy-editing the text. My thanks are also owed to Dr Carly Jacobs for her careful and perceptive reading of the text's first draft. I am grateful to Alexandra Doyle, my research assistant, whose diligence, intellectual engagement, and organisational skills were indispensable at a crucial stage of the project. Alexandra first encountered CHIP as a student in my classroom. It has been rewarding to see her develop into a valued colleague and collaborator.

To the many students with whom I have had the privilege of exploring CHIP over the years, I wish to express my deep appreciation. Their curiosity, critical questions, and thoughtful reflections have continually enriched my understanding of this field. Indeed, many of their insights are reflected in the pages of this book. To them, I extend my heartfelt thanks.

Any remaining errors, omissions, or misjudgements are, of course, entirely my own responsibility. I genuinely welcome feedback from readers, whether corrections, further insights, or topic recommendations for future editions of this book. Most of all, I would love to hear how readers have been inspired by their engagement with conceptual and historical issues in psychology, just as I was as an undergraduate student encountering CHIP for the first time.

Geoff Bunn
Manchester Metropolitan University
July 2025

Introduction

For many years, a curious and revealing cartoon hung in the entrance hall of the Department of Psychology at University College London. Sketched in the 1930s by the Department's Technical Assistant, Mr Raper, the pencil drawing depicts three men standing around what appears to be an ordinary jam jar. The men would have been familiar to anyone who worked in the department: Mr Raper himself, holding a fishing rod and pointing to the sky; Dr S. J. F. Philpott, sporting an enormous head of hair and wearing a trim pair of shorts; and Professor Charles Spearman, the statistician and psychologist most famous for formulating the concept of general intelligence, *'g'*, his bulging eyes peering into the jar through a magnifying glass. Scribbled across the top of the cartoon is the caption: 'G Hunting'.

A gentle and affectionate joke, the cartoon is a profound commentary on the nature of psychological knowledge. 'G Hunting' was portrayed as an act of fishing in an invisible pond for an invisible fish. Spearman's *'g'*, the supposed general factor underlying all forms of intelligence, was never something that could be physically captured, observed, or caught on a hook. Despite decades of psychometric testing and mathematical labour, general intelligence, *'g'*, remained a psychological construct, a statistical abstraction inferred from patterns in test score data rather than a tangible object in the world.

'G Hunting' quietly communicates this crucial concession. Intelligence is not an entity like a fish plucked from a pond or an object preserved in a jar. It does not exist independently in the natural world, waiting to be discovered. Rather, it is a conceptual artefact assembled from the numerical patterns that emerge when lots of people are subjected to certain forms of psychometric testing. The elusiveness of intelligence, its invisibility, its reliance on statistical analysis, expresses something fundamental about psychology itself. Unlike disciplines such as chemistry, physics, or biology, where the basic units of reality, such as forces, chemicals, and cells, exist regardless of whether we observe them or not, psychology deals with categories that only exist because humans have created them, named them, and acted upon them. Biologists have neurons, we have 'neurosis'. Astronomers have the moon, we have (or did have) 'lunacy'. A broken bone and a broken heart are two very different sorts of things.

Psychology's categories are much more like broken hearts than they are like broken bones. Once they have materialised from language and history, psychological categories become powerful and consequential. They make sense of and shape our daily lives, our institutions, our politics, and our hopes and fears. They become real in their effects, even though their reality is different from that of mountains, molecules, or magnetic fields. This distinction sits at the very heart of psychology as a discipline and forms the foundation for the approach taken in *Conceptual and Historical Issues in Psychology: An Inclusive, Integrated and Critical Approach* (CHIP).

A Critical Approach

Psychology is a social science. CHIP takes that fact seriously. Unlike the situation in the natural sciences, psychology has no periodic table of psychological elements, no universal laws, and no standard units of measurement; no Newtons, Joules, or Volts immortalising its pioneers. Whereas the natural sciences discover features of the external world that exist independently of human foibles, psychological knowledge is fundamentally shaped by its historical, social, and political contexts. Adopting a critical approach means recognising this. Psychological knowledge has never arisen in an historical vacuum. Psychology developed in response to practical problems posed by the discipline's many clients: schools, the military, factories, governments, colonial administrations, and corporations.

This book traces how psychology, in its ambition to be both scientific and useful, generated a variety of methods, an explosion of theoretical models, diverse modes of power, and an elaborate taxonomy of person-types, labelling some as different, disordered, deficient, or deviant. A critical approach to this history moves beyond asking whether a psychological theory is simply true or false. It asks instead how psychological knowledge has been constructed, whose interests it has served, and in what ways it has been deployed in society.

These complexities become clear when we consider intelligence, one of psychology's most influential and contested concepts and the entity that inspired 'G Hunting'. The history of intelligence shows how it emerged not from scientific curiosity alone but from the social demands of expanding education systems that needed to sort and manage diverse populations of children. Psychology responded by constructing new personological categories, such as the gifted, the backward, the feebleminded, asserting that intelligence was a stable, measurable trait inherent to the individual. Its primary methodological tool, the IQ test, reduced complex cognitive processes to a number. The resultant knowledge helped place children into educational streams, often determining life chances under the guise of scientific fairness. Whether framed as supportive guidance or rigid classification, intelligence testing actively produced hierarchies of personhood that determined access to education, opportunity, and social mobility.

This is why a CHIP book cannot simply recount psychology's history as a timeline of discoveries. It must examine how psychology's past continues to shape its present categories, practices, and assumptions, and how the discipline might be practised differently in the future. University College London's famous 'G Hunting' cartoon was more than a departmental in-joke; it offers an insight into psychology's deeper history. With ironic humour, it portrays a discipline repeatedly attempting to trap the invisible, to capture an intangible construct while risking the classic error of mistaking the jar for the fish; confusing the tools of measurement with the reality they claim to capture.

Three Questions

Curious children often ask three simple but profound questions: 'What is it?' 'How do you know?' and 'Why should I?' These are not just the questions of youthful inquisitiveness; they are the foundational questions at the heart of both philosophy and psychology. Each corresponds to a major domain of philosophical inquiry. 'What is it?' is the question of *ontology*, the study of what exists, what kinds of things are real, and how we categorise and define the world. 'How do you know?' is the question of *epistemology*, the study of how knowledge is generated, what counts as evidence, and how claims about the world are justified. 'Why should I?' is the question of *power*, an ethical and political question that concerns what is at stake, who benefits from knowledge, and how that knowledge is used to shape behaviour, manage populations, and justify interventions.

These three questions are inescapable in all areas of psychology. Whether psychology is practised in a classroom, a courtroom, a clinic, or a research laboratory, or whether it claims to be a pure science divorced from application, every psychological theory, experiment, diagnostic tool, and therapeutic intervention rests on implicit assumptions about what a person is, how that can be known, and what should be done with that knowledge. Psychology's three fundamental questions are the foundational concerns of this book, making an appearance in every chapter.

Questions concerning epistemology, ontology, and power form a structure akin to the three connected hoops of a Borromean knot, in which no single ring holds the structure together, but all three are interlocked so tightly that if one is severed, the entire structure collapses. In all psychology, pure or applied, ontology, epistemology, and power are distinct yet inseparable issues. This is why a critical approach is necessary. It is not enough to ask whether psychological knowledge is true or not. We must also examine how psychology's ways of knowing, its definitions of personhood, and its exercises of authority are fundamentally entangled, and how, together, they shape the real lives of those who are subject to its gaze.

1 How Do You Know?

The Issue of Epistemology

For many students, psychology can initially feel fragmented, an overwhelming patchwork of subfields that seem, at first glance, to have little in common. Social psychology studies groups, identity, and attitudes. Cognitive psychology investigates memory, perception, and attention. Clinical psychology focuses on mental health, diagnosis, and therapy. Biological psychology studies the brain and nervous system. Developmental psychology traces how individuals change across the lifespan. Each of these subfields seems to speak its own language, use its own models, and operate with its own assumptions, research designs, and evidence standards.

What can seem like fragmentation, however, is actually a form of diversity, a strength rather than a weakness. This diversity is a direct consequence of psychology's history as a discipline that developed in response to the varied needs of its clients and the many social projects it served. Psychology exerted an enormous influence on the modern world not simply because it pursued abstract scientific knowledge but because it was useful.

A range of clients presented psychology with an array of problems. Factory owners sought to optimise productivity, minimise fatigue, and select the most suitable workers: psychologists responded with time-and-motion studies, fatigue measurements, and performance metrics. Military strategists needed to select officers, assess morale, and predict resilience under stress: psychologists developed group intelligence tests, leadership inventories, and psychological screening procedures. Educational policymakers required ways to sort students, diagnose learning difficulties, and manage classroom diversity: psychologists devised IQ tests, reading assessments, and behavioural diagnostics. Medical authorities asked for techniques for diagnosing mental disorders and planning treatment regimes. Colonial administrators turned to psychology for ways of understanding, managing, and controlling Indigenous populations.

Each client posed a different version of the same epistemological challenge: how can we know people well enough to predict, classify, influence, rehabilitate, or manage them? As a result, psychology developed not one method but many. It became a discipline boasting an extraordinarily flexible and expansive methodological toolkit: laboratory experiments, field studies, longitudinal research, surveys, interviews, observational techniques, projective tests, focus groups, time-and-motion studies, computational modelling, and brain imaging, among many others.

Every methodological innovation reflected the requirements of a particular client, problem, or social context. A factory cannot use the same methods as a clinic; a courtroom cannot rely on the same tools as a school; a military recruitment office demands different forms of knowledge to those used in a nursery. Each institution requires a specific form of psychological knowledge that is actionable, reliable, and appropriate to its goals.

This book treats these epistemological questions as central. CHIP examines how psychologists, across different times and places, have devised methods to answer the question of how we can know what kind of person someone is, what they can become, and what should be done about it. Without understanding the epistemological foundations of psychology, it is impossible to understand the discipline's ontological claims.

2 What Is It?

The Issue of Ontology

Psychology is not only a science of methods; it is also a science of categories, entities, theories, models, and concepts. It is a discipline devoted to inventing, defining, and refining ideas about what kinds of people there are, what kinds of minds there are, and what counts as *psychology*. Over its history, psychology has generated a staggering variety of person-types, mental constructs, diagnostic labels, developmental stages, syndromes, typologies, and personality traits. These categories did not emerge naturally, nor were they discovered in the laboratory. They were constructed in response to the demands of psychology's clients; those organisations and institutions that each had their own missions, problems, and populations to manage.

Advertising and consumer research needed to understand motivation: psychology responded with categories such as the persuadable consumer, the impulse buyer, the status-seeker, and the brand loyalist. Clinics needed ways to diagnose suffering: psychology offered categories such as the hysteric, the neurotic, the schizophrenic, the depressed, the maladjusted, and the Borderline Personality. The military embraced categories such as the resilient soldier, the charismatic leader, and the psychologically unfit. Schools adopted psychological categories such as the gifted student, the remedial learner, and the hyperactive child.

Psychology has to be ontologically generous. The demands of modern societies, particularly the needs of institutions to sort, select, train, diagnose, rehabilitate, or manage populations, required psychology to produce an ever-expanding repertoire of person-types and mental constructs. Psychological categories shape how people are perceived by others, how they are treated by institutions, what opportunities are available to them, and how they come to understand themselves. To be classified as gifted, subnormal, depressed, maladjusted, neurodivergent, or antisocial is to be positioned within a powerful social ontology that structures everyday life.

This is why a CHIP book cannot restrict itself to a history of methods or pioneers. It must also examine ontology, the question of what kinds of entities psychology creates, defines, and acts upon. It must ask explicitly: what is it that psychology claims to study? Moreover, by examining the discipline's ontological generosity, we can understand how it exercises power.

3 Why Should I?

The Issue of Power

Psychology has never been simply a neutral or detached observer of human nature. From its earliest emergence as a scientific enterprise in the late nineteenth century, it has been deeply intertwined with power. Psychological expertise has consistently been mobilised by powerful institutions seeking to solve practical problems, whether in education, health, criminal justice, colonial administration, military recruitment, workplace management, or consumer behaviour. This does not mean that psychology is necessarily oppressive or inherently manipulative; rather, it means that psychological knowledge has always operated within larger networks of authority, serving to guide, manage, sort, rehabilitate, persuade, optimise, and liberate people.

Throughout its history, psychology adapted itself to the needs of the customer, shifting its modes of power accordingly. In factories, it aligned itself with *disciplinary power*, measuring and correcting worker behaviour to maximise productivity. In clinics and counselling settings, it adopted *pastoral power*, offering therapeutic guidance, support, and adjustment. Through public health campaigns and workplace wellness initiatives, psychology engaged in *biopower*, encouraging populations to self-regulate their mental health, productivity, and resilience in line with societal norms. When embedded in HR departments, consultancy firms, or educational testing bodies, psychology operated as *technocratic power*, using data and diagnostics to sort, manage, and optimise human resources. More recently, it has embraced the language of *empowerment*, offering tools for self-actualisation, growth, and resilience, particularly within coaching, positive psychology, and the well-being industry.

Whether the goal was to sort, train, heal, control, motivate, or rehabilitate, psychology aligned itself with the ambitions of those who were paying for its services. This cheerful adaptability has been central to psychology's social success, but it has also raised unavoidable ethical and political questions about the discipline's complicity in systems of control, governance, and inequality. Psychological knowledge is never just about what is *true*; it is always also about what is done with that truth, how it is used, whose interests it serves, and whose lives it shapes.

Psychology's entanglement with power has at times been creative, productive, and even liberatory. But it has also been damaging, exclusionary, and oppressive, especially when its categories have been grounded in racist assumptions, gender bias, class prejudice, ableism, or outdated conceptions of what counts as normal. This is why CHIP must confront directly the ethical and political dimensions of psychology's practices. Without addressing the power question, there is no meaningful way to understand what psychology is, who it includes, and who it excludes.

An Inclusive Approach

Psychology is a science of boundaries; boundaries between what is considered normal and abnormal, sane and insane, capable and deficient, acceptable and deviant. These boundaries have never been purely technical or scientific. They have always reflected the values, anxieties, and priorities of the institutions and clients that psychology served. In aligning itself with the needs of schools, clinics, prisons, factories, militaries, colonial governments, and corporations, psychology became not only an instrument of knowledge but also an agent of exclusion, defining who belonged and who did not, who was considered normal and who was rendered other.

The process of exclusion has taken many forms. Psychology reinforced racial hierarchies by classifying racialised groups as cognitively inferior, emotionally immature, or temperamentally deficient, offering scientific validation for colonialism and racism. It pathologised women, framing femininity as a form of deviance from a male norm, characterising women as unstable hysterics, intellectually limited, and too emotional to exercise rational thought or provide leadership. It categorised disabled people as feebleminded, deficient, or abnormal, contributing to their institutionalisation, exclusion, and eugenic targeting. It treated sexual and gender minorities as mentally ill, diagnosing homosexuality as a disorder and framing transgender identities as pathological deviations from normative gender binaries. Working-class people were frequently defined through the lens of moral weakness, lack of intelligence, bad habits, and poor parenting, with poverty framed as a personal failing rather than a structural condition. Psychology directly supported colonial projects by portraying Indigenous peoples as mentally undeveloped, emotionally volatile, and in need of governance by supposedly the more civilised.

This pattern of othering was not a mistake or an accidental by-product of bad science. It was structural, incorporated into psychology's service relationship with institutions that were themselves hierarchical, patriarchal, colonial, and capitalist. To be useful, psychology had to help define which kinds of people were manageable, salvageable, or employable, and which were dangerous, deviant, or irredeemably defective.

It is essential to recognise whose voices were excluded, whose experiences were pathologised, erased, or distorted, and how those absences fundamentally shaped psychology's knowledge, theories, and power structures. This is why this book takes an inclusive approach. It does not present psychology as a linear narrative of discoveries made by great men but as a contested history, one shaped as much by what was left out as by what was included. It is committed to retrieving lost voices, hearing the perspectives of those historically classified as deficient, deviant, or dangerous, and understanding how their exclusion structured the very foundations of psychological knowledge. CHIP's mission is to engage in an act of retrieval, seeking historical justice for the silenced and marginalised. Psychology cannot be fully understood, nor meaningfully reimagined, without reckoning with those it left out. This book is an invitation to rethink psychology: to interrogate not only the knowledge it produced but also the categories it created, the people it excluded, and the alternative psychologies that remain possible.

An Integrated Approach

CHIP does not aim to chart psychology's march towards progress or to congratulate the discipline on its gradual accumulation of timeless truths. It is not a greatest-hits compilation of landmark experiments, heroic discoveries, or celebrated pioneers. Instead, it is an argument for doing psychology differently, an invitation to think, inclusively, historically, and critically, about how psychological knowledge has been constructed, deployed, remembered, and, at times, conveniently forgotten. It is inclusive because it retrieves the voices, experiences, and perspectives that psychology has historically pathologised or erased. It is integrative because it insists that psychology's categories, methods, and power relations are not separable: they are fundamentally entangled, each shaping and reinforcing the others. And it is critical because it questions what counts as knowledge and asks who decides.

Across its chapters, this book describes a set of tools for critical thinking that will equip you to think about psychology not as a fixed body of facts but as a contested, evolving, and deeply human project. Psychology is not simply a mirror reflecting reality; it is a cultural, social, and political practice that actively participates in shaping the world it claims to describe.

CHIP does not position itself outside psychology, passing judgement from a distance. It is psychology at its most reflexive, rigorous, and responsible. It treats psychology as a profoundly human, social, and political discipline, one that has always been shaped by the priorities of its times, by its clients and by power, and by the processes of exclusion. And it shows that psychology, in turn, has always shaped the lives, identities, and futures of the people it has studied. CHIP is about reclaiming psychology's complexity, its plurality, and its contested legacy. This book argues that to be a good psychologist you must also be a historian, a philosopher, and a critic. Psychology's future depends on how honestly it can reckon with its past, and how boldly it can imagine doing things differently. This is the purpose of *Conceptual and Historical Issues in Psychology*. This is the journey this book invites you to begin.

1 The Contours of Murder

Phrenology and the Logic of Reductionism

Chapter Overview

This chapter critically examines the rise and fall of phrenology, a nineteenth-century system that claimed mental faculties could be localised in specific brain regions and revealed through the shape of the skull. Positioned at the intersection of medicine, education, political reform, and science, phrenology provides a rich case study for exploring the concept of *reductionism* in the history of psychology. The chapter introduces key figures such as Franz Joseph Gall, Johann Spurzheim, George Combe, and the Fowler brothers, who popularised and commercialised phrenological theory and practice across Europe and America.

The chapter examines how phrenology gained legitimacy, how it naturalised social hierarchies, and why it eventually lost scientific credibility. Despite being discredited, phrenology's historical echo continues to inform debates around psychological testing, brain-based explanations of psychological functioning, and the limits of biological determinism. In this chapter readers are encouraged to consider what counts as science, and who decides what science is, and to critically reflect on the enduring appeal of simplified, measurable models of the mind. By revisiting this early psychological movement, the chapter cultivates historical literacy, critical thinking, and ethical awareness about the uses and misuses of psychological knowledge.

The Contours of Murder

On 28 January 1829, a large crowd gathered in Edinburgh to witness the execution of William Burke, one half of the infamous Burke and Hare duo. The previous year, Burke and his accomplice had murdered at least 16 people, selling their bodies to the anatomist Dr Robert Knox for dissection. Hare turned informant, Burke was sentenced to hang. But even death did not end his usefulness to science. The next day, Burke's body was publicly dissected by Professor Alexander Monro at the University of Edinburgh. Thousands filed through the anatomical theatre to glimpse the corpse. During the demonstration, Monro dipped his pen into Burke's blood and wrote a chilling line: 'This is written in the blood of William Burke, who was hanged at Edinburgh on 28 Jan. 1829 for the murder of Mrs Campbell of Docherty. The blood was taken from his head on the 1 Feb. 1829.' A plaster cast of Burke's head was then made, to be displayed in the meeting rooms of the Edinburgh Phrenological Society. There, alongside those of poets, paupers, and

DOI: 10.4324/9781003565482-1

criminals, Burke's skull was offered as physical proof of phrenological claims. The Society's members and curious visitors were encouraged to feel the contours of the murderer's head, to locate the cranial 'organs' of Destructiveness, Secretiveness, and Amativeness that phrenologists believed foretold his crimes in bumps. In this moment, when the boundary between science and spectacle became blurred, the public touched a murderer's skull in search of hidden truths. Could criminality really be read in bumps and ridges?

Chapter Contents

- The rise and fall of phrenology as a scientific and cultural movement.
- Key figures and their influence on nineteenth-century science, society, and reform.
- Critical thinking tool: how phrenology illustrates the risks of reductionism.

Chapter Objectives

- To understand the historical development and social impact of phrenology.
- To evaluate how phrenology shaped and was shaped by broader cultural and scientific assumptions.
- To apply the critical thinking tool of reductionism to assess the simplification of complex psychological phenomena.

CRITICAL THINKING TOOL
REDUCTIONISM

In psychology, *reductionism* refers to the process of explaining complex human thoughts, emotions, and behaviours in terms of simpler, more fundamental elements, whether they are biological, neurological, or mechanistic. While reductionism can offer clarity and precision, it often comes at a cost: it risks oversimplifying the richness and complexity of human life. In the history of psychology, reductionism has frequently shaped both scientific theory and public discourse, sometimes with troubling consequences.

Phrenology is a compelling historical case study in reductionist thinking. Emerging in the early nineteenth century, phrenology proposed that the brain is composed of discrete 'organs' responsible for different traits and capacities, and that the shape of the skull could reveal the development of these faculties. A person's character, morals, and mental faculties, it was claimed, could be read from the bumps and contours of the head.

At first glance, phrenology appeared to be an objective effort to map the mind onto the brain; an early neuropsychology perhaps. But this mapping was starkly reductionist: it translated the full richness of human character into physical anatomy, and individual worth into cranial measurements. Phrenology thus collapsed the psychological into the physical. It replaced dialogue and context with diagnosis and categorisation. Critically examining phrenology through

the lens of reductionism encourages us to reflect not only on historical practices of the self but also on present-day assumptions about the relationship between body and mind. The temptation to reduce the mind to the brain is noticeable in many areas of contemporary psychology. In doing so, to what extent do we risk overlooking the richness of subjective experience, the role of culture and context, and the complexity of human meaning-making?

Introduction

Few psychological theories have enjoyed such an explosive popularity, or such a dramatic decline, as phrenology. Emerging in the early nineteenth century, phrenology was presented as a science of the mind, a method for understanding a person's character and mental capacities by examining the bumps and shape of their skull. Phrenology captivated the public imagination, spread rapidly across Europe and America, and left its imprint on everything from recruitment practices to criminal profiling. And yet, within decades, it was widely discredited in scientific circles as pseudoscience.

This chapter examines phrenology not just as a failed theory but as a window into psychology's deeper struggles with reductionism, authority, and identity. Why did so many people, including respected physicians, educators, and political reformers, believe in it? What can phrenology teach us about the early entanglement of psychology with medicine, ethnic differences, and social control?

For psychology students, phrenology offers more than a historical curiosity. It provides an opportunity to reflect on the enduring allure of biological explanations and the danger of oversimplifying the human mind. Phrenology may have become a historical curiosity, but the questions it raises about what counts as science, who decides, and what is at stake in reducing people to measurements are more relevant than ever.

Historical Issues

Phrenology emerged at a moment of profound transformation in European thought. In the late eighteenth and early nineteenth centuries, Enlightenment ideals of reason and progress were reshaping the systematic study of the natural world, while Romanticism was urging attention to individuality and inner life. In this productive context, the idea that the mind could be studied empirically, even mapped onto the body, seemed both radical and enticing.

The Austrian physician Franz Joseph Gall laid the groundwork for phrenology with the claim that the brain consists of distinct areas responsible for different mental faculties. Gall's collaborator, Johann Spurzheim, popularised and systematised these ideas under the name 'phrenology', a term derived from the Greek for 'mind' (*phren*) and 'discourse' (*logos*). Gall and Spurzheim proposed that the skull's shape reflected the underlying development of these brain regions, allowing the phrenological expert to assess a person's character and mental faculties through physical examination.

Phrenology appealed to progressive educators, social reformers, and a curious public. In an era of social upheaval and growing urbanisation, phrenology promised to make sense of human differences and to offer practical tools for understanding, improving, and managing individuals.

By the mid-nineteenth century, phrenological societies had formed in cities from London to New York. Travelling lecturers delivered demonstrations to packed audiences, and phrenological busts became common in homes and classrooms. The movement intersected with broader social trends, including temperance, criminal rehabilitation, and early public health reform.

George Combe's *The Constitution of Man* (1828) sold more than 200,000 copies in Britain and over 300,000 worldwide by the mid-1850s, making it one of the bestselling scientific works of the era. Meanwhile, American phrenological journals enjoyed circulations of around 20,000 subscribers, reflecting the transatlantic reach of the movement. In Britain, phrenology drew extraordinary public interest: historical records show that the Manchester Mechanics' Institution hosted a phrenology exhibition in 1842 to 1843, which attracted over 100,000 visitors. At the height of its influence, phrenology captivated the public imagination, drawing vast crowds and enjoying remarkable appeal across science, popular entertainment, education, and self-improvement culture.

However, cracks in the theory soon began to show. Anatomical evidence failed to support its claims, and phrenologists struggled to standardise its measurements. By the 1870s, phrenology had lost scientific credibility and was increasingly associated with quackery. Nevertheless, its influence lingered on, in popular culture, in the emerging disciplines of criminology and psychiatry, and in the persistent temptation to reduce the mind to matter.

Key Individuals

Phrenology was a movement shaped by a cast of characters, scientists, showmen, reformers, and entrepreneurs, each of whom added momentum and made a unique contribution. At its centre was Franz Joseph Gall (1758–1828), the founder of what he called *organology*. Gall's early work was rooted in anatomical observation. He believed that specific mental faculties, such as language, memory, or 'combativeness', were located in distinct regions of the brain, and that the size of each area in any particular individual corresponded to its strength. Crucially, he argued that these differences could be read on the external surface of the skull. This idea introduced a radical new claim: that one could objectively analyse a person's character by assessing the bumps and hollows on their head.

Gall's student and eventual rival Johann Spurzheim (1776–1832) played an essential role in turning organology into the system of phrenology. Spurzheim was a gifted communicator and populariser. He expanded and refined Gall's list of faculties, and gave the theory a more optimistic, moralistic tone. Whereas Gall had been relatively deterministic, Spurzheim believed that phrenology could aid moral and social reform by identifying and nurturing positive traits. Spurzheim toured widely across Europe and America, spreading phrenology to new audiences and helping to establish it as a self-contained system of self-knowledge.

In Britain, George Combe (1788–1858) became the most prominent and influential voice of phrenology. A Scottish lawyer turned intellectual and educator, Combe saw phrenology as the foundation of a new moral and scientific worldview. His 1828 book *The Constitution of Man* became a huge bestseller, integrating phrenology with utilitarian ethics, natural theology, and social improvement. Combe was also instrumental in founding the Edinburgh Phrenological Society, which became a key institution in promoting and legitimising phrenology as a respectable science.

Across the Atlantic, American phrenology had a distinctly commercial and democratic character. Here, Orson Squire Fowler (1809–1887) and his brother Lorenzo Niles Fowler (1811–1896) turned phrenology into a thriving business. The Fowler brothers offered personal head readings, published widely read journals and manuals, and produced phrenological busts and measuring tools. Their New York offices became a hub for curious citizens seeking self-understanding and life advice, reinforcing phrenology's appeal as a tool for individual empowerment.

Phrenology also attracted women and reformers who found in it a language of agency and empowerment. Lydia Folger Fowler (1823–1879), for instance, was the first American woman to receive a medical degree and a key figure in popularising phrenology among female audiences. She lectured widely on education, health, and women's roles, linking phrenological ideas to emerging feminist concerns.

Yet not all of phrenology's advocates were benign. Some used its claims to justify slavery, colonialism, and criminal punishment. James Cowles Prichard (1786–1848), a physician and anthropologist, attempted to reconcile phrenology with ethnology, reinforcing ideas of racial hierarchy. Similarly, some criminologists and early psychiatrists used phrenological principles to identify supposedly 'degenerate' types, particularly in asylums and prisons.

As phrenology declined scientifically, it retained a ghostly presence through these institutional pathways. As we shall see in Chapter 3, Cesare Lombroso (1835–1909), the founder of the Italian school of criminal anthropology, echoed phrenological logic in his claims that criminality could be read from physical features, a legacy that would later feed into eugenics and forensic profiling.

These individuals demonstrate the complex, contradictory legacy of phrenology. It was a scientific curiosity and a social movement, a platform for self-help and a tool of moral regulation. The appeal of its key figures, such as Gall's anatomical precision, Spurzheim's reformist zeal, Combe's rational morality, and the Fowlers' entrepreneurial flair, reminds us that scientific ideas do not spread by truth alone but by personal charisma, political context, and cultural enthusiasm.

Epistemological Issues

Phrenology styled itself as the science of character, a bold claim in an era when psychology had yet to establish itself as an academic discipline. Its proponents argued that, unlike metaphysical speculation or religious dogma, phrenology offered an empirical, observable, and testable approach to the human mind. Following phrenology's decline, psychology's ambitions to orientate itself towards the natural sciences reflected a broader epistemological drive: the pursuit of knowledge claims that aim to be reliable, objective, and authoritative.

At the heart of phrenology's epistemology was a faith in measurement. By examining the skull using fingers or callipers, phrenologists believed they could assess the mind's capacities and proclivities. Bumps and indentations were interpreted as indicators of developed or underdeveloped mental faculties, as if the brain were a landscape with measurable hills and valleys. This move from internal experience to external observation was deeply reductionist, collapsing the complexity of thought and emotion into surface anatomy. It echoed the Enlightenment belief that human nature could be known through classification, comparison, and quantification.

The epistemological weaknesses of phrenology soon became apparent. The identification and localisation of faculties were inconsistent across practitioners. Different phrenologists assigned different mental traits to similar cranial regions, and no standardised method of measurement existed. It seemed to be more of an art than a science. Furthermore, phrenological assessments often relied on confirmation bias, selecting evidence that fit the desired interpretation, and lacking any robust experimental verification. As critics pointed out, phrenology could not reliably *predict* future behaviour or differentiate cause from correlation.

Despite these flaws, phrenology succeeded epistemologically in another sense: it *felt* scientific. It used diagrams, busts, and technical language. It claimed empirical foundations. It offered a sense of order and control. This rhetorical power, its ability to *simulate* science, conferred credibility in the public eye, especially during an era when psychology's boundaries with medicine, anthropology, and philosophy remained porous.

Phrenology's story reminds us that epistemology is about how we come to believe that something counts as knowledge. It highlights that what counts as evidence in the human sciences is historically and culturally contingent, shaped by prevailing norms and practices. It reveals that the authority to decide what constitutes legitimate knowledge is often held by those in positions of institutional or scientific power. And it shows how easily the authority of science can be mimicked, and misused, by practices that adopt its language and appearance without its rigour.

Ontological Issues

Ontology concerns the nature of being, what kinds of things exist and how they are structured. In psychology, ontological questions often focus on what the 'mind' is, how it relates to the body, and what it means to be a person. Phrenology offers a fascinating case of an ontology of the self before psychology itself had become consolidated as a discipline. Phrenology assumed not only that the mind exists as a corollary of the body but that it is material, divisible, and measurable.

According to phrenology, the mind was not an immaterial soul or a single unified entity. Instead, it was understood as a set of distinct faculties, each with its own moral, emotional, or intellectual function, and each rooted in a specific region of the brain. This modular view of the mind had major ontological implications. It suggested that human nature could be broken down into discrete parts such as 'benevolence', 'destructiveness', and 'self-esteem', and that each of these parts could be independently assessed. This reductionist ontology simplified human psychology into a system of inner mental 'organs' with outer expressions.

Importantly, phrenology *naturalised* the mind. That is, it suggested that traits such as ambition, religiosity, or criminality were biologically ingrained and physically inscribed in the brain's anatomy. In doing so, phrenology blurred the line between the moral and the biological, treating character as something both inborn but also malleable. This helped to justify social hierarchy and inequality, but it also encouraged self-help. If one's intelligence or moral worth could be read from the skull, then social outcomes could be reinterpreted as natural facts or personal failings rather than as matters of opportunity.

Phrenology also reimagined the self as *transparent*, as something that could be read, assessed, and categorised by others. This ontological stance undermined traditional notions of interiority, agency, and privacy. The self was no longer mysterious or hidden; it was written on the body, available to scientific inspection.

Even as phrenology faded, its ontological claims lingered. The idea that personality is biologically determined, or that traits can be localised in the brain, re-emerged in twentieth-century psychometrics and persists today in fields like neuropsychology and behavioural genetics.

Power

Phrenology was never just about understanding the mind. It was also a technology of power, a way of knowing that enabled new ways of sorting, judging, and governing people. Presented as a scientific tool, phrenology offered apparent objectivity in the assessment of character, morality, and intellect. But behind the promise of neutral measurement lay a powerful apparatus for reinforcing social hierarchies and legitimising inequality.

One of the most striking aspects of phrenology's appeal was its capacity to authorise judgement. By claiming that mental traits could be read from the skull, it allowed employers, doctors, educators, and even parents, to assess others with a semblance of objectivity. Phrenology was used to select job candidates, determine educational paths, and identify potential criminals. In each case, it translated complex social and ethical questions into physical measurements, aligning closely with the logic of *disciplinary power*, Michel Foucault's term for the use of scientific knowledge to manage, regulate, and normalise populations.

Phrenology was also entangled with racism, sexism, and colonialism. It was frequently employed to justify the supposed inferiority of non-European peoples, claiming that African, Indigenous, or Asian skulls revealed lower faculties or moral deficits. These claims were central to phrenology's practice, reinforcing the colonial ideology of the 'civilising mission' and the apparently scientific classification of people into racial types. Similarly, some phrenologists argued that women had underdeveloped intellectual faculties and enhanced emotional ones, reinforcing patriarchal norms.

Even progressive uses of phrenology were shaped by power. Reformers who used phrenology to promote education, prison reform, or temperance still accepted its core assumption: that people could and should be shaped according to their measurable potential. The tools of liberation and discipline were often indistinguishable.

By embedding itself in institutions such as schools, prisons, and medical practices, phrenology helped naturalise a model of personhood that was hierarchical and externally validated. It served as both a mirror and a motor of nineteenth-century power structures. Today, phrenology reminds us that psychological knowledge is never innocent. It exposes how certain individuals or groups are positioned as normal or deviant according to dominant social values. It reveals that the definitions of intellect and morality are controlled by those with cultural and scientific authority. And it demonstrates how science can become complicit in systems of domination by reinforcing existing hierarchies under the guise of objectivity.

Chapter Summary

Phrenology is often remembered as a cautionary tale, an example of how science can go wrong. Its central claim, that the mind could be read from the shape of the skull, has long been debunked. But to dismiss phrenology simply as pseudoscience is to miss its deeper significance. It was a powerful cultural force that helped shape the emerging field of psychology and the public's understanding of what it means to be a person.

Throughout this chapter, we have seen how phrenology exemplifies the dangers and temptations of *reductionism*. Phrenology reduced the richness of human experience to physical measurements, collapsing morality into morphology and identity into anatomy. In doing so, it promised clarity, certainty, and control. Yet this clarity was an illusion, built on insecure empirical foundations and deeply implicated in systems of social control.

Phrenology emerged during a period of rapid change, when new scientific methods were being used to make sense of a world marked by industrialisation, migration, and colonialism. It thrived because it spoke to people's hopes and anxieties, offering self-understanding, social order, and moral improvement. It was seductive because it *felt* scientific, even as it reinforced old prejudices in new, technical terms.

The individuals who promoted phrenology, namely Gall, Spurzheim, Combe, and the Fowlers, were not charlatans. They were, in many cases, sincere believers in science and reform. But sincerity does not guarantee truth. Their efforts remind us that science is a human activity, shaped by cultural assumptions, institutional interests, and historical contexts.

The ontological and epistemological foundations of phrenology may have crumbled, but its legacy endures in subtle forms. The desire to map personality onto biology lives on in modern neuroscience, psychometrics, and even corporate personality testing. The authority of 'objective' psychological assessment continues to shape education, employment, and criminal justice.

For psychology students today, phrenology is not just a curious relic. It can act as a mirror that reflects psychology's ongoing struggles with its identity, its methods, and its moral responsibilities. To study phrenology critically is to become more alert to the history of ideas, more cautious about claims to objectivity, and more aware of the ethical stakes of psychological knowledge.

In the end, perhaps nothing captures phrenology's unsettling afterlife more vividly than the fate of William Burke's skull. Removed from his body after execution, it was measured and displayed as scientific evidence in the meeting rooms of the Edinburgh Phrenological Society. Once a man, now a specimen, Burke's skeleton today hangs in the Anatomical Museum at the University of Edinburgh. It stands as a haunting reminder that the tools of psychological science can illuminate or dehumanise, and that what we choose to preserve in our museums speaks as much about the present as it does about the past.

Reflective Questions

1. In what ways did phrenology reflect both Enlightenment ideals and nineteenth-century social anxieties?
2. Why was phrenology so compelling to different groups, including reformers, scientists, entrepreneurs, and the general public?
3. What does phrenology teach us about the risks of reductionism in psychology?
4. How did phrenology contribute to, and benefit from, existing power structures such as racism, sexism, and colonialism?
5. Can you think of contemporary examples where psychological or neuroscientific claims might be reductionist in a similar way?

Suggested Reading

Combe, G. (1828). *The Constitution of Man Considered in Relation to External Objects*. Edinburgh: Maclachlan & Stewart.

Eling P., & Finger, S. (2020). Franz Joseph Gall's non-cortical faculties and their organs. *Journal of the History of the Behavioural Sciences, 56*(1), 7–19. https://doi.org/10.1002/jhbs.21994.

Finger, S. (2019). Mark Twain's life-long fascination with phrenology. *Journal of the History of the Behavioural Sciences, 55*(2), 99–121. https://doi.org/10.1002/jhbs.21960.

Finger, S., & Eling, P. (2022). The quest for objectivity and measurements in phrenology's 'bumpy' history. *History of Psychology, 25*(3), 211–244. https://doi.org/10.1037/hop0000213.

Lilleleht, E. (2015). 'Assuming the privilege' of bridging divides: Abigail Fowler-Chumos, practical phrenology, and America's Gilded Age. *History of Psychology, 18*(4), 414–432. https://doi.org/10.1037/a0039476.

Lilleleht, E. (2022). *An Organ of Murder: Crime, violence, and phrenology in nineteenth-century America.* Rutgers University Press.

Parker Jones, O., Alfaro-Almagro, F., & Jbabdi. S. (2018). An empirical, 21st century evaluation of phrenology. *Cortex, 106,* 26–35. https://doi.org/10.1016/j.cortex.2018.04.011.

Poskett, J. (2019). *Materials of the Mind: Phrenology, race, and the global history of science, 1815–1920.* Chicago, IL: University of Chicago Press.

Sysling, F. (2021). Phrenology and the average person, 1840–1940. *History of the Human Sciences, 34*(2), 27–45. https://doi.org/10.1177/0952695120984070.

Van Wyhe, J. (2004). *Phrenology and the Origins of Victorian Scientific Naturalism.* Aldershot: Ashgate.

Key Terms

Confirmation Bias The tendency to interpret evidence in a way that confirms pre-existing beliefs; often seen in phrenological assessments and diagnoses.

Craniometry The measurement of the skull, used in phrenology (and later in eugenics) to make claims about intelligence, character, and race.

Critical Thinking Tool A conceptual lens used throughout the chapter to encourage analysis and reflection; in this chapter, the focus is on *reductionism.*

Disciplinary Power A term coined by Michel Foucault to describe how scientific knowledge is used to regulate and control populations; phrenology served as an early example.

Empiricism A philosophical approach that emphasises observation and experience as the primary sources of knowledge; used by phrenologists to claim scientific status.

Modular Mind The belief that the mind is composed of separate faculties or functions, each with its own location or 'module' in the brain; a foundational idea in phrenology.

Naturalisation The process by which social or moral traits are presented as biologically fixed and inevitable, often used in phrenology to justify inequality.

Organology An early term for the idea that the brain is composed of distinct 'organs' or areas, each responsible for specific mental faculties; the foundation of phrenological theory.

Phrenology A nineteenth-century theory claiming that mental faculties are localised in specific brain regions, and that the shape of the skull can reveal traits such as character and intelligence.

Reductionism The practice of explaining complex psychological phenomena by reducing them to simpler elements such as biology or neurology, often at the cost of nuance and context.

FREE INSTRUCTOR & STUDENT RESOURCES

ONLINE RESOURCES

Visit the Instructor & Student Resources website at routledgelearning.com/bpscoretextbooks for free digital resources, including:

- Interactive quizzes and flashcards to test your knowledge
- Links to useful websites and videos
- Instructor manual, lecture slides, and course guide to enhance teaching and save instructors time

2 Darwin's Shadow

Evolution and the Naturalisation of Mind

Chapter Overview

This chapter explores how evolutionary theory and scientific naturalism shaped the development of psychology from the late nineteenth century onward. Using naturalism as a critical thinking tool, students are introduced to the idea that human actions, emotions, and cognitions came to be studied using the same principles that govern the natural world. Beginning with Charles Darwin's theories of natural selection, emotional expression, and human descent from common ancestors, the chapter examines how these ideas led to the formation of new psychological areas and principles, such as comparative psychology, psychometrics, and functionalism.

Influential figures such as Herbert Spencer, Francis Galton, William James, and G. Stanley Hall are discussed alongside under-recognised psychologists such as Leta Stetter Hollingworth and Margaret Floy Washburn. The chapter offers a critical analysis of how evolutionary ideas were used to justify gender, racial, and class hierarchies. It also briefly considers the rise of sociobiology and evolutionary psychology in the late twentieth century.

Darwin's Shadow

When the Mexican performer Julia Pastrana died in Moscow in 1860, she might have hoped to rest in peace. Instead, her body was embalmed and exhibited across Europe for decades. Born with hypertrichosis and a rare gum condition, Julia had toured internationally in life as a 'bearded lady,' billed in freak shows and 'scientific' exhibitions alike as the *Ape Woman*, *Bear Woman*, and *Hybrid Between Human and Orangutan*. But Julia Pastrana was not just a sideshow act. She sang, she danced, she spoke several languages. Her husband, the showman Theodore Lent, continued to display her body after her death, parading her corpse before physicians, naturalists, and thrill-seeking audiences under the guise of science. Even into the twentieth century, her remains were kept in museum storage, until they were finally repatriated and buried in her native Sinaloa, Mexico, in 2013. What was it about her body that fascinated nineteenth-century scientists and audiences so deeply? At the heart of their obsession was a single question: where do humans end, and animals begin? Misunderstood and misrepresented, Julia Pastrana was treated as a kind of living fossil, a bridge species, a grotesque echo of some imagined ancestral past. Darwin himself said that 'her face had a gorilla-like appearance'. Her story

DOI: 10.4324/9781003565482-2

reveals the dark underside of Darwin's cultural legacy: how evolutionary theory, taken up beyond the pages of Darwin's *On the Origin of Species* (1859), was used to justify a hierarchy of minds and bodies, races and sexes, civilisations and savageries. Psychology, as it emerged from Darwin's shadow, did not stand apart from this. Psychology sought to explain the human mind in naturalistic terms. But in doing so, it cast its scientific gaze unevenly, illuminating certain bodies and lives while rendering others invisible, marginal, or monstrous. When we use biology to explain the mind, what, and who, becomes the object of study, and who is left in the shadows?

Chapter Contents

- The influence of evolutionary theory on the development of psychological subfields, including comparative psychology, psychometrics, and developmental psychology.
- A critical examination of naturalism as both a scientific method and ideological framework in psychology.
- The enduring impact of evolutionary theory on biological psychology, and its role in shaping assumptions about race, gender, and intelligence.

Chapter Objectives

- To explain how evolutionary theory shaped key concepts, methods, and assumptions in the history of psychology.
- To introduce naturalism as a critical thinking tool for evaluating the biological and ideological dimensions of psychological science.
- To encourage students to critically reflect on the role of naturalism in framing human behaviour, emotion, and cognition.

CRITICAL THINKING TOOL
NATURALISM

In the history of psychology, *naturalism* refers to the idea that human beings can be studied using the same methods that scientists have used to study the natural world. Rooted in Enlightenment ideals and given new intensity by Darwinian evolutionary theory, naturalism helped establish psychology as a biological science. The naturalistic perspective assumes that human development, actions, thoughts, and feelings are shaped by natural laws, such as those of inheritance, adaptation, and evolution.

But naturalism is more than a straightforward scientific principle; it is also a philosophical and ideological stance. To think critically about naturalism means asking not only *what it explains* but also *what it excludes*. What is lost when psychological questions are answered solely in terms of biological mechanisms or evolutionary principles? What kinds of explanations become dominant, and which ideas are marginalised or ignored?

In the context of this chapter, naturalism will help us explore how evolutionary ideas influenced psychology by encouraging reductionist, functionalist, and often deterministic models of mind and behaviour. Through the lens of naturalism, psychologists interpreted intelligence, emotion, development, morality, and even race, gender, and class, as natural phenomena that could be classified, measured, and often ranked.

By tracing the naturalistic turn in psychology, we can understand how science made human nature *knowable*, but also how this knowledge was shaped by power, culture, and assumptions about what counts as 'normal' or 'natural'. Naturalism remains central to modern biological psychology, but a historical approach invites us to question its limitations and explore alternative frameworks for understanding human experience.

Introduction

The integration of evolutionary theory into psychology provided an organising framework that reshaped how psychologists understood the mind, behaviour, and development. This transformation was deeply tied to the idea that human beings, like all other living creatures, could be studied using the methods of the natural sciences. Evolutionary theory gave this idea both scientific credibility and cultural power. Evolutionary theory was both an empirical demonstration of the continuity between nature and human nature and the theoretical justification and legitimation of the human sciences.

Charles Darwin's work redefined humanity's place in the natural world. His theory of descent with modification suggested that traits such as emotion, memory, and intelligence were not uniquely human but had evolved through the process of natural selection. In *The Descent of Man* (1871), Darwin acknowledged the tension between humanity's 'noble qualities' and its 'lowly origin', challenging earlier religious and philosophical accounts of mind and morality. His companion work, *The Expression of the Emotions in Man and Animals* (1872), argued that emotional expressions were biologically inherited and universally shared, reinforcing the evolutionary continuity between species.

Historical Issues

The influence of evolutionary theory on psychology emerged within a broader nineteenth-century shift towards naturalistic explanations of human nature. Darwin's theory of natural selection, published in *On the Origin of Species* (1859), challenged long-held assumptions about human uniqueness by asserting biological continuity between humans and other animals. This revolutionised how psychologists understood human development.

This shift towards naturalism involved a move away from supernatural interpretations towards a scientific understanding of the human mind. Moralistic or religious explanations located the cause of 'madness', for example, in the realm of sin, spiritual forces, or moral weakness, often prescribing remedies focused on religious practices or moral reform. Naturalistic explanations on the other hand sought the origins of mental illness in the physical body, heredity, environment, and psychological processes, paving the way for medical and psychological treatments.

The dominant popular and scientific evolutionary framework in the late nineteenth century was not Darwinian in a strict natural selection sense. Lamarckian and progressive evolutionary models were more widely accepted by many scientists, educators, and psychologists. Darwin's own theory of pangenesis (inherited bodily changes via 'gemmules') kept Lamarckian inheritance alive well into the 1880s. These ideas provided a more humanistic and purposeful view of evolution, which made them appealing to psychologists, especially those interested in development, learning, and moral education.

Darwin's idea of descent, namely that humans evolved from common ancestors shared with other species, helped create the field of comparative psychology. Figures such as George Romanes and Conwy Lloyd Morgan attempted to trace the mental evolution of humans by studying animals. Romanes focused on the continuity of emotions and cognitive capacities, albeit with an anthropomorphic lens, while Lloyd Morgan introduced the principle of parsimony (Lloyd Morgan's Canon), arguing that animal behaviour should be explained using the simplest possible mechanisms before invoking higher mental competencies. These debates reflected early struggles attempting to balance empirical rigour with evolutionary interpretation.

The emphasis on variation within species, a core Darwinian concept, was taken up by Darwin's cousin Francis Galton, who applied it to humans. Galton's studies of individual differences gave rise to psychometrics, but also to the ideology of eugenics, which aimed to 'improve' the human species by encouraging the reproduction of the most 'fit'. Here, naturalism was used not simply as a scientific framework but as a political and moral rationale, a way of naturalising existing social hierarchies as biologically inevitable.

Darwinian ideas also inspired theories of recapitulation, particularly in G. Stanley Hall's developmental psychology. Hall believed that children passed through evolutionary stages in their development, echoes of the species' biological past. Childhood thus became a window into evolution, and education a tool for steering it.

Meanwhile, the progressive ideal of evolutionary advance was shadowed by fears of degeneration, especially in the writings of Cesare Lombroso and Gustave Le Bon, who linked criminality, madness, and crowd behaviour to 'primitive instincts'. These ideas, aligned with Social Darwinism, framed lower social classes, racialised groups, and women as biologically less evolved. In all these cases, evolutionary theory aligned with naturalism to reframe human difference as a natural fact, observable and measurable, a pattern that remains influential in contemporary biological psychology.

Key Individuals

The evolutionary turn in psychology was shaped by a diverse set of thinkers who approached the relationship between mind, behaviour, and biology from different perspectives. Some, such as Herbert Spencer and Francis Galton, used evolutionary ideas to justify social hierarchies; others sought more adaptive and democratic interpretations. While many of these figures were prominent, it is also important to recognise those who challenged the naturalistic assumptions of their time, especially women who resisted biologically deterministic views of gender and intelligence.

Herbert Spencer (1820–1903), a philosopher and early populariser of evolutionary ideas, coined the term 'survival of the fittest'. He extended Darwinian concepts to society, arguing that competition and natural selection explained social progress. Spencer's Social Darwinism presented inequality as a natural outcome of evolutionary processes, framing poverty, criminality, and social unrest as signs of evolutionary inferiority. His ideas were influential in both psychology and sociology but have since been widely criticised for conceptualising injustice as a feature of nature.

Francis Galton (1822–1911), Darwin's cousin, took a more empirical approach. He founded differential psychology and psychometrics, seeking to investigate human 'natural ability' with the help of statistical tools. Believing that mental traits were hereditary, Galton developed the concept of eugenics, the idea that society could be improved by selectively breeding human beings for desirable traits. Galton's work contributed to the scientific foundations of psychology, but it also reinforced racist and classist ideologies, illustrating the double-edged legacy of psychological naturalism.

William James (1842–1910), a leading American psychologist, was strongly influenced by Darwin's approach. He believed that mental states such as fear or will should be studied in terms of their adaptive function. James argued that consciousness evolved to help humans navigate complex environments and solve problems. His approach, known as functionalism, became a core foundation for biological psychology. James's emphasis on pragmatism (truth is what works) aligned closely with the adaptive principles of evolution.

G. Stanley Hall (1846–1924), the first president of the American Psychological Association (1892), introduced Darwin's idea of recapitulation into developmental psychology. He believed that childhood development mirrored evolutionary history, with adolescence representing a transitional phase from primitive to civilised states. Hall's evolutionary views shaped early child psychology, educational theory, and even eugenic thought, particularly in the classification of 'normal' and 'abnormal' development.

James Mark Baldwin (1861–1934) offered an important Lamarckian-inflected alternative to deterministic models through his theory of organic selection, later known as the Baldwin effect. He argued that learned behaviours could influence evolutionary change, not by altering genes directly but by shaping who survives to pass them on. Baldwin's work bridged the divide between learning and evolution, and offered a more dynamic model of development, one with important implications for both biological psychology and education.

While many of these figures advanced psychology through their engagement with evolution, several female psychologists used naturalistic methods to challenge biological determinism. Leta Stetter Hollingworth (1886–1939) tested and refuted claims that women were biologically inferior to men. Her work demonstrated that many apparent sex differences were due to social roles, not biology. Margaret Floy Washburn (1871–1939), the first woman to earn a PhD in psychology, integrated evolutionary ideas into her comparative psychology, yet resisted drawing simplistic conclusions about human hierarchy from animal studies.

Epistemological Issues

The emergence of evolutionary psychology brought with it a significant shift in the epistemological foundations of psychology; that is, the ways psychologists sought to acquire and justify knowledge. Grounded in naturalism, evolutionary psychology assumed that human mental life could be studied using the same empirical methods employed by the natural sciences. This assumption drove a wave of efforts to observe, measure, and categorise psychological phenomena, particularly through biology-based methodologies.

One of the earliest examples of this was the work of George Romanes (1848–1984), who compiled narratives of animal behaviour in *Animal Intelligence* (1882) to demonstrate mental continuity between species. His method, rooted in comparative psychology, treated animal behaviours as windows into the evolutionary history of human thought. Romanes relied heavily on anecdotal evidence and anthropomorphic interpretation, projecting human mental states onto animals.

A corrective came in the form of C. Lloyd Morgan's 'Canon', an epistemological rule which held that animal behaviour should not be explained using higher mental processes if simpler explanations were sufficient. This principle laid the groundwork for more rigorous, observational, and behaviourist methods. Lloyd Morgan's approach reflected a broader trend in psychology: to secure scientific legitimacy by adopting methods that mirrored those of biology and physiology.

The influence of Francis Galton further formalised this trend. In his 'Anthropometric Laboratory', Galton used reaction times, sensory acuity, and statistical tools to quantify individual differences. He operationalised abstract traits such as intellect and sensory ability in measurable, testable terms.

Meanwhile, functionalists such William James emphasised pragmatic, real-world approaches to cognition. They investigated how mental processes evolved to meet adaptive challenges, linking thought directly to behaviour and survival. Their work marked a shift from introspection to adaptive epistemology, focusing on function rather than structure.

These contrasting approaches, ranging from anecdotal to experimental, introspective to quantitative, and interpretive to functional, demonstrate how evolutionary thinking shaped not only the subjects that psychologists chose to study but also their assumptions about how valid knowledge should be generated.

Ontological Issues

Evolutionary theory not only reshaped psychology's methods of inquiry but also transformed its ontology; that is, its assumptions about the nature of the mind, behaviour, and what kinds of entities psychological science studies. Influenced by naturalism, psychologists increasingly came to view the human mind as part of a biological continuum, subject to the same evolutionary forces as other species. This shift displaced older dualistic models and theological principles that separated mind from body and reason from instinct. Instead, mental processes were now seen as evolved adaptations, shaped by natural selection to meet environmental challenges.

One major ontological implication of this view was reductionism, the belief that complex human behaviours and experiences could ultimately be explained in terms of simpler, physical, or biological processes. Emotions, for example, were redefined as inherited traits linked to survival rather than as moral, cultural, or spiritual experiences. The study of instinct, especially in comparative psychology and ethology, further supported the idea that behaviour could be broken down into biologically preprogrammed responses.

This naturalistic ontology came with limitations. Critics argued that subjective experience, sociability, and moral reasoning resist neat biological explanation.

While evolutionary psychology offers powerful tools for understanding adaptation, its ontological assumptions can obscure the richness and variability of human life, especially when they treat behaviour as biologically determined rather than socially and historically situated.

Power

While evolutionary theory helped establish psychology as a scientific discipline, it also became a vehicle for the legitimation of power. The assumption that human traits and behaviours could be explained biologically made it easier to argue that social inequalities were natural and inevitable. This conflation of scientific description with social prescription, known as the naturalistic fallacy, allowed psychology to acquire moral and political dimensions.

In the late nineteenth and early twentieth centuries, evolutionary ideas were frequently employed to justify systems of gender inequality, racial hierarchy, and class division. The belief that certain groups were biologically less evolved, whether women, people of colour, or the working class, was used to rationalise their exclusion from education, political life, and intellectual labour. Social Darwinism, promoted by figures such as Herbert Spencer, merged natural selection with 'laissez-faire' ideology, suggesting that the 'fittest' individuals naturally rose to the top while others fell behind due to hereditary inferiority.

Female psychologists such as Leta Stetter Hollingworth and Margaret Floy Washburn actively resisted these ideas. They conducted empirical studies to disprove claims of female inferiority that were often rooted in evolutionary or biological arguments. Hollingworth, for example, challenged the 'variability hypothesis', which suggested that men had greater intellectual range due to natural selection. Her data showed no significant differences in variability between men and women, arguing instead that opportunity shaped achievement.

Power in evolutionary psychology operates through what appears natural, and thus unchangeable. The challenge for contemporary biological psychology is to remain alert to how naturalistic frameworks can mask cultural bias and reproduce historical inequalities, often under the guise of objectivity. Recognising these dynamics is essential to ensuring that evolutionary theory is used to understand human diversity, not to rank it.

Chapter Summary

Darwin's emphasis on descent, variation, and natural selection laid the foundations for key areas of psychological research. Comparative psychology explored mental continuity across species; developmental psychology traced the evolution of the child; psychometrics and eugenics attempted to quantify and control human difference. Functionalism, championed by figures such as William James, reframed consciousness as a tool for survival. Later, sociobiology and evolutionary psychology extended these principles into the domains of social behaviour, morality, and mating strategies, often provoking controversy when biological explanations were applied to complex social issues.

The integration of evolutionary theory into psychology represented a defining moment in the discipline's conceptual and methodological development. Under the influence of naturalism, the human mind, its development and disorders, came to be studied not as something separate from nature but as a product of the same evolutionary pressures that shape all life. This shift brought new scientific authority to psychology, aligning it with evolutionary biology and transforming it into a discipline capable of explaining behaviour, cognition, and emotion in naturalistic and adaptive terms.

But the legacy of naturalism is not neutral. As this chapter has shown, evolutionary frameworks have been used both to expand scientific understanding and to justify inequality. The naturalistic fallacy, confusing what *is* with what *ought to be*, has repeatedly allowed psychology to mask cultural values as biological facts. This was particularly evident in claims about gender and race, where naturalistic explanations often served to reinforce existing power structures.

Yet not every psychologist accepted the determinism that early evolutionary theory seemed to demand. The work of pioneers like Leta Stetter Hollingworth and Margaret Floy Washburn shows that naturalism can be a starting point rather than an endpoint. These women engaged with Darwinian ideas to challenge the status quo, questioning assumptions about sex differences, intelligence, and instinct. Their efforts carved out space for more pluralistic, socially responsive interpretations of human behaviour. Their legacy lives on in feminist psychology, critical developmental theory, and intersectional approaches to psychological science.

For students of biological psychology, this history is foundational. Evolutionary thinking provides powerful insights into behaviours such as attachment, aggression, and cooperation. But these insights are never neutral. They come embedded in cultural assumptions, social hierarchies, and political consequences. A critical understanding of naturalism enables us to ask not just how behaviours evolved but why we explain them in the way we do, and whose perspectives are included, or excluded, in that explanation.

This chapter began with the haunting story of Julia Pastrana, a woman exhibited as a monstrous hybrid between human and animal. Her body was once held up as proof of degeneracy, as a living argument for racial hierarchy and biological fatalism. But her life also reveals something more profound: the danger of mistaking scientific categories for moral truths. In psychology, as in biology, the temptation to naturalise social prejudice remains strong. The task of the critical psychologist is not to abandon science but to scrutinise its metaphors, its models, and its silences. Naturalism is not just a scientific position; it is a moral stance. And it demands, above all, that we remember the human costs of forgetting our own humanity.

Reflective Questions

1. What is naturalism, and in what ways did it help establish psychology as a science?
2. How did Darwinian theory contribute to both the scientific credibility and the social power of psychology?
3. In what ways did early female psychologists challenge the naturalistic fallacy, and why was this important for the development of a more inclusive psychological science?
4. How does the Baldwin effect complicate the nature-versus-nurture debate in evolutionary psychology?
5. What lessons can contemporary biological psychology learn from the historical misapplications of naturalism?

Suggested Reading

Barnes, J. (2021). Revisiting the 'Darwin–Marx correspondence': Multiple discovery and the rhetoric of priority. *History of the Human Sciences, 35*(2), 29–54. https://doi.org/10.1177/09526951211019226.

Bradley, B. (2020). *Darwin's Psychology*. Oxford: Oxford University Press. https://doi.org/10.1093/oso/9780198708216.001.0001.

de Carvalho, V. O., & Coelho, N. E. (2024). Freudian naturalism and the assessment of psychoanalysis as a natural science: Psychic phenomenon as process. *Theory & Psychology, 34*(2), 170–190. https://doi.org/10.1177/09593543241229047.

Goetz, A. T., & Shackelford, T. K. (2006). Modern application of evolutionary theory to psychology: Key concepts and clarifications. *The American Journal of Psychology, 119*(4), 567–584. https://doi.org/10.2307/20445364.

Jarrett, S. (2020). Consciousness reduced: The role of the 'idiot' in early evolutionary psychology. *History of the Human Sciences, 33*(5), 110–137. https://doi.org/10.1177/0952695120911557.

Malone, J. C. (2021). Darwin, Darwinism, and psychology. *Behavior and Philosophy, 49*(24), 1053–8348. https://www.jstor.org/stable/27204272.

Pichel, B. (2016). From facial expressions to bodily gestures: Passions, photography and movement in French 19th-century sciences. *History of the Human Sciences, 29*(1), 27–48. https://doi.org/10.1177/0952695115618592.

Racine, T. P. (2021). The rhetorical use of B. F. Skinner in evolutionary psychology. *Theory & Psychology, 32*(1), 61–81. https://doi.org/10.1177/09593543211030342.

Richards, R. J. (1987). *Darwin and the Emergence of Evolutionary Theories of Mind and Behavior*. Chicago, IL: University of Chicago Press.

Richardson, A. (2013). *After Darwin: Animals, emotions, and the mind*. Rodopi.

Wackers, G. (2025). Digital phenotyping of the mind: From biology to psychoinformatics. *Theory & Psychology, 35*(2), 141–162. https://doi.org/10.1177/09593543251322116.

Key Terms

Adaptation A trait or behaviour that has evolved because it increases an organism's chance of survival and reproduction in its environment. In psychology, adaptation refers to mental or behavioural traits shaped by evolutionary pressures.

Baldwin effect A theory proposed by James Mark Baldwin suggesting that learned behaviours can influence evolutionary outcomes over generations. Individuals who adapt successfully through learning may be more likely to survive and pass on traits that support such learning.

Comparative Psychology A branch of psychology that studies the behaviour and mental processes of animals to understand the evolutionary roots of human psychology. It is grounded in the assumption of continuity between species.

Eugenics A movement associated with Francis Galton that aimed to improve the genetic quality of human populations through selective breeding. It misused evolutionary theory to justify racist, sexist, and class-based hierarchies.

Evolutionary Psychology A modern field that explores how psychological traits and behaviours evolved to solve problems faced by our ancestors. It applies principles of natural selection to cognition, emotion, and social behaviour.

Functionalism A school of psychological thought influenced by Darwin, which focuses on the purposes of mental processes—how they help individuals adapt to their environments.

Lamarckian Inheritance The (now outdated) idea that traits acquired during an individual's life can be passed on to their offspring. Though discredited in biology, it influenced early psychological theories of development and learning.

Morgan's Canon A principle proposed by C. Lloyd Morgan stating that animal behaviour should not be explained by higher mental faculties if simpler explanations suffice. It helped define more rigorous, observational methods in comparative psychology.

Naturalism The belief that human psychology can be studied using the same methods and principles as the natural sciences. It assumes that mental life is a natural phenomenon and can be explained in biological terms.

Naturalistic Fallacy The logical error of equating what is natural with what is morally or socially right. In psychology, this fallacy often appears when evolutionary explanations are used to justify inequality or discrimination.

Recapitulation Theory The now-discredited idea that the development of the individual recapitulates the evolutionary history of the species. Popularised by G. Stanley Hall in child psychology.

Social Darwinism An ideological application of Darwinian theory to human society, often used to justify imperialism, economic inequality, and racial hierarchies under the guise of 'survival of the fittest'.

FREE INSTRUCTOR & STUDENT RESOURCES

ONLINE RESOURCES

Visit the Instructor & Student Resources website at routledgelearning.com/bpscoretextbooks for free digital resources, including:

- Interactive quizzes and flashcards to test your knowledge
- Links to useful websites and videos
- Instructor manual, lecture slides, and course guide to enhance teaching and save instructors time

3 The Skull That Sparked a Theory

Criminality and the Allure of Natural Kinds

Chapter Overview

This chapter explores the emergence of criminal anthropology in the late nineteenth century and its legacy in the psychological sciences. Focusing on the work of Cesare Lombroso and his critics, including Frances Kellor and Charles Goring, the chapter examines how scientific claims about criminality were constructed through a combination of biological, social, and moral assumptions. Lombroso's theory of the 'born criminal' treated criminality as a biologically fixed and measurable condition, while Kellor's feminist and sociological critique argued for understanding criminality as something shaped by environment, society, and cultural forces.

Using the critical thinking tool of natural kinds and human kinds, students are encouraged to question how knowledge in psychology is produced and how classification systems both reflect and reinforce structures of power. Through historical case studies, theoretical contrasts, and contemporary relevance, this chapter deploys the conceptual tools to critically assess the history of criminological thought, and to reflect on the ethical and political implications of categorising people in psychological science.

The Skull That Sparked a Theory

In 1870, Italian physician Cesare Lombroso conducted an autopsy on Giuseppe Villella, a notorious outlaw. As he examined the skull, Lombroso noticed an unusual indentation at its base, a feature he claimed resembled that of 'inferior animals, especially rodents'. 'At the sight of that skull,' he later wrote, 'I seemed to see all of a sudden, lighted up as if by a flash of inspiration, the problem of the nature of the criminal'. From this discovery, Lombroso developed his infamous theory of the 'born criminal': the idea that some individuals were biologically predisposed to commit crimes, not out of circumstance, desperation, or moral failure, but because they were evolutionary throwbacks. This was *Homo criminalis*, Criminal man, imprisoned in a primitive developmental stage of humanity. A sloping forehead, a jutting jaw, asymmetrical ears, long arms, or even tattoos were, for Lombroso, the bodily signatures of degeneracy and savagery. Southern Italians, women accused of sex work, people with epilepsy and even anarchists were all swept into his classificatory net. He published tables of physical indicators and cranial measurements, creating a taxonomy of criminal bodies. Lombroso's early work blended Darwinian

DOI: 10.4324/9781003565482-3

evolution, medical positivism, and a macabre fascination with bodily difference to advance a simple yet dangerous idea: some people were *born to be bad*. Criminology, as an emergent science, embraced this new natural kind of *Homo criminalis*, a biologically distinct and diagnosable human type. It was a seductive promise. But it came at a high cost. Lombroso's science was presented as neutral, objective, and data-driven. But it projected the fears, prejudices, and class anxieties of his era onto the bodies of the socially undesirable.

Chapter Contents

- The rise and fall of criminal anthropology and Lombroso's biological 'born criminal' theory.
- The distinction between natural kinds and human kinds as a framework for understanding criminality.
- Feminist and sociological critiques of biological determinism, including the work of Frances Kellor.

Chapter Objectives

- To explain the historical emergence of criminal anthropology and the theory of the 'born criminal'.
- To critically assess the distinction between natural kinds and human kinds as applied to psychological categories.
- To evaluate how theories of criminality have been shaped by scientific, political, and cultural forces.

CRITICAL THINKING TOOL
HUMAN KINDS AND NATURAL KINDS

Philosophers and scientists have often classified the world into kinds of things: elements, species, diseases, personalities. But not all categories are created equal. Philosophers of science distinguish between *natural kinds*, categories that exist independently of human judgement, such as chemical elements or biological species, and *human kinds*, categories that are shaped by social norms, language, and history. This distinction matters in psychology, especially when we try to decide whether something like 'criminality' is an objective biological category, or a social label shaped by policy and power.

The nineteenth-century science of criminal anthropology treated criminality as a natural kind. Pioneers such as Cesare Lombroso argued that criminals could be identified through biological features, such as the shape of the skull or facial asymmetry. This approach assumed that criminality was innate, measurable, and essential, a biological fact. But critics such as Frances Kellor, working from a more sociological and feminist perspective, rejected this view. For her, criminality was a human kind: a category produced by social conditions, moral expectations, and social forces linked to race, class, and gender.

This distinction between natural and human kinds runs through the history of criminology and continues to shape the field today. The way criminality is categorised, whether as an innate biological fact or as a socially constructed identity, has direct consequences for how individuals are policed, punished, and perceived. These frameworks influence not only criminal justice practices but also psychological theories about behaviour, responsibility, and deviance. Throughout this chapter, the critical thinking tool of natural versus human kinds will help us unpack the ontological and epistemological assumptions that underpin both historical and contemporary approaches to criminal behaviour.

Introduction

Criminal anthropology emerged in the late nineteenth century as a hybrid science that aimed to explain criminal behaviour naturalistically, not as a moral failure or a legal violation but as a biological condition, something rooted in human physiology and evolutionary development. Its central claim was that criminality could be studied, predicted, and even prevented through the empirical analysis of the body. By measuring skulls, cataloguing facial features, and analysing physical anomalies, its early proponents sought to establish criminality as a natural kind, an objective category akin to a disease or biological species.

The field gained momentum during a period of rapid social change. Industrialisation, urbanisation, and migration were transforming cities across Europe and North America, generating widespread concern about public disorder, poverty, and crime. In this context, criminal anthropology promised a scientific solution to the problem of crime: to identify the criminal body, and through it, the criminal mind. But this promise was also its problem. Critics soon challenged the field's reliance on biological determinism, its dehumanising practices, and its role in reinforcing existing hierarchies of race, class, and gender.

In this chapter, we explore how the idea of criminality shifted from being conceptualised as a natural kind to one understood as a human kind, and how the legacy of that shift continues to influence the discipline of psychology today.

Historical Issues

Criminal anthropology emerged in the second half of the nineteenth century, part of a wider intellectual movement to apply Darwinian evolutionary theory to the study of human society. Its leading figure, Cesare Lombroso, claimed that criminality was a biological fact. Some individuals, he argued, were 'born criminals', identifiable by measurable physical traits such as facial asymmetry, sloping foreheads, or protruding jaws. His theory of atavism suggested that these criminals were evolutionary throwbacks, degenerate remnants of a more primitive phase of human development.

This idea gained momentum during a period of dramatic scientific discovery. In 1856, fossilised bones found in Germany's Neander Valley were eventually identified as belonging to *Homo neanderthalensis*, a human species distinct from modern *Homo sapiens*. Further discoveries in France, Belgium, and Java (*Homo erectus* in 1891) confirmed that human history stretched back hundreds of thousands of years, and that our species had evolved through complex, branching pathways. These shocking revelations supported Darwin's theory of natural selection (1859), which proposed that all life, including humans, evolved gradually over time.

But evolution was not always imagined as progress. By the late nineteenth century, the idea of degeneration, that individuals or societies could go into evolutionary reversal and devolve into more primitive forms, began to trouble scientists and popular writers alike. Criminal anthropology was shaped by these anxieties. If some people could advance through evolution, others, it was feared, might regress. Lombroso's work attempted to locate that regression in the criminal body, reinforcing the view that criminality was a natural kind: fixed, measurable, inherited, and degenerate.

These themes filtered into culture as well as science. In Robert Louis Stevenson's *Dr. Jekyll and Mr. Hyde* (1886), the civilised doctor transforms into a violent, ape-like figure, implying a thin boundary separating morality from savagery. In Bram Stoker's *Dracula* (1897), the aristocratic vampire masks his primitive, predatory instincts behind a façade of culture. Such stories reflected a widespread fear that beneath modernity lay ancient, uncontrollable forces, criminality, madness, and desire, all imagined as throwbacks to an earlier stage of human evolution. H. G. Wells's *The Time Machine* (1895) added a futuristic dimension to these anxieties, depicting a world divided into the delicate and feeble Eloi and the subterranean, bestial Morlocks. The Morlocks in particular echoed Lombroso's *Homo criminalis*, an underground race defined by physical brutality and evolutionary regression, imagined through the lens of degeneration theory.

Key Individuals

Cesare Lombroso (1835–1909), the Italian physician and criminologist, is widely credited with founding the discipline of criminal anthropology. Lombroso's work combined anatomical investigation with an encyclopaedic ambition to catalogue human deviance. Drawing on hundreds of prison autopsies, case studies, and measurements, he attempted to build a comprehensive taxonomy of criminal types, each associated with particular physical, psychological, and even moral traits. His vast data collection, although lacking in statistical rigour by modern standards, reflected the positivist ideal of the time: that society's deepest problems could be solved through careful observation and classification. Lombroso did not confine his interest to violent crime; he proposed typologies of political criminals, prostitutes, and 'insane criminals', extending his framework into law, psychiatry, and moral philosophy. His work became a cornerstone of forensic science and criminological training across Europe and beyond, shaping policing practices, prison architecture, and even public perceptions of criminality.

Lombroso's theories extended beyond the male criminal. In *La Donna Delinquente* (*The Female Offender*, 1895), co-authored with Guglielmo Ferrero, he applied the same biological determinism to women, claiming that female criminals were doubly deviant, not only criminal but unnatural in their failure to conform to feminine norms of passivity and morality. His work drew heavily on essentialist ideas about gender and race, linking criminality to non-European ancestry, mental illness, and sexual transgression. His methods constructed an ideal of the white, bourgeois male as the evolutionary standard, pathologising those who deviated from it.

Enrico Ferri (1856–1929), Lombroso's student and collaborator, was a pivotal figure in the transition from biological to sociological criminology. Although he accepted the biological dimensions of criminal anthropology, Ferri introduced a broader framework that considered social and environmental factors in shaping criminal behaviour. A committed socialist, he argued that crime could be influenced by factors such as poverty, lack of education, and working conditions. In this way, Ferri helped push the field towards a more interdisciplinary approach, though he remained committed to a vision of crime as a scientifically manageable phenomenon. His work reflects an early move away from strict natural kinds, and towards a more complex understanding of human kinds shaped by both biology and environment.

Frances Kellor (1873–1952) offered one of the most sustained early critiques of criminal anthropology, grounded in both sociological reasoning and feminist insight. In her *Experimental Sociology* (1899), Kellor directly challenged Lombroso's claims, arguing that the assumption of biological inferiority in criminals was unsupported by evidence. Her research on sensory perception found that delinquents did not possess heightened physical senses, as Lombroso had suggested, but rather displayed no significant physiological abnormalities. 'Instead of proving . . . that the criminal is allied to the savage,' she declared in 1899, 'I found them to disprove it.'

Epistemological Issues

Criminal anthropology's epistemological framework rested on positivism, the philosophical position that claims true knowledge comes only from observable, measurable facts. By treating criminal behaviour as a biological phenomenon, researchers such as Lombroso attempted to build a scientific taxonomy of deviance, grounded in anatomical detail. This approach drew heavily from the emerging methods of physiology which sought to understand behaviour through the study of the brain, nervous system, and physical traits.

For Lombroso and his followers, criminality was a condition legible on the surface of the body, particularly in the face and skull. He drew mimetic comparisons between criminals and animals, arguing that certain anatomical features, such as protruding jaws, large canine teeth, flattened noses, and long arms, resembled those of apes, rodents, or reptiles. These physiognomic traits were, in his view, not only signs of evolutionary regression but also indicators of atavism: the reappearance of traits from a more primitive stage of human development. Criminals, he claimed, mimicked the physical appearance of animals lower on the evolutionary scale, a resemblance that confirmed their moral and psychological inferiority.

Lombroso extended this logic to include tattoos, which posed a conceptual challenge to his biological determinism. Tattoos, unlike skull shape or jaw structure, were not inherited or congenital. Yet he interpreted them as spontaneous expressions of the criminal's primitive instincts. To Lombroso, the decision to tattoo the body revealed an underlying psychological disposition, an aversion to social norms, an affinity with tribal or savage customs, and a disregard for pain or future consequences. In this way, even voluntary bodily markings were reabsorbed into a deterministic framework: outward signs of an innate, deviant nature.

A striking example of this epistemology in action comes from a case recorded in 1911 at Mantellate prison in Italy. Professor Salvatore Ottolenghi, a prominent criminal anthropologist, summoned a 28-year-old prisoner convicted of wife beating to serve as a living case study for a class of police administrators. In front of the class, Ottolenghi measured and scrutinised the man's body. He drew attention to his 'antieurhythmic' (disharmonious) face, receding forehead, enlarged cheekbones, and protruding bones. Scars or callouses were interpreted as further signs of a violent disposition. Ottolenghi also questioned the inmate about his childhood and health history, concluding that the man was 'un tipo inferiore', an inferior type, biologically predisposed to violent behaviour. He even linked this disposition to 'morbid epileptic rage'.

This example reveals the core epistemological assumption of criminal anthropology: that criminality could be objectively known through the body, measured like any other natural phenomenon. Yet as critics would later point out, this supposed objectivity often masked deep social and cultural biases. By treating criminality as a natural kind, the discipline obscured the role of poverty, inequality, and power in shaping who was labelled 'criminal', and how that knowledge was produced.

Frances Kellor was especially critical of how women were judged within criminological frameworks, in theory and in method. Where Lombroso relied on skull measurements and anatomical charts, Kellor turned to qualitative data, letters, interviews, case records, and observational reports in order to understand the lived experiences of women labelled as criminal. Her critique extended beyond scientific frameworks to the patriarchal values embedded within them. By foregrounding cultural expectations, structural inequalities, and the moral lens through which women's behaviour was interpreted, Kellor advanced an understanding of criminality as socially constructed, historically contingent, and responsive to context. In doing so, she positioned herself within a tradition of theorising criminality as a human kind, shaped by norms rather than by nature.

From an entirely different epistemological position again, Charles Goring (1870–1919), a British prison doctor, offered one of the most damaging refutations of Lombroso's theory. In *The English Convict* (1913), Goring conducted statistical studies comparing thousands of convicts with members of the general population. He found no consistent physical differences between the two groups, directly undermining Lombroso's claim that criminality could be identified through the body. Goring concluded that criminal behaviour was more closely linked to mental traits and social disadvantage than to biology alone. While Goring still made generalisations about 'inferior intelligence', his work marked a major epistemological shift: away from anatomical measurement, and towards psychological and statistical methods of understanding criminal behaviour.

Ontological Issues

Criminal anthropology was shaped by a set of deep ontological assumptions, ideas about what kinds of things exist in the world, and what kind of thing criminality is. At its core was the belief that criminality was a biological essence: an inherited and intrinsic part of certain individuals' nature. This essentialist view held that some people were simply born criminal, and that this condition could be observed, classified, and predicted through signs on the body.

The search for such signs animated the work of figures such as the Scottish psychiatrist Thomas Clouston. In 1894, Clouston posed the question: 'Have we among us men and women whose mental cortex is of such quality that in ordinary environment their conduct must necessarily be antisocial and lawless? And if so, what anatomical, physiological, and psychological signs are there to distinguish this criminal and his cortex?' For Clouston, if no such biological signs existed, then criminal anthropology had no foundation. The very existence of the discipline depended on the belief that criminality had material, organic roots, particularly in the brain.

Clouston's ontology extended even to minute anatomical details. He remarked on 'a curious and in itself an unimportant change in the hard palate', found so frequently in criminals, as well as 'idiots, congenital imbeciles, epileptics, and the adolescent insane', that it seemed to confirm the idea of a fundamental defect in brain development. In such accounts, the boundary between criminality, madness, and degeneracy collapsed into a single biological inferiority.

This view of criminality denied the relevance of free will, social structure, or moral reasoning. It replaced agency with anatomy. By reducing the criminal to a pathological body, criminal anthropology helped shape a tradition that sought to locate behaviour solely in brain and body. sometimes at the cost of social context, meaning, and justice.

Power

At the heart of criminal anthropology lies not only a theory of crime but a theory of power: who has the authority to define deviance, and whose bodies and behaviours are subject to surveillance, classification, and control. Cesare Lombroso's model of the 'born criminal' gave scientific legitimacy to pre-existing social hierarchies, reinforcing the marginalisation of the poor, immigrants, women, and racialised groups. By treating criminality as a natural kind, biological and fixed, this approach made criminal status seem inevitable and unchangeable, something to be measured, managed, and punished, rather than understood or reformed.

Frances Kellor challenged this model by shifting the gaze of criminology from the body to the social environment. She rejected the deterministic logic that underpinned Lombroso's science, arguing that crime was a product of poverty, inequality, and exclusion. Her critique was scientific and political. In her 1899 work *Experimental Sociology*, she tested Lombroso's claim that criminals were 'allied to the savage' by examining their sensory capacities. Far from finding enhanced perceptual abilities, she discovered that delinquents performed worse than students on tests of smell and taste. This directly undermined the theory that criminals possessed primitive, animal-like instincts, a trope often used to justify their dehumanisation.

Kellor's research examined the ways criminalised women were described, evaluated, and morally positioned by institutions and society. She argued that female criminality was frequently exaggerated due to prevailing ideals of womanhood. Behaviours such as smoking, swearing, or asserting independence were interpreted as signs of deviance in women, though the same behaviours were normalised or overlooked in men. 'We say woman is worse,' she wrote, 'but we judge her so by comparison with the ideal of woman, not with a common ideal.' Kellor's work demonstrates that the act of defining criminality was itself a form of power. Labelling behaviour as 'natural' served to reinforce social hierarchies and suppress alternative explanations. Her legacy reminds us that psychological classifications do not simply reflect the world; they participate in shaping it. Through naming and categorising, psychology exerts influence over how individuals are understood, governed, and treated.

Chapter Summary

The history of criminal anthropology offers a powerful case study in how scientific knowledge is shaped by cultural assumptions, political contexts, and underlying theories of human nature. In its nineteenth-century origins, criminal anthropology sought to explain crime by seeking evidence in physical features. Influenced by evolutionary theory and driven by the belief in biological determinism, early criminologists such as Cesare Lombroso treated criminality as a natural kind, a fixed and measurable category that could be identified through physical traits.

But this account was never without its critics. Figures such as Frances Kellor challenged the epistemological assumptions, ontological claims, and the political implications of criminal anthropology. For Kellor, criminality was a human kind, a social category produced by economic hardship, cultural norms, and institutional inequality. Her work redirected attention from bodies to environments, from pathology to power. Where Lombroso saw criminality in bone structure, Kellor saw it in the social structure.

The ambivalent relationship between natural kinds and human kinds runs throughout the history of psychology. It shapes how we define mental illness, intelligence, gender, and personality. And it continues to shape contemporary psychology, aspects of which remain invested in understanding the links between brain, body, and behaviour. While today's research methods are more rigorous and sensitive to context, the legacy of early criminal anthropology lingers in debates about neurocriminology, risk prediction, and behavioural genetics. The question remains: when we look to biology to explain crime, what do we gain, and what might we overlook?

At the beginning of this chapter, we encountered Lombroso hunched over the skull of Giuseppe Villella, struck by what he took to be the mark of a born criminal. In that moment of apparent revelation, 'lighted up as if by a flash of inspiration', Lombroso believed he had glimpsed the true nature of crime etched into bone. But what he also revealed was the extraordinary power of psychology not just to describe people but to define them. Villella's skull became more than evidence; it became a symbol, a justification, a warning. Today, we no longer read criminality in the curve of a forehead or the slope of a jaw. But we must still ask: where else might we be looking for it? In a brain scan? A genetic marker or a risk algorithm? The history of criminal anthropology reminds us that every act of classification, every label, every measure, carries with it the weight of interpretation. Psychology, at its best, can illuminate. But it must also learn from the shadow it once cast.

Reflective Questions

1. What does it mean to classify criminality as a 'natural kind', and how did Cesare Lombroso use this classification to support his theory of the born criminal?
2. How did Frances Kellor's sociological approach challenge the assumptions of criminal anthropology?
3. Why is the distinction between natural kinds and human kinds important in understanding the history of psychological science?
4. What role did power play in the formation and application of early criminological theories?
5. How do the historical debates around criminal anthropology continue to shape contemporary biological psychology and criminology today?

Suggested Reading

Fitzgerald, D. (2019). What was sociology? *History of the Human Sciences, 32*(1), 121–137. https://doi.org/10.1177/0952695118808935.

Gurley, J. R. (2009). A history of changes to the criminal personality in the DSM. *History of Psychology, 12*(4), 285–304. https://doi.org/10.1037/a0018101.

Hacking, I. (2007). Kinds of people: Moving targets. *Proceedings of the British Academy, 151*, 285–318. https://doi.org/10.5871/bacad/9780197264249.003.0010.

Hofman, E. (2022). A useful science: Criminal interrogation and the turn to psychology in Germany around 1800. *Journal of the History of the Behavioural Sciences, 58*(3), 319–334. https://doi.org/10.1002/jhbs.22193.

Karstedt, S. (2007). Explorations into the sociology of criminal justice and punishment: Leaving the modernist project behind. *History of the Human Sciences, 20*(2), 51–70. https://doi.org/10.1177/0952695107076199.

Kellor, F. (1899). *Experimental Sociology: Descriptive and analytical*. New York: Macmillan.

King, A. (2006). Serial killing and the postmodern self. *History of the Human Sciences, 19*(3), 109–125. https://doi.org/10.1177/0952695106066544.

Lišková, K., & Moravanská, L. (2021). From class origins to individual psychopathology: Spousal murder according to state socialist Czechoslovak criminology. *History of the Human Sciences, 35*(3–4), 237–259. https://doi.org/10.1177/09526951211027724.

Lombroso, C. (1876/2006). *Criminal Man*. (M. Gibson & N. Rafter, trans.). Durham, NC: Duke University Press.

Molina, J. (2024). British criminology, undercover policing, and racist attacks: Notes on the 'law and order' information infrastructure. *History of the Human Sciences, 38*(2), 56–74. https://doi.org/10.1177/09526951241278590.

Rafter, N. (1997). *Creating Born Criminals*. Urbana: University of Illinois Press.

Rose, N. (2010). 'Screen and intervene': Governing risky brains. *History of the Human Sciences, 23*(1), 79–105. https://doi.org/10.1177/0952695109352415.

Key Terms

Atavism A theory introduced by Lombroso suggesting that criminals are evolutionary throwbacks with physical traits linked to more 'primitive' humans.

Biological Determinism The belief that human behaviour, including criminal behaviour, is controlled by biological or genetic factors rather than by social or environmental influences.

Born Criminal Lombroso's concept of an individual who is biologically predisposed to commit crimes, identifiable by physical characteristics.

Criminal Anthropology A nineteenth-century field that attempted to study criminality through biological and anatomical features, especially of the skull and face.

Criminality The quality or state of being criminal; a concept debated as either biologically innate or socially constructed.

Degeneration Theory The belief that individuals or societies could regress or devolve over time, often used to explain perceived moral or social decline.

Empiricism A method of knowledge based on observation and measurement, central to the positivist scientific approach of criminal anthropology.

Epistemology The branch of philosophy concerned with how we come to know things, how criminality is known or claimed to be known through science.

Essentialism The view that certain traits or behaviours are fixed, natural, and inherent in a group or individual, rather than shaped by context.

Human Kind A social category created by human interaction, culture, and institutions, fluid, contextual, and responsive to change.

Natural Kind A category believed to reflect a real, fixed type in nature, such as a species or chemical element, discovered rather than invented.

Ontological Assumption A belief about the nature of reality, such as whether criminality is an inherent trait or a socially constructed label.

Positivism A scientific approach based on measurable facts and observable phenomena, which shaped criminal anthropology's methods.

Power The capacity to define, judge, and control others, especially through scientific and legal systems that labelled people as criminals.

ONLINE RESOURCES

Visit the Instructor & Student Resources website at routledgelearning.com/bpscoretextbooks for free digital resources, including:

- Interactive quizzes and flashcards to test your knowledge
- Links to useful websites and videos
- Instructor manual, lecture slides, and course guide to enhance teaching and save instructors time

4 Remembering Herculine

The Looping Effects of Sexuality

Chapter Overview

This chapter critically explores how sexuality emerged as a central concept in psychology, medicine, and society thought during the second half of the nineteenth century. Moving beyond a biological understanding of sex, the chapter traces the historical construction of sexuality as a site of identity, regulation, and scientific interest. Drawing on Michel Foucault's *History of Sexuality* (1978), it challenges the assumption that sexuality was simply repressed in the Victorian era, instead highlighting the production of sexuality through the proliferations of discourse, classification, and control.

The chapter introduces key sexologists such as Richard von Krafft-Ebing, Magnus Hirschfeld and Havelock Ellis, whose work transformed sexual behaviours into medical and legal categories. These scientific frameworks are contrasted with the erotic arts, artistic and spiritual traditions (*ars erotica*, e.g. the *Kama Sutra*) that understood sexuality to be a form of expression and experience rather than as a potential pathology.

Building on the distinction between natural and human kinds, the chapter introduces Ian Hacking's concept of the looping effect. The chapter concludes by showing how scientific classifications of sexuality shaped, and were reshaped by, the individuals they described, illustrating the complex interplay between knowledge, power, and identity in psychological thought.

Remembering Herculine

On 8 November 1838, in the small French town of Saint-Jean-d'Angély, a child named Herculine Barbin was born and assigned female at birth. Raised and educated in a convent school, Barbin trained as a teacher and lived in a deeply religious, all-female environment. But by the time Barbin was in her early twenties, things began to change. Barbin developed facial hair, a deeper voice, and increasing discomfort with a body that did not conform to a single, culturally legible sex. Barbin had also fallen in love with a fellow teacher, Sara, prompting scandal. In 1860, under pressure from religious authorities and physicians, Barbin underwent a medical examination. The doctors concluded that she was 'really' a man, though modern medicine would likely classify Barbin as intersex, having traits that did not align with binary sexual categories. Barbin's life, caught between categories, speaks to the violence of a culture unable to recognise or accommodate ambiguity, where living between genders was pathologised rather than

DOI: 10.4324/9781003565482-4

protected. Following a court ruling, Herculine was legally reclassified as male and forced to adopt the name Abel. Removed from the convent, separated from the only community they ever knew, and no longer able to live openly with Sara, Barbin drifted into poverty and isolation in Paris. In 1868, at the age of just 29, Herculine was found dead in a boarding house room, having died by suicide. Beside their bed was a poignant memoir, later published as *Herculine Barbin: Being the Recently Discovered Memoirs of a Nineteenth-Century French Hermaphrodite*.

Chapter Contents

- A historical and philosophical account of how sexuality became a scientific category in the nineteenth-century human sciences.
- An exploration of the *looping effect* of human kinds and the ways classifications influence identity.
- A critical comparison of medical, legal, artistic, and spiritual approaches to sexuality and its regulation.

Chapter Objectives

- To understand how sexuality was historically constructed as a category of scientific and psychological inquiry.
- To analyse the distinction between natural kinds and human kinds, and how these frame and form sexual identities.
- To describe and explain Ian Hacking's *looping effect* as a conceptual tool for understanding the feedback between classification, identity, and power and its role in 'making up people'.

CRITICAL THINKING TOOL
THE LOOPING EFFECT

In psychology, some categories don't merely describe people, they *change* people. Canadian philosopher of science Ian Hacking introduced the concept of *the looping effect* of human kinds to explain how classifications in the human sciences can create the very individuals they are meant to study.

Unlike *natural kinds* (e.g. water, gravity, electricity), which exist independently of our theories about them, *human kinds* (e.g. 'homosexuals', 'fetishists', 'nymphomaniacs') are classifications of people that are embedded in social and historical contexts. These categories are not discovered; they are created through scientific, legal, and cultural discourse. Once created, they begin to loop.

How does the loop work?

1. Experts create a classification: for example, nineteenth-century sexologists labelled certain sexual behaviours as 'deviant' and classified individuals who displayed them under new terms such as 'homosexual' or 'pervert'.

2. Once a label exists, individuals begin to see themselves through that lens. People recognise themselves in the category and adopt it. What was once simply an unremarkable behaviour becomes part of an identity.
3. People change in response to the category. Some conform, some resist, and some organise politically around the identity, adopting the category, forming communities around it, and challenging the original meaning of the label.
4. The category evolves. As people respond to the classification, the category itself changes, creating a feedback loop between knowledge, identity, and behaviour. Experts change their minds. Eventually, for example, homosexuality's pathological origins are abandoned and it becomes normalised.

This chapter shows how sexuality in the nineteenth century was constructed through discourses of medicine, law, and science. Classifications such as 'homosexual' were not simply medical diagnoses, they were *identity forming*. These new human kinds created lived realities: people came to live their labels. 'Homosexual' was initially a clinical label, but it eventually became a rallying point for LGBTQIA+ identity, pride, and political activism. Hacking's looping effect captures this co-constructed interaction between psychological knowledge and personal experience.

Introduction

Sexuality is a central aspect of human life, shaping personal identity, social relationships, cultural expression, and power dynamics. Its significance lies not only in the physical dimension of sex but in how societies have understood, regulated, and discussed it throughout history. As a concept, sexuality transcends biological sex and intersects with morality, law, psychology, medicine, and art. Understanding the historical and conceptual development of sexuality allows us to explore how science, the state, the medical and legal professions, and religious institutions have influenced personal and collective perceptions of desire, behaviour, and identity.

The nineteenth century marked a critical period when sexuality became a formal category of scientific inquiry, particularly through the work of a new category of experts called sexologists. Sexuality became an object of knowledge, social control, and moral regulation. One unintended consequence was that the proliferation of diverse identities provided a foundation for modern debates on sexual rights and freedoms. By examining the history of sexuality, we gain a deeper understanding of contemporary struggles around sexual identity, sexual health, and the politics of bodily autonomy.

Historical Issues

The concept of sexuality as a fundamental aspect of personal identity as distinct from mere biological reproduction began to take shape in the mid- to late nineteenth century. Before this, sex was primarily understood in terms of its biological and reproductive function, with cultural variations in how it was framed by religious, moral, and social norms. However, as the state began to take a greater interest in the health, fertility, and morality of the population, sexuality became a focal point of scientific and medical inquiry. This shift from sex to sexuality introduced new ways of thinking about human desire, identity, and behaviour.

Michel Foucault argues in *The History of Sexuality* (1978) that the nineteenth century did not *repress* sexuality, as was often thought, but in fact *constructed* it. Through legal, medical, and moral discourses, sexuality became an object of study, a category thought to be able to illuminate a variety of social concerns. Foucault argued that rather than hiding sexuality, societies such as those in Victorian Britain systematised and classified it, creating not only the scientific study of sexual behaviour but also new forms of identity in the process.

Institutions, including medicine, the emerging human sciences, and the law, began to develop detailed taxonomies of sexual behaviour. What were once seen as isolated immoral acts became categorised as intrinsic sexual identities, with terms such as 'homosexual', 'nymphomaniac', 'fetishist', and 'pervert' entering the medical lexicon. Although sexuality began to take shape as a medico-scientific category in Europe and North America, elsewhere it remained a source of morality and pleasure in religion and the erotic arts.

Key Individuals

Richard von Krafft-Ebing's (1840–1902) *Psychopathia Sexualis* (1886) systematically categorised sexual behaviours and established many of the terms still used in discussions of sexual identity today. Krafft-Ebing was particularly concerned with what he called sexual 'perversions', including homosexuality, fetishism, and sadomasochism. He viewed these behaviours as inherent deviations from the sexual norm, often linking them to biological or hereditary causes. His work helped lay the foundation for later studies of sexual pathology and psychiatry, making sexuality a legitimate subject of medical and psychological study.

Sigmund Freud (1856–1939), the inventor of psychoanalysis, developed influential theories about the relationship between sexuality and the unconscious in books such as *The Interpretation of Dreams* (1899) and *Three Essays on the Theory of Sexuality* (1905). He argued that sexuality was central to human development and introduced concepts such as the Oedipus complex. His theory of psychosexual development suggested that early childhood experiences profoundly influenced adult sexual behaviour. Freud's ideas on sexuality profoundly shaped not only psychology but also broader cultural understandings of sexual identity, repression, and development.

Ida Craddock (1857–1902) was an American sexologist and mystic who advocated for sexual reform and education, especially for women. She wrote about the spiritual dimensions of sexual intercourse, arguing that it could be a divine and transformative experience. Her works include *Heavenly Bridegrooms* (1894) and *The Wedding Night* (1900). Her work was considered obscene by authorities, and she faced repeated legal challenges. Persecuted by zealous anti-obscenity crusader Anthony Comstock, in 1902 she was convicted under US federal obscenity laws for distributing sex-education material through the mail. Following years of harassment, she was devastated by the prospect of five years' imprisonment. On the day before she was due to report for her sentence, Craddock died by suicide on 16 October 1902. She left behind two letters, one for her mother, and one for the public, in which she defended her work and condemned Comstock. Her suicide note was widely reprinted in newspapers, turning her into a tragic martyr for the cause of sexual reform. Her works on women's sexual autonomy and pleasure influenced later feminist discussions on sexual ethics and spirituality.

Havelock Ellis (1859–1939) was an English physician, writer, and one of the most influential early figures in the study of human sexuality. Trained in medicine, Ellis was part of the broader fin-de-siècle movement that sought to challenge Victorian moral rigidity through science, art, and psychology. His most famous work, the multivolume *Studies in the Psychology of Sex* (1897–1928), broke significant ground in bringing topics such as masturbation, homosexuality, and erotic fantasy into the realm of scientific inquiry. Ellis approached sexuality as a natural, diverse, and essential part of human life. Although he used the term 'inversion' to describe homosexuality (common at the time), he saw sexual variation as part of a continuum rather than a deviation. He also promoted the term 'uranism', an attempt to frame male same-sex attraction in classical terms, a rhetorical move to shift its meaning away from criminality or medicalised deviance. Ellis was also one of the first sexologists to take women's sexuality seriously, advocating for greater sexual freedom and exploring female desire without the heavy moralism typical of his era. Ellis's interest in eugenics evidences the connection between sexuality and biopower.

Albert Moll (1862–1939) furthered Krafft-Ebing's ideas by emphasising the biological and psychological dimensions of sexuality. He asserted that sexual behaviours were integral to human life and that deviations from normative heterosexuality were natural variations rather than moral failings. In his *The Sexual Life of the Child* (1908), one of the earliest works on childhood sexuality, Moll advised parents to provide sex education to their children. He also contributed to the understanding of sexual diversity, moving the conversation away from the religious or purely moral realm into the scientific.

Magnus Hirschfeld (1868–1935), a German physician, is considered one of the most important early advocates for the rights of sexual minorities. He was the author of *The Homosexuality of Men and Women* (1914). He founded the Scientific-Humanitarian Committee in 1897, which aimed to decriminalise homosexuality, and was a co-founder of The Institute for Sexual Science in Berlin, which became a hub for research on gender and sexuality until it was closed by the Nazis in 1933. His theory about sexuality emphasised that it was an innate characteristic, moving away from the idea that homosexuality was a disease.

Marie Stopes (1880–1958), one of the few prominent pioneering female sexologists, made significant contributions to discussions of female sexuality and reproductive rights. Her *Married Love* (1918) was groundbreaking for its open discussion of female sexual pleasure and contraception, topics that were taboo at the time. Stopes's advocacy for birth control and sexual education made her a controversial figure, but she remains an important voice in the history of sexuality, particularly regarding women's autonomy over their bodies. Unlike some of her male contemporaries, Stopes's focus on female pleasure challenged the dominant narrative that framed women as passive sexual beings.

Epistemological Issues

The study of sexuality in the nineteenth century diverged sharply between scientific and artistic traditions, although there were overlapping structures of meaning. The classificatory scientific approach relied on case studies, medical reports, and psychiatric evaluations to define sexual norms and deviations. Scientific sexology sought to establish a taxonomy of sexual behaviours, categorising them as either healthy, deviant, normal, or abnormal, based on biological, psychological, and hereditarian theories. In this tradition, sexuality was viewed as something that could be measured, analysed, and corrected, making it an object of scientific control. Foucault, somewhat controversially, highlighted how a sex act that might have been considered a relatively inconsequential 'bucolic pleasure' at one time became the object of legal and medical intervention at another, leading to the nineteenth-century French farmhand Charles Jouy being labelled and incarcerated as a 'dangerous individual'.

Written by 'Walter', *My Secret Life* (1888–1894) is an autobiographical, multivolume work that recounts in graphic detail the anonymous author's extensive sexual exploits. According to Foucault, Walter's obsessive detailing of his erotic and sexual life parallels the rise of scientific and medical interest in sexuality, where sexual behaviours were categorised, analysed, and pathologised. Just as sexologists systematically documented and classified sexual deviance in medical texts, Walter, in his own way, contributed to the construction of a detailed narrative about sexuality, despite operating outside official, scientific discourse.

Foucault contrasted the development of a science of sex (*'scientia sexualis'*) in North America and Europe with the history of the erotic arts (*'ars erotica'*) in Eastern cultures such as India. This latter approach appreciated sexuality from an experiential and expressive angle. Written between the second and fourth centuries CE by Vātsyāyana, the *Kama Sutra* is a Sanskrit text on love, relationships, and social conduct. It is a sophisticated approach to desire, seeing it as integral to achieving a balanced life in harmony with the other goals of duty, prosperity, and spiritual liberation. Similarly, the erotic carvings found on Indian temples, such as those at Khajuraho (ninth to tenth centuries CE) and the Sun Temple at Konark (thirteenth century CE), depict explicit sexual acts as part of a broader visual narrative that includes gods, daily life, and mythological scenes. These carvings are linked to tantric traditions, where sexual union symbolises cosmic creation and spiritual awakening.

The epistemological divide between these traditions reflects broader tensions in the nineteenth century: while science sought to regulate and control human bodies and behaviours, art emphasised expression, liberation, and the individual's relationship to their desires. As always, the human sciences developed by integrating insights from both approaches.

Ontological Issues

Both scientific texts and Walter's autobiographical narrative evidence Foucault's 'incitement to discourse' thesis because they created a form of documentation and categorisation of sexual acts and identities, which in turn produced a knowledge, and then an experience, of sexuality. For Foucault, this process is not repressive but productive, because it leads to the construction of sexuality as both an object of discourse (an epistemology) and a form of being (an ontology). Walter's compulsive record-keeping mirrored the scientific obsession with analysing and cataloguing sexual behaviour, highlighting how, even in personal and illicit contexts, discourse about sexuality proliferated during this era.

If sex is a natural kind, generated by evolution, then sexuality is a human kind, a cultural construct. The scientific tradition of the nineteenth century however approached sexuality through an ontological framework that conceptualised sexual behaviour *as though it were* a natural kind, a fixed category determined by biology or heredity. According to this view, people were inherently predisposed to certain sexual behaviours, whether 'unnatural' or 'deviant', and these behaviours could be objectively studied and classified. This reductionist ontology assumed that there was a natural order to human sexuality, with heterosexuality as the normative default and deviations such as homosexuality, fetishism, and nymphomania as biologically determined aberrations.

On the other hand, artistic and some religious traditions viewed sexuality as a human kind, shaped by culture, experience, and individual expression. In this framework, sexuality was not a fixed biological reality but a fluid and dynamic aspect of human life, capable of evolving with cultural norms, personal experiences, and social contexts. The erotic arts of Eastern tradition, for example, conceptualised sexuality as a vital part of human existence, intertwined with pleasure, morality, and spirituality. This ontology allowed for a more diverse and inclusive understanding of sexual practices and desires, rejecting the rigid classifications imposed by the scientific tradition. It is important to note that because human kinds are social-historical constructs they generate looping effects, whereas natural kinds do not.

Power

Michel Foucault offered a profound critique of how societies construct and regulate sexuality. He argued that sexuality is not a natural given but a historical construct, shaped by power relations. This makes sexuality an interesting phenomenon (and explains why Foucault dismissed sex as 'boring'). Medical, psychiatric, and legal discourses, together with anxieties about birth rates and moral campaigns against prostitution, inspired a collective 'polymorphous incitement to discourse'. People were encouraged to talk about their sexual desires, which were then classified and controlled. Whereas mechanisms of power must merely *accommodate* natural kinds, power can *construct* human kinds in alignment with various social and political agendas. This is why looping effects are deeply intertwined with power.

Throughout history, sexuality has been subjected to many forms of power. Two salient examples are what Michel Foucault described as disciplinary power and biopower. Disciplinary power seeks to classify, regulate, and normalise sexual behaviours, to enforce social norms. Biopower on the other hand links individual health and reproduction to the well-being of the population. Discourses about sexuality proliferated, not through repression but as a means to categorise 'normal' and 'abnormal', enabling the state and institutions to intervene in individual lives and manage the population's biological capacity for control and productivity.

Chapter Summary

Unlike the concept of sex, sexuality, as we understand it today, did not simply evolve from nature; it was constructed, codified, and circulated through nineteenth-century institutions, disciplines, and discourses. This chapter explored how medical, legal, and psychological frameworks redefined sexual acts into sexual identities, turning private behaviours into matters of public concern and clinical scrutiny. Drawing on Foucault's challenge to the 'repressive hypothesis', we have seen how sexuality was not in fact silenced in the Victorian era but rather was produced and proliferated through confession, surveillance, and classification.

Using the critical thinking tool of Ian Hacking's looping effect, we examined how the scientific invention of categories such as 'homosexual' or 'invert' had reflexive power: once named, individuals began to inhabit, resist, or transform these impositions. Hacking's notion of 'making up people' refers to the process by which new categories of human beings are created through scientific, medical, or legal classifications, and how people come to see themselves through these newly created categories. The result is a dynamic process where people do not just fit into categories, they inhabit them and change them. As identities are made and remade, the boundary between pathology and pride, stigma and solidarity, becomes historically contingent and politically charged. What begins as a form of control becomes, paradoxically, a source of selfhood. Sexuality, then, is not a fixed essence but a mutable history of how people are seen, see themselves, and are seen anew.

And yet history is never abstract. The life of Herculine Barbin reminds us that psychological categories had, and still have, consequences. Born in 1838 and reclassified against their will, Barbin's body became a battleground between religion, medicine, and identity. Today, Herculine's birthday, 8 November, is marked as Intersex Day of Remembrance, a quiet tribute to those whose lives have been shaped by the politics of sexuality.

Reflective Questions

1. How does Michel Foucault's critique of the 'repressive hypothesis' change the way we understand Victorian sexuality?
2. In what ways did early sexologists like Krafft-Ebing and Havelock Ellis contribute to both the medicalisation and normalisation of sexuality?
3. What is the difference between a natural kind and a human kind, and why is this distinction important when studying sexuality?
4. What does Ian Hacking's concept of the 'looping effect' reveal about the relationship between classification and self-identity?
5. How do artistic and spiritual traditions (such as *ars erotica* and the *Kama Sutra*) offer alternative understandings of sexuality compared to scientific sexology?

Suggested Reading

Brinkmann, S. (2005). Human kinds and looping effects in psychology: Foucauldian and hermeneutic perspectives. *Theory & Psychology*, *15*(6), 769–791. https://doi.org/10.1177/0959354305059332.

Csányi, G. (2025). Demography, pleasure, state, and market in socialist sexology: Medical-sexological and sexual-psychological public discourse in socialist Hungary through counselling books from a social-political perspective. *Journal of the History of the Behavioral Sciences*, *61*(1), e70015. https://doi.org/10.1002/jhbs.70015.

Fischer, N., & Seidman, S. (2016). *Introducing the New Sexuality Studies: 3rd edition* (Third ed.). Abingdon, Oxon: Routledge, Taylor & Francis Group.

Foucault, M. (1990). *The History of Sexuality*. Vol. 1, *The Will to Knowledge*. Harmondsworth: Penguin.

Hacking, I. (1986). Making up people. In T. C. Heller, M. Sosna, & D. E. Wellbery (Eds), *Reconstructing Individualism: Autonomy, individuality and the self in Western thought* (pp. 222–236). Stanford, CA: Stanford University Press.

Hacking, I. (1995). The looping effects of human kinds. In D. Sperber, D. Premack, & A. J. Premack (Eds), *Causal Cognition: A multidisciplinary debate*. Oxford: Clarendon Press.

Healy-Cullen, S., & Morison, T. (2024). Extending sexual scripting theory through critical discursive psychology: An analytical approach to explore the performance of sexual identities. *Theory & Psychology, 34*(6), 757–776. https://doi.org/10.1177/09593543241282330.

Leng, K. (2015). The personal is scientific: Women, gender, and the production of sexological knowledge in Germany and Austria, 1900–1931. *History of Psychology, 18*(3), 238–251. https://doi.org/10.1037/a0039519.

Leng, K., & Sutton, K. (2020). Histories of sexology today: Reimagining the boundaries of *scientia sexualis*. *History of the Human Sciences, 34*(1), 3–9. https://doi.org/10.1177/0952695120927172.

Marrow, E. (2023). 'Why should other people be the judge': The codification of assessment criteria for gender-affirming care, 1970s–1990s. *History of Psychology, 26*(3), 210–246. https://doi.org/10.1037/hop0000238.

McCarthy, T. (1981). Freud and the problem of sexuality. *Journal of the History of the Behavioral Sciences, 17*, 332–339. https://doi.org/10.1002/1520-6696(198107)17:3<332::AID-JHBS2300170304>3.0.CO;2-I.

Rutherford, A., & Pettit, M. (2015). Feminism and/in/as psychology: The public sciences of sex and gender. *History of Psychology, 18*(3), 223–237. https://doi.org/10.1037/a0039533.

Weeks, J. (2009). *Sexuality* (Third ed.). Abingdon, Oxon: Routledge.

Key Terms

Ars Erotica A tradition found in Eastern cultures that treats sexuality as an art form concerned with experience, pleasure, and spiritual fulfilment.

Biopower Michel Foucault's concept of power that regulates populations through institutions such as medicine, education, and public health.

Disciplinary Power Power that works at the individual level to shape behaviour, norms, and identity through surveillance and categorisation.

Erotic Arts Creative expressions—such as literature, sculpture, and visual art—that explore themes of desire, pleasure, and sexuality.

Fetishism A sexual attraction to specific objects, materials, or body parts, often pathologised in early sexology.

Homosexuality Historically, a term used in medical and legal contexts to categorise same-sex desire; later reclaimed as a positive sexual identity.

Human Kind A category of people created through social, cultural, or scientific classification, which can influence behaviour and self-identity.

Looping Effect A concept by Ian Hacking describing how people change in response to the categories used to describe them, which in turn changes the category itself.

Making Up People Hacking's term for how scientific or bureaucratic labels create new types of identities, shaping how individuals understand themselves and behave.

Medicalisation The process by which non-medical experiences (such as sexuality) are classified and treated as medical conditions or disorders.

Natural Kind A category that exists independently of social context, such as chemical elements or biological traits, assumed to be objectively discovered.

Nymphomania A historical term used to pathologise women's sexual desire, especially when it deviated from expected norms.

Pathologisation The framing of certain behaviours or identities as abnormal or diseased, often leading to their regulation or treatment.

Psychosexual Development A theory by Sigmund Freud suggesting that human sexuality develops through a series of stages during early childhood.

Scientia sexualis Michel Foucault's term for the Western scientific discourse that seeks to uncover the 'truth' of sex through confession, classification, and regulation.

Sex A biological classification based on physical characteristics such as chromosomes, hormones, and reproductive organs.

Sexology The scientific study of human sexual behaviour, function, and identity, especially popularised in the nineteenth century.

Sexuality The socially and historically constructed understanding of sexual behaviour, identity, and desire; shaped by culture, science, and power.

FREE INSTRUCTOR & STUDENT RESOURCES

ONLINE RESOURCES

Visit the Instructor & Student Resources website at routledgelearning.com/bpscoretextbooks for free digital resources, including:

- Interactive quizzes and flashcards to test your knowledge
- Links to useful websites and videos
- Instructor manual, lecture slides, and course guide to enhance teaching and save instructors time

5 The Queen of Hysterics

Hysteria and the Mimetic Body

Chapter Overview

This chapter explores the historical diagnosis of hysteria and its transformation from being understood as a neurological condition to being theorised as a psychological and symbolic disorder. Focusing on the work of Jean-Martin Charcot, Sigmund Freud, and Hippolyte Bernheim, it traces shifts in how hysteria was conceptualised, observed, and treated. Charcot's emphasis on visual diagnosis and theatrical demonstrations gave legitimacy to hysteria but reinforced patriarchal structures of power. Freud's focus on repressed trauma and unconscious symbolism introduced psychoanalytic concepts, while Bernheim's work on suggestion opened new ways of thinking about the condition.

The chapter introduces the critical thinking tool of mimesis, inviting a critical interpretation of hysterical symptoms as performances shaped by social constraint. Women's suffering is positioned not only as individual pathology but also as embodied protest within a restrictive gender order. By interrogating epistemological, ontological, and power dynamics, readers are encouraged to think critically about how psychological categories are constructed and how they function within broader cultural narratives. The historical lens invites reflection on contemporary issues, such as gendered diagnoses, medical authority, and the social shaping of distress, making hysteria a powerful case study in the psychology of society.

The Queen of Hysterics

She was called the Queen of Hysterics. Each week in the 1880s, Marie 'Blanche' Wittman was wheeled into the cavernous lecture hall of the Salpêtrière Hospital in Paris, watched by a rapt crowd of doctors, journalists, and artists. Under the clinical gaze of Dr Jean-Martin Charcot, Blanche would enter a trance. Her body writhed and contorted into dramatic poses of ecstasy, terror, and collapse, symptoms, it was said, of a damaged nervous system. Flashbulbs popped. Sketches were made. We know this scene not just through texts but through images. In André Brouillet's iconic 1887 painting, *A Clinical Lesson at the Salpêtrière*, Blanche is frozen in one of her dramatic poses, supported by a nurse, while Charcot lectures with calm authority. The room is filled with the faces of men who would go on to shape neurology and psychiatry: Georges Gilles de la Tourette, who would lend his name to the syndrome of involuntary tics; Joseph Babinski, future describer of the reflex that bears his name; and Paul Richer, an artist-physician who would help codify the visual language of hysteria. The painting captures not just a medical demonstration but a moment of cultural production, where the female body became spectacle, specimen, and symbol. Originally admitted to the Salpêtrière as a troubled domestic servant, Blanche quickly became

DOI: 10.4324/9781003565482-5

one of Charcot's favourite patients. Her 'attacks' under hypnosis became more stylised over time, eerily consistent with the hysterical sequences outlined by Charcot himself. Critics began to ask whether these episodes were not spontaneous at all but learned, possibly even rehearsed. In this world of white coats and male stares, suffering could be theatrical, even empowering. Perhaps her seizures were not simply symptoms but responses, imitative displays shaped by what the doctors wanted to see. Her body may have been considered pathological but it also became iconic, immortalised in medical atlases, art, and even poetry. Long after her symptoms faded, Blanche remained a spectral presence in the history of psychology, a reminder that trauma does not always speak in words, and that diagnosis may sometimes silence more than it discloses.

Chapter Contents

- Traces the development of hysteria from the nineteenth to the early twentieth century, focusing on Charcot, Freud, and Bernheim.
- Critically explores how hysterical symptoms mirrored and resisted social expectations of femininity and power.
- Introduces the critical thinking tool of mimesis to understand hysteria as a symbolic, embodied protest.

Chapter Objectives

- To understand how hysteria was diagnosed and treated differently across time and place, with attention to cultural and gender norms.
- To analyse the role of mimesis as a critical lens through which hysterical symptoms can be interpreted as social performances.
- To reflect on the power dynamics between doctors and patients and consider how these shaped historical and contemporary understandings of psychological distress.

CRITICAL THINKING TOOL
MIMESIS

In the history of psychology, *mimesis* refers to imitation, but not in a simple or mechanical sense, for example, when children copy each other in play. Mimesis (a word related in meaning to *mime* and *mimic*) is the deep, embodied symbolic process of expressing what cannot be said in words. In the context of hysteria, particularly in the nineteenth century, mimesis becomes a tool for understanding how symptoms might have *imitated* or *mimicked* the social, emotional, and political conditions in which women lived. When women in patriarchal societies were denied the right to speak openly, make choices, or express discontent, their bodies sometimes 'spoke' for them through paralysis, fainting, aphasia, or convulsions. These behaviours were not random or meaningless; they mimicked the limitations society imposed on them. In acting out these cultural scripts, hysterical woman were tragic performers of their own repression.

By thinking mimetically, we can approach hysteria not as a straightforward medical disorder but as a socially embedded drama of expression and resistance. Hysterical symptoms were often theatrical, emotional, and physically striking, qualities that mirrored the extreme binaries of femininity in Victorian culture: the saintly, passive 'angel' versus the uncontrollable, deceptive 'devil'. Mimesis helps us explore how social norms, expectations, and power relations become inscribed in the body. It remains relevant today in helping us understand psychosomatic illness, gender norms, and collective behaviour.

Introduction

Originating in ancient Greek medicine, *hystera* meaning 'uterus', hysteria was long believed to be a disorder specific to women. By the late nineteenth century, however, hysteria had become a subject of serious scientific inquiry, particularly across France, Germany, Britain, and the United States. It was marked by a striking array of symptoms: fainting, paralysis, mutism, convulsions, and dramatic displays of emotion.

At the Salpêtrière Hospital in Paris, neurologist Jean-Martin Charcot redefined hysteria as a biological disorder. Through visual observation, photography, and hypnosis, he made hysteria visible, both clinically and theatrically. Among his students was Sigmund Freud, who spent several months with Charcot in 1886. Freud, who was also influenced by Hippolyte Bernheim's work on suggestion, reinterpreted hysteria as a psychological phenomenon, proposing that hysterical symptoms were symbolic expressions of repressed trauma, psychic wounds made visible through the body.

Although the term *hysterical* still appears in everyday language to describe someone perceived as irrational or emotionally out of control, the medical diagnosis of hysteria disappeared from the medical literature before the outbreak of the First World War. Yet, far from a historical curiosity, hysteria played a foundational role in the emergence of psychological approaches to mental illness. Its study helped transform understandings of mind, body, and behaviour, influencing both clinical practice and cultural imagination.

Historical Issues

By the late nineteenth century, hysteria had become a notorious, contested, and charismatic diagnosis. In different cultural and medical contexts, it revealed as much about prevailing social attitudes as it did about individual patients. While understood in general terms as a disorder of the nerves marked by symptoms such as paralysis, emotional instability, and convulsions, its causes and treatments varied dramatically across national settings.

In Britain, physicians such as George Savage and Henry Maudsley framed hysteria within a moral discourse shaped by Victorian ideals of discipline, rationality, and emotional control. Hysteria was often interpreted as a failure of willpower, particularly in women. Treatments sought to restore order through isolation, routine, and rest, with some resorting to controversial surgical procedures. The emphasis on self-regulation reflected a broader concern with social respectability and gendered ideals of emotional restraint.

In Germany, medical figures such as Wilhelm Griesinger and Emil Kraepelin viewed hysteria as a symptom of inherited degeneration. Rooted in biological and hereditary explanations, their approach contributed to the development of scientific psychiatry but also reinforced stigma. German theories drew a sharper line between neurology and emerging psychological approaches, treating hysteria more as a sign of social decay than individual distress.

Across the Atlantic, American neurologist Silas Weir Mitchell promoted the 'rest cure', a regime of enforced inactivity aimed at quieting the 'nervous' female body. This treatment was famously critiqued by Charlotte Perkins Gilman in *The Yellow Wallpaper* (1892), which portrayed how the rest cure could intensify, rather than relieve, women's psychological suffering. In the United States, hysteria was shaped by cultural ideals of femininity, domesticity, and productivity, reflecting anxieties about women's changing roles in a rapidly industrialising society.

Beyond the clinic, hysteria became a cultural mirror. It reinforced gendered assumptions about irrationality and emotional excess, while also capturing broader fears about modernity, urban stress, technological change, and shifting gender dynamics. The figure of the hysterical woman appeared in literature, art, and theatre, symbolising both vulnerability and defiance. The history of hysteria thus tells us not only about medicine but also about power, gender, and the limits of social conformity.

Key Individuals

At the Salpêtrière Hospital in Paris, neurologist Jean-Martin Charcot (1825–1893) transformed hysteria into a legitimate object of medical study. He rejected older theories that attributed hysteria to the 'wandering uterus', arguing instead that it had a neurological basis. Charcot was renowned for his theatrical clinical demonstrations, often involving patients such as Augustine, whose seizures, mutism, and postures became semi-public spectacles. Using hypnosis and photography, Charcot created a visual taxonomy of hysteria, where symptoms were made visible, classifiable, and dramatic. His work medicalised the condition and reinforced the mimetic nature of hysterical symptoms: patients appeared to 'perform' their suffering in response to medical and social expectations.

Hippolyte Bernheim (1840–1919), A contemporary of Charcot, took a sharply contrasting approach. Whereas Charcot saw hypnosis as a sign of neurological abnormality, Bernheim viewed it as a psychological state that anyone could enter. He introduced the idea that *suggestion*, both verbal and social, played a central role in hysteria. For Bernheim, symptoms were not hardwired in the brain but shaped by the meanings and expectations imposed by others. Freud's rejection of the visual approach to hysteria can be traced to his meeting with Bernheim in 1889.

In Vienna, Josef Breuer (1842–1925) developed the therapeutic principle of *catharsis*, the idea that expressing previously repressed emotions could alleviate psychological symptoms. His treatment of Bertha Pappenheim, known as *Anna O.*, is often seen as the foundational case of psychoanalysis. Under hypnosis, Breuer encouraged Anna O. to speak about her traumatic experiences. As she verbalised her memories, her symptoms seemed to diminish. This led to the now-famous term *talking cure*, coined by Pappenheim herself, which would become a central pillar of psychoanalytic therapy. Breuer's emphasis on emotional expression rather than neurological classification marked a pivotal epistemological shift in understanding hysteria.

Sigmund Freud (1856–1939) collaborated with Breuer on *Studies on Hysteria* (1895), expanding and deepening the psychological interpretation of the disorder. Initially influenced by Charcot's use of hypnosis, Freud gradually abandoned hypnosis in favour of free association, dream analysis, and the systematic uncovering of unconscious conflict. He argued that hysterical symptoms were symbolic expressions of repressed trauma, often rooted in sexuality and early childhood experience. In *The Aetiology of Hysteria* (1896) Freud proposed that these symptoms were linked to repressed memories of sexual trauma. Though he later rejected the politely named 'seduction theory', the symbolic reading of bodily symptoms as disguised expressions of unconscious desire would remain central to psychoanalysis. In Freud's hands, hysteria became a mimetic performance of inner psychological conflict.

Though best known by her pseudonym Anna O., Bertha Pappenheim (1859–1936) was more than a case study. A highly intelligent and creative woman, she suffered from a range of psychosomatic symptoms in her early twenties, namely paralysis, hallucinations, and mutism, which she described with vivid metaphors and imaginative insight. Her collaboration with Breuer gave birth to the idea that repressed emotions could be 'spoken out' through therapy. After her recovery, Pappenheim became a pioneering social reformer, feminist, and writer. Her later life challenges the image of the passive female patient and offers a counternarrative of resilience and resistance.

In the United States, Charlotte Perkins Gilman (1860–1935) transformed her personal experience with hysteria into one of the most enduring critiques of patriarchal medicine. Diagnosed with 'nervous exhaustion', she was subjected to Silas Weir Mitchell's 'rest cure', a treatment that advised against reading, writing, and intellectual activity. The cure worsened her condition and inspired her 1892 short story *The Yellow Wallpaper*, in which a woman descends into madness under similar treatment. Gilman's work illustrates how hysteria functioned as a social metaphor. In her hands, hysteria was a mimetic expression of the psychological consequences of enforced passivity and domestic imprisonment.

Louise Augustine Gleizes (c. 1861–unknown), known as Augustine, was one of Jean-Martin Charcot's most celebrated and visually exploited patients at the Salpêtrière Hospital in Paris during the 1870s. Sexually abused as a child and raped by her mother's uncle at age 13, Augustine became a key figure in Charcot's theatrical demonstrations of hysteria. Her image was disseminated widely through photographs that depicted her in hypnotically induced spasms and convulsions, her body arched, eyes rolling, limbs contorted in what Charcot categorised as the stages of a 'hysterical attack'. Though presented as objective clinical evidence, these iconic images were carefully staged.

Epistemological Issues

The study of hysteria provides a vivid illustration of how different ways of producing and validating knowledge can shape the direction of psychological theory and practice. In the case of hysteria, we see a dramatic epistemological shift from *looking* to *listening*, from a framework grounded in visual empiricism to one based on verbal interpretation, from the body as a site of knowledge to language as a source of meaning.

Jean-Martin Charcot exemplified a visual, observational approach to hysteria. Trained in medicine and originally interested in art, Charcot relied on detailed visual inspection, photography, and public demonstrations to classify and diagnose symptoms. He treated the patient's body as something to be displayed, observed, and interpreted. Knowledge was generated through observation of physical signs and the visible effects of hypnosis. For Charcot, hysteria was a neurological phenomenon that could be understood through visual scrutiny.

In contrast, Sigmund Freud developed a radically different epistemology, one that prioritised the *spoken word* over the visible symptom. Freud's method of *free association* involved encouraging patients to say whatever came to mind without censorship, allowing unconscious conflicts to surface. Where Charcot observed the patient's body, Freud listened to her voice. Verbal expression became a therapeutic process in itself. This marked the emergence of psychoanalysis, with its emphasis on language, repression, and the interpretations of symbols.

Hippolyte Bernheim offered a third perspective that further blurred the boundary between body and mind. He argued that hypnosis and hysteria were not signs of neurological abnormality but products of suggestion, a psychological and social process. Bernheim's emphasis on the power of suggestion helped open psychology to questions of social influence and subjectivity.

All three clinicians engaged, implicitly or explicitly, with the logic of mimesis: the notion that symptoms could *imitate* both personal conflict and cultural expectation. This idea challenged the notion of purely objective symptoms and opened a new space in psychology for understanding how knowledge of the self is always filtered through bodily expression, language, and social expectations.

Ontological Issues

The history of hysteria is not just a story about changing treatments or theories. It is also a history of shifting *ontologies* or claims about what kind of thing hysteria *is*. For Jean-Martin Charcot, hysteria was a physical disorder rooted in the nervous system. He believed that symptoms such as paralysis, convulsions, and catalepsy had neurological causes that could be directly observed, manipulated, and documented. In this view, the body was the site of truth, and hysteria a dysfunction of the nervous system that manifested through visible, often dramatic, signs. His ontology located hysteria firmly within the material realm of medicine, anatomy, and physical intervention.

Freud, in contrast, shifted the ontological focus from the body to the psyche. For him, hysteria was not a disorder of the nerves but of the unconscious mind. Symptoms were bodily expressions of repressed desires, traumatic memories, and unresolved conflicts. Hysteria became a symbolic condition of the *unseen*, one that required interpretation, not just observation. Freud's approach redefined the ontology of hysteria as psychological rather than neurological.

Hippolyte Bernheim also rejected the neurological model but framed hysteria as a psychological phenomenon shaped by suggestion. For Bernheim, the mind could generate or resolve symptoms through belief, expectation, and social influence. His ontology highlighted the dynamic interplay between individual psychology and social interaction.

The concept of mimesis helps us interrogate these ontologies more critically. Rather than accepting hysteria as a biological defect, *mimetic thinking* invites us to see symptoms as *performances*, embodied expressions of social constraint. It is not the illness in a biological sense that is real, as such, but rather it is the performance that deserves ontological respect. Writers such as Charlotte Perkins Gilman challenged the idea that women were naturally predisposed to mental illness. Instead, they suggested that hysteria mirrored women's immobilisation, silencing, and loss of agency in patriarchal societies. In a world where women could not speak freely, their bodies became the site of protest. Ontologically, then, hysteria was a symbolic and cultural phenomenon, where personal suffering reflected broader systems of power.

Power

The diagnosis and treatment of hysteria in the nineteenth and early twentieth centuries were deeply embedded in the power structures of patriarchal society. At the heart of this discourse was a rigid cultural binary that reduced women to either *angels*—pure, passive, morally upright—or *devils*—dangerous, hypersexual, and untrustworthy. This reductionist framing of femininity shaped how physicians understood hysteria, reinforcing societal anxieties about women's sexuality, independence, and emotionality.

Medical interpretations of hysteria often aligned with this dichotomy. Women seen as repressed or sexually inhibited, the 'angelic' hysterics, were thought to suffer from a lack of sexual release. Treatments included genital massage, sometimes carried out by physicians using their hands, or, later, mechanical vibrators. British doctor Joseph Mortimer Granville, for instance, reputedly developed the electromechanical vibrator as a therapeutic tool to induce 'hysterical paroxysms', orgasms, in other words, believed to relieve symptoms. These interventions were often medicalised and sanitised despite their intimate nature, and reflect the unequal power dynamic in which the female patient was seen as both irrational and unknowing.

Conversely, women deemed 'hyper-sexual' or morally suspect, the 'devilish' hysterics, were subjected to far more invasive procedures. English physician Isaac Baker Brown notoriously promoted clitoridectomy as a cure for hysteria, epilepsy, and masturbation. His belief that female sexual arousal was pathological illustrates how medicine occasionally became a mechanism for enforcing sexual conformity. Although Baker Brown was eventually expelled from the Obstetrical Society of London, his practices highlight how medical authority could be used to regulate women's bodies under the guise of care.

Power also operated in more symbolic and institutional ways. Charcot's demonstrations at the Salpêtrière Hospital turned female suffering into public spectacle. In lecture halls filled with male medical students, women such as Augustine and Blanche Wittman were hypnotised into adopting indicative poses and performing dramatic seizures. These events functioned as a theatre of science, part diagnosis, part entertainment, focusing the male gaze and reinforcing the authority of the physician over the patient. Women's bodies became visual texts onto which medical meaning was inscribed.

Freud, though more private in method, also operated within this power dynamic. His early 'seduction theory' proposed that repressed memories of childhood sexual abuse were the root of hysteria, but he later retracted this view in favour of internal psychic conflict. Critics, including feminist scholars, have argued that this retreat masked the realities of patriarchal violence and child sexual abuse, privileging psychoanalytic theory over patient testimony. Freud's shift illuminates how psychological knowledge is not only shaped by unconscious dynamics but also by the wider forces that determine what can be acknowledged and what must remain unsaid.

Chapter Summary

The history of hysteria demonstrates a striking evolution in how psychological suffering has been conceptualised, categorised, and controlled. Charcot cast it as a neurological condition that could be witnessed through the spectacular body. Freud shifted the focus from the body to the mind, from physiology to narrative. He saw hysteria as a language of the unconscious, a symbolic enactment of trauma that could be deciphered through the analysis of symbols. A significant moment in the invention of psychoanalysis, Freud's abandonment of the seduction theory remains one of the most contested moves in the history of psychotherapy.

The symptoms of hysteria imitated, enacted, and protested the restricted conditions of women's lives. Hysteria was a psychosomatic protest, a mimetic critique of the structures that confined, silenced, and pathologised female subjectivity. To study hysteria is to ask whose suffering has been seen, whose stories have been heard, and whose knowledge has been authorised. It reminds us that psychological categories are shaped by those who define them, the gazes that interpret them, and the silences that surround them.

But psychological categories are also shaped by those who endure them. And this returns us to Augustine, Charcot's star patient, so often photographed in mid-spasm, her body contorted into the syntax of male medical authority. One night in 1880, disguised in men's clothing, Augustine slipped unnoticed past the Salpêtrière gates and vanished into the streets of Paris. She was never seen again. Her disappearance remains one of the most enduring gestures of resistance in the history of psychological medicine, a young woman who refused to be performed, studied, and displayed any longer. In that quiet escape, she left behind more than a diagnosis. Her legacy is a question that still lingers: what truths are lost when suffering slips out of sight?

Reflective Questions

1. How did cultural assumptions about femininity shape the diagnosis and treatment of hysteria in the nineteenth century?
2. In what ways can hysteria be understood as a form of social protest?
3. Compare and contrast Charcot's and Freud's approaches to hysteria. What do their methods reveal about changing ways of knowing in psychology?
4. Why was the abandonment of Freud's seduction theory controversial, and what does it suggest about the politics of psychological knowledge?
5. How does the history of hysteria remain relevant to social psychology today?

Suggested Reading

Arnaud, S. (2015). *On Hysteria: The invention of a medical category between 1670 & 1820.* Chicago, IL: The University of Chicago Press.

Breuer, J., & Freud, S. (1895/2004). *Studies in Hysteria* (New ed.) (N. Luckhurst, trans.). Harmondsworth: Penguin.

de Marneffe, D. (1991). Looking and listening: The construction of clinical knowledge in Charcot and Freud. *Signs, 17*(1), 71–111. http://www.jstor.org/stable/3174446.

Hajek, K. M. (2021). Félida, doubled personality, and the 'normal state' in late 19th-century French psychology. *History of the Human Sciences, 34*(2), 66–89. https://doi.org/10.1177/0952695120980648.
Hustvedt, A. (2011). *Medical Muses: Hysteria in nineteenth-century Paris*. London: Bloomsbury.
Kanaan, R. A. A., & Wessely, S. C. (2010). The origins of factitious disorder. *History of the Human Sciences, 23*(2), 68–85. https://doi.org/10.1177/0952695109357128.
Kimball, M. M. (2000). From 'Anna O.' to Bertha Pappenheim: Transforming private pain into public action. *History of Psychology, 3*(1), 20–43. https://doi.org/10.1037/1093-4510.3.1.20.
Kovalets, A. (2025). Hysteria and the birth of the new. *British Journal of Psychotherapy, 41*(2), 320–334. https://doi.org/10.1111/bjp.12953.
Micale, M. S. (1995). *Approaching Hysteria: Disease and its interpretations*. Princeton, NJ: Princeton University Press.
Ropper, A. H., & and Burrell, B. D. (2020). *How the Brain Lost its Mind: Sex, hysteria, and the riddle of mental illness*. London: Atlantic Books.
Scull, A. (2009). *Hysteria: The biography*. Oxford: Oxford University Press.
Showalter, E. (1985). *The Female Malady: Women, madness and English culture, 1830–1980*. London: Virago.

Key Terms

Angel-Devil Binary A cultural framework in nineteenth-century Western thought that positioned women as either morally pure and passive ('angelic') or sexually dangerous and manipulative ('devilish'), influencing medical interpretations of female behaviour.

Catharsis A therapeutic concept introduced by Josef Breuer and developed by Sigmund Freud, referring to the emotional release that occurs when repressed feelings are brought to consciousness and expressed.

Charcot's Lectures Public medical demonstrations conducted by Jean-Martin Charcot at the Salpêtrière Hospital in Paris, where female patients were hypnotised and exhibited symptoms of hysteria to audiences of mostly male physicians and students.

Clitoridectomy The surgical removal of the clitoris, historically used in some cases to treat hysteria or female sexual 'deviance' reflecting extreme and patriarchal medical practices aimed at controlling women's bodies.

Hysteria A historical psychological diagnosis, now obsolete, associated with dramatic physical symptoms—such as paralysis or fainting—with no apparent organic cause, and often interpreted as psychosomatic responses to psychological or social pressures, particularly in women.

Mimesis A concept meaning imitation or symbolic representation. In this chapter, it is used to explain how hysterical symptoms might mimic or embody social oppression, functioning as a form of non-verbal protest or cultural performance.

Rest Cure A nineteenth-century treatment for hysteria and other 'nervous' conditions, especially in women, which involved isolation, bed rest, and prohibition of intellectual activity. It was popularised by American neurologist Silas Weir Mitchell.

Seduction Theory Sigmund Freud's early theory that hysteria was caused by childhood sexual abuse, later replaced by his theory of internal unconscious conflict. The abandonment of the seduction theory remains controversial in the history of psychoanalysis.

Suggestion A psychological process in which symptoms or beliefs are shaped or induced by external influence, often unconsciously. This concept was central to the work of Hippolyte Bernheim, who emphasised the role of verbal suggestion in hysteria.

Talking Cure A term coined by Bertha Pappenheim (Anna O.) to describe the therapeutic process of verbalising repressed thoughts and emotions to relieve psychological symptoms—foundational to psychoanalytic therapy.

FREE INSTRUCTOR & STUDENT RESOURCES

ONLINE RESOURCES

Visit the Instructor & Student Resources website at routledgelearning.com/bpscoretextbooks for free digital resources, including:

- Interactive quizzes and flashcards to test your knowledge
- Links to useful websites and videos
- Instructor manual, lecture slides, and course guide to enhance teaching and save instructors time

6 Pursuing Beauty

Psychological Laboratories and the Metaphysics of Measurement

Chapter Overview

This chapter explores the early development of the psychological laboratory by comparing the contrasting approaches of Francis Galton and Wilhelm Wundt, with a focus on how each attempted to render measurable various mental attributes. The chapter argues that decisions about what to measure in psychology, whether as consciousness, reaction time, intelligence, visual acuity, and so on, are never purely objective. Rather, they are shaped by personal, philosophical, and cultural factors. Wundt's laboratory was devoted to gaining introspective access to universal mental processes, while Galton assembled a laboratory packed with a variety of scientific instruments, ultimately aimed at assessing individual differences. Drawing on Joel Michell's critique of measurement in the human sciences, the chapter introduces the idea that psychology's embrace of quantification was founded not on empirical demonstration but on metaphysical assumptions; that is, deeply held but untested beliefs about the nature of psychological phenomena. Michell argues that figures such as Wundt and Galton simply assumed, rather than actually proving, that mental attributes were capable of being quantified. This assumption underpinned entire measurement systems, even though there was little justification for treating psychological faculties as possessing numerical magnitude. By situating these measurement practices within the imaginary of the laboratory, the chapter shows how early psychology functioned as both an empirical science and a system of social classification. Psychological laboratories were not just spaces of discovery but institutions that helped define what counts as normal, deviant, intelligent, or conscious. Through this critical lens, measurement is revealed not as the mirror of nature but as a tool of power.

Pursuing Beauty

In the late nineteenth century, the streets of Britain became the unconventional laboratory of Sir Francis Galton, a man driven by a relentless pursuit of quantification that extended even to the ephemeral quality of beauty. A cousin of Charles Darwin and a fervent proponent of eugenics, Galton believed that desirable traits, including physical attractiveness, were heritable and vital to the improvement of the British population. Thus, he embarked on a clandestine mission to map the distribution of female beauty across the British Isles. Concealed within his pocket was a peculiar instrument, 'a needle mounted as a pricker, wherewith to prick holes,

DOI: 10.4324/9781003565482-6

unseen, in a piece of paper, torn rudely into a cross', which he used to surreptitiously assess the faces of passing women. Galton meticulously recorded each fleeting glance, his subjective impressions translated onto his improvised scale, 'classifying the girls I passed in streets or elsewhere', he later wrote in his memoirs, 'as attractive, indifferent, or repellent'. His findings, which he presented as objective statistical insights, purported to reveal a 'beauty map' of the British Isles, with London allegedly radiating the highest concentration of female beauty while Aberdeen was deemed comparatively less aesthetically blessed. This peculiar endeavour, a fusion of statistical method and personal judgement, starkly illustrates Galton's ambition to impose a numerical order on the subjective realm of human attributes. His investigation serves as a potent historical reminder that the tools and methodologies of science are never truly neutral but rather bear the indelible imprint of their creators' historical context and personal prejudices, a lesson that continues to hold critical relevance in our increasingly data-driven world. Galton's 'beauty map' raises a profound and unsettling question that still resonates: what are the ethical implications of reducing human qualities to mere data points?

Chapter Contents

- A comparison of Francis Galton's and Wilhelm Wundt's laboratories and their differing approaches to psychological measurement.
- An exploration of how psychological measurement has always been shaped by personal values, philosophical assumptions, and broader cultural forces.
- A critical investigation of the *metaphysics of measurement* as a conceptual tool to understand how psychological categories are constructed and legitimised, prior to their measurement.

Chapter Objectives

- To understand how Wundt and Galton contributed to the emergence of the psychological laboratory as a site of scientific inquiry.
- To evaluate the conceptual and political implications of psychological measurement using historical and contemporary examples.
- To apply the critical thinking tool of the metaphysics of measurement to examine how assumptions about human nature shape what is studied, measured, and normalised in psychology.

CRITICAL THINKING TOOL
THE METAPHYSICS OF MEASUREMENT

This chapter will explore the philosophical assumptions underlying psychological measurement, using the contrasting approaches of Wilhelm Wundt and Francis Galton to illustrate how decisions about what to measure in psychology are shaped by personal, social, and cultural

forces. Measurement in psychology will not be treated as a neutral or purely technical activity but rather as a process that reflects specific assumptions about human nature, the purpose of science, and the legitimacy of certain forms of knowledge.

Through the comparison of Wundt's experimental small-scale studies of consciousness with Galton's large-scale statistical investigations into individual differences, it will become apparent that different methods of measurement presuppose different ontological and epistemological assumptions. These assumptions will be shown to influence not only the design of experiments but also the interpretation of the resulting data and the kinds of conclusions that are drawn from them. Galton's emphasis on quantifying human variation will be examined alongside his promotion of eugenics, while Wundt's reliance on trained introspection will be situated within a broader philosophical tradition that valued precision measurement.

The chapter will highlight how laboratories function not only as sites of scientific inquiry but also as institutions of classification, standardisation, and control. *The metaphysics of measurement* will be shown to shape what is considered normal, valuable, or pathological within a given social setting. This critical perspective will encourage reflection on the ways in which psychological knowledge has been historically constructed, and how it continues to be shaped by choices about what, and whom, to measure.

Introduction

The experimental method is a fundamental approach to gaining knowledge in science. It involves the systematic manipulation of variables to observe their effects and draw conclusions about causal relationships. In its simplest form, an experiment consists of establishing two conditions (the 'independent variable', or stimulus) and measuring an outcome (the 'dependent variable', or response). This method helps researchers to limit the influence of complicating factors, allowing them to propose cause-and-effect relationships with the confidence that other research methods such as observational studies or correlational analyses cannot produce.

In psychology, the experimental method has played a crucial role in advancing our understanding of behaviour and mental processes. Psychologists use experiments to test hypotheses about how people think, feel, and behave. By isolating specific variables, researchers aim to establish patterns that can be generalised across populations. However, applying the experimental method to people introduces unique challenges. Human beings are complex and capricious. They bring individual differences and subjective experiences to any social situation, including psychological experiments. These complicate the researcher's goal of achieving objectivity and precision.

This chapter explores the foundations of experimental and laboratory-based psychology through the work of Wilhelm Wundt and Francis Galton. It examines how these pioneers approached the scientific study of human action and mental processes, albeit with different methodologies and objectives. Wundt focused on understanding universal aspects of consciousness through controlled experiments and introspection, while Galton emphasised differences between people and populations through a project of mass data collection.

The chapter highlights the challenges faced in applying experimental methods to psychology, including ontological problems of defining what to study, epistemological issues related to the nature of psychological experiments, and ethical concerns arising from human experimentation. Wundt and Galton both sought to study people scientifically, but their divergent approaches reflected fundamentally different assumptions about human nature and the proper focus of psychological inquiry. Their work laid the groundwork for modern psychology while also revealing the complexities and limitations of studying human behaviour through experimental methods.

Historical Issues

The historical context of early experimental psychology was marked by the tension between different approaches to studying human nature under controlled conditions. Wundt hoped that specifically focusing on a person's 'reaction-time' to an event would help him build a model of consciousness. Precision scientific instruments enabled him to seek accuracy and control in the laboratory. His experimental programme required working patiently with small groups of specially trained collaborators ('subjects') who could reliably report their perceptual experiences to him. In contrast, Galton collected data from over 9,000 members of the public, each of whom paid him a small fee in return for their data. Galton measured 17 different physical and mental abilities to generate insights into to distribution of human variation across the population.

These divergent approaches reflected broader scientific trends of the time, with Wundt representing a more traditional, philosophically informed approach to psychology, inspired by physiology, while Galton embodied the rising influence of statistical methods and evolutionary theory. The historical development of experimental psychology was also shaped by technological limitations such as the availability of precision measurement devices, and by the broader cultural context, including the growing emphasis on the credibility of empirical methods in the human sciences.

Key Individuals

Gustav Theodor Fechner (1801–1887) is often credited as the founding figure of *psychophysics*, the scientific attempt to relate physical stimuli to psychological experience through mathematical laws. His landmark text, *Elemente der Psychophysik* (1860), proposed that the mind could be studied quantitatively by linking external physical inputs (such as light or sound intensity) to internal sensations. Fechner proposed that sensation increased logarithmically with stimulus intensity, an effect that became known as the Weber–Fechner law.

Fechner's method did not establish that psychological magnitudes were genuinely quantitative in the mathematical sense. Rather, he *assumed* quantifiability and built a formal structure around that assumption, a move that has shaped the discipline ever since. From the standpoint of the politics of measurement, Fechner's psychophysics illustrates how scientific authority can rest not on demonstrable natural laws but on the persuasive power of method, metaphor, and numbers. What was measured, and whether it was even truly measurable, was as much a metaphysical and rhetorical decision as a scientific one.

Wilhelm Wundt (1832–1920) was a German physician and philosopher. Wundt is known for founding the first formal laboratory for psychological research at the University of Leipzig in 1879. This act is often seen as the official beginning of psychology as a distinct field of study, separate from philosophy and physiology. Wundt's experimental approach to psychology was a significant departure from the philosophical approach that previously dominated the study of the mind. He sought to understand the workings of consciousness by examining its basic structural elements, an approach that came to be known as *structuralism*. Wundt's method involved the careful observation and recording of thoughts and sensations through a process known as introspection. By measuring the time (in milliseconds) it took a person to react to a stimulus (such as the sound of a metal pellet hitting a plate), Wundt believed he could uncover the basic components of human thought processes, such as sensations and perceptions.

In addition to structuralism, Wundt also contributed to *voluntarism*, the theory that humans are active participants in organising their thoughts and experiences, driven by motives and attention. He emphasised the role of consciousness in shaping human experience, differentiating his ideas from deterministic approaches to psychology. Wundt devoted the last quarter of his life to 'völkerpsychologie', an entirely non-experimental form of psychology that involved the qualitative study of language, myth, folklore, and culture.

Francis Galton (1822–1911) was an English polymath whose influence extended across numerous fields, including psychology, statistics, heredity, criminology, and anthropology. A half-cousin of Charles Darwin, Galton was profoundly inspired by the theory of evolution and sought to apply the principles of natural selection to the study of human abilities. His work laid the groundwork for the psychology of individual differences, particularly through his study of mental and physical variation. Galton's most significant contribution to psychology was his pioneering work in *psychometrics*, the measurement of psychological capacities and attributes. His fascination with measurement led him to develop tests of sensory acuity, physical capacity, reaction time, memory, and perception, which he believed were indicative of a person's underlying intellectual ability. Galton established an Anthropometric Laboratory in 1884 in London, where he amassed vast data sets of people's physical and mental attributes. Though later research showed that these measures were not accurate reflections of general intellect as he had hoped they might be, Galton's belief in the importance of quantifying psychological traits had a lasting impact on psychology.

Galton was the first to introduce the concept of applying statistical methods to the study of human intellect and developing the statistics of the normal distribution curve to analyse data on human traits. His book *Hereditary Genius* (1869) was an early attempt to study the inheritance of personal qualities, marking the beginning of his lifelong interest in *eugenics*, a field he would later instigate with the goal of improving the quality of the human population through selective breeding.

Edward Bradford Titchener (1867–1927) was a British psychologist best known for his development of structuralism, a theory of consciousness that sought to analyse the mind into simplest components. A devoted student of Wundt, Titchener exported Wundt's ideas to the United States and became the leading proponent of experimental psychology in the English-speaking world. However, despite his deep admiration for Wundt, Titchener ultimately rebelled against his mentor's approach. He repudiated Wundt's thinking by rejecting his mentor's cultural psychology, *völkerpsychologie*, which Wundt viewed as essential for understanding higher mental processes. Titchener argued that psychology should focus solely on individual, conscious experiences and their elements through introspection. This starkly contrasted with Wundt's more holistic perspective.

James McKeen Cattell (1860–1944) was an American psychologist who played a pivotal role in establishing psychology as a scientific discipline in the United States. Cattell's work was heavily influenced by both Wundt and Galton. He studied under Wundt in Leipzig, where he developed his experimental skills and became interested in measuring mental processes. Cattell visited England in 1884 and subjected himself to Galton's anthropometric tests. His exposure to Galton's work led him to focus on applying statistical methods to psychological traits. Cattell named one of his daughters 'Psyche'. Psyche Cattell went on to become a psychologist in her own right, developing the Cattell Infant Intelligence Scale (1940), one of the first tests for measuring early childhood intelligence.

Epistemological Issues

Wundt's and Galton's approaches to acquiring psychological knowledge were significantly different. Wundt's epistemology was grounded in the belief that scientific knowledge about consciousness could be obtained through the careful use of 'brass instruments' and the precise measurement of a person's reaction time using a chronoscope. He emphasised the importance of trained observers who could reliably report their mental experiences, reflecting a view that psychological knowledge required both objective measurement and subjective reporting. Galton on the other hand believed that knowledge about human nature could be derived from measuring and comparing individual differences across populations. His epistemological framework prioritised the statistical analysis and graphical representation of large data sets.

Both approaches faced challenges. Wundt's reliance on introspection raised questions about the reliability and objectivity of both subjective reports and his scientific instruments, while Galton's focus on measurable traits overlooked the complexity and subjective nature of human experience. He was not interested in what people said about their experiences of taking part in his studies. These epistemological differences reflected broader questions about what constitutes valid psychological knowledge, how it can be obtained, and the ambitions that motivate its collection.

Ontological Issues

Wundt's and Galton's ontological assumptions also differed significantly, specifically with respect to the issue of human variation. Wundt saw differences between people as secondary to universal structures of consciousness, reflecting an ontology that emphasised the common features of human mental experience. He viewed the mind as active and organising, with consciousness composed of universal elements, common to all human beings, that were dynamically combined through mental processes.

Galton's ontology, conversely, placed individual differences at the centre of his programme. He conceptualised human nature in terms of an inherent and inescapable variability, with this variation being primarily determined by heredity. His ontological perspective viewed human abilities and traits as distributed along a spectrum, with some individuals naturally more gifted than others due to their biological inheritance. In this sense, Galton's horizontal spectrum of difference was also a vertical hierarchy of value, with white upper-class males like himself positioned at the top.

These contrasting ontological positions had profound implications for their respective approaches to psychological research. Wundt's focus on universal mental processes led to detailed studies of individual consciousness using a small group of trusted participants. Galton's emphasis on variation drove his interest in measuring and comparing large numbers of individuals. These differing ontological assumptions not only shaped their research methods, their broader understanding of human nature, and the goals of psychological science; they were also, in turn, shaped by their respective moral values.

Power

Unlike experiments in the natural sciences, where objects of knowledge exist independently of human foibles, psychological experiments are social situations in which the objects of knowledge are themselves human characteristics. This reflexive loop means that power is inevitably an ever-present feature of each and every psychological investigation of any kind. In Wundt's laboratory, the power dynamic was somewhat minimised as experimenters often served as subjects, creating a collaborative environment and a shared purpose.

Galton's approach involved more explicit power imbalances, with the researcher holding authority over the participants, who were charged a sum in return for their data. Galton and the visiting public had quite different agendas. Galton's commitment to eugenics further complicated these power dynamics because his scientific work was linked to social theories about human worth and potential biological engineering.

Galton was fascinated by the image of the *normal distribution* (the 'bell curve') and its associated statistic, the standard deviation, which expresses mathematical deviations from the average. In the context of a critical understanding of power, *normalisation* refers to the process by which certain behaviours, practices, or beliefs become to appear as normal or natural within a society. This concept is central to critical theories of power, particularly in the work of Michel Foucault, who explored how power operates not just through laws and authority but also through subtler, everyday practices, including measurement, that shape individuals' sense of what is normal, moral, or socially acceptable.

Normalisation does not simply prohibit or restrict behaviours; it actively produces and encourages certain ways of thinking and acting. Power, in this sense, is not only something that stops people from doing things but it is also something that creates norms, shaping what is seen as ideal, healthy, morally good, or socially sanctioned. For example, societal norms around gender identity, body image, or even mental health can be seen as products of normalisation.

Institutions such as schools, prisons, hospitals, and the mass media play a central role in normalisation. They establish standards of behaviour, knowledge, and identity that individuals come to accept, adopt, and internalise. Schools may normalise the wearing of uniforms, or certain forms of discipline or knowledge, while hospitals can normalise definitions of health and illness. These institutions are therefore vectors of power that subtly enforce conformity to social norms. Through normalisation, those who do not conform to social norms are labelled as deviant. This reinforces the power of the norm, as individuals strive to avoid being marginalised. Deviance becomes a way of distinguishing between normal and abnormal, further entrenching power structures.

Chapter Summary

Psychological experiments differ significantly from those in the natural sciences because of the reflexive nature of the subject and the entities being studied. Psychological experiments are not neutral environments in which 'natural' behaviour can simply be observed. Rather, they are highly structured social situations, embedded in sets of social rules, expectations, and power dynamics between the experimenter and the participant. When a person is placed in a laboratory setting, they are acutely aware of being observed and assessed. This complicates the notion that experiments can yield truly objective knowledge about human behaviour.

Wundt and Galton grappled with the problem of how to quantify and study mental processes that are not directly observable. Wundt addressed this through reaction-time experiments and introspection, while Galton treated physical and sensory traits as proxies for mental abilities. Wundt faced tremendous difficulties in achieving consistent results, partly because his instruments had to be repeatedly re-calibrated, but also because of irregular performances exhibited by his human subjects. Galton's anthropometric devices produced inconsistent results and were often damaged and had to be regularly repaired.

While ambling around Victorian Britain, Francis Galton silently scored the women who passed him as 'attractive, indifferent, or repellent'. This unsettling image of a man reducing women to a private taxonomy of worth opened this chapter, not for its disconcerting quaintness but because it captures something enduring about the politics of psychological measurement. Galton's beauty map was a crystallisation of the impulse to measure, classify, and hierarchise human difference.

This chapter has traced two divergent paths into the psychological laboratory, one marked by Galton's cold arithmetic of difference, the other by Wundt's search for universal structures of thought. Both were ambitious, flawed, and shaped by metaphysical assumptions. As psychology continues to refine its methods and expand its reach, it is worth asking: what are we choosing to measure, and why? As Galton showed with his pocket pricker and scrap of paper, what we decide to count sometimes reveals more about us than about those we are observing.

Reflective Questions

1. What is meant by the 'metaphysics of measurement' and how does this concept challenge the idea that psychological traits are naturally quantifiable?
2. How do the laboratories of Wilhelm Wundt and Francis Galton reflect different views about what psychology should be studying?
3. In what ways can the act of measurement in psychology be considered to be influenced by power?
4. What role did the concept of 'normality' play in Galton's work, and how does Foucault's idea of 'normalisation' help us to critically understand it?
5. Why might early psychological experiments be better understood as social performances rather than as purely objective scientific investigations?

Suggested Reading

Benschop, R., & Draaisma, D. (2000). In pursuit of precision: The calibration of minds and machines in late nineteenth-century psychology. *Annals of Science, 57*(1), 1–25. https://doi.org/10.1080/000337900296281.

Bringmann, L. F., & Eronen, M. I. (2015). Heating up the measurement debate: What psychologists can learn from the history of physics. *Theory & Psychology, 26*(1), 27–43. https://doi.org/10.1177/0959354315617253.

Danziger, K. (1990). *Constructing the Subject: Historical origins of psychological research.* Cambridge: Cambridge University Press.

Evrard, R., Gumpper, S., Beauvais, B., & Alvarado C. S. (2021). 'Never sacrifice anything to laboratory work': The 'physiological psychology' of Charles Richet (1875–1905). *Journal of the History of the Behavioral Sciences, 57*(2), 172–193. https://doi.org/10.1002/jhbs.22086.

Galton, F. (1885). On the Anthropometric Laboratory at the Late International Health Exhibition. *The Journal of the Anthropological Institute of Great Britain and Ireland, 14,* 205–221. https://doi.org/10.2307/2841978.

Hasselman, F. (2023). Going round in squares: Theory-based measurement requires a theory of measurement. *Theory & Psychology, 33*(1), 145–152. https://doi.org/10.1177/09593543221131511.

Michell, J. (2005). *Measurement in Psychology: A critical history of a methodological concept.* Cambridge: Cambridge University Press.

Michell, J. (2021). 'The art of imposing measurement upon the mind': Sir Francis Galton and the genesis of the psychometric paradigm. *Theory & Psychology, 32*(3), 375–400. https://doi.org/10.1177/09593543211017671.

Saint-Mont, U. (2012). What measurement is all about. *Theory & Psychology, 22*(4), 467–485. https://doi.org/10.1177/0959354311429997.

Key Terms

Anthropometry The measurement of human physical characteristics, often used by early psychologists and anthropologists to draw conclusions about intelligence and racial difference.

Epistemology The branch of philosophy concerned with the nature and limits of knowledge; in psychology, it refers to how knowledge about the mind and behaviour is produced.

Eugenics A social movement and pseudoscience developed by Francis Galton that aimed to improve the genetic quality of human populations through selective breeding.

Experimental Method A scientific approach involving the manipulation of variables under controlled conditions to establish cause-and-effect relationships.

Individual Differences Variations among people in terms of their abilities, behaviours, or psychological traits, often measured statistically in psychology.

Introspection A method of self-observation developed by Wilhelm Wundt, where participants report their inner experiences in response to controlled stimuli.

Metaphysics of Measurement A concept that encourages reflection on the underlying assumptions of measurement in psychology, especially the unproven belief that psychological traits are inherently quantifiable.

Normal Distribution (Bell Curve) A statistical model that shows how traits or test scores are spread across a population, with most people clustering around the average.

Normalisation A process identified by Michel Foucault, in which certain behaviours, identities, or characteristics become constructed as 'normal' and others as 'deviant' through subtle forms of institutional power.

Ontological Assumptions Beliefs about what kinds of things exist; in this chapter, it refers to what psychologists assume about the nature of the mind and mental traits.

Psychometrics The field of psychology concerned with the measurement of psychological traits such as intelligence or personality.

Psychophysics The scientific study of the relationship between physical stimuli and the sensations and perceptions they affect, pioneered by Gustav Fechner.

Reflexivity The idea that psychological research is shaped by the social roles and expectations of both researchers and participants, making it different from research in the natural sciences.

Structuralism A school of psychology that aimed to break down mental processes into their most basic components, associated with Wilhelm Wundt and later with Edward Bradford Titchener.

Völkerpsychologie A cultural psychology developed by Wilhelm Wundt to study higher mental functions such as language and myth through non-experimental methods.

FREE INSTRUCTOR & STUDENT RESOURCES

ONLINE RESOURCES

Visit the Instructor & Student Resources website at routledgelearning.com/bpscoretextbooks for free digital resources, including:

- Interactive quizzes and flashcards to test your knowledge
- Links to useful websites and videos
- Instructor manual, lecture slides, and course guide to enhance teaching and save instructors time

7 The Cat's Cradle

Untangling the Psychological Complex

Chapter Overview

This chapter explores how psychological knowledge was shaped by the institutional and spatial contexts in which it was produced by the first generation of people who called themselves 'psychologists'. Focusing on four key settings—laboratory, clinic, factory, and school—the chapter reveals how each space gave rise to distinct psychological methods, concepts, and subjects. Drawing on Donna Haraway's concept of *situated knowledge*, it challenges the idea that psychology discovers universal truths, showing instead how the production of knowledge is contingent on social context, institutional purpose, and power relations. In the history of psychology, the concept of situated knowledge helps us think critically about claims of universality, objectivity, and scientific neutrality. It remains vital for understanding how context shapes everything from identity to behaviour. The chapter traces the work of key figures such as W. H. R. Rivers, Hugo Münsterberg, Lightner Witmer, Sigmund Freud, Alfred Binet, and Cyril Burt, and connects their contributions to broader epistemological and ontological shifts. Each setting, whether producing introspective data, confessional narratives, efficiency metrics, or intelligence test scores, constructed the psychological subject differently and served different 'clients' of knowledge. The chapter aims to inspire critical thinking about how context continues to shape what psychology conceptualises, studies, and claims to know. It reveals that psychology is a flexible, powerful, and deeply situated field of knowledge, a 'complex' tangled up like a cat's cradle with governance, identity, and the social order.

The Cat's Cradle

In the sweltering heat on Mabuiag Island in the Torres Strait in 1898, British psychologist W. H. R. Rivers found himself captivated not by the grand rituals nor exotic artefacts he had anticipated but by the delicate dance of fingers weaving loops of string into intricate patterns. Among the Torres Strait Islanders, these string figures, known locally as *warru warru*, were more than mere games; they were storytelling devices, mnemonic tools, and embodiments of cultural knowledge. One such cat's cradle, referred to as the 'Crab', depicted the creature's movements and was accompanied by narratives about its role in local ecology and mythology. Another, the 'Turtle', was not only a representation of the animal but also a conduit for stories about navigation and survival. These figures served as a means of transmitting complex information across generations, blending play with education. Rivers's engagement with these practices marked a turning point in his academic journey. Initially trained in the empirical traditions of Western psychology, his

DOI: 10.4324/9781003565482-7

experiences in the Torres Strait challenged his assumptions about the universality of psychological processes. He began to appreciate the profound ways in which culture and cognition are intertwined, leading him to advocate for a more holistic approach that considered the situated nature of knowledge. However, the expedition was not without its ethical complexities. The Islanders, while often cooperative, were subjects of a study that sought to categorise and analyse their lives through a foreign lens. This encounter with the Torres Strait Islanders and their string figures invites us to reflect on the broader implications of cross-cultural research. It challenges us to consider how knowledge is constructed, who gets to construct it, and the responsibilities that come with that power.

Chapter Contents

- Explores how psychology between 1890 and 1930 operated in four key institutional spaces: the laboratory, the clinic, the factory, and the school.
- Examines how each space generated specific psychological knowledge, practices, and power relations.
- Introduces *situated knowledge* as the chapter's critical thinking tool, questioning the idea of universal psychological truth.

Chapter Objectives

- To help students critically assess how psychology's methods and assumptions are shaped by institutional and historical contexts.
- To deepen understanding of the epistemological and ontological diversity across psychology's early institutional spaces.
- To apply *situated knowledge* as a tool for analysing how psychological knowledge varies according to space, purpose, and power.

CRITICAL THINKING TOOL
SITUATED KNOWLEDGE

What we know depends on where we are and what we can see. That is the basic idea behind *situated knowledge*, a term coined by feminist philosopher of science Donna Haraway (1988) to challenge the idea that science produces objective, view-from-nowhere truths. Instead, Haraway argues that all knowledge is *partial*, *positional*, and *produced in context*. Scientific facts emerge from specific people, in specific places, using specific tools, for specific purposes. Psychology is no exception. This chapter explores how psychological knowledge was, and still is, shaped by its institutional settings. The psychology produced in laboratories or clinics differs from the psychology produced in factories or schools. Each setting not only invites different research methods but also produces different kinds of psychological subjects, relationships, and

dynamics of power. In other words, psychology is not just *applied* to the world; it is *constructed* in the world, with specific ambitions in mind. Situated knowledge helps us see that psychology is a flexible discipline but not a neutral one. It adapts to different social spaces and the needs of different clients of its expertise: military generals, school administrators, factory owners, medical professionals, and beyond. It also reminds us to ask critical questions: who is producing this knowledge and for whom? Under what assumptions are they doing so and to what effect?

Introduction

Psychology is often taught as if it were a universal science, patiently discovering timeless truths about human nature. But this chapter takes a different view. It argues that psychology has always been entangled with the productive spaces in which it operates. From laboratories and clinics to factories and schools, psychology has been shaped by the problems it is asked to solve, the people it has been commissioned to serve, and the institutions that fund it. These are not neutral settings. They are spaces of ambition, expectation, and power. This chapter introduces the idea of *the psychological complex*, a term adapted from Nikolas Rose (1985) to describe how, since the late nineteenth century, psychology became woven into the fabric of modern society. It did so by generating different kinds of truths in different contexts.

Each space explored in this chapter—the laboratory, the clinic, the factory, and the school—will show how psychology produces specific knowledge, serves specific functions, and constructs specific kinds of subjects. Using the concept of *situated knowledge* we will ask: what kind of psychology is made in each space and who benefits from it?

Historical Issues

By the end of the nineteenth century, psychology was not only defining itself as a new science of the mind, it was also attaching itself to the emerging institutions of modernity. As industrial capitalism, mass education, colonial administration, and clinical medicine expanded, psychology found a role to play in each setting. Its knowledge, far from universal, began to take shape in specific places, each associated with its own methods, subjects, and assumptions.

The laboratory, exemplified by Wilhelm Wundt's institute in Leipzig (1879), was the birthplace of modern experimental psychology. Inspired by physiology and the natural sciences, Wundt and his colleagues used controlled conditions to measure perception, attention, and reaction times. But this 'pure' psychology was already situated. Its subjects were often students or trained observers; its procedures favoured standardisation and repetition. The truths it generated were not timeless discoveries but carefully produced constructs.

A particularly revealing episode in the history of psychology's expansion beyond the laboratory was the 1898 Cambridge Expedition to the Torres Straits, led by anthropologist A. C. Haddon and psychologists W. H. R. Rivers and Charles S. Myers. This was an attempt to bring experimental methods, such as chronoscopes, colour wheels, and memory tasks, into the field, to test whether the mental processes of Indigenous people matched those of Europeans. But the field would not behave like the laboratory. The instruments faltered, the assumptions of universality were challenged, and the researchers themselves began to question whether psychology could ever be detached from its cultural context. The Torres Straits expedition marks an early and profound confrontation with *situated knowledge*, a moment when psychology's tools revealed their limitations when deployed in unfamiliar terrain.

At the same time, psychology was taking root in the clinic. Figures such as Sigmund Freud, Pierre Janet, and Lightner Witmer developed therapeutic approaches grounded in candid confession, narrative interpretation, and expert judgement. In these intimate spaces, psychology became a guide to personal conduct in an increasingly complicated society, not a discoverer of universal laws. In the school and factory, psychologists such as Alfred Binet and Hugo Münsterberg adapted their methods to sort, assess, and optimise human performance at scale. These were different articulations of power.

Psychological knowledge is built by people, in specific places, to solve certain problems. The people in the following section each contributed to the formation of modern psychology, but more importantly, they each worked in distinct settings—field stations, factories, clinics, and schools—where they developed methods and ideas suited to their specific environments. What they produced was not a single unified psychology but a range of psychologies, each shaped by its space of origin. Their work shows, in practice, how psychological knowledge is always situated.

Key Individuals

W. H. R. Rivers (1864–1922) attempted to take psychology out of the laboratory and into the world. A trained neurologist and experimental psychologist, Rivers joined the 1898 Cambridge Anthropological Expedition to the Torres Straits with the aim of testing whether so-called 'primitive' peoples had the same perceptual abilities as Europeans. He brought with him a portable laboratory: instruments for measuring visual acuity, colour sensitivity, and memory. It was a challenging to operate delicate scientific instruments on a tropical island. The florid context altered the findings, and Rivers found himself questioning the assumption that Western psychological categories could be universally applied. Later in life, Rivers turned to anthropology and the study of culture, and after serving as a military psychiatrist in the First World War he became a critic of institutional power. His journey reflects a broader truth: psychology's methods are never neutral; they are shaped by where and how they are deployed.

Hugo Münsterberg (1863–1916) embraced psychology's practical applications within the industrial economy. A student of Wundt, he moved to the United States where he became a leading figure in the development of industrial psychology. In *Psychology and Industrial Efficiency* (1913) he argued that psychology could be used to match workers to tasks, reduce error rates, and improve productivity. Münsterberg designed tests to select streetcar drivers, telephone operators, and factory workers. His tests were based on reaction times, attention, and sensory discrimination. His model was the factory: standardised, rational, and oriented towards output. His vision of the mind was functional and fragmented, understood through measurable components rather than personal meaning. For Münsterberg, psychology was a tool of optimisation, shaped by the values of efficiency and utility.

Lightner Witmer (1867–1956) shaped a very different space for psychology in the clinic. In 1896, he founded the first psychological clinic at the University of Pennsylvania, where he focused on helping children with learning difficulties and behavioural problems. Witmer's methods were less about experimentation and more about collecting detailed case histories, making observations, and devising therapeutic interventions. His approach combined medical, educational, and psychological tools. His patients were often working-class children whose struggles were interpreted through both individual and social lenses. The clinic, as a space, demanded a psychology of care and correction, not abstraction and generalisation. Witmer's work laid the foundations for school psychology, further blurring the boundary between knowledge and application.

The clinic-as-confessional reached its most elaborate form in the work of Sigmund Freud (1856–1939). Freud did not observe bodies or measure minds; he listened to what his patients were saying. Through dreams, slips of the tongue, and free association, he interpreted symbols of the psyche, unconscious forces shaping thought and behaviour. His consulting room was a private, ritualised space of disclosure. Patients, often women, were encouraged to speak freely, while Freud, positioned like a secular rabbi, offered interpretive insights. Psychology here was about the inner life, and its relation to moral, sexual, and familial codes. Inspired by the Jewish mystical tradition, the truths Freud uncovered revealed how deeply psychology was entangled with culture, gender, and patriarchal authority.

Alfred Binet (1857–1911), working in Paris, developed the first practical intelligence test in 1905 to help identify children in need of special educational support. Binet believed intelligence was complex and malleable, and he resisted the idea that a single score could define a person. His methods were nuanced and contextual. But when Binet's ideas were adopted in Britain and the United States, they were simplified and standardised, especially by Cyril Burt (1883–1971), who became a key figure in British educational psychology. Burt, who was once referred to as 'the first official psychologist in the world', advocated intelligence testing on a mass scale, using IQ scores to sort children into academic or vocational tracks. His work aligned psychology with national education policy (such as the creation of the 11+ Exam), turning psychological insight into institutional decision-making. In Burt's hands psychology became a gatekeeping tool, one that claimed objectivity but often reinforced class stratification.

Epistemological Issues

Epistemology refers to how we know what we know, in this case how psychology has historically defined, pursued, and legitimised knowledge about the mind and behaviour. The history of psychology reveals not one unified epistemological framework but multiple ways of knowing, each emerging from specific spaces of practice. These spaces, including the laboratory, factory, clinic, and school, actively shaped psychology's methods, aims, and assumptions about knowledge.

In the laboratory, the acquisition of psychological knowledge was modelled on the methods of the natural sciences. Researchers sought universal laws of perception, attention, or memory through controlled experiments. The epistemology here was a positivist one: knowledge was considered reliable if it was replicable, measurable, and free from subjective bias. Wundt's introspection protocols exemplified this approach. But, as seen in Rivers's work on the Torres Straits, once laboratory methods moved into the field, their reliability and meaning weakened. What counted as 'data' in the lab became unstable outside it, an early warning that objectivity is always contextual.

In the factory, knowledge was instrumental. Münsterberg's industrial psychology aimed not to explain mental life but to predict and control behaviour. The epistemology here was pragmatic and technocratic: knowledge was valid if it increased productivity or reduced error. Psychological truth was judged by its utility, not its depth, nor even its truth. Human variability was treated as noise to be managed or excluded.

In the clinic, psychology became interpretive. Freud and Witmer sought understanding, not prediction. Their methods, including free association, life histories, and behavioural observations, produced knowledge that was narrative, symbolic, and situated in personal and social contexts. The epistemology here was idiographic: it valued depth over generality, and meaning over measurement.

In the school, epistemology was bureaucratic. Binet's nuanced tests were recast by Burt and others into tools of classification. Intelligence was reduced to a number, a score, a rank. Knowledge was administrative: it enabled sorting, planning, and policy. Applying the critical thinking tool of situated knowledge demonstrates that the truth of an IQ test resides not in the test itself but in how and where it is used.

Ontological Issues

Ontology asks what kind of thing the mind is, what counts as psychological reality. In different historical spaces, psychology studied different minds and produced different kinds of subjects. The laboratory, the factory, the clinic, and the school each invited a different configuration of the psyche, one shaped by the demands, values, and relationships of that setting.

In the laboratory, the mind was conceptualised as a system of internal processes, perception, memory, and attention that could be analysed, measured, and mapped. The psychological subject here was assumed to be universal, abstract, and decontextualised. Participants were often adult male students trained to introspect under strict conditions. This produced an image of the mind as orderly, mechanistic, and detached from culture or identity, a 'view from nowhere' that, ironically, could only be achieved in the artificial setting of the laboratory.

In the factory, the mind was fragmented into functional capacities: attention span, speed of response, fatigue resistance. The worker became a *bundle of traits*, assessed for their usefulness within the machinery of industrial production. Ontologically, the mind was reduced to a tool to be calibrated, optimised, or discarded. There was little interest in inner life or complexity; what mattered was performance. The psychological subject here was a productive unit, a cog in a larger capitalist machine.

In the clinic, the mind was something hidden and conflicted, a depth to be explored rather than a mechanism to be tested. Freud's unconscious and Witmer's developmental case histories both treated the self as *contextual, moral, and historical*. The psychological subject was a storyteller, a patient, a person in crisis. Ontology here was rich but unstable: the mind could not be standardised because it was shaped by biography, family, and trauma.

In the school, the child was imagined as a future to be managed. The mind was treated as having measurable potential; quantifiable, developmental, and ranked. Psychological subjects here were pre-adults, destined for places in society based on scores and classifications. The school naturalised difference through numbers, producing minds that were measured and managed.

Power

Power does not so much repress as it shapes and produces. In each of the four sites of the cat's cradle of the psychological complex, psychology did more than uncover the mind; it helped define who could speak, who was examined, and who was classified. Its knowledge was not neutral but tied to systems of control, guidance, and normalisation. Through *situated knowledge*, we can see how power flows differently through each space, shaping what psychology could see, do, and say.

In the laboratory, power operated through standardisation and exclusion. Experimental psychology depended on the ability to isolate variables, control environments, and produce replicable data. But in doing so, it excluded those who didn't conform to the model of the rational, male, introspective subject. The lab privileged certain kinds of minds, those that could be trained, abstracted, and made to fit the apparatus. This space enacted what Foucault called *disciplinary power*: producing docile subjects by creating norms and opposing deviations.

In the factory, psychology became an agent of *economic governance*. Münsterberg's tests helped employers select the most efficient workers, often to the detriment of those deemed slow, distracted, or unsuitable. Here, power was exercised through measurement and sorting. Workers were *managed*. Psychology functioned as a handmaiden to capitalism, aligning mental traits with the logic of the assembly line.

In the clinic, psychology embodied *pastoral power*, a benevolent form of power that listens, diagnoses, nurtures, and guides. Freud's consulting room or Witmer's child clinics solicited confession in exchange for care. Patients were invited to reveal themselves, but under terms set by the therapist. The goal was not liberation as such but adjustment to norms of health, behaviour, and family. Psychology here operated as a benevolent moral authority.

In the school, psychology was enlisted in the management of populations. Intelligence testing sorted children into streams, sets, and classes, envisaging different opportunities, and futures for all. Burt's vision of inherited IQ helped justify educational inequality as natural difference. Schools became sites where psychology was embedded in policy, where students were not just taught but *known*. This was *biopower*: governing life by classifying it.

Chapter Summary

Psychology, as this chapter has shown, is not simply a science of the mind; it is also a *social technology*, forged in response to the needs of specific institutions and historical moments. From the laboratory to the clinic, from the factory to the school, psychology has adapted itself to different problems, different clients, and different forms of power. It has been a science of attention and introspection, of confession and control, of efficiency and exclusion, and of classification and care. And in each case, the kind of knowledge it produced was shaped by the context in which it was situated.

This is the central insight of *situated knowledge*: psychology does not describe the world from nowhere. It is always produced *somewhere*, by someone, for someone, and within specific material and institutional conditions. The epistemologies of the laboratory do not travel easily to the field. The truths discovered in the clinic may not apply in the classroom. The mind studied by experimental psychologists is not the same mind diagnosed by therapists or managed by educators.

For students of psychology, it is vital to understand that the discipline has always navigated a tension between the pursuit of universal laws and the reality of situational particularity. The study of human behaviour has always involved specific people, in specific places, under specific conditions, and in the service of particular interests. This remains just as true today, as psychology expands into digital classrooms, corporate HR systems, and AI-driven diagnostics. What psychology claims to know is inseparable from where that knowledge is produced, how it is validated, and whom it serves. To think critically about psychology's history is to understand the spaces from which it emerges.

On a beach in the Torres Straits in 1898, British psychologists invited Indigenous Islanders to play cat's cradle, observing the intricate string figures woven between their fingers. They were searching for cognitive universals, but what they found was something more profound: the entanglement of play, culture, knowledge, and place. That fragile web of string, suspended between hands, speaks still to the complexity of psychology's endeavour. Its truths are never floating free; they are stretched between bodies, anchored in context, and spun from the threads of power, place, and imagination.

Reflective Questions

1. How does the concept of *situated knowledge* challenge the idea that psychology is a universal science?
2. What ethical tensions are revealed by the Torres Straits expedition, and how does it illustrate the problem of applying laboratory methods in the field?
3. In what ways did psychology contribute to social sorting and classification in schools and factories during the early twentieth century?
4. What kind of subject (or 'self') is constructed in each of the psychological spaces explored in this chapter?
5. Why is this history relevant for social psychology today?

Suggested Reading

Colombo, M. (2020). Who is the 'other'? Epistemic violence and discursive practices. *Theory & Psychology, 30*(3), 399–404. https://doi.org/10.1177/0959354320923758.

Elgaard Jensen, T. (2019). Exploring the knowledge practices of psychology: Reflections on a field study. *Theory & Psychology, 29*(4), 466–483. https://doi.org/10.1177/0959354319853630.

Haraway, D. (1988). Situated knowledges: The science question in feminism and the privilege of partial perspective. *Feminist Studies, 14*(3), 575–599.

Held, B. S. (2019). Epistemic violence in psychological science: Can knowledge of, from, and for the (othered) people solve the problem? *Theory & Psychology, 30*(3), 349–370. https://doi.org/10.1177/0959354319883943.

Herle, A., and Rowse, S. Eds. (1998). *Cambridge and the Torres Strait: Centenary essays on the 1898 anthropological expedition.* Cambridge: Cambridge University Press.

Kontopodis, M., & Jackowska, M. (2019). De-centring the psychology curriculum: Diversity, social justice, and psychological knowledge. *Theory & Psychology, 29*(4), 506–520. https://doi.org/10.1177/0959354319858419.

Kvale, S. (2003). The church, the factory and the market: Scenarios for psychology in a postmodern age. *Theory & Psychology, 13*(5), 579–603. https://doi.org/10.1177/09593543030135005.

Lehmbrock, V. (2025). From intellectual imperialism to open system: Reassessing the 'Americanization' of social psychology through Festinger's frustration with the SSRC's project on transnational social psychology. *History of Psychology, 28*(2), 73–91. https://doi.org/10.1037/hop0000274.

Pouw, W. T. J. L., & Looren de Jong, H. (2015). Rethinking situated and embodied social psychology. *Theory & Psychology, 25*(4), 411–433. https://doi.org/10.1177/0959354315585661.

Rose, N. (1985). *The Psychological Complex: Psychology, politics and society in England, 1869–1939*. London: Routledge & Kegan Paul.

Shephard, B. (2014). *Headhunters: The search for a science of the mind*. London: The Bodley Head.

Ward, T., Sullivan, J., & Durrant, R. (2024). Epistemic disagreement in psychopathology research and practice: A procedural model. *Theory & Psychology, 34*(4), 484–507. https://doi.org/10.1177/09593543241263806.

Key Terms

Biopower A concept introduced by Michel Foucault to describe how modern societies regulate populations through scientific, medical, and psychological knowledge, often by classifying and managing life.

Clinic An institutional space where psychology is practised through therapeutic, diagnostic, and interpretive methods, often involving moral judgement and forms of pastoral power.

Epistemology The branch of philosophy concerned with knowledge—how we come to know things, what counts as evidence, and how truth is established in psychology.

Factory A site where psychology was used to enhance productivity, efficiency, and worker selection—shaping a functional, measurable view of the human mind.

Intelligence Testing A psychological method developed to assess mental capacity, often used in schools to sort children by perceived ability, but also implicated in social stratification.

Laboratory A controlled environment where early psychologists aimed to study universal mental processes using experimental methods such as introspection and reaction time.

Ontology The study of what exists; in psychology, this refers to assumptions about the nature of the mind or person being studied—whether fixed, fluid, individual, or relational.

Pastoral Power A form of subtle authority, historically associated with religious care, which in psychology refers to the therapist's or clinician's role in guiding, correcting, and shaping the individual.

Psychological Complex A term adapted from Nikolas Rose to describe the network of institutions, practices, and authorities through which psychology became embedded in modern society.

Psychometrics The branch of psychology concerned with the design and use of tests to measure mental capacities, traits, and behaviours.

Situated Knowledge A concept from Donna Haraway that argues that all knowledge, including psychological knowledge, is produced from a specific position, shaped by context, perspective, and power.

Torres Straits Expedition An 1898 research trip led by W. H. R. Rivers and colleagues to study Indigenous cognition using experimental tools; it exposed the limits of transferring laboratory psychology into the field.

FREE INSTRUCTOR & STUDENT RESOURCES

ONLINE RESOURCES

Visit the Instructor & Student Resources website at routledgelearning.com/bpscoretextbooks for free digital resources, including:

- Interactive quizzes and flashcards to test your knowledge
- Links to useful websites and videos
- Instructor manual, lecture slides, and course guide to enhance teaching and save instructors time

8 A Troubled Cure for a Troubled Mind

Psychology's Mastery of Metaphor

Chapter Overview

This chapter introduces metaphor as a critical thinking tool, encouraging us to question how metaphors shape what can be known, who can be known, and whose knowledge counts. Focusing on the work of William James and Sigmund Freud, it shows that metaphor is not merely a stylistic device but a constitutive element of knowledge, a way of constructing, not just describing, the mind. Through the contrasting metaphors of the 'stream of consciousness' and the 'iceberg model' of the unconscious, James and Freud created conceptual worlds that have profoundly influenced psychology's epistemological foundations. Alongside these canonical figures, the chapter recovers two lesser known but intellectually formidable psychologists: Karen Horney and Leta Hollingworth. Horney challenged Freud's gendered metaphors, proposing instead a dynamic, relational model of identity shaped by social pressure and cultural contradiction. Hollingworth used empirical data to dismantle the metaphor of female inferiority, replacing it with metaphors of growth, continuity, and potential. Their contributions highlight how metaphor operates as a site of both exclusion and resistance. In examining psychology's mastery of metaphor, the chapter challenges the neutrality of scientific language and reveals how metaphor encodes gendered, cultural, and philosophical assumptions.

A Troubled Cure for a Troubled Mind

In the early 1880s, two men who would go on to shape the future of psychology were experimenting with drugs. Not as recreational hedonists but as scientists trying to chart the limits of human experience. The American philosopher William James began experimenting with nitrous oxide gas around 1882. Grappling with depression, James was seeking to bridge the chasm between science and religion. Under the influence of nitrous oxide, he experienced what he called a 'tremendously exciting sense of an intense metaphysical illumination'. He described the gas as a solvent, dissolving ordinary consciousness and revealing hidden perspectives. James came to believe that altered states of consciousness offered profound insight into knowledge. Mystical revelation, pluralistic truths, and the primacy of subjective experience were rooted in those drug-induced numinous moments. For James, the psychedelic was a revelatory window to a new reality. Inspired by nitrous oxide, metaphor became the foundation for his experiential philosophy of psychology.

DOI: 10.4324/9781003565482-8

The Austrian neurologist Sigmund Freud turned to cocaine in 1884. Ambitious to distinguish himself in Viennese medical circles, he believed he had discovered a miracle drug. Cocaine, he wrote, was an 'absolutely harmless, marvellous treasure', a metaphor of alchemical promise. At first, the drug lifted his mood, sharpened his thoughts, and bolstered his confidence. But tragedy followed. Freud recommended cocaine to relieve a friend's chronic pain, believing it to be a harmless remedy. But the experiment ended in tragedy when the friend became addicted and died. Freud was deeply shaken. The metaphor changed. Cocaine was no longer a treasure but a poison, a false route towards liberation. Freud abandoned pharmacology and turned inward, towards the mind's own defences. He came to see repression not as something that must inevitably be dismantled but as a necessary function of the balanced mind. Releasing traumatic contents of the unconscious could be dangerous; they had to be revealed cautiously, symbolically, through free association and the analysis of dreams.

Chapter Contents

- How James and Freud used metaphor to shape foundational models of the mind.
- How metaphor encodes power, gender norms, and cultural assumptions in psychology.
- Exploring metaphor not as poetic decoration but as a constitutive form of psychological knowledge.

Chapter Objectives

- To compare the use of metaphor in the psychological theories of Sigmund Freud, William James, Karen Horney, and Leta Hollingworth.
- To critically assess how gendered metaphors shaped the development of psychological theory.
- To explore the role of metaphor as a critical thinking tool, enabling students to question how psychological concepts are constructed and framed.

CRITICAL THINKING TOOL
METAPHOR

Metaphor works by transferring meaning from one domain of experience to another. It occurs when a familiar or concrete concept (such as a 'stream', 'battlefield', or 'mirror') is used to describe and make sense of a more unfamiliar or abstract one (such as consciousness, emotion, or identity). This process is not simply decorative because metaphors shape the way we think, allowing us to organise complex or elusive ideas by anchoring them in more intuitive, bodily, or everyday experiences. In psychology, metaphor is especially important because most of its core subjects, such as the mind, memory, self, or trauma, are not directly observable. Metaphor

becomes a necessary tool for formulating intelligible models of such elusive phenomena. 'The attempt at introspective analysis,' William James wrote about this reflexive paradox, 'is in fact like seizing a spinning top to catch its motion, or trying to turn up the gas quickly enough to see how the darkness looks.' Metaphors carry embedded assumptions, cultural values, and theoretical commitments that must be examined critically.

James argued that the creation of new knowledge is essentially all about finding new metaphors. From James's perspective, metaphor functions as a perspectival shift: the world remains the same, but we suddenly see it through a different lens. Meanwhile, Sigmund Freud's entire psychoanalytic architecture rests on several clusters of metaphor; of archaeology, of pressure and release, of theatre, of conflict, and of movies. Dreams are 'the royal road' to the unconscious, repression operates like a 'dam', and the self protects itself through 'projection'. The psychological is rendered knowable through such metaphorical staging. Metaphor, then, is far from an innocent literary device. The metaphors that dominate psychology reflect deeper assumptions about the mind and the person. They also reflect who has the power to coin them. As we shall see, the metaphors employed by Freud and James often bear masculine, hierarchical, or mechanistic values, contrasted strikingly with the more relational or situated metaphors invoked by lesser known figures.

Introduction

Psychotherapy has been described as a conflicted 'battlefield', identity as an 'actor on a stage', and consciousness as a 'stream'. The mind has been likened to a house with a staircase leading down to a dark cellar. Each of these images offers a different understanding of what the mind *is*. But none are literal truths. They are metaphors, imaginative tools that do more than illustrate; they shape psychological knowledge itself.

This chapter compares two towering figures in the history of psychology: William James and Sigmund Freud. Both were prolific users of metaphor, and both understood that to speak of the mind at all required metaphoric language. Yet their metaphors pointed in sharply different directions. Freud's were mechanical, spatial, and hierarchical; he saw the mind as akin to a hydraulic pressurised system, riddled with conflict and repression. James, in contrast, imagined consciousness as a flowing stream, a fluid and ever-shifting experiential torrent. His metaphors were natural, organic, and perspectival. 'Our mental life,' he wrote, 'like a bird's life, seems to be made of an alternation of flights and perchings.'

Alongside these canonical figures, we also explore two critical but often overshadowed voices: Karen Horney and Leta Hollingworth. Their work, too, was rich in metaphor, but often emphasised growth, relation, and social context, a quiet rebellion against the heroic conquest metaphors of early psychology.

Historical Issues

William James and Sigmund Freud were near-contemporaries, both born in the nineteenth century: James in 1842 in New York, Freud in 1856 in what is now the Czech Republic. Yet their intellectual worlds, while overlapping, were shaped by markedly different historical forces. James emerged from the American pragmatic tradition, steeped in Protestant liberalism, Darwinian pluralism, and a spirit of philosophical openness. Freud, by contrast, came of age in fin-de-siècle Vienna, a city marked by repression, antisemitism, and the rigid hierarchies of the Austro-Hungarian Empire. Each thinker responded to their historical moment by crafting psychological theories steeped in metaphor that carried the traces of their respective cultures.

James' metaphors resonated with American ideals of freedom, individuality, and pluralism. His famous 'stream of consciousness' metaphor, first articulated in *The Principles of Psychology* (1890), rejected the reductionism of Wundt's structuralist psychology and invited readers to imagine thought as a continuous, flowing whole. James drew on evolutionary theory, religious experience, and literary narrative to construct a psychology of the open self; dynamic, unfinished, and perspectival.

Freud's metaphors reflected a mechanistic worldview inherited from nineteenth-century physics and neurology. Influenced by Helmholtzian energetics and Charcot's neurological theatre, he imagined the mind as a closed system of forces: libido, repression, cathexis, resistance. His clinical observations were rendered through metaphors of pressure, depth, conflict, and release. Freud's psychology mirrored the bourgeois, patriarchal family and the political tensions of empire where order had to be maintained, often through the subjugation of unruly forces.

As we saw in their different responses to their drug experiences, their metaphors reveal contrasting commitments; Freud to control and containment, James to movement and multiplicity. Their metaphorical repertoires also illustrate how psychology at the turn of the twentieth century was a cultural enterprise grappling with new ways of knowing and being. It is in this fertile moment that Horney and Hollingworth later intervened, challenging not only theory but the very metaphors through which psychological life was imagined.

Key Individuals

William James (1842–1910) was a philosopher of organic flux. His central metaphor, the 'stream of consciousness', remains one of the most enduring in psychology, offering a counterpoint to the atomistic metaphors of his structuralist contemporaries. In James's hands, metaphor was an epistemological device. Knowledge, for James, emerges when we find the right metaphor to shift our perspective, when we redescribe the familiar using a new image. This idea of redescription, of metaphor as transformation, lay at the heart of James's pluralistic psychology. The mind was a living system, adaptive, open-ended, and contingent.

Sigmund Freud (1856–1939) was also a master of metaphor, though his metaphors often reinforced the very structures of authority and repression he sought to expose. The psyche, in Freud's model, is divided into regions: the ego, id, and superego, mapped like territories in a political landscape. Dreams are coded messages; symptoms are symbols; desires erupt like revolutionary forces. The therapeutic process becomes archaeological, peeling back psychic layers to expose hidden relics.

Freud's metaphors drew heavily on nineteenth-century science, but they are also gendered. The metaphor of repression is tied to the control of dangerous impulses, a notion entwined with contemporary ideas of masculinity, sexuality, and civilisation. Freud's conceptual world is filled with thresholds, locks, and paternal injunctions. The dream 'censor' performs the vital work of maintaining psychic stability. Freud's metaphors produce a mind at war with itself, a fortress under siege, requiring the analyst to serve as both archaeologist and military general.

Karen Horney (1885–1952) disrupted the metaphorical logic of Freudian orthodoxy by prioritising the relational, the social, and the fluid. Rejecting Freud's phallic metaphors of authority and penetration, Horney recast psychological development in terms of connection, safety, and anxiety. Rather than speaking of drives and defences as impersonal forces, she imagined the psyche as a dynamic field of self and other, a living organism responding to its environment. Horney's metaphors are organic and embodied: the child 'gropes' for affection, the self 'blooms' or 'shrivels' depending on interpersonal nourishment. She spoke of 'neurotic trends' not as defects but as directional movements shaped by unmet relational needs. Her language carries a gentle, care-infused tone, often maternal rather than paternal in texture.

Leta Hollingworth (1886–1939) is best known for her empirical refutations of early twentieth-century beliefs about female intellectual inferiority. She was also a subtle master of metaphor. In contesting the so-called variability hypothesis, the idea that men show greater extremes of genius and idiocy than women, Hollingworth identified how metaphors reified cultural bias. She challenged metaphors of male brilliance as natural eruptions and female intelligence as derivative or dulled by menstruation. Instead, she offered metaphors of cultivation, development, and potential. Hollingworth used the metaphor of 'functional periodicity' to critique deterministic biological narratives and repositioned menstruation not as a debility but as a rhythm. Hollingworth's work reveals how metaphor operates in scientific discourse in the mundane descriptions that shape expectations and exclude possibilities.

Epistemological Issues

Psychology's epistemology, its way of knowing, has always leaned heavily on metaphor. Because the mind cannot be directly seen or measured like physical matter can, psychologists have turned to language, imagery, and analogy to bridge the gap between subjective experience and scientific explanation. William James, Sigmund Freud, Karen Horney, and Leta Hollingworth each built their psychological theories around metaphoric structures, and in doing so shaped not only what could be known but how it could be known.

James's epistemology was pluralistic. He distrusted rigid systems in favour of pragmatism, the view that ideas are tools rather than truths. His 'stream of consciousness' metaphor resisted the atomism of associationist psychology, offering instead an image of the mind as continuous, personal, and dynamic. Truth, for James, was something lived, organic, and provisional. His metaphors were literary, expansive, and epistemologically generative.

Freud's epistemology, in contrast, was hermeneutic, a science of interpretation. His metaphors, of pressure, repression, and excavation, implied that truth was not observed but uncovered. Yet this method, for all its innovation, rested on a paternal epistemology: the analyst was the expert interpreter, the patient his text.

Karen Horney rejected Freud's reduction of female experience to lack and neurosis, and with it his epistemic authority. Her theory of neurosis as a response to cultural and relational pressures proposed a different metaphor: the self as a compromised identity, shaped by social demands and inner conflict. Horney's knowledge was grounded in lived experience, not in the search for a universal law. Her approach foregrounded empathy, context, and relational insight. These choices were epistemological: Horney believed that metaphor had the power to reframe psychological suffering, to make it comprehensible without pathologising it.

Leta Hollingworth also questioned dominant methods and metaphors. She exposed the pseudoscience of sex difference research, arguing that the apparent instability of women's intellect was constructed by flawed male assumptions. Her work introduced an empirical feminist epistemology: rigorous, data-driven, yet critically aware of bias. In place of metaphors of deficit, she insisted on metaphors of potential and continuity, particularly in relation to child development and giftedness.

Ontological Issues

To ask 'what is the mind?' is an ontological question. It asks us to define what kind of thing the mind is, what it is made of, and how it persists or changes over time. The psychologists discussed in this chapter each provided a different answer to this question, and each constructed their answer through metaphor. Their ontologies shaped what psychology studied, and how it conceptualised the human.

James envisioned the mind as process, not substance. He described the brain, for example, as being 'like the aurora borealis, its whole internal equilibrium shifts with every pulse of change'. Influenced by Darwin, Bergson, and mystical experience, he refused to pin down the self, instead offering a model of multiple overlapping selves: material and spiritual. His ontology mirrored his radical empiricism: reality is experience, and all experience counts. The self, in James's model, is always developing.

Freud, in contrast, proposed a mind structured by internal conflict. His topographical and structural models, conscious, preconscious, unconscious; id, ego, superego, cast the psyche as a terrain of drives and defences, shaped by past trauma and instinctual pressure. His metaphors of excavation, warfare, and machinery reflected a deterministic ontology: the psyche as a site of repression, hierarchy, and struggle.

Horney challenged Freud's conception of the self as a battlefield governed by phallic authority. Her ontology offered an alternative: the self as relational and adaptive, constantly contorting itself to meet social expectations. Her metaphors of movement and distortion conveyed a psyche shaped by cultural and interpersonal forces. For Horney, identity was both vulnerable and emergent, not hardwired nor biologically preordained. Central to her theory was the concept of 'The Tyranny of the Should', a powerful metaphor she used to describe the rigid, often unrealistic, and self-imposed demands that neurotic individuals place on themselves, acting like an internal, relentless dictator dictating how they 'should' be, feel, or act.

Horney frequently described neurosis as a process where individuals become increasingly disconnected or 'alienated' from their real self. In this state they construct an idealised self, based on neurotic needs, which becomes a 'mask' or a 'prison' that prevents genuine connection and fulfilment. Her most famous and pervasive metaphorical framework, 'Moving Towards, Against, and Away from People', further elucidated these neurotic coping strategies, illustrating how individuals navigate their basic anxiety through compliance, aggression, or detachment from others.

Hollingworth viewed the self through the lens of continuity and growth. Rejecting fixed notions of male and female intellect, she argued for a mind that developed through nurture, education, and opportunity. Her research on giftedness and child development framed psychological difference as potential, not deficiency. Her ontological vision was optimistic, plastic, and generative. 'Isolation is the refuge of genius,' she wrote, 'not its goal.'

Hollingworth's metaphors aimed to provide accurate and empowering ways of understanding human development, particularly for marginalised groups such as women and gifted children. She used striking analogies to convey her scientific observations, such as her assertion that 'Mediocre or dull parents can no more produce a brilliant child than a tomato plant can produce a plum', succinctly highlighting her views on the distinct nature of giftedness and its hereditary components.

Power

Psychology has never been untouched by power. From its origins, it has been entangled in systems that classify, exclude, nurture and normalise. The metaphors psychologists use, such as kaleidoscopes, electric currents, stages, hierarchies, energy, and balance, are expressions of the power relations embedded in psychological theory. Across the work of James, Freud, Horney, and Hollingworth, we see how metaphor operates as a masterful technology of power, orienting knowledge in certain directions.

William James saw psychology as a site of epistemological liberation. His metaphors were democratic and organic: 'As a snowflake crystal caught in the warm hand is no longer a crystal but a drop,' he wrote, referring to thought, 'we find we have caught some substantive thing, usually the last word we were pronouncing . . . with its function, tendency and particular meaning in the sentence quite evaporated.'

Freud's psychoanalysis emerged from and contributed to pastoral power, as described by Foucault. It produced knowledge through an ethic of care, by diagnosing symptoms and by extracting hidden truths through analytic confession. Psychoanalysis operated like a secular priesthood, offering absolution through language while placing the analyst in a position of interpretive dominance. Freud's metaphors, of repression, neurosis, and inner conflict, reflected a model of the subject as fractured, guilty, and subordinate. His own position, as a Jewish outsider in Catholic Vienna, complicated this authority: he challenged bourgeois norms even as he sought respectability within them.

Karen Horney directly challenged the power embedded in Freudian metaphor. She rejected the psychoanalytic view of women as biologically inferior, exposing how Freud's metaphors of castration, lack, and envy served to naturalise patriarchal power. Horney reimagined neurosis as a reaction to cultural contradictions, a psychological protest against impossible social demands. Her work can be seen as a form of resistant biopower: seeking not to regulate the individual but to reframe the systems in which identity is formed.

Leta Hollingworth, too, refused the authority of male science. Her empirical dismantling of the 'variability hypothesis', the belief that women were less intellectually consistent than men, revealed the deep biases in psychological measurement and metaphor. In place of metaphors of instability and weakness, she substituted images of continuity, development, and potential. She used institutional science as a platform to critique its own exclusions, subtly asserting pastoral authority in the service of those denied it.

Chapter Summary

To understand psychology is to understand its mastery of metaphor. Metaphors are not merely ornamental flourishes whose function is simply to explain. They also create. This chapter has shown how metaphors shape the very structure of psychological thought, guiding what can be imagined, studied, or believed.

In the early 1880s, Freud and James each turned to drugs in search of insight. For James, nitrous oxide dissolved the rigid walls of consciousness and revealed new vistas of pluralistic truth. His metaphors flowed from that experience, liquid, luminous, open. For him, altered states were invitations. For Freud, cocaine seemed at first a miracle, a cure. But it ended in loss. A friend dead. A hope destroyed. And with that rupture came new metaphors, of battle, barrier, repression. The mind, in Freud's hands, became a locked room that only careful interpretation could unlock.

For William James, nitrous oxide was itself a metaphor. The drug's effects, loosening the boundaries of thought and perception, mimicked the mind's ability to shift perspective and reveal deeper truths. For James, altered states of consciousness were not dangerous, they were meaningful. Freud, on the other hand, believed that the mind should be explored with care and expertise, not through chemicals. For Freud, cocaine was not a useful metaphor, it was a dangerous distraction. Real insight, he believed, came through talking, analysing, and interpreting, not through intoxication.

Later thinkers such as Horney and Hollingworth revealed how gendered James and Freud's metaphors were, how power was hidden in the very images used to describe the psyche. They offered alternatives: of growth, safety, rhythm, and relation. To uncover psychology's mastery of metaphor therefore is to reveal its archaeology. Within every layer lies lived experience, the longing for truth, curative dreams. And it is in metaphor, chosen, inherited, or resisted, that the soul of psychology quietly resides.

Reflective Questions

1. How does metaphor shape what psychology is able to see and study?
2. In what ways do Freud's and Horney's models of the psyche reflect different views on gender and power?
3. What role does biography play in shaping psychological theory?
4. Can psychology ever be free of metaphor? Should it be?
5. Why is it important to recover the work of psychologists like Horney and Hollingworth?

Suggested Reading

Draaisma, D. (2000). *Metaphors of Memory: A history of ideas about the mind.* Cambridge: Cambridge University Press.

Green, C. D. (2019). Where did Freud's iceberg metaphor of mind come from? *History of Psychology, 22*(4), 369–372. https://doi.org/10.1037/hop0000135_b.

Harris, B. (2021). Eugenics, social reform, and psychology: The careers of Isabelle Kendig. *History of Psychology, 24*(4), 350–376. https://doi.org/10.1037/hop0000200.

Johnston, E., & Johnson, A. (2017). Balancing life and work by unbending gender: Early American women psychologists' struggles and contributions. *Journal of the History of the Behavioral Sciences, 53*(3), 246–264. https://doi.org/10.1002/jhbs.21862.

Knowles, E. S., & Sibicky, M. E. (1990). Continuity and diversity in the stream of selves: Metaphorical resolutions of William James's one-in-many-selves paradox. *Personality and Social Psychology Bulletin, 16*(4), 676–687. https://doi.org/10.1177/0146167290164008.

Leary, D. E. (1990). *Metaphors in the History of Psychology*. Cambridge: Cambridge University Press.

Leary, D. E. (1992). William James and the art of human understanding. *American Psychologist, 47*(2), 152–160. https://doi.org/10.1037/0003-066X.47.2.152.

Richards, G. (1991). James and Freud: Two masters of metaphor. *British Journal of Psychology, 82*(2), 205–215. https://doi.org/10.1111/j.2044-8295.1991.tb02395.x.

Ruck, N., Luckgei, V., Rothmüller, B., Franke, N., & Rack, E. (2022). Psychologization in and through the women's movement: A transnational history of the psychologization of consciousness-raising in the German-speaking countries and the United States. *Journal of the History of the Behavioural Sciences, 58*(3), 269–290. https://doi.org/10.1002/jhbs.22187.

Rutherford, A. (2017). 'Making better use of U.S. women': Psychology, sex roles, and womanpower in post-WWII America. *Journal of the History of the Behavioural Sciences, 53*(3), 228–245. https://doi.org/10.1002/jhbs.21861.

Soyland, A. J. (1994). *Psychology as Metaphor.* Thousand Oaks, CA: Sage.

Sullivan, P. (2017). Towards a literary account of mental health from James' *Principles of Psychology, New Ideas in Psychology, 46*, 31–38. https://doi.org/10.1016/j.newideapsych.2016.02.003.

Key Terms

Castration Anxiety A metaphor used by Sigmund Freud to theorise male anxiety about loss of power, often criticised for reinforcing patriarchal assumptions and gendered interpretations of mental life.

Dream of Irma's Injection A foundational Freudian dream analysis that illustrates how metaphor, bodily imagery, and self-justification operate in the unconscious. Frequently used as an example of the metaphorical richness of dream life.

False Self A metaphor used by Karen Horney to describe the compromised identity a person adopts in response to cultural or interpersonal pressure, masking their authentic needs and feelings.

Iceberg Model Sigmund Freud's metaphor for the psyche, where the visible conscious mind floats above the much larger, submerged unconscious, a model that suggests repression and hidden forces drive behaviour.

Metaphor A figure of speech that frames one thing in terms of another. In psychology, metaphor is not merely decorative but fundamental to theory-making. It shapes how the mind is conceptualised, from William James's 'stream' to Sigmund Freud's 'iceberg'.

Penis Envy A Freudian concept and metaphor describing a girl's supposed unconscious desire for male power and status. Widely criticised by feminist psychologists as a culturally biased, patriarchal narrative.

Royal Road Sigmund Freud's famous metaphor for dreams, describing them as the primary path to understanding the unconscious mind.

Stream of Consciousness William James's metaphor for the continuity and fluidity of thought, used to reject mechanistic or atomistic models of the mind and to promote a psychology grounded in lived experience.

Variability Hypothesis A nineteenth-century pseudoscientific belief that men are more variable—and therefore more likely to be geniuses or failures—than women. Leta Hollingworth empirically disproved this idea.

FREE INSTRUCTOR & STUDENT RESOURCES

ONLINE RESOURCES

Visit the Instructor & Student Resources website at routledgelearning.com/bpscoretextbooks for free digital resources, including:

- Interactive quizzes and flashcards to test your knowledge
- Links to useful websites and videos
- Instructor manual, lecture slides, and course guide to enhance teaching and save instructors time

9 The BITCH Bites Back

Categorisation and the Invention of Intelligence

Chapter Overview

This chapter examines the emergence of 'intelligence' as a dominant psychological category and uses the critical thinking tool of *categorisation* to interrogate how psychology selects, constructs, and institutionalises the concepts it uses to make sense of human difference. Around 1900, concepts such as instinct, reason, and intellect competed to define mental variation. By 1910, intelligence had taken their place, not because it was discovered in a scientific sense but because it became socially and institutionally useful, especially in education, the military, and eugenics. This chapter traces this shift through key figures, including Francis Galton, Alfred Binet, Charles Spearman, William Stern, Cyril Burt, and James Flynn. It highlights the role of measurement and mimicry in turning intelligence from an abstract idea into a reified quantifiable entity. The use of IQ tests to sort children, classify soldiers, and exclude immigrants is presented as an example of psychology functioning as a tool of power. Challenging the idea that intelligence is a stable, biological entity, the chapter introduces alternative perspectives such as the *Flynn Effect* and Ken Richardson's metaphor of *social distance*. It also foregrounds inclusive contributions, including Robert L. Williams's BITCH-100 test, which exposed cultural bias in standardised testing. Ultimately, the chapter invites students to rethink intelligence not as a natural kind but as a human kind, a historically contingent category that reveals more about society's priorities than the structure of the human abilities.

The BITCH Bites Back

For decades, standard IQ tests, widely used for educational and vocational gatekeeping, consistently revealed a stark and troubling pattern: African Americans, on average, scored lower than their white counterparts. This deeply problematic discrepancy fuelled damaging stereotypes and actively perpetuated systemic inequalities, leading to low academic expectations and limited opportunities. But in 1972 there came a groundbreaking challenge to this entrenched orthodoxy. Dr. Robert L. Williams, a pioneering African American psychologist and a founder member of the Association of Black Psychologists, introduced a revolutionary instrument designed to expose the profound cultural biases embedded within IQ tests. He provocatively named it the Black Intelligence Test of Cultural Homogeneity, or BITCH-100. Williams's own academic journey had been shaped by the sting of a biased IQ test that wrongly suggested he was suited for manual labour rather than intellectual pursuits. It was an audacious reversal of the status quo from a man who became a Professor of Psychology and African-American Studies at Washington

DOI: 10.4324/9781003565482-9

University in St Louis. Unlike traditional IQ tests that implicitly favoured white, middle-class experiences and vocabulary, the BITCH-100 was deliberately constructed from the rich tapestry of African American vernacular; slang, historical references, and everyday life scenarios. Questions featured terms such as 'alley apple' or 'boogie jugie', and situations familiar to Black communities. The results were a seismic shock: African American participants scored significantly higher than their white counterparts, unequivocally demonstrating how dramatically cultural context influences test performance. This provocative experiment was a potent, undeniable demonstration that the very tools of psychological assessment, far from being universal measures of intelligence, were often complicit in misrepresenting the cognitive abilities of those from different backgrounds. The BITCH-100 ignited critical reflection and forced psychology to confront an uncomfortable question: how do psychology's most trusted instruments of assessment inadvertently perpetuate systemic biases, shape destinies, and reinforce inequality?

Chapter Contents

- Traces the emergence of intelligence as a psychological category, replacing earlier concepts such as instinct, intellect, and reason.
- Critically examines how intelligence testing became central to individual differences psychology and the management of populations.
- Introduces *categorisation* as a critical thinking tool to analyse the historical, cultural, and political functions of psychological concepts.

Chapter Objectives

- To explore how intelligence emerged as a dominant psychological category in the twentieth century and to examine the forces that shaped its construction.
- To critically assess the methods and metaphors used to define, measure, and reify intelligence.
- To apply the critical thinking tool of *categorisation* to evaluate the historical and political work that psychological concepts perform.

CRITICAL THINKING TOOL
CATEGORISATION

In psychology, categories do more than organise knowledge; they make certain ways of thinking possible. The decision to group people by 'intelligence' rather than, say, by 'instinct' or 'reason' is not neutral. It reflects a series of historical, political, and epistemological choices about what matters, who counts, and how difference should be managed. *Categorisation*, then, is a critical tool for thinking about the construction of psychological knowledge. It invites us to ask: why this category, at this time, and for what purpose?

In this chapter, categorisation is used to explore how 'intelligence' emerged in the early twentieth century as a dominant psychological category. Around 1900, psychologists and

social reformers had many terms to choose from: reason, intellect, instinct, even divine intelligence. But by 1910, the now secularised concept of 'intelligence' had become the key label for describing and measuring individual mental differences. Its victory was not inevitable, it was strategic. Intelligence was elastic enough to fit new scientific ambitions, biological enough to match evolutionary thinking, and versatile enough to serve bureaucratic systems such as schools, armies, and immigration services.

Psychological categories are not discovered in the way physical scientists discover particles or genes. Instead, they are constructed, negotiated, and institutionalised. In a sense they are social achievements. Categorisation allows us to see that intelligence is not a timeless truth but a historically contingent way of sorting people, one that emerged when it became socially beneficial to do so. This chapter uses categorisation as a lens to re-examine how psychology has defined, measured, and managed mental difference.

Introduction

In the early twentieth century, psychology began to treat intelligence as if it were a real, measurable thing, like blood pressure or temperature, rather than a complex and contested idea. This process of turning a fuzzy concept into a fixed attribute is known as reification. Intelligence became something you could be said to 'have', and crucially, to have more or less of, because psychology decided to build measuring tools around it. These tools, such as IQ tests, were guided by operationalism, the belief that a concept is only meaningful if it can be measured. As a result, tests were designed to mimic what they aimed to assess: children's intelligence tests looked like puzzles and toys; adult ones like workplace tasks. This mimicry reinforced the illusion that intelligence existed as a natural entity (a natural kind), rather than as a human invention (a human kind).

Intelligence test scores improved dramatically across the twentieth century, with average IQs rising by over 25 points between 1950 and 2000. One consequence of this is that IQ tests must be recalibrated (i.e. made more difficult) every few years to ensure that the population's mean intelligence remains standardised at 100. This phenomenon, known as the Flynn Effect, challenges the idea that intelligence is fixed, inherited, or timeless. It suggests instead that intelligence may be a cultural artefact, something shaped by education, opportunity, and social life. This chapter begins from that finding.

Historical Issues

Psychology stood at a crossroads at the turn of the twentieth century. The word 'intelligence' had not yet secured its modern meaning, and alternative categories competed for dominance. In James Mark Baldwin's *Dictionary of Philosophy and Psychology* (1902), for example, there is no separate entry for 'intelligence'. Readers are referred to 'Intellect', which itself is described only as 'the faculty or capacity of knowing'. The absence is revealing. Psychology had not yet fixated on intelligence as its master category of individual difference.

This fixation emerged rapidly in response to new social demands. Three powerful forces, of compulsory education, the management of the so-called feeble-minded, and the pressures of military selection, combined to make intelligence testing not just useful but necessary. Schools needed to sort children efficiently, identifying those who could thrive in academic settings and those who should be diverted into vocational training. Governments sought to prevent the 'unfit' from reproducing, drawing on eugenic ideologies that categorised people as 'idiots', 'imbeciles', and 'morons' (terms made infamous by Henry Goddard). And during wartime, the military required a swift, scalable method to allocate recruits to roles of appropriate complexity.

Although Francis Galton never used the term 'intelligence' in the modern sense, he set the stage. Inspired by Darwin, he imagined a world in which mental abilities were biological and inheritable. Galton hoped to measure 'civic worth' using physical traits such as height, eyesight, and reaction time, assuming these were proxies for mental power. While his precise ambitions failed, his eugenic dream of a measurable hierarchy of minds flourished, particularly in the United States, Scandinavia, and Nazi Germany.

The emergence of intelligence as a psychological category was not the outcome of scientific 'discovery'. It was a convergence of institutional needs, the embedding of a particular metaphor, and cultural anxiety. Psychology responded by selecting 'intelligence' over other categories, because it could do multiple kinds of work: quantify, compare, sort, and exclude. In this sense, categorisation was not so much a scientific practice as it was a political decision.

Key Individuals

Francis Galton (1822–1911) is often remembered as the founder of differential psychology, but his categories were not yet those of IQ. Galton was preoccupied with hereditary genius and 'mental power', a metaphor he borrowed from physics to imagine minds as measurable forces. He aimed to connect physical traits (such as reaction time, grip strength, lung capacity) to civic value, assuming these were proxies for mental power. He failed to establish a true psychometric science on these terms, but his ideological legacy endured: especially the belief that mental difference was biological, measurable, and heritable.

In 1904, Charles Spearman (1863–1945) proposed the existence of a general intelligence factor ('g') which he argued underpinned all intellectual performance. Spearman's methods were mathematical: he used factor analysis to reduce complex test scores to a single, underlying dimension. For him, intelligence was like gravity: unseen but omnipresent. This shift marks a crucial point in the reification of intelligence. What had once been a cluster of overlapping abilities became a single, latent trait, embedded in the individual.

Alfred Binet (1857–1911), working in France, took a very different approach. Commissioned by the Ministry of Education to devise a tool for identifying children needing extra support, Binet saw intelligence not as fixed trait but as developmental. His 'mental age' scores were pragmatic tools, not ontological statements. Binet's philosophy and approach were fundamentally at odds with the idea of reducing intelligence to a single, fixed, reified score.

William Stern (1871–1938) invented the Intelligence Quotient (IQ), which divided mental age by chronological age. The innovation marked the moment when a diagnostic aid became an instrument of selection, exclusion, and control.

Cyril Burt (1883–1971) popularised intelligence testing in schools, most notably through the 11+ examination which was introduced in the UK as part of the 1944 Education Act. Burt's work was influential in embedding intelligence as a fixture in British educational policy. Yet his legacy is complicated by accusations of data fabrication and a rigid belief in the genetic basis of intelligence. Burt represents the full institutionalisation of the intelligence category: from a scientific hypothesis to an apparatus of population selection by the state.

John C. Raven (1902–1970) developed the Progressive Matrices test, intended to measure abstract reasoning without relying on language or cultural knowledge. This test, used across the world, appeared to offer a 'culture-free' measure of general intelligence. Ironically, it is precisely this test that showed the most dramatic Flynn Effect gains over the twentieth century, demonstrating that whatever Raven was measuring, it was far from biologically fixed.

James R. Flynn (1934–2020), the political philosopher who first documented intergenerational IQ gains, challenged the biological model. Intelligence, he argued, is not inherited in any simple sense; it responds to schooling, complexity, urbanisation, and even media exposure. Flynn's work is central to understanding intelligence as a historical category. He reframed IQ not as a property of minds but as a marker of changing environments.

Robert L. Williams (1930–2020) was a pioneering African American psychologist, educator, and outspoken critic of cultural bias in psychological testing. Born in Little Rock, Arkansas, Williams earned his PhD in clinical psychology in 1961 and went on to become a prominent figure in both Black psychology and educational reform. He was a founding member, and later President, of the Association of Black Psychologists, an organisation established in 1968 to challenge the racism embedded within mainstream psychology and to promote psychological approaches rooted in African American experience. Williams is perhaps best known for creating the Black Intelligence Test of Cultural Homogeneity (BITCH-100) in 1972.

In the history of intelligence testing, some individuals, such as Spearman and Stern, worked to stabilise the intelligence category, to make it unitary, measurable, and predictive. Others, including Binet, Flynn, and Gardner, destabilised it, exposing its cultural, developmental, and political contingencies. The history of intelligence is a field of contestation, shaped by decisions about what should count, what can be measured, and what kinds of people psychology should serve.

Epistemological Issues

Psychology has always struggled with questions concerning the kind of knowledge it wants to produce, and how it can acquire that knowledge. This struggle has been especially intense in the case of intelligence. From the beginning, intelligence has been an epistemologically divided category; at once concrete and abstract, numerical and metaphorical, biological and behavioural. Its apparent clarity rests not on what it *is* but on how it has been operationalised to be measured.

Psychometric tests are cultural artefacts built to simulate what they claim to reveal. Children's IQ tests, for example, mimic puzzles and games; adult tests often imitate real-world tasks such as recognising patterns or following instructions. As mimicry, these tests give the illusion of transparency: that intelligence simply shines through. But this is a performance, not a revelation. Psychologists design tests based on what they *think* intelligence looks like, and then use those tests to confirm its presence.

Operationalism is the idea that a psychological construct is defined by the way it is measured. In the 1930s, S. S. Stevens declared that intelligence is 'what the tests test'. This neat phrase sidesteps the difficult question of whether intelligence exists independently of our definitions of it. Yet it also allows psychology to treat invented metrics as if they were natural facts. The danger is that the existence of a measurement technique can mislead us into assigning an unwarranted status to the thing being measured.

In psychology, whether a category can be measured or not depends on convention. With respect to intelligence, the deeper question is whether intelligence is even a quantitative variable in the first place. Psychologist Joel Michell has argued that psychometrics never *proved* that its constructs are measurable in the strict, additive sense. They behave more like conventions than quantities.

Despite these criticisms, intelligence testing remains central to the field of individual differences psychology, where it continues to influence educational policy, workplace selection, and even mental health diagnosis. Yet if psychology is to be intellectually honest, it must constantly revisit its epistemological assumptions.

Ontological Issues

To ask about the ontology of intelligence is to ask: what kind of thing is it? Is it a fixed trait inside the head? The history of psychology shows that intelligence has been theorised in multiple and often contradictory ways. Is it a power present in all actions, or social aptitude? Each way of conceptualising intelligence carries its own implications, not just for what is measured but for who gets to be seen as possessing it, and who does not.

In the early twentieth century, intelligence was often described as a kind of mental power, a force-like metaphor inspired by physics. Galton, Spearman, and their followers imagined intelligence as an invisible mental property that governed performance across all tasks. Like gravity or voltage it could be stronger or weaker, but always present. This metaphor lent scientific authority to the idea of fixed, inherited ability. Once intelligence was reified in this way, people could be ranked, compared, and assigned different opportunities and jobs.

Yet intelligence has also been theorised very differently. Ken Richardson (2002) has argued that 'mental power' is the wrong metaphor for intelligence. Instead, he proposes *social distance*, the idea that performance on intelligence tests reflects how far individuals are from the norms, values, and language of the test-makers. On this view, intelligence is a product of the environment. It reflects culture and life opportunity.

These competing ontologies matter. If intelligence is understood as a *concrete thing* people possess, then it justifies selection, tracking, and exclusion. If it is seen instead as a *social artefact*, then the focus shifts to context, inequality, and reform. In the context of individual differences, this ontological instability is critical. The field seeks to explain variation among individuals, but if the very categories it uses are historically and socially contingent, then those explanations require ongoing scrutiny. Intelligence may look like a scientific object, but its nature, what it *is*, remains a vital question.

Power

Intelligence, as a psychological category, is a technology of classification that has long served institutional and political purposes. From its inception, intelligence testing has been entangled with the exercise of power: the power to sort, to rank, to include and to exclude. In this sense, it operates as a form of what Michel Foucault called *disciplinary power*: the regulation of people and populations through normalisation.

The emergence of intelligence testing coincided with the rise of the normal distribution curve, a statistical device that appeared to map ability onto a natural bell curve shape. Once intelligence was imagined as something measurable and normally distributed, it was possible to draw thresholds: to declare some children 'gifted', others 'average', and still others 'feeble-minded'. These categories carried profound consequences. They determined access to schooling, jobs, even reproductive rights. In the early twentieth century, so-called feeble-minded individuals were institutionalised, sterilised, or denied citizenship, all under the guise of science.

The 11+ exam in the UK is a good example of power operating through measurement. It was designed to divide children at age 11 into different educational pathways: grammar school, technical school, or secondary modern school, based on their performance on an intelligence test. The assumption was that intelligence was fixed and measurable by age 11. But in practice, the test mirrored and reinforced class structures, presenting social inequality as natural difference. Middle-class parents ensured that their children were given extensive instruction in how to pass the 11+.

In the United States, psychometric testing was used to justify immigration quotas, military rank, and voting restrictions. The early IQ tests, including those developed by Lewis Terman and used by the Army Alpha project, helped classify recruits during the First World War. These tests helped define what it meant to be fit to serve, to lead, and to learn. Seen this way, intelligence is a mechanism for managing populations. In individual differences psychology, this is a central tension: the field seeks to explain variation, but it also produces tools that sort people into hierarchies. Intelligence becomes a gateway, and a gatekeeper, to life chances.

Chapter Summary

Psychology's category of intelligence never merely described minds. From its entrance into the psychological lexicon in the early twentieth century, intelligence served social and institutional needs. Mass schooling, industrial warfare, and eugenic ambitions demanded tools for classifying people. Psychology delivered. Intelligence, in this historical sense, was engineered to function at the heart of a psychological complex.

The rise of Spearman's 'g' transformed intelligence into an apparent essence: innate, quantifiable, and unevenly distributed. This idea aligned comfortably with a hierarchical society obsessed with legitimacy and order. In Britain, the 11+ Exam, in the United States, IQ-based military selection, both embedded the notion that life chances could be assigned by number. Intelligence was fixed early, ranked on a curve, and naturalised as destiny.

But intelligence has never been destiny. The twentieth century's steady rise in global IQ scores, the Flynn Effect, revealed just how sensitive intelligence is to culture, context, and change. Alternative metaphors and models such as intelligence as social competence and multiple or emotional intelligence redefined what it meant to be 'clever'. These shifts forced psychology to confront a fundamental truth: intelligence is not a neutral measure of value. It is a historically contingent construct, shaped by power, and open to challenge.

In 1972, Robert Williams issued one such challenge. His Black Intelligence Test of Cultural Homogeneity (BITCH-100) not only tested differently, it asked who gets to define intelligence in the first place. The test did not seek to fix intelligence but to free it. Tools once used to exclude can be reclaimed, reimagined, and redeployed. Psychological tests can bite back.

Reflective Questions

1. Why did psychology settle on 'intelligence' as a key category, rather than instinct, reason, or intellect?
2. What does it mean to say that intelligence is a 'constructed' rather than a 'discovered' category?
3. How does the metaphor of 'social distance' challenge traditional views of intelligence testing?
4. In what ways has intelligence testing acted as a form of power in shaping people's life chances?
5. What lessons can the history of intelligence testing teach us about contemporary psychological practices?

Suggested Reading

Danziger, K. (1997). *Naming the Mind: How psychology found its language*. Thousand Oaks, CA: Sage.

Fancher, R. E. (1998). Biography and psychodynamic theory: Some lessons from the life of Francis Galton. *History of Psychology*, *1*(2), 99–115. https://doi.org/10.1037/1093-4510.1.2.99.

Franz, D. J. (2021). 'Are psychological attributes quantitative?' is not an empirical question: Conceptual confusions in the measurement debate. *Theory & Psychology*, *32*(1), 131–150. https://doi.org/10.1177/09593543211045340.

Michell, J. (2005). *Measurement in Psychology: Critical history of a methodological concept*. Cambridge: Cambridge University Press.

Michell, J. (2021). 'The art of imposing measurement upon the mind': Sir Francis Galton and the genesis of the psychometric paradigm. *Theory & Psychology*, *32*(3), 375–400. https://doi.org/10.1177/09593543211017671.

Richardson, K. (2002). What IQ tests test. *Theory & Psychology*, *12*(3), 283–314. https://doi.org/10.1177/0959354302012003012.

Richardson, K. (2017). *Genes, Brains, and Human Potential: The science and ideology of intelligence*. New York: Columbia University Press.

Schregel, S. (2020). 'The intelligent and the rest': British Mensa and the contested status of high intelligence. *History of the Human Sciences*, *33*(5), 12–36. https://doi.org/10.1177/0952695120970029.

Wackers, G. (2025). Digital phenotyping of the mind: From biology to psychoinformatics. *Theory & Psychology*, *35*(2), 141–162. https://doi.org/10.1177/09593543251322116.

Williams, R. L. (1972). The BITCH-100: A culture-specific test. Paper presented at the American Psychological Association Annual Convention.

Winston, A. S. (2018). Neoliberalism and IQ: Naturalizing economic and racial inequality. *Theory & Psychology*, *28*(5), 600–618. https://doi.org/10.1177/0959354318798160.

Key Terms

11+ Examination A UK educational test introduced in the mid-twentieth century used to determine secondary school placement, based on assumed fixed intelligence measured at age 11.

Biopower A term from Michel Foucault describing how institutions regulate populations through scientific categorisation and measurement, such as intelligence testing.

BITCH-100 The Black Intelligence Test of Cultural Homogeneity, developed by Robert L. Williams in 1972 to expose the cultural bias in traditional IQ testing.

Categorisation The psychological and political process of selecting, defining, and institutionalising categories—like intelligence—to make human differences legible and manageable.

Flynn Effect The substantial rise in average IQ scores observed globally over the twentieth century, challenging the view that intelligence is fixed or purely genetic.

General Intelligence (g) A theoretical core mental ability proposed by Charles Spearman that underlies performance across all cognitive tasks.

Hereditary Genius A concept proposed by Francis Galton suggesting that intellectual ability is inherited and unevenly distributed across the population.

Individual Differences Psychology A core area of psychology concerned with measuring and explaining how and why individuals vary in traits such as intelligence or personality.

Intelligence Quotient (IQ) A score derived from standardised tests, originally calculated by dividing mental age by chronological age and multiplying by 100.

Mental Age A concept developed by Alfred Binet and Théodore Simon indicating the intellectual performance level of an individual relative to average performance at a given age.

Multiple Intelligences A theory proposed by Howard Gardner suggesting that intelligence is not unitary but consists of various distinct forms (e.g. linguistic, musical, spatial).

Operationalism The belief that psychological concepts are meaningful only when defined by the operations used to measure them.

Psychometrics The field of psychology devoted to the theory and technique of psychological measurement, including intelligence, aptitude, and personality tests.

Reification The process of treating an abstract concept (like intelligence) as if it were a real, tangible thing.

Social Distance (Metaphor) A concept proposed by Ken Richardson to explain test performance as a function of cultural distance from the norms of the test designers, rather than innate ability.

FREE INSTRUCTOR & STUDENT RESOURCES

ONLINE RESOURCES

Visit the Instructor & Student Resources website at routledgelearning.com/bpscoretextbooks for free digital resources, including:

- Interactive quizzes and flashcards to test your knowledge
- Links to useful websites and videos
- Instructor manual, lecture slides, and course guide to enhance teaching and save instructors time

10

After the Flood

Companion Species and the Co-production of Psychology

Chapter Overview

This chapter reconsiders the role of animals in the development of psychological science through the critical lens of Donna Haraway's concept of *companion species*. Moving beyond the view of animals as passive tools or experimental objects, the chapter argues that animals have consistently shaped psychological knowledge as active participants, resisting, adapting, and interacting in ways that challenge traditional models of objectivity and control.

Through a re-examination of iconic experiments, including Pavlov's dogs, Harlow's monkeys, Köhler's apes, and Skinner's pigeons, the chapter demonstrates how animals' individual behaviours often disrupted the assumptions of behavioural psychology. Historical shifts are traced from anecdotal approaches to standardised experiments, culminating in contemporary insights from thinkers such as Peter Godfrey-Smith.

The chapter introduces key epistemological and ontological issues concerning the role of animals in psychological research. It examines how knowledge is produced with animals and explores the assumptions psychological methods make about what kinds of beings animals are. These concerns are situated within broader debates about power, ethics, and replicability. The chapter concludes by arguing that taking animals seriously, as companions in knowledge production, is ethically essential and methodologically and conceptually transformative. It encourages students to engage in critical, reflective, and ethically grounded thinking about the future of psychological science.

After the Flood

On a grey September day in 1924, the River Neva burst its banks in Saint Petersburg and flooded Ivan Pavlov's laboratory. The dogs, his most devoted experimental collaborators, were trapped in rising water. Panicked and howling, they clawed at the iron walls of their kennels while assistants waded through the chaos, submerging each animal to release them one by one. They survived, but the damage had been done. In the days that followed, the same dogs who had salivated to metronomes, buzzers, and harmoniums no longer did so. Some refused food. Others cowered at once-familiar sounds. The conditional reflex had not failed, it had been erased. Trauma had changed them. Contrary to modern myth, Pavlov never trained a dog to salivate to a bell. Nor did he ever utter the Russian equivalent of the phrase 'conditioned reflex'. 'Only one thing in life is of essential interest for us,' he observed, 'our psychical experience.' For him, animals were not machines, they were personalities: cowards, heroes, loners, neurotics. 'That which I see in dogs,' he once

DOI: 10.4324/9781003565482-10

reflected, 'I immediately transfer to myself.' For Pavlov, the great terror of life was *sluchainosti*: accidents, chaos, the unpredictability of fate. His science, grounded in methodological regularity, was an effort to impose law and order on chance. But in the aftermath of the flood, the dogs revealed what he most feared: that no laboratory procedure or scientific principle was immune to abrupt modification. Established facts could no longer be trusted. This chapter begins in that moment of rupture. What happens when the animals we study refuse to comply with our experimental procedures? What if they are not tools of knowledge but co-authors of it? In the stories of Pavlov's dogs, and of the many other animals who made psychology possible, we find a hidden history of the minds of others meeting across species lines, not always in harmony but always in relation.

Chapter Contents

- Explore the historical use of animals in psychological research, from Thorndike's cat to Godfrey-Smith's octopus.
- Analyse the concept of companion species and its challenge to behaviourist and mechanistic models of mind.
- Examine epistemological, ontological, and power-based issues in the co-production of psychological knowledge across species.

Chapter Objectives

- To understand how animals have shaped the development of psychological knowledge as experimental participants and epistemological collaborators.
- To assess the limitations of traditional behaviourist methods in light of emerging research on animal cognition, emotion, and communication.
- To apply the critical thinking tool of 'companion species' to reframe psychological experimentation as a relational and co-constituted process.

CRITICAL THINKING TOOL
COMPANION SPECIES

What if the animals in psychological experiments were not just passive subjects but active collaborators? That is the provocative question posed by Donna Haraway's concept of *companion species*. Introduced in her *Companion Species Manifesto* (2003), this idea challenges how we think about human–animal relations as deeply entangled partnerships. A *companion species* is more than a pet, and more than an experimental subject. It is a being whose life and intelligence are intertwined with ours, helping to co-shape meaning, knowledge, and even our scientific methods. Haraway's favourite example is the dog; loyal pet, worker, communicator, and fellow traveller through human history. In her view, dogs and humans have evolved together, mutually shaping each other's capacities and cultures. This concept offers a powerful critique of the traditional use of animals in psychology. Instead of viewing rats, pigeons, or monkeys as passive subjects in stimulus–response experiments, the lens of companion species emphasises

the collaborative nature of knowledge-making. It highlights how research outcomes are shaped by animals' individual quirks, their resistances, and their relationships with experimenters.

Haraway also calls for *situated knowledge*, a rejection of the so-called 'god trick' of scientific objectivity. That means we cannot pretend to observe animals from a detached, all-seeing vantage point. Our own position, expectations, and cultural assumptions matter. So too does the animal's individuality. The behaviour of a single chimpanzee in a problem-solving task might reflect not just universal 'chimp' cognition but also a specific, co-created moment in an interspecies relationship.

Introduction

Psychology has long relied on animals to build theories of learning, emotion, and intelligence. When animals are recognised as active partners in knowledge production, the nature of psychological inquiry shifts. This chapter explores several iconic moments in the history of psychology to demonstrate that animal minds were never merely objects of study. Instead, they actively shaped the very theories devised to explain them.

Far from being mechanical responders to stimuli, Pavlov's dogs reacted to the specific presence and behaviour of experimenters. Pavlov named his dogs, acknowledging their distinctiveness. Their so-called reflexes were relational, not just automatic. In Harry Harlow's work on maternal deprivation, infant monkeys formed bonds not predicted by theory, resisting the experimental set-up itself. The data demanded new ways of thinking about love and care. Köhler's chimpanzees demonstrated problem-solving that required human observers to rethink cognition itself. Skinner's pigeons, trained under strict behavioural conditions, nonetheless invented their own quirky routines, what Skinner called 'superstitions'. Even when they were operating within systems of control, animals pushed back.

Historical Issues

The use of animals in psychology predates the discipline itself. In the late nineteenth century, George Romanes laid the groundwork with *Animal Intelligence* (1882), offering a series of vivid anecdotes that attributed mental capacities such as reasoning and empathy to various non-human creatures. While often dismissed today as overly anthropomorphic, Romanes's work foregrounded animals as expressive, intentional beings, a theme that would later be sidelined in favour of more experimental approaches. That shift came with Edward Thorndike, whose puzzle box experiments with cats in the 1890s aimed to strip away speculation about mind and seek behavioural laws instead. Thorndike sought quantifiable results: how long a cat took to escape, how often it repeated successful actions, and framed learning as a gradual, mechanical process of trial and error. Animals became data points.

This mechanistic approach intensified with the rise of behaviourism. Rats in mazes became the gold standard and cartoon cliché of psychological science, their navigations interpreted as pure stimulus–response sequences. Pavlov's dogs, famously salivating at the sound of a bell, were seen as confirming that reflexes could be conditioned, yet even Pavlov noted that individual dogs responded differently to different experimenters. Such inconsistencies were often smoothed out in published reports but provide evidence of animals' relational capacities.

By the mid-twentieth century, B. F. Skinner was placing pigeons in operant chambers to explore schedules of reinforcement. He aimed for standardisation, but again, animal idiosyncrasy emerged. Pigeons developed strange ritual behaviours, turning in circles, bobbing heads, not explicitly reinforced by the experiments. Meanwhile, Harry Harlow's maternal deprivation studies with rhesus monkeys in the 1950s and 1960s produced unexpected results, as infant monkeys formed attachments to cloth 'mothers' and displayed social pathologies not easily explained by behaviourist models.

Wolfgang Köhler's chimpanzees, by contrast, were celebrated for their ingenuity. His early twentieth-century studies suggested that non-human primates could demonstrate 'insight' learning, problem-solving with apparent intentionality. These findings challenged simplistic stimulus–response paradigms.

Peter Godfrey-Smith's work with octopuses has reignited interest in the alien yet intelligent minds of animals. Godfrey-Smith traces the evolutionary split between vertebrates and cephalopods to over 500 million years ago. This vast separation means that the octopus's mind evolved in an entirely different environment and biological context. Unlike the centralised brain of mammals, the octopus's nervous system is radically distributed, with more than half of its neurons located in its arms, allowing for decentralised processing. In his words, octopuses 'have minds in their arms'. This challenges psychology's implicit model of the mind as a singular, centralised processing unit.

Key Individuals

George Romanes (1848–1894), a close associate of Charles Darwin, pioneered the comparative study of animal minds in *Animal Intelligence* (1882). He collected stories about animal cleverness, from dogs rescuing drowning humans to elephants solving mechanical puzzles, to argue that animals shared mental capacities with humans. Often critiqued for anthropomorphism and lack of rigour, Romanes was nonetheless one of the first to treat animals as sentient beings with minds worth taking seriously.

Ivan Pavlov (1849–1936) was a Russian physiologist turned psychologist. Pavlov is famous for his experiments on classical conditioning. While his dogs are often presented as machines trained to salivate at bells, Pavlov's lab notes suggest a more complex picture. He named and described individual dogs, noting how some were nervous, others sociable. Their behaviour changed in response to the presence or mood of the experimenter. These overlooked relational dynamics hint at animals as participants, responders to the human world around them.

Edward L. Thorndike's (1874–1949) puzzle box experiments with cats stimulated the emergence of behaviourism. His 'Law of Effect', that behaviours followed by satisfying outcomes are more likely to recur, was derived from watching animals learn through trial and error. Thorndike minimised the inner lives of animals, focusing on quantifiable inputs and outputs. His cats became prototypes for a theory of learning that would dominate twentieth-century psychology.

Wolfgang Köhler (1887–1967) worked with chimpanzees on the island of Tenerife. Köhler investigated 'insight' learning. He observed chimps stacking boxes or using sticks to reach bananas. This kind of behaviour resisted simple stimulus-response accounts and suggested a more holistic, Gestalt approach to cognition. Köhler's work reintroduced intentionality into animal psychology. His chimps were problem-solvers, a finding that resonates strongly with the idea of animals as co-constructors of experimental meaning.

B. F. Skinner's (1904–1990) behaviourist empire rested on the operant conditioning chamber, or 'Skinner Box'. Here, pigeons and rats learned to press levers or peck keys for food. Skinner prided himself on control and replicability, yet his own experiments betrayed complexity. In the 'superstition' study, pigeons developed rituals unrelated to reinforcement, perhaps trying to make sense of their environment. Skinner interpreted this within his framework, but others saw signs of animal agency, quirks and patterns not fully reducible to the schedule of reinforcement.

Harry Harlow's (1905–1981) studies on maternal deprivation, attachment, and affection in rhesus monkeys are infamous and influential. His work showed that infant monkeys clung to soft, cloth 'mothers' even when they offered no food, suggesting that love and comfort were psychologically primary. While often criticised for ethical reasons, Harlow's work forced psychology to reckon with emotional needs and social bonds. His monkeys disrupted the logic of behaviourism by demonstrating preferences, sufferings, and desires.

Barbara Smuts (b.1950) is a primatologist and anthropologist whose work radically reoriented how researchers understand animal minds through empathy, intimacy, and mutual recognition. Conducting long-term fieldwork with baboons and chimpanzees, Smuts rejected the distanced, behaviourist framework of much psychological science in favour of what she later described as *intersubjective fieldwork*. She argued that animals are not mere subjects of human observation but intentional beings capable of forming genuine relationships, including friendship. Her approach embodies the spirit of *companion species* thinking by refusing to see animals as tools or mirrors of the human, instead recognising them as co-participants in the making of meaning.

Peter Godfrey-Smith (b.1965) is a philosopher of science and scuba diver. Godfrey-Smith brings new insights to animal minds through his work on octopuses. In *Other Minds* (2016), he explores the radically different embodiment of cephalopods, creatures whose intelligence may be decentralised, fluid, and tactile. His reflections invite psychology to stretch its assumptions as to what counts as mind, intelligence, and selfhood. By diving repeatedly into the same octopus habitats, Godfrey-Smith adopts an immersive, ethological method closer to field primatology or Barbara Smuts's work with baboons than to traditional lab-based comparative psychology. His methodology is guided by empathy, patience, and attention to individual differences in behaviour.

Epistemological Issues

The methods psychologists use to study animals shape that knowledge. Every apparatus, protocol, and framework carries assumptions about what animals are capable of and how they should behave. Whether it's a maze, a puzzle box, or a reinforcement schedule, the experimental setup frames animals as either responsive machines or intelligent agents. But what if we took seriously the idea that knowledge in these contexts is co-produced, that the animal is a partner in shaping the experimental outcome?

Much of twentieth-century animal psychology relied on the idea of the 'blank slate' animal: a generalised, interchangeable organism that could be used to extract universal laws of behaviour. This assumption suited behaviourism, which sought regularities that could be mapped across species and contexts. Rats, pigeons, and dogs became stand-ins for the generalised organism, stripped of context or individuality. Yet even under strict experimental control, animals displayed variability. Some rats learned faster, some pigeons developed idiosyncratic rituals, and some monkeys rejected the parameters of the experiment altogether.

Different animals are suited to different tasks, not just because of their evolutionary history but because of their history with humans. Dogs, for example, have evolved in intimate cohabitation with humans; their responsiveness to gaze, gesture, and voice makes them ideal for studying social cognition. Octopuses, by contrast, resist domestication and standardisation. Their behaviours are highly contextual, fluid, and often difficult to interpret. This does not mean that they are less intelligent, only that our methods might not be suited to recognising their intelligence.

The companion species approach reframes epistemology by focusing on how knowledge is produced and with whom it is produced. It positions experiments as interspecies encounters shaped by dynamics such as trust, fear, familiarity, and communication. A monkey in a laboratory cage does not simply respond to isolated stimuli; it responds to the total situation, its confinement, its prior experiences, and the presence of the researcher.

Ontological Issues

Animals in psychological science have been variously conceptualised as machines, minds, and assemblages of reflexes. The question of animal ontology, what animals are, has often been answered implicitly through the design of experiments. Behaviourism, for example, positioned animals as organismic black boxes: entities that respond to inputs with observable outputs, without requiring speculation about their inner experiences. This ontology aligned with the scientific aspiration for objectivity and control.

By bracketing out the animal's mental life, psychology could be modelled on physics, seemingly untroubled by questions of subjectivity. But that bracketing was always a fiction. Harlow's monkeys displayed yearning, grief, and playfulness. Köhler's chimpanzees solved problems. Skinner's pigeons behaved unpredictably. Each time, the animal's being-in-the-world resisted reduction. Animals demonstrate the subjectivity of 'the other'. Their actions were not fully explicable by the categories available to us, pushing us to revise our ontological assumptions.

Alex, the African Grey parrot, not only named objects and colours but also appeared to display humour, emotional attachment, and the rudiments of syntax. His final words, 'You be good. See you tomorrow. I love you', unsettled traditional boundaries between animal instinct and emotional subjectivity. Similarly, Washoe, the first chimpanzee taught American Sign Language, signed over 250 words and once labelled a swan 'water bird', a potentially creative act of recombination. Whether or not it meets the criteria of syntax, Washoe's communication suggested the presence of symbolic intent and intersubjective awareness.

Donna Haraway's idea of *companion species* demands that we reconsider animals as beings that we cannot fully understand using our categories but that nevertheless demonstrate agency, emotion, and memory. This reframing moves us beyond a flat ontology of 'the animal' and towards a richer, more layered understanding of animal minds. Ontological questions also matter when we consider cross-species comparisons. Can we meaningfully compare the intelligence of an octopus and a dog? Their minds are shaped by radically different evolutionary histories and habitats. The octopus's nervous system is distributed through its arms; the dog's is centralised and socially attuned to humans. Both are intelligent, but in ways shaped by their embodiment, environment, and relational histories.

To treat animals as companion species is to accept that their being is not fully knowable through experimental abstraction. Their minds emerge through interactions: with humans, environments, and other animals. This makes psychological knowledge about animals more complex, but also more truthful to the messy, relational nature of mind itself.

Power

The history of animals in psychology is also a history of power, of cages, control, conditioning, and compliance. Traditional experimental paradigms position the human researcher as sovereign and the animal as subject: controlled, measured, manipulated. The case of Peter the dolphin, raised in a language research experiment in the 1960s, shows the ethical entanglements of researcher–subject intimacy. When Peter formed a strong bond with a human researcher, one that crossed conventional boundaries of care, the experiment highlighted not only the depth of interspecies connection but also the fragility of objectivity. Peter's life ended tragically, but his story endures as a cautionary tale of emotional overreach in the name of science.

The concept of *companion species* allows us to reconceive power as co-constituted, not just imposed. Animals are not passive experimental subjects. They bring histories, personalities, resistances, and affective presences. A monkey who refuses to engage with a surrogate mother, a pigeon who develops a 'superstitious' dance, an octopus who ambushes a lab assistant with a well-aimed squirt, these are acts that reconfigure the flow of power in the lab. They remind us that even under conditions of confinement, animals have agency.

If knowledge emerges from these interspecies dynamics, then power is not something to eliminate; it is something to account for. Haraway's notion of *situated knowledges* teaches us that objectivity is not the absence of perspective but the responsible acknowledgement of it. The researcher's body, mood, and actions matter. So too does the animal's individuality. A standardised experiment may still yield divergent results, not because of error but because the relation itself is irreducible.

Power also threads through the politics of replication. If experimental outcomes depend on the unique relationship between a particular researcher and a particular animal, then results may not be easily generalised. This undermines one of psychology's cherished ideals: that findings are universal and reproducible. But perhaps that ideal needs rethinking. In a world of companion species, knowledge is always partial, always relational. To study animals, then, is to enter a field of power—not only over them but *with* them. Recognising this does not weaken science; it makes it more honest. It invites a psychology that is about connection.

Chapter Summary

Animals have always been part of psychology's story, but they have rarely been granted agency, and almost never been centred on their own terms. They have been used as models, proxies, metaphors, and tools, silent stand-ins for human processes. Yet, as this chapter has shown, animals have also shaped, disrupted, and co-authored the very knowledge systems designed to study them. They are active participants in meaning-making encounters.

To revisit the iconic experiments, from Pavlov's dogs to Harlow's monkeys, from Skinner's pigeons to Köhler's apes, is to recover moments of resistance, unpredictability, and profound relationality. These interspecies dramas were saturated with emotion, ethics, and interpretation. Knowledge was always made together.

Donna Haraway's concept of companion species urges us to move beyond the binaries that have long structured psychological thought: subject and object, human and animal, reason and instinct. It encourages us to think instead in terms of co-evolution, co-agency, and entanglement. Psychology, through this lens, becomes a relational discipline grounded in mutual responsiveness and situated understanding.

This reframing calls for a transformation in method, attitude, and imagination. Psychology must become attuned to the lived particularities of other species: to their ways of knowing, sensing, and relating. The shift is already underway in comparative cognition, animal-assisted therapy, and multispecies ethnography. But the deeper revolution lies in rethinking what knowledge is, and with whom it can be made.

That revolution originated in crisis. On a September morning in 1924, the River Neva flooded Pavlov's laboratory. The dogs, once perfectly conditioned, stopped salivating. Their learned reflexes disappeared. Something had been undone; to the animals and to science. In that moment of flood and rupture, the myth of control gave way to a fragile recognition that no laboratory can fully understand the life of others. To take animals seriously is not a sentimental gesture, it is a conceptual revolution. One that invites psychology to be not only more ethical but more curious, more humble, and more attuned to the multiple forms of intelligence that share our world.

Reflective Questions

1. What does the concept of 'companion species' reveal about the relationship between researcher and animal in psychology?
2. In what ways did Pavlov's dogs—and their reactions after the flood—disrupt the assumption that conditioning is purely mechanical?
3. Can animals be considered co-authors of psychological knowledge? If so, what are the implications for experimental design and scientific ethics?
4. To what extent has psychology managed to avoid anthropomorphism (the interpretation of animal behaviour in terms of human qualities)?
5. How might Barbara Smuts's or Jane Goodall's approach to animal research exemplify the idea of 'situated knowledge'?

Suggested Reading

Adams, M. (2020). The kingdom of dogs: Understanding Pavlov's experiments as human–animal relationships. *Theory & Psychology*, *30*(1), 121–141. https://doi.org/10.1177/0959354319895597.

Brantz, D. (2010). *Beastly Natures: Animals, humans, and the study of history*. Richmond: University of Virginia Press.

Gillaspy, J. A., Jr., Brinegar, J. L., & Bailey, R. E. (2014). Operant psychology makes a splash—in marine mammal training (1955–1965). *Journal of the History of Behavioral Sciences.*, *50*(3), 231–248. https://doi.org/10.1002/jhbs.21664.

Godfrey-Smith, P. (2016). *Other Minds: The octopus, the sea, and the deep origins of consciousness*. New York: Farrar, Straus and Giroux.
Haraway, D. J. (2003). *The Companion Species Manifesto: Dogs, people, and significant otherness*. Chicago, IL: Prickly Paradigm Press.
Haraway, D. (2008). *When Species Meet*. Minneapolis: University of Minnesota Press.
Kirk, R. G. W. (2014). In dogs we trust? Intersubjectivity, response-able relations, and the making of mine detector dogs. *Journal of the History of the Behavioural Sciences, 50*(1), 1–36. https://doi.org/10.1002/jhbs.21642.
Linge, I. (2020). The potency of the butterfly: The reception of Richard B. Goldschmidt's animal experiments in German sexology around 1920. *History of the Human Sciences, 34*(1), 40–70. https://doi.org/10.1177/0952695119890545.
Smuts, B. (2001). Encounters with animal minds. *Journal of Consciousness Studies, 8*(5/7), 293–309.
Sorabji, R. (1993). *Animal Minds and Human Morals: The origins of the Western debate*. Ithaca, NY: Cornell University Press.
Wilson, D. (2001). A 'precipitous *dégringolade*': The uncertain progress of British comparative psychology in the twentieth century. In G. C. Bunn, A. D. Lovie, & G. Richards, Eds., *Psychology in Britain: Historical essays and personal reflections*. British Psychological Society.

Key Terms

Animal Agency Recognition that animals are not passive subjects but beings capable of resisting, adapting, or disrupting experimental conditions in ways that shape outcomes.

Anthropomorphism The attribution of human traits to non-human entities—often viewed critically in science, but reassessed here as part of the relational interpretation of animal minds.

Behaviourism A psychological approach that focuses on observable behaviours and conditioning rather than internal mental states, often criticised for reducing animals to machines.

Companion Species A concept developed by Donna Haraway to describe animals, not as tools or pets but as co-constitutive partners in human lives, cultures, and knowledge systems.

Conditioned Reflex A learned response to a previously neutral stimulus, famously investigated by Ivan Pavlov, though he used the term 'conditional reflex' to emphasise its context dependency.

Co-production of Knowledge The idea that scientific knowledge is not simply discovered but shaped through dynamic relationships, here, between experimenters and animals.

Ethology The study of animal behaviour in natural settings, often involving long-term, empathetic observation and emphasising the individuality and agency of animal subjects.

Intersubjectivity A mutual, relational understanding between beings, used here to describe emotionally and cognitively meaningful relationships between humans and animals.

Reflexivity The process by which researchers examine how their presence, assumptions, and methods affect the outcomes of experiments, in this case with animal subjects.

Situated Knowledge The idea that all knowledge is shaped by the specific context, perspective, and position of the knower, used in this chapter to challenge claims of objectivity in animal research.

Trauma and Unlearning Refers to the psychological effects of environmental stress or harm on learned behaviours, as in the aftermath of the 1924 flood in Ivan Pavlov's lab.

FREE INSTRUCTOR & STUDENT RESOURCES

ONLINE RESOURCES

Visit the Instructor & Student Resources website at routledgelearning.com/bpscoretextbooks for free digital resources, including:

- Interactive quizzes and flashcards to test your knowledge
- Links to useful websites and videos
- Instructor manual, lecture slides, and course guide to enhance teaching and save instructors time

11 Pigeons Play Ping Pong

Behaviourism and the Crisis of the Paradigm

Chapter Overview

This chapter explores the rise, dominance, and decline of behaviourism in twentieth-century American psychology, using Thomas Kuhn's concept of the *scientific paradigm* as a critical thinking tool. It traces how behaviourism redefined psychology as the study of observable behaviour, rooted in empiricism, environmental determinism, and prediction and control. Through the work of key figures such as John B. Watson, B. F. Skinner, Edward Tolman, and John Garcia, the chapter examines how behaviourism functioned as a paradigm that shaped research questions, methods, and assumptions about human and animal nature. The chapter discusses how *anomalies*, including Chomsky's critique of language acquisition, Tolman's theory of cognitive maps, and Garcia's findings on biological constraints, challenged the coherence of the behaviourist model. These tensions culminated in the replacement of behaviourism with a new paradigm centred on internal mental processes and symbolic representation: the cognitive revolution. In addition to tracing this epistemological and ontological shift, the chapter also interrogates behaviourism's alignment with systems of power and discipline, drawing on Michel Foucault's concepts of social control. While behaviourism no longer dominates psychology, its legacy persists in applied fields such as behaviour therapy, education, and artificial intelligence. The chapter invites us to reflect critically on how scientific frameworks both reflect and shape the societies in which they arise.

Pigeons Play Ping Pong

In the 1950s, visitors to B. F. Skinner's Harvard laboratory were treated to a strangely mesmerising sight: two pigeons standing at either end of a miniature ping pong table, pecking a tiny ball back and forth with uncanny coordination. The demonstration, designed to amuse and impress, was more than a curiosity. It was Skinner's proof that complex behaviour, including competitive games, turn-taking, strategy even, could be broken down into simple units of reinforcement. With no need for thoughts, intentions, or inner drives, the pigeons became paradigm cases of a wider vision: a world where all behaviour, human and animal, could be predicted and controlled through the careful calibration of consequences. For Skinner, this was a blueprint for society. In *Walden Two* (1948), his fictional utopia, people were no more free than pigeons; they were simply better conditioned. This playful demonstration, however, had a serious and unsettling precursor in Skinner's earlier, secretive wartime project: *Project Pigeon*. In this covert programme, pigeons were trained to peck at images of targets displayed on screens mounted inside the nose cones of missiles, effectively steering the weapons towards their destination. Yet even as

DOI: 10.4324/9781003565482-11

behaviourism reached its technical zenith in these bizarre military applications, deeper tensions were surfacing. The same logic used to guide a missile was being applied to explain how a child learns to speak, how a person might lie, resist, or rebel. Love, morality, memory, and madness were being redefined within a framework that refused to open the black box of the mind. The pigeons kept pecking. But outside the lab, psychology was beginning to shift. Not all behaviour could be engineered, it seemed, and not all minds could be ignored. This chapter begins at the moment of apparent triumph, when psychology's vision of prediction and control seemed closest to realisation, and asks why, so soon after, the vision disappeared.

Chapter Contents

- The rise and fall of behaviourism as a dominant psychological paradigm in the twentieth century.
- The use of Thomas Kuhn's theory of scientific paradigms to examine the development, crisis, and decline of behaviourism.
- Critical reflections on epistemological, ontological, and power structures that shaped and challenged the behaviourist movement.

Chapter Objectives

- Explain how behaviourism redefined psychology as a science of observable behaviour and why it initially succeeded as a dominant paradigm.
- Apply Thomas Kuhn's theory of the scientific paradigm to understand how behaviourism functioned as 'normal science' and how its decline illustrates a paradigm shift.
- Critically evaluate the epistemological assumptions, ontological commitments, and institutional uses of behaviourism, especially in relation to power and social control.

CRITICAL THINKING TOOL
THE SCIENTIFIC PARADIGM

The term *scientific paradigm* is central to the work of philosopher Thomas Kuhn, who argued that science does not progress in a straight line but rather advances through a series of revolutions. A *paradigm* is more than just a theory; it is a shared framework that shapes how scientists see the world, the kinds of questions they ask, the methods they use, and what counts as valid knowledge. It is a kind of mental model or lens through which a scientific community interprets reality.

In the history of psychology, behaviourism functioned as a dominant paradigm for much of the twentieth century. It defined what counted as scientific psychology, focusing on observable behaviour, controlled experiments, and measurable outcomes, while rejecting mental states as

either unscientific or irrelevant. Within this paradigm, key concepts such as stimulus–response learning, reinforcement, and conditioning structured how research was designed and interpreted.

Kuhn also introduced the idea of *paradigm shifts*. Over time, all paradigms accumulate anomalies, observations, or findings that don't quite fit. If enough of these anomalies accumulate, they can lead to a crisis, the rejection of the old paradigm, and the adoption of a new paradigm. This is what happened when behaviourism was challenged by cognitive psychology. Anomalies such as language acquisition, cognitive maps, and biological limits to learning could not be explained within the behaviourist framework. The result was a paradigm shift: the rise of cognitivism, with its emphasis on mental representation, information processing, and internal states.

Introduction

Behaviourism was one of the most influential paradigms in twentieth-century psychology, particularly in the United States. Emerging partly as a reaction against introspectionist and psychoanalytic traditions, it redefined psychology as the scientific study of observable behaviour. Advocating objective measurement, experimental control, and environmental determinism, behaviourists sought to align psychology with the natural sciences. In his 1913 manifesto *Psychology as the Behaviourist Views It,* John B. Watson formally established this paradigm, insisting that only measurable behaviour, and not thoughts or feelings, should form the basis of scientific psychology.

The behaviourist paradigm thrived for several decades, evolving through figures such as B. F. Skinner, Clark Hull, and Edward Tolman. It shaped experimental methods and influenced social and educational policies. Yet, as Thomas Kuhn argued, all paradigms encounter inexplicable apparent glitches, or weird anomalies. By the mid-twentieth century, challenges to behaviourism, such as Noam Chomsky's critique of language learning and John Garcia's findings on biological constraints to learning, signalled the beginning of a paradigm shift.

This chapter uses Kuhn's concept of the scientific paradigm to explore the rise, crisis, and decline of behaviourism. In doing so, it also notes behaviourism's continuing influence, particularly in cognitive behaviour therapy, where questions of conditioning, reinforcement, and behaviour modification remain central.

Historical Issues

The early twentieth century was fertile ground for a new scientific psychology. Industrialisation, the rise of statistical thinking, and the valorisation of engineering efficiency created a cultural climate in which the measurement and control of human behaviour became both scientifically respectable and socially desirable. Behaviourism emerged into this context. It provided an experimental system that was suited to the growing demand for practical solutions in education, labour management, and governance. It offered a vision of psychological science that was orderly, mechanistic, and productive. This was *mature normal science*, according to Kuhn, doing research and solving problems within a shared matrix of understanding.

By the 1930s and 1940s, behaviourism had consolidated its institutional power in American psychology. Its models were codified in textbooks, its methods formalised in laboratory protocols, and its researchers well positioned within influential departments. Federal and military funding during and after the Second World War accelerated this consolidation, particularly as behaviourist methods proved adaptable to large-scale psychological testing, pilot training, and behavioural conditioning programmes. During the Cold War, behaviourism's reputation for predictive control aligned it with national interests in security, education, and technological advancement.

However, behaviourism never achieved the same hegemony outside the United States. In Europe, competing schools of thought held sway. Gestalt psychology, with its emphasis on holistic perception and cognitive organisation, flourished in Germany. In France and the UK, Freudian psychoanalysis remained dominant in clinical settings. The ethological studies of Konrad Lorenz and Nikolaas Tinbergen introduced biologically grounded models of behaviour, based on evolution, adaptation, and innate mechanisms. These approaches all challenged behaviourism's environmental determinism.

Findings in language development, neurobiology, and ethology exposed weaknesses in the stimulus-response framework. Once seemingly complete, behaviourism began to appear narrow and insufficient. The cognitive revolution changed psychology's questions and realigned its sympathies towards fields such as neuroscience and sociobiology. It was a paradigm shift in the very nature of what psychology could be.

Key Individuals

Although Ivan Pavlov (1849–1936) was a Russian physiologist rather than a psychologist, his work on conditioning deeply influenced the development of behaviourism. Pavlov demonstrated that dogs could learn to associate a neutral stimulus with a biologically significant one (food), producing a conditioned response (salivation). Pavlov's simple (and misunderstood) principles became foundational to behaviourist thought, especially in Watson's early work. Pavlov's model fitted neatly with the behaviourist emphasis on learning as a passive, automatic response to the environment. Yet it also raised deeper biological questions. Pavlov's interest in reflexes, neural pathways, involuntary responses, and indeed the psyche, foreshadowed later developments in biological psychology, even if behaviourism would later strip away many of those physiological concerns in favour of purely environmental explanations.

John B. Watson's (1878–1958) 1913 manifesto *Psychology as the Behaviourist Views It* launched behaviourism as a full-blown scientific revolution in American psychology. Rejecting introspection and mentalism, and inspired by the experimental precision of physics, Watson proposed a psychology based exclusively on observable behaviour. He positioned psychology as a branch of natural science, capable of predicting and controlling behaviour through experimental observation. Watson's infamous Little Albert experiment (1920), though later criticised for its unethical frightening of an infant, became a paradigmatic case study. It illustrated how even emotional responses could be learned through classical conditioning. As Kuhn would have put it, this experiment served as an exemplar for normal science within the behaviourist paradigm. Although Watson's academic career was cut short by a sexual scandal, he continued to influence public life through advertising, showing how behaviourist principles could shape consumer behaviour on a mass scale.

B. F. Skinner (1904–1990) carried behaviourism to its logical conclusion with his theory of *radical behaviourism*, which rejected internal mental states as unnecessary for understanding behaviour. While Watson emphasised stimulus–response associations, Skinner introduced *operant conditioning*, a model in which behaviour is shaped and maintained by its consequences. His operant conditioning chamber, the Skinner Box, allowed precise control over reinforcement schedules, transforming behaviourist research into a highly replicable, data-driven enterprise. Skinner exemplified Kuhn's notion of normal science: he was not challenging the paradigm but refining and extending its internal logic. His work focused on the puzzle-solving tasks of adjusting reinforcement patterns and modelling learning across species. However, his reluctance to engage with cognition left behaviourism vulnerable to critique. *Walden Two* (1948), Skinner's utopian vision of a society governed by reinforcement principles, showcased both the ambition and the limits of radical behaviourism. As questions of language, representation, and human agency became harder to ignore in the 1960s, Skinner's approach began to feel increasingly out of step with emerging scientific sensibilities.

Often described as a *cognitive behaviourist*, Edward C. Tolman (1886–1959) introduced early challenges to the behaviourist orthodoxy. His experiments with rats navigating mazes revealed that learning could occur without reinforcement, a process he termed *latent learning*. More provocatively, he argued that rats developed *cognitive maps*, internal representations of their environment. While Tolman still adhered to many behaviourist methods, his findings presented anomalies that behaviourism could not easily explain. According to Kuhn, such anomalies are the seeds of discontent that lead to rebellion. Tolman's work foreshadowed the cognitive revolution, and his emphasis on purpose and mental representation opened the door to new questions about agency, memory, and motivation.

Clark Hull (1884–1952) attempted to turn behaviourism into a mathematically rigorous science. His *hypothetico-deductive model* aimed to predict behaviour using formal equations based on *drive reduction theory*, the idea that learning occurs as organisms act to reduce biological needs. Hull's meticulous use of logic and operational definitions gave behaviourism a technical precision that aligned closely with biological psychology, particularly in its treatment of drives and internal physiological states. Hull's influence peaked in the 1940s but his theories eventually proved too rigid. As the complexity of human cognition came into view, Hull's formulas could not keep pace. His work remains important, however, for establishing the value of formal modelling in psychology, a legacy continued in both cognitive science and computational neuroscience.

John Garcia (1917–2012) was an American psychologist whose groundbreaking research in the 1960s exposed deep flaws in the dominant behaviourist paradigm. Garcia's most famous work emerged from applied research funded by the US military, where he was studying how to prevent radiation sickness. During these experiments, he discovered that rats exposed to radiation developed aversions to the flavours they had consumed before falling ill, even when hours separated the stimulus (taste) and the consequence (nausea). This was revolutionary. Behaviourist orthodoxy, rooted in the work of Watson and Skinner, insisted that learning required *multiple* pairings of stimulus and response, and that reinforcement had to be immediate. Garcia showed that one-trial learning could occur with long delay, and, more radically, that not all associations were equally learnable. Rats easily linked taste with sickness but not sound or light, undermining the behaviourist principle of equipotentiality. Garcia's findings suggested that biology mattered, that organisms came pre-equipped with evolved predispositions for learning certain things. This was heresy to behaviourism's assumption that organisms were 'blank slates' when it came to their tendencies. His initial findings were rejected, his research dismissed, and for years Garcia was largely ignored by mainstream psychology. Yet his work ultimately helped precipitate the paradigm crisis Kuhn described, hastening the fall of behaviourism and the rise of cognitive and evolutionary approaches.

Epistemological Issues

A scientific paradigm is fundamentally an epistemological framework: it determines what counts as knowledge, how that knowledge is produced, and which empirical questions are seen as legitimate. Behaviourism's epistemology was built on the foundations of empiricism and positivism, prioritising observation, measurement, and experimental control. Its central claim was that psychology could only be scientific if it focused exclusively on observable behaviour, rejecting mental states as unmeasurable and therefore irrelevant.

Key to behaviourism's epistemology was the principle of operationalism, the idea that psychological concepts must be defined in terms of observable operations. Terms such as 'motivation', 'intention', or 'drive' were either rephrased behaviourally or discarded altogether as unmeasurable or metaphysical. This made behaviourism scientifically persuasive, but it also led to epistemological narrowing: anything not directly observable risked being excluded from inquiry. As a result, behaviourism struggled to account for complex, internal, or emergent behaviours.

Anomalies accumulated. Noam Chomsky's critique of Skinner's *Verbal Behavior* (1959) exposed behaviourism's inability to explain the generativity of language. Edward Tolman's work on latent learning and cognitive maps showed that organisms could acquire knowledge without reinforcement, suggesting that internal cognitive processes played a role. John Garcia showed that rats could form powerful aversions after a single pairing of taste and illness, even with hours between the stimulus and response, violating the behaviourist assumption of temporal contiguity. Garcia's findings pointed to biological constraints on learning, revealing inconsistencies in behaviourism's epistemological foundations.

Meanwhile, research in ethology demonstrated that many animal behaviours were innate and evolutionarily programmed, not acquired through conditioning. These findings, alongside developments in artificial intelligence and cognitive modelling, contributed to a Kuhnian paradigm shift. By the 1970s, behaviourism's epistemology had been largely displaced by cognitive psychology, which reintroduced mental representation, information processing, and symbolic reasoning as central to psychological science.

Ontological Issues

Every scientific paradigm carries with it not only rules for acquiring knowledge but assumptions about what the world is fundamentally made of. These assumptions, its ontological claims, define what entities exist, how they behave, and what kinds of explanations are permissible. The ontology of behaviourism was unapologetically mechanistic and deterministic. From Watson's early formulations to Skinner's radical behaviourism, human and animal organisms were seen as passive systems, wholly shaped by their environments through conditioning and reinforcement. Mental states were treated either as unknowable or irrelevant, mere by-products of behavioural processes, not causes.

This worldview reflected a broader materialist and positivist tradition. Organisms, like machines, were assumed to respond automatically to environmental contingencies. The 'black box' metaphor summed it up: behaviourists studied the inputs and outputs to and from the organism but not what lay in between. The concept of free will was seen as a metaphysical illusion, and internal processes such as memory, intention, and thought were excluded from serious scientific inquiry. For decades, this ontological simplicity allowed behaviourism to flourish as a model of scientific rigour.

But as Kuhn's model suggests, anomalies accumulate not only at the level of data but at the level of fundamental assumptions. By the 1960s, behaviourism's core ontology was under strain, thanks to the work of Tolman, Chomsky, and Garcia. Advances in neuroscience underscored the causal role of internal processes, memory, representation, and problem-solving, reintroducing consciousness into the scientific imagination. By the early 1970s, behaviourist's ontology could no longer accommodate these aberrations.

Power

Scientific paradigms are never just systems of knowledge; they are also expressions of power. As Michel Foucault argued, scientific practices are deeply entangled with mechanisms of discipline and social control. Behaviourism, with its emphasis on prediction, conditioning, and environmental determinism, exemplified this dual function. It was a method of regulating, normalising, and optimising human conduct in ways that aligned closely with institutional priorities.

Nowhere was this clearer than in education, where B. F. Skinner's model of *programmed instruction* proposed a mechanised vision of learning. By delivering small units of information, followed by immediate feedback and reinforcement, Skinner aimed to maximise efficiency and minimise error. Yet this system also positioned students as objects of behavioural engineering, subjects to be modified. In workplaces, behaviourist principles were built into productivity metrics and performance management systems, which rewarded compliance and corrected deviation through quantifiable feedback loops.

Behaviourism's power was magnified during the Cold War, when its principles were absorbed into military and governmental institutions. Behavioural psychology offered tools for training, persuasion, propaganda, and even interrogation. These applications blurred the line between science and control, and raised ethical questions about autonomy, manipulation, and consent. Critics, especially from humanistic and existential psychology, viewed behaviourism as complicit in a technocratic vision of society. Its denial of agency and interiority aligned with systems that sought to standardise human behaviour for institutional ends, rather than support personal freedom or psychological depth.

Kuhn's concept of the paradigm shift helps explain the social dynamics of behaviourism's decline. Paradigm change is not driven by data alone; it is also a generational struggle. Older scientists who have invested much time and effort into building the dominant framework passionately defend it. Younger and less prejudiced researchers, exposed to innovative technologies, different values, and new theoretical tools, become the agents of revolution. In the 1960s and 1970s, psychology experienced just such a shift. The rise of cognitive science restructured the field, replacing engineers of behaviour with architects of mental representation. Yet even as behaviourism fell from theoretical dominance, its techniques of control persisted, embedded in the fabric of educational systems, corporate environments, and therapeutic practices. Power, like paradigms, is not easily surrendered.

Chapter Summary

In a laboratory built for certainty, two pigeons played ping pong. Their game was precise, almost comical, yet behind the scenes it revealed something deeper: a vision of psychology that aimed to predict and control behaviour with the elegance of mechanical cause and effect. This was the promise of behaviourism. In the twentieth century, behaviourism redefined psychology as a science of observable actions, grounded in experimentation, measurement, and environmental conditioning. By purging the inner life from psychological theory, it sought legitimacy among the empirical sciences, offering a paradigm of methodical rigour and practical application.

According to Kuhn's model of scientific revolutions, all paradigms face their moment of crisis. For behaviourism, this came in the form of anomalies it could not explain: language acquisition, internal reasoning, spontaneous learning. The cognitive revolution displaced behaviourism and reintroduced the mind as an object of study, reinstating cognition, memory, and representation at the heart of psychological science.

Yet behaviourism never truly vanished. Its experimental ethos, its tools, and even its metaphors live on in forms like applied behaviour analysis (ABA), cognitive behaviour therapy (CBT), and reinforcement learning in artificial intelligence. These afterlives speak to behaviourism's enduring practical legacy, even as its theoretical dominance has waned.

The pigeons kept playing, long after the world outside had changed. Their game is a metaphor not just for behaviourism but for the back-and-forth process of science itself, caught between precision and mystery, method and meaning, control and the unpredictable stirrings of life, where even the most conditioned movements can carry echoes of something uncanny and absurd.

Reflective Questions

1. Why did behaviourism become so dominant in American psychology, and what cultural or institutional factors helped sustain it?
2. How does Thomas Kuhn's concept of a 'paradigm' help us understand the rise and fall of behaviourism?
3. What were the main epistemological assumptions of behaviourism, and how did they limit what counted as psychological knowledge?
4. In what ways did behaviourism act as a form of disciplinary power, and how might we critically assess its social uses?
5. How did the work of John Garcia disrupt behaviourist assumptions, and why was his research initially ignored?

Suggested Reading

Braat, M., Engelen, J., van Gemert, T., & Verhaegh, S. (2020). The rise and fall of behaviorism: The narrative and the numbers. *History of Psychology, 23*(3), 252–280. https://doi.org/10.1037/hop0000146.

Clark, D. O. (2023). A science of adaptation: The transnational origins of the American functional behaviorism of the 20th century. *Revista de Historia de la Psicología, 44*(3), 11–18. https://doi.org/10.5093/rhp2023a10.

Green, C. D., Feinerer, I., & Burman, J. T. (2013). Beyond the Schools of Psychology 1: A digital analysis of *Psychological Review*, 1894–1903. *Journal of the History of the Behavioural Sciences, 49*(2), 167–189. https://doi.org/10.1002/jhbs.21592.

Harris, B. (2011). Letting go of little Albert: Disciplinary memory, history, and the uses of myth. *Journal of the History of the Behavioral Sciences, 47*(1), 1–17. https://doi.org/10.1002/jhbs.20470.

Kontopodis, M., & Jackowska, M. (2019). De-centring the psychology curriculum: Diversity, social justice, and psychological knowledge. *Theory & Psychology, 29*(4), 506–520. https://doi.org/10.1177/0959354319858419.

Link, A. (2016). Documenting human nature: E. Richard Sorenson and the National Anthropological Film Centre, 1965–1980. *Journal of the History of the Behavioral Sciences, 52*(4), 371–391. https://doi.org/10.1002/jhbs.21813.

Lubek, I., & Apfelbaum, E. (1987). Neo-behaviourism and the Garcia effect: A social psychology of science approach to the history of a paradigm clash. In M. G. Ash & W. R. Woodward (Eds.), *Psychology in Twentieth-Century Thought and Science* (pp. 59–91). Cambridge: Cambridge University Press.

Murray, S. O. (1988). W. I. Thomas, behaviourist ethnologist. *Journal of the History of the Behavioural Sciences, 24*(4), 381–391. https://doi.org/10.1002/1520-6696(198810)24:4<381::AID-JHBS2300240405>3.0.CO;2-K.

O'Donohue, W., Ferguson, K. E., & Naugle, A. E. (2003). The structure of the cognitive revolution: An examination from the philosophy of science. *The Behavior Analyst, 26*(1), 85–110. https://doi.org/10.1007/BF03392069.

O'Neil, W. M. (1995). American behaviorism: A historical and critical analysis. *Theory & Psychology, 5*(2), 285–305. https://doi.org/10.1177/0959354395052008.

Prilleltensky, I. (1994). On the social legacy of B. F. Skinner: Rhetoric of change, philosophy of adjustment. *Theory & Psychology, 4*(1), 125–137. https://doi.org/10.1177/0959354394041006.

Rutherford, A. (2009). *Beyond the Box: B. F. Skinner's technology of behaviour from laboratory to life, 1950s–1970s*. Toronto, Ont: University of Toronto Press.

Torracinta, S. (2022). Maps of desire: Edward Tolman's drive theory of wants. *History of the Human Sciences, 36*(1), 3–30. https://doi.org/10.1177/09526951221135852.

Key Terms

Applied Behaviour Analysis (ABA) A therapeutic approach derived from behaviourist principles, especially operant conditioning, used to modify behaviour in clinical and educational settings.

Black Box A metaphor used by behaviourists to describe the mind as unknowable or irrelevant to scientific psychology; only observable inputs (stimuli) and outputs (responses) are considered legitimate data.

Classical Conditioning A learning process where a neutral stimulus becomes associated with a reflexive response through repeated pairings with an unconditioned stimulus.

Cognitive Revolution The shift in psychology during the mid-twentieth century away from behaviourism towards approaches that emphasised internal mental processes, such as memory, perception, and language.

Contiguity The behaviourist principle that learning occurs when a stimulus and a response are closely paired in time.

Determinism The belief that behaviour is entirely shaped by environmental causes, with no role for free will or internal agency.

Equipotentiality The behaviourist assumption that any stimulus can be equally associated with any response, regardless of biological or cognitive constraints.

John Garcia Effect Also known as conditioned taste aversion; Garcia's discovery that animals can form strong associations between taste and illness, even with a long time delay—contradicting core behaviourist principles.

Normal Science According to Thomas Kuhn, the routine, puzzle-solving work done within the boundaries of an accepted scientific paradigm. Behaviourist psychology in the mid-twentieth century is an example of normal science.

Operant Conditioning A type of learning where voluntary behaviours are shaped by reinforcement or punishment, introduced by B. F. Skinner.

Operationalism The view that scientific concepts must be defined in terms of the operations or procedures used to measure them. Central to behaviourist methodology.

Paradigm In Thomas Kuhn's theory, a shared framework of theories, methods, and assumptions that shapes what is considered legitimate science at a given time.

Paradigm Shift A fundamental transformation in the assumptions and practices of a scientific field, occurring when existing paradigms can no longer accommodate accumulating anomalies.

Power (Foucauldian) In psychology, the ways in which knowledge production and behavioural techniques can be used to discipline, control, and normalise individuals and populations.

Radical Behaviourism B. F. Skinner's version of behaviourism, which claimed that all behaviour—including language and thought—could be explained through operant conditioning without reference to internal mental states.

Reinforcement A consequence that increases the likelihood of a behaviour being repeated. Can be positive (adding something desirable) or negative (removing something undesirable).

Stimulus-Response (S-R) The foundational behaviourist model in which a specific stimulus elicits a specific behavioural response through conditioning.

FREE INSTRUCTOR & STUDENT RESOURCES

ONLINE RESOURCES

Visit the Instructor & Student Resources website at routledgelearning.com/bpscoretextbooks for free digital resources, including:

- Interactive quizzes and flashcards to test your knowledge
- Links to useful websites and videos
- Instructor manual, lecture slides, and course guide to enhance teaching and save instructors time

2 'Three Generations of Imbeciles Are Enough'

Psychology, Biopower, and the Apparatus of Eugenics

Chapter Overview

This chapter explores the entanglement between psychology and the eugenics movement in the early twentieth century. It examines how psychological science became a mechanism through which people and populations were categorised, evaluated, and managed. Psychologists developed tools such as intelligence tests, classification systems, and statistical models which, far from being neutral instruments, became technologies of power. These methods legitimised policies of segregation, institutionalisation, immigration control, and forced sterilisation. The chapter introduces Michel Foucault's concept of biopower as its critical thinking tool. Biopower refers to the way modern states regulate life through expert knowledge, including psychological expertise, in order to exert control over biological processes. The chapter uses this concept to analyse how psychological ideas about intelligence and deviance were embedded in institutional practices across Britain, the United States, and Scandinavia. While highlighting the central roles played by psychologists, the chapter also includes critical voices that questioned biological determinism and emphasised the role of environment and social inequality. Through a critical historical lens, the chapter invites us to reflect on psychology's complicity in exclusionary systems of power and its legacy in contemporary debates around intelligence, genetics, and social policy. It argues that understanding this history is essential not only for ethical reflection but also for reimagining the role of psychology in promoting equity and justice.

'Three Generations of Imbeciles Are Enough'

In 1927, a young woman named Carrie Buck stood at the very centre of a trial that would chillingly shape the lives of tens of thousands across America. Aged just 17, Carrie had been institutionalised at the Virginia State Colony for Epileptics and Feebleminded, a facility where those deemed 'socially inadequate' were confined. Her confinement was not for any diagnosed medical condition but because she had become pregnant while in foster care. The official records labelled her 'promiscuous' and 'feebleminded', language that obscured a far darker truth: she had likely been raped by a member of her foster family. Rather than investigate this horrific crime, the state chose to pursue a different, more convenient, narrative. Her pregnancy became the supposed 'evidence' of her moral and intellectual deficiency, justifying her permanent confinement and a far more invasive procedure. This narrative was cemented by the fact that her mother, Emma Buck, had already been institutionalised for similar

DOI: 10.4324/9781003565482-12

reasons, and even Carrie's infant daughter, Vivian, was declared 'likely defective'. This was not a criminal trial designed to seek justice but a eugenic one, orchestrated to validate state power over individual bodies. The fundamental question before the court was whether the state had the right to forcibly sterilise Carrie Buck without her consent. The case advanced to the U.S. Supreme Court, where the perceived authority of psychology loomed large. The rigid, hierarchical classification system for intelligence, namely 'idiot', 'imbecile', 'moron', developed by influential psychologist Henry Goddard, heavily underpinned the legal reasoning. Justice Oliver Wendell Holmes Jr. delivered the court's decision with clinical finality, uttering the chilling words: 'Three generations of imbeciles are enough.' Carrie's sterilisation went ahead, a profound violation of her bodily autonomy. Over 60,000 Americans, disproportionately those from impoverished backgrounds, individuals with disabilities, and many who were racialised or simply nonconforming to societal norms, would be forcibly sterilised in the name of eugenics, psychological science, and population control. This dark chapter forces us to confront not only the profound human cost of such policies but also the devastating consequences when scientific authority is wielded to define, categorise, and ultimately control human worth.

Chapter Contents

- The rise of eugenics as a psychological and political movement in the late nineteenth and early twentieth centuries.
- Psychology's role in developing and applying tools such as intelligence testing and statistical classification to support eugenic policy.
- Critical analysis of eugenics through the lens of biopower, showing how psychological knowledge became a mechanism for governing populations.

Chapter Objectives

- To examine how psychology became instrumental in constructing and legitimising eugenic ideas and practices across Britain, the United States, and Scandinavia.
- To identify the ways psychological methods, such as IQ testing, mental classification, and statistical modelling, were used to justify exclusion, institutionalisation, and sterilisation.
- To introduce and apply the critical thinking tool of biopower, enabling students to reflect on the relationship between scientific knowledge, state policy, and the management of human life.

CRITICAL THINKING TOOL
BIOPOWER

The history of psychology is not just a history of ideas; it is a history of power. One of the most illuminating tools for understanding this is *biopower*, a concept developed by the philosopher Michel Foucault. Biopower refers to the way modern societies exercise control over life, not

just through coercion or force but also through the management of populations, bodies, and behaviours via institutions like medicine, education, and science. Unlike earlier forms of power that focused on punishment or death, biopower operates by defining norms, monitoring health, measuring intelligence, and regulating reproduction.

In the early twentieth century, psychology became a key instrument of biopower. As a new science of the mind and behaviour, psychology offered techniques for categorising individuals, diagnosing abnormalities, and predicting social outcomes. These tools—standardised tests, mental classifications, statistical norms—gave psychologists a powerful role in defining who was considered healthy, productive, or intelligent, and who was not. Under the banner of eugenics, this knowledge was used to justify policies such as forced sterilisation, racial segregation, immigration control, and the institutionalisation of people deemed 'unfit'.

Biopower helps us understand why these developments were not just 'bad science' but forms of governance through knowledge. Psychology's biological explanations became entangled with political projects that sought to shape society by managing who could live, reproduce, or be educated. The history of eugenics is therefore not simply a story of scientific error but of a discipline being recruited into a much larger machinery of control.

In this chapter, biopower will guide our critical analysis of how psychology helped produce categories of normality and deviance, and how those categories were used to serve political ends.

Introduction

In the late nineteenth and early twentieth centuries, the rise of psychology as a scientific discipline corresponded with the emergence of eugenics as a powerful social and political movement. Eugenics, the belief that the human population could be improved through selective breeding, was widely accepted across Europe and North America, endorsed by scientists, reformers, and politicians from both the left and the right of the political spectrum. At a time of rapid industrialisation, urbanisation, and imperial expansion, and prior to the emergence of national insurance and social security, eugenics offered an evidently scientific response to anxieties about poverty, crime, disability, and degeneration.

Psychologists played a central role in shaping and legitimising eugenic thinking. Through intelligence testing, studies of heredity, and the classification of 'mental defect', psychology lent scientific credibility to exclusionary policies such as institutionalisation, forced sterilisation, and immigration control. In the UK, the Mental Deficiency Act of 1913 marked a turning point in the institutionalisation of eugenic thinking within law and policy. It classified individuals as 'idiots', 'imbeciles', 'feebleminded', and 'moral defectives', enabling their segregation in asylums and institutional 'colonies'. Psychological assessments played a central role in populating these categories, reinforcing the idea that certain lives were biologically inferior and socially dangerous. In the United States, eugenic policies disproportionately targeted African American women, many of whom were sterilised without consent under state-run programmes throughout the twentieth century. These acts were often justified using psychological diagnoses of feeblemindedness or moral degeneracy. Across the British Empire, colonial psychiatry used eugenic frameworks to pathologise colonised populations, treating indigenous ways of life as signs of arrested mental development and using intelligence testing to assert racial hierarchies.

Historical Issues

The historical relationship between psychology and eugenics is one of considerable interconnection. Psychology did not simply echo the eugenic ideas of its time; it actively constructed and legitimised them. As psychology emerged as a scientific discipline in the late nineteenth century, it was shaped by widespread anxieties about degeneration, criminality, and the supposed decline of the imperial or national 'stock'. Psychologists responded by developing new tools to measure and categorise human difference, tools that were quickly deployed in education, medicine, criminal justice, and social policy.

A pivotal example is the development of intelligence testing. In Britain, Charles Spearman's theory of a general intelligence factor (g) and Cyril Burt's twin studies advanced the idea that intelligence was largely hereditary. These findings helped justify the channelling of children into different educational pathways, an approach that naturalised class-based inequalities. In the United States, Lewis Terman's adaptation of the Binet-Simon test into the Stanford-Binet IQ test enabled the widespread classification of individuals by 'mental age', and had real-world consequences for military placement, immigration restriction, and institutionalisation.

Psychology's close relationship with statistics further reinforced its role in eugenics. Karl Pearson, Francis Galton's friend and collaborator, and a key figure in both statistics and psychology, used psychometric data to argue for population-level control through differential reproduction. Statistical tools created norms, and those who fell outside those norms were often labelled as 'defective' or 'unfit'.

These ideas were not confined to the classroom or laboratory. In the United States, psychological testimony helped legitimise the forced sterilisation of institutionalised women in the infamous *Buck v. Bell* case (1927). In Scandinavia, eugenics was implemented within progressive welfare states. Sweden's State Institute for Racial Biology (1922), led by Herman Lundborg, used psychological and anthropological tests to target ethnic minorities, especially the Sami and Finns. Across Sweden, Denmark, Norway, and Finland, IQ tests, behavioural assessments, and psychiatric diagnoses were used to justify sterilisation, institutionalisation, and marginalisation. These cases reveal the disciplinary power of psychology, and how even democratic societies used psychological science to govern the boundaries of life, worth, and citizenship. In Nazi Germany, from 1939, psychological theories of hereditary mental illness underpinned the T4 euthanasia programme in which thousands of disabled people were systematically murdered, a precursor to the Holocaust.

Key Individuals

Francis Galton (1822–1911) was a polymath whose contributions spanned statistics, anthropology, and criminology. He coined the term 'eugenics' in 1883 and was one of the first to argue that intelligence and moral character were biologically inherited. In his book *Hereditary Genius* (1869), Galton proposed a system where society would encourage 'the more suitable races or strains of blood a better chance of prevailing speedily over the less suitable'. He suggested monetary incentives for what he considered 'judicious marriages', unions between individuals deemed to have superior inherited endowments. Galton also pioneered the use of correlation and regression, tools that would become foundational to psychological testing.

Galton's intellectual heir Karl Pearson (1857–1936) was instrumental in institutionalising eugenics in Britain. He became the first Chair of Eugenics at University College London and directed the Galton Laboratory, which developed statistical tools for studying human heredity (including 'Pearson's r' correlation coefficient). Pearson believed fervently in the biological basis of intelligence and criminality, and his work was used to promote policies aimed at limiting reproduction among the working classes and the 'socially unfit'.

Charles Spearman (1863–1945) introduced the concept of the general intelligence factor, or g, which became central to psychometric theory. Although he was not an outspoken eugenicist, his statistical methods, especially factor analysis, were easily appropriated by those who wished to rank human worth according to IQ. Spearman's model of intelligence supported the notion that cognitive ability was fixed and heritable, helping to fuel racial and class-based interpretations of intellectual potential.

A leading figure in British psychology, Cyril Burt (1883–1971) conducted influential twin studies that purported to show a high heritability of intelligence. His findings played a key role in the 1944 Education Act, which stratified children into grammar, technical, and secondary modern schools based on an IQ test performance. Burt's legacy was later clouded by allegations of data fabrication, but his impact on the institutionalisation of eugenic ideas in education was significant.

In the United States, Lewis Terman (1877–1956) was a central figure in translating eugenic ideas into educational and military policy. He adapted Alfred Binet's intelligence test into the Stanford-Binet scale, which he used to argue for the biological basis of intelligence. Terman's IQ tests became tools for educational tracking, immigration restriction, and military placement. During the First World War, he contributed to the development of the Army Alpha and Beta tests, which reinforced ethnic and class biases. He believed that those with low IQs posed a threat to national efficiency and advocated for their exclusion from mainstream society.

Henry Goddard (1866–1957) introduced IQ testing into American public institutions and popularised the classification of 'morons' as a distinct category of mental defect. His work at the Vineland Training School and his studies of heredity among the 'Kallikak' family provided a scientific rationale for sterilisation and institutionalisation. Goddard's ideas influenced the 1924 Immigration Act, which sought to limit entry to the United States from Southern and Eastern Europe. Although he later modified his views, his work laid the groundwork for the large-scale application of psychological testing in the service of eugenic policy.

Herman Lundborg (1868–1943) was a Swedish physician and racial biologist whose work exemplified the connections between psychological classification and state power. As the founding director of the *Statens institut för rasbiologi* (Swedish State Institute for Racial Biology), established in 1922, he led research into heredity and intelligence that targeted the country's ethnic minorities. Lundborg used anthropometric measurements, IQ testing, and behavioural assessments to create detailed racial typologies. His work provided the scientific justification for Sweden's compulsory sterilisation policies, which remained in force until 1975.

Epistemological Issues

At the heart of eugenic psychology lies a particular epistemology: the belief that human worth can be objectively measured, categorised, and hierarchised. Psychologists claimed to discover truths about people through intelligence tests, statistical measures, and diagnostic classifications, yet these tools were far from neutral. They were embedded in the cultural anxieties and political ideologies of their time, particularly those related to race, class, gender, and ability.

A central epistemological problem was the reification of intelligence. Psychologists treated intelligence as a fixed, biologically inherited property, something that could be measured and ranked with precision. Standardised IQ tests presented this as scientific fact, but they privileged culturally specific forms of reasoning and language use. These tests were designed by, and for, members of dominant social groups. As such, they systematically disadvantaged immigrants, working-class children, and ethnic minorities, transforming social inequalities into apparent biological deficiencies.

Statistical methods further obscured these biases. Correlation coefficients, heritability estimates, and normal distribution curves gave a sheen of objectivity to what were fundamentally normative judgements. The language of averages and deviations implied that those who did not conform to statistical norms were not just different but deficient. In doing so, psychology became a powerful mechanism for classifying individuals in ways that supported social exclusion.

Ontological Issues

The ontology of eugenics, the assumptions it makes about what people are and how they can be known, relied on a deeply reductionist view of human nature. It posited that individuals could be categorised into fixed biological types, that traits like intelligence, morality, and mental capacity were essentially inherited, and that these traits defined a person's worth. Such ontological commitments underpinned the division of humanity into binaries: fit and unfit, normal and deviant, valuable and expendable.

In this worldview, individuals were no longer seen as complex beings shaped by context, relationships, and culture. Instead, they were treated as bearers of inherited essence, carriers of value or degeneration. Psychology, with its growing authority in testing and classification, helped reduce people to data points in a biological ledger. Mental deficiency, once a vague and contested label, was reframed as a measurable, diagnosable condition with fixed consequences for a person's place in society. These assumptions were not confined to theory. They justified institutionalisation, sterilisation, and exclusion. Fixed racial hierarchies rationalised colonial rule; classifications of mental defect legitimised lifelong confinement. In both cases, the person was flattened into a set of inherited traits, denying the possibility of transformation, education, or growth.

Within psychology, this ontological framework fed directly into wider projects of control, towards the management and purification of populations. Essentialist views of mind and self became tools of social engineering. Today, we recognise that identity, ability, and development are plastic, context-dependent, and relational. But understanding this earlier ontological framework helps us see how easily psychological science can be co-opted into systems of exclusion, especially when it treats people as fixed biological entities rather than as dynamic, lived selves.

Power

Eugenics marks a moment in history where psychology became fully enmeshed in the exercise of biopower. This concept, introduced by Michel Foucault, refers to the ways in which modern societies govern populations not through violence or law alone but by managing the vital processes of life, through intervening in birth, death, reproduction, and health. Psychology, with its authority to define and measure the human, became a key tool in this project.

Through intelligence testing, psychological classification, and statistical norms, psychology offered a language and a method for deciding whose lives were valuable, productive, and fit for society. Those who did not conform to these norms, such as immigrants, the working class, ethnic minorities, and people with disabilities, were often labelled as biologically inferior. These classifications justified sweeping interventions, including segregation, sterilisation, institutionalisation, and, in extreme cases as in Nazi Germany, elimination.

The power of psychology lay in its ability to naturalise inequality. Biopower did not need to appear cruel to be effective. It worked through the logic of care, protection, and efficiency. Psychological assessments were used to rationalise who should be educated, who could immigrate, and who could reproduce. In doing so, psychology became a science of population management. Across the early twentieth century, countries, including the United States, Germany, Sweden, Denmark, Norway, and Finland, enacted eugenic policies legitimised by psychological science. The reach of biopower was not confined to authoritarian regimes; it shaped liberal democracies too, under the guise of health and social improvement.

Importantly, not all psychologists accepted this role. Leta Hollingworth (1886–1939), an American psychologist and pioneer of gifted education, challenged the idea that intelligence tests revealed innate ability. She argued that poverty, gender discrimination, and lack of opportunity distorted outcomes and warned that psychology was being misused to justify inequality. Franz Boas (1858–1942) was arguably the most significant scientific opponent of eugenics and scientific racism in the United States. His core argument was that culture and environment primarily shaped human behaviour, intellect, and social organisation. He systematically dismantled the concept of fixed racial types and hierarchies through empirical research, particularly his studies on immigrant children, showing how their physical characteristics changed over generations in response to environmental factors. These figures remind us that resistance was always possible, and that psychological knowledge can be mobilised to challenge, rather than enforce, social hierarchies.

Chapter Summary

The history of eugenics in psychology is not merely a catalogue of flawed ideas or outdated methods. It is a haunting reminder of how knowledge, when aligned with state power, can be used to categorise, control, and diminish human life. From the late nineteenth to the mid-twentieth century, psychologists in Britain, the United States, Europe, and the Nordic countries participated in building a vision of society in which human worth could be measured and managed. Armed with IQ tests, behavioural assessments, and statistical techniques, psychology did not simply observe the world, it helped shape it. These tools created thresholds of normality and deviance, reinforcing hierarchies of race, gender, class, and ability.

Eugenics was not the domain of fringe extremists. It was supported by liberal reformers and conservative elites alike, legitimised by scientific institutions, and codified into laws that governed reproduction, education, and institutionalisation. For many, it was seen as a rational, even benevolent, application of scientific principles to social problems. But in retrospect, it marks one of psychology's deepest ethical failings.

Foucault's concept of biopower helps us see that psychology was a mechanism for governing life and health. It helped determine who could be born, who could learn, who was fit to work, and who could be loved. These decisions had devastating consequences.

Declared 'feebleminded' and forcibly sterilised in 1927, Carrie Buck died in a Virginia nursing home in 1983. Near the end of her life, legal scholar Paul Lombardo interviewed her and found her to be of ordinary intelligence. She regretted never having the chance to have more children. Few attended her funeral. In 2002, when a historical marker was placed at her birthplace, the Governor of Virginia issued 'a sincere apology for Virginia's forced participation in eugenics'.

It came too late for Carrie, but not too late for us. The language and logic of eugenics still echo in contemporary debates over intelligence, genetics, and disability. As we move into an era of AI-driven assessment, genetic selection, and behavioural prediction, we must ask again: what kind of psychology do we want? Carrie Buck's story compels us to choose wisely.

Reflective Questions

1. What does the concept of biopower help us understand about psychology's role in eugenics?
2. In what ways did intelligence testing support systems of social inequality in the twentieth century?
3. How did eugenics operate differently in Britain, the United States, and Scandinavia?
4. Why is it important to include dissenting voices, like Leta Hollingworth's, in the history of psychology?
5. What are the legacies of eugenic thinking in psychology today?

Suggested Reading

Bangham, J. (2015). What Is Race? UNESCO, mass communication and human genetics in the early 1950s. *History of the Human Sciences, 28*(5), 80–107. https://doi.org/10.1177/0952695115600581.

Beccalossi, C., Fisher, K., & Funke, J. (2023). Sexology and development. *History of the Human Sciences, 36*(5), 3–14. https://doi.org/10.1177/09526951231213970.

Broberg, G., & Roll-Hansen, N. (2005). *Eugenics and the Welfare State: Sterilization policy in Denmark, Sweden, Norway, and Finland*. Ann Arbor: Michigan State University Press.

Germann, P. (2021). Race in post-war science: The Swiss case in a global context. *History of the Human Sciences, 35*(1), 216–241. https://doi.org/10.1177/09526951211010385.

Jarska, N., Lišková, K., & Wahl, M. (2024). Early state socialism and eugenics: Premarital medical certificates in Czechoslovakia, East Germany, and Poland in the aftermath of World War II. *History of the Human Sciences, 38*(1), 51–77. https://doi.org/10.1177/09526951241270931.

Kelly, E., Manning, D. T., Boye, S., Rice, C., Owen, D., Stonefish, S., & Stonefish, M. (2021). Elements of a counter-exhibition: Excavating and countering a Canadian history and legacy of eugenics. *Journal of the History of the Behavioral Sciences, 57*(1), 12–33. https://doi.org/10.1002/jhbs.22081.

Kevles, D. J. (1985). *In the Name of Eugenics: Genetics and the uses of human heredity*. Cambridge, MA: Harvard University Press.

Lombardo, P. A. (2022). *Three Generations, No Imbeciles: Eugenics, the Supreme Court, and Buck v. Bell*. Indiana, IN: Johns Hopkins University Press.

Pilgrim, D. (2023). Verdicts on Hans Eysenck and the fluxing context of British psychology. *History of the Human Sciences, 36*(3–4), 83–104. https://doi.org/10.1177/09526951221143888.

Sims-Schouten, W. (2021). 'A troublesome girl is pushed through': Morality, biological determinism, resistance, resilience, and the Canadian child migration schemes, 1883–1939. *History of the Human Sciences, 35*(1), 87–110. https://doi.org/10.1177/09526951211036553.

Stern, A. M. (2016). *Eugenic Nation: Faults and frontiers of better breeding in modern America* (Second ed.). Berkeley, CA: University of California Press.

Teicher, A. (2022). How family charts became Mendelian: The changing content of pedigrees and its impact on the consolidation of genetic theory. *History of the Human Sciences, 37*(3–4), 85–105. https://doi.org/10.1177/09526951221107558.

Weizmann, F. (2010). From the 'Village of a Thousand Souls' to 'Race Crossing in Jamaica': Arnold Gesell, eugenics and child development. *Journal of the History of the Behavioral Sciences, 46*(3), 263–275. https://doi.org/10.1002/jhbs.20440.

Key Terms

Biopower A concept developed by Michel Foucault referring to the way modern states govern populations through the regulation of health, reproduction, and behaviour. In psychology, biopower describes how tests, diagnoses, and classifications are used to define and control who is considered normal, intelligent, or fit.

Buck v. Bell (1927) A landmark U.S. Supreme Court case that upheld the constitutionality of forced sterilisation. Psychological testimony was used to declare Carrie Buck 'feebleminded', legitimising a broader eugenics policy across many states.

Eugenics A scientific and political movement that aimed to improve the human population by encouraging the reproduction of the 'fit' and limiting the reproduction of the 'unfit'. Supported by many early psychologists, it led to policies such as forced sterilisation, institutionalisation, and immigration restriction.

Intelligence Testing The practice of using standardised assessments to measure cognitive ability. Originating in early twentieth-century psychology, intelligence testing became closely tied to eugenic ideology and was often used to justify exclusionary policies.

IQ (Intelligence Quotient) A numerical score derived from standardised intelligence tests, used to rank cognitive ability. IQ scores became central to eugenic arguments about heritability and were used to justify exclusionary social policies.

Mental Deficiency Act (1913) A British law that allowed for the segregation of people labelled 'feebleminded' or 'morally defective'. Psychological assessments were used to classify individuals, legitimising their removal from society and institutional confinement.

Psychometrics The branch of psychology concerned with measuring mental traits and abilities. In the context of eugenics, psychometrics became a tool for classifying people as intelligent, average, or deficient.

Statistical Norms The idea that psychological traits like intelligence follow a normal distribution, with most people falling around an average. Used in eugenics to pathologise deviation from the norm and to justify interventions against those who fell outside the statistical 'ideal'.

FREE INSTRUCTOR & STUDENT RESOURCES

ONLINE RESOURCES

Visit the Instructor & Student Resources website at routledgelearning.com/bpscoretextbooks for free digital resources, including:

- Interactive quizzes and flashcards to test your knowledge
- Links to useful websites and videos
- Instructor manual, lecture slides, and course guide to enhance teaching and save instructors time

3 Broken Bodies, Wounded Souls

The Psychosomatic Protest of Shell Shock

Chapter Overview

This chapter explores the history of shell shock during the First World War as a moment of profound crisis in psychology, culture, and medicine. Drawing on the concept of psychosomatic protest, it examines how trauma manifested differently in officers and ordinary soldiers, shaped by class, power, and military expectations. Officers were often haunted by moral injury, while lower-ranked men exhibited physical symptoms such as paralysis or mutism, bodily expressions of suffering that could not be spoken about, let alone discussed. The chapter contrasts the empathetic therapeutic methods of W. H. R. Rivers with the punitive disciplinary approach of Lewis Yealland, revealing how social hierarchies were reproduced through psychological treatment. It also briefly explores the cultural afterlife of shell shock through interwar literature and poetry and connects these early twentieth-century debates to later understandings of psychological trauma, including Post-Traumatic Stress Disorder (PTSD). Ultimately, shell shock is presented not simply as a medical condition but as a politically and symbolically charged episode in the history of psychology, one that continues to shape how we think about trauma, masculinity, and the ethics of care.

Broken Bodies, Wounded Souls

At dawn on 18 October 1916, Private Harry Farr was led into a field near Carnoy on the Western Front. He was tied to a wooden post, blindfolded, and executed by a firing squad made up of his fellow soldiers. His crime: refusing to return to the front line. This was a stark end for a soldier whose conduct had previously been exemplary, serving faithfully since before the Great War began and enduring the brutality of combat without a blemish on his record. What the court martial had not fully acknowledged, or refused to understand, was that Farr had already endured over two years of shellfire and had been hospitalised several times for what was then called 'nervous debility'. He had collapsed, shaken uncontrollably, and complained of persistent tremors and ringing in his ears. His medical records described him as 'unable to stand the strain of shellfire'. But Farr had no visible wounds. The military authorities interpreted his condition not as trauma but as cowardice. In a brutal system more concerned with discipline than diagnosis, Farr was made an example of, one of over 300 British soldiers shot for 'desertion' or 'cowardice' during the First World War. His execution silenced the evidence of his

DOI: 10.4324/9781003565482-13

suffering. It was not until 2006 that Harry Farr was officially pardoned, following decades of campaigning by his family and military historians. Farr's story reveals how the early psychological casualties of war were punished rather than treated, their symptoms misunderstood, misdiagnosed, or ignored altogether. In the eyes of the state, broken bodies could be repaired, but wounded souls were expendable.

Chapter Contents

- Explores the historical, psychological, and cultural origins of shell shock during the First World War.
- Analyses how class, power, and gender shaped the diagnosis, treatment, and interpretation of shell shock.
- Introduces the critical thinking tool of psychosomatic protest to examine how symptoms can be understood as embodied resistance.

Chapter Objectives

- To understand the emergence of shell shock within the context of industrialised warfare and medical modernity.
- To critically evaluate different therapeutic and disciplinary responses to shell shock and their implications.
- To apply the critical thinking tool of psychosomatic protest to interpret the symbolic meaning of psychological symptoms in a historical and social context.

CRITICAL THINKING TOOL
PSYCHOSOMATIC PROTEST

Psychosomatic protest refers to the phenomenon in which psychological distress is expressed through bodily symptoms, often when no other form of expression, resistance, or protest is available. It draws attention to the symbolic and embodied dimensions of suffering, particularly in situations where speech, refusal, or emotional expression are suppressed or impossible. In the context of the First World War, this concept helps us make sense of the extraordinary range of symptoms associated with shell shock: trembling hands, frozen limbs, mutism, paralysis, hysterical blindness, and nightmares. For many soldiers, particularly those in the lower ranks, these symptoms were not just evidence of neurological breakdown or emotional collapse but an involuntary form of resistance, a protest issued by the body itself. These men were often expected to endure the unendurable in silence: relentless shellfire, death, mud, lice, the stench of decay, and the dehumanising machinery of industrial warfare. Class played a central role. While officers sometimes developed neurotic symptoms related to guilt and responsibility, such as nightmares, insomnia, or hallucinations, ordinary soldiers often exhibited uncontrollable shaking or loss of speech, symptoms that can be understood as the body's rebellion in the absence of permission to rebel in any other way. Psychosomatic protest challenges the traditional mind–body division that has long dominated Western psychology. It insists that

symptoms are not merely failures of the individual psyche or body but are deeply embedded in social, cultural, and political contexts. This makes it a powerful critical tool for psychologists and historians alike. When we look at the history of shell shock using this critical concept, we begin to see trauma as a political and cultural message, something embodied when it cannot be spoken, enacted when it cannot be refused. Symptoms, in this sense, become forms of protest and meaning-making.

Introduction

The concept of shell shock emerged during the First World War, a conflict that profoundly reshaped how psychological trauma was understood, both medically and socially. Several historical conditions of possibility contributed to its visibility. One major shift was in the nature of warfare. Unlike the mobile battles of the Boer War (1899–1902), the First World War introduced an industrialised war machine. Soldiers endured months in the trenches under constant bombardment, surrounded by death, mud, and decay. This unrelenting sensory and emotional assault produced a level of psychological strain never encountered in battle before.

Thousands of men broke down not from physical wounds but from overwhelming psychological trauma that manifested in paralysis, mutism, hallucinations, and tremors. At first, doctors believed these symptoms were caused by physical damage from shell blast waves. But as the war continued, it became clear that something more complex was occurring. This chapter explores shell shock through the lens of psychosomatic protest, a concept that helps us read these symptoms not just as medical conditions but as embodied expressions of suffering, resistance, and the deep psychic wounds inflicted by war.

Historical Issues

Shell shock was made possible by a convergence of historical, technological, cultural, and ideological forces that shaped the psychological experience of soldiers prior to and during the war. In contrast to earlier conflicts such as the Boer War (1899–1902), which involved smaller-scale battles, cavalry manoeuvres, and single-shot rifles, the First World War introduced an unprecedented scale of mechanised violence. Machine guns, long-range artillery, poison gas, tanks, and barbed wire turned the battlefield into a machine for crushing, suffocating, and grinding bodies. Soldiers were confined for weeks or months in cold, wet trenches, constantly exposed to the sights, sounds, and smells of mass death. This continuous sensory onslaught created conditions of unrelenting psychological stress, contributing to the emergence of what came to be known as shell shock.

Beyond the battlefield, powerful cultural forces shaped the mental vulnerability of those who enlisted. Wartime propaganda played a role, portraying military service as a noble duty full of adventure, masculinity, and honour. Recruitment posters appealed to national pride, religious virtue, and romanticised visions of manhood, while concealing the reality of industrial slaughter. Many young men, particularly from working-class backgrounds, were seduced by these images and joined up with little understanding of what they would face. Those who hesitated were often publicly shamed. The White Feather Campaign, which used women to hand out white feathers to men who were not in uniform, branded them as cowards and traitors. In a society that equated masculinity with stoicism and sacrifice, such shame could be psychologically devastating.

Meanwhile, existing theories of psychiatric illness further constrained how shell shock was understood. Medical thinking at the time was heavily influenced by theories of biological degeneration, applied to criminals, the working class, and the 'feebleminded', and by ideas of hysteria, which were primarily associated with women. Many doctors interpreted psychological collapse in male soldiers as evidence of unmanly weakness or malingering. These assumptions, rooted in classism, sexism, and moral judgement, left little room to view trauma as a rational and understandable response to unbearable conditions. Shell shock emerged as both a crisis of war and a crisis of psychological meaning.

Key Individuals

British anthropologist and psychiatrist W. H. R. Rivers (1864–1922) tried to understand and treat shell shock humanely. Working at Craiglockhart War Hospital near Edinburgh, Rivers treated some of the most well-known shell shock patients of the First World War, including the war poets Siegfried Sassoon and Wilfred Owen. Rivers rejected punitive treatments in favour of what he called the 'talking cure', a psychoanalytic approach that encouraged soldiers to confront, rather than repress, their fears and guilt. Drawing on Freudian theory and his own anthropological research, Rivers saw shell shock as a meaningful psychological response to intolerable conditions. His work prioritised patient recovery over military efficiency, though he did still hope to return men to active duty. What made Rivers remarkable was his capacity to interpret psychological symptoms as signs of suffering rather than moral failure.

In contrast, Lewis Yealland (1884–1954), a Canadian-born neurologist at the National Hospital for the Paralysed and Epileptic in London, embodied the disciplinary approach to shell shock. Yealland believed symptoms such as mutism, paralysis, and tremors were failures of will power rather than expressions of trauma. He applied harsh techniques, most notoriously electric shock therapy, to 're-educate' a soldier's nervous system and enforce military discipline. His treatments aimed not to understand the suffering of his patients but to silence it, often literally. Yealland resisted psychological explanations, fearing they might excuse what he perceived as malingering. His methods, though reportedly effective in the short term, were widely criticised for their cruelty and lack of long-term follow-up.

Between these extremes was Arthur Hurst (1879–1944), a British neurologist who treated shell shock patients at Seale Hayne Military Hospital in Devon. Hurst used a wide range of methods, including hypnosis, physical therapy, drama-based re-enactments, and reintegration activities, to address both psychological and physical symptoms. His patients often presented with movement disorders such as repetitive 'tics' and paralysis, despite having no evident physical injury. Hurst's use of film to document before-and-after treatment sessions remains one of the earliest and most influential visual records of psychotherapy. Although some have critiqued his reliance on spectacle and the ethical implications of re-enactment, Hurst's approach reflected a growing belief that recovery could be achieved through empathetic, patient-focused care, especially when the body itself became the site of protest.

British psychologist Charles S. Myers (1873–1946) first introduced the term 'shell shock' into the medical literature in 1915. Initially believing the condition was caused by blast-related physical injury to the brain, Myers later realised that psychological factors were central. Despite this insight, he struggled to implement meaningful reforms within a military system that prioritised functionality over recovery. His 1940 book, *Shell Shock in France, 1914–1918*, was an eleventh-hour effort to advocate for the psychological needs of soldiers.

William McDougall (1871–1938), a prominent British American psychologist, significantly shaped how shell shock was understood. His hugely influential instinct theory, outlined in his 1908 work *An Introduction to Social Psychology*, argued that human behaviour was fundamentally driven by a set of innate, inherited tendencies, each linked to a specific emotion. Within this perspective, shell shock could be seen as the 'unmanly' instinct of flight overwhelming the expected 'courageous' instincts of combat or self-assertion. This provided a psychological justification for views that often linked shell shock vulnerability to a perceived lack of masculinity or the failure of a soldier's will to suppress 'weaker' emotions, thereby contributing to the stigmatisation of those suffering from psychological trauma.

The psychological experience of war was also captured in poetry. The war poets of the First World War offered some of the most poignant testimonies of trauma. Wilfred Owen (1893–1918) used poetry to depict the horror of gas attacks and the moral obscenity of war. In *Dulce et Decorum Est*, he viciously dismantled the patriotic myth that it was 'sweet and fitting' to die for one's country. Siegfried Sassoon (1886–1967), a patient of Rivers, channelled his anger into biting satire in poems like *The General*, condemning military incompetence and the needless sacrifice of soldiers. Isaac Rosenberg (1890–1918), from a working-class Jewish background, infused his poetry with existential and spiritual themes, as in *Break of Day in the Trenches*. And Ivor Gurney (1890–1937), both a poet and composer, struggled with mental illness long after the war, haunted by the persistent sorrow and abandonment felt by many survivors.

Epistemological Issues

Shell shock was first identified in 1915 by British psychologist C. S. Myers, who observed soldiers suffering from tremors, paralysis, nightmares, and memory loss, often in the absence of physical injury. At a time when psychology lacked robust frameworks for understanding trauma, shell shock posed serious epistemological challenges. The condition was initially approached through observational methods, patient interviews, and rudimentary neurological tests, but its symptoms defied standardisation. Without physical markers to measure, doctors struggled to define, diagnose, or explain what they were seeing.

Many early theories attributed shell shock to blast-related brain damage, suggesting that the concussive force of explosions caused microlesions in the nervous system. Yet soldiers who had never been near an explosion also exhibited symptoms, forcing a gradual shift towards psychological explanations. The subjective nature of trauma, particularly symptoms such as mutism, dissociation, or flashbacks, meant that shell shock did not easily fit into established diagnostic models. It was not easily measured, and this led to debates over its legitimacy. Some military authorities accused soldiers of malingering or cowardice, especially when symptoms seemed to lack a visible cause.

Complicating matters further was the emergence of what we now call moral injury: the psychological harm caused by acting against one's ethical beliefs, or by being betrayed by authority. Soldiers faced harrowing choices: killing at close range, watching comrades die, or following orders they believed to be futile or cruel. The impact of these experiences could not be captured by neurological tests. The emotional fallout, including guilt, shame, grief, and rage, challenged prevailing understandings of traumatic experience.

Ontological Issues

Shell shock posed a crisis for how trauma was understood, forcing competing interpretations to emerge. Some viewed it as a neurological injury, others as a psychological breakdown, and still others as a social or cultural expression of distress. One of the striking features of shell shock was how differently it manifested according to rank. Officers often experienced nightmares, flashbacks, and profound moral injury, haunted by their responsibility for sending men to their deaths. These symptoms reflected internal conflict, guilt, and the unbearable weight of leadership under impossible conditions.

Ordinary soldiers, by contrast, more commonly displayed physical symptoms: paralysis, tremors, mutism, and shaking, often with no discernible physical cause. These can be interpreted as a form of *psychosomatic protest*, in which the body acts out suffering that cannot be consciously spoken or resisted. Trapped in trenches, exposed to mud, death, hunger, and terror, the bodies of these men seemed to rebel against the inhuman conditions. Their symptoms were symbolically resonant: a protest enacted through the body in the absence of any permitted refusal.

This difference in symptom clusters highlights that understandings of what shell shock was were shaped by power and class. Officers' trauma was interpreted in moral or psychological terms, while the breakdown of ordinary soldiers was often seen as mechanical or disciplinary. Traditional ideals of masculinity and military duty left little room for vulnerability, pushing emotional suffering beneath conscious awareness. Shell shock became the space where this cultural contradiction played out, an affliction that had to be explained without undermining the very values of endurance and heroism the military relied upon.

Over time, the ontological framing of shell shock shifted. Influenced by figures such as W. H. R. Rivers and Charles Myers, and informed by emerging psychoanalytic ideas of repression and trauma, the condition came to be seen less as physical injury and more as psychological collapse. Yet this interpretation was deeply contested. To acknowledge psychological vulnerability was to threaten the ideals of the war itself. Shell shock exposed the fragility of the categories used to contain and explain such vulnerability.

Power

Understanding shell shock through the lens of power relations reveals how psychological breakdown was not only treated differently depending on the patient's symptoms but was also shaped by their rank, class, gender, and perceived social value. Treatment approaches were embedded in military and social hierarchies, drawing on both disciplinary and pastoral forms of power. These differing modes of control help explain the stark contrast between how ordinary soldiers and officers were managed, guided, or corrected.

Disciplinary power is concerned with regulating individuals through coercion, surveillance, and correction, aiming to produce obedient, functional bodies. This was exemplified by the work of Lewis Yealland, whose treatment of shell shock at London's National Hospital reflected a rigidly disciplinary ethos. Yealland's patients, primarily drawn from the lower ranks, were subjected to electric shock therapy, verbal command, and routinised procedures designed to eliminate symptoms quickly and return men to the front. His approach positioned psychological suffering as a form of defiance or weakness to be stamped out, not a condition to be explored or understood. In this model, shell shock was a failure of discipline. Yealland's interventions reinforced military authority through fear and bodily control.

Pastoral power, by contrast, seeks to guide and care for individuals, cultivating their inner capacities through empathy and insight. This approach was embodied in the work of W. H. R. Rivers at Craiglockhart War Hospital, where he treated officers including war poets Siegfried Sassoon and Wilfred Owen. Rivers's therapeutic methods were grounded in talking cures, psychoanalytic principles, and a deep respect for his patients' emotional suffering. Rather than punishing symptoms, he encouraged reflection, memory, and meaning-making, fostering psychological healing in those burdened with moral injury and existential guilt. Pastoral power is no less a form of governance, but it works through care rather than command. It was largely reserved for men of rank and education.

This division reflects the broader inequalities of wartime psychological treatment. Officers were treated as minds in crisis; working-class soldiers were treated as malfunctioning bodies. The management of shell shock was also a theatre of power.

Chapter Summary

The experience of shell shock left an indelible mark on those who survived the war. Many soldiers returned home not only with psychological trauma but with a profound sense of moral injury, a deep, corrosive distress caused by actions they were forced to take or witness, and by the betrayal of values they had believed in. They had killed at close range, watched comrades die, and endured dehumanising conditions for a cause they were told was noble. Yet when they returned, they often met with silence, suspicion, or scorn. Accused of cowardice or malingering, many veterans were left to suffer in isolation, their wounds invisible and illegible to a society still clinging to heroic ideals of war and masculinity.

Shell shock's moral injury reflected a broader failure of recognition. The same propaganda that had recruited them with promises of glory made no room for the broken, grief-stricken men who came back. The psychological cost of war, largely unacknowledged by military authorities and civilian institutions, left a legacy of alienation that extended far beyond the battlefield. The trauma of these men was compounded by a social failure to understand it.

Yet shell shock did not disappear. Its legacy echoed throughout the interwar years, not only in hospitals and military manuals but in the literature and culture of the time. Writers and poets gave form to the psychological wounds that medicine struggled to name. Works such as Rebecca West's *The Return of the Soldier* (1918), Virginia Woolf's *Mrs Dalloway* (1925), and Erich Maria Remarque's *All Quiet on the Western Front* (1929) brought the inner lives of traumatised veterans into public consciousness, shaping how war was remembered and understood. These narratives offered what the official record often denied: a space for suffering to be witnessed.

Nevertheless, societal resistance to acknowledging psychological trauma persisted. In 1940, Charles Myers, who had coined the term 'shell shock', felt compelled to revisit the issue in his book *Shell Shock in France, 1914–1918*, a sobering reflection on the failure to learn from the past. His call for more humane treatment of psychological injury remained urgently relevant as the world braced for yet another war. The story of shell shock is a lesson in what happens when society refuses to listen to the voices of those with broken bodies and wounded souls.

Reflective Questions

1. What does the concept of 'psychosomatic protest' reveal about the meaning of shell shock symptoms?
2. How did class and military rank influence the diagnosis and treatment of shell shock during the First World War?
3. In what ways did the treatment approaches of Rivers and Yealland reflect broader systems of power and control?
4. How does the concept of moral injury help us understand the long-term psychological impact of war on soldiers?
5. What role did literature and poetry play in shaping public understanding of shell shock?

Suggested Reading

Barham, P. (2004). *Forgotten Lunatics of the Great War.* New Haven, CT: Yale University Press.

Brunner, J. (1991). Psychiatry, psychoanalysis, and politics during the First World War. *Journal of the History of the Behavioral Sciences, 27*(4), 352–365. https://doi.org/10.1002/1520-6696(199110)27:4<352::AID-JHBS2300270404>3.0.CO;2-9.

Carden-Coyne, A. (2014). *The Politics of Wounds: Military patients and medical power in the First World War.* Oxford: Oxford University Press.

Downing, T. (2016). *Breakdown: The crisis of shell shock on the Somme, 1916.* London: Little, Brown.

Jones, E. (2018). Trans-generational transmission of traumatic memory and moral injury. *Military Behavioral Health, 6*(2), 134–139. https://doi.org/10.1080/21635781.2018.1454362.

Jones, E., & Wessely, S. (2005). *Shell Shock to PTSD: Military psychiatry from 1900 to the Gulf War.* Bristol: Psychology Press.

Leuenberger, C. (2003). Beyond invisible walls: The psychological legacy of Soviet trauma. *Journal of the History of the Behavioural Sciences, 39*(2), 183–184. https://doi.org/10.1002/jhbs.10071.

Mather, R., & Marsden, J. (2004). Trauma and temporality: On the origins of post-traumatic stress. *Theory & Psychology, 14*(2), 205–219. https://doi.org/10.1177/0959354304042017.

Shephard, B. (2001). *A War of Nerves: Soldiers and psychiatrists in the twentieth century.* Cambridge, MA: Harvard University Press.

Showalter, E. (1987). *The Female Malady: Women, madness and English culture, 1830–1980.* London: Virago.

Trembinski, D. (2011). Comparing premodern melancholy/mania and modern trauma: An argument in favor of historical experiences of trauma. *History of Psychology, 14*(1), 80–99. https://doi.org/10.1037/a0020430.

Zait, J. (2024). 'I'm not a person anymore': The 'survivor syndrome' and William G. Niederland's perception of the human being. *History of Psychology, 27*(2), 121–138. https://doi.org/10.1037/hop0000250.

Key Terms

Craiglockhart War Hospital A military psychiatric hospital in Edinburgh where Rivers treated shell-shocked officers, including poets Siegfried Sassoon and Wilfred Owen.

Disciplinary Power A concept from Michel Foucault describing power exercised through coercion, correction, and bodily control, often applied to lower-ranked soldiers.

Firing Squad A method of military execution used during the First World War, including for soldiers accused of cowardice or desertion—some of whom likely suffered from untreated shell shock.

Hysteria A psychological diagnosis historically associated with women, but influential in shaping how early psychiatrists interpreted the symptoms of shell shock in men.

Instinct Theory A psychological theory, notably advanced by William McDougall, that behaviour is driven by innate, inherited tendencies, each linked to a particular emotion.

Moral Injury A deep psychological wound caused by witnessing or participating in actions that violate one's ethical or moral beliefs, often associated with war.

Pastoral Power Michel Foucault's term for a form of power that operates through care, guidance, and therapeutic attention, typically applied to officers in contexts like Craiglockhart.

Psychosomatic Protest The idea that the body expresses psychological suffering through physical symptoms when emotional protest is not socially or psychologically possible.

Shell shock A term used during the First World War to describe psychological breakdown in soldiers, often marked by paralysis, mutism, or tremors, and initially thought to result from physical blast exposure.

Trench Warfare A brutal and static form of combat characteristic of the First World War, involving prolonged exposure to artillery fire, death, and extreme living conditions.

War Neuroses A broader category used during and after the First and Second World Wars to describe psychological disorders arising from the stresses of combat.

War Poets A group of soldier poets, including Wilfred Owen and Siegfried Sassoon, who wrote vivid, often critical, reflections on the trauma of war.

FREE INSTRUCTOR & STUDENT RESOURCES

ONLINE RESOURCES

Visit the Instructor & Student Resources website at routledgelearning.com/bpscoretextbooks for free digital resources, including:

- Interactive quizzes and flashcards to test your knowledge
- Links to useful websites and videos
- Instructor manual, lecture slides, and course guide to enhance teaching and save instructors time

4 The Secrets of Black Magic

Industrial Psychology's Technologies of the Self

Chapter Overview

This chapter explores the emergence and evolution of industrial psychology as a form of applied psychological science closely tied to the needs of capitalism. Beginning in the early twentieth century, psychologists such as Hugo Münsterberg, Lillian Gilbreth, Kurt Lewin, and Elton Mayo developed psychological techniques, not simply to describe workers but to shape them. Industrial psychology helped determine who was employable, trainable, efficient, and obedient, making psychology a crucial part of the machinery of modern labour.

The chapter introduces the critical thinking tool *technologies of the self*, drawing on Michel Foucault's idea that people are not just governed externally but come to govern themselves through scientific categories, norms, and reflexive techniques. Industrial psychology created the conditions for workers to internalise identities like 'productive', 'suitable', or 'motivated' based on psychological evaluations.

This chapter invites us to critically reflect on how psychology functions as a social technology, and how it has historically served the needs of industry by shaping the very selves it claims to study. In doing so, it points to the legacy of workplace testing and behavioural surveillance in contemporary management, human resources, and employee profiling.

The Secrets of Black Magic

Throughout the austere years of the early 1930s, amidst the Great Depression, Britain was exhausted by economic despair. Rowntree's, the venerable Quaker chocolate manufacturer in York, was struggling. Yet, amidst the hardship, a craving for small luxuries persisted, a desire for a moment of affordable escape. Rowntree's desperately needed a new product to compete with rivals such as Cadbury's. But how could a chocolate company understand what a nation wanted? Rowntree's was a forward-thinking company with a faith in the potential of industrial psychology to improve business efficiency. In 1933, Seebohm Rowntree, the company's chairman, commissioned the National Institute of Industrial Psychology (NIIP) to undertake an unprecedented exercise in consumer research. The NIIP embarked on a vast investigation into what people desired in a box of chocolates. The psychologists interviewed thousands of shopkeepers and surveyed over 7,000 consumers across Britain, meticulously documenting their preferences for chocolate types, fillings, textures, and even the aesthetics of packaging. The end product of this research, launched in 1933, was Black

DOI: 10.4324/9781003565482-14

Magic chocolates, the first assortment to be developed to order for a mass market. The dark, mysterious box and sophisticated name hinted at romance and allure, tailored with precision to the psychological finding that 60 per cent of chocolate boxes were bought by men as gifts for women. Black Magic was a case study in psychological engineering: how industrial psychology could not only shape consumer habits but subtly rewrite the rituals of love and courtship. Its runaway success opened the door to other Rowntree innovations, Kit Kat, Aero, and Smarties, each infused with the sweet authority of market research and behavioural insight. But beneath the charm lies something more unsettling. If a chocolate box could be reimagined to engineer desire, could it be that our private habits, sumptuary pleasures, and personal desires have also been shaped by the unseen hand of psychological expertise?

Chapter Contents

- Explores the historical development of industrial psychology from the early twentieth century, including the work of Münsterberg, Gilbreth, Lewin, and Mayo.
- Critically examines the role of psychological testing and behavioural science in shaping worker identity, productivity, and compliance.
- Introduces the critical thinking tool of *technologies of the self* to analyse how psychological categories operate as tools of governance.

Chapter Objectives

- To explain how industrial psychology developed in tandem with changing economic and managerial practices in the workplace.
- To evaluate how psychological tools such as tests, profiles, and performance measures became embedded in the regulation of workers' behaviours and identities.
- To apply the critical thinking tool *technologies of the self* to understand how psychological expertise shapes people's internal sense of who they are and what they are capable of.

CRITICAL THINKING TOOL
TECHNOLOGIES OF THE SELF

Coined by the philosopher Michel Foucault, the phrase *technologies of the self* refers to the ways people are encouraged, or compelled, to shape their own behaviour, habits, thoughts, and identities in line with dominant social expectations. These 'technologies' are not just devices or methods; they are subtle systems of self-regulation that work through *internalisation*. People are taught to monitor themselves, to correct themselves, and to make themselves into better or more efficient versions of who they already are.

The concept is especially powerful in the history of industrial psychology. The field was never simply about measuring productivity or selecting the best worker for the job. It was about

shaping individuals, mentally, physically, and emotionally, to get them to fit into the industrial world. Psychology did not just train or assess the worker from the outside. It invited workers to think of themselves in new ways: as profiles, as types, as optimisable units of labour. It introduced tests, surveys, interviews, and morale-building exercises that weren't merely descriptive or diagnostic, they were formative. They taught people how to see themselves.

This chapter traces how industrial psychology became a toolkit of technologies of the self; how it entered the factory, the office, and the test room not only to measure people but to make them up, through tests, profiles, interviews, and morale programmes. It's a story that reveals the field's remarkable adaptability, and its complicity with systems of power. And we'll ask: when psychology helps people 'fit in', what is it asking them to leave out?

Introduction

Industrial psychology emerged in the early twentieth century as an active collaborator in the shaping of the modern worker. Hugo Münsterberg in the United States, for example, promised that industrial psychology could enhance productivity, reduce accidents, and help business run more efficiently. From the start, industrial psychology aligned itself with the priorities of management and the logic of capitalism, offering tools to measure performance and to mould behaviour in accordance with business objectives.

In the United States, scientific management and time-motion studies reflected a mechanical view of human labour. In Europe, *psychotechnics* sought to shape individuals for the needs of national and industrial systems. From its inception, industrial psychology was a shape-shifting discipline, evolving alongside the machinery of capitalism. As mass production accelerated in the early twentieth century, psychology found fertile ground in the factory. The central question was not whether psychology should serve industry, it was how thoroughly it could do so.

Historical Issues

With the publication of Hugo Münsterberg's *Psychology and Industrial Efficiency* (1913), psychology became a tool for selecting the right workers, training them properly, and designing the environment to optimise their output. The goal was not just to fix inefficient systems but to produce the kind of worker industry required. Over time, the psychological apparatus expanded to include everything from aptitude tests and performance evaluations to morale programmes and worker counselling.

Elton Mayo's work emerged as a reaction, or perhaps an evolution, from this purely mechanistic view. Mayo acknowledged that workers were not just driven by financial incentives or physical comfort but also by complex social and emotional needs. The challenge then became how to manage these invisible, subjective forces. Kurt Lewin placed a greater emphasis on democratic ideals, participation, and the complexities of organisational change. As organisations grew in size and complexity, there was a need for more sophisticated models of intervention that could deal with group dynamics and the fostering of commitment rather than mere compliance.

Industrial psychology was more paternalistic in Britain. Charles S. Myers, co-founder of the NIIP in 1921, offered expertise in vocational guidance and workplace welfare. Aiming to balance the needs of capital and labour, psychology intervened not to challenge the industrial order but to stabilise it. A particularly revealing example was at Rowntree's Cocoa Works in York, where the first British industrial psychologist Victor Moorrees applied psychology to improve staff selection, reduce fatigue, and boost morale.

The cumulative effect of these interventions was the creation of a new kind of psychological subject: one who internalised the values of productivity, teamwork, and personal responsibility. Through these technologies of the self, psychology subtly redirected dissatisfaction, boredom, or resistance away from collective critique and towards individual adjustment.

Key Individuals

Hugo Münsterberg (1863–1916) was one of the first to articulate a vision of psychology as a business asset. In *Psychology and Industrial Efficiency* (1913), he proposed that psychological principles could be used to hire the best workers, design optimal work environments, and reduce waste. But beneath this pragmatic framing was a deeper shift. Münsterberg helped redefine the worker as a *mental object*, someone whose inner life, their attention, fatigue, and willpower, could be shaped for maximum efficiency. His influence endures in the idea that the self could be trained to serve the system.

Walter Dill Scott (1869–1955), a pioneer in advertising and personnel selection, injected psychology directly into the heart of American capitalism. His work translated complex human attributes into scalable, measurable traits. He developed rating scales and testing procedures during the First World War that were later repurposed for industrial use. Scott's genius was in making psychology managerial. But his tools did not just help employers select workers; they also taught workers how to see themselves: as types, as profiles, in terms of test results. In doing so, he helped make self-assessment a form of compliance.

Charles S. Myers (1873–1946) co-founded the British National Institute of Industrial Psychology (NIIP) and played a pivotal role in adapting psychology to the needs of British industry. A veteran of the First World War and a former experimental psychologist, Myers shifted his focus from the laboratory to the shop floor. He advocated for welfare programmes, rest pauses, and accident prevention to maintain morale and productivity. Myers encouraged managers and workers to think of fatigue, frustration, and inefficiency as *psychological* problems.

Henri Piéron (1881–1964) exemplified the European tradition of *psychotechnics*, which sought to match individuals to roles through testing and vocational guidance. Working in postwar France, Piéron developed a battery of tests that measured everything from reaction time to logical reasoning. These tools were designed not only to classify people but also to channel their energies into socially useful employment. Piéron's psychotechnical laboratories blurred the distinction between diagnosis and discipline: the test was both an evaluation and a prescription. In this model, to *know oneself* was to *accept one's place*, a defining feature of psychological governance.

Lillian Moller Gilbreth (1878–1972) brought a humanistic veneer to the cold calculus of Taylorism. Alongside her husband, Frank Gilbreth, she conducted time-and-motion studies that dissected every movement a worker made. But

Lillian went further: she considered worker satisfaction, fatigue, and even emotion. Her innovations in ergonomics and kitchen design, often targeted at female labour, extended industrial psychology into the domestic sphere. Gilbreth's contribution was to make self-optimisation seem natural, even compassionate. By helping workers become more efficient, she helped inscribe industrial values into the rhythms of everyday life.

George Elton Mayo (1880–1949), an Australian psychologist and industrial researcher, rose to prominence through his central involvement in the Hawthorne Studies (1924–1932) at the Western Electric Company. His key contribution was to shift the focus of industrial efficiency from purely physical and cognitive aspects to the psychological and social management of the worker's subjectivity. Mayo's early background in psychopathology may have primed him to perceive industrial issues through the lens of psychological adjustment. He famously observed that changes in worker productivity were significantly influenced by social attention and the development of informal group norms, the famous 'Hawthorne Effect.' This revealed the critical importance of the 'emotional self' and the 'social self' as new, crucial sites for organisational intervention.

Kurt Lewin (1890–1947), a German-American psychologist, was a foundational figure in social, organisational, and applied psychology. His influence on 'technologies of the self' stems from his development of field theory, action research, and his model of group change dynamics. Lewin highlighted the fluid and context-dependent nature of the individual self, constantly shaped by its social and psychological surroundings. Lewin's contribution was less about fixed traits and more about understanding the forces and tensions that dynamically shape human behaviour within a given 'life space', a concept readily applied to organisational environments.

Epistemological Issues

Industrial psychology did not apply experimental techniques to industrial problems, but instead shaped its knowledge practices to reflect what industry needed, and, crucially, what made sense to industry. If the factory required efficient bodies, psychology developed time-and-motion studies; if it needed adaptable minds, it developed aptitude tests. Knowledge was constructed in the image of utility. The methods were deeply mimetic. Münsterberg's tests for trolley bus drivers, for example, mimicked the demands of real-world driving by measuring speed of perception, accuracy of judgement, and responsiveness under pressure, so that psychological assessment mirrored the operational challenges of the industrial workplace.

In Europe, *psychotechnics* exemplified this adaptive epistemology. Psychologists such as Henri Piéron built test environments that mimicked real-world tasks: textile workers had to thread beads, office clerks had to sort items under time pressure, machine operators had to manipulate levers. These methods created an illusion of realism but they were also a subtle form of prescription. They told workers not only what they could do but what they should do.

Observation, too, became a method of power. Time-and-motion studies, morale surveys, and interview protocols were not just about gathering data, they were about encouraging self-regulation. In the famous Hawthorne experiments, productivity increased not because of lighting changes but because workers knew they were being watched. This became the model for a new kind of psychological intervention: one that influenced through awareness, attention, and participation.

Mayo's approach was primarily empirical and observational, akin to an ethnographic study of the workplace. The Hawthorne researchers meticulously observed worker interactions, conducted interviews, and documented informal group norms. While not explicitly therapeutic, the counselling programmes provided a novel space for workers to express grievances and sentiments. This approach created new forms of data collection (qualitative observations and interview transcripts) that offered insights into the 'inner life' of the worker. The knowledge produced was descriptive and diagnostic, aiming to uncover the latent social and emotional dynamics that influenced productivity. The underlying epistemological assumption was that these subjective states, once understood, could then be influenced or 'managed' to align with organisational goals.

Lewin's epistemology was fundamentally experimental, interventionist, and action-oriented. His concept of 'action research' embodied a commitment to knowledge production through active engagement and planned intervention. Rather than merely observing, Lewin believed that true understanding of social phenomena, including the self in organisational contexts, came from attempting to change them. His methods involved *empirical experimentation* (studies on leadership style); *collaborative inquiry* (involving workers and managers as participants in the research process); and *feedback loops* (plan-act-observe-reflect). Lewin's epistemology sought not only to understand the *nature* of the self in a group but also to provide replicable methods for *reshaping* that self through structured interventions and guided reflection.

Industrial psychology thus forged a hybrid form of knowledge: empirical and managerial, descriptive and normative. It helped produce workers who knew themselves through tests, aligned themselves with expectations, and managed themselves accordingly.

Ontological Issues

Industrial psychology did more than measure skills or recommend training regimes; it helped define what a worker *was*. In doing so, it produced a set of implicit ontologies: ideas about human nature, the limits of subjectivity, and the forms of selfhood suitable to modern industry. These were evolving constructs that mirrored the needs of the economic system.

At the dawn of the twentieth century, the dominant model was the worker-as-machine. Influenced by Taylorism and early efficiency studies, psychologists viewed labour as a system of bodily movements to be optimised. Time-and-motion studies, such as those performed by Frank and Lillian Gilbreth, turned workers into collections of measurable gestures. Fatigue became a mechanical breakdown, error a misalignment of parts.

Later, the psychometric turn reimagined the worker as a set of traits, aptitudes, and profiles. Intelligence tests, vocational guidance tools, and personality inventories offered new ways to classify individuals. But classification is also an act of creation. These instruments encouraged workers to see themselves as types: 'introverts', 'clerical thinkers', 'average intelligences'. In this ontology, the worker was knowable, sortable, and ideally, placeable. Identity became a form of utility.

What unites these models was not just their prescriptiveness but their normativity. Workers were expected to internalise these ontologies, to shape themselves in accordance with them. A good worker was one who *fitted*, who did not just perform well but accepted the psychological model offered to them as a kind of truth.

In this way, industrial psychology helped install technologies of the self at the deepest level: by offering models of personhood that shaped how individuals thought about their own abilities, limits, and aspirations. It defined not just what work was but what kinds of people were *worthy* of doing it. The 'technologies of the self' deployed by Mayo and Lewin reveal contrasting yet complementary understandings of the worker's fundamental nature (ontology) as conceived within Industrial/Organisational psychology (I/O) psychology.

For Mayo, the worker transitioned from being primarily a rational-economic being (as in Taylorism) or a physiological machine (as in early fatigue studies) to an inherently social and emotional being. The Hawthorne studies unveiled an ontology where the worker was motivated by wages and physical comfort, and by the need for belonging and recognition. Lewin's ontology of the worker was more dynamic and less fixed, conceptualising the individual as an agent capable of change and self-organisation within a social field. While acknowledging the influence of individual traits, Lewin's field theory emphasised the 'person-in-environment' dynamic: the worker was constantly interacting with and being shaped by their psychological environment, the 'life space' of the organisation.

Both Mayo and Lewin contributed to an ontology of the worker that was fundamentally psychological and social, moving away from purely physical or economic determinism. This opened up new territories for the exercise of managerial power through the manipulation and cultivation of both the inner and the social self.

Power

The power of industrial psychology was never solely in its methods or theories; it lay in its ability to govern conduct, both at the level of the individual and the population. The field operated at the intersection of two powerful dynamics: what Michel Foucault called *technologies of the self* and *biopower*. While the former shaped how individuals saw and managed themselves, the latter concerned the regulation of bodies, capacities, and life itself across whole workforces.

Through interviews, tests, training programmes, and morale initiatives, industrial psychology invited workers to become self-regulating subjects. Productivity, punctuality, and emotional stability were not simply imposed, they were internalised. Workers learned to view lateness as a failure of discipline, fatigue as a personal deficiency, and success as a matter of psychological adjustment. These are the classic hallmarks of *technologies of the self*: modes of power that operate with the psyche, not against it.

The contributions of both Mayo and Lewin, when viewed as technologies of the self, represented sophisticated expansions of organisational power, moving beyond overt coercion to more subtle forms of shaping and normalisation. Mayo and Lewin significantly expanded the scope and sophistication of power within organisations, moving from overt control of the body and task to the subtle yet profound shaping of the worker's emotional, social, and psychological self, ultimately producing subjects better fitted for the demands of industrial capitalism.

Chapter Summary

Industrial psychology did more than study the workplace, it helped invent it. From its earliest interventions on the shop floor, psychology offered itself not as a dispassionate science but as a willing accomplice to industrial capitalism. It profiled workers, streamlined routines, and engineered morale. It advised managers not only on who to hire but how to shape those hires into docile, productive selves. The factory may have built products, but psychology helped build the people inside it.

At its core, this was a project of profound intimacy. Under the guise of efficiency, psychology invited itself into the body, the mind, and the soul of the worker. Through technologies of the self, aptitude tests, personality scales, feedback sessions, and guidance schemes, it taught people to monitor themselves, regulate their moods, and align their identities with the logic of the firm. Fatigue was no longer a symptom of exploitation but a personal failing. Alienation became poor adjustment. Resistance was pathologised as low morale.

It was the same genius that reinvented a box of chocolates. *Black Magic*, with its sleek black casing and seductive branding, turned gift-giving into psychological theatre. Designed using consumer research by industrial psychologists, it not only appealed to taste; it rewrote the rituals of courtship. The pleasure was not in the chocolate. It was in the feeling of having made the right, romantic choice. Just as in the workplace, desire was no longer spontaneous; it was orchestrated, by design.

Today, the tools have evolved—behavioural nudges, algorithmic profiling, workplace wellness apps—but the dynamic endures. Psychology continues to whisper in the ear of power, offering insights, metrics, and human tweaks. It continues to shape how we work, but also how we love, relate, and see ourselves.

This chapter asks you not just to understand and critically approach industrial psychology. To see it not as a mirror of the human condition, but as a machinery of shaping. The question is no longer just how psychology serves the workplace but what kinds of people it helps produce. And whether we are still receiving gifts we never asked for.

Reflective Questions

1. How did early industrial psychologists shape the definition of a 'productive' worker?
2. In what ways were psychological tests in the workplace mimetic rather than objective?
3. What does Foucault's idea of 'technologies of the self' reveal about the power of psychological classification?
4. How did gender influence the design and application of industrial psychology, especially in the work of Lillian Gilbreth?
5. Can contemporary workplace assessments—such as psychometric profiling or performance targets—be understood as continuations of early industrial psychology?

Suggested Reading

Ackers, P. (2006). The history of occupational psychology: A view from industrial relations. *Journal of Occupational and Organizational Psychology, 79*(2), 213–216. https://doi.org/10.1348/096317906X100666.

Baritz, L. (1960). *The Servants of Power: A history of the use of social science in American industry*. Hanover, NE: Wesleyan University Press.

Bryan, L. K., & Vinchur, A. J. (2025). *Key Thinkers in Industrial and Organisational Psychology*. Abingdon, Oxon: Routledge.
Endrejat, P. C., & Burnes, B. (2022). Kurt Lewin's ideas are alive! But why doesn't anybody recognize them? *Theory & Psychology, 32*(6), 931-952. https://doi.org/10.1177/09593543221118652.
Foucault, M. (1988). *Technologies of the Self: A seminar with Michel Foucault* (L. H. Martin, H. Gutman, & P. H. Hutton, Eds.). Amherst: University of Massachusetts Press.
Havoc, R. C., & Woody, W. D. (2025). The shrouded self: Racial passing as a tool of survival in early 20th century psychology. *History of Psychology, 28*(2), 170–178. https://doi.org/10.1037/hop0000277.
Hodgetts, D., Sonn, C., Li, W., & Groot, S. (2020). What does Theory & Psychology have to offer community-orientated psychologists? *Theory & Psychology, 30*(6), 852–863. https://doi.org/10.1177/0959354320947821.
Hollway, W. (2016). Efficiency and welfare: Industrial psychology at Rowntree's Cocoa Works. *Theory & Psychology, 3*(3), 303–322. https://doi.org/10.1177/0959354393033002.
Luks, T. (2020). Building the 'House of Industry': Factory citizenship and gendered spaces at Cadbury's and Rowntree's. *Labour History Review, 85*(3), 233–252. https://www.liverpooluniversitypress.co.uk/doi/10.3828/lhr.2020.10.
Rose, N. (1999). *Governing the Soul: The shaping of the private self* (Second ed.). London: Free Association Books.
Schmidt, M. A. (2017). Planes of phenomenological experience: The psychology of deafness as an early example of American Gestalt psychology, 1928–1940. *History of Psychology, 20*(4), 347–364. https://doi.org/10.1037/hop0000074.
Vinchur, A. J. (2018). *The Early Years of Industrial and Organizational Psychology*. Cambridge: Cambridge University Press.

Key Terms

Aptitude Testing Standardised tests developed to assess an individual's potential for particular types of work. These were used to sort, select, and train workers according to perceived 'fit' with industrial roles.

Behavioural Science A broad term encompassing psychology, sociology, and related disciplines that study human actions. In industrial contexts, it was used to shape and control behaviour in workplaces.

Human Engineering An early term for ergonomics or applied psychology in the workplace, concerned with designing tools, tasks, and environments to optimise human performance.

Industrial Psychology A branch of applied psychology that developed in the early twentieth century, focused on improving workplace efficiency, selection, and productivity by studying worker behaviour, aptitude, and performance.

Mimesis A term meaning imitation or mirroring. In this context, it refers to how psychological tests were designed to mimic the tasks and demands of industrial work, rather than measuring universal traits.

Psychotechnics A psychological method of applying experimental knowledge to practical problems in industry, such as selecting workers or designing interfaces. Popular in continental Europe in the early twentieth century.

Scientific Management A management theory developed by Frederick Winslow Taylor that emphasised standardisation, control, and measurement of labour to maximise industrial efficiency.

Subjectification A Foucauldian term describing the process by which individuals become subjects through internalising external norms, roles, and categories. In this context, it refers to how psychology shaped workers' sense of self.

Technologies of the Self A concept developed by Michel Foucault, referring to the ways individuals come to understand and shape themselves through scientific, cultural, and institutional norms. In industrial psychology, it describes how workers internalised psychological categories like 'motivated', 'productive', or 'unfit'.

Time-and-Motion Studies A technique used to analyse and optimise physical labour, pioneered by Frank and Lillian Gilbreth. It involved breaking down tasks into discrete motions and timings to improve workplace efficiency.

ONLINE RESOURCES

Visit the Instructor & Student Resources website at routledgelearning.com/bpscoretextbooks for free digital resources, including:

- Interactive quizzes and flashcards to test your knowledge
- Links to useful websites and videos
- Instructor manual, lecture slides, and course guide to enhance teaching and save instructors time

5 Duty, Uses, and Abuses

Personality Psychology's Modal Selves

Chapter Overview

This chapter offers a critical historical account of the history of personality through the lens of the *modal self*, the culturally dominant model of personhood in any given era. Tracing a trajectory from the *moral self* of the nineteenth century, through the *modern self* of mid-twentieth-century psychometrics, to the *postmodern self* of the neoliberal age, the chapter explores how psychology has actively participated in constructing and legitimising different self-ideals. Drawing on Warren Susman's concept of the modal self, it argues that psychological theory has not merely described individuals but has helped shape the normative traits, behaviours, and affective styles that each historical era demands. Through an integrated analysis of epistemology, ontology, and power, the chapter shows how each modality of the self is produced through specific ways of knowing (moral judgement, psychometric testing, performance metrics), assumptions about human nature (virtue, fixity, adaptability), and disciplinary techniques (pastoral power, classification, self-optimisation). Key theorists are situated within these cultural transformations. Ultimately, the chapter reveals how the psychology of the self is deeply entwined with political economy, reinforcing values such as moral discipline, industrial efficiency, and neoliberal adaptability in shaping the human subject.

Duty, Uses and Abuses

On 3 September 1934, an 18-year-old exile, fleeing the ideological extremism of Nazi Germany, arrived in Britain. Hans Eysenck would later recount that his subsequent resolve as a psychologist was profoundly shaped by this experience, a flight not merely from fascism but from irrationalism itself. His self-appointed duty was to turn psychology into a rigorous, empirical science, purged of what he considered the excesses of introspection, speculative theory, and political distortion. Over the ensuing decades, Eysenck became the most cited psychologist in Britain, achieving considerable public recognition through writing bestsellers such as *Uses and Abuses of Psychology* (1953). He established a psychometric research programme at the Institute of Psychiatry in London, based on the assumption that the essence of human personality could be rendered into statistically validated traits. Personality stood at the very centre of Eysenck's scientific programme, serving as the central construct through which he sought to establish psychology as a rigorous, biologically grounded discipline.

And yet, the very methodological rigour that once secured Eysenck global acclaim could not protect him from the sweeping cultural and epistemological shifts that came to redefine psychological science. His controversial claims, that smoking-related cancers were driven more by personality traits than tobacco use, or that racial differences in intelligence were innate, were later revealed to rest on studies entangled

DOI: 10.4324/9781003565482-15

with ethically compromised funding sources, including covert support from the tobacco industry and The Pioneer Fund, a eugenics-linked organisation. In 2019, King's College London formally condemned over 20 of his publications and raised concerns about dozens more. But Eysenck's fall was not solely the result of dubious data or political entanglements. It marked the fading authority of a psychology rooted in the belief that personality could be fixed, measured, and rendered in clean statistical lines. His eclipse symbolised something larger: the collapse of a solid modernist vision of the self, displaced by a liquid era in which psychology became more attuned to precarity, performance, and plurality. Eysenck's legacy serves as a cautionary tale about the fate of paradigms whose scientific aspirations become unmoored from the changing moral and social currents they once presumed to master.

Chapter Contents

- The chapter traces the historical evolution of personality psychology through the lens of the modal self, from moral character to neoliberal optimisation.
- It critically examines the epistemological, ontological, and political foundations underpinning the construction of personality in different eras.
- The critical thinking tool explores Warren Susman's concept of the modal self and its implications for understanding culturally dominant models of personhood.

Chapter Objectives

- To introduce students to the historical modalities of the self, moral, modern, and postmodern, and link them to corresponding psychological theories of character and personality.
- To critically analyse the role of psychology in shaping and legitimising normative selfhood through institutions, testing, and ideology.
- To explore the critical thinking tool of the modal self, encouraging students to reflect on how prevailing cultural values define what counts as a 'normal' or 'desirable' personality.

CRITICAL THINKING TOOL
THE MODAL SELF

The cultural historian Warren Susman argued that the history of the self since the nineteenth century can be divided into two broad epochs. The dominant model in the nineteenth century was the *character* ideal: a moralised sense of self rooted in virtue, duty, inner restraint, and adherence to social norms. But from the early twentieth century, Susman argued, there emerged a new dominant ethos: the *personality* ideal. This new modality prioritised charm, sociability, self-presentation, and emotional appeal. Where *character* was about who one *was*, *personality* became about how one *appeared to be*. Susman's concept of *the modal self* suggests that

different historical moments tend to elevate different constellations of qualities, behaviours, and affective norms as the cultural standard of personhood. These are not merely individual but rather representative, that is, *modal*; valued, encouraged, and performed collectively, through education, the mass media, work, and bureaucracy. In this view, psychological theories of the self are never neutral; they reflect and reinforce prevailing social ideals. Whether in the form of the Victorian gentleman, the 1950s organisation man, or the contemporary entrepreneurial self, these models of selfhood reveal how psychology is always entangled with cultural values. This chapter explores how these shifting self-ideals shaped the study of character, personality, and selfhood in psychology, from moralistic origins to scientific systems of trait measurement, culminating with contemporary forms of selfhood organised around performance and presentation.

Introduction

The psychological study of the self may seem like a twentieth-century innovation, but its roots reach deep into older traditions of character, virtue, and temperament. From the medieval alignment of the four humours, to Renaissance theories of physiognomy, and up to nineteenth-century phrenological theories, the Western philosophical tradition long sought to map mental or spiritual qualities onto corporeal features. Religion, astrology, and moral philosophy offered early frameworks for understanding the self, often centred on virtue and sin. By the late nineteenth century, however, moralistic notions of *character*, as something built through discipline and duty, were beginning to give way to the more modern, secular conception of *personality*. A new modal self has emerged in the last half century: the entrepreneurial neoliberal self.

The conceptualisation of the self is not a static or linear scientific endeavour, but a dynamic process deeply embedded within prevailing historical, economic, and political contexts. This chapter argues that societies, at different junctures, valorise distinct ideal types of individuals, giving rise to what can be termed a 'modal self'. Such a perspective, informed by the work of cultural historian Warren Susman, allows for a critical examination of how psychological theories of the self have not merely described but actively participated in the construction and normalisation of these dominant self-ideals.

The chapter explores three distinct historical modalities of the self: the moral self (character), the modern self (personality), and the postmodern (entrepreneurial) self. We will analyse the historical underpinnings for each modality, examine the contributions of key theorists, elucidate its specific epistemological foundations, articulate its ontological premises, and demonstrate the mechanisms through which power operates to shape and manage it. This integrated and critical approach aims to provide students with a nuanced understanding of personality's historical contingency and its ongoing interrelationship with broader societal forces.

Historical Issues

The historical trajectory of Western societies reveals a succession of dominant self-ideals, each shaped by particular economic structures and political imperatives.

Understanding these historical backdrops is crucial for comprehending the specific forms that psychological inquiry into personality assumed. The initial phase, spanning the late nineteenth to the mid-twentieth century (c.1860–1940), fostered the moral self. This period was characterised by the consolidation of industrial capitalism, demanding a disciplined, punctual, and reliable workforce for increasingly complex factory systems. Economically, the Protestant work ethic provided a powerful cultural scaffolding, linking diligent labour and asceticism to moral virtue and spiritual salvation, thereby internalising economic imperatives. The title of Samuel Smiles's 1870 book *Character* captured the moral ideal of the Victorian age. For Smiles, 'character' reflected a deep commitment to discipline, self-restraint, and moral virtue.

In an era that equated personal worth with industriousness and respectability, *Character* helped shape a view of the self as something to be built, measured, and judged. Politically, this was an era of extensive imperialism and a pervasive concern with social control. Governments and influential institutions actively promoted public morality, such as temperance societies, viewing national strength and social order as intrinsically linked to the moral rectitude and character of individual citizens. This backdrop emphasised self-discipline and adherence to external moral standards as central to one's being.

Following this, the era of high modernity (c.1940–1980) gave rise to the modern self. If Samuel Smiles's *Character* (1870) distilled the Victorian ideal of moral selfhood, then Gordon Allport's *Personality: A Psychological Interpretation* (1937) heralded the modern scientific turn. Allport's book recast the self not as a moral project but as a psychological construct, complex, dynamic, and measurable, marking the beginning of psychology's sustained efforts to map individual difference without moralising it.

Economically, this period was dominated by Fordism and Taylorism, which standardised mass production and consumption. Large, hierarchical corporations and state bureaucracies emerged, necessitating the efficient management of vast workforces through scientific principles. Stable employment and predictable career paths were common, reinforcing the notion that people should be 'square pegs in square holes'; individuals fitting well into defined occupational roles. Politically, the ascendancy of 'cradle-to-grave' welfare state central planning and the exigencies of the Cold War fostered a focus on national efficiency. Governments sought systematic methods for classifying and deploying individuals in optimal roles within complex bureaucratic structures, leading to the institutionalisation of psychometric assessment for personnel selection and national security.

Finally, the neoliberal era (c.1980–present) cultivated the postmodern self. Economically, this period is defined by accelerated globalisation, the rise of the knowledge economy, and the increasing precariousness of work. De-industrialisation in many Western nations, coupled with the dominance of financial capital, has necessitated continuous innovation and reskilling, 'lifelong learning'. Individuals are increasingly expected to be 'entrepreneurial' with respect to their own careers, and health and welfare, and to navigate unpredictable economic landscapes. If Allport's *Personality* (1937) promised scientific understanding of individual difference, Daniel Goleman's *emotional intelligence* (1995) translated the self into emotional capital.

In the age of neoliberalism, the self must not only know and improve itself but do so flexibly, affectively, and performatively, because success, now, is not about being good or consistent but being adaptable. Politically, the prevailing neoliberal ideology emphasises individual responsibility, free markets, and a reduced role for state welfare. This fosters a pervasive culture of self-optimisation, where individuals are compelled to demonstrate continuous adaptability, flexibility, and resilience to remain competitive in a rapidly evolving global market. These demands, critics argue, constitute significant abuses of the self, as individuals are continually pressured to commodify their identities, internalise systemic failures as personal inadequacies, and perform an endless, exhausting labour of self-regulation and reinvention, all while social safety nets erode and collective responsibility is denied.

Key Individuals

The Moral Self

Samuel Smiles (1812–1904) was a Scottish author, physician, and social reformer best known for his influential Victorian moral treatises. Smiles rose to prominence with *Self-Help* (1859), a bestselling manual that preached industriousness, perseverance, and moral discipline as the key ingredients of success. The book was a cultural sensation, widely read across Britain and its empire, and became a cornerstone of the Victorian belief in individual responsibility and moral character. His later work, *Character* (1870), extended these ideas, arguing that integrity, self-restraint, and self-control were the true foundations of both personal advancement and national strength.

A. F. Shand's (1858–1936) *The Foundations of Character* (1914) directly addressed the scientific study of moral character. He meticulously detailed how sentiments, conceived as organised and enduring systems of emotions and volitional tendencies, constitute the stable core of an individual's self. Shand argued that these integrated sentiments (e.g. the sentiment of justice, the sentiment of honour) provided consistency and predictability to one's moral life.

William McDougall (1871–1938) developed a theory of instincts, propensities, and sentiments. In his *An Introduction to Social Psychology* (1908), he argued that innate human tendencies become organised into stable 'sentiments' (e.g. love, hate, reverence) through social interaction. Crucially, McDougall explicitly theorised the process of 'moralisation', whereby individuals' raw instincts are channelled and transformed by societal influence into altruistic and duty-bound sentiments.

The Modern Self

Gordon Allport (1897–1967), a foundational figure in trait theory, provided the conceptual framework for modern selfhood. He defined personality as a 'dynamic organisation within the individual of those psychophysical systems that determine his characteristic behaviour and thought'. Allport posited that individuals possess stable, enduring traits, consistent internal predispositions, which reliably guide their behaviour across diverse situations.

Raymond Cattell (1905–1998) advanced the psychometric project of solidifying personality. Employing rigorous factor analysis, he systematically reduced a vast array of personality descriptors to 16 fundamental personality factors (the 16PF). These factors were conceptualised as stable, measurable source traits that constituted the underlying structure of personality. Cattell's ambition was to create a comprehensive, empirically derived, and universally applicable taxonomy of fixed personality dimensions.

Hans Eysenck (1916–1997) was a highly influential advocate for a biological trait theory, proposing that personality could be largely understood through three broad, inherited supertraits: Psychoticism, Extraversion, and Neuroticism. His work emphasised the genetic and physiological underpinnings of these dimensions, arguing for their fundamental and relatively immutable nature. Eysenck's scientific rigour (though later subject to controversy) and prolific output made him a key figure in establishing the notion of personality as a stable, biologically determined entity.

The Postmodern Self

Martin Seligman (b.1942), often credited as the founder of Positive Psychology, reshaped the discipline by redirecting attention from dysfunction to *flourishing*. With an emphasis on *resilience, learned optimism, strengths*, and *subjective well-being*, Seligman's vision appealed to both the public and policymakers during a period marked by economic uncertainty, workforce precarity, and the medicalisation of stress. Positive Psychology presents the self as a *project to be managed*: capable of continual improvement through cognitive reframing, gratitude practices, and the pursuit of personal meaning. In this sense, it offers a set of tools for thriving in neoliberal conditions.

Daniel Goleman (b.1946), a psychologist and science journalist, is best known for popularising the concept of *emotional intelligence* (EQ) in his bestselling 1995 book. Goleman defined EQ as a suite of abilities, such as self-awareness, emotional regulation, empathy, motivation, and social skill, that are essential for personal and professional success. His work emerged precisely as the global economy was transitioning towards precarious, flexible, and affectively demanding forms of work. In an era of project teams, client-facing roles, and emotional branding, the emotionally intelligent subject is calm under pressure, attuned to others, and perpetually self-managing, an ideal worker in the knowledge economy.

Paul Costa (b.1942) and Robert McCrae (b.1949) developed and refined the *Five-Factor Model* of personality, commonly known by the acronym OCEAN (Openness, Conscientiousness, Extraversion, Agreeableness, Neuroticism), a taxonomy that has become a global standard for understanding the contemporary self. Their *NEO Personality Inventory*, first published in 1985, offered a structured and empirically validated approach to measuring personality traits across cultures and life stages. The Big Five has become a cornerstone of applied psychology in education, employment, and personal development. Personality traits are not simply measured but increasingly managed, precisely because the factors are flexible and malleable.

Epistemological Issues

Prior to the twentieth century, knowledge about the moral self was primarily derived from moral and religious authority, alongside public observation of an individual's conduct and their social reputation. Truth about character was not empirically discovered in a scientific sense but was revealed through adherence to virtues, fulfilment of duty, and often through divine or communal judgement. Evidence lay in demonstrating consistent virtuous behaviour, disciplined self-control, having a good *character*, and the maintenance of a good standing within the community. Self-knowledge was often attained through introspection guided by religious tenets or moral codes, leading to an understanding of one's own struggles with temptation and adherence to ethical ideals.

The modern self of the twentieth century was understood through a positivist, scientific epistemology of objective measurement and quantification. Truth about *personality* was conceived as quantifiable, generalisable, and statistically verifiable. The primary methods involved psychometric tests, standardised questionnaires and inventories, factor analysis, and controlled observational studies. These techniques aimed to uncover stable, underlying structures (traits or types) that could be reliably measured and correlated with predictable behaviours. What constituted valid evidence were numerical scores, statistical significance, and consistent behavioural patterns observed across various assessments, thereby establishing a seemingly objective, scientific basis for personality.

The postmodern self operates within an epistemology of continuous assessment, performance metrics, and perpetual feedback, emphasising ongoing reflexivity and optimisation. Truth about the self is no longer a fixed measurement but a dynamic, evolving narrative of growth, adaptability, and continuous improvement through personal reflection. Knowledge is acquired through regular performance reviews, '360-degree feedback', personal development plans, and self-assessment tools. Evidence is manifested in demonstrated adaptability, resilience in the face of change, the capacity to acquire new skills, effective self-management, and positive feedback from peers or supervisors, all geared towards maintaining an optimal profile for competitive advantage in a fluid, performance-driven world.

Ontological Issues

The moral self was ontologically grounded in the concept of character as a moral and often spiritual essence. It was conceived as a moral agent possessing willpower and conscience, capable of choosing between good and evil, yet inherently prone to temptation. At its core, character was understood as an integrated, relatively stable set of moral habits, virtues, and duties. The self's fundamental nature was intrinsically tied to its ethical standing and its relationship with a moral, social, or divine order, making it an entity whose very being was defined by its active adherence to internalised moral imperatives and its struggle against perceived moral failings.

The modern self was ontologically understood as a fixed, quantifiable entity composed of stable traits, types, or biologically determined predispositions. Its essence was perceived as an enduring, internal structure, an almost immutable psychological architecture that could be objectively measured and categorised, akin to a physical object. The self was assumed to possess an inherent, biologically fixed core that determined consistent patterns of thought, emotion, and behaviour. This view posited a predictable, somewhat static 'solid modern' individual, ideal for precise placement within the rigid, hierarchical structures of modern industrial and bureaucratic systems.

The postmodern self is ontologically conceived as a dynamic, highly adaptable, and continuously optimising agent. Its essence resides not in having a fixed core but in its inherent capacity for transformation, learning, and fluidity. It is a 'work-in-progress', a portfolio of evolving competencies, and an active 'human capital' asset to be perpetually invested in and refined. This 'liquid modern' self is expected to constantly mould itself to external demands, viewing its very being as malleable and responsive, driven by the imperative to remain relevant and competitive in an ever-shifting economic, social, and technological landscape.

Power

The moral self was subjected to *pastoral paternalistic power*, primarily through moral authority and social pressure. This involved religious doctrine, sermons, and prayer, techniques which instilled guilt and promoted virtuous conduct. Moral education in schools and families aimed to cultivate self-discipline and suppress undesirable impulses. Social shaming and ostracism were powerful tools, because reputation was paramount. Individuals were normalised by their adherence to an ideal moral archetype (the diligent worker, the pious citizen). Deviation was framed as a moral failing or sin, requiring spiritual guidance, social correction, or sometimes institutionalisation in morally corrective environments.

The modern self was governed through *discipline*, exercised through scientific expertise and bureaucratic control. The key mechanisms were psychological testing, selection, and classification. Individuals were subjected to standardised assessments to identify their 'fixed' traits or types, allowing for their optimal placement and allocation within large organisations (factories, military, government). Power operated by defining and sorting individuals into pre-defined roles, ensuring predictability and efficiency. Normalisation occurred through statistical fit to ideal profiles or average scores for specific positions. Deviance was viewed as a 'misfit' or an 'abnormality' requiring adjustment or different placement, rather than as a moral defect.

The postmodern self is governed through *empowerment*. It is increasingly exercised through internalised self-management and the pervasive pressure for continuous optimisation. Mechanisms include constant performance assessment, 360-degree feedback, coaching, and the adoption of entrepreneurial thinking applied to the self. Individuals are compelled to engage in lifelong learning and self-improvement to remain competitive. Normalisation occurs through demonstrated adaptability, resilience, and a commitment to perpetual growth. Deviation is seen as a lack of flexibility, resistance to change, or a failure of personal responsibility, leading to obsolescence in the job market. This power operates through the internalisation of market logic and the relentless drive for competitive advantage.

Chapter Summary

This chapter has provided a critical historical overview of personality psychology through the lens of the modal self, demonstrating that our understanding of 'who we are' is not a static scientific truth but a dynamic construct deeply influenced by historical, economic, and political forces. We have explored the evolution from the moral self of the Victorian era, defined by character and duty, through the solid modern self of high modernity, characterised by fixed, measurable traits, to the contemporary liquid modern self, valorising flexibility and continuous adaptation.

The chapter has demonstrated how psychological concepts of the self are intimately tied to their social contexts. This analysis reveals psychology not merely as a descriptive science but as a discipline actively engaged in shaping the ideal human being of its time. This critical perspective encourages a more nuanced and inclusive understanding of theories of the self, acknowledging their historical contingency and ongoing interaction with broader social and cultural forces. As the rise and fall of Hans Eysenck so starkly reminds us, even the most celebrated architects of psychological truth can find their legacies undone when the values underpinning their science shift beneath their feet.

Reflective Questions

1. How has the dominant psychological model of the self changed from the nineteenth to the twenty-first century, and what social or economic factors have driven this shift?
2. What does Warren Susman's concept of the 'modal self' help us understand about the relationship between psychology and culture?
3. To what extent can contemporary personality assessments (e.g. the Big Five, emotional intelligence) be seen as tools of empowerment versus tools of conformity?
4. How do different psychological models define what it means to be a 'normal' person? What assumptions do they make about gender, race, class, or ability?
5. What forms of power operate through personality psychology, and how have they shifted across the moral, modern, and postmodern eras?

Suggested Reading

Banicki, K. (2017). The character–personality distinction: An historical, conceptual, and functional investigation. *Theory & Psychology, 27*(1), 50–68. https://doi.org/10.1177/0959354316684689.

Bullard, A. (2005). The critical impact of Frantz Fanon and Henri Collomb: Race, gender, and personality testing of North and West Africans. *Journal of the History of the Behavioural Sciences, 41*(3), 225–248. https://doi.org/10.1002/jhbs.20102.

Cieciuch, J. (2012). The Big Five and Big Ten: Between Aristotelian and Galilean physics of personality. *Theory & Psychology, 22*(5), 689–696. https://doi.org/10.1177/0959354311432904.

Danziger, K. (1997). *Naming the Mind: How psychology found its language*. Thousand Oaks, CA: Sage.

Dumont, F. (2010). *A History of Personality Psychology: Theory, science, and research from Hellenism to the twenty-first century*. Cambridge: Cambridge University Press.

Fierro, C. (2022). How did early North American clinical psychologists get their first personality test? Carl Gustav Jung, the Zurich School of Psychiatry, and the development of the 'Word Association Test' (1898–1909). *History of Psychology, 25*(4), 295–321. https://doi.org/10.1037/hop0000218.

Gibby, R. E., & Zickar, M. J. (2008). A history of the early days of personality testing in American industry: An obsession with adjustment. *History of Psychology, 11*(3), 164–184. https://doi.org/10.1037/a0013041.

Hajek, K. M. (2021). Félida, doubled personality, and the 'normal state' in late 19th-century French psychology. *History of the Human Sciences, 34*(2), 66–89. https://doi.org/10.1177/0952695120980648.

Percival, T., & Bergstrom-Katz, S. (2025). The material force of categories. *History of the Human Sciences, 38*(2), 3–17. https://doi.org/10.1177/09526951251318223.

Pilgrim, D. (2023). Verdicts on Hans Eysenck and the fluxing context of British psychology. *History of the Human Sciences, 36*(3–4), 83–104. https://doi.org/10.1177/09526951221143888.

Susman, W. (1984). *Culture as History: The transformation of American society in the twentieth century*. New York: Pantheon.

Treviño, A. J. (2023). Talcott Parsons on building personality system theory via psychoanalysis. *Journal of the History of the Behavioural Sciences, 59*, 417–432. https://doi.org/10.1002/jhbs.22257.

Key Terms

Big Five Personality Traits A widely used model of personality comprising Openness, Conscientiousness, Extraversion, Agreeableness, and Neuroticism. Promoted as stable, measurable traits, often applied in employment and personal development contexts.

emotional intelligence (EQ) A concept popularised by Daniel Goleman, referring to the ability to manage one's own emotions and social relationships. Seen as crucial in the flexible, emotionally demanding workplaces of liquid modernity.

Entrepreneurial Self A term used to describe the idealised neoliberal subject who self-manages, self-optimises, and continuously adapts in order to remain market-relevant.

Liquid Modernity A term coined by Zygmunt Bauman to describe the contemporary social condition where identities, careers, and institutions are fluid, temporary, and in constant flux.

Modal Self A critical concept developed by Warren Susman. Refers to the dominant, culturally constructed ideal of the self in any given historical era, which individuals are encouraged to embody.

Pastoral Power A form of power described by Michel Foucault, in which individuals are guided and shaped through moral or religious authority, often under the guise of care and salvation.

Positive Psychology A movement led by Martin Seligman that focuses on well-being, resilience, and human flourishing, often linked to neoliberal imperatives for self-optimisation.

Self-optimisation The imperative to constantly improve and adapt oneself—psychologically, emotionally, and professionally—often in response to neoliberal values of performance and flexibility.

FREE INSTRUCTOR & STUDENT RESOURCES

ONLINE RESOURCES

Visit the Instructor & Student Resources website at routledgelearning.com/bpscoretextbooks for free digital resources, including:

- Interactive quizzes and flashcards to test your knowledge
- Links to useful websites and videos
- Instructor manual, lecture slides, and course guide to enhance teaching and save instructors time

6 'An Ego that Only Desires Pleasure'

Psychoanalysis, Phallocentrism, and the Maternal Metaphor

Chapter Overview

The history of psychoanalysis, while groundbreaking, has traditionally been told predominantly by men, often obscuring or downplaying the profound contributions of women. This chapter re-tells that history, focusing specifically on the pivotal roles women played in shaping and, at times, radically transforming psychoanalytic theory and practice. We will explore how these women psychoanalysts reacted to, adapted, and ultimately challenged the prevailing paternal metaphor that dominated early Freudian thought. By centring the maternal metaphor, encompassing themes of relationality, attachment, development, empathy, and the embodied experience of care, this chapter argues that women brought crucial dimensions to the understanding of the psyche. Their work critiqued the limitations of a phallocentric framework and introduced nuanced perspectives on human development, psychopathology, and the therapeutic process itself, thereby re-gendering the very fabric of psychoanalytic inquiry and making it more inclusive and comprehensive.

'An Ego that Only Desires Pleasure'

In 1904, a severely distressed young Russian woman was admitted to the Burghölzli Mental Hospital in Zurich. Sabina Spielrein was tormented by violent fantasies, uncontrollable tics, and a near-total withdrawal from speech. She was placed under the care of a talented but unconventional young psychiatrist: Carl Jung. What followed was an analysis so intense, so boundary-crossing, that it unsettled the conventional roles of doctor and patient. By today's standards, Jung and Spielrein's romantic connection breached therapeutic ethics. Nevertheless, their relationship evolved into an emotionally charged intellectual connection that would influence the very foundations of psychoanalytic thought. Emerging from her own psychic suffering, Spielrein articulated complex theoretical insights, not only as a patient but as a theorist in her own right. She developed a radical idea, years before Freud articulated his own concept of 'the death instinct', that destruction can serve as a necessary precursor to psychological transformation.

Spielrein's 1912 essay, 'Destruction as the Cause of Coming into Being', reimagined psychic life through a maternal framework, as something born through

DOI: 10.4324/9781003565482-16

rupture, loss, and renewal. 'A wish for self-injury, a joy in pain, is, however, thoroughly incomprehensible,' she wrote, 'if we believe merely in the existence of an ego that only desires pleasure.' In this, she offered a metaphor of the psyche that challenged the dominant, paternalistic structure of early psychoanalytic theory. Spielrein's original insights were profoundly rooted in her embodied, gendered experience as a woman. Yet for decades she had been forgotten, her name relegated to a footnote in the histories of Freud and Jung. It was only in the late twentieth century that psychoanalytic scholars and feminist historians began to recover the significance of her contributions. Her vision of the psyche, forged in the crucible of pain and connection, offered a maternal metaphor of psychic life: as a process of separation, vulnerability, and creative becoming. Her story invites us to ask not only what psychoanalysis has said about women but also what it has failed to hear.

Chapter Contents

- A critical exploration of the role of women in psychoanalysis as both analysands and analysts.
- The development of psychoanalytic theory through case studies and feminist critique.
- A focus on the critical thinking tool 'the maternal metaphor' and how it illuminates issues of gender, power, and subjectivity.

Chapter Objectives

- To examine how psychoanalysis has historically constructed the feminine as Other, and how women have reclaimed voice and agency within this tradition.
- To introduce students to key female figures in psychoanalysis and to analyse their contributions and challenges to mainstream theory.
- To engage students with the critical thinking tool, the maternal metaphor, by encouraging reflection on epistemology, ontology, and power in psychological discourse.

CRITICAL THINKING TOOL
THE MATERNAL METAPHOR

The Oedipus complex, as formulated by Freud, refers to a child's unconscious desire for the opposite-sex parent and rivalry with the same-sex parent, typically resolved through identification with the latter. It is a cornerstone of Freud's theory of psychosexual development and underpins his account of gender identity, desire, and repression. This formulation, deeply embedded in a patriarchal society, forms the bedrock of the paternal metaphor in psychoanalysis. Feminist critics have profoundly challenged the Oedipus complex, arguing that it presumes a universal male subject, marginalises women's experiences, and positions female development as a fundamental lack or deviation. This critique highlights the need for an alternative approach, one that better captures the full spectrum of human development and relationality.

The maternal metaphor serves as a powerful critical tool for re-examining the history and theory of psychoanalysis. It refers to the conceptual emphasis on aspects traditionally associated with the maternal function and early mother–infant relations: relationality, empathy, intersubjectivity, embodied experience, primary attachment, and nurturing. This stands in contrast to a paternal metaphor, which typically prioritises the symbolic order, individuation, law-giving, and intellectual mastery, often reflecting a phallocentric worldview. Utilising the maternal metaphor allows us to identify how various psychoanalytic theories either foreground or marginalise these relational and pre-verbal dimensions of human development and therapeutic change. It helps uncover hidden biases in established narratives, highlight the theoretical and clinical innovations that emphasised connection and care, and provide a framework for understanding how female psychoanalysts enriched and expanded the scope of psychoanalytic thought beyond its initial patriarchal foundations.

Introduction

Psychoanalysis has long been described as a 'talking cure', a discipline of listening. But whom does it listen to? This chapter invites us to consider not only *what* is said in psychoanalysis but *who* gets to speak. In the psychoanalytic tradition, the patient, especially the female patient, often appears as an enigma: a figure to be interpreted, decoded, or explained. She is not simply the speaker but the spoken-about. In philosophical terms she is the *Other*: not quite subject, not quite object, always filtered through someone else's gaze.

Traditionally, psychoanalysis has been seen as a male-authored discourse, shaped by theorists who interpreted women more than they listened to them. But this chapter centres women not only as patients (or 'analysands') but also as analysts, thinkers, writers, and theorisers of their own experience. It challenges us to read psychoanalytic history critically, attending to both the presence and absence of women's voices. What can we learn by listening differently to the hesitations, interruptions, and resistances that mark the voice of the Other?

Historical Issues

Psychoanalysis emerged into a world steeped in hierarchies, of class, gender, and knowledge. Fin-de-siècle Vienna, with its strict codes of bourgeois morality and anxieties about modernity, was fertile ground for new ways of understanding the mind. Hysteria, in particular, became a diagnostic label for women whose bodies expressed conflicts that had no socially acceptable outlet. These women were often treated as spectacles of dysfunction, figures to be managed, studied, or cured.

The historical landscape of early psychoanalysis was complex, marked by both radical intellectual ferment and entrenched societal patriarchy. Sigmund Freud's earliest predominantly female case studies were instrumental in the formation of psychoanalytic theory. But these women were also theorised through male frameworks. Freud's initial formulations, while revolutionary, emerged from and largely reflected the Victorian patriarchal norms of his time. Concepts such as the Oedipus complex, penis envy, and the primacy of the phallus positioned the male as the normative human subject, often pathologising or marginalising female experience. This created an intellectual environment where women analysts, despite their presence from the earliest days of the movement, often faced significant challenges in having their theoretical contributions recognised. Many early women analysands, such as Anna O. and Dora, were interpreted in a way that overlooked their relational distress or agency, often reducing their symptoms to unresolved sexual conflicts or a failure to adapt to prescribed gender roles.

Despite the patriarchal structures of the early psychoanalytic movement, several women became analysts. Anna Freud built a career in child psychoanalysis and ego psychology. Melanie Klein developed a radically different approach to the inner lives of infants and mothers. Sabina Spielrein, once Jung's analysand, formulated her own influential theory of the death drive, pre-dating Freud's. These women were not just footnotes to Freud; they were formative contributors to psychoanalytic knowledge, often working under institutional pressures that marginalised their contributions. Their contributions, therefore, represent a quiet revolution, introducing ideas that gradually shifted the field's focus towards the vital role of early relationships, the pre-Oedipal realm, and the complex lived experience of women and children.

Key Individuals

Melanie Klein (1882–1960) revolutionised psychoanalysis by shifting its focus to the earliest stages of infant development and the profound impact of pre-Oedipal object relations. Klein's emphasis on maternal ambivalence and early psychic conflict challenged Freud's developmental timeline. Her theories of the paranoid-schizoid and depressive positions, primitive phantasies, and the intense emotional world of the infant, dominated by the internal representation of the mother's body and breast, are direct articulations of the maternal metaphor. Her emphasis on early aggression, envy, and the capacity for reparation profoundly deepened the understanding of the most primal aspects of the psyche.

Joan Riviere (1883–1962) was an influential British psychoanalyst. Riviere's 1929 essay, 'Womanliness as a masquerade', offered a profound challenge to normative understandings of femininity. She proposed that womanliness could function as a defensive performance, a conscious or unconscious act designed to conceal anxieties about occupying traditionally masculine spheres of knowledge or power. By foregrounding the performative nature of gender, Riviere anticipated critical insights in later gender theory and queer studies. Her work complicates the simple notion of identity as authentic or stable, effectively deconstructing the prescriptive roles often imposed by the paternal metaphor and hinting at the underlying anxieties and subjective struggles beneath outward appearances.

Sabina Spielrein (1885–1942) was a Russian-Jewish physician, theorist, and one of the first female psychoanalysts. Initially a patient of Carl Jung, Spielrein later became his colleague and intellectual peer. Her work on the 'destructive instinct' and transformation preceded Freud's death drive and Jung's concept of the shadow. Her ideas about the ambivalent interplay of creation and destruction offered a dynamic and nuanced alternative to orthodox psychoanalysis. Her emphasis on transformation, disintegration, and psychic re-creation can be seen as resonant with the cyclical, often generative and regenerative processes associated with the maternal metaphor, moving beyond a purely linear, Oedipal progression. Despite her profound influence, Spielrein was largely erased from official psychoanalytic histories.

Karen Horney (1885–1952) was a fierce critic of Freud's phallocentric views, challenging the concept of penis envy by reinterpreting it as 'womb envy' or a broader societal struggle for power and recognition. She emphasised the importance of social and cultural factors in shaping personality and neurosis, moving away from purely biological drives. Her focus on relational dynamics, basic anxiety arising from inadequate parental care, and the self's pursuit of real versus idealised self-images resonates with the maternal metaphor by highlighting the impact of early relational environments.

While remaining more aligned with her father's psychoanalysis, Anna Freud's (1895–1982) pioneering work in child analysis inherently engaged with the maternal metaphor. Her clinical innovations in adapting analytic technique for children, her detailed observations of developmental lines, and her focus on the ego's defensive functions implicitly acknowledged the centrality of the early caregiving environment and the child's relational world in shaping psychological health. Her emphasis on the child's need for a stable, nurturing environment in therapeutic work further underscored this.

Margarete Mahler (1897–1985) was a key figure in ego psychology. Mahler's groundbreaking research on the separation-individuation process in infants and toddlers directly elucidated the crucial stages by which a child psychologically 'hatches' from symbiotic union with the mother. Her work mapped the intricate dance between connection and autonomy, explicitly placing the mother–infant dyad at the heart of early self-development, thereby providing a robust theoretical framework for the 'maternal metaphor'.

Although a male analyst, Donald W. Winnicott's (1896–1971) concepts were deeply steeped in the maternal metaphor. His ideas of the 'good enough mother', the 'holding environment', and the 'transitional object' articulated the absolute necessity of a responsive, adaptive maternal presence for the development of a true self. His work emphasised care, attunement, and the creation of a safe space for spontaneous being, reflecting the foundational aspects of maternal care.

Luce Irigaray (b.1930) is a seminal philosopher and psychoanalyst. Irigaray is renowned for her incisive critique of the pervasive phallocentrism embedded within Western thought, including both Freudian and Lacanian psychoanalysis. She forcefully introduced the concept of sexual difference as a fundamental philosophical and ethical imperative, arguing for a recognition of the feminine as a distinct and irreducible subjectivity, not merely a derivative of the male. Her poetic, non-linear writing style often performs the very feminine voice she theorises, resisting the linear logic associated with the paternal metaphor. Irigaray stands as a central figure in feminist reimaginings of psychoanalysis, seeking to articulate a feminine symbolic realm rooted in the embodied and relational, thereby offering a radical expansion and re-gendering of the maternal metaphor within the realm of language and thought.

Epistemological Issues

Epistemological issues in psychoanalysis concern how analysts know what they claim to know, the nature of truth within the analytic setting, and the methods by which knowledge is acquired and validated. The paternal metaphor in early psychoanalysis often leaned towards a positivist epistemology, seeking universal, objective truths derived from a Freudian metapsychology that prioritised innate drives and linear developmental stages. Knowledge was largely seen as being 'uncovered' or 'discovered' by the analyst who held epistemic authority, interpreting the patient's words against a pre-established theoretical framework. In the classical psychoanalytic tradition, the female patient often emerges not as a subject of knowledge but as its object. Her symptoms, hysteria, repression, and anxiety are treated as puzzles to be solved, evidence to be interpreted, and signs of deeper, unconscious truths.

To Freud, case studies were a means of accessing the unconscious, but they were also stylised narratives authored by the analyst. In texts such as *Dora: An analysis of a case of hysteria* (1905), we do not hear Dora's voice directly; we encounter her as filtered through Freud's interpretations. Her refusals and resistances are read as further symptoms rather than as acts of epistemic agency. Feminist critics have asked whether such texts represent listening at all, or whether they enact a kind of epistemic violence, transforming women's experiences into material for male theory-making.

Ida Bauer (1882–1945, 'Dora'). Freud interpreted Ida Bauer's symptoms through a rigid Oedipal framework, seeing her distress as a result of repressed sexual desires towards her father and Herr K. He largely ignored the complex relational dynamics and betrayals within her family, particularly her mother's absence and her father's problematic behaviour. Her famous premature termination of analysis can be reread not as 'resistance' to truth (a paternal-authoritarian view) but as a healthy assertion of her subjective experience against an analyst who failed to provide genuine relational understanding.

Bertha Pappenheim (1859–1936, 'Anna O.'). Pappenheim's initial treatment by Josef Breuer, focusing on cathartic release of repressed memories, aligns with an early proto-paternal metaphor of uncovering individual 'facts' or 'drives'. However, a re-reading of her case through the maternal metaphor highlights the profound relational deprivation and psychic collapse she experienced while caring for her dying father. Her symptoms can be seen as a desperate communication of unmet relational needs and a lack of psychic holding rather than just unresolved 'traumatic memories'. Pappenheim's later life as a feminist and social reformer powerfully embodies a reclaiming of agency and a focus on collective care and societal well-being, a broader, activated 'maternal' drive for social connection and amelioration that transcended her individual pathology.

The contributions of women psychoanalysts, through the lens of the maternal metaphor, introduced significant epistemological shifts. They challenged the idea of a singular, objective truth, arguing instead for a more intersubjective, relational, and co-created understanding of the analytic process. This shift emphasises that knowledge emerges from the unique relational dynamic between analyst and analysand rather than being imposed from an external, authoritative source. Epistemologically, this means: (1) an emphasis on empathy and attunement with the patient's subjective experience; (2) recognising that the analyst is an active participant whose own subjectivity shapes the therapeutic encounter; (3) prioritising the patient's narrative truth over a rigid adherence to theory; and (4) valuing experiential knowledge and embodied understanding alongside intellectual insight.

Ontological Issues

In psychoanalytic theory, the self is never whole. It is fragmented, divided between conscious and unconscious, desire and repression, self and Other. This split self is forged through relationships, through the internalisation of others, through loss, fantasy, and identification. Psychoanalysis reveals the self as *relational* at its core: a subject who emerges in response to, and in tension with, the Other.

For women in psychoanalytic theory, this relational ontology is fraught. Classical Freudian models frame femininity through absence and lack, defined not by what it is but by what it is not. The female child is said to experience *penis envy*, marking her as forever missing something. Ontological issues in psychoanalysis pertain to the very nature of being, what it means to be human, and the fundamental structure of the self. Early Freudian psychoanalysis, bewitched by the paternal metaphor, often presented human nature as rooted in a fixed ontology of instinctual drives. The self was understood primarily as an ego negotiating between id, superego, and external reality.

The maternal metaphor, championed by women psychoanalysts, introduced a radically different ontology, foregrounding the relational and developmental aspects of being. This perspective proposes that: (1) the self is fundamentally relational, constituted through its earliest relationships; (2) being is co-created, continuously formed through interactions with others; (3) the pre-Oedipal phase is crucial for development; (4) subjectivity is not solely a cognitive process but is deeply rooted in the body; and (5) the self is seen as fluid, dynamic, and capable of transformation throughout the lifespan.

This ontological shift moved psychoanalysis from a purely phallic drive-based model to one that profoundly emphasises the human need for connection, recognition, and the intersubjective ground of existence, fundamentally reshaping our understanding of what it means to be a person.

Power

Psychoanalysis presented itself as a space of listening, but it was never a neutral space. The analytic relationship is built on asymmetry: one person speaks, the other interprets; one is vulnerable, the other possesses expertise; one is the subject of the case, the other is its author. When the analysand is not only a patient but also a woman, a poet, Jewish, a dissident, or all these together, the asymmetry is intensified. She becomes the cultural Other, spoken for, spoken about, but rarely allowed to speak in her own right.

The dimension of power within psychoanalysis is multifaceted, encompassing individual, institutional, and societal dynamics. Early psychoanalysis, steeped in the paternal metaphor, often mirrored and reinforced patriarchal power structures. The analyst, typically male, held a position of epistemic authority and paternalistic-pastoral power, guiding, interpreting, and ostensibly leading the analysand towards insight and conformity with social norms. This dynamic, particularly in the case of female analysands, could perpetuate a disempowering narrative in which female subjectivity was pathologised or reframed to fit a male-centric understanding.

The contributions of women psychoanalysts significantly disrupted this power dynamic. By deploying the maternal metaphor, they challenged the traditional power imbalance in several ways: (1) challenging the analyst's authority by emphasising intersubjectivity and the co-creation of meaning; (2) shifting the focus from the patient conforming to a societal norms (often male-defined), to fostering the patient's own authentic agency; (3) exposing how the paternal metaphor functioned as a form of symbolic biopower, subtly shaping and regulating female bodies and subjectivities to align with societal expectations; and (4) valuing relational power, the generative power inherent in relational connection, empathy, and mutual recognition.

This re-evaluation of power dynamics by women analysts has been crucial in leveraging psychoanalysis into a more ethically conscious and liberating practice, attuned to the complexities of power in both individual and social contexts.

Chapter Summary

To listen to women in psychoanalysis is to listen differently. Their voices have too often been interpreted, translated, or dismissed rather than heard on their own terms. This chapter has explored a feminist and critical re-reading of psychoanalysis, foregrounding the maternal metaphor as a counterpoint to the dominant phallocentric paternal framework. Rather than tracing a lineage of founding fathers, we have followed the contributions of women who reshaped psychoanalytic theory through their insights into care, desire, relationality, and embodied subjectivity.

These women challenged the epistemological pretence of objectivity, foregrounding narrative, intersubjectivity, and the co-creation of meaning in the analytic encounter. Ontologically, they reimagined the self as relational and evolving, not fixed by drives or typologies. In doing so, they also reconfigured power, offering a more ethical, responsive vision of analytic practice rooted in mutual recognition rather than authority.

Spielrein's voice, however, was not just overshadowed, it was eventually extinguished. After a pioneering career as a child analyst in the Soviet Union, she and her two daughters were murdered in 1942 by an SS Einsatzgruppe in Rostov-on-Don, alongside thousands of other Jewish victims. Her death, like her life, stands as a haunting reminder of how voices that speak from the margins can be lost, not only through theoretical omission but through historical violence. Her story must inspire us to ask: what other ways of knowing have been silenced or erased altogether by history?

Reflective Questions

1. How does the concept of 'the Other' help us reinterpret the voices of female analysands in early psychoanalysis?
2. What does it mean to treat a psychoanalytic case study as a 'dialogic performance' rather than a scientific report?
3. In what ways did Sabina Spielrein's contributions challenge the dominant, male-authored psychoanalytic canon?
4. How do feminist critiques of the Oedipus complex destabilise Freudian theories of gender and development?
5. What power dynamics are at play in the relationship between analyst and analysand, especially when the analysand is culturally or politically marginalised?

Suggested Reading

Angel, K. (2012). Contested psychiatric ontology and feminist critique: 'Female Sexual Dysfunction' and the *Diagnostic and Statistical Manual*. *History of the Human Sciences, 25*(4), 3–24. https://doi.org/10.1177/0952695112456949.

Borbely, A. F. (2008). Metaphor and psychoanalysis. In R. W. Gibbs (Ed.), *The Cambridge Handbook of Metaphor and Thought* (pp. 412–424). Cambridge: Cambridge University Press.

Bueskens, P. (2014). *Mothering and Psychoanalysis: Clinical, sociological and feminist perspectives*. Coe Hill, ONT: Demeter Press.

Copperman, J., & Chaney, S. (2024). The politics of recovery: Women's mental health activism in the UK, 1986–2002, with a focus on Bristol Crisis Service for Women. *History of the Human Sciences*. https://doi.org/10.1177/09526951241289061.

Haaken, J. (2008). When White Buffalo Calf Woman meets Oedipus on the road: Lakota psychology, feminist psychoanalysis, and male violence. *Theory & Psychology, 18*(2), 195–208. https://doi.org/10.1177/0959354307087881.

Harris, B. (2021). Eugenics, social reform, and psychology: The careers of Isabelle Kendig. *History of Psychology, 24*(4), 350–376. https://doi.org/10.1037/hop0000200.

Hubbard, K. (2017). Queer signs: The women of the British projective test movement. *Journal of the History of Behavioural Sciences, 53*(3), 265–285. https://doi.org/10.1002/jhbs.21863.

Johnston, E., & Johnson, A. (2017). Balancing life and work by unbending gender: Early American women psychologists' struggles and contributions. *Journal of the History of the Behavioural Sciences, 53*(3), 246–264. https://doi.org/10.1002/jhbs.21862.

Kontopodis, M., & Jackowska, M. (2019). De-centring the psychology curriculum: Diversity, social justice, and psychological knowledge. *Theory & Psychology, 29*(4), 506–520. https://doi.org/10.1177/0959354319858419.

Launer, J. (2014). *Sex versus Survival: The life and ideas of Sabina Spielrein*. London: Gerald Duckworth.

Rowold, K. (2024). Child psychology from Vienna to London: Charlotte Bühler, concepts of childhood, and parenting advice in interwar Britain. *History of the Human Sciences, 38*(1), 3–25. https://doi.org/10.1177/09526951241289028.

Rutherford, A. (2018). Feminism, psychology, and the gendering of neoliberal subjectivity: From critique to disruption. *Theory & Psychology, 28*(5), 619–644. https://doi.org/10.1177/0959354318797194.

Spielrein, S. (1912/1994). Destruction as the cause of coming into being. *Journal of Analytical Psychology, 39*(2), 155–186. https://doi.org/10.1111/j.1465-5922.1994.00155.x.

Stone, A. (2011). *Feminism, Psychoanalysis, and Maternal Subjectivity*. Abingdon, Oxon: Taylor & Francis.

Key Terms

Abjection Julia Kristeva's concept describing the psychic process of separating from what is deemed impure or threatening to identity, often linked to the maternal.

Analysand The person undergoing psychoanalysis; their speech, symptoms, and subjectivity are central to the analytic process.

Case Study A detailed narrative account of a patient's psychoanalytic treatment, often blending clinical observation with interpretive theory.

Destruction and Creation Sabina Spielrein's psychoanalytic idea that inner psychic development involves a destructive impulse that makes way for renewal.

Hysteria A historically gendered diagnosis in psychoanalysis, frequently associated with women and used to pathologise emotional and bodily expression.

Masquerade A concept introduced by Joan Rivière suggesting that femininity may be performed to conceal masculinity or power.

Maternal Metaphor A conceptual framework highlighting maternal themes (e.g. care, absence, embodiment) in the construction of psychoanalytic theory.

Phallic Lack A Freudian notion positing that femininity is defined through the absence of the phallus, critiqued by feminist theorists.

The Other A philosophical and psychoanalytic concept referring to individuals or groups perceived as different from the dominant self, often marginalised or silenced.

Voice Used metaphorically in this chapter to represent agency, speech, and the power to be heard and recognised as a subject.

FREE INSTRUCTOR & STUDENT RESOURCES

ONLINE RESOURCES

Visit the Instructor & Student Resources website at routledgelearning.com/bpscoretextbooks for free digital resources, including:

- Interactive quizzes and flashcards to test your knowledge
- Links to useful websites and videos
- Instructor manual, lecture slides, and course guide to enhance teaching and save instructors time

7 The Wisdom of the Crowd

Reification and the Authority of Statistics

Chapter Overview

This chapter explores the historical and conceptual development of statistics in psychology, focusing on how numerical tools such as correlation, regression, the Analysis of Variance (ANOVA), and significance testing (p-values) became central to psychological inquiry. Beginning in the nineteenth century with figures such as Francis Galton and Karl Pearson, the chapter traces how early efforts to quantify human differences led to the formalisation of key statistical methods. It examines the innovations of influential statisticians, including William Gosset and Ronald Fisher, highlighting how their solutions to specific methodological challenges shaped modern psychology. Central to the chapter is the critical concept of reification: the tendency to treat abstract constructs (such as intelligence, anxiety, or personality) as if they were fixed, measurable entities. Drawing on Joel Michell's critique of measurement in psychology, the chapter examines the epistemological, ontological, and political risks of treating statistical abstractions as psychological realities. It also explores how statistical reasoning granted psychology institutional power, but at the cost of potential conceptual distortion. The chapter invites us to interrogate not only how psychologists use statistics but also what those numbers are presumed to represent.

The Wisdom of the Crowd

In 1906, amidst the livestock and lively chatter of a bustling agricultural fair in Plymouth, England, Francis Galton was meticulously collecting scraps of paper. Now in his mid-eighties, Galton was an intensely curious Victorian polymath and inventor. His lifelong obsession was quantifying human traits and understanding heredity. He was not there for the prize-winning pigs, however. He was captivated by a peculiar competition. Participants had paid sixpence to guess the weight of a slaughtered and dressed ox. The closest guess would win a prize. Galton saw a unique opportunity to test the collective wisdom of what he usually dismissed as the 'ignorant multitude'. Galton assumed that only a select few people possessed the right intellectual acuity, members of the local landed gentry perhaps, or gentlemen farmers from 'good stock', to guess the correct weight. The average guess would be ridiculously inaccurate, he thought. What he discovered, therefore, astonished him. When he painstakingly calculated the average guess from all 787 tickets, the result was 1,197 pounds, only one pound off the ox's actual dressed weight of

DOI: 10.4324/9781003565482-17

1,198 pounds. This finding wasn't the chaotic roar of the ignorant masses after all; it was the remarkably precise collective wisdom of the crowd.

This simple finding illuminates several themes in the history of psychological statistics. It highlights the issue of random variation across all the competitors (the problem of individual differences), yet also points to the surprising power of aggregating those differences to produce new knowledge: the mean. It shows how seemingly abstract mathematical concepts such as the average can cut through individual variation to reveal a hidden truth. It also showcases Galton's pioneering attempt to quantify the unquantifiable and his role in establishing the groundwork for understanding relationships between numbers, such as the distribution of guesses around a mean value. The anecdote also introduces the subtle power and inherent risk of *reification*: while the average guess was spot-on, no single person's guess *was* the average. The average or mean number is a powerful summary, but it is not 'real' in an empirical sense. This unexpected outcome at a rural fair encapsulates how the development of powerful statistical tools revolutionised our understanding of how human beings could be studied scientifically.

Chapter Contents

- The historical development of statistical thinking in psychology.
- Critical perspectives on measurement, including Joel Michell's challenge to psychological operationalism.
- The role of reification in shaping how psychological constructs are measured, interpreted, and institutionalised.

Chapter Objectives

- To trace the emergence and evolution of statistical methods in psychology, including key tools like ANOVA, correlation, and factor analysis.
- To examine the philosophical and methodological debates around the measurement of psychological constructs.
- To introduce and apply the critical thinking concept of *reification* as a tool for evaluating the scientific authority of statistics in psychology.

CRITICAL THINKING TOOL
REIFICATION

Reification is a concept used in the social sciences to describe the tendency to treat abstract ideas, theoretical constructs, or statistical models *as if they were* concrete, real, and independent entities. In psychology, this tendency manifests when complex human experiences, such as thought, emotion, or personality, are translated into numerical scores, categories, or diagnostic labels. While this process facilitates analysis, comparison, and prediction, it also carries epistemological risks. By reducing lived experience to measurable variables, reification can obscure the cultural assumptions, theoretical frameworks, and methodological choices that shape those variables in the first place.

The history of psychology offers clear examples of this process. In the nineteenth century, phrenologists claimed that moral and intellectual traits could be read from the shape of the skull. They treated abstract qualities, such as 'Philoprogenitiveness' or 'Secretiveness', as spatially locatable on the skull. Although phrenology has since been discredited, the impulse to map psychological categories onto measurable surfaces persists. In contemporary psychological science, constructs such as 'intelligence', 'self-esteem', and 'executive function' are routinely quantified through IQ tests, Likert scales, and statistical techniques such as factor analysis. These constructs are frequently treated as though they refer to stable, discoverable entities within individuals.

This subtle and overlooked transformation, from concept to quantity, from model to reality, is the essence of reification. Once a person is assigned a numerical score for an attribute such as anxiety, that score can come to stand in for the person themselves. The number appears to confirm the existence of the trait, even though it is a product of measurement decisions, theoretical assumptions, and a specific social situation.

Recognising reification as a methodological and conceptual risk does not mean abandoning measurement altogether. Rather, it calls for critical attention to the distinction between models and reality, between symbolic indicators and the phenomena they are intended to represent. By remaining alert to this distinction, we can better evaluate the validity of psychological claims and resist the seductive power of numbers.

Introduction

Psychology, as it developed in the nineteenth century, was drawn to the promise of scientific legitimacy but lacked reliable tools for moving beyond philosophical speculation. The challenge of quantifying subjective phenomena such as thought, emotion, or behaviour led the first generation of psychologists to seek methods for comparison, classification, and inference. Over time, their efforts gave rise to the statistical techniques that would become central to the discipline. These tools, tables of data, p-values, regression equations, are now firmly embedded in the language and practice of psychological science. Yet their development was shaped by complex histories of ingenuity, ambition, and conceptual compromise.

According to Joel Michell, psychology appropriated the authority of measurement from the physical sciences without meeting its central requirement: the demonstration that any psychological category possessed an underlying quantitative structure. Demonstrating measurability prior to measurement, in other words. Scientific measurement, in this view, requires evidence of ratios, intervals, and stable magnitudes corresponding to real-world properties (such as height and weight). Psychological constructs do not in fact exhibit such properties. Despite this, psychologists routinely applied statistical tools such as ANOVA, t-tests, and p-values, treating constructs *as if they were* genuinely measurable entities.

This conceptual sleight of hand was formalised by S. S. Stevens in 1946, when he redefined measurement as the assignment of numerals according to rules. Stevens's pragmatic definition allowed psychology to proceed without first validating whether its variables possessed quantity. For Michell, this marked a shift away from scientific coherence: a move that prioritised methodological convenience over epistemological clarity. By turning operations into definitions and statistics into truths, psychology installed reification, the treatment of abstract constructs as concrete realities, at the heart of its methodological identity. Michell wants us to resist this.

Historical Issues

The historical origins of psychological measurement are closely tied to efforts to manage human error. In the nineteenth century, astronomers developed statistical techniques to address discrepancies in human observation, particularly when measuring celestial events. These methods, concerned with variation, distribution, and the modelling of error, were gradually adapted for use in the human sciences. A nineteenth-century Belgian astronomer and statistician, Adolphe Quetelet, applied mathematical techniques to the study of human populations. He introduced the idea of the 'average man' and was among the first to use the bell-shaped curve to represent how values (such as height or weight) tend to cluster around a mean in large populations. Quetelet used this model to argue that individual differences were not errors or anomalies but part of predictable statistical patterns (the famous 'normal distribution'). Galton suggested that traits such as intellect, criminality, or physical attractiveness could be similarly understood as statistically regular phenomena.

Before these statistical tools could be fully integrated into psychology, however, the field faced several conceptual and methodological challenges. Psychology emerged from a tradition of philosophical inquiry, and its early methods relied heavily on introspection, anecdotal reporting, and speculation. This reliance gave rise to what might be termed the problem of subjectivity: the difficulty of producing reliable knowledge from private mental states. Gustav Fechner's pioneering work in psychophysics demonstrated that mental and physical events could be related mathematically, yet the elusive and constructed nature of psychological variables remained unresolved. Even the controlled experiments of Wilhelm Wundt's laboratory, while more systematic, had to confront the unpredictability and variability of human experience, much to Wundt's annoyance.

At the same time, researchers confronted the problem of chance: the need to distinguish meaningful effects from random fluctuations in data. In applied contexts, such as quality control in industry, they also encountered the problem of small samples, where reliable conclusions had to be drawn from limited data. These practical and philosophical dilemmas created the conditions for psychology's embrace of statistical reasoning. While statistics offered the promise of empirical rigour, they also introduced new conceptual risks, most notably the tendency to conflate mathematical structure with psychological reality. This tension lies at the heart of all psychological measurement.

Key Individuals

Francis Galton (1822–1911) was Charles Darwin's half-cousin and a maverick explorer of individual differences. Obsessed with quantification, his eccentric data collection, from the Anthropometric Laboratory to the Beauty Map of England, fuelled his interest in eugenics. Galton grappled with the problem of how to describe how two different human traits relate, especially across generations, and how to predict future traits, such as whether tall parents would have tall children.

His solution involved introducing the concepts of 'co-relation', the forerunner of modern correlation, and 'regression', describing the tendency for extreme values to (sadly, according to Galton) move towards the average in successive generations. However, Galton's work often carried a significant reification risk, as he tended to treat complex traits like 'genius' or 'ability' as inherited elements, rather than as multifaceted constructs influenced by environment.

Building on Galton's insights was Karl Pearson (1857–1936), his intellectual successor and a brilliant mathematician who led the 'Biometric School'. Pearson formalised the statistical methods necessary for understanding relationships and analysing categorical data. He tackled the problem of how to mathematically describe the strength and direction of a linear relationship between two continuous variables such as height and weight. His solution was the development of the Pearson Product-Moment Correlation Coefficient (Pearson's r) in 1896. He also addressed the problem of how to determine if observed frequencies in different categories truly differed from what one might expect by chance, or if two categorical variables were independent; for instance, whether an association existed for one ice cream flavour between boys and girls. His answer was the creation of the Chi-Squared ($\chi 2$) test in 1900, used to assess the 'goodness of fit' between observed and expected frequencies.

As a chemist working for the Guinness Brewery in Dublin, William Gosset (1876–1937) faced the practical problem of how to derive meaningful insights from small samples (of beer), when the population's true variability was unknown and unmeasurable due to its sheer volume. Because his employer's strict secrecy rules prevented him from publishing under his real name, Gosset released his groundbreaking work under the pseudonym 'Student'. Gosset's insight lay in realising that small samples have different statistical properties to those of the larger population, necessitating a new approach. His solution was the development of the t-distribution and Student's t-test in 1908. While the t-test itself is not primarily about reifying psychological constructs, its widespread adoption contributed to the reification of 'statistical significance' as a binary 'truth' or 'no truth' decision, often divorced from practical importance.

A gifted, if sometimes combative, statistician based at Rothamsted Experimental Station, Ronald Fisher (1890–1962), tackled the complex problem of how to statistically compare more than two groups and examine the effects of multiple factors simultaneously. One afternoon in the early 1920s at Cambridge, a lady, believed to be Dr Muriel Bristol, claimed she could tell whether milk had been poured into a cup before or after the tea. Fisher, intrigued, saw an opportunity to demonstrate the principles of experimental design. He proposed a randomised experiment: the lady would be given eight cups of tea, four of each type, presented in random order, and asked to identify which was which. Fisher calculated the probability of her achieving various outcomes by chance. This example became a cornerstone in the illustration of formal hypothesis testing. Fisher's formulation of Analysis of Variance (ANOVA), first published in 1918 and popularised through his later work, enabled the efficient comparison of multiple group means and the assessment of complex experimental designs with multiple variables.

Epistemological Issues

The adoption of statistical methods marked a profound transformation in how psychology sought to produce knowledge. Whereas early psychological inquiry was rooted in philosophical speculation, introspection, and anecdotal observation, the rise of statistics offered a new epistemological foundation grounded in empirical analysis and mathematical inference. This shift enabled psychologists to move beyond the study of individual cases or subjective experiences and instead to identify patterns across large populations. Through techniques such as sampling, estimation, and hypothesis testing, psychologists were now able to make generalisations based on limited data, ushering in a move from deterministic to probabilistic modes of thinking.

This transformation introduced new epistemological tensions. A statistically 'significant' finding might suggest that an observed effect is unlikely to have occurred by chance, but whether it meant anything was open to question. For Ronald Fisher, statistical inference involved assessing the strength of evidence against a null hypothesis. Other statisticians later framed significance testing as a decision-making procedure, balancing the risk of different types of error. These competing interpretations laid the groundwork for an ongoing debate about the meaning, reliability, and limits of statistical evidence in psychological research.

Compounding these challenges was the increasing reliance on statistical techniques to operationalise and measure abstract psychological constructs such as self-esteem, impulsivity, and attachment style. Through repeated use in testing and research, psychology's constructs acquired an unjustified aura of objectivity and stability. Their validity as measurable psychological entities often rested on unexamined assumptions. The use of techniques and tools such as factor analysis and Likert scales allowed psychologists to reduce complex mental and emotional phenomena to quantifiable variables. In doing so, however, they risked reifying provisional constructs, treating them not as heuristic models but as real, discoverable properties of the individual. This process blurs the line between measurement and invention, with important consequences for how psychology claims to know what it knows.

Ontological Issues

The application of statistical methods in psychology fundamentally reshaped what was thought to exist in the psychological realm. Statistical reasoning, particularly in the hands of early figures such as Francis Galton, brought into focus the concept of individual differences. Galton's efforts to quantify traits such as sensory acuity, aptitude, and mental imagery contributed to the view that these attributes were not only measurable but also inherent and stable properties of individuals. This marked a pivotal ontological shift: behaviours and tendencies that might once have been viewed as contextually shaped or relationally dynamic, thanks to statistics, came to be understood as personological *traits*, internal, quantifiable, and enduring.

This way of thinking laid the groundwork for the construction of a host of contemporary psychological constructs, including locus of control, resilience, and executive function. Each of these terms began as theoretical frameworks designed to describe how individuals respond to their environments. However, once operationalised through questionnaires, behavioural tasks, and statistical models, they came to be treated as if they referred to concrete, pre-existing entities within the individual. A score on a resilience scale, for example, is often interpreted as an index of a person's core psychological strength, rather than as a situational or socially constructed appraisal.

This tendency to treat statistical constructs as ontologically real is a core manifestation of reification. Factors derived from psychometric analysis, such as impulsivity or working memory capacity, are rarely observable in any direct sense, yet are frequently discussed as if they have physical or even neurological essences. The same dynamic can be seen in the interpretation of statistically significant effects in clinical trials, where a treatment's probabilistic outcome under experimental conditions is reified into an inherent and universal effect of the therapy itself. In such cases, the risk is both epistemological and ontological: statistical abstractions are mistaken for psychological realities. This conflation can obscure the complexity, variability, and embeddedness of human experience, replacing it with a model that is numerically elegant but conceptually fragile.

Power

The rise of statistical methods endowed psychology with epistemic, institutional, and reputational power, both within academia and across wider society. The adoption of quantitative techniques lent the discipline scientific legitimacy, aligning it with the perceived rigour of biology, chemistry, and physics. This methodological alignment established statistics as a gatekeeping device, determining what counted as credible research and shaping the allocation of funding, publication opportunities, and professional advancement. Over time, statistical significance became reified as the ultimate indicator of scientific truth, leading to entrenched practices such as p-hacking, publication bias, and over-reliance on narrow thresholds for legitimacy, patterns that would later contribute to the so-called replication crisis.

This statistical authority also positioned psychology as a key agent in the exercise of social power. Galton's analyses helped construct binary distinctions between the 'fit' and the 'unfit', and were instrumental in legitimising the eugenics movement, which sought to regulate the reproduction of human populations through sterilisation, segregation, and other coercive policies. Eugenics exemplified the logic of biopower, in Foucault's sense: the statistical categorisation and management of populations based on hereditary traits.

In the twentieth century, intelligence testing became a major site of disciplinary power, another Foucauldian concept related to the normalisation and regulation of individuals through subtle institutional mechanisms. The statistical validation of IQ tests, initially developed by Alfred Binet and later widely standardised, enabled psychologists to sort individuals within schools, military organisations, and immigration systems. IQ scores, increasingly treated as stable and objective indices of mental worth, were used to justify educational tracking, employment selection, and social exclusion. In this way, measurement tools became instruments of knowledge and control.

Even in clinical psychology, where statistics inform decisions about treatment efficacy and diagnostic validity, there is a persistent risk of reifying diagnostic categories, transforming fluid, context-dependent phenomenological experiences such as 'bipolar disorder' into rigid identities. Understanding this historical interplay between statistics and power across the domains of knowledge production, population governance, and individual subject formation is essential for developing an ethically reflective and critically informed psychology.

Chapter Summary

The story of statistics in psychology is one of ingenuity, ambition, and far-reaching consequence. Early psychology struggled with profound challenges, how to measure intangible experiences, distinguish real effects from chance, and generalise from limited data. These obstacles inspired pioneers such as Francis Galton, who introduced regression and sought patterns in human traits, and Karl Pearson, who formalised correlation and developed tools such as the correlation coefficient and the Chi-squared test.

William Gosset, working under the pseudonym 'Student' in a brewery, developed the t-Test to address the problem of small samples. Ronald Fisher revolutionised experimental design with ANOVA, making it possible to evaluate multiple factors at once, epitomised by the tea-tasting lady's challenge. Each innovation pushed psychology further into the realm of empirical science.

But with these tools came a powerful tendency towards reification: the transformation of abstract statistical constructs into assumed realities. This chapter has shown how reification affects both epistemology and ontology, shaping how we know and what we think exists. To understand statistics in psychology is not merely to learn formulas but to question how knowledge is made. That critical spirit takes us back to Galton at the Plymouth agricultural fair in 1906, where he famously predicted the weight of an ox by averaging the guesses of hundreds of fair-goers. The result was uncannily accurate, an emblem of statistical wisdom, and a reminder that sometimes, truth emerges not from the authorities but from the crowd.

Reflective Questions

1. What is reification, and why is it particularly relevant to the measurement of psychological constructs?
2. How did statistical tools like the normal distribution and factor analysis influence the development of psychological theory and practice?
3. In what ways did the work of figures like Galton and Fisher both advance and compromise the ethical standing of psychology?
4. How does Joel Michell's critique challenge the legitimacy of psychological measurement?
5. How can recognising the role of reification help students become more critical consumers of psychological research today?

Suggested Reading

Boudewijnse, G.-J. A., Murray, D. J., & Bandomir, C. A. (2001). The fate of Herbart's mathematical psychology. *History of Psychology, 4*(2), 107–132. https://doi.org/10.1037/1093-4510.4.2.107.

Cowles, M. (2001). *Statistics in Psychology: An historical perspective.* New York: Lawrence Erlbaum.

Crone, G., & Green, C. D. (2025). Tools of the data detective: A review of statistical methods to detect data and result anomalies in psychology. *Theory & Psychology, 35*(3), 359–380. https://doi.org/10.1177/09593543241311861.

Danziger, K. (1990). *Constructing the Subject: Historical origins of psychological research.* Cambridge: Cambridge University Press.

Friendly, M., & Denis, D. (2005). The early origins and development of the scatter-plot. *Journal of the History of the Behavioural Sciences, 41*(2), 103–130. https://doi.org/10.1002/jhbs.20078.
Gigerenzer, G., Swijtink, Z., Porter, T., Daston, L., Beatty, J., & Krüger, L. (1989). *The Empire of Chance: How probability changed science and everyday life*. Cambridge: Cambridge University Press.
Lamiell, J. T. (2018). Re-centering psychology: From variables and statistics to persons and their stories. *Theory & Psychology, 29*(2), 282–284. https://doi.org/10.1177/0959354318766714.
Lovie, S., & Lovie, P. (2004). A privileged and exemplar resource: Traumatic avoidance learning and the early triumph of mathematical psychology. *History of Psychology, 7*(3), 248–264. https://doi.org/10.1037/1093-4510.7.3.248.
Lusinchi, D. (2022). Kiær and the rebirth of the representative method: A case-study in controversy management at the International Statistical Institute (1895–1903). *Journal of the History of the Behavioral Sciences, 58*(2), 163–182. https://doi.org/10.1002/jhbs.22145.
Michell, J. (1997). Quantitative science and the definition of measurement in psychology. *British Journal of Psychology, 88*(3), 355–383. https://doi.org/10.1111/j.2044-8295.1997.tb02641.x.
Morozova, S. V. (2022). How statistics became a 'forbidden trick' for Soviet psychologists. *History of Psychology, 25*(2), 121–142. https://doi.org/10.1037/hop0000204.
Salsburg, D. (2013). *The Lady Tasting Tea: How statistics revolutionized science in the twentieth century*. New York: Henry Holt and Company.
Uygun Tunç, D., Tunç, M. N., & Lakens, D. (2023). The epistemic and pragmatic function of dichotomous claims based on statistical hypothesis tests. *Theory & Psychology, 33*(3), 403–423. https://doi.org/10.1177/09593543231160112.

Key Terms

Analysis of Variance (ANOVA) A statistical technique developed by Ronald Fisher that allows researchers to compare means across multiple groups to determine whether observed differences are likely due to chance.

Biopower A concept from Michel Foucault describing the way institutions use statistical knowledge and measurement to regulate populations, particularly in areas like health, education, and reproduction.

Construct An abstract psychological concept (e.g. intelligence, anxiety, resilience) that is operationalised and measured through specific procedures, often treated as if it refers to a stable, real trait.

Disciplinary Power A Foucauldian concept referring to the subtle, institutional means by which individuals are classified, normalised, and regulated—often through testing, diagnosis, and statistical comparison.

Epistemology The branch of philosophy concerned with the nature and limits of knowledge; in psychology, it refers to the theories and assumptions that underlie how we know what we claim to know.

Factor Analysis A statistical method used to identify latent variables or 'factors' that explain patterns of correlations among observed variables, widely used in intelligence and personality testing.

Inferential Statistics Techniques that allow researchers to draw conclusions about populations based on data from samples, including tests of significance such as the t-test, chi-square, and p-value analysis.

Normal Distribution A bell-shaped curve representing the distribution of a trait or variable in a population; widely used in psychology to describe 'average' behaviour and to identify statistical outliers.

Operationalism A methodological stance, associated with S. S. Stevens, that defines scientific concepts in terms of the procedures used to measure them, allowing psychology to sidestep deeper philosophical questions about what is being measured.

P-value A statistical index that quantifies the probability of obtaining a result at least as extreme as the observed one, assuming the null hypothesis is true; often misinterpreted as a direct measure of truth or effect size.

Quantification The process of assigning numerical values to psychological phenomena, making them amenable to statistical analysis; central to the transformation of psychology into a data-driven science.

Reification The critical thinking tool of the chapter; it refers to the tendency to treat abstract concepts or statistical constructs as if they were real, tangible entities (e.g. treating 'IQ' as a fixed property rather than as a measurement output).

FREE INSTRUCTOR & STUDENT RESOURCES

ONLINE RESOURCES

Visit the Instructor & Student Resources website at routledgelearning.com/bpscoretextbooks for free digital resources, including:

- Interactive quizzes and flashcards to test your knowledge
- Links to useful websites and videos
- Instructor manual, lecture slides, and course guide to enhance teaching and save instructors time

8 The Machine That Knew Too Much

The Lie Detector and the Discursive Production of Truth

Chapter Overview

This chapter explores the lie detector as a case study in the history of applied psychology, critically examining how it emerged as a cultural and scientific artefact in the United States during the period prior to the start of the Second World War. Rather than asking whether the polygraph 'really works', the chapter applies the tool for critical thinking of discourse analysis to investigate how the lie detector came to signify truth, objectivity, and guilt. Through an exploration of historical context, key individuals, and the socio-technical development of the polygraph, students are introduced to the ways in which psychological tools are shaped by, and help shape, the discourses of science, justice, and emotion. Focusing on the competing visions of William Moulton Marston and Leonarde Keeler, the chapter uncovers the ideological contradictions embedded in early lie detection discourse, including the tension between mechanical objectivity and human interpretation. It analyses the subject positions (expert, suspect, machine), interpretative repertoires (truth machine versus performance), and ideological dilemmas (science versus spectacle) that structure the polygraph's authority. The chapter concludes by showing how the lie detector functioned as a technology of power: as a tool of police discipline, therapeutic intimacy, and spectacular cultural performance. Ultimately, the polygraph is revealed to be not merely a machine but a discourse: it was a way of thinking, seeing, and acting that reshaped ideas about truth, guilt, and psychological expertise. By applying discourse analysis, students are invited to question how psychological knowledge is produced, validated, and operationalised in both science and society.

The Machine That Knew Too Much

On a cold March night in 1937, Joseph Rappaport sat in a cell at Cook County Jail in Chicago, waiting to hear whether the Governor would spare his life. Rappaport had been convicted of murdering Max Dent, a government informant, but he insisted he was innocent. The trial had been murky, the evidence contested. Governor Henry Horner was not entirely convinced of the case against him. Now, in a final effort to tip the scales, Rappaport had agreed to something unprecedented:

DOI: 10.4324/9781003565482-18

a lie detector test. The machine was new, experimental, but surrounded by hype. Its advocates claimed it could read the truth written on the body, in the flicker of a heartbeat, the tightening of the breath, the sweat on the skin. 'Judge in the Test,' the *New York Times* reported, 'was Professor Leonarde Keeler of the Scientific Crime Detection Laboratory of Northwestern University, inventor of the lie detector, scientifically known as a polygraph.' Keeler put an odd-looking black box-like machine on the table and then tightened a rubber tube around Rappaport's chest. The interrogation began.

Keeler asked the crucial question: 'Do you know who shot Max Dent?' 'No', Rappaport replied. Keeler studied the jagged lines on the graph paper, then delivered his judgement: guilty. Governor Horner had already granted Rappaport four reprieves, unsure whether to commute the sentence, although he had confessed to being a 'great believer' in the lie detector's abilities. The machine had spoken, and its verdict tipped the balance. Hours later, Rappaport was dead, executed in the electric chair. The lie detector had transformed bodily signals into a declaration of guilt. A chart of lines and pulses stood in for a confession. This is the story of the lie detector: a device born from ambition, fear, and the dream of perfect honesty. But behind the wires and the graphs lies a more tangled story, a story of power, persuasion, spectacle, and belief. The polygraph was not just a machine; it was an entire discourse.

Chapter Contents

- The cultural and scientific history of the lie detector from 1910 to 1950.
- Competing subject positions, repertoires, and ideological dilemmas surrounding lie detection.
- Discourse analysis as a critical tool for understanding truth, power, and psychological authority.

Chapter Objectives

- To examine the historical development of the lie detector within the context of early twentieth-century American psychology and policing.
- To critically analyse how lie detection was constructed through discourse, including popular culture, legal practice, and psychological theory.
- To introduce discourse analysis as a critical thinking tool for interrogating the epistemological, ontological, and power dynamics of applied psychological technologies.

TOOL FOR CRITICAL THINKING
DISCOURSE ANALYSIS

Discourse analysis is a powerful tool for critical thinking in psychology. It focuses on the ways that systems of language, imagery, and representations shape our understanding of the world.

A discourse is not simply a set of statements or ideas; it is a complex social practice composed of symbols, speech acts, behavioural routines, and patterns of meaning that structure what can be said, by whom, and with what authority. Unlike a 'paradigm', which tends to refer to scientific consensus within a discipline, a discourse encompasses both explicit, often contradictory, claims and implicit assumptions, working across cultural, social, and institutional boundaries. Discourses are epistemological: they shape how knowledge is defined and legitimised. They are also ontological: they construct what counts as a subject, an object, or a fact. And they are saturated with power: they regulate behaviour, normalise assumptions, and create hierarchies of knowledge and expertise.

Discourse analysis typically attends to three key features. First, *subject positions*: who is allowed to speak and act, and what authority they claim. In psychology, for example, this might involve the authoritative voice of the 'expert' versus the client commissioning a report, or the pathologised voice of a 'patient'. Second, *interpretative repertoires*: the clusters of metaphors, tropes, phrases, and images used to make arguments persuasive, such as 'the brain is a computer' or 'emotions are chemical imbalances'. Third, *ideological dilemmas*: the contradictions and tensions within discourses, such as psychology's simultaneous commitment to objectivity and empathy, or the conceptualisation of a psychological category as a human kind or natural kind. These three features of discourse analysis will be central to our analysis of the history of the lie detector.

Introduction

The history of the lie detector is a compelling episode in the broader story of applied psychology. Between 1910 and 1950, psychologists claimed to have invented a machine that could detect lies, a feat that, if true, would revolutionise law enforcement, personal relationships, and the nature of truth itself. This device, commonly known as the polygraph, measures physiological responses such as blood pressure, heart rate, respiration, and perspiration, which were assumed to change under the stress of telling a lie. But what the polygraph could do, in fact, was much more than 'detect a lie'. Lie detector discourse was a carefully constructed discourse of language and behaviour, science and spectacle.

In this chapter, we will explore the history of the lie detector through the lens of discourse analysis. Rather than asking whether the polygraph 'really works' in the simple sense of it being able to detect lies, we will examine how it came to be seen as having authoritative magical powers. We will investigate how its advocates framed the machine as a scientific breakthrough, how it was received by police departments and the public, and how it emerged in popular culture as a near-mystical device for revealing hidden truths.

This is a story about applied psychology, but it's also about trust, fear, and power. It reveals how discourses of science and justice can produce instruments that shape, and sometimes distort, reality.

Historical Issues

The early twentieth century in the United States was a period marked by rapid change, uncertainty, and anxiety. Industrialisation had brought millions of people into urban centres, producing expanding cities and complex new forms of social organisation. Alongside these transformations came new forms of perceived threat: rising crime rates, high-profile robberies and murders, and widespread social unrest. The introduction of Prohibition in 1920 exacerbated the situation. By criminalising alcohol, a substance embedded in the social life of millions, the Volstead Act inadvertently fuelled organised crime, bootlegging, and a flourishing black market. A sensationalist press depicted law enforcement as weak and overwhelmed.

At the same time, the police themselves were undergoing transformation. The brutal, confession-by-force tactics of the nineteenth century were increasingly seen as outdated and unprofessional. A new ethos of scientific policing was emerging, promising to replace brute force with reason, and arbitrary suspicion with the systematic gathering of measurable evidence. The burgeoning field of forensic science, including fingerprinting, ballistics, and crime scene analysis, was part of this shift. So too was psychology, ever eager to demonstrate its social utility. Into this context emerged the lie detector's seductive promise: to reveal the truth not through coercion or intuition but through objective and measurable bodily signs.

The period also witnessed a conceptual shift in how criminality was understood. In earlier eras, crime had often been attributed to immutable personal traits, as in the domain of the 'born criminal', as theorised by Cesare Lombroso. But as the twentieth century progressed, criminality became increasingly framed as something hidden, internal, and potentially universal. Anyone might be guilty. The challenge was how to find out who was harbouring guilty knowledge. The lie detector emerged from this epistemic fault line. It offered a new way of thinking about deception, responsibility, and truth itself.

Key Individuals

The history of the lie detector is, to some extent, the story of two men: the psychologist William Moulton Marston (1893–1947) and the criminologist Leonarde Keeler (1903–1949). Both were pivotal in the invention and popularisation of polygraphic lie detection, yet they approached the technology from radically different worldviews. Their lives reveal much about the ideological contradictions embedded in the discourse of psychological truth detection.

Harvard graduate William Moulton Marston was a psychologist, lawyer, and self-styled moral philosopher. He is most famous today as the creator of the comic book character *Wonder Woman*, whose magic lasso compels truth-telling, a fictional echo of Marston's own vision. For Marston, the lie detector was not simply a technique for solving crime but a means to access deeper psychological truths. In his 1917 doctoral research which Hugo Münsterberg had supervised, he proposed that systolic blood pressure rose during deception, laying the theoretical foundation for what he called the 'systolic blood pressure deception test'. Crucially, Marston believed that lies were psychological symptoms, emotionally charged distortions of the self, which the sphygmomanometer could reveal.

Marston tested his device in universities, psychiatric clinics, and even on potential romantic partners. He claimed that the lie detector could help lovers reveal their true feelings, and that women were more honest, more emotionally intelligent, and more trustworthy than men, a belief he later wove into the origin myth of *Wonder Woman*. For Marston, the polygraph was a device of pastoral power: it offered liberation through emotional truth, guided by a benevolent psychologist-priest.

Leonarde Keeler, by contrast, was a pragmatist and a showman. Keeler developed the 'Keeler Polygraph' and took out a commercial patent on his device. Unlike Marston, Keeler worked directly with law enforcement, first in Berkeley, California, under the influential criminologist August Vollmer. Vollmer was a key figure in the professionalisation of American policing. He viewed Keeler's device as part of a broader shift towards scientific crime detection. In this context, the polygraph was not so much a therapeutic instrument as a disciplinary one: its role was to extract confessions, support convictions, and deter wrongdoing.

Keeler understood that the lie detector's secret power lay in its psychological effect on the suspect. The spectacle of the machine, the wires, the needles, the slow-moving paper chart, created an atmosphere of surveillance and scientific inevitability. Recommending that suspects spent the night in the cells prior to an encounter with the machine the following day, suspects were often intimidated into confessing before the test had even begun. Keeler capitalised on this performative aspect, training polygraph examiners to act with confidence and authority. He taught them how to perform a sleight-of-hand card magic trick on the suspect to establish the machine's uncanny abilities. He also promoted the device relentlessly, appearing in newspapers, magazines, and even a Hollywood movie, *Call Northside 777*.

Keeler blurred the lines between science, spectacle, and commerce. He sold polygraphs to police departments and trained operators in their use, creating a new professional niche: the expert polygrapher. Whereas Marston framed the device in terms of moral introspection and personal reform, Keeler embedded it in the machinery of the state, marketing the lie detector as both a deterrent and a tool of justice.

The contrast between Marston and Keeler reveals a deep ideological dilemma at the heart of lie detection. Was the polygraph a neutral scientific tool, or a theatrical performance? Was it a path to inner truth. or a coercive mechanism of confession? Was the psychologist a healer, or an enforcer? These tensions were never resolved because the discourse was capable of absorbing all of them at once. Such contradictions coexisted, generating competing interpretative repertoires and unstable subject positions.

It is tempting to see Marston and Keeler as embodying opposing archetypes: the idealist and the pragmatist, the academic and the entrepreneur. Yet their stories also overlap. Both were invested in the authority of science, the power of psychological expertise, and the cultural allure of machines that promise to reveal unseen truth. Both contributed to the enduring myth of the lie detector as a device that could penetrate deception and produce truth, a myth that was never quite as stable or scientific as it seemed.

Epistemological Issues

At the heart of the lie detector discourse lies a fundamental epistemological question: how can we know whether someone is lying? The polygraph was offered as a solution to this problem: here was an objective, scientific instrument that could bypass fallible human judgement and access truth directly. But the reality was more ambiguous. The history of lie detection reveals a deep and enduring tension between two modes of knowledge production: mechanical objectivity and human interpretation.

On the one hand, the polygraph appeared to provide a form of visual truth. As the machine traced the suspect's blood pressure, respiration, and galvanic skin response onto a slowly moving chart, it generated a record that looked technical, detached, and unbiased. This was the epistemological appeal of the graph, the idea that the machine itself could 'do the knowing'. The graph was treated as a kind of psychological seismograph, registering disturbances that pointed to underlying deception. Within this framework the polygraph was imagined as a neutral arbiter, free from bias or prejudice.

Yet in practice, the graph was never self-interpreting. Although polygraphers were trained to read subtle fluctuations in the lines, they were also encouraged to interpret the demeanour, posture, and speech patterns of the subject. The reading of the graph was inseparable from a broader performance of expertise. The examiner's interpretative work became central to the process: deciding which interrogation questions were relevant, judging when a response was suspicious, and ultimately determining whether the suspect had lied. As such, the machine was not an autonomous truth-teller but part of a wider system of meaning-making, one that ultimately depended on human judgement and rhetorical authority.

This ambiguity gave rise to competing epistemological claims. The lie detector was both an automatic mechanical oracle *and* a tool that only worked in the hands of a skilled interpreter. The discourse of lie detection did not reconcile these positions, relying on the illusion that no contradiction existed. This unresolved tension, between mechanical objectivity and human interpretation, reveals the epistemological fragility at the core of psychological expertise in the courtroom, the police station, and the public imagination.

Ontological Issues

The history of the lie detector is a story about what kinds of things are made *real* through discourse. The polygraph played an active role in constructing 'the lie' as a measurable psychological phenomenon. This ontological shift, from lie as sin, to lie as symptom, to lie as signal, was a key part of the lie detector's discursive power.

In the nineteenth century, criminality was often seen as a biological fate, an inherited flaw located in the skull, the bloodline, or in the race, as in Lombroso's 'born criminal'. But by the early twentieth century, crime had been reframed as a behavioural choice. Because anyone could lie, anyone could be a suspect. The polygraph emerged within this new ontology of universality: the criminal was no longer a monstrous Other but potentially your neighbour, your colleague, or even yourself. The polygraph's task was to differentiate between the truthful and the deceptive, not through moral judgement but through bodily signs.

But deception had to be ontologically stabilised before it could be detected. In other words, the lie had to become a 'thing', a deviation from an imagined baseline of honesty, conveniently encoded by the body's physiology. This was a discursive achievement. Polygraph examiners assumed that physiological arousal indicated anxiety, and that anxiety indicated deception. Yet fear, embarrassment, confusion, and many other emotional states could produce similar bodily effects. Nonetheless, the discourse of lie detection equated arousal with lying, thereby producing the 'lie' as a measurable event.

Importantly, the goal of the polygraph was not always punishment. For Keeler, the ultimate objective was the confession: a moment of psychological resolution and institutional closure. The lie produced the truth. For Marston, however, truth-telling was the starting point for a therapeutic encounter. The polygraph enabled personal insight, especially in intimate relationships. In both cases, the machine summoned truth into being. This is the ontological sleight-of-hand at the heart of the lie detector: it created the very truths it claimed only to discover.

Power

The lie detector emerged as an instrument of power, in every sense of Michel Foucault's conceptualisations. Far from being a neutral device for measuring deception, the polygraph operated within complex networks of authority, surveillance, and truth production. These dynamics of power were not incidental; they were integral to the lie detector's meaning and function.

The first and most obvious form of power at work was disciplinary power. The polygraph was used by police forces, often in the absence of clear evidence, to exert control, intimidate suspects, and extract confessions. Its very presence created a coercive atmosphere. Wired to a machine, under interrogation, the suspect became both object of suspicion and source of confession. This was power enacted through procedure, routine, and institutional legitimacy, the same kind of power that ran through the modern prison and the psychiatric ward.

Yet alongside this carceral logic was a more intimate form of power: pastoralism. William Moulton Marston framed the lie detector as an instrument of emotional revelation. He used it to mediate romantic relationships, to resolve conflicts between lovers, and to promote psychological honesty among politicians. In this framework, the polygraph was less about surveillance and more about salvation, a tool to uncover the 'real feelings' hidden beneath social masks. The psychologist in this role did not punish but guided, comforted, and interpreted. The goal was not justice but healing.

Finally, the lie detector operated through spectacular power. Keeler and Marston both understood the visual and symbolic appeal of the machine, its wires, dials, graphs, and blinking lights. It featured prominently in films, pulp novels, and comic books. Marston's own creation, *Wonder Woman*, embodied this power. Her lasso of truth was a mythic translation of the polygraph: a magical device that compelled honesty. Here, the lie detector became a symbol of psychological modernity: mysterious, powerful, and incontrovertible.

Chapter Summary

The lie detector has long occupied a peculiar space in the history of psychology: part machine, part myth, and part mirror. It claimed to reveal the truth, yet its very functioning depended on a discursive web of assumptions, performances, and rhetorical manoeuvres. In this chapter, we have used discourse analysis to reframe the polygraph as a product of historically contingent ways of thinking, speaking, and acting.

Discourse analysis demonstrates that scientific knowledge emerges through systems of representation, social practice, and power. The polygraph helped operationalise criminality, define what a lie was, decide who was likely to tell one, and determine which forms of truth mattered. It created *subject positions*: the suspect, rendered visible and vulnerable; the expert examiner, cloaked in authority; the machine itself, often treated as sentient. It mobilised *interpretative repertoires* that cast lie detection as both science and theatre, both liberation and coercion. And it embodied *ideological dilemmas,* naturalised contradictions that remained unresolved: objectivity versus interpretation, discipline versus care, justice versus spectacle.

This critical approach also reveals how material culture is never neutral. The polygraph was a cultural artefact loaded with meaning. It appeared in courtrooms, detective fiction, comic books, and even domestic settings, shaping public imagination far beyond the realm of science. Its power lay in what it promised to measure. The promise of a mechanical path to moral clarity made it both compelling and dangerous.

The lie detector emerged from a specific historical moment: a time of rising faith in science, anxiety about crime, and the transformation of the police from capricious thugs to scientifically informed professionals. It was a solution to a cultural problem as much as a technical one. Discourse analysis can reveal how psychology operates within and through language, image, and behaviour, shaping our most fundamental understandings of truth, personhood, and power. In the end, the story of the lie detector not only tests the suspect; it reveals how psychology itself functions.

Reflective Questions

1. How did the lie detector reflect the changing understanding of criminality in early twentieth-century America?
2. In what ways did William Moulton Marston and Leonarde Keeler represent different visions of psychological expertise?
3. How does discourse analysis help us understand the lie detector not as a neutral device but as a cultural artefact?
4. What forms of power operated through the use and popularisation of the lie detector, and how were these legitimised?
5. What does the history of the lie detector reveal about the relationship between psychology, science, and public trust?

Suggested Reading

Alder, K. (2002). A social history of untruth: Lie detection and trust in twentieth-century America, *Representations, 80*(1), 1–33. https://doi.org/10.1525/rep.2002.80.1.1.

Alder, K. (2007). *The Lie Detectors: The history of an American obsession*. New York: Free Press.

Balmer, A. S., & Sandland, R. (2012). Making monsters: The polygraph, the plethysmograph, and other practices for the performance of abnormal sexuality. *Journal of Law and Society, 39*(4), 593–615. https://doi.org/10.1111/j.1467-6478.2012.00601.x.

Balmer, A. S. (2018). *Lie Detection and the Law: Torture, technology and truth*. Abingdon, Oxon: Routledge.

Bunn, G. C. (2007). Spectacular science: The lie detector's ambivalent powers. *History of Psychology, 10*(2), 156–178. https://doi.org/10.1037/1093-4510.10.2.156.

Bunn, G. C. (2012). *The Truth Machine: A social history of the lie detector*. Baltimore, MD: Johns Hopkins University Press.

Bunn, G. C. (2019). 'Supposing that truth is a woman, what then?': The lie detector, the love machine, and the logic of fantasy. *History of the Human Sciences, 32*(5), 135–163. https://doi.org/10.1177/0952695119867022.

Derksen, M. (2012). Control and resistance in the psychology of lying. *Theory & Psychology, 22*(2), 196–212. https://doi.org/10.1177/0959354311427487.

Foucault, M. (1980). *Power/Knowledge: Selected interviews and other writings 1972–1977* (C. Gordon, Ed.). New York: Pantheon.

Littlefield, M. M. (2011). *The Lying Brain: Lie detection in science and science fiction*. Ann Arbor: University of Michigan Press.

Scott, P., & von Unger, H. (2021). Discourses on im/migrants, ethnic minorities, and infectious disease: Fifty years of tuberculosis reporting in the United Kingdom. *History of the Human Sciences, 35*(1), 189–215. https://doi.org/10.1177/09526951211015886.

Sims-Schouten, W., Riley, S. C. E., & Willig, C. (2007). Critical realism in discourse analysis: A presentation of a systematic method of analysis using women's talk of motherhood, childcare and female employment as an example. *Theory & Psychology, 17*(1), 101–124. https://doi.org/10.1177/0959354307073153.

Viner, R. (1996). Melanie Klein and Anna Freud: The discourse of the early dispute. *Journal of the History of the Behavioural Sciences, 32*(1), 4–15. https://doi.org/10.1002/(SICI)1520-6696(199601)32:1<4::AID-JHBS1>3.0.CO;2-Y.

Key Terms

Disciplinary Power Power enacted through institutional surveillance, regulation, and correction, such as in the prison, the clinic, or the police station.

Discourse A system of language, symbols, and practices that shapes how we understand, talk about, and act upon the world, including what counts as truth, knowledge, and authority.

Discourse Analysis A method of critical inquiry that examines how meanings, subject positions, and power relations are constructed and contested through language and symbolic practices.

Ideological Dilemma A contradictory or tension-laden feature of discourse where conflicting beliefs or values are naturalised and made to coexist.

Interpretative Repertoire A recurring set of metaphors, narratives, and linguistic resources used to describe or explain a phenomenon, often revealing cultural assumptions.

Mechanical Objectivity The belief that machines or instruments can produce unbiased, neutral knowledge free from human interpretation or error.

Pastoral Power A form of power concerned with care, guidance, and emotional truth-telling, often associated with therapeutic or intimate contexts.

Polygraph Also known as the lie detector, a device developed in the early twentieth century to measure physiological responses such as blood pressure and respiration, believed to indicate deception.

Spectacular Power The symbolic and theatrical dimension of power, where authority is reinforced through visual display, drama, and cultural representation.

Subject Position The socially and discursively constructed role a person occupies within a given context, such as 'expert examiner', 'suspect', or 'truth machine'.

FREE INSTRUCTOR & STUDENT RESOURCES

ONLINE RESOURCES

Visit the Instructor & Student Resources website at routledgelearning.com/bpscoretextbooks for free digital resources, including:

- Interactive quizzes and flashcards to test your knowledge
- Links to useful websites and videos
- Instructor manual, lecture slides, and course guide to enhance teaching and save instructors time

9 Into the Dome

The Material Culture of Child Psychology

Chapter Overview

This chapter explores the material foundations of developmental psychology, focusing on how tools, technologies, and objects have shaped our understanding of the child. Beginning with a vivid historical case, namely the use of Arnold Gesell's photographic dome at Yale, it examines how supposedly neutral scientific environments actively produce psychological knowledge. By following the history of cots, domes, toys, observation rooms, standardised tests, and other artefacts, the chapter shows that developmental psychology is not only theoretical but fundamentally material. Figures such as Margaret Lowenfeld, John Bowlby, and Kenneth and Mamie Clark are discussed in terms of the physical cultures they created around children. The chapter introduces the critical thinking tool of material culture, highlighting how instruments of observation shape what development means. Drawing on epistemological, ontological, and power-based critiques, the chapter considers how norms of childhood have been constructed through selective sampling, biopolitical agendas, and assumptions about race, gender, and class. Ultimately, the chapter encourages students to see developmental psychology not as a passive window onto childhood but as an active participant in constructing what childhood is and ought to be.

Into the Dome

On 17 May 1927, four-week-old Edward Calhoun was carried in his mother's arms into a steel and glass hemispheric dome at the heart of Yale University's Psycho-Clinic. From the outside, the dome looked like a futuristic observatory: smooth, sealed, and silent. From the inside, it was a dazzling theatre of light and surveillance. The walls were curved inwards like a planetarium, the lighting artificially suffused to mimic daylight. In the centre was a cot, precisely marked to ensure identical object placement for every infant who would follow. Two hidden cameras, outside the dome, tracked the baby's every gesture. A small team of observers, along with Edward's mother, now separated from her child behind a specially constructed one-way screen, watched what they believed was natural, unguarded behaviour. A man with white hair and wearing a white coat greeted the child with a whisper: 'Teddy.'

The man was Dr Arnold Gesell, renowned child psychologist. He had designed the dome's austere architecture himself. This was no ordinary laboratory. It was an immersive environment designed for making normal development visible to science. Teddy was neither ill, troubled, nor abnormal. Quite the opposite. He had been chosen precisely because he was ordinary: white, healthy, and of middle-class

DOI: 10.4324/9781003565482-19

standing. In fact, he was the prototype for a new kind of scientific knowledge, a frame-by-frame record of normal development. The cameras rolled. Teddy reached for the toys. His mother, unseen behind the glass, looked on with a mixture of pride and apprehension. This was the first filmed trial in an ambitious programme to define the stages of normal child development. Was Teddy about to reveal a natural law of development? Or was the dome, and its cinematic staging and dramatic lighting, constructing the very norms it claimed to observe?

Chapter Contents

- The case study of Arnold Gesell's photographic dome as a material apparatus of developmental psychology.
- How objects, technologies, and settings, such as cots, toys, and observation rooms, shaped scientific views of the child.
- How material objects influence the conceptual frameworks of developmental psychology.

Chapter Objectives

- To introduce students to the material culture of developmental psychology and its influence on theory and method.
- To examine key historical figures and technologies that have shaped how childhood is scientifically understood.
- To apply the critical thinking tool of material culture to understand the history of child psychology.

CRITICAL THINKING TOOL
MATERIAL CULTURE

The history of developmental psychology is often told as a sequential narrative of evolving theories, pioneering experiments, and influential figures. Yet, this traditional account risks overlooking a crucial, tangible dimension that profoundly shaped this enterprise: *material culture*. Far from being a mere backdrop or supporting prop, material culture, encompassing objects, spaces, and technologies, is an indispensable tool for critical thinking. This is particularly true for child psychology because infants and very young children are largely non-verbal or possess limited verbal ability. Researchers have consequently been obliged to follow a mimetic strategy, utilising familiar objects, such as toys and games and carefully constructed environments, as the primary means to observe, measure, and infer children's inner worlds, cognitive processes, and emotional states.

This obligation, however, had a profound unintended consequence: the very tools and techniques employed to study the non-verbal child came to exert a formative influence on how the child itself came to be conceptualised. Methodology shaped theory. Developmental psychology's material culture provides a compelling illustration of Gerd Gigerenzer's powerful 'tools-to-theories' argument that scientific instruments and methodologies do not merely *test* pre-existing theories but actively *shape* new theoretical metaphors and conceptualisations of the human being, or, in this case, human development. In examining objects such as observational tools, standardised tests, therapeutic toys, and surrogate mothers, we can see that these were not just aids to research. They helped shape core ideas about what a child *is*, embedding assumptions, biases, and power relations into the foundations of developmental psychology.

Introduction

Even before the advent of experimental psychology, material culture shaped the moral and cognitive landscape of childhood. Victorian schools, with their regimented rows of desks facing the teacher, high windows to prevent distraction, and austere interiors, were designed not only for instruction but for moral regulation. These spaces reflected a deeply held belief that the environment could instil discipline, respectability, and industriousness, qualities considered essential to the proper development of children. The schoolroom was a material technology for enacting the moral order. This chapter embarks on a critical exploration of the history of developmental psychology from this observation, employing material culture as its primary analytical framework.

From the earliest scientific observations to contemporary digital landscapes, the physical world has been an active participant in shaping psychological discourse, influencing research paradigms, and embodying society's values concerning children. We will explore how specific material artefacts, such as observational domes, standardised tests, therapeutic toys, and even the dolls used in groundbreaking studies about identity, actively co-constructed the very definitions of 'the child' and 'normal development'. This approach allows us to unearth the implicit biases, structures of power, and epistemological challenges woven into the fabric of developmental psychology, revealing the profound interplay between the material world, knowledge production, and the lived experiences of children across the twentieth century.

Historical Issues

The twentieth century witnessed transformative changes that profoundly influenced child development research, moving from largely anecdotal observations, such as those made by Charles Darwin about his own children in the late nineteenth century, to more systematic investigations. Early in the century, the burgeoning child study movement in the United States, spearheaded by figures such as G. Stanley Hall, began collecting vast amounts of data on children, often through questionnaires that were themselves material artefacts. This shift from anecdote to data aimed to bring scientific rigour to the understanding of childhood, departing from purely philosophical or pedagogical interests. The emergence of experimental psychology, with its emphasis on controlled environments and measurable phenomena, significantly impacted the tools and spaces used in child research. Laboratories became specialised material sites, designed to isolate variables and standardise observation.

Following the two World Wars, especially in the UK, a heightened awareness of children's welfare in the wake of widespread traumatic displacement spurred greater public and professional interest in children's development. This period saw the rise of studies of institutions, where the material conditions of orphanages and hospitals became subjects of intense scrutiny, directly influencing theories of attachment and early care. Concurrently, the postwar economic boom in both countries fuelled a consumer culture that increasingly targeted children, creating a vast industry of toys, books, and media, a material culture that profoundly shaped childhood experiences and became new sites of psychological inquiry. The latter half of the century witnessed criticisms concerning the pernicious effects of comic books and television on impressionable minds. Throughout these shifts, material objects and research spaces actively framed and shaped research questions, methodologies, and prevailing conceptions of childhood.

Key Individuals

Arnold Gesell (1880–1961) believed that children underwent an innate developmental sequence. His most iconic material contribution was the Gesell Dome, a specially designed one-way observation environment that allowed researchers to observe children without being seen themselves. The Dome embodied Gesell's epistemological commitment to objective observation, seeking to minimise external interference and reveal the 'natural' unfolding of developmental stages. Crucially, Gesell extensively utilised filming technology to capture precise, sequential developmental milestones. The use of film to record and analyse these behaviours, facilitated by the controlled environment of the Gesell Dome and standardised test materials, directly contributed to Gesell's view of development as an orderly, predetermined, and *filmic progression* of innate maturational stages. The measurement tool became the metaphor for the developmental process.

Margaret Lowenfeld (1890–1973) developed material tools with which to understand and communicate with children in a therapeutic context. Frustrated by the limitations of talking therapies, Lowenfeld introduced her 'World Technique' in the 1930s. This involved a large, rectangular sand tray and a collection of miniature objects such as toy figures, animals, buildings, and natural features which children could imagine and build their own 'worlds' with. These objects expressed the child's symbolic language, a tangible medium through which children could communicate their inner emotional landscapes, conflicts, and experiences that words often failed to capture. The open-ended, symbolic nature of the sand tray led Lowenfeld to conceptualise the child's psyche as a complex, dynamic, and symbolically expressive world that could be actively constructed and explored through material means, a clear instance of her tools shaping her understanding of the child.

Lev Vygotsky (1896–1934) profoundly influenced developmental psychology in Europe and North America, particularly through his emphasis on the role of culture and social interaction. For Vygotsky, development was fundamentally mediated, not just by social interaction but critically by tools, both material (e.g. a hammer or an abacus) and psychological (such as language and symbols). He argued that human beings transform their environment and themselves using these tools. Vygotsky's emphasis on material and psychological tools as mediators of action and thought led him to the theory of the child as fundamentally a *socio-cultural being*, whose mind and development are actively constructed through purposeful interaction with culturally shaped material artefacts. The very tools children learn to manipulate and the cultural artefacts they engage with are seen as constitutive of their developing cognitive processes and identity.

Jean Piaget (1896–1980) likewise relied heavily on material interaction. Piaget's ingenious experiments often involved children manipulating simple, everyday objects such as blocks, water containers of different shapes, clay, marbles, and coins. These materials were carefully chosen for their ecological validity and their evident ability to reveal children's underlying cognitive structures and logical operations. Piaget's conservation tasks, involving the pouring of water between differently shaped glasses, or the rearrangement of objects, directly utilised the physical properties of these items to probe children's understanding of quantity and invariance. Piaget's experimental design, which relied on children's active manipulation of simple, everyday objects to reveal their reasoning, shaped his view of the child as an *active constructor of knowledge*, whose cognitive development unfolds through stages characterised by evolving logical operations performed through interaction with the material world.

Kenneth (1914–2005) and Mamie Phipps (1917–1983) Clark conducted groundbreaking research that compellingly demonstrated the psychological harm of racial segregation, using material culture as their central investigative tool. Their iconic doll studies involved presenting Black children with both black and white dolls and asking them questions about racial preference and self-identification. The dolls were potent material artefacts that served as direct mirrors for children's racial perceptions and internalised self-esteem. The children's responses, frequently showing a preference for the white dolls and attributing negative characteristics to the black dolls, provided tangible, observable evidence of the psychologically damaging effects of growing up in a racist society. The Clarks' use of these racially differentiated dolls as direct probes led them to conceptualise the child's ethnic identity as a deeply socially and materially constructed aspect of being, vulnerable to the damaging impact of negative cultural representations found in their material world.

John Bowlby (1907–1990), the architect of attachment theory, developed his ideas largely in response to the profound impact of material deprivation on children's emotional development during the Second World War. His early work involved observing children in institutional settings such as orphanages, hospitals, and residential nurseries whose very architecture and lack of personalised material possessions were central to his observations. The absence of stable, individualised material environments (such as a familiar bed, or personal toys and clothes) was inextricably linked to the emotional distress and developmental difficulties he documented. Bowlby's theory emphasised the child's need for a secure base, a concept rooted in the consistent presence of a caregiver and, by extension, a predictable, nurturing material environment. Bowlby's observations of children in materially deprived and unstable institutional environments moved him to articulate a theory where the child is fundamentally a relational being, whose healthy emotional development is contingent upon a secure, consistent bond.

Mary Ainsworth (1913–1999), a key collaborator with Bowlby, designed the influential 'Strange Situation' procedure to empirically test attachment theory. A masterclass in the deliberate use of material culture to elicit specific behaviour, the 'Strange Situation' was a meticulously designed laboratory environment. The layout of the room, the specific chairs for the parent and stranger, and crucially the selection of toys available for the child to explore, were all carefully chosen material elements. The systematic presence and absence of the caregiver, and the introduction of a stranger, were choreographed interactions within this fixed material and mimetic space. The child's interaction with the available toys during the parent's absence and return, and their use of the physical space of the room, were central to the classification of their attachment style. Ainsworth's 'Strange Situation' enabled her to conceptualise the child as possessing distinct, observable attachment 'styles', revealing individual differences in security of emotional connection expressed through interaction patterns during separation and reunion.

Epistemological Issues

In the history of child development, material culture provides a useful lens through which to critically examine epistemological questions. The very tools and apparatus psychologists used actively shaped what could be observed and, consequently, what counted as knowledge. For example, Gesell's pursuit of objective observation was deeply embedded in the design of the Gesell Dome and the use of one-way mirrors, filming equipment, and the temporary removal of the mother from her child. These material devices were intended to minimise experimenter bias and capture 'pure' behaviour, yet they simultaneously imposed a highly controlled, artificial environment, raising questions about the ecological validity of the protocol. Such procedures, being inherently limited or biased by their design, invariably influenced the scope and nature of the resulting knowledge.

The drive for standardisation, evident in the widespread use of normalised tests, developmental scales, and diagnostic manuals (all material artefacts), also profoundly impacted epistemology. These printed, codified materials created uniform methods for data collection, supposedly enhancing reliability and comparability. However, they also established specific criteria for 'normal' development, subtly defining who counted as 'typical' and who might be regarded as abnormal. The laboratory itself, as a physical space, embodied a particular epistemological commitment to controlled experimentation, often privileging quantitative data and experimental manipulation over qualitative observation in naturalistic settings. By critically examining these material dimensions, we can assess the validity, biases, and inherent limitations of the knowledge claims made throughout the history of child psychology, recognising that the medium of knowledge production inevitably shapes the message.

Ontological Issues

Material culture is a fundamental tool for critically understanding the history of child and developmental psychology. By shifting our gaze from abstract theories to the concrete objects, spaces, and technologies of childhood and its study, we can generate a richer, more nuanced historical narrative. The true force of this approach lies in its ability to reveal how the material culture of developmental psychology directly influenced how researchers came to see the ontology of child development itself. The history of developmental psychology is a compelling example of Gigerenzer's argument that the instruments and environments used to gather knowledge not only shape the nature of the knowledge produced but also inform the theoretical concepts used to make ontological claims.

Gesell's reliance on filming technology as a mode of investigation directly contributed to his conceptualisation of development. By capturing and analysing developmental sequences frame-by-frame, Gesell and his researchers came to see development as an orderly, predetermined, and filmic progression of innate maturational stages. The Dome's capacity for sequential capture became the theory's inherent structure.

Margaret Lowenfeld's open-ended World Technique sand tray fostered an ontology where the child's psyche was seen as a complex, dynamic, and symbolically expressive world that could be actively constructed through material means. Likewise, Vygotsky's emphasis on material and psychological tools led him to an ontology where the child is fundamentally a socio-cultural being, whose mind is constructed through interaction with culturally shaped artefacts. Piaget's experiments with simple, manipulable objects shaped his concept of the child as an active constructor of knowledge, whose cognitive development unfolds through engagement with the material world.

The Clarks' use of racially differentiated dolls inspired their theory that racial identity was a deeply socially and materially constructed aspect of being, vulnerable to cultural representations. Bowlby's observations in materially deprived institutional environments led him to a view of the child as a relational being, reliant on consistent material surroundings for secure attachment. Ainsworth's meticulously controlled 'Strange Situation' laboratory setup enabled her to conceptualise distinct attachment styles and emotional connections expressed through structured material interaction in the laboratory that mimicked the world outside.

Power

Power, in the context of developmental psychology, is intrinsically linked to material culture, manifesting in who defines, controls, and benefits from the objects and environments that shape children's lives and their study. One key aspect is the power of expertise. Psychologists gain authority through their ability to design, produce, market, and disseminate specific research tools, diagnostic materials, and therapeutic interventions. The creation and widespread adoption of a standardised test, for example, grants immense power to its creators to define 'normal' and 'abnormal' development, influencing educational policy and clinical practice. The very architecture and design of clinics and university laboratories physically embody this professional authority, establishing spaces where specific types of knowledge are sanctioned and produced.

The history of child development is also entangled with the logics of biopower, a concept articulated by Michel Foucault, which describes the strategic management of population health through the pervasive regulation of individual bodies and capacities. Within this framework, developmental psychology has often positioned the child not merely as an object of care or curiosity, but as a critical carrier of the 'race' or nation, a biological vessel through which the future health, intelligence, and moral fitness of a population are perceived to be secured. The meticulous observation and categorisation of children thus became integral to broader societal projects of optimising human potential.

This entanglement is starkly evident in the work of figures such as Arnold Gesell. As a pioneer of normative developmental schedules, Gesell's scientific endeavour was rooted in a commitment to identifying and charting typical developmental trajectories. Gesell was also a committed eugenicist, aligning his work with the widespread early twentieth-century movement aimed at 'improving' the human gene pool. He believed in the importance of understanding and, where possible, promoting so-called superior traits through early psychological observation. His meticulously designed Gesell Dome, a tool for purportedly neutral scientific observation, was a component of a broader biopolitical project to survey, measure, and ultimately optimise human potential by identifying developmental 'deviations' that might signal 'unfit' individuals. Gesell's work, through its very methods of precise measurement and categorisation, contributed to the establishment of developmental benchmarks that implicitly defined what was desirable or undesirable in a population, laying groundwork for interventions aimed at managing human traits.

The influence of biopolitical thought extended even to therapeutic innovations within the field. Margaret Lowenfeld, known for her humanistic approaches and material-based therapies such as the World Technique, had a direct familial connection to prominent figures in population planning. Her sister, Helena Wright, was a highly influential British physician and a leading advocate for birth control and family planning, notably involved in the establishment of the International Planned Parenthood Federation. These familial and ideological proximities underscore how developmental psychology, even in its most humanistic or therapeutic forms, existed within and could inadvertently contribute to the broader realm of biopolitical governance.

Chapter Summary

This chapter has demonstrated that material culture is a fundamental tool for critically understanding the history of developmental psychology. By shifting our gaze from abstract theories to the concrete objects, spaces, and technologies of childhood and its study, we unveil a richer, more nuanced historical narrative. The true force of this approach lies in its ability to reveal how the material culture of developmental psychology, its very epistemological devices, directly influenced how researchers came to see the ontology of human development itself. This resonates with the 'tools-to-theories' thesis, where the material cultures used to gather knowledge fundamentally shape the nature of the knowledge produced.

Perhaps nowhere is this more hauntingly visible than in the image of the Gesell Dome: a stark, hemispherical bubble of one-way glass, behind which the child sits, plays, cries, or fidgets, clearly visible to the scientific gaze. In 1927, a small boy named Edward became its first inhabitant, his every movement meticulously recorded by silent observers beyond the mirrored surface. Inside, the Dome transformed childhood into data; outside, it turned psychologists into disembodied eyes, detached, clinical, and omnipresent. The Dome was an architecture of surveillance, a technology for gathering developmental norms. It captured not only Edward's behaviour but also a vision of the child as a measurable, knowable, and ultimately governable being. The history of the Gesell Dome reminds us that material culture defines the very possibilities of what psychology can know, and indeed who we can become.

Reflective Questions

1. What role did the photographic dome play in shaping the concept of 'normal' child development?
2. How does the idea of 'tools-to-theories' challenge traditional views of objectivity in developmental psychology?

3. In what ways can developmental psychology be seen as a form of biopower?
4. How have material objects such as toys or test kits embodied assumptions about gender, class, or race?
5. What lessons can be drawn from historical practices in child psychology for today's digital tools for child monitoring and assessment?

Suggested Reading

Bultman, S. (2020). Seeing inside the child: The Rorschach inkblot test as assessment technique in a girls' reform school, 1938–1948. *History of Psychology, 23*(4), 312–332. https://doi.org/10.1037/hop0000167.

Burman, E. (2017). *Deconstructing Developmental Psychology* (Third ed.). Abingdon, Oxon: Routledge, Taylor & Francis Group.

Gigerenzer, G. (1992). Discovery in cognitive psychology: New tools inspire new theories. *Science in Context, 5*(2), 329–350. https://doi.org/10.1017/S0269889700001216.

Harris, B. (2011). Arnold Gesell's progressive vision: Child hygiene, socialism and eugenics. *History of Psychology, 14*(3), 311–334. https://doi.org/10.1037/a0024797.

Moro, C. (2016). To encounter, to build the world and to become a human being. Advocating for a material-cultural turn in developmental psychology. *Integrative Psychological and Behavioral Science, 50*(4), 586–602. https://doi.org/10.1007/s12124-016-9356-4.

Ossmer, C. (2020). Normal development: The photographic dome and the children of the Yale Psycho-Clinic. *Isis, 111*(3), 515–541. https://doi.org/10.1086/711127.

Ratcliff, M. J. (2024). Jean Piaget and the autonomous disciples, Alina Szeminska and Bärbel Inhelder: From the 'critical method' to the appropriation of research culture. *History of Psychology, 27*(4), 317–332. https://doi.org/10.1037/hop0000261.

Rietmann, F. E. (2023). Mother-blaming revisited: Gender, cinematography, and infant research in the heyday of psychoanalysis. *History of the Human Sciences, 37*(2), 87–116. https://doi.org/10.1177/09526951231187556.

Rowold, K. (2024). Child psychology from Vienna to London: Charlotte Bühler, concepts of childhood, and parenting advice in interwar Britain. *History of the Human Sciences, 38*(1), 3–25. https://doi.org/10.1177/09526951241289028.

Sims-Schouten, W. (2021). 'A troublesome girl is pushed through': Morality, biological determinism, resistance, resilience, and the Canadian child migration schemes, 1883–1939. *History of the Human Sciences, 35*(1), 87–110. https://doi.org/10.1177/09526951211036553.

Skagius, P. (2019). Brains and psyches: Child psychological and psychiatric expertise in a Swedish newspaper, 1980–2008. *History of the Human Sciences, 32*(3), 76–99. https://doi.org/10.1177/0952695118810284.

van der Horst, F. C. P., van Rosmalen, L., & van der Veer, R. (2019). Research notes: John Bowlby's critical evaluation of the work of René Spitz. *History of Psychology, 22*(2), 205–208. https://doi.org/10.1037/hop0000127b.

Key Terms

Biopower A term from Michel Foucault, referring to the ways modern institutions manage populations through the regulation of bodies, health, and development—often by defining what is 'normal'.

Developmental Psychology The field of psychology focused on how humans grow and change across the lifespan, particularly in childhood and adolescence.

Developmental Schedule A standardised timeline outlining the expected milestones in a child's cognitive, physical, and emotional growth, often based on selective data.

Material Culture The physical objects, tools, and spaces through which psychological knowledge is created, observed, and reproduced.

Normativity The cultural and scientific process of defining what is typical, healthy, or desirable, often disguising power and bias as objectivity.

Observational Science A branch of psychology that relies on structured, often technologically mediated, observation of behaviour to draw conclusions about mental life.

Photographic Dome A specially designed dome-shaped observation chamber developed by Arnold Gesell at Yale to film and analyse infant behaviour in a controlled setting.

Play Therapy A psychological approach that uses toys and play as a medium for understanding and treating children's emotional and developmental issues.

Surrogate Mother An artificial or substitute maternal figure used in psychological experiments, especially those testing attachment and dependency in Harlow's infant primate studies.

Tools-to-Theories A concept introduced by Gerd Gigerenzer, describing how the instruments used in psychological research often influence or shape the theories that emerge from that research.

FREE INSTRUCTOR & STUDENT RESOURCES

ONLINE RESOURCES

Visit the Instructor & Student Resources website at routledgelearning.com/bpscoretextbooks for free digital resources, including:

- Interactive quizzes and flashcards to test your knowledge
- Links to useful websites and videos
- Instructor manual, lecture slides, and course guide to enhance teaching and save instructors time

20

A Most Haunted House

Parapsychology's Boundary-work

Chapter Overview

This chapter explores the haunted margins of psychology by tracing its complex and often contradictory relationship with parapsychology. Using the concept of 'boundary-work' as its tool for critical thinking, the chapter investigates how psychology has historically defined itself by what it excludes, particularly the paranormal. Through compelling case studies, including Borley Rectory and the medium Leonora Piper, the chapter examines how psychology's scientific identity has been shaped by the very phenomena it seeks to dismiss. It offers a historical analysis from the late nineteenth century until after the Second World War, revealing shifting attitudes toward apparitions, telepathy, and extrasensory perception. Alongside biographical sketches of key figures such as Frederic Myers, William James, J. B. Rhine, and Carl Jung, the chapter interrogates the epistemological, ontological, and power dynamics that underpin psychology's disciplinary boundaries. Ultimately, it argues that parapsychology has functioned as a kind of 'constitutive other' for psychology: never fully accepted, yet never entirely absent, and often responsible for shaping the very tools and methods of psychological science.

A Most Haunted House

On 12 June 1929, Harry Price, charismatic, controversial, and already something of a showman in psychical research circles, arrived at a red-brick Victorian house nestled in a quiet Essex village. Built in 1862, Borley Rectory had already acquired whispers of a reputation. Price's arrival turned it into a national conversation. He brought with him thermographs, cameras, spirit-writing planchettes, and a keen eye for a spectacle. What followed was a flurry of dramatic claims: unexplained footsteps echoing in empty halls, ghostly coaches glimpsed in the moonlight, cryptic messages scrawled by unseen hands, and above all, the apparition of a sorrowful nun said to have been entombed in the cellar walls. Price documented these phenomena in vivid detail, claiming to have physical and photographic evidence, and fed it all to a hungry press. Borley, he declared, was the most haunted house in England. But scientific renown, like a séance, can quickly sour into suspicion. As Price's stories grew more elaborate, members of the Society for Psychical Research, the organisation founded to study such anomalies, began to grow uneasy. Questions were raised about his methods, his interpretations, even his honesty. After his death in 1948, the SPR launched a full re-investigation, culminating in the infamous *Borley Report*. It accused Price of methodological negligence, selective reporting, and possibly outright deception. Once-hailed evidence was reclassified as coincidence, hoax, or error. The Rectory was reimagined, not as

DOI: 10.4324/9781003565482-20

a site of paranormal eruption but as a psychological case study in suggestibility, credulity, and the mechanics of belief. The Borley Rectory affair thus became more than a ghost story. It was a drama about scientific identity, staged on the contested boundary between psychology and parapsychology. At its heart was a deeper anxiety: about what kinds of things could be studied, what kinds of knowledge could be trusted, and how a science built on the invisible could protect itself from becoming indistinguishable from illusion. Borley Rectory came to embody the uneasy spectrality of psychology itself: forever negotiating what counts as legitimate knowledge and what does not.

Chapter Contents

- Traces the historical relationship between psychology and parapsychology, focusing on three key periods of boundary negotiation.
- Profiles key individuals, including William James, J. B. Rhine, and Leonora Piper, to illustrate how psychological knowledge was produced, resisted, and shaped.
- Introduces the critical thinking tool of 'boundary-work' to explore how psychology defines legitimate knowledge by excluding the paranormal.

Chapter Objectives

- To examine how parapsychology has historically challenged and shaped the scientific identity of psychology.
- To evaluate the epistemological, ontological, and power issues involved in excluding certain phenomena and individuals from mainstream psychology.
- To understand and apply the concept of 'boundary-work' as a critical tool for analysing how disciplines protect, patrol, and perform their limits.

TOOLS FOR CRITICAL THINKING
BOUNDARY-WORK

The history of psychology cannot be fully understood without examining how it defines what belongs inside the discipline, and what must be excluded. The concept of *boundary-work*, developed by sociologist Thomas Gieryn, refers to the rhetorical, institutional, and methodological labour that disciplines undertake to mark out the limits of legitimate knowledge. For psychology, these boundaries have shifted over time, reflecting not only changing theories and methods but also broader cultural anxieties about what counts as rational, scientific, and acceptable data.

Parapsychology is the study of phenomena such as telepathy, apparitions, precognition, and hauntings. The discipline occupies a particularly provocative place in the process of demarcating between truth and error. From the late nineteenth century onwards, psychology has often defined itself against the paranormal, portraying psychical research as unscientific,

superstitious, or credulous. And yet, paradoxically, this act of exclusion has been deeply productive. In its effort to distance itself from the paranormal, psychology has developed many of the very features it associates with scientific legitimacy: experimental control, statistical inference, randomisation, and replicability. The paranormal has thus operated as what historians of science sometimes call a 'constitutive other', a domain that psychology needs in order to articulate what it is *not*. This chapter demonstrates that the line between science and non-science is historically contingent, and often haunted by the very phenomena it tries to exclude.

Introduction

Psychology, from its earliest incarnations, was never an orderly affair. It was born not in the glare of pure reason but in a dimly lit parlour, half laboratory, half séance, where the empirical and the uncanny brushed against one another like invisible presences. In 1886, the publication of *Phantasms of the Living* by The Society for Psychical Research offered more than just a catalogue of ghost stories. It was a bold attempt to summon the invisible into visibility, to gather apparitions and premonitions into the sphere of systematic inquiry. The book's authors, Frederic Myers, Henry Sidgwick, and Edmund Gurney, were prominent intellectuals, animated by the belief that consciousness itself might stretch across space, time, and death.

The early discipline was alive with such spectral possibilities. William James, ever the philosophical medium, channelled radical empiricism into a form of intellectual clairvoyance, seeing value in phenomena others dismissed as noise. He studied mediums as conduits, liminal figures through whom new models of mind might emerge. To James, psychology was not merely a science of observable behaviour but a field charged with latent energy, flickering at the edges of the measurable.

But over time, this openness became a site of disturbance. Psychology, increasingly anxious to secure its place among the sciences, began a quiet exorcism. Apparitions were reclassified as hallucinations, telepathy as error, spiritual phenomena as delusion. The once-invited spirits of inquiry were banished. Yet something lingered. The field continued to be haunted by the subliminal, the anomalous, the excluded. Like ectoplasm, unpleasant traces remained.

Historical Issues

The boundary between psychology and the paranormal has always flickered and periodically shifted like a presence glimpsed in peripheral vision, always just at the edge of certainty. Across its history, psychology has performed a kind of disciplinary séance, invoking and then banishing the uncanny to affirm its scientific legitimacy. In this section, we trace three key historical phases: an early openness when the field was still in an ontological trance; a postwar demarcation, where experimental rigour became a tool of exorcism; and a late century scepticism, where the paranormal re-emerged as epistemological residue.

In its earliest phase in the late nineteenth century, psychology's identity was porous, its methods diverse, its ontology unsettled. Founders such as Frederic Myers and William James acted as mediums between traditions, transmitting ideas from philosophy, spiritualism, medicine, and theology. Founded in 1882, The Society for Psychical Research was a credible platform where topics such as spiritualism, theories of the subliminal self, telepathic communion, and the survival of consciousness after death were earnestly debated. Psychology during this era conducted something close to a séance with the unknown: willing to listen, to wait in the darkness, to treat the whisper as data. It was a period of ontological pluralism.

The Great War brought mass trauma and mass grief. Spiritualism surged as families sought contact with the dead, and psychology was asked to choose sides. The newly professionalised discipline, now associated with laboratories, universities, and a growing anxiety about legitimacy, responded with sceptical solemnity. The behaviourists launched a full-blown exorcism: no more introspective ghosts, no subliminal selves, no paranormal leaks from mind to world. Consciousness was shackled to stimulus and response. What could not be operationalised was swiftly dematerialised during this shift towards methodological demarcation.

In this effort to confine the psychological to the visible, new methodological forces stirred. J. B. Rhine's experiments in extrasensory perception at Duke University, using Zener cards, randomisation protocols, and statistical significance thresholds, were attempts to bring clairvoyance under laboratory control. In doing so, Rhine's lab unwittingly conjured some of the future tools of mainstream psychological science. The boundary may have closed, but its contours were etched by the very phenomena it sought to repel.

In the postwar years, parapsychology, now marginalised in the academy, resurfaced in the cultural unconscious: in film, in television, in Cold War research into mind control, telekinesis, spoon-bending, and remote viewing. Psychology, meanwhile, had entered its cognitive phase, cautiously returning to the terrain of mind and belief. But now, the paranormal was processed as pathology: apparitions became perceptual errors; mediumship, a dissociative coping mechanism; haunting, an unresolved trauma.

Key Individuals

Frederic Myers (1843–1901) is a ghostly presence in the history of psychology. A founding member of The Society for Psychical Research, he was deeply invested in the subliminal, those buried, disarticulated aspects of mind that might surface through dreams, trance states, séances, or telepathy (a term he coined). He conceived of the self as an open channel, susceptible to distant impressions and ancestral memories. Myers theorised the psyche as an apparition-producing system. Though his work was later eclipsed, it never completely vanished, continuing to influence conceptions of unconscious life.

Leonora Piper (1857–1950) was a Boston-born trance medium whose apparent communications with the dead captivated and confounded the leading psychologists and psychical researchers of the late nineteenth and early twentieth centuries. She was studied extensively by figures such as William James and Oliver Lodge, and her séances became a testing ground for the boundary between psychology and spiritualism. Piper became a subject of long-term experimental observation by The Society for Psychical Research in both the United States and UK. Her trance states, spirit 'controls', and messages from beyond the grave were treated by researchers as legitimate data. Under the gaze of science, Piper remained a passive subject rather than a co-creator of knowledge. Her life highlights how women could be central to the production of psychological insight while being structurally excluded from its authorship.

William James (1842–1910) was a philosopher of haunted boundaries. In his investigation of mediumship, especially the case of Leonora Piper, James displayed an almost extrasensory attunement to anomaly. He was less concerned with proving the existence of spirits than with challenging psychology's refusal to see what was already there, treating psychic experiences as having an uncanny validity. James operated like a kind of academic remote viewer: scanning the outer limits of experience to bring back intelligence that the central command of psychology would later disavow.

William McDougall (1871–1938) occupied a more conflicted role. His early work on instinct and volition had offered a spirited resistance to behaviourist reductionism. At Duke University, he acted as the telekinetic link between psychology and parapsychology (a term he coined), lending institutional weight to Rhine's early ESP research. Yet McDougall always walked a delicate line: he supported anomalous inquiry, such as studies into Lamarckian inheritance, without ever fully crossing over into the supernatural. He was, in effect, a controlled dissociator, holding opposing beliefs in tension without collapsing into contradiction.

Carl Jung (1875–1961) opened a wormhole in the psychological cosmos. His theory of synchronicity was an 'acausal connecting principle' that allowed for meaningful coincidences. Jung's ontology was never rigid. For him, the psyche extended beyond the body, weaving together archetypes, dreams, the distant past, and inexplicable but meaningful chance events. He was haunted by alchemy, painting mandalas, consulting the I Ching, and encountering what he described as spirits during his famed *Red Book* period of spiritual crisis.

J. B. Rhine (1895–1980) is perhaps the most remarkable conjurer of credibility in the history of parapsychology. Through methodical experimentation and the development of tools such as Zener cards, Rhine sought to give form to the formless, to record the intangible, to map the mind's extrasensory reach. His laboratory was a careful attempt to measure the unmeasurable, extrasensory perception (a term he coined). And yet, despite his devotion to scientific rigour, Rhine remained a marginal figure, a spectre lingering in the shadows of institutional respectability.

Epistemological Issues

Psychological evidence is materialised, interpreted, filtered, and at times dismissed like a suspect voice in a darkened room. The history of parapsychology throws this into stark relief. No other domain of psychology has so persistently tested the limits of what psychologists are willing to recognise as data; no other field so vividly exposes the conventions, rituals, and taboos of psychological science. In its attempts to capture the invisible, parapsychology has inadvertently revealed the apparatus of exclusion: a kind of epistemological séance in which some voices are invited to speak in the room, while others are left knocking from the other side of the door.

In the nineteenth century, evidence was broad and inclusive. Testimony, introspection, and case reports were quite admissible. When Frederic Myers or William James recounted a dream, a premonition, or a moment of telepathic impression, it was treated as meaningful data. These early psychologists were surveyors of the soul: reviewing meaning from fleeting impressions, strange coincidences, and the psychic residue of the dead.

But by the early twentieth century, psychology had begun a process of epistemic exorcism. The ghosts were still there but the rules had changed. Behaviourism demanded clean lines, repeatability, quantification. Apparitions, trances, and out-of-body phenomena were uninvited spirits, reclassified as inadmissible. The shift was methodological and metaphysical. What was no longer experimentally testable was deemed no longer real.

Yet in trying to banish the paranormal, mainstream psychology found itself drawing on its tools. J. B. Rhine developed randomisation protocols to avoid unconscious influence, double-blind designs to eliminate telepathic leakage, and significance testing to detect patterns invisible to chance. Rhine was inventing the conditions under which ESP might be demonstrated. His experiments, however contested, brought statistical inference into mainstream psychology. After Rhine, psychologists no longer sought to prove the reality of anomalous phenomena but to explain their persistence in belief. The question shifted from 'Is this real?' to 'Why do people believe this is real?' In this reframing, the paranormal became a fog of biases, heuristics, perceptual errors, and false memories that distorted rational thought.

Ontological Issues

Psychology has always had an uneasy relationship with the unseen. The science of mind has long policed the borders of what kinds of minds, what kinds of realities, and what kinds of evidence it will admit. Parapsychology, as both a domain and a provocation, exposes psychology's ontological fault lines. It asks questions concerning what kinds of things we are allowed to imagine exist. And it reminds us that exclusion is an ontological performance: a sealing of portals, a refusal to let in certain entities.

In the late nineteenth century, figures such as Frederic Myers theorised the subliminal self as literal structure, something porous, multileveled, and open to influence from beyond. The psyche could receive distant impressions, host apparitions, or become the site of possession. This was an age of ontological openness: trances, automatisms, séances, and telepathic exchanges were treated as clues to a larger, stranger reality. The unconscious was not yet domesticated. It shimmered with mystery, haunted by archetypal memories not of one's own.

Then came the great closing of the doors. In the interwar period, the rise of behaviourism, and later cognitive science, reduced the self to a set of mechanisms and rules. Minds became machines, and the soul was not exorcised so much as bureaucratically reassigned, marked as 'non-observable', filed under 'subjective', quietly dismissed. Apparitions were reinterpreted as hallucinations, mediumship as dissociation, synchronicity as mere coincidence after all. The psyche was pulled back into the body, tethered to the nervous system, stripped of clairvoyance.

Yet the boundaries never held completely. Carl Jung, with his doctrine of synchronicity, insisted that causality was not the only thread connecting events, that meaning could leak between minds and world like a cold draught under a locked door. Psychoanalysts offered cold readings of uncanny poltergeist phenomena, suggesting that the noisy spirits haunting family homes might in fact be unconscious traumas made kinetic, psychic wounds expressed through crashing plates and inexplicable cold spots. In this vision, the poltergeist was a psychological entity, still ghostly but now a function of repression rather than death.

Contemporary psychology, in contrast, tends to tolerate the paranormal only as epistemic error. Ghosts are perceptual illusions. Telepathy is pattern-matching. Out-of-body experiences are neural failures of proprioception. The phenomena may be reported but their reality is not entertained. The haunted house is still studied, but only as a theatre of suggestibility, group dynamics, sleep paralysis, cognitive error, or electro-magnetic warping. And yet the paranormal persists: in popular culture, clinical encounters, dreams, family stories, and sudden moments of inexplicable intuition. Psychology's ontology, for all its claims of closure, remains riddled with cracks. Experiences seep in through those gaps, bringing an uncanny sense of unease.

Power

The boundary between psychology and parapsychology has always been more than a line on a map. It is a contested frontier patrolled by institutions, reputations, and ideological gatekeepers, a space where careers can be made or destroyed, where scientific identities must be fiercely defended against contamination. To believe, or to appear to believe, in the paranormal has often been to risk a kind of intellectual possession by stigma, derision, and disciplinary exile.

From the beginning, psychical researchers walked this line. They occupied a space between the drawing room and the laboratory, between séance and symposium. Their methods were often rigorous, their intentions sincere. But the legitimacy they sought was elusive. The Society for Psychical Research attempted to base its investigations on methodological clarity, but it was frequently cast in the role of the mesmerist's apprentice, entertaining illusions, consorting with the irrational. The more it tried to summon credibility, the more it found itself surrounded by sceptics.

The spectacle of the paranormal also intersects with the politics of belief. Gender, class, and cultural capital all shape who gets to see spirits and who gets to study them. Mediums were often working-class women; their voices were filtered through male investigators who transcribed, interpreted, and frequently pathologised. The paranormal became a site of projection: a space where anxieties about gender, race, and the irrational could be staged under the guise of neutral inquiry. In this way, the haunted house was always more than haunted, it was ideologically furnished.

Power also operates through what remains unpublished, what grants are denied, what doctoral projects are quietly redirected. J. B. Rhine himself was never discredited, but nor was he embraced. His ESP studies floated in disciplinary limbo: always almost legitimate, never quite institutionalised. Ultimately, the boundary between psychology and parapsychology has always been one of surveillance. Those who crossed it without permission were marked, sometimes indefinitely. And yet, those very borderlands have also produced methodological innovation, resilience, and the capacity to glimpse not only what is hidden but what has been wilfully forgotten.

Chapter Summary

Psychology, for all its ambitions to clarity and order, has always been shadowed by the uncanny. Even as it emerged to claim its status as a modern science, armed with statistical tests, experimental controls, and randomisation, it could never entirely silence the whispers from its own margins. Parapsychology, anomalous experiences, and psychical research were symptoms of a deeper uncertainty within the discipline itself: about the limits of perception, the reach of the psyche, and the nature of reality.

This chapter has traced the boundary-work psychology has undertaken to keep such phenomena outside its remit. It has exorcised ghosts, reclassified visions, and quarantined the inexplicable under the banners of delusion, error, and belief. And yet, the house remains haunted. The very act of exclusion leaves traces, residues of fascination, fragments of possibility, and, crucially, methods that persist long after their original subjects have been dismissed. In this way, psychology is not only haunted by the paranormal; it is partially built from it.

The return of the paranormal in new guises, such as dream research, anomalistic psychology, and cognitive explanations of belief, suggests that what has been repressed may sometimes return. Boundary-work is never finished. But the more carefully the line is drawn, the more it reveals the discipline's own haunted architecture: its discomfort with uncertainty, its longing for certainty, and its reliance on rituals of validation no less performative than the séances it once disavowed. Perhaps the most unsettling truth is one Harry Price perhaps glimpsed at the most haunted house in England: sometimes the ghosts we are searching for are ones we have made for ourselves.

Reflective Questions

1. How has psychology historically used parapsychology to define its own disciplinary boundaries?
2. Why might figures such as Leonora Piper be considered both central and marginal to the development of psychological knowledge?
3. In what ways did J. B. Rhine's methods in parapsychology contribute to mainstream psychological science?
4. What does the chapter suggest about the ontological status of paranormal phenomena in psychology's history?
5. How might the concept of a 'haunted discipline' help us understand the lingering presence of excluded ideas in contemporary psychology?

Suggested Reading

Asprem, E. (2010). A nice arrangement of heterodoxies: William McDougall and the professionalization of psychical research. *Journal of the History of the Behavioural Sciences, 46*(2) 123–143. https://doi.org/10.1002/jhbs.20422.

Blum, D. (2014). *Ghost Hunters: William James and the search for scientific proof of life after death*. Harmondsworth: Penguin Books.

Cypert, R., & Petro, M. S. (2024). A faith in science: Gardner Murphy and parapsychology. *History of the Human Sciences, 38*(1), 78–98. https://doi.org/10.1177/09526951241280534.

Evrard, R., Pratte, E. A., & Cardeña, E. (2018). Pierre Janet and the enchanted boundary of psychical research. *History of Psychology, 21*(2), 100–125. https://doi.org/10.1037/hop0000086.

Gieryn, T. F. (1983). Boundary-work and the demarcation of science from non-science: Strains and interests in professional ideologies of scientists. *American Sociological Review 48*(6), 781–795. https://doi.org/10.2307/2095325.

Gyimesi, J. (2012). Sándor Ferenczi and the problem of telepathy. *History of the Human Sciences, 25*(2), 131–148. https://doi.org/10.1177/0952695111434253.

Hacking, I. (1988). Telepathy: Origins of randomization in experimental design. *Isis, 79*, 427–451. http://www.jstor.org/stable/234674.

Kloosterman, I. (2012). Psychical research and parapsychology interpreted: Suggestions from the international historiography of psychical research and parapsychology for investigating its history in the Netherlands. *History of the Human Sciences, 25*(2), 2–22. https://doi.org/10.1177/0952695111421580.

Lachapelle, S. (2005). Attempting science: The creation and early development of the Institut Métapsychique International in Paris, 1919–1931. *Journal of the History of the Behavioral Sciences, 41*(1), 1–24. https://doi.org/10.1002/jhbs.20061.

Lamont, P. (2013). Spiritualism and a mid-Victorian crisis of evidence. *Historical Journal, 56*(3), 833–860. https://doi.org/10.1017/S0018246X04004030.

Mülberger, A., & Balltondre, M. (2012). Metaphysics in Spain: Acknowledging or questioning the marvellous? *History of the Human Sciences, 25*(2), 108–130. https://doi.org/10.1177/0952695112439374.

Owen, A. (1989). *The Darkened Room: Women, power and spiritualism in late nineteenth century England*. London: Virago.

Parra, A. (2025). Spiritualism and psychology in Argentina: The inception of parapsychology in the scientific mainstream (1948–1955). *Journal of the History of the Behavioural Sciences, 61, e70035*. https://doi.org/10.1002/jhbs.70035.

Sommer, A. (2012). Psychical research and the origins of American psychology: Hugo Münsterberg, William James and Eusapia Palladino. *History of the Human Sciences, 25*(2), 23–44. https://doi.org/10.1177/0952695112439376.

Wolffram, H. (2006). Parapsychology on the couch: The psychology of occult belief in Germany, c. 1870–1939. *Journal of the History of the Behavioural Sciences, 42*(3), 237–260. https://doi.org/10.1002/jhbs.20171.

Wooffitt, R., & Allistone, S. (2005). Towards a discursive parapsychology: Language and the laboratory study of anomalous communication. *Theory & Psychology, 15*(3), 325–355. https://doi.org/10.1177/0959354305053218.

Key Terms

Apparition A perceived ghostly figure or presence, often central to paranormal claims; treated historically as either spiritual evidence or psychological hallucination.

Boundary-Work A concept from the sociology of science, describing how disciplines construct and defend their borders by defining what counts as legitimate knowledge.

Constitutive Other An excluded category or domain that paradoxically helps define and stabilise the identity of a discipline by providing a contrast or counterexample.

Extrasensory Perception (ESP) The claimed ability to acquire information without using the known senses, studied under experimental conditions by J. B. Rhine.

Koestler Chair An academic position in parapsychology at the University of Edinburgh, symbolising both institutional recognition and marginalisation of anomalous research.

Parapsychology The study of alleged psychic phenomena such as telepathy, clairvoyance, and psychokinesis; often positioned at the margins of psychological science.

Phantasms of the Living An 1886 publication by The Society for Psychical Research documenting telepathic and apparitional experiences, marking an early attempt to scientifically catalogue the paranormal.

Poltergeist A type of haunting characterised by physical disturbances; interpreted in psychology as possible expressions of repressed trauma or family dynamics.

Séance A spiritualist ritual intended to communicate with the dead, historically entangled with early psychological investigations into consciousness and mediumship.

Subliminal Self Frederic Myers's concept of a layered psyche, receptive to impressions from beyond conscious awareness or even beyond death.

Synchronicity Carl Jung's idea of meaningful coincidence without causal explanation, often invoked in discussions of the paranormal and subjective meaning.

Zener cards A set of 25 cards featuring five distinct symbols, designed in the 1930s by perceptual psychologist Karl Zener to test ESP in controlled laboratory experiments.

FREE INSTRUCTOR & STUDENT RESOURCES

ONLINE RESOURCES

Visit the Instructor & Student Resources website at routledgelearning.com/bpscoretextbooks for free digital resources, including:

- Interactive quizzes and flashcards to test your knowledge
- Links to useful websites and videos
- Instructor manual, lecture slides, and course guide to enhance teaching and save instructors time

21 Mad Travellers

Mad Travellers

The Historical Ontology of Psychological Categories

Chapter Overview

This chapter investigates the idea that psychological categories, such as hysteria, intelligence, and personality, are not timeless features of human nature but historically contingent constructs. Drawing on Ian Hacking's concept of 'historical ontology', it introduces the idea of human kinds as 'moving targets': they emerge, shift, and sometimes disappear in response to specific social, scientific, and institutional conditions. Through the metaphor of the 'ecological niche', the chapter examines how certain psychological categories became thinkable, diagnosable, and real in particular moments, only to fade when the historical conditions change. It compares abandoned categories such as fugue, neurasthenia, and drapetomania with enduring ones such as emotion, motivation, and intelligence, whose meanings have been radically redefined over time. In doing so, it interrogates how ways of being and forms of suffering are brought into existence through classification systems, diagnostic practices, and expert discourse. The chapter also addresses epistemological, ontological, and power-related issues, arguing that psychological categories are produced through historically situated knowledge practices, not simply discovered. By the end, students are encouraged to rethink the stability of the categories they study, recognising that psychology's objects of knowledge are co-produced by culture, history, the human sciences, and the people who live through them.

Mad Travellers

'It all began one morning last July when we noticed a young man of twenty-six crying in his bed', Dr Philippe Tissié recalled in his book *Les aliénés voyageurs* (1887). Tissié was the psychiatrist in charge of the young man, whom he had first met in 1886. 'He had just come from a long journey on foot and was exhausted, but that was not the cause of his tears. He wept because he could not prevent himself from departing on a trip when the need took him; he deserted family, work, and daily life to walk as fast as he could, straight ahead, sometimes doing 70 kilometers a day on foot, until in the end he would be arrested for vagrancy and thrown in prison.' The tearful man was Albert Dadas, a quiet, diligent gas fitter, who without warning had abandoned his job and family and set off walking. Not merely to nearby towns, but across borders and to another continent; to Prague, Vienna, Moscow, even as far as Algeria. These journeys, sometimes thousands of kilometres long, were undertaken with little money, few possessions, and no clear purpose. Albert travelled on foot, stowed away on trains, and wandered through towns and the countryside. When caught, often for vagrancy, he was bewildered, confused, and unable to recall where

DOI: 10.4324/9781003565482-21

he had been or why he had left. When finally returned home to Bordeaux in late 1887, Albert fell into the care of Dr Tissié, who documented his case for the medical profession. Dadas became the prototype of a new psychiatric identity: the fugueur, or 'mad traveller'. Soon, others like him appeared across France during the 1890s, young men, often labourers or soldiers, who vanished from their routines and reappeared hundreds of miles away, unable to account for their actions. By the turn of the century, fugue had entered the psychiatric lexicon as a recognised diagnosis, peaking in descriptions around 1910. Yet, a few decades later, it was gone. The epidemic had ended, and the diagnosis faded into obscurity. What happened to fugue? Had it been cured, debunked, or simply forgotten? More importantly, what does its rise and disappearance tell us about the nature of psychological reality itself?

Chapter Contents

- Explores how psychological categories are historically constructed and subject to change.
- Introduces the critical thinking tool of *historical ontology* to question assumptions of fixed psychological reality.
- Analyses key categories that have either disappeared or shifted over time, such as fugue, hysteria, intelligence, and motivation.

Chapter Objectives

- To examine the concept of *historical ontology* and its implications for understanding psychological categories as contingent and dynamic.
- To analyse specific examples of psychological categories that have emerged, transformed, or disappeared, highlighting the fluidity of psychological knowledge.
- To describe and explain the influence of epistemology, ontology, and power in shaping what counts as psychological reality.

CRITICAL THINKING TOOL
HISTORICAL ONTOLOGY

The story of Albert Dadas and his fellow 'mad travellers' invites us to consider that psychological categories are shaped by history, culture, and the practices that name them. The critical thinking tool of *historical ontology* proposes that psychological categories are not timeless, immutable features of human nature but are rather dynamic constructs whose existence, meaning, and reality are historically contingent. Exploring this and other psychological categories, the chapter argues that these categories are *made real* through specific historical processes, intellectual frameworks, and socio-cultural contexts. Once those contexts disappear, the constructs disappear with them.

As Ian Hacking argued, a psychological category requires an 'ecological niche' to emerge and thrive. This isn't a biological niche but a specific constellation of historical conditions: a

receptive medical taxonomy, prevailing cultural anxieties, observable symptoms, and often a paradoxical form of social release or recognition. When these conditions shift, the category itself moves, either transforming into something new or, like fugue, largely disappearing. It becomes a 'moving target'. Historical ontology challenges the illusion of permanence, urging us to examine the very foundations of psychological knowledge as a fluid, co-produced reality between the classified and the classifier.

Introduction

We typically experience psychological categories, such as depression, intelligence, or personality, as stable, universal aspects of the human mind, discovered rather than constructed. This chapter opposes that perception, arguing that the language of our inner lives is fundamentally ontologically insecure. We will explore how some categories have emerged, gained a robust reality, and then largely disappeared, while others have persisted but undergone profound transformations in meaning and status. By adopting an historical ontological perspective, this chapter invites a critical re-evaluation of what we assume to be natural and permanent in psychology, revealing the profound fluidity of the human psyche as understood through its own changing definitions.

The historical backdrop is crucial for understanding why certain psychological categories emerge and others fade. The nineteenth and twentieth centuries witnessed a dramatic shift towards the medicalisation of deviance, where human qualities previously understood through moral, religious, or criminal frameworks became subjects of scientific inquiry. This transition, fuelled by Enlightenment ideals of progress and a growing faith in scientific rationality, provided a new interpretive framework for human suffering and nonconformity. The rise of modern psychiatry, with its emphasis on classification, and the establishment of asylums and clinics across Europe and North America created new institutional and conceptual spaces for observing, diagnosing, and managing individuals.

The decline of older frameworks for understanding the self is epitomised, for example, by the distinction between pre-modern *melancholy* and modern *depression*. For centuries, explanations for temperament, personality, and mental illness were dominated by the humoural system. This ancient medical theory, stretching from Hippocrates and Galen well into the early modern period, posited that the human body's functioning was determined by four fundamental fluids or 'humours': blood ('sanguine', hot and wet), yellow bile ('choleric', hot and dry), black bile ('melancholic', cold and dry), and phlegm ('phlegmatic', cold and wet). The balance of these humours, which were themselves embedded in a wider cosmology, was believed to determine an individual's temperament, health, and predisposition to disease. An excess of any humour could lead to specific physical ailments and mental woes.

Within this system, melancholy was understood as an excess of 'black bile', believed to arise from the spleen. This was not merely a mood; it was a profound, systemic imbalance thought to affect the entire body and mind, manifesting as dejection, rumination, fear, or even stupor. This complex, holistic framework, where feelings were inseparable from bodily fluids and cosmic influences, stands in contrast to the later psychologised concept of depression as primarily a mental or neurochemical disorder.

The disappearance of melancholy as a dominant diagnostic category, along with the humoural system itself, powerfully demonstrates how profoundly the historical-ecological niche dictates the very existence and nature of psychological categories.

Industrialisation and urbanisation in the nineteenth and twentieth centuries introduced new stressors and anxieties, leading to the conceptualisation of new forms of 'nervous' disorders. 'Neurasthenia', for example, expressed overwhelming weariness with modern life. Simultaneously, the burgeoning field of psychometrics sought to quantify human abilities, giving rise to categories such as 'feeble-mindedness', driven by societal needs for sorting and control within burgeoning educational and military systems. These macro-historical forces, from the secularisation of explanations for suffering, to the policy of mandatory schooling, not only influenced *how* we understood psychological states; they actively contributed to the *making* of these states as distinct objects of psychological knowledge, creating the specific 'ecological niches' in which these categories could flourish and generate lived experience.

Key Categories

Our investigation into moving targets reveals two primary modes of transformation: categories that have largely disappeared, and those that persist but have fundamentally changed their meaning.

Categories that Emerged and Disappeared

These categories illustrate how particular forms of human experience or suffering, or specific theoretical constructs used to explain them, were once formalised as diagnostic or central conceptual entities but now hold little to no clinical or theoretical reality in their original form.

Accidie: Once a significant spiritual or moral failing (spiritual sloth) in medieval Christian thought, accidie was a profound spiritual apathy or torpor. Its decline reflected the secularisation and medicalisation of inner experience, as explanations shifted from theological justifications to psychological and biological ones.

Drapetomania: Coined by American physician Samuel A. Cartwright in 1851, drapetomania ('runaway madness') was meant to account for why enslaved Americans wanted to escape captivity. Designed to pathologise the desire for freedom among black slaves in the American South, drapetomania is a stark example of a psychological concept fabricated explicitly for the purposes of social control.

The Will/Conation: Central to nineteenth-century faculty psychology, 'The Will' or 'Conation' was considered to be a distinct mental faculty responsible for conscious striving and intention, a cornerstone of psychological understanding. Its abandonment as a singular, unified psychological entity reflects a shift towards more complex, fragmented, and empirically grounded understandings of motivation and agency.

Hysteria: A pervasive diagnosis, particularly in the late nineteenth century, hysteria encompassed a vast array of physical and psychological symptoms, strongly associated with femininity. Its elaborate manifestations at the Salpêtrière in Paris and its eventual decline reflect changing gender roles, neurological theories, and the rise of psychoanalysis, illustrating a 'form of life' that faded as its specific ecological niche disappeared.

Neurasthenia: Prevalent in the late nineteenth and early twentieth centuries, this diagnosis clustered symptoms such as fatigue and anxiety, attributed to the stresses of modernity, rapid industrialisation, urban life, and perceived 'overwork'. Its eventual fragmentation into more specific modern diagnoses (e.g. chronic fatigue syndrome, anxiety disorder) demonstrates how broad 'nervous' conditions were disaggregated as the understanding of specific biological and psychological mechanisms advanced.

Fugue: As seen with Albert Dadas, fugue represented a distinct nineteenth-century transient disorder, a compulsive wandering linked to specific ideas about automatism. Its transient nature highlights how a category's reality can be profoundly tied to its historical and cultural moment.

Feebleminded/Moron/Imbecile: Central to the early twentieth-century eugenics movement, these labels, tied to early IQ testing in the United States and Europe, were used for social control, leading to institutionalisation and forced sterilisation. Their abandonment (and later replacement by 'intellectual disability') reflects a shift away from eugenic ideology and a more ethical understanding of human variation.

Drive: Clark Hull's highly influential mid-twentieth-century behaviouristic drive-reduction theory posited that 'drives' (hunger, thirst) were fundamental, mechanistic motivators reducible to physiological needs, and central to explaining all learned behaviour. Hull's mathematical concept of drive (D) was one component of his equation predicting 'reaction potential' (sEr), where sEr = (sHr x D x K x V) – (sIr + Ir) +/– sOr. After his death, former colleagues described Hull's mathematico-deductive system as 'just silly'.

Hormic: William McDougall's early twentieth-century hormic psychology emphasised instincts ('horme' meaning urge or impulse) as the primary, purposive drivers of all human behaviour. This grand theoretical system, with its specific catalogue of instincts, while influential for a time, disappeared soon after McDougall's death.

Categories that Persist but Have Transformed

These categories remain in use, but their core definitions, theoretical underpinnings, and ontological status have undergone radical historical shifts.

Emotion: Once understood using the language of 'passions' (external forces affecting the soul) or humoural theories (which linked feelings to the cosmos via four bodily fluids), 'emotion' only emerged as a distinct, psychologised internal state in the mid-nineteenth century. Reinforced by Darwin's work on expression and the rise of physiological psychology, this shift created a new object of psychological inquiry, defined as distinct from reason.

Motivation: From earlier philosophical concepts of 'the will', a faculty of rational choice, 'motivation' evolved into a scientific construct. This transformation was influenced by industrial psychology's need to understand worker productivity and later by psychoanalytic theory and Maslow's hierarchy of needs. Its meaning has continually adapted to new explanatory and societal demands, transitioning from philosophical inquiry to scientific measurement and management.

Intelligence: The reification of 'intelligence' into a single, measurable quantity (the IQ score) in the early twentieth century, particularly through the work of Binet and Terman, profoundly shaped educational and social policy. Its origins were often intertwined with eugenics and the desire for social sorting. Despite ongoing debates about its definition, cultural bias, and the concept of 'multiple intelligences', its continued re-evaluation highlights its constructed and contested nature.

Personality: The shift from older concepts of 'character' (which had a strong moral dimension) and 'temperament' (often linked to predispositions) to modern, trait-based 'personality' (e.g. the 'Big Five' traits) is a testament to the influence of psychometrics. The desire to quantify individual differences for purposes like selection in the military or industry profoundly shaped how we conceive of a stable self, moving towards more empirical and less moralistic frameworks.

Multiple Personality Disorder: This striking phenomenon gained significant clinical attention in the late nineteenth century, often linked to the exploration of hypnosis and hysterical dissociation by figures such as Jean-Martin Charcot and Pierre Janet. Characterised by distinct alternate identities within one individual, it became a rare diagnosis for much of the early to mid-twentieth century before its later resurgence, finding a new ecological niche among victims of child sexual abuse.

Epistemological Issues

The historical ontology of psychological categories is deeply intertwined with epistemological issues, questions about how we come to know and classify the psyche. The very act of diagnosis, often perceived as a neutral recognition of pre-existing conditions, is a powerful act of *making* categories real. Classification systems, most notably the *Diagnostic and Statistical Manual of Mental Disorders* (DSM), not only describe mental illness; they actively shape its observable manifestations, influencing how individuals experience their own suffering and how clinicians perceive symptoms. This dynamic process leads to Hacking's 'looping effect', where classifying individuals can change how they behave or present, thereby altering the very category itself.

The challenges of defining and measuring internal states, such as emotions, thoughts, or motivations, profoundly influence category construction. Psychologists and psychiatrists rely on subjective reports, observable behaviours, and neurobiological markers, all of which are subject to interpretation from within certain theoretical frameworks. Furthermore, dominant scientific paradigms, from behaviourism's focus on observable stimuli and responses to cognitive science's emphasis on mental processes, and increasingly neuroscience's biological frameworks, determine what counts as valid psychological knowledge and, consequently, which categories emerge or are prioritised.

Ontological Issues

Beyond how we know, ontological issues concern the very nature of existence of psychological categories. The disappearance of categories such as fugue and hysteria demonstrates that what was once a clinically and socially recognised way of being can cease to exist in that form, not because the underlying human suffering vanished but because its specific conceptualisation and recognition faded. These categories did not simply *describe* kinds of people; they actively *created* specific kinds of people and kinds of suffering, with distinct forms of lived experience, presentation, and treatment. This is historical ontology.

When an 'ecological niche' for a category disperses into history due to shifts in medical theory, social norms, or technological advancements, a specific way of *being* mad or *experiencing* psychological distress also fades. A compelling illustration of this fluid ontology is Multiple Personality Disorder (MPD), later re-conceptualised as Dissociative Identity Disorder (DID). After a period of prominence in the late nineteenth century, MPD largely disappeared from clinical view for decades. However, it saw a dramatic resurgence in the late twentieth century, spurred by bestselling books, media attention, changes in diagnostic criteria (e.g. in the DSM), and shifts in therapeutic approaches (e.g. a focus on repressed trauma such as sexual abuse). This is an example of Hacking's 'looping effect': as the diagnosis became more widely known and discussed, individuals learned to present symptoms in ways that fitted the category, and therapists, seeking to identify it, inadvertently shaped its manifestations. The 'kind of person' with MPD/DID thus became ontologically 'real' in a new way, demonstrating that while the underlying suffering from trauma is undeniable, the specific *form* it takes and how it is named is profoundly contingent upon its historical and social ecological niche.

Power

The construction and transformation of psychological categories are never value-neutral; they are profoundly shaped by mechanisms of power. Diagnostic labels often function as tools of social control, enabling the medical profession and broader society to pathologise, contain, and normalise certain behaviours.

Drapetomania stands as a stark testament to this, an egregious example of medical authority being explicitly used to justify the oppression of enslaved people. The category of 'feeblemindedness' provided justification for the eugenics movement in the early twentieth century, leading to coercive institutionalisation, forced sterilisation, and strict immigration policies. The gendered nature of hysteria reflected a historical power imbalance, where the female body was medicalised as a disorder rooted in a 'wandering womb' or emotional instability rather than being attributed to legitimate social grievances.

The curious trajectory of MPD further underscores the power of psychiatric attention and classification. After its initial nineteenth-century phase, MPD largely receded from clinical prominence for decades, becoming almost unthinkable within mainstream psychiatry. Its dramatic late twentieth-century resurgence, however, under the new label of DID, depended on psychiatry taking notice of it once again, under different circumstances.

MPD illustrates the formidable power of the psy-sciences to grant 'thinkability' and, by extension, reality to a psychological category, making it a prominent feature of clinical and public discourse following a period of near-oblivion. The power of experts to define and legitimate reality, through diagnostic manuals and theoretical frameworks, imbues certain perspectives with authority while marginalising others. This ethical dimension is critical: understanding these power dynamics is crucial for critically assessing the classifications that shape our understanding of the human mind and for recognising whose realities are prioritised or silenced.

Chapter Summary

This chapter has explored psychological categories as 'moving targets', demonstrating that our understanding of the psyche is a fluid, dynamic, and historically contingent construct rather than a stable, natural reality. The chapter introduced historical ontology as a critical thinking tool, revealing how psychological categories are *made real* within specific historical ecological niches shaped by scientific, social, and cultural forces.

We first examined abandoned categories that once held robust diagnostic reality but that have largely disappeared. The compelling case of Albert Dadas vividly illustrated this phenomenon, highlighting how specific forms of madness can emerge and recede. Similarly, hysteria faded with changing gender roles and shifting medical paradigms, while drapetomania was almost immediately satirised, particularly in the Northern United States. Neurasthenia, feeblemindedness, the will, and so on further demonstrated how diagnostic and theoretical categories are products of their time, reflecting prevailing anxieties and modes of explanation.

Concepts such as emotion, motivation, personality, and intelligence, commonly perceived as universal, were shown to be historical constructs. Their evolution reveals shifts from philosophical or moral understandings to psychologised, often quantified, entities, influenced by introspection, industrial needs, psychometrics, and social sorting.

Finally, we highlighted the pervasive influence of power. Categories are not just descriptive; they are vehicles of meaning, agents of control, used to normalise and manage individuals and populations. In a more mundane sense, psychological categories help us make sense of our experience. Adopting a historical ontological perspective urges us to view psychological reality with critical humility. It challenges the assumption of fixed, universal categories, encouraging us to recognise the ongoing co-production of knowledge and reality within psychology. This understanding fosters a more nuanced appreciation of human experience, acknowledging its profound historical and cultural variations and preparing us for the ongoing movement of the human psyche's definitions.

New forms of experience are continually being named into existence, often shaped by institutional needs and cultural anxieties. To adopt a historical ontological perspective is to invite us to view psychological categories as constantly on the move. This perspective cultivates critical humility, reminding us that the knowledge we produce about the mind is inseparable from the world in which we produce it. It challenges us to remain attentive to the ways in which our diagnostic practices are co-produced with the social realities they claim to describe. In doing so, we not only gain a richer understanding of past psychologies but we also equip ourselves to interrogate the present. What forms of experience today are being named into existence? What kinds of people are we creating through our categories of mind? And what might disappear tomorrow, like fugue, quietly disappearing into history following in the footsteps of Albert Dadas?

Reflective Questions

1. What does the concept of 'historical ontology' reveal about the way psychological categories are created and maintained?
2. Why did 'fugue' as a psychological category appear and then vanish from psychiatric discourse?

3. How does Ian Hacking's 'looping effect' challenge our understanding of diagnosis and classification in psychology?
4. In what ways do power dynamics influence which psychological categories become legitimate or dominant?
5. How have categories such as 'emotion' or 'intelligence' changed over time, and what does this suggest about their ontological status?

Suggested Reading

Brinkmann, S. (2005). Human kinds and looping effects in psychology. *Theory & Psychology, 15*(6), 769–791. https://doi.org/10.1177/0959354305059332.

Danziger, K. (1997). *Naming the Mind: How psychology found its language*. Thousand Oaks, CA: Sage.

Hacking, I. (1992). Multiple personality disorder and its hosts. *History of the Human Sciences, 5*(2), 3–31. https://doi.org/10.1177/095269519200500202.

Hacking, I. (2002). *Historical Ontology*. Cambridge, MA: Harvard University Press.

Hacking, I. (2002). *Mad Travelers: Reflections on the reality of transient mental illnesses*. Cambridge, MA: Harvard University Press.

Harper, D. J. (1994). Histories of suspicion in a time of conspiracy: A reflection on Aubrey Lewis's history of paranoia. *History of the Human Sciences, 7*(3), 89–109. https://doi.org/10.1177/095269519400700304.

Kimball, M. M. (2000). From 'Anna O.' to Bertha Pappenheim: Transforming private pain into public action. *History of Psychology, 3*(1), 20–43. https://doi.org/10.1037/1093-4510.3.1.20.

Knight, I. F. (1984). Freud's 'project': A theory for Studies on Hysteria. *Journal of the History of the Behavioural Sciences, 20*(4), 340–358. https://doi.org/10.1002/1520-6696(198410)20:4<340::AID-JHBS2300200404>3.0.CO;2-L.

Low, K. G. (1997). Mad, but not crazy. *Theory & Psychology, 7*(2), 282–284. https://doi.org/10.1177/0959354397072014.

Rae, G. (2025). From reason to madness and back: Critiquing reason through the Derrida–Foucault debate. *History of the Human Sciences, 38*(3–4), 175–194. https://doi.org/10.1177/09526951251337677.

Sass, L. A. (1994). Civilized madness: Schizophrenia, self-consciousness and the modern mind. *History of the Human Sciences, 7*(2), 83–120. https://doi.org/10.1177/095269519400700206.

Smith, R. (2005). The history of psychological categories. *Studies in History and Philosophy of Biological and Biomedical Sciences, 36*(1), 55–94. https://doi.org/10.1016/j.shpsc.2004.12.006.

Key Terms

Diagnosis The process of identifying and naming a psychological condition, which can shape both the behaviour of individuals and how they are perceived.

Drapetomania A fabricated psychological disorder used in the nineteenth century to pathologise the desire of enslaved people to escape captivity.

Ecological Niche The specific historical, cultural, and institutional conditions that allow a psychological category to emerge, flourish, or disappear.

Feeblemindedness A historical label used to classify people with low intelligence, often tied to eugenics and social control.

Fugue A once-recognised psychological condition involving compulsive wandering and amnesia, prominent in the late nineteenth century but now largely obsolete.

Historical Ontology A way of thinking about how psychological categories are made real through historical, cultural, and scientific processes rather than being discovered as natural facts.

Hysteria A now-discredited diagnosis, historically applied primarily to women, that included a wide range of physical and psychological symptoms.

Looping Effect A concept developed by Ian Hacking to describe how people classified under certain psychological categories begin to change in response to that classification, which then alters the category itself.

Moving Targets A metaphor describing psychological categories as unstable and shifting over time, rather than fixed or permanent.

Multiple Personality Disorder (MPD) A diagnosis involving the presence of distinct identities within a single individual, now largely replaced by Dissociative Identity Disorder (DID).

Neurasthenia A nineteenth-century diagnosis referring to nervous exhaustion caused by modern life, later replaced by more specific terms such as anxiety and chronic fatigue.

Power In the context of psychology, the ability of experts and institutions to define, control, and legitimate what counts as 'normal', 'mad', or 'disordered'.

Psychometrics The field of psychology concerned with measuring mental traits such as intelligence and personality through standardised tests.

FREE INSTRUCTOR & STUDENT RESOURCES

ONLINE RESOURCES

Visit the Instructor & Student Resources website at routledgelearning.com/bpscoretextbooks for free digital resources, including:

- Interactive quizzes and flashcards to test your knowledge
- Links to useful websites and videos
- Instructor manual, lecture slides, and course guide to enhance teaching and save instructors time

22

Behind the Mask

Psychological Diagnosis and the Politics of Interpellation

Chapter Overview

This chapter explores psychological diagnosis as a site of power, identity, and negotiation, using the concept of *interpellation* to examine how individuals are 'hailed' into diagnostic categories, and how they may resist, reinterpret, or reclaim these labels. The chapter shows how the removal of homosexuality from the DSM exemplifies diagnosis not as a neutral classification but as a dynamic and contested social act. Through historical analysis and five key case studies (PTSD, ADHD, autism, schizophrenia, and CFS/ME), the chapter traces how diagnoses are shaped by expert authority, political activism, and lived experience. It examines the epistemological frameworks used to construct diagnostic knowledge, the ontological consequences of being named, and the power struggles that determine what counts as a disorder. By drawing on the dialectical model of interpellation, the chapter invites a critical engagement with diagnosis as a process of naming and being named, a two-way conversation between clinicians, patients, institutions, and communities. Diagnosis, it argues, is a cultural and political performance that shapes who we are and who we are allowed to become.

Behind the Mask

On 2 May 1972, a man wearing a grotesque rubber mask, an ill-fitting tuxedo, and carrying a voice modulator, stepped onto the stage at the annual meeting of the American Psychiatric Association in Dallas, Texas. He introduced himself as 'Dr Henry Anonymous'. His distorted voice boomed into the room: 'I am a homosexual. I am a psychiatrist.' No one knew who he was. If they had, his career would have been over. At that moment, homosexuality was still classified as a mental disorder in the APA's *Diagnostic and Statistical Manual of Mental Disorders* (DSM-II), listed under 'sexual deviations' alongside paedophilia and fetishism. Throughout the 1960s and 1970s, gay and lesbian activists increasingly challenged the authority of psychiatry to define and pathologise their lives. By 1972, it was five years since the British government had decriminalised homosexuality through an Act of Parliament. In the United States, however, nationwide decriminalisation would not happen until 2003. But in 1972, according to American psychiatry, to be gay was to be sick. And for the man behind the mask, Dr John Fryer, a gay psychiatrist, this meant living in fear not just of social exclusion but of professional censure. The room fell silent. It was an unsettling moment, not just because of the mask but because of what it revealed: that psychiatry itself had become a mechanism of silencing, surveillance, and stigma. Dr Fryer's appearance, as Dr Henry Anonymous, was both a confession and a protest, a radical intervention in the machinery of

DOI: 10.4324/9781003565482-22

classification. Less than two years later, the APA voted to remove homosexuality from the DSM, a landmark moment in the history of psychological diagnosis. This chapter begins with this story because it exemplifies its central argument: psychological diagnosis is a dynamic negotiation, a struggle over meaning, authority, and identity. The language of disorder is always situated, always shaped by the voices of both those who speak it and those who are spoken of. As we will see, this dialectic between hailing and counter-hailing is fundamental to the history, construction, and contestation of psychological diagnosis.

Chapter Contents

- Explores the role of interpellation in shaping psychological diagnosis as a two-way social and political process.
- Traces the historical development of psychiatric classification systems and introduces key diagnostic debates.
- Analyses five case studies (PTSD, ADHD, autism, schizophrenia, and CFS/ME) to demonstrate how diagnoses are shaped by institutions, activism, and lived experience.

Chapter Objectives

- To introduce the concept of interpellation and apply it as a critical thinking tool for understanding psychological diagnosis.
- To examine the historical evolution of psychiatric categories and their social consequences.
- To evaluate the epistemological, ontological, and power dimensions of diagnostic practice through contemporary and historical examples.

CRITICAL THINKING TOOL
INTERPELLATION

The term *interpellation* originates in the work of Marxist theorist Louis Althusser, who used it to describe the process by which individuals are 'hailed' into subject positions by ideological structures. In psychological diagnosis, this process becomes vividly apparent. When a clinician declares a person 'depressed', 'schizophrenic', or 'autistic', they are not merely describing; they are performing a hailing, a request to embrace a particular identity, with its associated expectations, behaviours, and social consequences.

Yet interpellation is not a one-way transmission of authority. It is dialectical. The person being hailed is an active participant in the process of subjectification. Some may accept the diagnosis, finding it a meaningful framework through which to understand their experience. Others may resist or reshape it, offering alternative narratives, critiques, or identities. This resistance constitutes a form of 'counter-hailing', a reflexive, and often collective, re-articulation of what it means to be named.

This two-way process means that diagnostic categories are mutable constructs negotiated in practice. The rise of activist movements, peer-support groups, and alternative epistemologies, from the psychiatric survivor movement to neurotribes, illustrates how counter-hailing can reshape clinical language, challenge power, and redefine the boundaries of what is considered normal. Interpellation helps us grasp diagnosis not as the discovery of pre-existing conditions but as an active, contested social process, an ongoing dialogue between the voices that diagnose and the voices that speak back.

Introduction

Psychological diagnosis is one of the most powerful acts in the human sciences. It can offer clarity, relief, and a path to treatment, but it can also constrain, mislabel, and silence. At its core, diagnosis is a form of classification that carries the weight of authority. Diagnoses do not simply describe; they also prescribe. They name, define, and delimit what it means to be a person in psychological distress. Yet this process does not always go unchallenged

This chapter explores diagnosis through the lens of interpellation, a concept that frames diagnosis as a two-way encounter. On one side are the 'hailers', the clinicians, institutions, and practice manuals that define and categorise psychological experience. On the other are the 'hailed', those who receive, accept, contest, or resist these definitions. Diagnosis, in this framing, is an evolving negotiation between expert knowledge and lived experience.

To make this argument, the chapter traces the historical development of diagnostic authority, analyses five key case studies (PTSD, ADHD, autism, schizophrenia, and CFS/ME), and unpacks the epistemological, ontological, and political stakes of diagnosis. In doing so, it invites us to view psychological categories not as static facts but as dynamic, socially constructed forms of power and identity.

Historical Issues

Long before the advent of modern psychiatry, societies found ways to 'hail' those who deviated from normative expectations of behaviour or emotion. In the pre-medical era, 'madness' was often interpreted through religious, moral, or supernatural frameworks. Individuals were confined, exorcised, punished, or ostracised, not necessarily because of health but to maintain the social order. These early forms of interpellation were unsystematic but no less powerful, naming individuals as deviant or dangerous and embedding them within rigid social hierarchies.

The nineteenth century brought a decisive epistemological shift. As medicine professionalised and psychiatry emerged as a distinct discipline, the language of pathology replaced that of sin or superstition. Emil Kraepelin's classificatory system laid the groundwork for thinking about mental illness as a set of discrete, biologically determined entities. He distinguished between two major categories of severe mental illness: Dementia Praecox (later renamed schizophrenia), and Manic-Depressive Insanity (including what we now call bipolar disorder and major depression). The rise of diagnostic manuals, culminating in the DSM's publication in the twentieth century, marked the consolidation of a medical model that formalised psychological 'hailing' into categories backed by institutional authority.

This medical model positioned diagnosis as a one-way act: experts identified disorders, and patients received labels. The early DSMs codified this asymmetry, offering little room for the perspectives or experiences of those diagnosed. To be named was to be positioned within a system that claimed scientific neutrality but often reflected cultural and political assumptions.

By the mid-twentieth century, however, this unilateral power began to fracture. Figures such as Thomas Szasz argued that mental illness was a myth, a socially constructed tool for controlling undesirable behaviour. R. D. Laing challenged the biological determinism of schizophrenia, framing it instead as a rational response to an irrational world. These voices constituted early forms of philosophical 'counter-hailing', rejecting the diagnostic gaze and reclaiming meaning from the margins. These developments marked the beginning of a more dialectical understanding of diagnosis. No longer simply imposed, diagnostic categories were now subject to challenge and reinterpretation. The emergence of activism, advocacy, and lived experience narratives in the late twentieth century further destabilised the expert monopoly, setting the stage for diagnosis as an arena of negotiation rather than prescription.

Key Diagnoses

Post-Traumatic Stress Disorder (PTSD)

The diagnosis of PTSD emerged directly from grassroots pressure. Although trauma-related symptoms had long been observed in war veterans under terms such as 'shell shock' or 'combat fatigue', they were often framed as moral weakness, cowardice, or malingering. Following the Vietnam War, thousands of veterans returned with debilitating psychological distress, yet found themselves misdiagnosed or dismissed. It was their collective action, alongside supportive clinicians and researchers, that reframed their experiences as legitimate psychological injury. By lobbying the American Psychiatric Association and organising protests, these veterans forced the inclusion of PTSD into the DSM-III in 1980. This was a paradigmatic case of counter-hailing: those once pathologised for weakness redefined their suffering as a consequence of violence and moral injury.

Autistic Spectrum Disorder

Autism was initially described in the 1940s by Leo Kanner and Hans Asperger, and for decades was understood through narrow medical and behavioural frames, often attributing blame to so-called refrigerator mothers. Starting in the 1980s, parental advocacy groups began to push back against these dehumanising narratives, demanding better educational provision and diagnostic clarity. By the early twenty-first century, a new counter-hailing emerged: the neurodiversity movement. Autistic individuals began speaking for themselves, rejecting the pathology model and asserting autism as a difference, not a disorder. (As symbolised by the difference between being called 'an autistic person' or 'a person with autism'.) This rearticulation of diagnosis challenged core ontological assumptions about normality and impairment. The diagnostic category expanded and softened, becoming more inclusive but also more contested.

Attention-Deficit/Hyperactivity Disorder (ADHD)

ADHD provides one of the most intricate illustrations of interpellation as a networked, multi-stakeholder process. Originally framed as 'minimal brain dysfunction' and later as 'hyperkinetic reaction of childhood', ADHD was rebranded in the late twentieth century as a neurodevelopmental disorder involving deficits in attention, impulse control, and executive functioning. Importantly, diagnosis rarely arises from a single clinical encounter. It typically involves teachers flagging behavioural issues, parents raising concerns, psychologists conducting assessments, and medical professionals prescribing medication. Each party contributes to a distributed act of hailing, drawing on different institutional logics, education, parenting, psychiatry, and pharmacology.

This diffusion of diagnostic power renders the process both more inclusive and more unstable. ADHD is widely seen as over-diagnosed in some populations and under-diagnosed in others, especially in girls and adults, whose symptoms may diverge from the hyperactivity model initially developed around young boys. In recent years, a new wave of adult self-diagnosis and neurodivergent activism has counter-hailed the deficit and dysfunction narrative, reframing ADHD as cognitive difference shaped by capitalist norms of productivity and discipline. This movement brings into focus the wider ideological backdrop: the diagnosis of ADHD reflects a set of cultural values about time, attention, and behaviour. As such, ADHD exemplifies how diagnosis is entangled with education, social control, economic productivity, and self-governance.

Schizophrenia

Few diagnoses have been as stigmatised or contested as schizophrenia. Historically seen as a chronic, biologically determined illness, it was framed by early psychiatry as a loss of reality and reason. The language of 'disorder' was definitive and exclusionary. In recent years, however, alternative framings have gained ground. The British Psychological Society's 2014 report proposed a 'psychosocial formulation' that places emphasis on trauma, meaning-making, and social context, offering an explicit challenge to the biomedical model. This was a significant act of professional counter-hailing: rather than rejecting the diagnosis outright, it sought to reimagine its conceptual foundations. Although resistance from mainstream psychiatry remains, the BPS's intervention marks an institutional rethinking of how schizophrenia is understood and explained, a shift born of pressure from service users, researchers, and critical clinicians alike, a looping effect in action.

Chronic Fatigue Syndrome/Myalgic Encephalomyelitis (CFS/ME)

CFS/ME exemplifies a different but no less urgent form of diagnostic struggle: the battle for recognition. Marked by persistent fatigue, cognitive impairment, and post-exertional malaise, the condition has often been dismissed as psychosomatic or misattributed to anxiety or depression. For decades, patients, often women, were either denied a diagnosis or subjected to treatments that worsened their symptoms. This pattern of mis-hailing was met with sustained counter-hailing: patient-led advocacy groups challenged public health guidance, demanded research funding, and lobbied for the legitimisation of CFS/ME as a biomedical condition. Although official guidelines in the UK and elsewhere have begun to shift, the category remains unstable and contested. CFS/ME reveals how the absence of institutional recognition can itself be a form of diagnostic violence, and how counter-hailing is often the precondition for being heard at all.

Epistemological Issues

The construction of psychological diagnoses rests on particular epistemological foundations; that is, on specific ways of producing and validating knowledge. In the case of the DSM, this foundation has shifted over time towards what is often called an 'atheoretical' model. Rather than being based on causal theories, diagnoses are now defined by clusters of observable symptoms. This symptom-based, checklist approach claims to be neutral and pragmatic, designed to maximise reliability between clinicians. Yet this very neutrality is deceptive. The criteria are not found; they are decided by panels of experts, working within particular historical, cultural, and institutional constraints.

The power to define what counts as a 'disorder' is thus tightly controlled. Committees determine thresholds, subtypes, and exclusions, often drawing on clinical consensus rather than experimental verification. This process raises serious questions about whose experiences are considered valid, and which forms of suffering are rendered visible, or invisible, within the diagnostic frame. Conditions affecting women, ethnic minorities, or those outside Euro-American cultural contexts have often been misclassified, underdiagnosed, or pathologised according to biased assumptions.

Moreover, diagnosis is rarely epistemologically pure. It is shaped by external forces, including the priorities of funding agencies, research institutions, and, significantly, the pharmaceutical industry. The expansion of categories such as ADHD or bipolar disorder has coincided with the development and aggressive marketing of corresponding drug treatments. In such cases, diagnostic criteria may follow the commercial imperatives of pharmaceutical companies rather than empirical imperatives.

Concerns about reliability and validity persist. Despite attempts to systematise diagnosis, studies repeatedly show that different clinicians may assign different labels to the same person, depending on their own training or cultural expectations. What appears to be scientific classification is often a judgement call, imbued with tacit knowledge, institutional norms, and broader social narratives. The epistemology of diagnosis is less about discovering objective truths and more about codifying a working consensus.

Ontological Issues

A psychological diagnosis can profoundly shape the way individuals understand themselves. A person leaves the doctor's surgery a slightly changed person if a diagnosis of 'clinical depression' was considered during the consultation. To be diagnosed is to be interpellated into a particular mode of being. This can bring clarity, validation, and access to support. But it can also bring stigma, alienation, or constraint. Diagnosis, in this sense, becomes ontological: it helps describe and constitute a state.

For many, receiving a diagnosis is a moment of recognition. It names what was previously chaotic, offering a vocabulary for suffering and a framework for action. But this act of naming can impose limitations on identity, inviting the person to see themselves through the lens of disorder or dysfunction. The risk is that the diagnosis becomes totalising, transforming complexity and nuance into pathologised typology.

Yet the hailed do not always remain silent. Across the diagnostic landscape, individuals and communities have resisted these imposed identities and generated their own meanings. Movements such as neurodiversity, mad pride, and peer-led recovery initiatives have redefined what it means to live with a diagnosis. Rather than accepting the category passively, they have repurposed it, challenging its medical assumptions, reframing it in terms of diversity or social struggle, and building new forms of collective belonging.

This counter-hailing transforms diagnosis from a private, clinical matter into a shared cultural and political project. Online forums, advocacy organisations, and identity-based communities provide spaces where alternative narratives are forged. Here, the meaning of a diagnosis is debated, reclaimed, or even rejected. Such ontological shifts are significant. They reconfigure what it means to be a person with a diagnosis, an agent of meaning-making. When the hailed speak back, they resist and reauthor their being. Diagnosis, then, becomes less a sentence and more a site of negotiation over the self.

Power

Power inevitably enters the diagnostic process because there are, as yet, no biological tests or definitive biomarkers for psychological disorders. Unlike natural kind-based diagnoses in the biological sciences, such as tuberculosis or diabetes, mental health conditions are categories whose boundaries, meanings, and implications are shaped by human interpretation, context, and response; they are human kinds. This makes diagnosis inevitably political and relational. It is a matter of navigating competing narratives, values, and experiences. In the case of ADHD, for instance, diagnosis is rarely made by a single clinician alone. It typically involves multiple authorities: the child themselves, their parents, teachers, Special Educational Needs Coordinators (SENCOs), general practitioners, and psychological specialists. Each brings their own expectations and assumptions, making the diagnostic act a microcosm of broader social negotiations. Far from being a neutral classification, diagnosis becomes a space where the very meaning of disorder is worked out between people.

Psychological diagnosis is a locus of power. It operates through institutions, professions, manuals, and protocols, but also through the intimate terrain of selfhood and identity. The clinician's pronouncement of a diagnosis carries with it social, legal, and psychological consequences: access to care, eligibility for benefits, pathways to treatment, and societal status. This authority is grounded in systems of expert knowledge, institutional validation, and cultural legitimacy. In Althusser's terms, it is the power to 'hail', to call someone into a position that they may not have chosen but must now inhabit.

Yet this power is not absolute, and diagnosis is not a monologue. Patients and those around them do receive and actively respond to diagnoses. This response may be one of acceptance, but it can also involve reinterpretation, resistance, or radical refusal. In these moments, we witness counter-hailing: the assertion of alternative ways of understanding psychological difference, distress, and diversity.

This dialectical movement is especially evident in the rise of social movements and user-led advocacy. When veterans demanded recognition of PTSD, when autistic self-advocates reframed their neurology as difference rather than disorder, when patients with CFS/ME challenged their exclusion from medical legitimacy, they were all demanding epistemic and ontological recognition. They were rebalancing power. To understand diagnosis is therefore to understand power as the shifting field in which categories are constructed, identities are lived, and knowledge is continuously remade. Psychological diagnosis is never final. It is always a scene of potential transformation.

Chapter Summary

This chapter has explored psychological diagnosis as a dynamic, contested process shaped by power, negotiation, and identity. Using the concept of interpellation as a critical thinking tool, we have re-examined diagnosis as a two-way dialectic, an act of 'hailing' by professionals, institutions, and diagnostic systems, and a site of response, resistance, or redefinition by those being diagnosed.

Historically, we have traced the evolution of psychiatric diagnosis from early social control and moral condemnation through to the emergence of the medical model in the nineteenth and twentieth centuries. While this model brought formal classification systems and institutional legitimacy, it also imposed a top-down structure in which the experiences of the diagnosed were often marginalised or ignored. Critical voices such as those of Thomas Szasz and R. D. Laing marked the beginning of philosophical counter-hailing, challenging the authority of diagnosis itself.

In the case studies of PTSD, ADHD, autism, schizophrenia, and CFS/ME, we have seen how diagnostic categories are continuously redefined through struggle and participation. Veterans, parents, patient groups, and self-advocates have all played critical roles in reshaping the diagnostic landscape, demonstrating that what counts as 'disorder' constantly loops, a fluid, contested, and culturally embedded process.

This chapter has shown how diagnostic knowledge is constructed through expert consensus, institutional practice, and wider socio-cultural forces. Without definitive biological markers, psychological diagnoses rely on negotiated symptom criteria, shaped by assumptions about normality, dysfunction, and social value. Ontologically, we have explored how individuals internalise, resist, or reimagine their diagnostic identities, often moving from passive recipients to active reauthors of their experience. Dr John Fryer risked his career to speak an unspeakable truth: that diagnosis is a political act. His masked testimony was an act of radical disclosure. In naming himself, he made space for others to speak, and helped change the face of psychological diagnosis forever.

Reflective Questions

1. Why was Dr John Fryer's masked appearance at the 1972 APA meeting such a significant moment in the history of diagnosis?
2. What does the concept of interpellation reveal about the way psychological diagnoses are created and experienced?
3. How have patient advocacy and social movements contributed to changes in specific diagnostic categories such as PTSD or autism?
4. In what ways do epistemological assumptions shape who gets diagnosed, and whose experiences are excluded from diagnostic systems?
5. Why is it important to understand psychological disorders as 'human kinds' rather than as 'natural kinds'?

Suggested Reading

Angel, K. (2012). Contested psychiatric ontology and feminist critique: 'Female Sexual Dysfunction' and the Diagnostic and Statistical Manual. *History of the Human Sciences, 25*(4), 3–24. https://doi.org/10.1177/0952695112456949.

Brinkmann, S. (2016). Toward a cultural psychology of mental disorder: The case of attention deficit hyperactivity disorder. *Culture & Psychology, 22*(1), 80–93. https://doi.org/10.1177/1354067X15621485.

Frances, A. (2013). *Saving Normal: An insider's revolt against out-of-control psychiatric diagnosis, DSM-5, big pharma, and the medicalization of ordinary life*. London: HarperCollins.

Freeborn, A. (2025). Testing psychiatrists to diagnose schizophrenia: Crisis, consensus, and computers in post-war psychiatry. *History of the Human Sciences, 38*(2), 18–39. https://doi.org/10.1177/09526951241309504.

Healy, D. (2014). Psychiatric 'diseases' in history. *History of Psychiatry, 25*(4), 450–458. https://doi.org/10.1177/0957154X14543980.

Kornaj, J. (2024). 'It's a fight—the whole personality of the patient to win': The development of concepts of psychosis in the Jewish Hospital in Warsaw, 1898–1943. *Journal of the History of the Behavioral Sciences, 60*(4), e22328. https://doi.org/10.1002/jhbs.22328.

Mayes, R., & Horwitz, A. V. (2005). DSM-III and the revolution in the classification of mental illness. *Journal of the History of the Behavioral Sciences, 41*(3), 249–267. https://doi.org/10.1002/jhbs.20103.

Moncrieff, J. (2010). Psychiatric diagnosis as a political device. *Social Theory and Health, 8*(4), 370–382. https://doi.org/10.1057/sth.2009.11.

Moncrieff, J., & Timimi, S. (2010). Is ADHD a valid diagnosis in adults? No. *British Medical Journal, 340*, c547. https://doi.org/10.1136/bmj.c547.

Noll, R. (2018). Feeling and smelling psychosis: American alienism, psychiatry, prodromes and the limits of 'category work'. *History of the Human Sciences, 31*(2), 22–41. https://doi.org/10.1177/0952695117750341.

Pienkos, E. (2024). Understanding, schizophrenia, and the limits of phenomenology. *Theory & Psychology, 34*(4), 427–445. https://doi.org/10.1177/09593543241266618.

Pilgrim, D. (2014). Historical resonances of the DSM-5 dispute: American exceptionalism or Eurocentrism? *History of the Human Sciences, 27*(2), 97–117. https://doi.org/10.1177/0952695114527998.

Reichardt, E. M., Stam, H. J., & Tan-MacNeill, K. (2023). 'Mere guesswork': Clarifying the role of intelligence, mentality, and psychometric testing in the diagnosis of 'mental defectives' for sterilization in Alberta from 1929 to 1972. *History of Psychology, 26*(4), 283–313. https://doi.org/10.1037/hop0000236.

Young, A. (2001). *The Harmony of Illusions: Inventing post-traumatic stress disorder*. Princeton, NJ: Princeton University Press.

Key Terms

Chronic Fatigue Syndrome/Myalgic Encephalomyelitis (CFS/ME) A contested diagnosis involving chronic exhaustion and cognitive dysfunction, historically marginalised and reframed through sustained patient activism.

Counter-hailing The process by which individuals or groups respond to or resist interpellation, challenging imposed diagnostic identities and offering alternative narratives or meanings.

Diagnostic and Statistical Manual of Mental Disorders (DSM) The standardised classification system used by American psychiatry to define and categorise mental disorders, produced by the American Psychiatric Association.

Epistemology The branch of philosophy concerned with knowledge—how it is produced, validated, and limited. In this chapter, it refers to the methods and assumptions that shape diagnostic systems.

Human Kinds Categories that are not naturally occurring but socially constructed, whose meaning and boundaries change over time due to human interpretation and interaction.

Interpellation A concept from Louis Althusser describing how individuals are 'hailed' into social roles by ideological systems; in this chapter, used to understand how people are positioned and categorised through psychological diagnosis.

Natural Kinds Scientifically observed categories in the natural world, such as physical diseases with identifiable biological markers, which are presumed to exist independently of human interpretation.

Neurodiversity A social and political movement that frames neurological conditions such as autism and ADHD, not as disorders but as natural variations in human cognition and identity.

Ontology The philosophical study of being and identity. In this context, it explores how receiving a diagnosis can shape or transform an individual's sense of self and lived experience.

Post-Traumatic Stress Disorder (PTSD) A psychological diagnosis that emerged from the activism of Vietnam War veterans, used to describe ongoing psychological distress following traumatic events.

FREE INSTRUCTOR & STUDENT RESOURCES

ONLINE RESOURCES

Visit the Instructor & Student Resources website at routledgelearning.com/bpscoretextbooks for free digital resources, including:

- Interactive quizzes and flashcards to test your knowledge
- Links to useful websites and videos
- Instructor manual, lecture slides, and course guide to enhance teaching and save instructors time

23

Telling Tales

The Cold War Parables of Social Psychology

Chapter Overview

This chapter reimagines some of the most famous experiments in American social psychology as symbolic stories or 'parables' that captured the moral imagination of Cold War society. Focusing on studies such as Milgram's obedience experiment, Zimbardo's prison simulation, and the bystander apathy narrative that emerged from the murder of Kitty Genovese, it explores how these canonical pieces of research reflected the anxieties and aspirations of their historical moment. Drawing on the critical thinking tool of the parable, the chapter unpacks the ways in which these experiments were crafted, received, and mythologised. It asks students to consider how psychology became a powerful site of cultural storytelling, sometimes generating truths, sometimes reinforcing ideological narratives. Throughout, we invite the reader to approach these studies as fables that reveal the hopes and fears of their time, and perhaps of ours too.

Telling Tales

On the cold morning of 13 March 1964, New Yorkers awoke to a horrifying headline: *'37 Who Saw Murder Didn't Call the Police.'* The story, printed in the *New York Times*, told of Kitty Genovese, a 28-year-old woman who was brutally attacked and murdered outside her apartment in Queens, New York. The assault reportedly lasted for over half an hour. She screamed for help. Lights flicked on in neighbouring windows. And yet, according to the story, none of the 37 witnesses intervened. No one called the police. No one came to her aid. It was a story that seemed to confirm the darkest fears of modern urban life: that in the anonymity of the city, empathy dissolves. That people, surrounded by others, would still do nothing. The public response was immediate and visceral. Editorials condemned the moral decay of city dwellers. Psychologists mobilised to explain this shocking apathy. Within months, psychologists Bibb Latané and John Darley had begun to conduct studies identifying what would become known as the bystander effect, the idea that the more people there are present, the less likely any one individual is to help. But there was just one problem. The story wasn't true, not entirely. Later, investigations revealed that several neighbours *did* call the police. One friend even held Kitty in her arms as she died. The myth of the 37 silent witnesses was largely a fiction, exaggerated or invented by the press. And yet, this myth launched decades of psychological research, cementing an image of urban indifference that became a foundational story in social psychology. This chapter begins with the Kitty Genovese myth not to discredit the research it inspired but to ask a deeper question: what happens when psychology builds its science on symbolic stories, stories that tap

DOI: 10.4324/9781003565482-23

into cultural anxieties, tell moral lessons, and capture the public imagination, even if they are not entirely true? In what ways does psychology participate in creating modern parables, narratives that shape how we understand ourselves, our society, and each other?

Chapter Contents

- Introduces the concept of 'parable' as a critical lens for reinterpreting classic American studies in social psychology.
- Reconstructs the historical and cultural backdrop of the Cold War, exploring how social psychology responded to societal anxieties.
- Critically examines key studies, including Milgram, Zimbardo, Asch, Sherif, Bandura, and bystander apathy, as symbolic acts of storytelling.

Chapter Objectives

- To equip students with a critical framework for understanding the narrative structure and cultural function of classic experiments in social psychology.
- To foster an appreciation of how historical context, especially the Cold War era, shaped the design, interpretation, and reception of these studies.
- To introduce the critical thinking tool of *parable*, enabling students to identify how psychological knowledge can function both as explanation and myth.

CRITICAL THINKING TOOL
PARABLE

A *parable* is a short, symbolic story that teaches a moral lesson. But in this chapter we use the term more broadly to describe how certain psychological studies function like cultural parables, stories that resonate far beyond the laboratory. These are not just scientific experiments; they are symbolic texts that encapsulate deep social fears, desires, and beliefs. When we read Milgram's obedience experiment or Zimbardo's prison simulation as a parable, we are not asking whether the study was methodologically flawless or whether its findings can be replicated. Instead, we are asking: what does this study tell us about the cultural moment in which it appeared? What moral does it teach? Why did it capture the imagination of psychologists, the media, and the public so powerfully? Parables simplify and dramatise. They offer unambiguous lessons in situations that are far more complex in reality. In doing so, they can reproduce myths, about human nature, about morality, about society, that shape public understanding. But they also have critical value: they reveal what a culture finds urgent, threatening, or admirable. This lens does not dismiss the importance of the research; it reframes it. Reading psychological studies as parables allows us to see how science and storytelling collide, and how psychology participates in the construction of social meaning. In the chapter that follows, we will treat each classic experiment as a kind of modern parable, a fable through which postwar America narrated its deepest social and psychological anxieties.

Introduction

In the decades following the Second World War, American social psychology entered a golden age of experimentation. Seeking to understand the forces that drive human behaviour in social contexts, psychologists turned their attention to topics such as conformity, obedience, aggression, and group dynamics. The field promised scientific answers to some of the most troubling moral questions of the time: why do people follow orders? Why do they remain passive in the face of violence? How easily do people embrace assigned roles?

But these now-iconic studies, by Milgram, Zimbardo, Asch, Latané, and Darley, Sherif, and Bandura, did more than generate data. They became foundational stories, repeated in classrooms, textbooks, movies, comic books, and media reports. They offered powerful, emotionally charged lessons about human nature. In doing so, they crossed the boundary from science into myth.

This chapter invites you to re-examine these studies as modern parables. Each experiment, we will argue, reflects a particular cultural anxiety of Cold War America, about authority, community, individuality, and control. By reading them as symbolic narratives rather than as neutral observations, we can uncover their deeper social meanings and their ongoing influence. In the sections that follow, we will explore these studies as the fables we live by, illuminating, persuasive, sometimes misleading, but always revealing.

Historical Issues

To understand why classic American social psychology produced such enduring experiments, we must first understand the historical moment in which they emerged. The period from the 1940s to the 1970s was defined by profound social, political, and moral anxiety, a backdrop that both inspired and shaped the psychological imagination of the time.

In the immediate aftermath of the Holocaust, psychologists and the wider public grappled with the horrifying realisation that ordinary people could be complicit in extraordinary evil. The idea that blind obedience, not monstrous intent, could explain such atrocities became a central concern. This gave rise to Milgram's now-famous studies on obedience to authority, which tapped into a broader postwar reckoning with authority and the so-called banality of evil.

Simultaneously, the Cold War intensified fears of ideological conformity, surveillance, and loss of autonomy. American society was saturated with messages about loyalty, subversion, and the dangers of communism. It was no coincidence that Asch's conformity studies and Sherif's group conflict experiments gained traction at this time. They were responses to a cultural climate that feared the erosion of individual judgement in the face of groupthink.

The era also reflected a profound optimism in science. Behaviourism and positivism were ascendant, promising objective, universal truths about human nature. The social sciences aligned themselves with this model, favouring experiments that could produce 'laws of behaviour'. Yet in their pursuit of certainty, researchers often created highly artificial settings, generating dramatic outcomes that resonated culturally, even if their replicability was questionable.

Moreover, the ethical framework of the time was still evolving. In the absence of modern protocols for informed consent, techniques of deception and emotional manipulation were common features of research. The field was driven by a desire to create grand theories that could explain complex human phenomena, from genocide to social apathy, with a few powerful variables. These conditions created a fertile ground for psychological storytelling, where experiments became allegories.

Key Individuals

Muzafer Sherif (1906–1988) was a Turkish American social psychologist best known for the Robbers' Cave experiment (1954), which explored intergroup conflict and cooperation. Conducted in a summer camp setting, the study divided young boys into two groups, gradually escalating competition between them to provoke hostility, before later introducing superordinate goals to encourage cooperation. Sherif concluded that conflict arose not from individual pathology but from group structures and competing interests. The study fed into a broader Cold War concern with group processes and conflict resolution.

Solomon Asch (1907–1996) produced one of the most iconic experiments in social psychology: the conformity studies of the 1950s. Participants were asked to match the length of lines on cards, surrounded by confederates who intentionally gave wrong answers. Asch found that a significant proportion of participants conformed to the group's incorrect answer, even when the correct answer was obvious. The study crystallised fears of mindless conformity in a McCarthy-era America, when groupthink and the dangers of dissent were cultural flashpoints.

Stanley Milgram (1933–1984) followed in this lineage with his notorious obedience to authority experiments (1961–1963), conducted at Yale University. Believing they were administering real electric shocks to another person, participants continued to do so under the prodding of an authoritative experimenter, even when the 'learner' (a confederate) screamed in pain or fell silent. Milgram's conclusion was stark: ordinary people will commit inhumane acts when instructed to do so by authority. This study was often interpreted as offering insight into the Holocaust and the capacity for evil within modern bureaucracies. It remains one of the most cited and taught studies in psychology, often summarised with the claim that 'two-thirds of people will obey authority to the point of killing'.

Philip Zimbardo (1933–2024) pushed the narrative further with the Stanford Prison Experiment (1971), in which student volunteers were assigned to roles of guards and prisoners in a simulated prison. Within days, the experiment deteriorated as the 'guards' became abusive and the 'prisoners' showed signs of psychological distress. Zimbardo concluded that situational factors, not personality, drive behaviour, and, moreover, that people internalise their assigned roles with frightening ease. The study became a touchstone for understanding the corrosive effects of institutional power and was widely used to explain real-world atrocities in prisons and military settings, particularly following the abuses at Abu Ghraib.

John Darley (1938–2018) and Bibb Latané (b.1937) were central figures in the development of bystander apathy theory. Sparked by the widely reported (though later discredited) story of the 1964 murder of Kitty Genovese in New York, where 37 neighbours supposedly watched and did nothing, Darley and Latané conducted mimetic experiments that demonstrated a 'diffusion of responsibility' in group settings. Their smoke-filled room and seizure studies showed that people were less likely to help in emergencies when others were present. The studies were read as evidence of a fractured and individualistic society, seemingly apathetic in the face of others' suffering.

Albert Bandura (1925–2021) contributed a different kind of foundational tale with the Bobo Doll Experiment (1961), in which children who watched an adult model behave aggressively towards a doll were more likely to imitate that behaviour. Bandura's findings were interpreted as proof of the power of observational learning and mass media in shaping aggression. The experiment underpinned growing concerns about television violence and childhood behaviour, becoming part of a broader cultural anxiety about the influence of media.

Epistemological Issues

At the heart of these classic studies lies a pressing epistemological question: what kind of knowledge do they actually produce? Are they revealing fundamental truths about human nature, or constructing narratives that resonate with particular historical and cultural conditions? Many of these experiments took place in artificial settings, often involving deception, confederates, and tightly controlled conditions. Whether it was Asch's line-judging task or Milgram's electric shocks, the behaviour observed was shaped by highly specific and sometimes contrived scenarios. This raises concerns about ecological validity.

A related problem is demand characteristics, participants' tendency to guess what the study is about and to behave accordingly. In several cases the boundary between role-playing and genuine behaviour became blurred. Were participants demonstrating psychological truths, or responding to scripts and expectations they believed they were meant to perform?

Measurement is another issue. Terms such as 'obedience', 'conformity', or 'aggression' sound straightforward, but their operational definitions were often narrow or ambiguous. For instance, Milgram interpreted pressing a button on a fake shock machine as 'obedience', but later critics suggested that participants may have been cooperating with the experimenter, and not necessarily submitting to authority.

Perhaps most crucially, we must consider the role of the researcher as narrator. Each of these studies was framed, sometimes dramatically, by the researcher's interpretation. They shaped how the findings were presented to the public, often simplifying messy data into clean moral lessons. Rather than discovering immutable truths, these studies may have constructed compelling stories, stories that reflect more about the era's anxieties than about universal human psychology.

Ontological Issues

Solomon Asch's famed conformity experiments, so compelling in 1950s America, proved strangely unreproducible. British researchers who conducted a direct replication of Asch's experiment in the UK using science and engineering students found significantly lower levels of conformity (only 1 conforming response out of 396 trials). The social environment had changed: the deferential, postwar consensus of Asch's America had given way to a more individualistic, countercultural climate in 1970s Britain. In ecological terms, the niche that had allowed conformity to flourish, patriarchal authority, group loyalty, Cold War anxiety had eroded. Asch's 'discovery' was a parable of its historical moment. Once the cultural scaffolding was gone, the behaviour vanished with it.

Albert Bandura's Bobo Doll Experiments are often cited as empirical proof that children imitate aggressive behaviour modelled by adults. Yet anyone who has ever observed children at play knows that imitation is a foundational human capacity. From peekaboo to storytelling, mimicry saturates the social lives of children. What, then, did Bandura truly 'discover'? Was it that that aggression, when theatrically demonstrated in a context stripped of real-world consequences, might be echoed in toy-pummelling gestures? The experiment arguably revealed less about learning than about the psychology's desire to brand commonplace human behaviour as scientific novelty. In this sense, Bobo becomes another *parable*, this time about the fragility of the child's moral world and the supposed power of media and adult influence in shaping it. Bandura's study thus participates in a broader pattern: the transmutation of common sense into gold standard psychological science through the alchemy of experiment.

Recent scholarship by Stephen Gibson has radically reframed our understanding of the Milgram obedience experiments. Drawing directly from Milgram's own transcripts and archival recordings, Gibson challenged the canonical interpretation that participants blindly followed authority. Instead, he revealed a dynamic process in which many participants actively negotiated, resisted, and questioned the commands of the experimenter. Far from being passive conduits of obedience, these individuals displayed oppositional agency, a capacity to object, deflect, or reframe the situation. This re-reading unearths a crucial ontological oversight in Milgram's narrative: the erasure of the subject's active meaning-making. What emerges, then, is not a psychological discovery about innate obedience but a cultural parable about authority and submission, one whose lasting power depended precisely on the silencing of alternative subject positions within the experimental frame.

The Stanford Prison Experiment, often heralded as a revelation about the corrupting nature of power and roles, in fact staged an already-familiar cultural script. By the early 1970s, the American public had been repeatedly exposed to scenes of brutality by uniformed officers, on television, in the streets, and through civil rights reportage. The idea that authority corrupts, or that guards might abuse power, was hardly a novel psychological insight; it was long-standing social reality. Zimbardo's experimental theatre merely re-performed what was already known. Moreover, his active involvement in shaping the events, and the absence of methodological controls, undermine the claim that this was even a scientific experiment as such. It functioned more as a *morality play* for an anxious Cold War society, a symbolic dramatisation of authority and degradation whose power lay in its allegorical resonance.

In 2002, the BBC undertook a televised replication of Zimbardo's Stanford Prison Experiment under the guidance of social psychologists Alex Haslam and Steve Reicher. But instead of confirming Zimbardo's thesis, namely that ordinary people, when cast as guards, will readily abuse power, the study produced a radically different outcome. The guards, far from becoming authoritarian, struggled to form a coherent group identity or impose control. Meanwhile, the prisoners organised themselves, developed solidarity, and eventually overthrew the guards. What had once been interpreted as a natural psychological response to hierarchical roles now appeared contingent, fragile, and entirely reversible. The study's opposite findings, televised for a public audience, delivered an implicit critique of the original: that Zimbardo's experiment had staged a specific performance, one shaped by the cultural and institutional expectations of early 1970s America.

Power

Power saturates the classic experiments of American social psychology. It operates not just within the lab, indeed as an experimental variable in some cases, but also in the cultural narratives that grew around the studies and in the authority that psychology itself claimed as a discipline.

Power was deliberately structured within the experiments. Milgram's white-coated experimenter, Zimbardo's prison guards, the authority embedded in a clipboard or a stopwatch, each set the stage for participants to submit, resist, or perform. They were carefully designed to replicate asymmetries of control, mimicking wider societal hierarchies: teacher and learner, guard and prisoner, sane and insane. Often, the power of the setting itself, the institution, the role, the rules, overrode the power of conscience.

Power was not only enacted in the studies; it was also produced by them. The narratives that emerged, of blind obedience, of apathetic bystanders, of situational corruption, quickly entered public discourse. They became powerful explanations for disturbing social phenomena, offering comfort in simplicity. If people harm others because of 'the situation', then evil becomes situational too: manageable, explainable, even preventable. But this also carried the risk of absolving systems, institutions, and ideologies of deeper responsibility.

Finally, the parables these studies created often reflected and reinforced broader power structures. The fear of moral collapse, the pathologising of deviance, the emphasis on individual weakness in the face of social pressure, all echoed the ideological tensions of Cold War America. These were not just experiments on behaviour, they were cultural diagnostics, crafted in an era deeply concerned with conformity, control, and ideological loyalty.

Chapter Summary

This chapter has revisited some of the most iconic experiments in American social psychology as modern parables. These studies captivated the public imagination because they offered emotionally charged narratives about human nature, power, and morality. Their legacy lies less in the robustness of their data and more in the compelling stories they told.

Beginning with the myth of Kitty Genovese, we explored how a flawed media narrative launched an entire research tradition on bystander apathy. From there, we followed how Asch, Sherif, Milgram, Zimbardo, Latané and Darley, and Bandura crafted powerful fables about conformity, conflict, obedience, institutional cruelty, urban alienation, and imitation. Each study offered a moral shorthand, a simplified lesson about human behaviour, framed in binaries of good and evil, submission and resistance.

Using the critical concept of *parable*, we reframed these experiments as cultural artefacts shaped by the anxieties of Cold War America. In a time preoccupied with authoritarianism, conformity, and the fragility of the self, these studies resonated because they dramatised those very fears. But like all tidy stories, they also obscured complexity.

Epistemologically, these experiments were fraught with artificiality and fragile generalisability. Ontologically, they imagined people as passive subjects of social forces, an image as much a reflection of Cold War paranoia as of empirical truth. And in terms of power, they shaped the very definition of what psychology claimed to know.

To read them as parables does not diminish their significance but reveals it. Social psychology tells stories about the world, stories that explain, reassure, unsettle, and, above all, disclose more than they intend. Social psychology, in other words, is always telling tales.

Reflective Questions

1. What does it mean to describe classic social psychology experiments as 'parables'?
2. Why might the historical and political context of the Cold War have influenced the kinds of research questions social psychologists asked?
3. How does the Kitty Genovese story exemplify the role of myth in shaping psychological research?
4. What are the epistemological risks of assuming that laboratory behaviour reveals universal truths about human nature?
5. To what extent do experiments like Milgram's and Zimbardo's reinforce existing societal power structures rather than challenge them?

Suggested Reading

Brannigan, A. (2004). *The Use and Misuse of the Experimental Method in Social Psychology.* Abingdon, Oxon: Routledge.

Brannigan, A., Nicholson, I., & Cherry, F. (2015). Introduction to the special issue: Unplugging the Milgram machine. *Theory & Psychology, 25*(5), 551–563. https://doi.org/10.1177/0959354315604408.

De Vos, J. (2010). From Milgram to Zimbardo: the double birth of postwar psychology/psychologization. *History of the Human Sciences, 23*(5), 156–175. https://doi.org/10.1177/0952695110384774.

Drury, S., Hutchens, S. A., Shuttlesworth, D. E., & White, C. L. (2012). Philip G. Zimbardo on his career and the Stanford Prison Experiment's 40th anniversary. *History of Psychology, 15*(2), 161–170. https://doi.org/10.1037/a0025884.

Gibson, S. (2013). Milgram's obedience experiments: A rhetorical analysis. *British Journal of Social Psychology, 52*(2), 290–309. https://doi.org/10.1111/j.2044-8309.2011.02070.x.

Griggs, R. A., & Whitehead, G. I. (2015). Coverage of recent criticisms of Milgram's obedience experiments in introductory social psychology textbooks. *Theory & Psychology, 25*(5), 564–580. https://doi.org/10.1177/0959354315601231.

Herrera, C. D. (1997). A historical interpretation of deceptive experiments in American psychology. *History of the Human Sciences, 10*(1), 23–36. https://doi.org/10.1177/095269519701000102.

Hoffman, E., Myerberg, N. R., & Morawski, J. G. (2015). Acting otherwise: Resistance, agency, and subjectivities in Milgram's studies of obedience. *Theory & Psychology, 25*(5), 670–689. https://doi.org/10.1177/0959354315608705.

Manning, R., Levine, M., & Collins, A. (2007). The Kitty Genovese murder and the social psychology of helping: The parable of the 38 witnesses. *American Psychologist, 62*(6), 555–562. https://doi.org/10.1037/0003-066X.62.6.555.

Mastroianni, G. R. (2015). Obedience in perspective: Psychology and the Holocaust. *Theory & Psychology, 25*(5), 657–669. https://doi.org/10.1177/0959354315608963.

Perry, G. (2013). *Behind the Shock Machine: The untold story of the notorious Milgram psychology experiments*. New York: The New Press.

Shotter, J. (2014). Agential realism, social constructionism, and our living relations to our surroundings: Sensing similarities rather than seeing patterns. *Theory & Psychology, 24*(3), 305–325. https://doi.org/10.1177/0959354313514144.

Šikl, R., Preiss, M., & Hoskovcová, S. (2024). Between conformity and individuality: Psychologists in Czechoslovakia during normalization (1968–1989). *History of Psychology, 27*(2), 178–198. https://doi.org/10.1037/hop0000254.

Yanchar, S. C. (2020). Concern and control in human agency. *Theory & Psychology, 31*(1), 24–42. https://doi.org/10.1177/0959354320958078.

Key Terms

Allegory A symbolic story in which the characters, events, or settings represent abstract ideas or moral qualities. In this chapter, social psychology experiments are read as allegories that reflect societal anxieties.

Banality of Evil A concept introduced by political theorist Hannah Arendt to describe how ordinary people can commit horrific acts not out of fanaticism or cruelty but through unthinking conformity, obedience, and a failure to critically reflect on their actions within bureaucratic systems.

Bystander Effect A social psychological theory suggesting that individuals are less likely to offer help to a victim when other people are present. It emerged in the wake of the (misreported) Kitty Genovese case.

Cold War A geopolitical period following the Second World War, marked by ideological conflict between the United States and the Soviet Union. It fostered widespread societal fears—such as authoritarianism and conformity—which shaped psychological research.

Conformity The act of matching attitudes, beliefs, or behaviours to group norms. In the context of this chapter, it features in Asch's line-judgement experiments and is explored for its cultural and symbolic significance.

Critical Thinking Tool: Parable An interpretative device that helps students understand psychological experiments as symbolic stories with moral or ideological lessons. The chapter uses this tool to reframe classic studies in terms of their narrative power.

Ecological Validity The extent to which research findings can be generalised to real-world settings. The chapter critiques the lack of ecological validity in many classic laboratory studies.

Kitty Genovese A young woman whose 1964 murder in New York became a moral parable in psychology. The original story of public indifference was later shown to be largely false but profoundly influenced research.

Milgram Experiment A study conducted by Stanley Milgram (1963) to test obedience to authority. This chapter examines the moral and cultural narrative the experiment came to symbolise during the Cold War era.

Myth A story or idea that expresses deep cultural beliefs and is widely accepted, often without scrutiny. In this chapter, psychological studies are examined as modern myths that shape public perception.

Narrative Psychology An approach to psychology that focuses on how human beings make sense of their experiences through stories. This chapter invites readers to consider how experiments function as narrative devices.

Obedience Compliance with an order, request, or law. In social psychology, often studied in the context of authority figures, as in Milgram's experiments.

Parable A simple story used to illustrate a moral or philosophical lesson. The chapter applies this concept to psychological experiments, arguing that they convey more than empirical results—they tell cultural stories.

Power The ability to influence or control others, structures, or narratives. Explored in this chapter in relation to both the content of the experiments and the authority of psychological knowledge itself.

Replication Crisis A recent controversy in psychology concerning the difficulty of replicating many foundational studies. This issue is linked in the chapter to the constructed, context-dependent nature of knowledge.

Symbolic Function The role experiments play in conveying meaning beyond their data—through narrative, metaphor, or parable. A key concept in understanding psychology as a cultural practice.

Zimbardo Experiment Also known as the Stanford Prison Experiment (1971), this study explored the psychological effects of perceived power. This chapter critiques it as a pre-scripted performance with enduring mythic power.

ONLINE RESOURCES

FREE INSTRUCTOR & STUDENT RESOURCES

Visit the Instructor & Student Resources website at routledgelearning.com/bpscoretextbooks for free digital resources, including:

- Interactive quizzes and flashcards to test your knowledge
- Links to useful websites and videos
- Instructor manual, lecture slides, and course guide to enhance teaching and save instructors time

4 Hidden Treasures

Humanistic Psychotherapy and the Dialectic of Meaning

Chapter Overview

This chapter explores the rich and sometimes contradictory traditions of humanistic and existential counselling psychology. Emerging in the mid-twentieth century as a hopeful response to widespread alienation and the perceived dehumanisation of mainstream psychology, these approaches emphasised personal meaning, authenticity, emotional honesty, and the therapeutic relationship. Central to the chapter is the use of *hermeneutics*, the art and theory of interpretation, as a critical thinking tool. The traditions are read through a binary relationship: a *hermeneutics of trust*, which embraces their emancipatory and ethical potential, and a *hermeneutics of suspicion*, which interrogates how these same ideas may align with broader socio-political shifts, such as individualisation. Through the work of key figures, students are invited to consider how concepts such as self-actualisation, personal growth, and meaning-making have shaped both therapy and culture. Yet these ideals are not immune to critique. What appears liberating may, in some contexts, reinforce pressure to perform psychological well-being in ways that are aligned with political agendas.

Hidden Treasures

In 1967, Violet Oaklander was at a crossroads, even if she did not know it. A recently qualified graduate teaching elementary school in Long Beach, California, one day she played a Woody Guthrie protest song to her first-grade students. The children loved the song's rhythm and its raw, rebellious spirit. But within days, school authorities reported her as a communist. Violet was stunned. The song was meant to be a relationship bridge, a way of reaching children who rarely spoke, not a political broadcast. Yet now she faced a dilemma: to challenge the accusation politically, or to take stock, and to turn inwards towards something subtler but perhaps more enduring. She chose the second path. As Oaklander herself later reflected, 'I guess I was an alternative teacher before I knew what that meant.' That moment of censorship became, paradoxically, a source of inspiration. If the political content of the music was too threatening, perhaps the emotional content was where the real power lay. She began working with emotionally troubled children, drawn to Gestalt therapy, and bringing modelling clay, art materials, sand trays, and storytelling into her sessions. Over time, she found that what these children could not say in words, they could express through colour, shape, and play. The therapy room became her new home, one where inner meaning could be enacted without fear of institutional censorship. Years later, in her book *Hidden Treasure: A Map to the Child's Inner Self* (2006), she explored the profound inner riches submerged

DOI: 10.4324/9781003565482-24

beneath children's hushed worlds. If her own story was also a map of a personal journey, then it would chart how a public accusation gave rise to a private revelation and her choosing a different pathway. What seemed like political defeat became an existential shift, resistance through presence, not protest. Violet's story mimics the dilemma explored in this chapter: What should we do when we find meaning in both compassion and confrontation at the same time?

Chapter Contents

- The chapter explores the evolution of humanistic and existential approaches to counselling psychology in the context of twentieth-century cultural, philosophical, and therapeutic developments.
- Key figures are introduced, and their contributions critically examined.
- The chapter uses *hermeneutics*, particularly the dialectic of trust and suspicion, as a critical thinking tool to explore the meanings, promises, and limits of selfhood, freedom, and psychological healing.

Chapter Objectives

- To examine the historical, epistemological, ontological, and political dimensions of humanistic and existential counselling psychology.
- To assess the contributions of major figures in these traditions and to understand how their work responded to cultural and clinical needs.
- To apply the critical thinking tool of *hermeneutics* in analysing the dialectical tensions within these approaches, between liberation and constraint, authenticity and adaptation.

CRITICAL THINKING TOOL
HERMENEUTICS

Hermeneutics is the philosophical tradition concerned with interpretation: how we make sense of texts, experiences, and human meaning. Originating in the interpretation of the Bible and legal texts, hermeneutics argues that understanding meaning is never neutral or detached; rather, it is always situated in a historical and cultural context. The 'hermeneutic circle' captures this: we can only understand the parts of a story by grasping the whole, yet we only comprehend the whole through its parts. Interpretation is therefore a dynamic, reflexive process.

A *hermeneutics of trust* invites us to approach humanistic and existential psychology with empathy and generosity. It acknowledges that these traditions were born out of a sincere desire to alleviate suffering, to affirm the dignity of human experience, and to promote freedom, responsibility, and meaning. The founders of these approaches sought to humanise therapy, to attend to potential, growth, and the fullness of life, not just illness. A hermeneutics of trust urges us to understand these efforts on their own terms, as attempts to respond ethically and creatively to the challenges of modern existence.

By contrast, a *hermeneutics of suspicion* casts a critical eye. Drawing on thinkers such as Marx, Nietzsche, Freud, and more recently Jan De Vos, it examines what is obscured when psychology promises inner freedom. The language of self-actualisation and personal growth can shift attention away from structural injustice, reframing systemic problems as individual challenges. Rather than liberating the self, the hermeneutics of suspicion critically examines the extent to which these ideals may function as a cultural demand for the self to adapt to an increasingly individualised and competitive world.

Introduction

Humanistic and existential counselling psychology emerged in the mid-twentieth century as radical alternatives to the dominant currents of behaviourism and psychoanalysis. These movements placed human experience, meaning, and potential at the centre of psychological understanding. Rejecting the idea of people as passive, conditioned organisms or bundles of unconscious sexualised drives, humanistic and existential psychologists instead envisioned human beings as capable of choice, growth, and self-transcendence. Their approaches to therapy were rooted in empathy, authenticity, and a belief in the inherent dignity and agency of the person.

But as the language of meaning, authenticity, and self-actualisation has proliferated, so too have questions about the cultural function of humanistic psychology. Amid rising economic inequality and social disconnection, psychology has turned decisively towards the individual. Humanistic ideas, while noble in origin, have been accused of contributing to the wider cultural trend of placing the burden of happiness, success, and mental health squarely on the individual.

This chapter explores these tensions through a reflexive hermeneutic circle. A hermeneutics of trust seeks to understand humanistic and existential counselling as sincere efforts to promote psychological and ethical flourishing. A hermeneutics of suspicion, by contrast, interrogates the social and political implications of these same efforts. In doing so, we aim to deepen our understanding.

Historical Issues

The emergence of humanistic and existential counselling psychology must be understood in relation to the dramatic social and cultural shifts of the twentieth century. In the wake of two world wars, industrialisation, the decline of religious authority, and the fragmentation of traditional communities, the individual was increasingly left to navigate the question of meaning alone. In the United States, particularly after the Second World War, there was a widespread sense of spiritual exhaustion amid unprecedented material prosperity. In this context, humanistic and existential approaches offered a timely and hopeful response: psychology could serve as a guide to living well.

From a hermeneutics of trust perspective, this was a moment of ethical innovation. The breakdown of external structures, such as family, church, and class solidarity, created opportunities for a psychology that could affirm inner life, autonomy, and self-realisation. Influential voices, such as those of Abraham Maslow and Carl

Rogers, offered a language of human potential and purpose, speaking to a population desperate for depth during a period of conformity and obedience. In Cold War America, these ideas carried political weight: the emphasis on inner freedom and self-determination served as a cultural counterpoint to the perceived collectivism and authoritarianism of the Soviet Union. Humanistic psychology was, in part, a defence of liberal individualism, and of the dignity of the person.

Yet, from the perspective of the hermeneutics of suspicion, a different story emerges. As sociologist David Riesman lamented in *The Lonely Crowd* (1950), American society had shifted from tradition-directed and inner-directed modes of identity to a new, 'other-directed' personality type, one shaped by external approval, mass media, and corporate culture. A generation later, Christopher Lasch's *The Culture of Narcissism* (1979) argued that self-awareness was no longer a path to liberation but a coping mechanism for living in a world stripped of social solidarity. In *Bowling Alone* (2000), Robert Putnam detailed how civic life in the United States had entered a deep decline as social capital and collective belonging eroded, leaving individuals disconnected from meaningful community. From this perspective, humanistic and existential psychology may have helped reframe systemic social dislocation as personal crisis. The demand for self-actualisation and authenticity could, paradoxically, fuel anxiety and self-blame, especially as the responsibility for emotional well-being was gradually shifted away from community and state, and onto the individual.

Key Individuals

Abraham Maslow (1908–1970) was a founding figure of humanistic psychology. He was best known for his hierarchy of needs, a motivational model that culminates in 'self-actualisation'. Dissatisfied with psychology's emphasis on pathology, Maslow sought to understand psychological health, creativity, and fulfilment. His studies of exceptional individuals led him to identify 'peak experiences', moments of deep insight, joy, or transcendence, as central to well-being. Maslow argued that psychological science should concern itself with the full range of human potential.

Carl Rogers (1902–1987) revolutionised psychotherapy with his client-centred approach, which emphasised empathy, unconditional positive regard, and authenticity as the key conditions for psychological change. He believed that individuals possess an inherent tendency towards growth, and that therapeutic progress arises when people feel deeply heard and accepted. Rogers challenged both the interpretive authority of psychoanalysis and behaviourism's mechanistic reductionism, instead placing relational presence at the heart of therapy. His ideas extended into education, conflict resolution, and organisational development, shaping how we understand dialogue, respect, and the conditions under which people thrive.

Viktor Frankl (1905–1997) was a psychiatrist and Holocaust survivor who developed logotherapy, a form of existential psychotherapy grounded in the 'will to meaning'. Frankl argued that the search for purpose is the most fundamental human motivation, and that even profound suffering can be made meaningful if it is integrated into a life narrative shaped by values. His widely read book *Man's Search for Meaning* (1959, originally entitled *A Psychologist Experiences the Concentration Camp*) offered a compelling synthesis of existential philosophy and clinical insight, drawn from his experience of surviving Nazi concentration camps. Frankl emphasised that individuals are always free to choose their attitude, even in the most extreme conditions.

Rollo May (1909–1994) played a pivotal role in introducing existential ideas to American psychology. Influenced by European philosophy, he explored how anxiety, guilt, freedom, and destiny shape the human experience. May saw psychological suffering as part of the universal existential struggle rather than as a purely clinical problem. His books, including *The Meaning of Anxiety* (1950) and *Love and Will* (1989), offered a rich, literary approach to the dilemmas of modern life. May argued that creativity, courage, and myth are essential tools for navigating meaning in a fragmented world. He was also critical of superficial optimism in psychology, insisting that therapy should address moral and spiritual concerns.

Medard Boss (1903–1990) was a Swiss psychiatrist who, in collaboration with philosopher Martin Heidegger, developed Daseinsanalysis, a distinctive form of existential therapy. Rooted in Heidegger's concept of *being-in-the-world*, Boss challenged the medicalisation of mental distress and the abstract categorisation of people into diagnoses. He believed that psychological suffering could only be understood in relation to the person's lived context, their time, space, language, and relationships. Daseinsanalysis rejects the idea of the self as a hidden inner entity, focusing instead on how one exists and discloses meaning through everyday life.

Violet Oaklander (1927–2021) was a pioneering American therapist who transformed the field of child psychotherapy by integrating Gestalt principles with expressive and sensory-based methods. Initially trained in education and art, Oaklander entered the world of therapy through her work with emotionally distressed children during the late 1960s, a period marked by shifting cultural attitudes towards childhood, discipline, and emotional development. Rather than relying on verbal insight or behavioural management, she developed a multimodal approach that used creative media as pathways into a child's inner world. Her method respected the symbolic language of children, allowing them to express complex emotions, unresolved conflicts, and aspects of identity that could not yet be articulated in words.

Irvin D. Yalom (b.1931) is a leading existential psychotherapist whose work assimilates insights from philosophy, fiction, and clinical practice. He identified four 'ultimate concerns'—death, freedom, isolation, and meaninglessness—as the existential dilemmas underlying much psychological suffering. Yalom's therapeutic approach focuses on confronting these concerns directly, encouraging clients to live more authentically in light of their finitude. His accessible writing, especially *Love's Executioner* (1989) and *Staring at the Sun* (2008), brought existential therapy into popular awareness while retaining philosophical depth. Yalom is also known for his emphasis on the here-and-now in group therapy, and for modelling a transparent, relational stance.

Emmy van Deurzen (b.1951) is an existential psychotherapist and philosopher who helped establish existential therapy in the UK. She emphasises that therapy should not aim to 'fix' clients but to help them face life's fundamental dilemmas; freedom, mortality, meaning, and responsibility. Drawing on existential phenomenology, van Deurzen views psychological distress as a disruption in how people make sense of their world. Her books, including *Everyday Mysteries* (2010), have made existential theory accessible while maintaining philosophical rigour. Van Deurzen remains a leading advocate for a therapy of depth, values, and ethical reflection.

Linda James Myers (b.1948) is a pioneering African American psychologist best known for developing the theory of Optimal Psychology, a humanistic framework rooted in African and Afrocentric worldviews. Her work challenges the individualistic, materialist assumptions of Western psychology by affirming the interconnectedness of all life, the centrality of spiritual meaning, and the ethical imperative of communal harmony. Drawing from African philosophy, particularly the principle of *Ubuntu* ('I am because we are'), Myers redefines self-actualisation as a process of aligning with a higher, collective consciousness. In contrast to the Western emphasis on self as a bounded, autonomous agent, Myers presents the self as fundamentally relational, embedded in history, ancestry, and moral responsibility. Psychological health, in her view, is achieved through living in right relation, with others, with nature, and with one's purpose. Her work bridges the existential concern with meaning and the humanistic focus on potential while also offering a powerful critique of the colonial and racial biases embedded in mainstream psychology.

Epistemological Issues

At its heart, humanistic and existential counselling psychology represents a challenge to dominant epistemologies in psychology, especially the legacy of positivism. Rather than seeking universal laws, statistical regularities, or observable behaviours, these traditions argue that psychological understanding begins with the lived experience of the individual. The self is not a variable to be measured but a subject to be understood.

From a hermeneutics of trust perspective, this epistemological reorientation can be seen as both radical and necessary. Rogers' emphasis on empathy was an epistemology: we can know and understand others best when we are present, receptive, and open to their frame of reference. Maslow rejected the idea that psychology should just study illness or ordinary behaviour, insisting instead that the exceptional, the transcendent, and the fulfilled were also worthy of scientific attention. Existential and humanistic psychologists have embraced philosophy and literature, qualitative methods, phenomenology, and first-person narratives as additional ways of grasping the complexity of human meaning.

From a hermeneutics of suspicion perspective, this valorisation of subjectivity raises significant concerns. When experience is the primary site of truth, it becomes difficult to adjudicate between competing claims, or to recognise when an individual's perception is shaped by ideology, trauma, or power. The emphasis on 'your truth' or 'my truth' may, at its extreme, slide into epistemological relativism, a condition where shared realities dissolve, and all critique risks being seen as invalidating.

Moreover, the centrality of individual meaning-making can support a psychologised framing of social issues. If a person's suffering is interpreted only in terms of their unique worldview, there may be little space to discuss the structural forces that shape that worldview in the first place. In works such as *Psychologization and the Subject of Late Modernity* (2013), De Vos warns that psychologisation often begins at the epistemic level, when psychology's interpretive gaze becomes the only lens through which experience is rendered intelligible. In this light, the very tools that seek to liberate the individual may obscure the social, cultural, and political matrices that underlie suffering.

Ontological Issues

Humanistic and existential counselling psychology rests on a distinctive and optimistic ontology: a belief in the human being as meaning-seeking, free, and fundamentally capable of growth. Unlike deterministic models that reduce behaviour to conditioning or biology, these approaches hold that individuals are not simply products of their environments or histories; they are also agents of their own becoming. Psychological distress is often framed as a response to the challenge of living authentically in a complex world. While existential and humanistic therapies offer a powerful reassertion of the person's depth and potential, they may also carry, unwittingly, the burden of idealised personhood.

For the hermeneutics of trust, this ontology is liberating. Maslow's concept of self-actualisation, Rogers' faith in the actualising tendency, and Frankl's insistence on the will to meaning all assert that human beings have ethical and existential depth. Rollo May's emphasis on will, destiny, and myth positioned psychological work as a moral enterprise, one that affirms freedom, responsibility, and the possibility of transformation. For many clients and therapists, this vision remains profoundly empowering. It validates the desire to live with purpose, to make choices in the face of uncertainty, and to find coherence in suffering.

Yet for the hermeneutics of suspicion, this ontology invites critical scrutiny. The emphasis on freedom, agency, and authenticity can obscure the structural conditions that delimit choice. In the context of poverty, systemic racism, or intergenerational trauma, exhortations to 'take responsibility' or 'find your own truth' can seem like empty directives. When therapy presents freedom as a universal given, it risks becoming a site where failure is silently moralised. If you are unhappy, the implication may be that you are insufficiently aligned with your 'authentic self'.

Power

Power, as Michel Foucault argued, is not always repressive; it can be productive, relational, and benevolent. It shapes what we take to be normal, desirable, or even possible. In this light, therapy is a site where subjectivities are formed, guided, and governed.

From a hermeneutics of trust perspective, humanistic and existential therapy can be understood as an ethical mode of power, what Foucault called *pastoral power*. Originating in religious traditions, pastoral power is exercised through care: it seeks the good of the other, guiding them, with grace, towards self-realisation, insight, or salvation. In therapy, the client is gently supported, even cherished. The therapist, like the shepherd, provides a safe horizon within which the individual may reflect, choose, and grow. Core conditions, dignity in suffering, and philosophical companionship, are all expressions of a trust-based relationship that aims to empower the client while respecting their autonomy. Such power is personal, sustained, and deeply relational; it rests on the faith that healing occurs through guided dialogue.

From a hermeneutics of suspicion perspective, this very language of *empowerment* becomes problematic. Empowerment, in contemporary therapeutic culture, often implies that individuals must take full responsibility for their well-being, self-identity, and life outcomes. What appears as liberation may function as *responsibilisation*, a process by which individuals are quietly burdened with managing structural problems as if they were personal challenges. If you are anxious, unfulfilled, or lost, it becomes your task to fix yourself, perhaps with therapeutic assistance but always within the logic of self-improvement.

Chapter Summary

This chapter has explored humanistic and existential counselling psychology as a tradition defined by a central tension, a *dialectic of meaning*, between care and critique, presence and politics. Using a hermeneutic lens, we traced how these approaches can be read both as sincere efforts to honour human dignity and as products of their historical moment, sometimes reinforcing individualism, responsibilisation, and subtle forms of power.

Emerging in the cultural aftermath of war and social upheaval, figures such as Abraham Maslow, Carl Rogers, Victor Frankl, and Irwin Yalom reframed psychological well-being as a quest for purpose, authenticity, and freedom. Yet the same ideals may also serve to obscure structural inequalities, transforming existential suffering into personal responsibility, a challenge taken up by Linda James Myers' Optimal Psychology, for example.

The chapter considered the epistemological shift towards subjectivity and lived experience and questioned whether the emphasis on personal meaning risks marginalising collective critique. It reflected on the empowering ontology of the self as agentic and unfolding while acknowledging its potential to moralise distress. And we examined the therapeutic space as a site where both liberation and normativity may quietly coexist.

Meaning does not always arrive, on time, with clarity or volume. It might not shout or even explain itself. Sometimes, as Violet Oaklander discovered in a moment of quiet defiance, it arrives in unexpected ways, through play, through symbol, or even through conflict. You have to pause. You have to wait. Sometimes, like Violet, you have to listen out for the faint echo of a distant song. What can you hear?

Reflective Questions

1. How do humanistic and existential therapies differ from earlier forms of psychotherapy, such as behaviourism or psychoanalysis?
2. In what ways might the concepts of 'self-actualisation' or 'personal growth' be seen as politically and culturally situated?
3. What is the significance of using 'hermeneutics'—especially the dialectic between trust and suspicion—as a critical thinking tool in this chapter?
4. How did therapists such as Violet Oaklander and Lydia James Myers expand the reach and inclusivity of humanistic psychology?
5. Can therapy be both a site of liberation and a form of social adaptation? How should we hold these tensions as future psychologists?

Suggested Reading

Amouroux, R., Gerber, L., & Aronov, M. (2022). Putting psychotherapy in its place: The regionalization of behaviour therapy in France, Switzerland, and Belgium, 1960s–1990s. *Journal of the History of the Behavioral Sciences*, *58*(1), 5–23. https://doi.org/10.1002/jhbs.22142.

De Vos, J. (2013). *Psychologization and the Subject of Late Modernity*. Basingstoke: Palgrave Macmillan.

Felder, A. J., & Robbins, B. D. (2011). A cultural-existential approach to therapy: Merleau-Ponty's phenomenology of embodiment and its implications for practice. *Theory & Psychology*, *21*(3), 355–376. https://doi.org/10.1177/0959354310397570.

Han, S. (2014). The illusion of autonomy: Locating humanism in existential-psychoanalytic social theory. *History of the Human Sciences*, *28*(1), 66–83. https://doi.org/10.1177/0952695114551655.

Harrist, S., & Richardson, F. C. (2012). Levinas and hermeneutics on ethics and the Other. *Theory & Psychology*, *22*(3), 342–358. https://doi.org/10.1177/0959354310389647.

Hîncu, A. (2022). Social science and Marxist humanism beyond collectivism in Socialist Romania. *History of the Human Sciences*, *35*(2), 77–100. https://doi.org/10.1177/09526951211069491.

Loewenthal, D. (2015). *Critical Psychotherapy, Psychoanalysis and Counselling: Implications for practice*. Basingstoke: Palgrave Macmillan.

Malone, K. R. (2007). The Subject as drop-out: Cultural accountability and the ethics of psychoanalysis and humanistic psychology. *Theory & Psychology*, *17*(3), 449–471. https://doi.org/10.1177/0959354307077291.

Marks, S. (2017). Psychotherapy in historical perspective. *History of the Human Sciences*, *30*(2), 3–16. https://doi.org/10.1177/0952695117703243.

Mather, R. (2008). Hegel, Dostoyevsky and Carl Rogers: Between humanism and spirit. *History of the Human Sciences*, *21*(1), 33–48. https://doi.org/10.1177/0952695107086151.

Rennie, D. L. (2000). Grounded theory methodology as methodical hermeneutics: Reconciling realism and relativism. *Theory & Psychology*, *10*(4), 481–502. https://doi.org/10.1177/0959354300104003.

Rowan, J. (2001). *Ordinary Ecstasy: The dialectics of humanistic psychology* (Third ed.). London: Routledge. https://doi.org/10.4324/9781315787794.

Totton, N. (2010). *The Problem with Humanistic Therapies*. London: Karnac.

Wharne, S. (2020). How is distress understood in existential philosophies and can phenomenological therapeutic practices be 'evidence-based'? *Theory & Psychology*, *31*(2), 273–289. https://doi.org/10.1177/0959354320964586.

Key Terms

Client-Centred Therapy Carl Rogers' non-directive therapeutic approach that emphasises empathy, unconditional positive regard, and authenticity as conditions for psychological change.

Existential Therapy A therapeutic tradition grounded in existential philosophy, focusing on themes such as death, freedom, isolation, and meaninglessness.

Gestalt Therapy A form of psychotherapy that emphasises holistic experience, present-moment awareness, and the integration of mind and body. It influenced Violet Oaklander's child therapy work.

Hermeneutics The theory and practice of interpretation, particularly of meaning-making in human experience. In psychology, hermeneutics highlights how understanding is shaped by context, language, and perspective.

Hermeneutics of Suspicion A critical interpretive stance that questions surface meanings to uncover hidden ideologies, power dynamics, or unconscious motives. Associated with thinkers such as Karl Marx, Sigmund Freud, and Michel Foucault.

Hermeneutics of Trust An interpretive approach that takes people's words and experiences at face value, seeking insight, connection, and authenticity. Often associated with the values of humanistic psychology.

Hidden Treasure A metaphor used by Violet Oaklander to describe the buried emotional truths that children—and perhaps all of us—can access through symbolic or creative expression.

Logotherapy Viktor Frankl's existential therapy based on the 'will to meaning'—the idea that people are fundamentally motivated by a search for purpose in life.

Pastoral Power A form of psychological power identified by Michel Foucault in which the therapist guides and shapes the client towards socially acceptable or 'healthy' forms of life under the guise of care.

Peak Experience A term coined by Abraham Maslow to describe moments of intense joy, insight, or connection, seen as vital expressions of psychological health.

Reflexivity The practice of critically examining one's own assumptions, values, and positionality in psychological theory or practice.

Self-actualisation A core concept in humanistic psychology, referring to the process of realising one's fullest potential, authenticity, and personal growth.

Subjectivity The lived, felt experience of being a person. Humanistic and existential psychologists view subjectivity as central to understanding psychological life.

Therapeutic Society A concept critiquing the cultural shift in which psychological discourse and self-help replace collective political action, turning social problems into individual emotional ones.

Ultimate Concerns Irvin Yalom's term for the fundamental existential issues all humans face: death, freedom, isolation, and meaninglessness.

FREE INSTRUCTOR & STUDENT RESOURCES

ONLINE RESOURCES

Visit the Instructor & Student Resources website at routledgelearning.com/bpscoretextbooks for free digital resources, including:

- Interactive quizzes and flashcards to test your knowledge
- Links to useful websites and videos
- Instructor manual, lecture slides, and course guide to enhance teaching and save instructors time

25

Speaking Truth to Power

Community Psychology's Critical Consciousness

Chapter Overview

This chapter explores the emergence of community psychology as a radical and ethically engaged response to the social and political crises of the twentieth century. Grounded in a commitment to social justice, it traces how psychologists working under conditions of dictatorship, marginalisation, and exile transformed the discipline by refusing to remain neutral in the face of oppression. At the heart of this transformation is the concept of *critical consciousness*, drawn from Paulo Freire's liberation pedagogy, and reworked into a psychological framework that foregrounds reflexivity, dialogue, and collective empowerment. The chapter introduces students to foundational figures such as Ignacio Martín-Baró, Carolyn Kagan, and Mark Burton, and demonstrates how their work exemplifies a psychology that speaks truth to power. Epistemological and ontological shifts are examined, especially in relation to participatory action research, community-based intervention, and the dismantling of the traditional expert–subject divide. Through a discussion of power, injustice, and resistance, the chapter invites students to imagine a psychology that is not only critical and inclusive but also transformative. In doing so, it offers a compelling account of how psychology can contribute to community resilience, solidarity, and emancipatory change, especially when it listens to the voices of those historically excluded from its gaze.

Speaking Truth to Power

On the early morning of 16 November 1989, amid the turmoil of El Salvador's civil war, soldiers from the Salvadoran Army's Atlácatl Battalion entered the campus of the Universidad Centroamericana (UCA) in San Salvador. Their mission was to eliminate six Jesuit priests perceived as subversive elements. Among the victims were Fathers Ignacio Ellacuría, Ignacio Martín-Baró, Segundo Montes, Amando López, Juan Ramón Moreno, and Joaquín López y López. Also killed were Elba Ramos, the housekeeper, and her 16-year-old daughter Celina, who were staying at the residence that night. Ignacio Martín-Baró, a Spanish-born Jesuit priest and social psychologist, was a prominent advocate for 'liberation psychology'. He contended that psychology should not remain neutral in the face of systemic oppression and state-sponsored violence. Trained in the United States, Martín-Baró critically examined traditional Western psychology's individualistic focus, arguing that mental distress in Latin America was deeply intertwined with socio-political

DOI: 10.4324/9781003565482-25

realities such as poverty, militarism, and colonialism. His work aimed to expose and challenge the ideologisation of reality, the narratives that justified injustice, and to foster critical consciousness among the oppressed. He believed that psychology must serve the marginalised, giving voice to the voiceless and speak truth to power. The assassination of Martín-Baró and his colleagues was a stark, brutal message. It was not only the catastrophic murder of several individuals but a violent attempt to silence intellectuals and activists who dared to align scientific inquiry with the pursuit of justice. Martín-Baró's legacy, though born from tragedy, remains a powerful testament to the transformative potential of a psychology deeply committed to human rights and liberation. His murder forces a profound reckoning: can psychology truly be apolitical when confronted with profound human suffering rooted in social injustice?

Chapter Contents

- An exploration of how community psychology emerged from a series of political, intellectual, and moral ruptures in the twentieth century, including exile, dictatorship, and social protest.
- Biographical case studies of key figures such as Ignacio Martín-Baró, Paulo Freire, and Carolyn Kagan, whose work redefined psychology as a form of political and ethical action.
- Examination of critical consciousness as a critical thinking tool, tracing its origins in education and its adaptation into psychology as a method for social transformation.

Chapter Objectives

- To understand how the history of community psychology is shaped by broader political struggles, including dictatorship, war, and collective resistance.
- To critically evaluate the role of epistemology and ontology in shaping participatory, socially engaged forms of psychological knowledge.
- To explore the concept of critical consciousness and its value as a critical thinking tool for interrogating the relationship between psychology, power, and community action.

CRITICAL THINKING TOOL
CRITICAL CONSCIENCE

Conscience is usually understood as an inner voice, a moral compass guiding individuals to distinguish right from wrong. However, in psychology, particularly within its critical and political forms, conscience transcends personal guilt or virtue. Instead, it becomes a fundamental question of how we comprehend and actively respond to the suffering experienced by others. *Critical conscience*, in this context, refers to the profound awareness that psychological

problems are not solely individual phenomena but are inextricably linked to social, political, and systemic forces. It necessitates recognising when concepts such as mental health are profoundly shaped by pervasive issues such as poverty, the impact of war, forms of oppression, or the alienation inherent in modern life. This recognition then compels a critical reflexive question: what is my responsibility, as a psychologist, scholar, or citizen, in the face of this suffering?

Psychology does not simply describe or explain, it intervenes. Every theory, test, and practice carries assumptions about what it means to be human, what counts as a problem, and who has agency and authority to address it. In this chapter, our critical vision is sharpened by six interrelated principles drawn from liberation psychology, as articulated by thinkers such as Paolo Freire, Ignacio Martín-Baró and developed by Mark Burton. The concept of critical consciousness (*conscientização*), as developed by Brazilian educator Paulo Freire, is the capacity of oppressed people to perceive the social, political, and economic contradictions of their reality, and to act against the oppressive elements of that reality. His radical pedagogy laid the foundation for liberationist models in education, theology, and psychology. Critical conscience is the ability to understand and critically analyse societal inequalities, particularly how power structures and systems of oppression impact individuals and communities.

Introduction

Conventionally viewed as a neutral science of the mind, psychology has always been deeply entwined with values, power, and ethics. Beyond its empirical pursuits, psychology bears a moral responsibility to address issues of justice, equity, and human dignity. This chapter explores the evolution of psychology's critical conscience, examining how historical events, key figures, and political movements have shaped its ethical compass. The chapter proposes that psychology is always political, whether it admits it or not. Its theories, methods, and applications often reflect and reinforce existing power structures or, conversely, challenge them. This sets the stage for understanding the motivations behind the movements discussed below, asserting that neutrality in psychology can often implicitly serve to maintain the status quo, making a conscious ethical stance crucial.

The chapter first explores the formation of the Society for the Psychological Study of Social Issues (SPSSI) during the tumultuous 1930s, highlighting its role in steering psychology towards social engagement. The Marienthal Study by Marie Jahoda will then serve as a case study in epistemological innovation, demonstrating how methodological approaches can reflect ethical commitments. Liberation psychology, emerging from Latin America, offers an ontological reimagining of psychological practice, centring the experiences of the oppressed. Finally, the development of community psychology in the UK exemplifies psychology's potential to challenge and redistribute power. Through these historical moments, the aim is to understand how psychology can move beyond individualistic assumptions to embrace a more socially conscious and ethically engaged practice.

Historical Issues

Founded in 1936 amid the Great Depression in the United States, the Society for the Psychological Study of Social Issues (SPSSI) emerged as a collective of psychologists committed to applying their expertise to pressing social problems. Recognising the limitations of a purely academic psychology, SPSSI members sought to address issues such as unemployment, racial discrimination, and war. By integrating psychological research with social activism, the SPSSI laid the groundwork for a discipline that acknowledged and acted upon its social responsibilities. This revolutionary proactive stance established a precedent for organised psychological advocacy directly challenging the notion of science detached from social responsibility. Kurt Lewin, a central figure in the SPSSI, famously declared, 'Research that produces nothing but books will not suffice.' The Society's primary goals were: (1) to encourage research on psychological issues most vitally related to modern social, economic, and political policies; and (2) to help the public and its representatives understand and use contributions from the scientific investigation of human behaviour in the formation of social policies.

The horrors of the Second World War, including propaganda, genocide, and the psychological trauma experienced by soldiers and civilians, profoundly impacted psychology, forcing practitioners to confront the destructive potential of human behaviour and the ethical dilemmas of their own work. Psychologists became involved in areas such as troop morale, the treatment of combat stress, and rehabilitation. This era directly spurred the formalisation of ethical guidelines, such as the American Psychological Association's (APA) first ethics code in 1953, aiming to prevent misuse and ensure responsible practice after observing the devastating consequences of psychological knowledge when misapplied or ignored.

In the aftermath of the war, understanding the psychological roots of fascism became paramount. *The Authoritarian Personality* (1950), led by Theodor Adorno and colleagues at the University of California, Berkeley, investigated the personality traits that predisposed individuals to authoritarianism and prejudice. The study identified characteristics such as rigidity, submissiveness to authority, and aggression towards out-groups. This work underscored the role of psychological factors in social phenomena and highlighted the importance of addressing underlying personality structures to combat authoritarian tendencies. It was a direct effort to use psychological insight to safeguard democratic values.

Key Individuals

Marie Jahoda (1907–2001) trained in Vienna. Jahoda collaborated on the Marienthal Study (1933), an extraordinary example of engaged social science. The research investigated the psychological and social impact of mass unemployment on a small Austrian town. Rather than blame individuals, it showed how structural poverty destroyed the perception of time, community bonds, and self-worth. The methodology, blending diaries, ethnographic observation, and quantitative data, reflected a commitment to understanding suffering in its lived context. After being imprisoned by the Austrofascists and then exiled, Jahoda took her ethical vision to the UK, where she worked on racial prejudice and youth development. Jahoda's work exemplified how personal experience with political upheaval and social injustice could directly inform an ethically committed research agenda.

Kurt Lewin (1890–1947), another émigré from Nazi Germany, transformed the study of group processes and social change. A founder member of the SPSSI, his notion of action research rejected the idea of detached observation. Instead, he argued that psychologists should intervene in real-world problems such as racism, authoritarianism, workplace injustice, and help solve them collaboratively with affected communities. His famous maxim, 'There is nothing so practical as a good theory', exemplified his belief that scientific knowledge should lead to practical change. Lewin's focus on democracy, group dynamics, and leadership shaped post-war efforts to combat prejudice and promote participatory citizenship.

Paulo Freire (1921–1997) was a Brazilian educator, philosopher, and political thinker whose ideas have profoundly shaped education, critical theory, and liberation psychology. Born in Recife, Brazil, Freire suffered poverty and hunger during the Great Depression, an experience that deeply influenced his later commitment to social justice. He is best known for his influential work *Pedagogy of the Oppressed* (1970), where he introduced the concept of 'conscientização' or critical consciousness. This refers to the process by which individuals develop an awareness of the socio-political conditions that shape their lives, enabling them to take transformative action. Although exiled during Brazil's military dictatorship, Freire's ideas spread globally, impacting grassroots movements, popular education, and critical pedagogy worldwide.

Ignacio Martín-Baró (1942–1989), a Jesuit priest and psychologist in El Salvador, created Liberation Psychology, a radical framework that prioritised the needs of oppressed communities. Working during a time of brutal military dictatorship, Martín-Baró argued that psychology should expose and challenge systemic violence. He developed concepts such as social trauma, critical consciousness, and de-ideologisation, encouraging psychologists to demystify the narratives that justified oppression. His work focused on concrete conditions of existence, including poverty, militarism, colonialism. In 1989, he was murdered by a death squad, a martyr to his commitment to a psychology of liberation. Martín-Baró's legacy is a powerful testament to the risks involved when psychology takes a definitive stance against state-sponsored violence and oppression, directly linking psychological theory to political activism.

Carolyn Kagan (b.1951) and Mark Burton (b.1952) are leading figures in the development of critical community psychology in the UK. Long-standing collaborators and partners in both academic and activist work, they exemplify a psychology grounded in social justice, systemic critique, and collaborative praxis. Their work not only shaped the field of community psychology but also offered a distinctively British contribution to the global movement for a more ethical and emancipatory psychology. Kagan was deeply committed to addressing marginalisation in all its forms, working with disabled people, refugees, young carers, and economically excluded communities. She believes psychology should be useful, accessible, and accountable, responsive to the needs of those most often silenced by dominant narratives. Burton began his career in clinical psychology but moved steadily towards systemic, organisational, and policy-focused work. Burton's intellectual range includes systems thinking, political economy, and Latin American liberation psychology.

Epistemological Issues

Marie Jahoda's Marienthal Study exemplified epistemological innovation by integrating diverse methodologies to capture the lived experiences of the unemployed, challenging the prevailing positivist approaches of the time. Conducted in the early 1930s, the Marienthal Study investigated the effects of unemployment on a small Austrian community. Led by Jahoda, Paul Lazarsfeld, and Hans Zeisel, the research employed a combination of quantitative data, qualitative observations, and ethnographic methods. Some of the fieldworkers moved into the village for several months. This methodological pluralism allowed for a nuanced understanding of how prolonged unemployment led to apathy, loss of purpose, and social disintegration. By prioritising the community's subjective experiences alongside statistical analysis, the study challenged the dominant paradigm that often overlooked the human aspects of social issues.

Embracing social conscience means rejecting the notion of a value-free science. Attempts at detached observation often implicitly uphold existing power structures, leading to an unconscious maintenance of the status quo. Instead, psychologists committed to social justice transparently adopt value-laden methodologies, openly stating their ethical commitments and working towards a more just society through their research and practice.

Originating in Latin America during the 1980s, liberation psychology emerged as a response to the inadequacy of traditional psychological models in addressing the lived realities of oppressed populations. Pioneered by Ignacio Martín-Baró, this approach emphasised the role of social, political, and economic structures in shaping individual and collective psychological experiences. Liberation psychology posits that psychological distress often stems from systemic oppression rather than from individual dysfunction. It advocates for a praxis-oriented epistemology, where psychologists engage directly with communities to co-create knowledge and foster empowerment.

Paulo Freire's notion of praxis, the iterative process of reflection and action, deeply resonated with the participatory and emancipatory goals of community psychology. Freire insisted that knowledge must emerge from lived experience, and that critical reflection is inseparable from the struggle for liberation. These insights guided community psychology's rejection of detached, top-down models of theory and intervention.

Community psychology in the UK developed as a transformative discipline dedicated to challenging individualistic models of mental health and reframing psychological knowledge as a tool for social justice. A key practice within the field is Participatory Action Research (PAR), which exemplifies this epistemological commitment. Rather than treating participants as passive data sources, PAR involves them as co-researchers in identifying problems, designing interventions, and interpreting findings. This approach directly contests hierarchical knowledge structures, valuing lived experience as equal to academic expertise. In doing so, community psychology disrupts traditional top-down models of research and clinical authority, seeking to redistribute the power of knowledge production.

Ontological Issues

A social conscience view fundamentally challenges an ontology of fixed, individualistic psychological reality. Instead, it argues that distress, identity, and behaviour are deeply shaped by social, economic, and political contexts. This ontological stance asserts that many psychological phenomena are socially constructed, meaning that experiences are products of social interaction and power relations.

This perspective leads to a crucial ontological shift away from locating problems solely within the individual ('mental illness is a brain disease'). Instead, it posits that much distress is a rational, human response to unjust or oppressive social conditions. This reframes suffering as a symptom of social dysfunction rather than solely individual deficit, demanding a broader, more systemic analysis.

A relational ontology of human being underpins the emphasis on community intervention and systemic change inherent in community and liberation psychologies. By situating psychological phenomena within broader socio-political contexts, liberation psychology challenges the ontological claims of mainstream psychology. It calls for a reimagining of the individual as a being in constant interaction with and shaped by their environment. This perspective encourages psychologists to address the root causes of distress and to work collaboratively towards social transformation.

To adopt a social conscience is to rethink the very nature of psychological reality. Ontology, the question of what kinds of beings we are, and what kind of world we inhabit, underpins every psychological theory, whether explicit or not. Traditional models often posit individuals as bounded, rational, and biologically determined entities. Socially conscious psychology contests this view, offering an alternative approach to psychological reality grounded in context, relationship, and structural forces.

Power

UK-based community psychologists such as Carolyn Kagan and Mark Burton have been instrumental in developing practices that attend to both systemic injustice and the psychological consequences of oppression. Their work highlights the dangers of decontextualised interventions and emphasises the need to locate distress within broader social, political, and economic frameworks. In contrast to both mainstream academic psychology and conventional community psychology, their approach is explicitly political, ethically grounded, and deeply reflexive. Drawing on decades of practical engagement and scholarship, especially from their work in Manchester, a city marked by industrial decline, social fragmentation, and economic inequality, they set out a distinctive model of community psychology rooted in social justice, systemic critique, and transformative practice.

Kagan and Burton define critical community psychology as a *praxis*, an integration of theory and action that seeks to transform oppressive structures rather than merely work around them. At the heart of this praxis is a commitment to what they call prefigurative action: the creation of alternative social forms and ways of being that embody the values of a more just society within the present, often hostile, context. For Kagan and Burton, critical community psychologists must engage not only with local needs but with the structural and ideological forces that generate inequality, capitalism, racism, ableism, and neoliberalism.

Kagan and Burton show how critical community psychology can be deeply embedded in real-world struggles, how it can draw inspiration from both global and local traditions, and how it can resist the depoliticisation and individualism that too often characterise psychological science. Kagan and Burton offer a vision of psychology that starts with the question not 'what is wrong with this person?' but 'what is wrong with this world, and how can we help to change it?'

Kagan and Burton's emphasis on *prefigurative practice*, the attempt to build alternative social relations in the here and now, closely aligns with Freire's idea that emancipation is both a goal and a method. Like Freire, they understood that power must be reconfigured through participatory processes that empower communities to name, understand, and transform their world.

Chapter Summary

This chapter has explored how psychology's social conscience emerged as both a critique and an alternative to the discipline's traditional focus on the individual. At key historical moments, psychologists have confronted the limitations of apolitical, individualistic models and turned towards approaches rooted in justice, community, and collective well-being.

The formation of SPSSI in the 1930s was an early recognition that psychology could not stand aside from the social crises of its time. Marie Jahoda's Marienthal Study challenged the discipline's reliance on detached positivism, showing that lived experience, context, and dignity must be central to psychological inquiry. In the aftermath of war and genocide, *The Authoritarian Personality* demonstrated that understanding prejudice and violence required psychology to grapple with the social conditions that produce them.

These developments were more than technical innovations; they represented a deeper epistemological shift. Knowledge was no longer seen as something produced *about* people from a distance, but created *with* communities. Liberation psychology, arising in Latin America, extended this shift into a radical ontological challenge. Psychological suffering, it argued, is not simply located within damaged minds but within broken societies. This demanded that psychologists become participants in the struggle against the causes of suffering.

Across the world, from the Marienthal Study to the Authoritarian Personality, from the work of Paolo Freire to UK critical community psychology, this movement has been animated by a refusal to accept the status quo. It insists that psychology is never neutral, and never has been. Either it serves the powerful, or it serves the oppressed.

That choice is not abstract. It is written, with devastating clarity, in the life and death of Ignacio Martín-Baró. His refusal to separate psychology from justice, his belief that psychology must stand with the poor and the persecuted, cost him his life. His legacy endures as a stark reminder that the work of speaking truth to power is never without risk, but that silence, too, is a choice.

Reflective Questions

1. What does it mean to say that psychology is never neutral, and how does community psychology exemplify this principle?
2. How does Paulo Freire's concept of 'critical consciousness' influence the theory and practice of community psychology?
3. In what ways does community psychology rethink the concept of power, and how is this rethinking reflected in its methods?
4. Why is the Marienthal Study considered a landmark in socially conscious psychological research?
5. How do the lives and work of key individuals like Ignacio Martín-Baró, Carolyn Kagan, and Mark Burton illustrate psychology's potential to contribute to social change?

Suggested Reading

Comas-Díaz, L., & Torres Rivera, E. (2020). *Liberation Psychology: Theory, method, practice, and social justice*. American Psychological Association.

Dutta, U. (2016). Prioritizing the local in an era of globalization: A proposal for decentering community psychology. *American Journal of Community Psychology*, *58*(3–4), 329–338. https://doi.org/10.1002/ajcp.12047.

Kagan, C., Burton, M., Duckett, P., Lawthom, R., & Siddiquee, A. (2020). *Critical Community Psychology: Critical action and social change* (Second ed.). Abingdon, Oxon: Routledge.

Kessi, S., Suffla, S., & Seedat, M. (2022). *Decolonial Enactments in Community Psychology*. London: Springer.

Martín-Baró, I., Aron, A., & Corne, S. (1994). *Writings for a Liberation Psychology*. Cambridge, MA: Harvard University Press.

Mills, J. A., & Harrison, T. (2007). John Rickman, Wilfred Ruprecht Bion, and the origins of the therapeutic community. *History of Psychology, 10*(1), 22–43. https://doi.org/10.1037/1093-4510.10.1.22.

Nelson, G. B., & Prilleltensky, I. (2010). *Community Psychology: In pursuit of liberation and well-being* (Second ed.). Basingstoke: Palgrave Macmillan.

Parker, H. (2023). The regional survey movement and popular autoethnography in early 20th-century Britain. *History of the Human Sciences, 36*(3–4), 3–26. https://doi.org/10.1177/09526951231167038.

Pettit, M. (2024). The racial economy of psychological care: Professionalism, social justice, and political action during American psychology's communitarian moment. *History of Psychology, 27*(3), 203–226. https://doi.org/10.1037/hop0000259.

Pols, H. (2001). Divergences in American psychiatry during the Depression: Somatic psychiatry, community mental hygiene, and social reconstruction. *Journal of the History of the Behavioral Sciences, 37*(4), 369–388. https://doi.org/10.1002/jhbs.1066.

Rodkey, K. L., & Rodkey, E. N. (2020). Family, friends, and faith-communities: Intellectual community and the benefits of unofficial networks for marginalized scientists. *History of Psychology, 23*(4), 289–311. https://doi.org/10.1037/hop0000172.

Sanscartier, S. (2023). Anatol Rapoport's social responsibility: Science and antiwar activism; 1960–1970. *History of Psychology, 26*(1), 29–50. https://doi.org/10.1037/hop0000223.

Sonn, C. C., Fox, R., Keast, S., & Rua, M. (2022). Fostering and sustaining transnational solidarities for transformative social change: Advancing community psychology research and action. *American Journal of Community Psychology, 69*(3–4), 269–282. https://doi.org/10.1002/ajcp.12602.

Wang, J., & Huo, Y. (2023). The diffusion of Bruner's psychological research in China and its impact. *History of Psychology, 26*(2), 164–182. https://doi.org/10.1037/hop0000232.

Key Terms

Community Psychology A branch of psychology that focuses on understanding individuals within their social, cultural, economic, and political contexts, emphasising empowerment and social change.

Critical Consciousness A concept developed by Paulo Freire referring to the ability to perceive social, political, and economic oppression and to take action against the oppressive elements of society.

Epistemology The study of knowledge—its nature, sources, limitations, and validity—particularly as it relates to how psychologists understand and research social phenomena.

Freirean Pedagogy An approach to education based on the work of Paulo Freire, emphasising dialogue, critical reflection, and education as a tool for liberation.

Liberation Psychology A movement within psychology, founded by Ignacio Martín-Baró, that focuses on addressing social injustices and empowering oppressed populations through psychological practices.

Ontology The philosophical study of being or existence; in community psychology, concerns assumptions about the nature of individuals, communities, and their relationships.

Participatory Action Research (PAR) A research approach that involves participants in the research process as co-researchers, aiming to produce knowledge that leads to social change.

Power In community psychology, refers to the capacity to influence others and control resources, often analysed in terms of who benefits and who is marginalised.

Reflexivity A critical practice in psychology and social research involving self-awareness about the researcher's positionality and the power dynamics inherent in knowledge production.

Social Justice A foundational goal of community psychology aimed at reducing inequality and promoting fair treatment and opportunities for all people.

FREE INSTRUCTOR & STUDENT RESOURCES

ONLINE RESOURCES

Visit the Instructor & Student Resources website at routledgelearning.com/bpscoretextbooks for free digital resources, including:

- Interactive quizzes and flashcards to test your knowledge
- Links to useful websites and videos
- Instructor manual, lecture slides, and course guide to enhance teaching and save instructors time

26

'You're All Wet!'

Evolutionary Psychology and the Pleasures of Fantasy

Chapter Overview

This chapter explores the emergence and cultural influence of sociobiology and evolutionary psychology from the 1970s to the present. It charts how evolutionary explanations of human behaviour have triggered intense scientific and political debate, especially around gender, sexuality, and power. The chapter describes how sociobiology's claims about kin selection, altruism, and sex differences evolved into the modular, mind-focused framework of evolutionary psychology. Through a cast of supporters and opponents of evolutionary psychology, readers are introduced to both the debates and ideological stakes of the field.

The chapter uses Slavoj Žižek's theory of *fantasy* as its central critical lens, showing how evolutionary psychology functions not only as a scientific paradigm but as a narrative that provides seductive, comforting explanations for complex social realities. These fantasies are shown to fulfil several functions, and to shape belief even when disavowed. Readers are encouraged to 'traverse the fantasy' by thinking critically about how scientific claims are constructed, received, and mobilised in culture.

'You're All Wet!'

On 15 February 1978, at the annual conference of the American Association for the Advancement of Science (AAAS) in Washington, DC, the normally polite rituals of academic discussion were dramatically disrupted. Edward O. Wilson, the Harvard biologist renowned for his work on ants and the author of the incendiary *Sociobiology: The new synthesis* (1975), had been invited to speak at a symposium. His book had ignited a firestorm by extending evolutionary explanations from the animal kingdom to human social behaviour, claiming that traits such as aggression, altruism, and even gender roles could be understood as evolutionary adaptations. As Wilson approached the lectern, he was intercepted by members of Science for the People, a group of feminist and Marxist scientists whose aim was to challenge what they saw as the book's covert endorsement of racism, sexism, and biological determinism. One protester stepped forward and poured a jug of iced water over Wilson's head, shouting: 'Wilson, you're all wet!' The water soaked his suit and notes. Momentarily stunned, Wilson composed himself, dried off as best he could, and carried on with his talk. The symbolism of the act, and the media attention it generated, lingered far longer than his presentation. From a psychoanalytic perspective this protest was more than a theatrical gesture; it symbolically disturbed the façade of disinterested science. The protesters had staged a rupture that punctured the fantasy of dispassionate, apolitical science. For them, sociobiology was

DOI: 10.4324/9781003565482-26

an ideological illusion that masked real social antagonisms. The water, cold and shocking, was a material metaphor of their critique: an attempt to cleanse the discourse, to expose what lay beneath its polished surface, and to force an encounter with the unconscious politics of knowledge.

Chapter Contents

- The opening anecdote of Edward O. Wilson's public dousing sets the stage for a critical examination of sociobiology and evolutionary psychology.
- Students are introduced to the scientific and ideological claims of evolutionary psychology, including how it evolved from sociobiology and the controversies it has provoked.
- The chapter uses Žižek's theory of fantasy as a critical thinking tool to explore the role of cultural narratives, ideology, and desire in the appeal of evolutionary explanations for human behaviour.

Chapter Objectives

- To trace the historical development of sociobiology and evolutionary psychology, focusing on their scientific claims and cultural impact.
- To examine the methods, figures, and criticisms that have shaped these fields, particularly in relation to gender, sexuality, and power.
- To apply the critical thinking tool of fantasy, as developed by Slavoj Žižek, to analyse how evolutionary psychology functions ideologically in both academic and popular settings.

CRITICAL THINKING TOOL
FANTASY

For Slavoj Žižek, *fantasy* is not merely an illusory escape from reality but a structuring force, something that gives coherence to our social world, our beliefs, and our assumptions. He proposes five key principles that can help reveal the ideological dimensions beneath even the most seemingly objective claims. First, fantasy supports ideology. It acts as an unconscious script that makes ideological positions feel natural, inevitable, even comforting. In evolutionary psychology, for example, the fantasy that human behaviour has been shaped by ancient prehistoric pressures can make gender roles or inequality appear biologically ordained rather than socially constructed. Second, fantasy conceals social antagonism. Rather than confronting uncomfortable contradictions in society, between equality and hierarchy, for instance, fantasy provides neat, evolutionary explanations that smooth over complexity and conflict. It protects us from encountering the instability or 'lack' at the heart of social life. Third, fantasy provides secret enjoyment, or *jouissance*. We derive a perverse satisfaction from some evolutionary narratives, such as the idea that aggression or promiscuity is 'natural', because they license trans-

gressive or cynical attitudes under the semblance of biological truth. Fourth, to 'traverse the fantasy' means to confront what the fantasy conceals: that the world is incoherent, that knowledge is partial, and that human behaviour is not fully determined. Traversing the fantasy is not about disbelieving science but seeing through its ideological use. Fifth and finally, fantasy operates even when disavowed. People may mock or criticise certain evolutionary claims but still behave *as if* they are true. This reveals fantasy's enduring grip, not just in what we say but in how we live.

Introduction

Why do humans cooperate or compete? Why do they fall in love, lie, or cheat? For proponents of sociobiology and evolutionary psychology, the answers lie in our distant evolutionary past. These fields aim to explain human behaviour by identifying the survival challenges faced by our ancestors hundreds of thousands of years ago. The argument is that many of our psychological traits evolved as adaptations to those environments and continue to shape our actions today.

Popularised by E. O. Wilson's *Sociobiology: The new synthesis* (1975), sociobiology sought to extend evolutionary principles from animal behaviour to human societies. While academically controversial, its influence was widespread. Works such as Desmond Morris's bestselling *Manwatching* (1977) introduced these ideas to mass audiences, presenting human behaviour through the frameworks of ethology and evolutionary biology.

By the 1990s, sociobiology had given way to evolutionary psychology, a more refined attempt to locate universal psychological mechanisms shaped in the ancestral struggle for survival. Rather than focusing directly on genes or outward behaviours, evolutionary psychologists proposed that the human mind was composed of domain-specific cognitive modules, mental adaptations sharpened in the prehistoric environment inhabited by our ancestors. Yet, despite these new methods and frameworks, many of the same questions, and the same criticisms, remained.

Historical Issues

As readers will recall from earlier chapters of this textbook, psychology was decisively shaped by the theory of evolution from its inception in the late nineteenth century. Charles Darwin's *On the Origin of Species* (1859) revolutionised biology and offered a new basis for understanding human psychology as the product of natural selection. Psychologists such as William James and G. Stanley Hall were profoundly influenced by evolutionary theory, viewing consciousness, emotion, and behaviour as functional responses to environmental challenges. The Darwinian legacy made evolutionary principles part of psychology's scientific DNA.

By the 1970s, psychology stood at a disciplinary crossroads. Behaviourism was in decline, cognitive science was on the rise, and a renewed interest in biology, including genetics and ethology, was influencing how psychologists thought about human nature. Against this backdrop, Edward O. Wilson's *Sociobiology: The new synthesis* (1975) sought to integrate ethology, ecology, population biology, and genetics to explain the biological basis of social organisation. Its final chapter, which extended these principles to Homo sapiens, sparked immediate controversy.

Wilson's book drew on the evolutionary principles of kin selection and reciprocal altruism. These ideas explained how apparently selfless behaviours could evolve if they enhanced the survival of shared genes or long-term cooperation. Wilson claimed that these principles could be extended to human aggression, altruism, mating patterns, and gender differences. Homosexuality, for example, might be explained through kin selection: individuals who do not reproduce themselves might still enhance their 'inclusive fitness' by investing in the survival and reproductive success of close relatives.

Critics accused Wilson of biological determinism, the notion that complex social behaviours could be reduced to genetic imperatives. Influential biologists such as Stephen Jay Gould and Richard Lewontin formed the Sociobiology Study Group of Science for the People to challenge what they saw as a reactionary ideology disguised as science. They accused sociobiology of reinforcing inequality, essentialising gender roles, and ignoring the social and historical dimensions of behaviour. Their critiques pointed to the 'naturalistic fallacy', the mistaken idea that what is natural must therefore be desirable.

A strategic shift occurred in the 1980s and 1990s in response to this backlash. Evolutionary psychology moved away from genes and towards *psychological mechanisms* shaped in the prehistoric environment inhabited by our ancestors. Rather than hardwired behaviours, they proposed evolved cognitive modules designed to solve ancestral problems.

Key Individuals

Ruth Hubbard (1924–2016) was the first woman to be granted a tenured biology professorship at Harvard University, Hubbard was also a fierce critic of sociobiology and a pioneer in feminist science critique. Her work exposed the ways in which supposedly neutral scientific practices were saturated with cultural assumptions, especially regarding gender and race. In her essays and public lectures, she argued that biological theories of human behaviour often reflected the ideological biases of their creators. Hubbard was also involved with the Science for the People group.

Edward O. Wilson (1929–2021) was a renowned biologist and expert in ant behaviour. Wilson's *Sociobiology: The new synthesis* (1975) became the lightning rod for the controversy surrounding sociobiology. Wilson argued that social behaviours, including those of humans, could be explained through evolutionary theory. Though only the final chapter in the book focused on humans, it was this one that provoked the most intense backlash. Wilson's vision of a biologically anchored human nature was read by critics as a reassertion of social hierarchies and gender norms under the guise of objectivity. Protesters doused him with ice water at the 1978 AAAS conference, an act that symbolised the battle between sociobiology and its critics.

Richard Lewontin (1929–2021) and Stephen Jay Gould (1941–2002), both Harvard University biologists, became the intellectual figureheads of the opposition to sociobiology. Influenced by Marxism and committed to an anti-reductionist science, Lewontin and Gould challenged both the scientific assumptions and the political implications of evolutionary explanations of human behaviour. Lewontin's book *Not in Our Genes* (1984), co-authored with

Steven Rose and psychologist Leon Kamin, was a brilliant critique of biological determinism. It targeted the misuse of IQ testing, eugenics, and the idea that biology determines intelligence or moral worth.

Steven Rose (1938–2025), a neurobiologist, and Hilary Rose (b.1935), a sociologist of science and feminist scholar, were among the most vocal and sustained critics of sociobiology and evolutionary psychology. Rose and Rose produced powerful critiques of biological determinism across several decades. They argued that sociobiology presented socially and politically loaded claims under the veil of scientific neutrality, and that such frameworks neglected history, culture, and agency. In addition to numerous essays and books, they were co-editors of *Alas, Poor Darwin: Arguments against evolutionary psychology* (2000).

Richard Dawkins (b.1941), a prominent British evolutionary biologist, became widely known for his 1976 book, *The Selfish Gene*. This influential work proposed a gene-centric view of evolution, positing that genes, not organisms, are the fundamental units of selection, and organisms are merely 'survival machines' for their propagation. In this context, 'selfish' describes the gene's drive to replicate itself; it is not a psychological or moral trait of any individual organism. Despite Dawkins's explicit caveat, the book's title and core metaphor were often misinterpreted. Many readers conflated 'gene selfishness' with human psychological egoism, leading to the pervasive notion that humans are inherently selfish and that such behaviour is biologically 'natural' and therefore justifiable.

Joan Roughgarden (b.1946) is a theoretical biologist and ecologist whose work challenges conventional Darwinian theories of sexual selection. A transgender woman, she brought a critical lens to evolutionary biology, especially around sex, gender, and sexuality. Her influential book *Evolution's Rainbow: Diversity, gender, and sexuality in nature and people* (2013), a foundational work in feminist and queer biology, critiques the standard narrative of sexual selection, where males compete for females, as narrow and ideologically loaded. Drawing on a wide range of animal studies, Roughgarden documents the prevalence of same-sex behaviour, gender variation, and cooperative social structures in nature. She argues that these patterns contradict the competitive, binary assumptions that underpin much sociobiology and evolutionary psychology. Instead, she proposes *social selection* as an alternative framework, where evolutionary success is driven by cooperation and social bonding rather than by dominance and reproductive rivalry.

David Buss (b.1953) is one of the leading empirical researchers in evolutionary psychology. Buss is best known for his work on mating preferences, sexual jealousy, and intersexual conflict. He has conducted large-scale cross-cultural studies and generated testable hypotheses about the evolved roots of mate selection. While his work is widely cited, it has also drawn criticism for essentialising gender roles and reinforcing patriarchal assumptions. Buss has defended evolutionary psychology as a rigorous empirical science but he remains a polarising figure in the field.

Steven Pinker (b.1954) is a cognitive psychologist and prolific popular writer, Pinker became one of the most prominent defenders of evolutionary psychology in the late twentieth and early twenty-first centuries. In books such as *How the Mind Works* (1997) and *The Blank Slate* (2002), Pinker argued that the human mind consists of evolved, domain-specific modules shaped in the ancestral prehistoric past. His work has been criticised for its sweeping claims, gender essentialism, and reliance on adaptationist logic. Pinker framed evolutionary psychology as a corrective to what he saw as naïve social constructivism, but many of his critics viewed his work as veiled ideology masquerading as science.

Epistemological Issues

To understand the epistemology of evolutionary psychology, it is important to ask how researchers in this field justify their claims. What counts as evidence, and by what logic are theories constructed and validated? Evolutionary psychology typically begins with what is known as *reverse engineering*. Researchers start by identifying a current human behaviour such as mate preferences, jealousy, or altruism, and then hypothesise what adaptive problem this behaviour might have solved in our ancestral past. From there, they propose an *evolved psychological mechanism* designed to solve that problem.

The next step is the generation of *testable predictions*. Researchers design mimetic experiments, surveys, or cross-cultural studies to determine whether behaviours conform to the hypothesised evolutionary function. David Buss's work on mate preferences, for example, predicted that men across cultures would place more emphasis on youth and physical attractiveness, while women would prioritise status and resources, traits said to reflect prehistoric reproductive challenges. The confirmation of such patterns is used to claim the existence of underlying evolved mechanisms.

Another important strand of evidence comes from *infant cognition studies*. Researchers observe the expectations, reactions, and problem-solving strategies of babies, often before the influence of formal socialisation, to infer what cognitive capacities may be innate. If infants consistently show preferences for fairness, for example, or a rudimentary understanding of physics or number, these are taken as possible indicators of evolved predispositions.

Evolutionary psychologists often rely on cross-species comparisons, examining similar behaviours in primates and other animals to infer evolutionary continuity. A key epistemological move involves appealing to *consilience*, the idea that an evolutionary hypothesis gains credibility when converging evidence appears across disciplines such as anthropology, biology, and psychology. However, critics note that this methodological strategy frequently depends on mimetic plausibility rather than direct empirical proof. Because we cannot directly observe ancestral environments or historical selection pressures, much of the evidence is inferential, shaped as much by present-day assumptions as by empirical data. From a Žižekian perspective, this very structure of reasoning may function as a fantasy, a narrative that retroactively stitches together disparate observations into the reassuring illusion that we have uncovered the deep truth of human nature. In this view, evolutionary psychology's appeal lies in the psychological comfort it offers.

Ontological Issues

Evolutionary psychology's ontological project, the question of what really exists in 'human nature', asserts that much of our psychology is universal, evolved, and rooted in ancestral adaptations. This vision of the human being is compelling but also contested. Evolutionary psychology assumes that core features of human behaviour, such as mate choice, aggression, parenting, jealousy, and cooperation, reflect adaptations shared across all humans. This sits in tension with the social sciences, where variation, cultural learning, and historical contingency are prioritised. Critics argue that evolutionary psychology's emphasis on universality neglects the fluidity, diversity, and situatedness of human subjectivity.

While most scientists agree that the physiology of Homo sapiens is a product of natural selection, evolutionary psychologists argue that the mind is composed of domain-specific modules, each evolved to solve distinct prehistoric challenges. If the mind is modular, then our behaviours are rooted in structures that may not align with the flexibilities demanded by modern life, raising ontological questions about mismatch, rigidity, and constraint.

Reductionism is another ontological tension. Critics argue that evolutionary accounts reduce complex phenomena, love, morality, even consciousness, to mechanistic functions driven by reproductive success. Such reduction can evacuate human experience of its ethical, existential, or cultural dimensions. Feminist critics have been especially vocal in challenging how claims about male dominance or female 'mate selection' are presented as natural, thereby essentialising political inequalities.

The most profound ontological issue lies in the opposition between the *natural* and the *social*. Evolutionary psychology seeks to explain social behaviour as an extension of biology (natural kinds), but in doing so risks erasing the very thing that makes social life complex: history, ideology, and meaning (human kinds). Žižek's notion of *fantasy* helps us see how the fantasy of a fixed human nature functions ideologically. It promises stability, identity, and coherence in a world that is in fact contingent and contradictory. The desire to locate timeless truths beneath human behaviour may reflect a disavowed anxiety about the fluidity of the self. In this way, evolutionary psychology may not only be describing reality but *creating* a fantasy to defend against its unsettling contingencies.

Power

The history of sociobiology and evolutionary psychology cannot be disentangled from questions of power, both in the Foucauldian sense of *power-knowledge*, and in the more direct ways that scientific claims have intersected with structures of gender, race, and class.

Michel Foucault argued that knowledge is never neutral: the production of scientific truth is always shaped by institutions, practices, and discourses that serve particular power relations. This is especially evident in the case of sociobiology, where scientific theories about human nature emerged alongside, and often reinforced, dominant ideologies. In the 1970s and 1980s, critics noted that claims about male aggression, female sexual selectivity, or the inevitability of competition seemed suspiciously aligned with patriarchal, capitalist, and heteronormative assumptions.

Feminist scientists were among the first to name these ideological functions. They argued that sociobiology often operated as a *science of the status quo*, providing what appeared to be natural justifications for deeply unequal power structures. Evolutionary accounts of gender roles, for example, could be used to legitimise workplace inequality, domestic labour divisions, or male dominance as biologically 'hardwired'.

This, in Žižekian terms, is the *ideological fantasy* at work: a fantasy that conceals the historical and political construction of social roles by presenting them as inevitable. It tells a comforting story: this is just how men and women are. The fantasy masks antagonisms, between men and women, and between dominant and marginalised groups, by displacing the source of social antagonisms onto 'nature'.

The authority of scientific discourse grants evolutionary theory extraordinary cultural weight. Evolutionary explanations often circulate far beyond the lab, in journalism, education, therapy, and even policy, where they shape how people understand themselves and others. This diffusion of power is subtle but pervasive. It does not command; it normalises. The act of critique, then, becomes a political act. To question evolutionary explanations is to disrupt the institutional and ideological arrangements such theories may support.

Chapter Summary

This chapter has traced the development of sociobiology in the 1970s and its transformation into evolutionary psychology by the 1990s. It introduced key figures and examined how evolutionary principles such as kin selection and reciprocal altruism were extended to explain complex human behaviours. The chapter also highlighted the contributions of feminist and Marxist scientists who offered pointed critiques of its reductionism and gender essentialism.

We explored the methodologies evolutionary psychologists have used to support their claims, from reverse engineering to infant cognition studies and appeals to consilience. While these methods aim to generate testable, empirical hypotheses, critics argue that much of the field remains speculative, especially when it comes to imaginatively reconstructing prehistoric environments. Epistemologically, evolutionary psychology operates on the boundary between scientific plausibility and ideological reassurance.

Slavoj Žižek's theory of *fantasy* as a critical lens has shown how scientific narratives about evolution can function as ideological fantasies. These fantasies support dominant beliefs, mask social antagonisms, and produce a perverse enjoyment in the revelation of 'truths' that often naturalise inequality. The ice water protest against E. O. Wilson in 1978 was a moment of rupture that exposed both the perils and the pleasures of scientific storytelling.

Reflective Questions

1. Why does the chapter begin with the anecdote of Edward O. Wilson being drenched with ice water?
2. How does the concept of fantasy, as used by Žižek, help us understand the enduring appeal of evolutionary psychology?
3. In what ways do critics argue that evolutionary psychology reinforces traditional gender roles?
4. How does the chapter contrast the approaches of Edward O. Wilson and Joan Roughgarden?
5. What role does popular science, such as Desmond Morris's *Manwatching*, play in shaping public attitudes towards evolutionary psychology?

Suggested Reading

Alter, S. G. (2007). Race, language, and mental evolution in Darwin's descent of man. *Journal of the History of the Behavioral Sciences, 43*(3), 239–255. https://doi.org/10.1002/jhbs.20238.

Brown, G. R., & Laland, K. N. (2024). *Sense and Nonsense: Evolutionary perspectives on human behaviour* (Third ed.). Oxford: Oxford University Press.
Dunbar, R. I. M. (2007). Evolution and the social sciences. *History of the Human Sciences, 20*(2), 29–50. https://doi.org/10.1177/0952695107076197.
Dunbar, R. I. M., & Barrett, L. (2007). *Oxford Handbook of Evolutionary Psychology*. Oxford: Oxford University Press.
Fisher, K., & Funke, J. (2023). 'All the progressive forms of life are built up on the attraction of sex': Development and the social function of the sexual instinct in late 19th- and early 20th-century Western European sexology. *History of the Human Sciences, 36*(5), 42–67. https://doi.org/10.1177/09526951231208992.
Jackson, J. P., Jr. (2023). Arthur Jensen, evolutionary biology, and racism. *History of Psychology, 26*(1), 1–28. https://doi.org/10.1037/hop0000221.
Jarrett, S. (2020). Consciousness reduced: The role of the 'idiot' in early evolutionary psychology. *History of the Human Sciences, 33*(5), 110–137. https://doi.org/10.1177/0952695120911557.
Peters, B. M. (2013). Evolutionary psychology: Neglecting neurobiology in defining the mind. *Theory & Psychology, 23*(3), 305–322. https://doi.org/10.1177/0959354313480269.
Racine, T. P. (2021). The rhetorical use of B. F. Skinner in evolutionary psychology. *Theory & Psychology, 32*(1), 61–81. https://doi.org/10.1177/09593543211030342.
Rose, H., & Rose, S. P. R. (2010). *Alas, Poor Darwin: Arguments against evolutionary psychology*. Vintage Digital.
Roughgarden, J. (2013). *Evolution's Rainbow: Diversity, gender, and sexuality in nature and people*. Berkeley: University of California Press.
Ruck, N. (2016). Controversies on Evolutionism: On the construction of scientific boundaries in public and internal scientific controversies about evolutionary psychology and sociobiology. *Theory & Psychology, 26*(6), 691–705. https://doi.org/10.1177/0959354316652968.
Segerstrale, U. (2001). *Defenders of the Truth: The sociobiology debate*. Oxford: Oxford University Press.
Žižek, S. (1997) *The Plague of Fantasies*. London: Verso.

Key Terms

Biological Determinism The belief that human behaviour is primarily or exclusively the result of biological factors such as genetics or evolutionary heritage, often criticised for ignoring cultural, historical, and political influences.

Evolutionary Psychology A branch of psychology that emerged from sociobiology in the 1990s, proposing that the human mind consists of evolved psychological mechanisms adapted to solve problems faced by our ancestors.

Fantasy Adapted from the work of Slavoj Žižek, fantasy is used in this chapter to describe the ideological stories we unconsciously tell ourselves to make sense of the world, especially when confronted with scientific uncertainty or contradiction.

Gender Essentialism The belief that men and women possess fixed, biologically determined traits and roles, often challenged by feminist critics as a cultural construction disguised as scientific fact.

Ideology In this chapter, ideology refers to the systems of belief that shape what we accept as 'natural' or 'scientific'—often masking power relations and reinforcing dominant cultural norms.

Inclusive Fitness A refinement of natural selection theory that accounts for an individual's genetic success through both direct reproduction and the support of relatives' reproductive success.

Kin Selection An evolutionary theory which suggests that behaviours that help genetic relatives survive and reproduce can be favoured by natural selection, even if they reduce the individual's own reproductive success.

Modularity of Mind The idea, central to some strands of evolutionary psychology, that the human brain is composed of specialised 'modules', each evolved to handle specific adaptive tasks such as mate choice or language.

Popular Science The dissemination of scientific ideas to general audiences, often simplified or exaggerated, which can influence public understanding and reinforce cultural narratives.

Reification The process of treating abstract concepts or theories (such as 'human nature') as if they were concrete, unchangeable facts.

Sexual Selection A concept in evolutionary theory, introduced by Charles Darwin, referring to the process by which certain traits become more or less common depending on an individual's success in mating and reproduction.

Sociobiology A field of study that emerged in the 1970s, associated primarily with Edward O. Wilson, which seeks to explain social behaviour in all species, including humans, through evolutionary theory and genetic selection.

FREE INSTRUCTOR & STUDENT RESOURCES

ONLINE RESOURCES

Visit the Instructor & Student Resources website at routledgelearning.com/bpscoretextbooks for free digital resources, including:

- Interactive quizzes and flashcards to test your knowledge
- Links to useful websites and videos
- Instructor manual, lecture slides, and course guide to enhance teaching and save instructors time

7 Language Games

The Cult of the Fact and the Enchantment of Discourse

Chapter Overview

Psychology was facing an intellectual and moral crisis by the 1970s. The experimental approach that had once promised objectivity and clarity now seemed reductive, irrelevant, and out of touch with lived experience. Amid this disillusionment a new approach emerged, one that turned its attention not inward to mental states but outward to language, context, and interaction. This chapter explores the rise of discursive psychology as a powerful response to the perceived failures of behaviourism and cognitive science. Anchored in the later philosophy of Ludwig Wittgenstein, particularly his concepts of 'language games' and 'forms of life', discursive psychology treats language not as a mirror of thought but as a social practice through which psychological reality is constituted.

Drawing on the work of several critical psychologists, this chapter explores how meaning, identity, and emotion are produced in language. It also considers how discourse, as a critical thinking tool, reveals the operations of power as something internal to language, performed and resisted through it. The chapter concludes by reflecting on the continued relevance and radical promise of discourse in reimagining what psychology is, and what it might become.

Language Games

In 1948, having resigned from his position as Professor of Philosophy at the University of Cambridge, Ludwig Wittgenstein went to Ireland, seeking isolation and hoping to complete his *Last Writings of the Philosophy of Psychology*. While staying near Dublin, he developed a routine: each day he would visit Bewley's Café in Grafton Street and sit quietly at his table. Without a word, the waitress would bring him his usual order: a coffee and an omelette. To most, this might seem like little more than the austere habit of a regular customer. But Wittgenstein was especially pleased by this simple gesture. (This was a man who thought nothing of serving his dinner guests powdered eggs, his culinary *pièce de résistance*.) In this silent ritual, we can see something profound about Wittgenstein's philosophy of language. No request was made, no words traded, yet the message was understood. The exchange worked because all parties were participating in a shared practice, a language game without words but one in which everyone knew the rules. This small scene captures the essence of Wittgenstein's later philosophy: meaning does not reside in words alone but in the activities, contexts, and expectations that surround them. Communication is not always verbal; it can be enacted through presence, routine, and mutual understanding. Wittgenstein called this a *form of life*, the rich, unspoken background of human customs that makes language possible. Even silence, then,

DOI: 10.4324/9781003565482-27

can be part of a language game if the rules are known, the roles understood, and the pattern sustained. The omelette and coffee arrived not because Wittgenstein *said* something but because he and the waitress both belonged to a pattern of life where meaning was already established. In psychology, this insight invites us to look beyond words as mere containers of thought and towards discourse as a social activity, a practice performed, patterned, and deeply embedded in the texture of everyday life.

Chapter Contents

- A critical exploration of discursive psychology as a response to the limitations of mainstream experimental psychology in the twentieth century.
- An introduction to Ludwig Wittgenstein's concept of 'language games' and its influence on psychological theory.
- A detailed investigation of the critical thinking tool of discourse, showing how language is used to construct psychological life and enact power.

Chapter Objectives

- To explain how the crisis of disillusionment in the 1970s led to the emergence of discursive approaches in psychology.
- To understand discourse as a contextual method in psychology and a constitutive aspect of the psychological.
- To identify key figures in discursive psychology and describe how their work challenged traditional epistemological and ontological assumptions in psychology.

CRITICAL THINKING TOOL
DISCOURSE

Discursive psychology is a way of studying psychology that treats language as an active force in constructing mental life. It assumes that psychological phenomena, such as thoughts, emotions, identities, and even the self, do not exist independently of the ways we talk about them. Instead, they are performed, negotiated, and contested through language.

Discourse analysis is the broader methodological approach that studies how language works in context. It explores the ways that talk and text shape our understanding of the world, influence social relationships, and sustain systems of power. While there are many varieties of discourse analysis (some rooted in linguistics, others in sociology or literary theory), discursive psychology brings this approach into the realm of psychological inquiry.

At its core, discursive psychology starts from three assumptions. First, that language is constitutive, not merely reflective: language brings the world into being. Second, that meaning is context-dependent: the same word or phrase can mean very different things depending on how, when, and by whom it is used. Third, that psychological life is socially enacted: thoughts

and feelings are not just internal states but public, discursive performances. Rather than looking inside the head for universal truths, discursive psychologists examine how people use language to make sense of their lives, position themselves and others, justify actions, and contest meanings.

Introduction

By the early 1970s, psychology was in crisis. Across classrooms, conferences, and journals, a wave of disillusionment was gathering. The grand promises of behaviourism and cognitive psychology were beginning to falter. For many, the discipline had become sterile, reductive, and alienating. Experiments often felt like artificial mimetic performances stripped of the richness of real-life contexts, and theories seemed to reduce people to data points, mental processes, or abstract variables.

In 1972, Paul Secord and Rom Harré argued that laboratory experiments often created artificial social situations where participants were essentially 'performing' for the researcher rather than exhibiting natural behaviour. The same year, Liam Hudson decried the 'cult of the fact', warning that psychology was chasing rigour at the expense of relevance. In an influential essay published the following year, Ken Gergen argued that social psychology produces knowledge that is historically contingent, reflecting the norms, values, and anxieties of the society that generates it. Many of the disillusioned contributors to Nigel Armistead's *Reconstructing Social Psychology* (1974) called for a more humane, more socially attuned psychology. Towards the end of the decade, Gordon Westland summarised the feeling of discontent in his nine *Current Crises in Psychology* (1978).

Beneath these frustrations was a growing sense that the discipline had taken a wrong turn, that it was ignoring the ways in which people make meaning, shape identities, and navigate social life. It was this concern that opened the door to radical new approaches. Alongside this shift, the work of philosopher Michel Foucault began to filter into psychological discourse. His analysis of power, knowledge, and discourse offered a powerful 'archaeological' framework with which to rethink how knowledge organises our lives, how it is connected to power, and what psychology might become if it took that framework seriously.

Historical Issues

At the centre of psychology's turn towards discourse was the work of Ludwig Wittgenstein (1889–1951), an enigmatic philosopher whose thinking transformed how language is understood as a public, rule-governed activity. His concept of 'language games' marked a departure from the idea that words derive meaning through logical reference or internal representation. Instead, Wittgenstein proposed that meaning arises from *use*, from what people conventionally do with words in specific social contexts. In discussion with Bertrand Russell at Cambridge, Wittgenstein challenged the idea of what it means to make a meaningful assertion. 'There is no rhinoceros in the room', Russell retorted. Wittgenstein, unfazed, started looking under the furniture, irritating Russell. To him, the sentence was logically true regardless of inspection. But Wittgenstein was making a deeper point: meaning does not exist in words alone, it emerges from their practical use within a certain context.

Wittgenstein developed this insight into a radical theory of language in his *Philosophical Investigations* (1953). He imagined a builder who shouts 'Slab!' to a co-worker. What does the word mean? It depends on the shared context, the task, the expectations, and the rules of interaction. The meaning is not inside the word but in how it functions as part of an activity, a language game where the players know the implicit rules. Crucially, these games are embedded in what he called 'forms of life', the social and cultural practices that make understanding possible.

By the 1970s, psychologists were growing increasingly dissatisfied with approaches that treated language as a transparent medium for inner mental states. The cognitive revolution, while displacing behaviourism, still assumed that the mind was best understood through the metaphor of 'information processor'. Internal states, mental schemas, and abstract constructs remained the focus. But what if psychological phenomena were not inner 'events' to be measured or inferred but rather actions performed through talk and interaction?

A pivotal text that brought these ideas into sharper focus within British psychology was *Changing the Subject: Psychology, social regulation and subjectivity* (1984), authored by Julian Henriques, Wendy Hollway, Cathy Urwin, Couze Venn, and Valerie Walkerdine. This interdisciplinary volume marked a major intervention in the field, linking power, knowledge, and subjectivity through a discursive and post-structural lens. The authors argued that psychology had not only measured and classified the self but had actively *produced* particular kinds of selves suited to the demands of modern society. *Changing the Subject* was an attempt to *rethink* what psychology could be if it took discourse, power, and history seriously.

Key Individuals

Rom Harré (1927–2019) was a central figure in challenging psychology's reliance on experimentalism and behaviourist models. A philosopher and psychologist trained in both sciences and the humanities, Harré argued that the discipline had lost sight of the human subject. In *The Explanation of Social Behaviour* (1972), co-written with Paul Secord, he advanced the idea that people should be understood not as bundles of stimuli and responses but as *persons*, beings who act for reasons, not just causes. Harré's emphasis on language as a medium for performing identity and agency laid crucial groundwork for discursive approaches.

Liam Hudson (1933–2005) was a sharp critic of psychology's methodological rigidity, Hudson's *The Cult of the Fact* (1972) delivered a damning verdict on the field's obsession with measurement. He argued that the quantification of human life stripped away richness, ambiguity, and moral relevance. For Hudson, psychology needed to attend to *how* people understand the world, not simply whether their responses to stimuli could be measured. His work anticipated many of the core insights of discourse analysis: that language is not neutral, that knowledge is perspectival, and that psychology must engage with meaning.

Kenneth Gergen (b.1935) is one of the most influential voices in introducing social constructionism into psychology. In his landmark essay 'Social psychology as history' (1973), Gergen argued that psychological knowledge is shaped by its social and historical context; it is not cumulative but interpretive. He challenged the discipline's obsession with generalisability and prediction, arguing that the very questions psychologists ask are products of cultural forces. In *The Saturated Self: Dilemmas of identity in contemporary life* (1991), Gergen explored how modern communication technologies and the proliferation of relationships contribute to a fragmented sense of self.

John Shotter (1937–2016) was deeply influenced by Wittgenstein, and brought a powerful emphasis on dialogue, social accountability, and the rhetorical construction of selfhood. For Shotter, psychological life is not contained within the individual but emerges in *relational space*, through conversations, conflicts, and shared narratives. His notion of the dialogical self reflects the idea that the self is not fixed but is continually being negotiated through discourse. Shotter's writing was often evocative, arguing for a psychology that was responsive, conversational, and contextually grounded.

Jonathan Potter (b.1956) was instrumental in formalising discursive psychology as a distinct approach. Drawing on conversation analysis, ethnomethodology, and Wittgenstein, Potter explored how psychological concepts, such as attitudes, beliefs, and even memory, are actively managed in *talk-in-interaction*. In *Discourse and Social Psychology: Beyond attitudes and behaviour* (1987), co-authored with Margaret Wetherell, he argued that what we call 'psychological states' are often better understood as rhetorical devices used to position and account for oneself in conversation.

Margaret Wetherell (b.1954) is a pioneering figure in the development of discursive psychology. Wetherell helped establish how discourse shapes identity, power, and meaning. Her work often focused on social categories such as gender, race, and class, and how these are produced and contested in language. In her joint work with Potter, and later in texts like *Identity in the 21st Century* (2009), Wetherell showed how language both reflects and constructs our social world. She has been especially influential in applying discourse analysis to real-world issues, including prejudice, inequality, and mental health.

Ian Parker (b.1956) has been one of the most influential and uncompromising voices in the development of critical discursive psychology. Drawing on Foucault, Lacan, Marxism, and post-structuralism, Parker's work has consistently foregrounded the political and ideological functions of psychological discourse. For Parker, discourse is a medium of communication and a technology of power. His subsequent work, especially *Discourse Dynamics* (1992) and *Revolution in Psychology* (2007), developed a critical methodology for analysing how psychological language disciplines thought and constrains alternative ways of being. Unlike more liberal discursive approaches, Parker insists on the need for ideological critique and political resistance, positioning discourse analysis as a tool not only for interpretation but for transformation.

Erica Burman (b.1960) has been a formidable critic of mainstream developmental psychology, particularly its failure to account for the ways power, gender, race, and class shape psychological knowledge. In her influential book *Deconstructing Developmental Psychology* (1994), Burman interrogated the seemingly neutral language of child development, revealing how psychological discourse often reinforces normative Western ideals of family, gender roles, and progress. Drawing on feminist theory, postcolonial critique, and discourse analysis, she exposed how categories such as 'normal development' marginalise women, working-class families, and people of colour.

Epistemological Issues

For much of its history, psychology operated within an epistemological framework shaped by positivism and empiricism. Knowledge, in this view, was something objective and discoverable through systematic observation, experiment, and measurement. The researcher was seen as a neutral observer, uncovering universal truths about human nature from a detached, impartial standpoint.

Discursive psychology fundamentally disrupts the empiricist picture. Instead of seeking decontextualised 'facts' or measuring 'variables', it insists that psychological inquiry should aim to account for the contextual, constructed, and contested. Meaning is not fixed in advance, waiting to be discovered; it is made, moment by moment, through language. Epistemologically, discursive psychology is not about prediction and control. Its aim is interpretation: to understand how psychological life is constituted through talk, and how that talk is shaped by history, power, and social norms. This means that what counts as 'psychological' is not something hidden inside individuals but something enacted through their speech, texts, and social practices.

For example, in analysing a transcript of a therapy session or a political speech, a discursive psychologist would not treat the language as merely expressing the speaker's attitudes or beliefs. Instead, they would ask: what is this speaker *doing* with their words? Are they justifying, blaming, resisting, persuading, or constructing an identity? In this way, language is not a window into the mind, it is a site of action and persuasion.

This shift brings with it new responsibilities for the researcher. No longer imagined as a passive recorder of facts or experimental manipulator, the psychologist is now understood as an active participant in constructing knowledge. Every research choice, of topic, language, interpretation, shapes what is seen as real. This aligns with broader critiques from feminist and postcolonial scholars who argue that mainstream psychological research often hides the politics of its own methods under a veneer of objectivity.

Ontological Issues

The dominant ontology of traditional psychology has assumed that psychological phenomena, such as emotions, attitudes, or mental disorders, are *internal* entities. These are imagined as residing inside individuals, hidden from view but measurable through tests, surveys, or observation. This model treats the mind as a container of thoughts and feelings, and the psychologist's task is to uncover what is already there.

Discursive psychology offers a very different ontological picture. It suggests that psychological phenomena are not simply discovered within the individual but are *brought into being* through language. That is, they are social accomplishments, constructed, performed, and made meaningful in talk and through the rules of interaction. This process can be seen in real-world examples. In therapy, clients rarely announce feelings with precision. Instead, they narrate stories, use metaphors, or describe bodily sensations. Through their exchanges with therapists, emotions such as grief or anger are not simply revealed, they are *co-constructed*. The emotion is not inside the person waiting to be found; it *emerges* through the interaction with the therapist.

Similarly, rather than measuring prejudice as a stable attitude, discursive psychologists analyse how speakers *manage* accusations of bias. When someone says, 'I'm not racist, but . . .', they are performing a social task: defending themselves, navigating accountability, and constructing a particular moral identity. Prejudice here is a discursive act, shaped by context.

Even identity, often treated in psychology as a constellation of fixed traits, is shown to be fluid and performed. In a classroom setting, a teacher may label a student as 'not a maths person', and students may internalise or resist these identities through everyday talk. These utterances *create* psychological reality.

In this framework, psychological concepts become outcomes of discourse. What counts as an 'emotion', a 'diagnosis', or an 'identity' is *made real* through language. Discursive psychology thus invites us to relocate the site of psychological life, not inside the head but within the unfolding practices of everyday communication.

Power

One of the most important consequences of psychology's turn to discourse was the realisation that discourse is never neutral. Language helps *shape* the world and our experiences of it. And in shaping it, language is deeply entangled with power.

This insight owes much to the work of French philosopher Michel Foucault (1926–1984). Trained as a clinical psychologist, Foucault's ideas about discourse and power/knowledge had a profound influence on critical psychology. For Foucault, power is not just something wielded by the sovereign, individuals or institutions; it operates through discourse via the rules, classifications, and assumptions that govern what can be said, by whom, and with what authority.

Discourses, in this sense, are more than just patterns of talk. They are systems of knowledge that define categories (such as 'madness', 'intelligence', or 'childhood'), legitimate certain practices (such as therapy or diagnosis), and exclude or silence others. In psychology, discourse shapes everything from who gets diagnosed to how normality is defined. To speak is to enter into a field of power.

Discursive psychology takes this seriously. It asks not just *what* people say but *what their saying does*, whose voices are heard, whose are marginalised, and what social arrangements are sustained or challenged through language. For example, analysing a clinical interview might reveal how a professional subtly positions a client as 'emotional and irrational' or 'co-dependent' through the structure of questioning, tone, or word choice. Alternatively, a study of everyday talk about immigration might show how prejudice is reproduced through seemingly 'reasonable' concerns about security or economy.

Importantly, discourse can also be a site of resistance. People are assumed to be able to contest dominant meanings, reinterpret them, or strategically subvert them. Feminist, postcolonial, and queer psychologists have shown how marginalised groups use language to reclaim identity, challenge stigma, and create new ways of speaking the self. Discursive psychology makes power visible, not as an external force acting upon individuals but as something produced and negotiated through language itself. By examining how psychological concepts are spoken, circulated, and contested, it reveals the politics embedded in what often passes as neutral science.

Chapter Summary

By the 1970s, psychology was facing a growing crisis of confidence. The discipline's allegiance to experimentation, quantification, and laboratory-based knowledge, what Liam Hudson called 'the cult of the fact', was beginning to unravel. Critics argued that psychology had become too enamoured with objectivity, too focused on controlling variables, and too detached from the complexities of real life. It was failing to ask the most human questions.

Into this space of disillusionment came a quiet revolution: a shift in attention from the hidden contents of the mind to the visible practices of language. Drawing on Wittgenstein's later philosophy, psychologists began to rethink what language is and what it does. No longer treated as a transparent medium for inner states, language came to be seen as a social activity, a game played within specific contexts and forms of life.

From this foundation, discursive psychology emerged as a disparate array of provocations, practices, and possibilities. Figures such as Rom Harré, Paul Secord, John Shotter, Kenneth Gergen, Liam Hudson, Jonathan Potter, Margaret Wetherell, and Erica Burman challenged the idea that psychology could uncover universal mental truths. Instead, they showed how psychological life is *made* in language, how emotions, identities, diagnoses, and prejudices are constructed, negotiated, and contested through talk and text.

Epistemologically, this meant abandoning the fantasy of the detached observer. Knowledge, they argued, is situated, constructed, and always bound up with the researcher's position and methods. Ontologically, it meant shifting from fixed internal entities to dynamic social performances. Power, meanwhile, was brought to the fore: language was no longer politically neutral but recognised as a tool for inclusion, exclusion, and resistance. In this way, discursive psychology reimagined the crisis of confidence in psychology in the 1970s. And in doing so, it opened the door to a more critical, inclusive, and interpretative psychology.

If the 'cult of the fact' had promised certainty, discourse offered enchantment. It invited psychologists to embrace the richness of lived experience by expanding what counted as psychological reality. In 1948, in a quiet Dublin café, where Wittgenstein received his daily omelette and coffee without uttering a word, we can glimpse the spark of this enchantment. Meaning is not hidden inside us waiting to be extracted but subsists between us all, in the shared, often unspoken, rhythms of our everyday lives.

Reflective Questions

1. What does Wittgenstein's concept of a 'language game' reveal about the relationship between language and meaning?
2. How did the crisis in psychology during the 1970s open the door for discursive approaches to emerge?
3. In what ways does discursive psychology challenge traditional ideas about the nature of psychological knowledge?
4. How is power understood and analysed in discursive psychology, particularly in relation to Michel Foucault's influence?
5. What are the implications of treating emotions, attitudes, and identities as discursive performances rather than as internal states?

Suggested Reading

Chouliaraki, L., & Fairclough, N. (1999). *Discourse in Late Modernity: Rethinking critical discourse analysis*. Edinburgh: Edinburgh University Press.

Coulter, J. (1979). *The Social Construction of Mind: Studies in ethnomethodology and linguistic philosophy.* Basingstoke: Palgrave Macmillan.
Harré, R. (1988). Wittgenstein and artificial intelligence. *Philosophical Psychology, 1*(1), 105–115. https://doi.org/10.1080/09515088808572928.
Hook, D. (2001). Discourse, knowledge, materiality, history: Foucault and discourse analysis. *Theory & Psychology, 11*(4), 521–547. https://doi.org/10.1177/0959354301114006.
Hudson, L. (1972). *The Cult of the Fact.* London: Jonathan Cape.
Kalis, A. (2019). No intentions in the brain: A Wittgensteinian perspective on the science of intention. *Frontiers in Psychology, 10*(946), 1–9. https://doi.org/10.3389/fpsyg.2019.00946.
Racine, T. P., & Müller, U. (2009). The contemporary relevance of Wittgenstein: Reflections and directions. *New Ideas in Psychology, 27*(2),107–117. https://doi.org/10.1016/j.newideapsych.2008.04.008.
Scott, P., & von Unger, H. (2021). Discourses on im/migrants, ethnic minorities, and infectious disease: Fifty years of tuberculosis reporting in the United Kingdom. *History of the Human Sciences, 35*(1), 189–215. https://doi.org/10.1177/09526951211015886.
Shotter, J. (1996). Living in a Wittgensteinian world: Beyond theory to a poetics of practices. *Journal for the Theory of Social Behaviour, 26*(3), 293–311. https://doi.org/10.1111/j.1468-5914.1996.tb00292.x.
Standish, P. (2022). Inner and outer, psychology and Wittgenstein's painted curtain. *Journal of Philosophy of Education, 56*(1), 115–123. https://doi.org/10.1111/1467-9752.12656.
van der Merwe, W. L., & Voestermans, P. P. (1995). Wittgenstein's legacy and the challenge to psychology. *Theory & Psychology, 5*(1), 27–48. https://doi.org/10.1177/0959354395051002.
Wetherell, M., & Potter, J. (2015). Discourse and social psychology, postmodernism, and capitalist collusion: An argument for more complex historiographies of psychology. *Theory & Psychology, 25*(3), 388–395. https://doi.org/10.1177/0959354314552009.
Willig, C. (2000). A discourse-dynamic approach to the study of subjectivity in health psychology. *Theory & Psychology, 10*(4), 547–570. https://doi.org/10.1177/0959354300104006.

Key Terms

Critical Psychology A field that challenges the assumptions of mainstream psychology, focusing on issues of power, ideology, and social justice in psychological theory and practice.
Discourse A system of language and social practices that shapes how we understand and organise the world; in psychology, discourse refers to the ways talk and text construct psychological realities.
Discursive Psychology An approach that treats psychological concepts as socially enacted through language rather than as internal mental states; it studies how talk and text perform actions such as justifying, blaming, or constructing identity.
Empiricism An epistemological stance that views knowledge as arising from sensory experience and observation, often associated with measurement and objectivity in psychology.
Form of Life Ludwig Wittgenstein's term for the broader cultural and social practices within which language games are played and made meaningful.
Interpretivism An epistemological position that sees knowledge as constructed and context-bound, requiring interpretation of meaning rather than discovery of universal facts.
Language Games A concept developed by Ludwig Wittgenstein to describe how words derive their meaning from use in specific social contexts and practices rather than from fixed definitions.

Power/Knowledge A term from Michel Foucault emphasising that knowledge is never neutral but is always entangled with power relations that determine what can be said, by whom, and with what effect.

Prejudice (Discursive Approach) Not a fixed internal attitude but a social action performed in talk, often managed through strategies of denial, justification, or identity positioning.

Subjectivity A term used to describe how people come to understand and experience themselves, especially as shaped by discourse, power, and social context.

FREE INSTRUCTOR & STUDENT RESOURCES

ONLINE RESOURCES

Visit the Instructor & Student Resources website at routledgelearning.com/bpscoretextbooks for free digital resources, including:

- Interactive quizzes and flashcards to test your knowledge
- Links to useful websites and videos
- Instructor manual, lecture slides, and course guide to enhance teaching and save instructors time

28 Unnatural Emotions

The Social Construction of Feelings

Chapter Overview

What if emotions were not just things we feel inside but ways we learn to live together? This chapter challenges the idea that emotions such as anger, sadness, or love are hardwired, universal responses. Instead, it shows how feelings are shaped by culture, language, history, and power. We begin on a small Pacific Island, where anthropologist Catherine Lutz was puzzled by a mother's tears, not of sadness, but something the Ifaluk people called *fago*, a feeling with no easy English translation. From there, we trace how the modern idea of 'emotion' replaced older ways of understanding human feeling, such as passions or affections. Scientists such as Darwin and Ekman tried to classify emotions as biological and universal but their theories have been questioned by anthropologists, feminist thinkers, and discourse psychologists who argue that emotions are learned, performed, and deeply political. Using social constructionism as our critical thinking tool, we ask: what counts as an emotion and who gets to feel it? Far from being private, emotions are public acts, expressed in speech, shaped by culture, and bound up with systems of power. By the end of this chapter you will see emotion not just as something we feel but as something we do.

Unnatural Emotions

One sunny afternoon in the late 1970s, on the coral atoll of Ifaluk in Micronesia, anthropologist Catherine Lutz sat quietly near a family hearth. A mother, her face calm but tired from a morning of collective labour, cradled her hungry child and softly coaxed him to eat. As the child accepted the food, tears slowly gathered in the mother's eyes. Lutz observed the moment closely but was unsettled. Was this an expression of sadness? Could it have been relief or even exhaustion? None of the Western emotional categories seemed to capture the scene. The woman did not speak, nor gesture dramatically. She simply rested her hand on the child's back, weeping quietly, and then returned to her tasks. Trained in Western psychological and anthropological traditions, Lutz initially struggled to make sense of what she had seen. There was no apparent crisis, no external drama, just a subtle but profound intensity of feeling. Over the following months, living closely with the Ifaluk community and listening to them with care, she began to grasp the cultural contours of a concept foreign to Western psychology. *Fago*, she came to understand, was a moral sentiment, a relational practice. The feeling combined sadness and love, vulnerability and duty. To feel *fago* was to care deeply about another's suffering and to express that care through quiet, embodied acts of attention. It was public, not private, and somehow moral. In time, Lutz realised that emotions like *fago* could not be captured neatly by Western taxonomies of inner states. They revealed something more radical: that emotion is always shaped by each

DOI: 10.4324/9781003565482-28

culture's specific moral economy. Lutz's fieldwork, which culminated in her 1988 book *Unnatural Emotions*, radically challenged Western psychological models of emotions as biological forces. From this profound starting point, we will ask: are emotions universal and internal, or are they, like *fago*, constructed, situated, and experienced through relationships?

Chapter Contents

- Explores how the concept of 'emotion' has shifted historically from a moral and religious concern to a scientific and psychological category.
- Examines key figures such as Catherine Lutz, Paul Ekman, and Arlie Hochschild to show how emotions are shaped by culture, language, and power.
- Introduces 'social constructionism' as a critical thinking tool for challenging the idea of universal, biologically fixed emotions.

Chapter Objectives

- To help students understand that emotions are not simply natural, universal states but are shaped by cultural, social, and historical forces.
- To introduce students to key thinkers and case studies in the anthropology, discourse analysis, and feminist psychology of emotion.
- To encourage students to use the critical thinking tool of social constructionism to question how psychological categories like 'emotion' are defined, applied, and naturalised.

CRITICAL THINKING TOOL
SOCIAL CONSTRUCTIONISM

Social constructionism emerged in psychology in the mid-twentieth century as a critical response to dominant positivist and empiricist approaches. It questioned the assumption that psychological phenomena, such as emotion, exist independently of the social worlds in which they are described. Instead, it drew on sociology, anthropology, and philosophy to examine how categories of mind and behaviour are shaped by culture, language, and power.

Social constructionism invites us to question what we take for granted. Rather than treating emotions as fixed, universal facts of nature, it encourages us to ask how emotional categories are shaped by culture, language, history, and social norms. From this perspective, emotions are constructed through shared practices, meanings, and institutions. Social constructionism allows us to see that what we call 'anger' or 'shame' is not merely a response to biological arousal but a concept shaped by a specific culture, in a particular time and place.

This approach challenges the idea that feelings such as anger or fear are biologically pre-given and instead frames them as concepts that emerge within specific social contexts. Emotional life, then, is a patterned form of expression and understanding shaped by time, place, and power. To think critically about emotion is to consider who defines it, how it is expressed, and whose voices are heard or silenced in the process.

Introduction

Emotion feels like one of the most immediate and natural aspects of human life. We know when we are angry, joyful, or afraid. And yet, the very idea of what counts as an emotion, how it is expressed, and what it means has shifted dramatically over time. In psychology, the category of 'emotion' has not always existed as a clearly defined object of study. It emerged slowly, through philosophical debate, scientific redefinition, and cultural negotiation. What we take for granted as human universal may, in fact, be deeply contingent on time and place.

This chapter argues that emotion is not simply a biological or cognitive event that happens inside the body. Instead, it is a social construct, something that is made, shaped, and performed through culture, history, language, and power. From the Western invention of the category 'emotion' to the cultural specificity of Ifaluk *fago* or Ilongot *liget*, we will explore how feelings are experienced and produced.

We begin by tracing the historical emergence of 'emotion' as a psychological object, then move through anthropological and feminist critiques, culminating in the discursive perspective. In doing so, we will see how emotion shifts from a natural kind concept to a human kind, and ultimately, to a political practice.

Historical Issues

The concept of emotion as we understand it today is a relatively recent invention. Prior to the nineteenth century, Western affective discourse focused on 'passions', 'affections', and 'sentiments', terms bound up with moral philosophy and religious life ('the passion of the Christ'). These categories were not yet seen as psychological states to be measured or diagnosed but as ethical experiences, linked to virtue and vice, self-discipline and spiritual struggle. In this context, feelings were to be cultivated or resisted as part of a spiritual life. Charles Taylor's *Sources of the Self* (1989) connected changes in affective rules with broader transformations of identity. He argued that the Protestant Reformation catalysed a deep restructuring of the emotional and moral self.

In his influential work *From Passions to Emotions: The creation of a secular psychological category* (2003), Thomas Dixon traced how the modern concept of emotion emerged in nineteenth-century Britain through the gradual dismantling of older religious and moral frameworks. For Dixon, this shift did not simply rename existing feelings, it fundamentally reclassified them. Where earlier traditions spoke of 'passions', 'affections', or 'moral sentiments', rooted in Christian theology and virtue ethics, the new language of 'emotion' marked a turn to the secular. Emotions became increasingly detached from moral judgement and theological meaning, and were reimagined as natural, internal responses amenable to scientific study. Crucially, Dixon argued that the new term 'emotion' allowed psychologists to bypass complex philosophical distinctions between reason, will, and appetite, instead offering a neutral-sounding category that could be studied empirically. Figures such as Alexander Bain, in *The Emotions and the Will* (1859), exemplified this move, bringing emotion into the realm of physiology and experimental psychology, further detaching it from its ethical and spiritual roots.

This move represented the 'naturalisation' of emotion. No longer a question of ethics or theology, emotion was reimagined as a biological response system, a reaction of the body to external stimuli. This redefinition made emotion into something measurable, observable, and scientifically legitimate. Charles Darwin's *The*

Expression of the Emotions in Man and Animals (1872) argued that certain emotional expressions were universal across species and cultures. He suggested that emotions were deeply rooted, originating in our evolutionary past, a 'natural kind'.

This essentialist trajectory found its fullest modern expression in the work of Paul Ekman, whose cross-cultural studies of facial expression in the 1970s claimed to confirm Darwin's thesis that six basic emotions are biologically hardwired and universally recognised. Ekman's emotion typology, widely adopted in psychological research, law enforcement training, and even Hollywood movies (notably in Pixar's *Inside Out*), reinforced the view that emotions are evolutionarily determined mechanisms that operate independently of culture or language. In this Darwinian framework, emotions are seen as inherited modules, biologically prepared for rapid deployment in the face of environmental threats or social stimuli.

Yet from the 1970s onward, this paradigm started to unravel. Feminist psychologists, social constructionists, and discourse theorists increasingly challenged the idea that emotion could be divorced from context, power, or politics. They argued that emotions were instruments of moral regulation, especially in patriarchal societies. Emotions such as shame, guilt, and anger became sites of critical inquiry, no longer simply inner states but socially sanctioned responses that maintained gendered hierarchies and constrained agency. Anthropologists, sociologists, and psychologists turned the study of emotion outward, examining how feelings were performed, policed, and made meaningful through cultural norms, discursive practices, and institutional structures. Rather than viewing emotion as a universal biological substrate, this new wave of theorists reframed it as a politically charged and socially constructed domain, one that demanded historical and critical analysis.

Key Individuals

The modern scientific study of emotion began with William James (1842–1910), whose 1884 essay 'What is an emotion?' consolidated the biological approach. James proposed that emotion was not a cause of bodily change but its effect: we feel afraid because we tremble, not the other way around. Emotion, in his theory, was a physical event, bodily arousal interpreted by the brain as a feeling. This reversed common sense and inaugurated a long-standing interest in the physiological basis of emotion. James's theory located emotion in the body, pre-conscious and automatic, reinforcing the idea that emotions are natural kinds, biological facts universal to all humans.

This view was modified by Stanley Schachter (1922–1997) and Jerome Singer (1924–2010), who proposed a 'two-factor theory' of emotion. The theory stated that participants who experienced arousal (artificially induced by adrenaline) but lacked an explanatory context attributed and labelled their emotion based on social cues. One participant might feel euphoria, for example, if surrounded by playful confederates; another might interpret the same bodily state as anger in a more threatening setting. Schachter and Singer thus redefined emotion as a combination of physiological arousal and cognitive appraisal.

A central figure in the biological tradition, Paul Ekman (b.1934), is best known for his cross-cultural research on facial expressions. Building on Darwin's legacy, Ekman argued that basic emotions (happiness, sadness, fear, anger, surprise, and disgust) are biologically hardwired and expressed similarly across cultures. His research involved showing participants photographs of posed facial expressions and asking them to identify the emotions depicted. Ekman's work gained significant influence in psychological science and beyond, impacting fields such as lie detection, national security, and Hollywood.

Philosopher and psychologist Rom Harré (1927–2019) was a leading figure in the social constructionist approach to emotion. The contributors to his edited volume *The Social Construction of Emotions* (1986), argued that emotions are cultural scripts that individuals learn through social interaction. Emotions, in this view, are shaped by language, norms, and social context. Harré emphasised that emotional episodes are public performances that position speakers, regulate interaction, and reproduce moral orders. This discourse-based view suggests that what counts as an emotion, how it should be expressed, and who is allowed to feel it are all historically and socially contingent.

From here, psychology began to confront cultural challenges. Anthropologist Renato Rosaldo (b.1941), in his work with the Ilongot people of the Philippines, offered a powerful critique of emotional universals. The sentiment of liget, for example, had no direct English equivalent, inadequately translated as energy, anger, passion, or vitality. It was associated with intense affective arousal, often linked to headhunting, masculine pride, grief, and existential restlessness. Rosaldo's insight was profound: what counts as an emotion, and how it is felt and enacted, is inseparable from a society's symbolic order and moral economy.

Catherine Lutz (b.1952) extended this insight in her groundbreaking work on the Ifaluk of Micronesia. She meticulously documented emotional terms and practices that bore little resemblance to Western categories. *Song*, an emotion often approximated as 'justifiable anger', was central to Ifaluk social life, reinforcing moral order and communal accountability. Yet, to translate song simply as 'anger' would miss its profound moral resonance and social texture. Lutz's book, *Unnatural Emotions* (1988), argued that Western psychology had fundamentally misunderstood emotion by abstracting it from the rich social and cultural worlds in which it is lived.

Feminist sociologist Arlie Hochschild (b.1940) provided a parallel critique of emotion's role in capitalist economies and gendered expectations. In *The Managed Heart* (1983), Hochschild introduced the concept of 'emotional labour' to describe how workers, especially women, are expected to manage and display emotions as part of their job. Flight attendants, for example, are expected to smile, soothe, and absorb frustration, often at personal emotional cost. Hochschild's analysis showed that emotional expression is gendered and commodified. Emotion is work, but work that is unequally remunerated.

Epistemological Issues

Early approaches to emotion, particularly those influenced by physiology and behaviourism, assumed that emotion could be known objectively: through bodily indicators, facial expressions, or observable behaviours. William James's theory, for instance, implied that emotional knowledge came through introspection guided by physiological changes. Later, researchers such as Paul Ekman attempted to classify emotion through 'universal' facial expressions, further reinforcing the belief that emotions could be directly photographed, coded, and universally recognised.

However, as psychologists turned towards cognitive and cultural models, these assumptions were called into question. Schachter and Singer's experimental research suggested that the same physiological state could be interpreted in multiple ways depending on social context. This raised a crucial epistemological problem: if emotions depend on interpretation, then they are not straightforwardly observable. Knowing an emotion requires understanding the cultural scripts, language, and norms that shape it. Emotion, in this view, becomes less an object to be detected and more a meaning to be decoded.

Anthropological research deepened the challenge to psychological universalism not only in its findings but in its methods. Researchers such as Catherine Lutz and Renato Rosaldo had to develop epistemological strategies suited to the task of understanding emotional life from within a culture rather than imposing external categories. Their work relied on participant observation, long-term immersion, language learning, and ethnographic interviewing to grasp the moral and relational logics embedded in everyday practices. These researchers collected examples of cultural variation and demonstrated that knowledge of emotion is situated, dialogical, and interpretive, an achievement of shared understanding. This made the pursuit of emotional knowledge into one that required humility, reflexivity, and a willingness to be transformed by the encounter.

This problem intensifies in discursive psychology, where emotion is conceptualised as something performed and made real through talk. To say 'I am angry' to take up a social position, to lay claim to a response, to demand justice, and perhaps to exert influence. Epistemologically, this collapses the distinction between knowing and doing. We co-create emotion in the process of naming and narrating. To know an emotion, then, is to participate in the discursive practices that bring it into being.

Ontological Issues

What *is* an emotion? This deceptively simple question lies at the heart of psychological inquiry, and the answers have shifted significantly depending on theoretical commitments and historical context. What kind of a thing emotion is moved from a natural kind ontology to a human kind one during the twentieth century.

The biological approach offered a clear ontological stance: emotions are internal, bodily events triggered by external stimuli. In this view, emotion exists as a discrete biological response, one that precedes cognition and is rooted in the body's automatic functions. Whether joy or fear, emotion is understood as a pre-social, natural state, something universal across human beings, and some animals, regardless of culture or context.

Cognitive theories unsettled this biological certainty. If emotion requires both physiological arousal and a cognitive label, then its ontological status becomes less fixed. It is no longer an internal object waiting to be uncovered but a relational phenomenon shaped by interpretation. Schachter's view implies that emotion *becomes* rather than *is*, a product of appraisal, meaning-making, and the interaction between individual and environment.

Anthropological research pushed this further. Rosaldo's and Lutz's accounts suggest that emotions are constituted through culturally specific practices. What counts as an emotion, how it is named, when it is appropriate to express, and what it means, these are all shaped by collective life. From this vantage point, emotions are forms of social participation and cultural identity.

Social constructionist research by Batja Mesquita has demonstrated that emotions such as *guilt* and *shame* are culturally patterned responses that reflect normative expectations. In individualistic societies, guilt is typically experienced as an internal failure of moral conscience, an individual deviation from personal standards. In contrast, in collectivist cultures, shame is relational and public, emerging when one's actions reflect poorly on the group. Emotional experience in this framework is context-dependent, shaped by socially acquired scripts. As Mesquita demonstrated in her book *Between Us: How cultures create emotions* (2022), immigrant populations demonstrate ontological shifts in their emotional repertoires as they move between cultures, suggesting that emotions themselves change, not just their expression. Here, emotion is ontologically reframed as a culturally variable mode of moral engagement.

From a discursive psychology perspective, as articulated by Margaret Wetherell in works such as *Affect and Emotion: A new social science* (2012), emotions such as *anger* are social actions constructed through language. Analyses of TV talk shows reveal how anger is used performatively to assert moral claims, manage accountability, and shape audience alignment. A guest might say, 'I'm angry that you've ignored my question' to reposition themselves as wronged and the other as morally suspect. These utterances function strategically, calibrated for effect, and evaluated by audiences in real time.

Power

Emotions are shaped, policed, and deployed within relations of power. While much of psychology has historically treated emotion as a private matter, something internal to the individual, the social constructionist perspective reveals emotion as a deeply political phenomenon. Power enters through how they are permitted, denied, or required.

Arlie Hochschild's concept of 'emotional labour' demonstrates this with striking clarity. In service professions, particularly those occupied by women, such as flight attendants, nurses, and customer service agents, workers are expected to display specific emotions regardless of how they feel. Smiling, calming, reassuring: these emotional displays are commodified, required as part of the job, although never remunerated. Workers are required to manage their emotional expressions to meet organisational expectations, often at great personal cost. The workplace, in this context, becomes a site where emotion is disciplined, gendered, and alienated.

This dynamic extends beyond the workplace. Social norms dictate which emotions are considered appropriate for men and women, children and adults, leaders and followers. Anger is often legitimised in men but pathologised in women; sadness in men may be read as weakness, while in women it can be romanticised. These norms reproduce inequalities and impose social expectations. Calling someone 'hysterical' or 'too emotional' delegitimises their claim, framing them as irrational, unstable, and feminine. Language, in this sense, is part of the machinery through which emotion is the agent for granting or denying social authority. In this view, emotion is a site of struggle. It reflects and reproduces the structures of gender, class, race, and institutional control.

Margaret Wetherell's work on romantic discourse adds further nuance, showing how love itself, often idealised as natural, authentic, and spontaneous, is structured by deeply gendered emotional scripts. Women are expected to perform emotional availability, care, and vulnerability in ways that reinforce heteronormative power dynamics. These emotional expectations are imposed through cultural norms that shape who women are permitted, and expected, to be.

Chapter Summary

This chapter has argued that emotion is not a universal biological given but a socially constructed phenomenon shaped by language, culture, and power. We explored how the modern category of 'emotion' emerged historically, replacing older moral and philosophical terms like 'passion'. This reclassification aligned with psychology's ambitions to become a science and led to a naturalised, internalised view of emotion, exemplified by William James. But this framework was challenged by Schachter and Singer's two-factor theory which emphasised social interpretation, and by feminist and discursive critiques that exposed how emotion is regulated, performed, and politicised.

Arlie Hochschild's work on emotional labour showed how feeling is governed by gendered power structures, while discursive psychology revealed that emotions are enacted in language. Anthropological research pushed the argument further, showing that emotional life is culturally specific. Understanding emotion, then, requires attention to the social and moral worlds in which feeling is made.

Emotions are built within specific moral and relational worlds. Just as Catherine Lutz once sat puzzled beside an Ifaluk mother whose quiet tears defied all Western categories, we too are reminded that to understand emotion is not to unlock a universal code but to listen, carefully and with humility, to the lives and languages through which feeling takes form.

Reflective Questions

1. What does the example of *fago* on Ifaluk tell us about the relationship between emotion and culture?
2. How did the transformation from 'passions' to 'emotions' change the way psychology approached human feeling?
3. In what ways did feminist theorists such as Arlie Hochschild challenge dominant understandings of emotion?
4. How do discursive psychologists argue that language shapes emotion?
5. What does the critical thinking tool of social constructionism help us uncover about emotion?

Suggested Reading

Ahmed, S. (2014). *The Cultural Politics of Emotion* (Second ed.). Edinburgh: Edinburgh University Press.

Dixon, T. (2003). *From Passions to Emotions: The creation of a secular psychological category.* Cambridge: Cambridge University Press.

Dupouy, S. (2011). The naturalist and the nuances: Sentimentalism, moral values, and emotional expression in Darwin and the anatomists. *Journal of the History of the Behavioural Sciences, 47*(4), 335–358. https://doi.org/10.1002/jhbs.20515.

Hutchinson, P. (2020). The 'placebo' paradox and the emotion paradox: Challenges to psychological explanation. *Theory & Psychology, 30*(5), 617–637. https://doi.org/10.1177/0959354320928139.

Larrain, A., & Haye, A. (2020). The dialogical and political nature of emotions: A reading of Vygotsky's *The Psychology of Art. Theory & Psychology, 30*(6), 800–812. https://doi.org/10.1177/0959354320955235.

Loaiza, J. R. (2025). Cultural variation of emotions and radical relativism. *Theory & Psychology, 35*(4), 444–465. https://doi.org/10.1177/09593543251332575.

Malekzad, F., Jais, M., Hernandez, G., Kehr, H., & Quirin, M. (2022). Not self-aware? Psychological antecedents and consequences of alienating from one's actual motives, emotions, and goals. *Theory & Psychology, 33*(4), 463–484. https://doi.org/10.1177/09593543221086598.

Mesquita, B., Boiger, M., & De Leersnyder, J. (2017). Doing emotions: The role of culture in everyday emotions. *European Review of Social Psychology, 28*(1), 95–133. https://doi.org/10.1080/10463283.2017.1329107.

Perrotta, D. (2025). Affective experience in neuroscience and phenomenology: An epistemological analysis of emotions and feelings. *Theory & Psychology, 35*(4), 466–487. https://doi.org/10.1177/09593543251336171.

Plamper, J. (2015). *History of Emotions: An introduction* (K. Tribe, Trans.; First ed.). Oxford: Oxford University Press.

Rose, A. C. (2012). Animal tales: Observations of the emotions in American experimental psychology, 1890–1940. *Journal of the History of the Behavioural Sciences, 48*(4), 301–317. https://doi.org/10.1002/jhbs.21562.

Sánchez, F., & Sebastián, C. (2024). Integrating affection, emotion, and aesthetics into a General Theory of Learning. *Theory & Psychology, 34*(2), 233–256. https://doi.org/10.1177/09593543241229740.

Wassmann, C. (2014). 'Picturesque incisiveness': Explaining the celebrity of James's Theory of Emotion. *Journal of the History of the Behavioural Sciences, 50*(2), 166–188. https://doi.org/10.1002/jhbs.21651.

Wetherell, M. (2012). *Affect and Emotion: A new social science understanding*. Thousand Oaks, CA: Sage.

Key Terms

Affect A broader category than emotion, encompassing pre-conscious intensities, moods, and embodied states that may not be easily named or verbalised.

Discursive Psychology A branch of psychology that analyses how people use language to perform psychological functions—including expressing and constituting emotions—within social interactions.

Emotion A historically constructed psychological category referring to feelings, often treated as internal states but increasingly understood as social, cultural, and political processes.

Emotional Labour A concept introduced by Arlie Hochschild, describing how people (especially in service roles) manage their feelings to meet the emotional expectations of their jobs.

Emotionology A term coined by Peter and Carol Stearns to describe the collective emotional norms of a culture and how societies manage emotional expression.

Ethnography A method of anthropological research involving deep immersion in a culture's everyday life, used by Catherine Lutz to study emotions in context.

Fago An Ifaluk emotion meaning something like 'compassionate love', combining sadness, care, and moral duty—demonstrating that emotions are culturally embedded.

Passions Pre-nineteenth-century term for strong feelings associated with moral and religious life, later replaced by the scientific category of 'emotion'.

Social Constructionism The critical thinking tool of this chapter; an approach that sees categories like emotion as created through language, culture, and power relations rather than discovered as natural kinds.

Speech Act An utterance that performs an action (e.g. 'I'm sorry', 'I'm afraid'); important in discursive psychology for understanding how emotions are enacted through language.

Universal Emotions Theory A theory associated with Paul Ekman and rooted in Charles Darwin, suggesting that certain emotions (e.g. anger, fear, happiness) are biologically hardwired and universally recognised.

Unnatural Emotions The title of Catherine Lutz's 1988 book; it challenges the assumption that emotions are natural, arguing they are shaped by cultural and moral systems.

FREE INSTRUCTOR & STUDENT RESOURCES

ONLINE RESOURCES

Visit the Instructor & Student Resources website at routledgelearning.com/bpscoretextbooks for free digital resources, including:

- Interactive quizzes and flashcards to test your knowledge
- Links to useful websites and videos
- Instructor manual, lecture slides, and course guide to enhance teaching and save instructors time

29 The Power Within

Cognitive Psychology's Embodied Cognition

Chapter Overview

This chapter challenges the assumption that cognitive psychology is a neutral, disembodied science of the mind. Instead, it reveals that cognitive psychology emerged from a particular time and place, shaped by the pressures of war, the demands of bureaucracy, and the technical metaphors of control, command, and computation. Beginning with the story of Kenneth Craik, a brilliant young psychologist whose wartime research helped lay the foundations for modern cognitive models, the chapter shows how metaphors of memory as storage, processing, and retrieval were never simply descriptive. They were imaginative projections of the environments and values in which psychologists themselves were embedded. Drawing on the critical thinking tool of embodied cognition, the chapter argues that thought is not abstract or free-floating but shaped by our physical bodies, our lived experiences, and our institutional contexts. It examines how cognitive psychology borrowed from engineering, telecommunications, and military systems. It concludes with a call to rethink metaphors of mind not as data manipulation but as embodied activity.

The Power Within

In the summer of 1936, Frederic Bartlett, Professor of Experimental Psychology at the University of Cambridge, was walking along a country road with James Drever, Professor of Psychology at the University of Edinburgh. Drever turned to Bartlett and announced: 'Next term, I am going to send you a genius.' The first time Bartlett met Drever's brilliant prodigy, in October 1936, the student conjured a working model of a combustion engine from his waistcoat pocket. 'He knew,' Bartlett later recalled, 'and within a very few minutes I knew, of the power that was within him.' Kenneth Craik was indeed a precocious and unique student, a polymath unafraid to trespass across intellectual and disciplinary boundaries, living and breathing philosophy, engineering, and physiology, and possessing an ability to tinker with gadgets of all kinds. 'He went to the Cambridge Technical School for a course on plumbing and welding,' Bartlett marvelled; 'He did a lot of physiology, and later on, brain anatomy.' By 1941, Craik was leading research at the newly formed Medical Research Council's Applied Psychology Unit (APU) in Cambridge. A direct response to wartime demands, established to study fatigue, vigilance, reaction time, and decision-making under extreme conditions, the APU was an institutional bridge between psychology and the military, and the new targets for psychological experiments were pilots, radar operators, and gunners. The goal was to simulate the mind's inner workings as though it were a machine. Here, already, was cognitive psychology's master metaphor: the mind is

DOI: 10.4324/9781003565482-29

an information-processing system. It was not an idea that had originated during late night philosophical debate; it had been forged under pressure amid the urgent and practical demands of war. The metaphor conscripted postwar cognitive psychology into an alignment with weapons design, communications theory, systems engineering, and eventually, artificial intelligence. Yet behind it all was a man with a bicycle, a pencil, and a restless intellect, living and working at the juncture of war, science, and the imagination.

Chapter Contents

- A critical evaluation of cognitive psychology's wartime and Cold War origins, including its ties to military research and command-and-control metaphors.
- Exploration of the careers and influence of key individuals, with emphasis on how their institutional and technological environments shaped their psychological theories.
- Introduction of *embodied cognition* as a critical thinking tool, used to interrogate the metaphors, models, and assumptions of mainstream cognitive psychology.

Chapter Objectives

- To examine how historical contexts, especially the Second World War and the rise of computer technologies, influenced the development of cognitive psychology.
- To analyse the lives and ideas of key figures in the cognitive tradition and understand how their work was shaped by institutional, technological, and military environments.
- To apply the critical thinking tool of *embodied cognition* to question how metaphor, environment, and embodiment influence psychological theories of the mind.

CRITICAL THINKING TOOL
EMBODIED COGNITION

Psychology often claims to study the mind in general. But minds are specific and are situated in certain places, embodying particular forms of life. This chapter uses the concept of *embodied cognition* as a critical thinking tool. This framing allows us to approach psychological theory as the cultural product of particular people living and working in a particular context.

For example, among Aboriginal Australians, memory is lived through the body, navigated by walking the land, inscribed in *song lines*: through movement, rhythm, and the physical environment. For the Pacific Island–dwelling Ifaluk to feel *fago*, a blend of love and sadness, is not only to think compassionately but to embody care through gentle posture, softened voice, and attentive bodily presence. Among flight attendants, emotional labour is taught and performed through the body, where smiling, posture, and tone become trained habits, shaping the way emotion itself is experienced.

One of the most striking ways embodied cognition reveals itself is through metaphor. The metaphors we habitually employ reflect how we live. When a soldier describes emotional resilience as 'armour', or when a psychiatrist views mental illness as a 'hormone imbalance', or when a game designer sees identity as a modifiable 'avatar', all are expressing how they also experience life themselves. The metaphors we use to describe mind, self, and identity are traces of embodied cognition.

In this chapter, we will examine the embodied cognitions of the cognitive psychologists. How did their lived experience influence their preferred metaphors? We will see that many of the most influential figures in cognitive psychology were men of war and industrial bureaucracy, individuals whose daily environments were saturated with military command structures, telecommunications system diagrams, and the mechanised logic of Cold War paranoia. Unsurprisingly, they came to see the human mind as a projection of those environments. Their metaphors, of executive control, input, processing, storage, and retrieval, did not parachute out of the sky. They were born of command centres, radar screens, air traffic control towers, and listening devices.

Embodied cognition allows us to view their favoured metaphors as traces of lives lived. They are components of what Wittgenstein called 'forms of life'. When cognitive psychologists likened the mind to a machine, they were communicating something about their worldview. In this chapter, we will read the history of cognitive psychology as a story of embodied cognition.

Introduction

Kenneth Craik's ideas were born in the cockpit, refined in the laboratory, and tested in the trenches of government bureaucracy. The Applied Psychology Unit in Cambridge was an innovative node in the military-industrial network of mid-twentieth-century Britain. The psychologists who worked there were technicians of control, engineering the human mind to work better under pressure, fatigue, and threat.

This history matters because it reveals something crucial about psychology: theories in psychology are shaped by metaphor, and metaphor is never innocent. In this chapter, we will critically examine how psychology's understanding of memory and attention, especially in cognitive psychology, has been constrained and animated by a particular form of metaphorical thinking. From the cockpit to the computer, we will trace the imaginative architecture of cognitive theory, arguing that metaphors generate scientific ideas.

Introduced by historian of psychology Kurt Danziger, a generative metaphor is productive. It organises knowledge, frames experiments, and channels entire research programmes. When a psychologist chooses to deploy a metaphor such as 'memory bank', 'filing system', or 'central executive', they are not just speaking poetically. Metaphors introduce a commitment to a model of the mind that communicates ethical, epistemological, and ontological values.

We will focus on figures such as Donald Broadbent, whose celebrated attention theory mirrored radar systems; and Alan Baddeley, whose influential working memory model emerged from a world of secretaries, executives, and filing cabinets, conceptual furniture drawn from battlefields and bureaucracies alike. We will explore how their elegant models, while constructed from substantial imaginations, were nonetheless built on rather light empirical foundations.

Finally, we will propose an alternative organic metaphor for memory. Drawing on the work of William Randall, we will conceptualise memory as a vital process of decay, transformation, and renewal. Human memory, unlike computer memory, degrades and decomposes over time. Randall's alternative metaphorical choice is a world away from precision and control servomechanisms.

Historical Issues

If the soul of cognitive psychology were to be traced, it would be located in the cockpit of a bomber or the console of a nuclear command centre. Forged in the heat of the Second World War and hardened in the paranoid logistics of the Cold War, cognitive psychology emerged from operational imperatives, as dictated from the communications bunkers, radar rooms, and cryptography labs of military intelligence.

Meanwhile, the Cambridge APU became a hub of state-sponsored psychological research. Funded by the Medical Research Council but operating in close collaboration with the Ministry of Defence, the APU studied vigilance, signal detection, decision fatigue, and communication breakdown, problems faced by pilots, operators, and military strategists. The newly emergent concept of information processing, adopted from communications theory, entered psychology through the work of radar operators, code-breakers, and systems designers. The goal was to enhance vigilance, reduce fatigue, and perfect machine–human interaction.

By the 1960s, the information-processing computer metaphor had become hegemonic in cognitive psychology. It aligned perfectly with the priorities of Cold War governments: prediction, control, optimisation, and command. The APU was funded by the Ministry of Defence, the Post Office, and other arms of the British state. Its work on working memory, vigilance, and task performance contributed directly to the military industrial complex. And crucially, these metaphorical choices had consequences. They shaped experimental protocols, justified funding, and excluded alternatives. If the mind is a computer, then memory must be about speed, capacity, and error correction, and not about meaning, emotion, or transformation. The metaphors not only described reality; they also generated it.

Key Individuals

Kenneth Craik's (1914–1945) engagement with the military bureaucracy was extensive: he was a member of the Vision Committee of the Flying Personnel Research Committee, the Military Personnel Research Committee where he worked on tanks, and the Servo-mechanisms Panel of the Ministry of Supply's Target Tracking Panel. His research encompassed critical wartime problems such as dark adaptation, night photometers, and the principles of radar display. Aiming to maximise the efficiency of the human factor in instrument control, Craik reframed the mind as an anticipatory, model-building system, a mechanical metaphor for the very essence of human thought.

Craik's most iconic contribution to the nascent field of cognitive psychology was his work on what became known as the 'Cambridge Cockpit'. Designed in 1943, this working simulation mimicked the intense perceptual and cognitive load faced by combat pilots. Originally dubbed the Fatigue Apparatus, the device was part machine, part experimental tool, and part provocation. Craik believed that to truly understand the human management of complex tasks, the mind can be understood as actively constructing inner models, dynamic simulations of the external world that allow us to anticipate, plan, and adjust. This vision was, in effect, one of the first computational models of the mind.

Donald Broadbent (1926–1993) was one of the most influential architects of early cognitive psychology. Working at the Medical Research Council's Applied Psychology Unit during the years after the Second World War, Broadbent was immersed in the language and logic of telecommunications, control rooms, and cockpit engineering. His most famous contribution, the Filter Model of Attention, proposed that the mind functions like a communication system, selectively passing information through a filter based on limited processing capacity. Broadbent's metaphors of buffer systems, channels, and bottlenecks were drawn from the technologies and infrastructures with which he worked. His book *Perception and Communication* (1958) contains the first box-and-arrow drawing of cognitive functioning, a diagram almost indistinguishable in form from wartime diagrams used in anti-aircraft command systems or radar coordination centres. Mechanistic, predictive, and unapologetically functional, his work illustrates the central claim of this chapter: that psychologists' metaphors, models, and theories are imaginative projections of their own embedded social and technological worlds.

George A. Miller (1920–2012) translated pressing wartime concerns into peacetime research in the United States, decisively shaping the landscape of cognitive psychology. At Harvard University he worked in the Psycho-Acoustic Laboratory researching military voice communications for the Army Signal Corps during the Second World War. His doctoral thesis, *The Optimal Design of Jamming Signals*, was classified top secret by the US Army. Like Broadbent, Miller was immersed in information theory, particularly the groundbreaking 'cynernetics' of Claude Shannon and Warren Weaver. Their model of communication, developed at Bell Labs, addressed fundamental problems of signal transmission, noise, and encryption, all essential components of Cold War intelligence and weapons systems. Miller's highly cited 1956 paper 'The magical number seven, plus or minus two' treats human memory capacity explicitly as a bandwidth problem: how many discrete units of information can be held and transmitted reliably without distortion? His famous answer—approximately seven—reframed human cognition as a channel with a known limit, a critical constraint that designers of systems, from fighter plane dashboards to command terminals, needed to accommodate.

During his formative years at the Cambridge Applied Psychology Unit, Alan Baddeley (b.1934) worked on diverse military and industrial applications for large bureaucracies such as the Ministry of Defence and the General Post Office. His PhD thesis had been inspired by Fletcher Pratt's *Secret and Urgent: The story of codes and ciphers* (1942). Graham Hitch (b.1946) had originally trained in physics before switching to psychology. When Baddeley and Hitch launched their highly influential model of working memory in 1974, it landed as an apparently objective theoretical map of the mind. Nevertheless, the model proposed a 'central executive' that coordinated two 'slave systems': the 'phonological loop', responsible for holding auditory information via an 'inner voice', and a 'visuo-spatial sketchpad'. Later, an 'episodic buffer' metaphor was added to integrate information across modalities.

While the vocabulary of their model appears scientific, its underlying logic is deeply bureaucratic and inherently militaristic. The 'central executive' echoes the top-down chain-of-command systems familiar to anyone operating within military or governmental hierarchies. More strikingly, the 'slave systems' (a term curiously unscrutinised for its ethical implications at the time) suggest unthinking, obedient units. Cognition is a command centre, reflecting the organisational priorities of the period. Baddeley's research focused on optimising human performance in complex systems: postal sorting, military communication chains, and attention under stress. The working memory model, therefore, reflected the pervasive organisational logic of the 1970s office or military HQ, complete with executive oversight, subservient 'secretaries', and filing systems. In this context, the metaphors embodied a specific set of values about how human cognition should be understood and managed.

Epistemological Issues

To understand the mind, cognitive psychology turned to machines. But in doing so, it ignored the hand that built the machine, the eye that observed it, and the body that operated it. Its elegant theories rested upon an epistemological sleight-of-hand: the belief that models of memory are discovered rather than designed, and such models emerge from the data rather than from metaphor, analogy, and value-laden imaginative projection.

The core data of Baddeley and Hitch's model of working memory, in part harvested from army recruits, consisted of reaction times and memory errors, somewhat weak signals from which to reconstruct the baroque edifice of central executives, slave systems, and visuospatial scratchpads. These theoretical components were not determined by the data; as ever, they were imposed upon it through a creative act of imagination. The metaphors did not emerge from the measurements; they were *mapped onto them*. There is no way to build a theoretical model other than by choosing an appropriate metaphor that sits comfortably within a particular form of life.

The choice of the computer as the central metaphor for the mind for mid-twentieth-century psychology expressed a deeply held set of values. Cognitive psychologists valued precision, control, modularity, and predictability. They enjoyed tinkering with machines. They admired the clarity of algorithms, the discreteness of storage units, the elegance of symbolic logic. They were, in effect, importing the *epistemology of engineering* into the study of mind.

Ontological Issues

If epistemology asks how we know, ontology asks what things are. And cognitive psychology has presented us with a curiously sterile image of what memory is: a storage unit, a filing system, a hard drive. In this architecture of mind, memories are discrete packets of data, encoded, stored, retrieved, occasionally corrupted. The metaphors are precise, efficient, and bloodless. The human organism becomes a kind of clerical assistant in its own mental bureaucracy: filing experiences, retrieving them on demand, and occasionally misplacing a document.

But what if memory is thought of in an entirely different way? In a bold departure from this barren vision, William Randall (2008) offers an alternative metaphor for memory, one that is organic, embodied, and alive: the compost heap. If there is one phenomenological fact about memory that everyone knows, it is that memory decays. The second truth, perhaps we all know, is that memory is an emotive issue. Like compost, memory is a process of decomposition and integration, where remnants of past experiences are broken down, fermented, and merged into the fertile substrate of the self. For Randall, a Professor of Gerontology, memory is about transformation. We do not retrieve memories so much as *grow* from them. They nurture us, decay within us, heat up and cool down, mingle with newer experiences, and form the nutrient-rich humus to sustain future meaning.

Ontologically, the compost heap metaphor is profoundly different from the computer metaphor. A compost heap is messy, unpredictable, and responsive to the environment. It makes room for emotion as part of the fermenting heat. It acknowledges forgetting not as system failure but as transformation. Some traumatic memories, as we know, stubbornly refuse to decay, such as an avocado stone in a compost heap. And it emphasises interconnectedness over compartmentalisation: old relationships nourish new ones; former selves transform into future identities.

The compost heap is a fundamentally different claim about what memory is. It resists reduction, embraces temporality, and foregrounds the dynamic, reconstructive, and often unconscious work of memory. Most crucially, it re-embeds memory in the living body, in the affective and sensory dimensions of experience, in the rhythms of deterioration, renewal, and growth. This stands in radical contrast to the disembodied formalism of the computer metaphor, which flattens time, ignores context, and sanitises affect. In a field long dominated by metaphors of precision and partition, the compost heap calls for an ethic of integration, slowness, and dirt. It reminds us that memory is muddy, slippery, and unpredictable.

Power

To define is to dominate. In psychology, perhaps more than in any other science, the metaphors we use to describe the mind create reality. They shape research programmes, funding priorities, and therapeutic norms. They dictate what counts as a good explanation, a valid intervention, and a credible self.

The information-processing metaphor of the computer succeeded because it was aligned with institutional power. It was funded by military contracts, legitimised by government laboratories, and elevated by its rhetorical status. When psychologists described the mind in terms of information, modules, and storage systems, they were speaking the language of postwar bureaucracies and Cold War technocracies. They were becoming legible, and useful, to the very institutions that shaped them.

In this way, metaphor functions as a political agent. It polices the boundaries of acceptable inquiry. It enshrines quantitative, disembodied, mechanistic kinds of knowledge as superior to others. And it silences alternatives, particularly those that arise from elsewhere, perspectives that recognise the entanglements of body, emotion, context, and memory.

Acknowledging that theory is an act of imagination, an embodied, historical, value-laden process, does not descend us into relativism. We ascend into responsibility. We become aware that every model is also a moral vision. And we reclaim the possibility of building models that honour complexity, embrace transformation, and centre the embodied, living human subject.

To describe the mind as being like a computer is not an innocent act. Nor is it inevitable, however. It is a choice, laden with consequences. It frames forgetting as failure, emotion as error, and subjective meaning as noise. It invites us to 'fix' malfunctioning memories like broken code rather than tending to them as wounds, transformations, or composting processes. The responsibility of the psychologist, then, is not merely to test hypotheses but to reflexively interrogate the metaphors that scaffold them.

Chapter Summary

Memory is never just one thing, an expression for storage, or its failure. It is always about something more. This chapter has been about memory and attention, but it is also about power, politics, and the stories psychology tells itself. Having employed embodied cognition as a tool with which to explore the history of cognition, this chapter has acted reflexively, as psychology itself should. When psychologists describe the mind, they describe themselves, their culture, their training, their tools.

For all its precision, the metaphor of the mind as a computer left something vital behind. It dislodged the mind from the body, stripped memory of emotion, and cast human beings as data processors in a world of control panels and circuit boards. This chapter has offered an alternative: a return to the grounded, lived, and tangled roots of thought. Embodied cognition reminds us that minds emerge from the fertile soil of human experience shaped by relationships, habits, and environments. They walk, breathe, age, and ache.

From this vantage point, we have revisited the rise of cognitive psychology as a story of metaphors forged in war and hardwired into bureaucracy. Baddeley and Hitch imagined memory through the machinery of their world: offices, command structures, and the cold rationality of systems. Memory became something to store, to retrieve, to fix.

In the shadows of this story stands Kenneth Craik. Dispatched to Cambridge with the prophetic words 'I'm sending you a genius', Craik imagined the mind as a model-maker, a forecaster, a planner, a mental experimenter. His ideas seeded the very foundations of cognitive science. But he also believed that thinking could not be separated from doing, from feeling, from experiencing the pressures of life as it is lived.

On 7 May 1945, a lorry knocked Craik off his bicycle outside his college. The following day, the very day the Second World War ended in Europe, he succumbed to his injuries. He was 32 years old. This chapter, then, is not only a critique of memory; it is also a quiet act of remembrance. Craik did not live to see the psychology that followed him, nor to challenge the metaphors that hardened in his absence. But in tracing the contours of thought, through bodies, metaphors, and machines, we honour the path he created. And perhaps, at last, we can come down from the control tower and return to the earth.

Reflective Questions

1. How did the military-industrial context of the 1940s and 1950s shape the development of cognitive psychology?
2. What does the concept of embodied cognition reveal about the limitations of the 'mind as computer' metaphor?
3. Why is Kenneth Craik considered such a pivotal figure in the emergence of cognitive psychology, and what aspects of his work remain overlooked?
4. In what ways can metaphor serve as both a creative and constraining force in psychological theory?
5. What might cognitive psychology have looked like if it had taken a more embodied or ecological direction earlier in its history?

Suggested Reading

Arrigo, J. M., Rockwood, L. P., O'Brien, J., Franz, D., DeBatto, D., & Kiriakou, J. (2022). A military/intelligence operational perspective on the American Psychological Association's weaponization of psychology post-9/11. *History of the Human Sciences, 35*(5), 51–79. https://doi.org/10.1177/09526951221121711.

Baddeley, A. D. (2001). 'Memories of memory research'. In G. C. Bunn, A. D. Lovie, & G. D. Richards (Eds.), *Psychology in Britain: Historical essays and personal reflections* (pp.344–352). Hoboken, NJ: BPS Books/Wiley.

Bloor, D. (2025). *The Cambridge Cockpit and the Paradoxes of Fatigue, 1940–1977.* Chicago, IL: University of Chicago Press.

Chen, W., Ping, X., & Dong, D. (2023). Filling in the vacuous flesh: Embodiment, constitution, and interoception. *Theory & Psychology, 33*(4), 515–534. https://doi.org/10.1177/09593543231169967.

Coulter, J. (2008). Twenty-five theses against cognitivism. *Theory, Culture & Society, 25*(2), 19–32. https://doi.org/10.1177/0263276407086789.

Danziger, K. (1990). Generative metaphor and the history of psychological discourse. In D. J. Leary (Ed.), *Metaphors in the History of Psychology* (pp. 331–356). Cambridge: Cambridge University Press.

Draaisma, D. (2000). *Metaphors of Memory: A history of ideas about the mind.* Cambridge: Cambridge University Press.

Hampe, B. (2017). *Metaphor: Embodied cognition and discourse.* Cambridge: Cambridge University Press.

Jackson, P. (2022). Theorising embodied interaction in coaching: A Merleau-Pontian perspective on embodied practice. *Theory & Psychology, 33*(1), 78–98. https://doi.org/10.1177/09593543221123970.

Jones, E. (2012). 'The gut war': Functional somatic disorders in the UK during the Second World War. *History of the Human Sciences, 25*(5), 30–48. https://doi.org/10.1177/0952695112466515.

Kölbl, C. (2023). Klaus Holzkamp smiled: Soviet psychology in the Federal Republic of Germany in the Cold War era. *History of Psychology, 26*(4), 314–333. https://doi.org/10.1037/hop0000243.

Ma, H. L., Dawson, M. R. W., Prinsen, R. S., & Hayward, D. A. (2022). Embodying cognitive ethology. *Theory & Psychology, 33*(1), 42–58. https://doi.org/10.1177/09593543221126165.

Nietzel, B. (2016). Propaganda, psychological warfare and communication research in the USA and the Soviet Union during the Cold War. *History of the Human Sciences, 29*(4–5), 59–76. https://doi.org/10.1177/0952695116667881.

Randall, W. (2007). From computer to compost: Rethinking our metaphors for memory. *Theory & Psychology, 17*(5), 611–633. https://doi.org/10.1177/0959354307081619.

Sampson, E. E. (1996). Establishing embodiment in psychology. *Theory & Psychology, 6*(4), 601–624. https://doi.org/10.1177/0959354396064004.

Wu, H. Y-J. (2020). Psychiatrists' agency and their distance from the authoritarian state in post-World War II Taiwan. *History of Psychology, 23*(4), 351–370. https://doi.org/10.1037/hop0000174.

Key Terms

Applied Psychology Unit (APU) A research institute founded in 1944 in Cambridge to support wartime needs, especially in aviation and communications. It became a major centre for the development of cognitive psychology in the UK.

Baddeley and Hitch Model A multi-component model of working memory that includes a central executive, a phonological loop, and a visuospatial sketch-pad, developed in the 1970s and shaped by bureaucratic and computational metaphors.

Box-and-Arrow Diagram A schematic style of representing mental processes using boxes (for stages or systems) and arrows (for flow or direction), influenced by cybernetics and command-and-control models in wartime contexts.

Cognitive Psychology A psychological approach that studies mental processes such as memory, perception, and problem-solving, often using metaphors drawn from computing, engineering, and bureaucracy.

Command and Control A metaphor derived from military and systems engineering that conceptualises human cognition in terms of information flow, regulation, and executive decision-making.

Embodied Cognition A theoretical framework which argues that cognition is grounded in bodily experience, physical interaction, and lived context rather than being abstract or disembodied.

Internal Model Kenneth Craik's term for the brain's capacity to create a mental simulation or small-scale representation of external reality in order to plan and act effectively.

Metaphor A figure of speech used in psychology not just for illustration but for shaping theory. In cognitive psychology, metaphors such as 'filing cabinet', 'processor', and 'cockpit' reveal the embodied and cultural contexts of theorists.

Working Memory A system for the temporary storage and manipulation of information, especially during reasoning or comprehension, central to modern models of cognition.

FREE INSTRUCTOR & STUDENT RESOURCES

ONLINE RESOURCES

Visit the Instructor & Student Resources website at routledgelearning.com/bpscoretextbooks for free digital resources, including:

- Interactive quizzes and flashcards to test your knowledge
- Links to useful websites and videos
- Instructor manual, lecture slides, and course guide to enhance teaching and save instructors time

0

A Cold of the Soul

Positive Psychology's Neoliberal Cure

Chapter Overview

This chapter offers a critical history of positive psychology, arguing that its rise must be understood within the broader framework of globalisation. While positive psychology began as a movement to shift attention from mental illness to well-being and human flourishing, it has become deeply entangled with political, economic, and institutional agendas. Drawing on the concept of neoliberal governmentality, the chapter explores how happiness is framed not just as a personal goal but as a moral obligation and economic asset.

The chapter interrogates how emotion is medicalised, commodified, and governed. Key figures such as Martin Seligman, Mihaly Csikszentmihalyi, and Geni Núñez are examined in relation to broader systems of power, including colonialism, militarism, and the global wellness industry. Students are introduced to the critical thinking tool of neoliberal governmentality, and encouraged to reflect on how psychological science can both obscure and reinforce structural inequality. Ultimately, the chapter invites students to consider whether unhappiness might not be a pathology but a rational response to social injustice, and whether the demand for happiness itself deserves greater scrutiny.

A Cold of the Soul

In the autumn of 2000, the Canadian psychiatrist Dr Laurence Kirmayer, one of the world's leading experts on cultural psychiatry, received a curious invitation. He was asked to join an elite panel of psychiatrists gathering in Kyoto, Japan. The all-expenses-paid invitation came with a first-class $10,000 plane ticket and the promise of a palatial suite in one of the city's most exclusive hotels. The meeting, hosted behind closed doors, would explore how culture shapes the experience of depression. It was funded by pharmaceutical giant GlaxoSmithKline (GSK). Kirmayer accepted the invitation. The sessions were civil, scholarly, and cautiously framed. 'The focus was not on medications,' he later recalled. 'They were not trying to sell drugs to us. They were interested in what we knew about how cultures shape the illness experience.' But beneath the surface, the agenda was clearer: GSK needed help to launch its antidepressant drug Paxil (paroxetine) in Japan. The Japanese, it turned out, had a fundamentally negative view of depression. The existing Japanese term for the condition, *utsubyō*, evoked intractability, psychosis, and social shame. It was seen as an incurable and inborn condition, not one that could be managed with a pill. To succeed in this enormous untapped market, GSK needed to invent a new metaphor. Working with advertising consultancies and local academics, they coined the phrase *kokoro no kaze*: 'a cold of the soul'. It was

DOI: 10.4324/9781003565482-30

brilliant marketing: depression was now gentle, temporary, and treatable. It suggested that anyone could get 'a cold of the soul', and more importantly, anyone could recover from it if prescribed the right medication. The reframing marked the start of a campaign to reshape public perception, make sadness eligible for pharmaceutical intervention, and expand the boundaries of what could be considered a disorder. Kirmayer left Kyoto feeling disturbed. He had apparently lent his expertise to a global project of affective re-engineering, where sadness was rebranded, and suffering had become a sales pitch. By 2008, Paxil sales in Japan exceeded $1 billion. This troubling story poses a deep question for psychology: what happens when sadness becomes a market opportunity, and happiness an industry?

Chapter Contents

- The story of how a pharmaceutical giant invented a new disorder to sell antidepression medication to a culture that had no need for it.
- A critical exploration of positive psychology through the lens of neoliberal governmentality, with a focus on history, epistemology, ontology, and power.
- Analysis of key individuals and how their work reflects or resists the logic of neoliberalism and the critical thinking tool of governmentality.

Chapter Objectives

- To examine the historical development of positive psychology and its emergence within the cultural climate of neoliberal individualism.
- To understand how epistemological and ontological assumptions within positive psychology shape the way happiness, sadness, and flourishing are defined and measured.
- To evaluate the field of positive psychology using the critical thinking tool of neoliberal governmentality, and to consider its implications for political agency, emotional life, and social justice.

CRITICAL THINKING TOOL
NEOLIBERAL GOVERNMENTALITY

To understand how positive psychology came to occupy such a prominent position in contemporary psychological discourse, we must first grasp the concept of *neoliberal governmentality*. This term fuses two powerful ideas: *neoliberalism* as a political-economic system, and *governmentality*, a term coined by Michel Foucault, to describe the ways in which power operates not merely through laws and institutions but through the shaping of human subjectivities.

Neoliberalism is an economic doctrine favouring free markets, privatisation, low taxes, and deregulation. It also encourages a psychological shift, in which individuals are positioned as self-entrepreneurs responsible for their own success, health, and happiness. Claiming penury, the state withdraws from the collective provision of social security, and instead encourages self-sufficiency, self-responsibility and resilience. Within this framework, people are no longer

governed directly by the state but indirectly through capitalist services that promise to nurture aspirations to be efficient, productive, and fulfilled.

Governmentality describes how power functions through such forms of self-governance. Under neoliberalism, individuals are encouraged to regulate themselves, to monitor their moods, track their goals, optimise their diets, and 'work on themselves' in ever more refined ways. Here, psychology becomes a key technology of governance, helping to produce subjects who are happy, resilient, and self-actualising; traits that align closely with the demands of a competitive, precarious, and market-driven society. Within this system, happiness and well-being become moral imperatives for some and economic opportunities for others. To be happy is to be a successful citizen. To be sad is not only to suffer but also to fail.

Introduction

Positive psychology emerged at the turn of the twenty-first century with an ambitious promise: to rebalance psychology by turning its attention away from pathology, dysfunction, and distress, and towards the study of human strengths, flourishing, and happiness. Led by figures such as Martin Seligman, this movement positioned itself as a corrective to what it saw as psychology's 'negative bias'.

But this chapter takes a more critical stance. It argues that the rise of positive psychology must be understood within the broad socio-political context of neoliberal governmentality, a system in which individuals are increasingly held responsible for their own well-being, productivity, and emotional regulation. Within this framework, happiness becomes a duty. Well-being becomes a metric of personal success and sadness, melancholy, or even grief, risk being pathologised as individual failure.

The chapter explores how scientific discourses, especially brain-based explanations of mood, combine with popular psychology to promote a vision of the self as a project to be managed and optimised. It critiques the explicit disavowal of politics within positive psychology and asks whether its valorisation of happiness ultimately serves to obscure the structural and economic sources of human suffering.

Historical Issues

The roots of positive psychology stretch back further than the term itself. Its intellectual precursors lie in the humanistic psychology of the mid-twentieth century, led by figures such as Abraham Maslow and Carl Rogers. Humanistic psychology sought to understand human potential, creativity, and self-actualisation, offering a more optimistic view of the person than the psychodynamic or behaviourist paradigms that had dominated earlier decades. However, while humanistic psychology was often critical of mainstream society and emphasised authenticity, autonomy, and human dignity, positive psychology would later reframe these themes in a more instrumental, managerial, and neoliberal register.

The postwar period saw the rapid expansion of psychology as a tool for diagnosis and treatment, especially in relation to mental illness. This focus was reinforced by the rise of the DSM method in psychiatry, the biomedical model, and the increasing role of pharmaceutical interventions. By the 1990s, the emphasis on disorder and dysfunction had become entrenched in clinical practice and public consciousness alike. Positive psychology positioned itself as a necessary correction to this medicalised view of the human mind, promising to restore balance by shifting attention to well-being and flourishing.

Starting in the late twentieth century, Western societies experienced a marked decline in collective structures of social support. Trade unions weakened, religious and community organisations lost influence, and the welfare state came under sustained attack from all sides. In their place arose a culture of individualism, self-help, and personal responsibility. In this cultural climate, the market for a psychology that emphasised personal growth, emotional intelligence, and inner strength grew substantially.

Positive psychology responded to this moment by offering a new framework for understanding the self: one that was hopeful but also highly individualised. It reassured people that they could, and should, cultivate happiness, resilience, and optimism, regardless of their external circumstances. In doing so, it mirrored and reinforced the neoliberal worldview that holds individuals responsible for their own fates, and often renders invisible the structural causes of distress.

Key Individuals

Aaron Beck (1921–2021), though not a figure of positive psychology per se, played a pioneering role in the development of cognitive therapy. Beck's approach focused on identifying and modifying dysfunctional thoughts, an intervention that helped pave the way for the now-dominant culture of individual self-management. His work underpins many cognitive-behavioural frameworks, including those that emphasise positive reframing and self-talk. In the neoliberal landscape, Beck's model has been widely applied as a quick, cost-effective solution to emotional distress, one that often bypasses social or structural explanations of suffering.

Mihaly Csikszentmihalyi (1934–2021) contributed the concept of phenomenological *flow*, a state of deep immersion and engagement in a task, often characterised by losing track of time and experiencing intrinsic satisfaction. His work, though less overtly political, nevertheless dovetails with neoliberal ideals by celebrating productivity, individual mastery, and performance. The 'flow state' has been embraced by corporate culture, athletic training, and productivity gurus alike, reinforcing the idea that optimal mental states should serve functional and goal-oriented outcomes. Flow offers peak efficiency, making it highly compatible with economic systems that value output over introspection or rest.

Martin Seligman (b.1942) is widely regarded as the founder of positive psychology. Early in his career, Seligman's research focused on *learned helplessness*, a model of depression derived from studies in which animals stopped trying to escape aversive conditions after repeated failures. In the original studies during the late 1960s, he and his colleagues subjected dogs to electric shocks from which they could not escape. After repeated exposure, many of the dogs stopped trying to avoid the shocks, even when escape later became possible. By the late 1990s, however, Seligman had pivoted to a more optimistic model: *learned optimism*. This reframing formed the intellectual and rhetorical foundation for positive psychology as a movement. Seligman promoted the idea that individuals could train themselves to become more resilient, optimistic, and flourishing. He institutionalised the field through his leadership at the American Psychological Association and his championing of the Positive Psychology Center at the University of Pennsylvania. Yet critics argued that his vision aligns seamlessly with neoliberal imperatives of workplace productivity, self-management, and emotional control, qualities prized by corporate and military institutions alike. Indeed, Seligman's direct involvement in US military resilience training programmes such as the Comprehensive Soldier Fitness (CSF) programme (later renamed 'Ready and Resilient') underlines the political alignment of his framework with state and economic power.

Laurence Kirmayer (b.1957) is a psychiatrist and medical anthropologist who has consistently challenged the universalisation of Western psychiatric categories. Kirmayer's work in cultural psychiatry reveals how emotional and mental experiences are always situated within cultural contexts. He warns against imposing one-size-fits-all Western psychological models onto diverse cultures. His critiques are particularly relevant when examining how positive psychology has been exported around the globe, often with little regard for local understandings of emotion, suffering, and resilience.

Geni Núñez (b.1991) is a Guarani-Kaiowá scholar, psychologist, and activist from Brazil whose work embodies a powerful decolonial critique of Western psychology and its complicity in systems of coloniality, racism, and neoliberal control. Grounded in Indigenous epistemologies and community activism, Núñez's scholarship reveals how institutions, such as marriage, mental health systems, and scientific discourse, serve as technologies of governmentality, producing compliant, self-monitoring subjects within white supremacist and capitalist structures. She exposes how emotional norms, such as those promoted by positive psychology, operate as tools of affective discipline, requiring individuals to perform happiness, resilience, and gratitude in ways that obscure ongoing histories of dispossession and violence. Her work challenges the psychologisation of social pain, instead asserting Indigenous ways of knowing, collective resistance, and ancestral memory as vital counterforces. Núñez does not seek to reform Western psychology; she seeks to unsettle it. Her inclusion in this chapter reminds us that the pressure to be 'happy' is political, and it is contested.

Epistemological Issues

Positive psychology often relies on quantitative tools such as self-report questionnaires and psychometric scales to assess well-being. These include instruments such as the PERMA model (Positive Emotion, Engagement, Relationships, Meaning, Accomplishment) developed by Seligman, and widely used happiness indices. While these tools offer apparent objectivity, they also drastically simplify and reify complex, culturally embedded experiences. Happiness becomes a number to be compared, tracked, and improved. Such metrics serve academic research programmes as well as corporate productivity reviews, government policy targets, and self-optimisation apps, where personal fulfilment becomes yet another key performance indicator.

This epistemological reductionism is compounded by the rise of affective neuroscience and the biological framing of emotion. Popular accounts describe happiness as a product of dopamine 'hits' or serotonin 'balance'. These narratives, although derived from real research, are often mythologised in their public translation. Brain-based explanations, while appealingly deterministic, occlude the relational, historical, and political dimensions of emotion. They support the idea that well-being is an internal state correctable by pharmacology or cognitive effort rather than something shaped by poverty, precarity, or discrimination.

Moreover, positive psychology often assumes a universalist epistemology. It tends to treat happiness and flourishing as stable, measurable constructs applicable across all cultures and contexts. This approach erases the plurality of emotional life and sidelines voices that understand well-being in collective, spiritual, or ecological terms. In this way, positive psychology's claim to science becomes a form of epistemic colonisation.

As Geni Núñez argues, the imposition of Euro-American psychological constructs, especially those wrapped in the neutral language of science, represents a form of epistemicide: the erasure of Indigenous ways of knowing, healing, and relating. For Núñez, Western psychology's obsession with measuring well-being fails on methodological, cultural, and ethical grounds. It displaces relational, spiritual, and land-based understandings of wellness with individualised, commodified metrics that serve colonial-capitalist interests.

Núñez argues that colonialism functions through the epistemological driver of monocausality, the positing of simple single explanations for complicated problems. Monoculture systems include monotheism, monogamy, and monosexism, all of which have in common the principles of exclusivity, non-concomitance, and non-coexistence. Indigenous non-monoculture, in contrast, looks to the forest as a sign of diversity and concomitance. As a result, Indigenous voices in the articulation of non-monogamous perspectives and anti-colonial struggles are prioritised, with the aim of working towards an emotional reforestation of relationships between humans and with the planet.

Ontological Issues

What does it mean to be human within the framework of positive psychology? This is the ontological question at the heart of the chapter, and the answer offered by positive psychology is a highly specific one: the ideal human is happy, resilient, self-optimising, and emotionally agile. To exist well is to flourish. To flourish is to be well-adjusted, forward-facing, efficient, and productive.

This construction of the 'happy subject' has profound implications. It creates a moral imperative that is difficult to oppose. Positive emotions are cast as desirable and expected. Individuals are encouraged to cultivate gratitude, optimism, and joy, often through repetitive techniques: journaling, affirmations, reframing, and mindfulness. Happiness becomes both a personal duty and a performance; one must feel good and be seen to feel good.

Conversely, sadness, melancholy, and grief are increasingly pathologised. While these are universal and normal aspects of the human condition, the dominant psychological discourse frames them as medicalised disorders: depression, dysthymia, anhedonia. Rather than recognising the political, historical, or relational context of sadness, the field tends to interpret it as a deviation from optimal functioning, something to be corrected through therapy, medication, or personal effort. The sad subject, in this context, is not only suffering but also failing.

Self-actualisation, once imagined by Maslow as a form of transcendence and existential fulfilment available only to a tiny minority of unique individuals, has become commodified and allegedly available to everyone. It is now marketed through life coaching, productivity regimes, wearable technology, and curated lifestyles. Flourishing has been stripped of its philosophical and existential roots and repackaged as a consumable goal. To become fully oneself increasingly requires an investment: in apps, courses, wellness spa retreats, or psychological services.

Crucially, this ontology neglects the collective, the relational, and the interdependent aspects of human life. Communities, solidarities, traditions, and political movements are largely absent from the positive psychological view of what it means to be human. In their place stands a self-monitoring individual, endlessly working on their mood, mindset, and metrics.

Geni Núñez draws attention to how the neoliberal imperative to 'be happy' functions as a form of affective control. It produces a moral economy in which pain, anger, grief, or resistance are rendered illegible or worse, punishable. In Indigenous communities, this imperative flattens emotional worlds that are deeply embedded in land, ancestry, and collective survival. The ontology of the 'happy, self-actualising individual' is a colonial imposition. By offering a restricted, normative model of the human, positive psychology constrains what kinds of lives are considered valuable and what kinds of suffering are rendered illegible.

Power

The rise of positive psychology cannot be disentangled from the power structures that enable, shape, and benefit from it. Far from being a neutral or purely academic endeavour, positive psychology functions as a subtle but effective form of neoliberal governance. It helps to produce citizens who are emotionally self-regulating, personally accountable, and economically productive, without requiring structural change or state support.

This is neoliberal governmentality in action. Instead of the state guaranteeing social security or justice through taxation, individuals are encouraged to manage their own well-being through their purchasing decisions. People struggling with life are encouraged to reframe their negative cognitions. Impoverished or insecure people are instructed to build resilience. The burden of adaptation is shifted from political systems to the individual self. In this sense, positive psychology acts as a technology of the self, the phrase Michel Foucault used to describe how individuals internalise norms and discipline themselves according to dominant imperatives.

Corporate and state institutions have eagerly adopted this model. Nowhere is this more evident than in the US military's deployment of Seligman's resilience training programme, which sought to inoculate soldiers against PTSD through mental conditioning. The logic is chilling: if trauma can be prevented by cultivating optimism, then structural critiques of war, violence, and exploitation are rendered unnecessary.

The pharmaceutical industry has also played a crucial role in constructing the biochemical narrative of mood. The infamous marketing of SSRIs in Japan in the 1990s, recasting everyday sadness as *kokoro no kaze*, a cold of the soul, illustrates how emotional life can be medicalised for market expansion. Meanwhile, the booming wellness industry has seized on positive psychology's rhetoric to sell products, services, and experiences promising fulfilment. Happiness becomes a purchasable good, whether through apps, gratitude journals, coaching sessions, or yoga retreats. Even Bhutan's Gross National Happiness Index, often cited as an alternative to GDP, risks being co-opted into a technocratic exercise in affective measurement, vulnerable to the same blind spots around justice and inequality.

Drawing on Foucauldian and postcolonial ideas, Geni Núñez has articulated how institutions, including the family, religion, and psychology, serve as sites of affective governmentality. She describes these as 'necropolitical' tools: not just regulating life but deciding which forms of life are worthy of protection and which are disposable. In this context, happiness makes a weaponised demand: be positive, or be excluded.

In this way, positive psychology contributes to the depoliticisation of suffering. It redirects attention away from the compromised economic and social structures that produce distress, and towards the self, creating the impression that happiness is simply a matter of better management.

Chapter Summary

Crucially, this chapter has underscored the disavowal at the heart of positive psychology: its refusal to acknowledge the political and economic conditions that shape mental health and emotional life. By focusing inward, on mindset, mood, well-being and attitude, positive psychology obscures structural challenges such as precarity, inequality, racism, and environmental collapse.

In a world increasingly demanding happiness, this chapter has asked a difficult but necessary question: what if our unhappiness is not a personal failure but a political cue? And what if, like Laurence Kirmayer, wrestling with his conscience in his hotel suite in Kyoto, we find ourselves in comforted complicity, invited to the table, flattered for our insight, unaware until too late that we are lending our names, our science, our silence to the rewriting of sadness for profit? Perhaps the most important task of psychology today is not to teach people how to be happy but to ask why they are being told to be happy in the first place. Who stands to gain, we should ask, when sadness is rebranded, medicated, and sold back to us as the new normal?

Reflective Questions

1. What is neoliberal governmentality, and how does it shape the way psychology defines and promotes happiness?
2. In what ways did the pharmaceutical industry reshape public attitudes towards depression in Japan using the phrase 'a cold of the soul'?
3. Why is Geni Núñez critical of Western psychological models of emotion and flourishing?
4. How do the key individuals discussed in this chapter reflect different relationships to power, resistance, and cultural values?
5. Is unhappiness always a problem to be solved, or can it be a legitimate response to structural injustice?

Suggested Reading

Becker, D., & Marecek, J. (2008). Positive psychology: History in the remaking? *Theory & Psychology, 18*(5), 591–604. https://doi.org/10.1177/0959354308093397.

Binkley, S. (2014). *Happiness as Enterprise: An essay on neoliberal life*. New York: State University of New York.

Cabanas, E. (2018). Positive psychology and the legitimation of individualism. *Theory & Psychology, 28*(1), 3–19. https://doi.org/10.1177/0959354317747988.

Christopher, J. C., & Hickinbottom, S. (2008). Positive psychology, ethnocentrism, and the disguised ideology of individualism. *Theory & Psychology, 18*(5), 563–589. https://doi.org/10.1177/0959354308093396.

Davidson, I. J. (2025). Well-being at the cost of welfare: Learned helplessness and responsibility in positive psychology and American policy. *History of the Human Sciences*. https://doi.org/10.1177/09526951251336898.
De La Fabián, R., & Stecher, A. (2017). Positive psychology's promise of happiness: A new form of human capital in contemporary neoliberal governmentality. *Theory & Psychology, 27*(5), 600–621. https://doi.org/10.1177/0959354317718970.
De La Fabián, R., & Stecher, A. (2018). Positive psychology and the enhancement of happiness: A reply to Binkley (2018). *Theory & Psychology, 28*(3), 411–417. https://doi.org/10.1177/0959354318772098.
Graiver, I. (2021). A historical perspective on mental health: Proposal for a dialogue between history and psychology. *History of Psychology, 24*(1), 1–12. https://doi.org/10.1037/hop0000139.
Jackson, M. (2012). The pursuit of happiness: The social and scientific origins of Hans Selye's natural philosophy of life. *History of the Human Sciences, 25*(5), 13–29. https://doi.org/10.1177/0952695112468526.
Martínez-Guzmán, A., & Lara, A. (2019). Affective modulation in positive psychology's regime of happiness. *Theory & Psychology, 29*(3), 336–357. https://doi.org/10.1177/0959354319845138.
Núñez, G. (2024). *Felizes por enquanto: Escritos sobre outros mundos possíveis*. Planeta.
Raffnsøe, S., Rosenberg, A., Beaulieu, A., Binkley, S., Kristensen, J. E., Opitz, S., Rabinowitz, M., & Holm, D. V. (2009). Neoliberal governmentality. *Foucault Studies*, 1–4. https://doi.org/10.22439/fs.v0i0.2464.
Sewaybricker, L. E., & Massola, G. M. (2022). Against well-being: A critique of positive psychology. *History of the Human Sciences, 36*(1), 131–148. https://doi.org/10.1177/09526951221114733.
Watters, E. (2010). *Crazy Like Us: The globalization of the American psyche*. New York: Free Press.

Key Terms

Affective Governance The regulation of emotion by social institutions, where particular emotional states (e.g. positivity) are encouraged or enforced as moral obligations or forms of civic virtue.

Epistemicide The erasure or marginalisation of alternative knowledge systems, especially Indigenous and non-Western ways of knowing, through the dominance of Euro-American scientific paradigms.

Flow A concept introduced by Mihaly Csikszentmihalyi describing a state of deep, enjoyable immersion in a task where time and self-consciousness seem to disappear.

Governmentality Michel Foucault's term describing how power operates not only through institutions but through the shaping of subjectivities and everyday behaviours, making individuals responsible for their own self-governance.

Gross National Happiness A national development philosophy adopted by Bhutan that attempts to measure well-being beyond GDP, though subject to critique for technocratic and depoliticised implementation.

Kokoro No Kaze A Japanese phrase meaning 'a cold of the soul', developed in the 1990s as part of a marketing strategy to medicalise depression and promote pharmaceutical treatment in Japan.

Learned Helplessness A concept developed by Martin Seligman in the 1970s to explain how repeated failure can lead individuals (and animals) to give up trying; later reworked into the more empowering concept of 'learned optimism'.

Monocausality A critique of oversimplified thinking that seeks single causes for complex problems, often linked to colonial systems that privilege singular narratives over plural, relational, or diverse explanations.

Neoliberal Governmentality A form of power described by Michel Foucault, where individuals are governed not through overt force but through internalised norms, especially those promoting self-optimisation, responsibility, and emotional regulation in line with market values.

PERMA An acronym developed by Martin Seligman to describe the five elements of well-being: Positive Emotion, Engagement, Relationships, Meaning, and Accomplishment.

Positive Psychology A psychological movement that emerged in the early twenty-first century focusing on human strengths, flourishing, and happiness, often framed in individualistic and empirically measurable terms.

Resilience Training Psychological interventions, often developed for military or corporate settings, designed to enhance individual coping and adaptation, sometimes criticised for shifting responsibility away from systemic conditions.

Self-Actualisation Originally proposed by Abraham Maslow as the pinnacle of psychological development, now often co-opted in consumer culture as a commodified goal of lifestyle and wellness industries.

Technologies of the Self Michel Foucault's phrase describing how people shape, monitor, and manage their own behaviours, emotions, and thoughts in accordance with cultural and institutional norms.

FREE INSTRUCTOR & STUDENT RESOURCES

ONLINE RESOURCES

Visit the Instructor & Student Resources website at routledgelearning.com/bpscoretextbooks for free digital resources, including:

- Interactive quizzes and flashcards to test your knowledge
- Links to useful websites and videos
- Instructor manual, lecture slides, and course guide to enhance teaching and save instructors time

31

Ghost Stories

Romantic Love from Courtship to Situationship

Chapter Overview

This chapter explores how the psychology of romantic love has changed from the age of long-term commitment to the fluid uncertainties of hookup culture. Anchored in Zygmunt Bauman's concepts of solid and liquid modernity, the chapter critically examines how love has transformed alongside broader social, economic, and technological shifts. Through the lens of the charismatic Reddit anecdote of a 'ghosted' dater, the chapter opens a conversation about how intimacy is now increasingly shaped by apps, feeds, and disappearing messages.

Tracing the history of love in psychology from early evolutionary and anthropological accounts to contemporary theories of attachment and affect, the chapter highlights key figures in the study of romantic love. The critical thinking tool of 'solid and liquid modernity' helps students assess epistemological and ontological shifts in the study of love, from stable binaries to proliferating fluidities. The chapter also foregrounds the power relations embedded in new romantic norms, especially those that govern availability, rejection, and self-presentation in the digital age.

Ghost Stories

In 2020, props89 posted to Reddit's *r/datingoverthirty*.[1] 'So, I've (30) been seeing a guy I met on Tinder for a couple of months. We'd been seeing each other once or twice a week, chatting daily, including starting to have the deeper talks about each other's life etc etc. All seems to be going well and then the Christmas holidays come and the slow fade begins.' Then, after New Year, the guy vanished. No warning, no explanation, just silence. Props89 sent a message asking if he fancied meeting up again. 'Left on read,' Props89 wrote, 'ghosted.' The sorrowful Reddit post hit a nerve, inspiring 198 sympathetic responses. People reacted with knowing solidarity. 'I agree with what you say here,' replied talkinhaikus108. 'My ghoster (god I can't believe I just use this term 'my ghoster' . . . =_=) is a very insecure person. Even I'm upset that he chose the worst way to end our relation, I can see where this action came from.' Others shared stories of dates that fizzled, and then fizzled out, passion that evaporated, weeks of intimacy erased by a blank screen. These accounts formed a collective terrain of disappointment, fragments of a culture built on indifference. Reddit, with its countless threads of fleeting attachments and failed matches, has become the lexicon of liquid love. There, in the subreddits of heartbreak and hookup, words gather around wounds: *ghosted, breadcrumbed, benched, paperclipped, wokefished, zombied*. These neologisms signify a shift in the grammar of intimacy. Props89 replied to the posts with gratitude. But it was a quiet

DOI:10.4324/9781003565482-31

comment near the end of the thread that captured the moment with devastating precision: 'Sorry, that's the new normal.' This chapter begins with that sentiment, with the inaudible violence of contemporary love unspoken and unravelling. In a world where commitment is suspended and romance now floats in the ever-refreshing feed of liquid modernity, we might ask: what kind of psychology can make sense of love in an age that forgets it so quickly?

Chapter Contents

- The psychology of romantic love from the nineteenth century to the digital age.
- Key individuals and theories in the psychological study of love.
- The shift from solid to liquid modernity as a critical thinking tool.

Chapter Objectives

- To examine how psychological theories of love have evolved over time.
- To evaluate how technological and social changes have reshaped romantic intimacy.
- To apply the critical thinking tool of 'solid and liquid modernity' to understand the conceptual transformation of love.

CRITICAL THINKING TOOL
SOLID AND LIQUID LOVE

To understand the changing psychology of love, we must first understand the changing nature of modernity itself. In his *Liquid Modernity* (2003), sociologist Zygmunt Bauman distinguished between two phases of modern life: *solid* modernity and *liquid* modernity. Solid modernity, roughly spanning the nineteenth to the mid-twentieth centuries, was characterised by institutional stability, long-term commitments, and fixed social roles. Identity was shaped largely by stable institutions such as family, religion, work, and nation. Love, within this framework, was imagined as monolithic; singular, enduring, and structured, typically culminating in marriage and children, and guided by cultural scripts that prioritised fidelity, duty, and sacrifice.

Liquid modernity, Bauman argued, emerged in the late twentieth century with the rise of globalisation, neoliberalism, and hyper-individualism. In this new condition, the permanence and solidity of social institutions gave way to fluidity, mobility, and relentless personal choice. Identities became self-curated projects, and love was increasingly defined by flexibility, autonomy, and consumption. Bauman described liquid love as a relationship form marked by ambivalence, ephemerality, and emotional insecurity, a shift from 'until death do us part' to 'until it stops working for me'.

Psychologists, too, have reflected and reinforced these historical shifts. From the standardised measurement of passionate love in the 1970s, to more recent explorations of polyamory, blended families, and LGBTQIA+ love, psychological theories have often mirrored the cultural zeitgeist. Where love was once treated as a stable trait that could be measured, scored, and predicted, it is now increasingly approached as a dynamic, relational, and discursively constructed phenomenon, reflexively shaped by power, culture, and context.

Introduction

Love has long preoccupied poets, philosophers, and ordinary citizens alike. But what is love, and how has our understanding of it changed over time? This chapter explores how the psychology of love, its theories, measurements, and cultural meanings, has evolved in response to shifting social and historical conditions. Drawing on Zygmunt Bauman's distinction between solid and liquid modernity, we examine how the psychological study of love has mirrored wider transformations in modern life: from enduring commitments rooted in duty and stability, to flexible, individualised, and often precarious relationships.

In the decades following the Second World War, love became a legitimate object of psychological inquiry. Early efforts sought to quantify it, understand its evolutionary function, and identify its psychological components. These approaches emerged during a time when love itself was imagined as structured, stable, and desirable, aligning with the broader ethos of solid modernity. But by the turn of the twenty-first century, love had become more fragmented. In a world increasingly defined by choice, mobility, and self-optimisation, the phenomenology of love shifted too, adopting new forms such as polyamory, blended families, hookup culture, and networked intimacy.

Throughout the chapter, we examine how key theorists, from Zick Rubin and Elaine Hatfield to contemporary researchers of love's diversity, responded to these changes. We explore whether psychology has helped liberate love from outdated norms, or whether it has adapted to the logics of neoliberal individualism. As the language of love has dematerialised into ghosts, vampires, and zombies, it becomes clear that romance in the twenty-first century is haunted by new forms of impersonal violence shapeshifting emotional, structural, and symbolic forms.

Historical Issues

For much of Western history, love was not seen as a proper subject for scientific inquiry. It belonged to the domains of poetry, theology, and mythology, where it was alternately idealised, feared, or moralised. Nowhere was this more vivid than in the courtly traditions of medieval Europe, where love was imagined as an exalted torment, an unattainable passion between the chivalric knight and his distant, idealised lady. In the Victorian era, love became domesticated and sentimentalised, celebrated through ritualised courtship, flowery prose, and mass-produced tokens of affection, such as the newly popular Valentine's Day cards that turned romantic devotion into a consumable spectacle.

In psychology's early years, love was marginalised, considered too subjective, too messy, or too moral to study scientifically. Yet in the mid-twentieth century, amid the optimism of the postwar years and with the rise of the welfare state, researchers began to take love seriously as an empirical topic. This historical moment coincided with what Bauman calls solid modernity: a time when romantic love was still imagined as a path to security, marriage, and family life.

Zick Rubin's seminal work in the 1970s was a turning point. His Love Scale sought to measure the emotional components of romantic attachment with scientific objectivity. Around the same time, Elaine Hatfield and colleagues developed the Passionate Love Scale, reflecting the growing belief that love could be quantified, predicted, and universalised. This was the rationalisation of romance, casting love as an emotional state amenable to psychometric measurement, cross-cultural comparison, and behavioural prediction.

Yet even as these tools gained traction, cracks were beginning to show. Feminist critics questioned the gendered and patriarchal assumptions behind romantic norms, and rising divorce rates confronted the ideal of lifelong love. By the 1990s, the forces of globalisation, digital communication, and neoliberalism began reshaping love into something more flexible, diverse, and unstable. The psychological study of love followed suit, shifting its focus from permanence to plasticity, from norms to narratives.

In solid modernity, relationships were often anchored by social scripts, rituals, and expectations. These offered both constraints and protection. Liquid love severs this historical continuity. Many young people cannot imagine lifelong commitment because they no longer see it. Love becomes unhistoricised, detached from both past and future. Liquid love fosters pseudo-intimacy: fast emotional connections with temporary security. The result is a form of emotional whiplash, where individuals feel closeness followed by sudden detachment. This erodes our ability to regulate attachment and detachment healthily, especially damaging for those with traumatic histories or insecure attachment styles.

Key Individuals

Edward Westermarck (1862–1939) was a Finnish philosopher, sociologist, and anthropologist whose work laid the foundations for a naturalistic and cross-cultural study of romantic love. He was one of the first scholars to apply Darwinian evolutionary theory to human social institutions. His landmark book *The History of Human Marriage* (1891) argued that love and pair bonding were natural instincts rooted in human biology and shaped by evolutionary pressures. He later developed this argument in *Marriage Ceremonies in Morocco* (1914), using ethnographic evidence from both Western and non-Western societies. His evolutionary and comparative framework challenged the prevailing notion that romantic love was a modern Western invention, insisting instead on its biological and cross-cultural universality.

Zick Rubin (b.1944) was among the first psychologists to treat romantic love as a measurable construct. In the early 1970s he developed the Love Scale, designed to distinguish between love and liking. Rubin's work was methodologically pioneering, conceptualising love as a psychological state that could be quantified. This effort reflected the ethos of solid modernity, which prized order, measurement, and predictive certainty. Love, in this context, was an enduring emotional bond, expected to culminate in long-term commitment and marriage. Rubin's scale, though foundational, was deeply reflective of its time: a heterosexual, monogamous model of romantic attachment framed within the psychology of stability.

Elaine Hatfield's (b.1937) early work extended Rubin's legacy, culminating in the widely used Passionate Love Scale (1986). Hatfield defined passionate love as a 'state of intense longing for union with another', and sought to capture its cognitive, emotional, and behavioural components. Her approach was notable for its cross-cultural validation and methodological rigour, making her a central figure in the scientific study of romantic emotion during the late solid modern period. Hatfield later questioned the limitations of quantitative scales, advocating for greater cultural sensitivity and narrative-based approaches.

Robert Sternberg (b.1949) whose three components of Triangular Theory of Love (1986) were intimacy, passion, and commitment. Different combinations of these elements generated different kinds of love: romantic, companionate, fatuous, and consummate. Like Rubin and Hatfield, Sternberg worked within the solid modern tradition of typologising and categorising love, aiming to provide clarity and guidance in a complex domain. Sternberg's model also retained normative elements: consummate love, which includes all three components, is implicitly valued as the most complete form. While still influential, the theory has been critiqued for assuming universality in the emotional architecture of love and for downplaying the effects of culture, gender, and power.

In the late 1980s, Cindy Hazan (b.1960) and Phillip Shaver (b.1944) applied Bowlby's attachment theory to adult romantic relationships. Their research suggested that people develop secure, avoidant, and anxious romantic attachment styles, based on early life experiences. Their work linked developmental psychology to adult love, offering a powerful explanatory framework for individual differences in intimacy and commitment. Attachment theory has proved highly durable. In its original form, it resonated with solid modern ideals of emotional consistency and relational security.

Eva Illouz (b.1961), a sociologist, has offered some of the most powerful critiques of the psychological study of love. In works such as *Consuming the Romantic Utopia* (1997) and *Why Love Hurts* (2012), Illouz argues that love has been commodified by capitalism and reframed by therapeutic culture. Modern individuals are encouraged to treat love as a project of self-actualisation, seeking fulfilment, not duty; satisfaction, not sacrifice. Illouz's work describes the liquid modern experience of love: emotionally ambivalent, consumer-driven, and marked by choice anxiety. Drawing on interviews, historical data, and cultural analysis, she shows how love has become entangled with market logic, especially through dating apps, therapy-speak, and lifestyle branding.

Epistemological Issues

Edward Westermarck's epistemology was grounded in comparative empiricism. He collected ethnographic and anthropological data from a wide range of cultures aiming to uncover recurring social patterns. He sought to understand romantic and sexual behaviour through observation, documentation, and the synthesis of diverse sources, from traveller accounts and colonial records to his own fieldwork. In this respect, he exemplified an early quasi-positivist approach, seeking to study human emotions using the tools of social science, believing that empirical data could reveal universal trends and natural instincts beneath surface differences.

In solid modernity, psychological knowledge about love was premised on the ideal of objectivity and universality. Researchers sought to pin love down, to define, classify, and measure it. This epistemological orientation mirrored the era's broader belief in scientific rationalism and standardisation. Rubin's Love Scale and Hatfield's Passionate Love Scale exemplify this approach: both were built on the assumption that love could be reduced to core psychological components and quantified across populations. Love was treated as a stable internal state, discoverable through well-constructed psychometric tools.

This approach had clear strengths: it allowed psychologists to study love systematically, compare findings across cultures, and bring empirical rigour to a topic once considered unscientific. However, it also reflected a narrow cultural framing, often heterosexual, monogamous, and Western in its assumptions. By focusing on universals, early research tended to overlook the social and historical variability of love and the ways in which it is shaped by language, ideology, and power.

The epistemological terrain began to shift in the late twentieth century. Researchers such as Eva Illouz, and Belli, Harré, and Íñiguez (2010) challenged the idea that love could be understood purely through measurement. Instead, they proposed that love is socially constructed and culturally mediated, a product of narrative, discourse, and material conditions. This move from positivism to constructivism and hermeneutics reflects the broader intellectual currents of liquid modernity, where fixed truths give way to multiple meanings and contested interpretations. This approach demands that psychologists attend to voice, context, and cultural specificity, and it invites critical reflection on the assumptions embedded in their own methods.

In the current era, the psychology of love is increasingly shaped by plural epistemologies: quantitative and qualitative, empirical and narrative, biological and discursive. What binds them is a reflexive recognition that how we know love depends on how we frame it. The sheer prolixity of neologisms—*ghosting, zombieing, paperclipping, situationships*—points to a landscape where hurt is normalised, routinised, and even aestheticised. The need to name so many micro-aggressions suggests a system that is inherently injurious. Each term masks deep emotional damage behind a euphemistic gloss. This insight is essential for any student of psychology navigating between the certainties of solid modernity and the fluid complexities of the present.

Ontological Issues

What is this *thing* called love? In the psychological traditions of solid modernity, love was often assumed to be a discrete, measurable, and universal phenomenon, a natural kind. Westermarck argued that emotions such as love are rooted in biology and evolved to serve adaptive purposes in relation to mating, reproduction, and kin bonding. For him, culture shaped the expression of love but not its origin. 'Love is a state of consciousness that may be excited by a great variety of causes,' he wrote, 'but in its most typical form, it is based on a natural impulse common to mankind.'

Later theories from Rubin, Hatfield, and Sternberg all rested on the ontological belief that love exists as an internal, individual state, a kind of emotional essence that can be isolated, examined, and categorised. Whether cast as passion, commitment, intimacy, or a combination thereof, love was treated as a bounded and identifiable construct, akin to an emotion like fear or joy. This ontological stability reflected wider cultural ideals. In a world oriented around lifelong partnerships, institutionalised marriage, and normative gender roles, it made sense to imagine love as a fixed emotional glue, fermented by evolution, that stuck people together. Attachment theory reinforced this picture by rooting adult romantic behaviour in early developmental templates, suggesting that love was part of the emotional architecture of the self.

But in liquid modernity, such firm ontologies began to come apart. Love no longer appeared as a singular essence but as a dynamic, situational, and negotiated process. Liquid love fosters pseudo-intimacy: fast emotional connections with no stable framework. The result might be energising but it fosters closeness followed by sudden detachment.

Eva Illouz's work redefines love as a social performance entangled in power and consumer culture. Similarly, Belli, Harré, and Íñiguez (2010) show that love is ontologically discursive: it emerges through language, culture, and interaction rather than existing prior to them. Love, in this view, is performed rather than possessed; it is something people enact, interpret, and contest.

This ontological fluidity certainly allows for the recognition of multiple forms of love: queer love, non-monogamous love, digital intimacy, and blended families. It invites psychology to shift from asking *what* love is to exploring *how* love is lived and narrated in diverse contexts. It also raises ontological questions about absence and failure: what does it mean to *not* be in love, or to love in ways that are illegible to dominant scripts?

Power

Love may feel personal but it is always political. In both solid and liquid modernity, the psychology of love has been shaped by powerful norms and ideologies about who may love, how, and under what conditions. In the solid modern world of the mid-twentieth century, love was tightly bound to reproduction, gender roles, the nuclear family, and economic security. Psychology played a supporting role in reinforcing attachment norms. It promoted stable heterosexual love as the psychological ideal, pathologising alternatives, from same-sex desire to extramarital longing, as deviant or dysfunctional.

In liquid modernity, the dynamics of power become more diffuse but no less coercive. Neoliberalism reframed love as personal fulfilment, choice, and optimisation. Individuals are encouraged to treat love as a project of self-development, a site for achieving happiness, identity, and emotional growth. This shift appears liberatory, but as Eva Illouz and others have shown, it also individualises responsibility for relationship failure and commodifies intimacy. Dating apps, therapy culture, and social media recast love as labour and lifestyle, often governed by algorithms and market logic.

The rise of polyamory, queer relationships, and blended families opens up spaces for relational diversity, but it also exposes people to precarity, emotional labour, and normative anxiety. In this context, psychology can either reinforce neoliberal ideals by assessing 'relationship satisfaction' or 'communication skills', or it can challenge them by attending to the structural conditions that make certain kinds of love more visible, legible, or liveable. In this way, love becomes a site of biopolitical management, where psychological knowledge helps shape populations, what Foucault might have called a governmentality of the heart.

In liquid love, individuals become *products* on a dating shelf. Apps such as Tinder gamify intimacy, encouraging people to shop for others, and to market themselves, like consumer goods. Affection is transactional, and partners are replaceable. As Bauman warned, this generates 'connections without consequences', where people are discarded like packaging after a brief use.

Chapter Summary

This chapter has explored how the psychology of romantic love has shifted from the structured certainties of solid modernity to the precarious fluidities of our liquid age. It has charted the development of scientific theories of love from the mid-twentieth century to the present, examining how ideas of attachment, passion, and intimacy have been shaped by changing cultural, social, and economic contexts. We have considered the ways in which love has been theorised, as biology, as affect, as choice, and how it has also been technologised, commodified, and destabilised.

Through the critical lens of Zygmunt Bauman's distinction between solid and liquid modernity, we have traced a movement away from enduring forms of courtship, commitment, and relational identity towards a more fragmented, transactional, and provisional emotional culture. In this world, the rituals of romance have not disappeared; they have multiplied. But instead of grounding us, they often disorient, hurt, or exhaust us. From ghosting and breadcrumbing to the algorithmic self, we see love becoming harder to hold onto and harder to name.

And yet, behind the vocabulary of wounds, a quieter longing remains. A hope, sometimes naïve, sometimes defiant, for something more lasting than a swipe right, more truthful than a profile, more human than a ghost. If love today is liquid, its ache may still be solid. Beneath the code, behind the glow of the screen, the question what love is endures. As props89 and hundreds like them quietly testify, we are still waiting for a reply.

Reflective Questions

1. What does Zygmunt Bauman mean by 'liquid modernity', and how does it help us understand changing patterns in romantic relationships?
2. How did early figures like Edward Westermarck and John Bowlby conceptualise love, and in what ways do their theories reflect the 'solid modern' mindset?
3. What is the significance of the new vocabulary emerging around dating (e.g. ghosting, breadcrumbing, zombied), and what does it suggest about the ontology of contemporary love?
4. How do power dynamics manifest in liquid relationships, particularly in digital spaces?
5. Can psychology offer a stable theory of love in an unstable world? Or must psychological knowledge evolve with culture?

Note

1 props89 (@props89), "Another ghosting story," r/datingoverthirty, n.d., https://www.reddit.com/r/datingoverthirty/comments/exlm34/another_ghosting_story/.

Suggested Reading

Alparone, D., Pozzetti, R., & Rizzo, A. (2024). Sexuality in the digital world: Treatment of a case of dating app addiction. *Theory & Psychology, 34*(5), 630–645. https://doi.org/10.1177/09593543241268499.

Bauman, Z. (2003). *Liquid Love: On the frailty of human bonds*. Bristol: Polity Press.

Belli, S., Harré, R., & Íñiguez, L. (2010). What is love? Discourse about emotions in social sciences. *Human Affairs, 20*(3), 249–270. https://doi.org/10.2478/v10023-010-0026-8.

Burge, A. (2018). The rough guide to love: Romance, history and sexualization in gendered relationship advice. *Journal of Gender Studies, 27*(6), 649–660. https://doi.org/10.1080/09589236.2017.1287065.

Chiang, H. H. (2010). Liberating sex, knowing desire: *Scientia sexualis* and epistemic turning points in the history of sexuality. *History of the Human Sciences, 23*(5), 42–69. https://doi.org/10.1177/0952695110378947.

Domínguez, G. E., Pujol, J., Motzkau, J. F., & Popper, M. (2017). Suspended transitions and affective orderings: From troubled monogamy to liminal polyamory. *Theory & Psychology, 27*(2), 183–197. https://doi.org/10.1177/0959354317700289.

Fisher, K., & Funke, J. (2023). 'All the progressive forms of life are built up on the attraction of sex': Development and the social function of the sexual instinct in late 19th- and early 20th-century Western European sexology. *History of the Human Sciences, 36*(5), 42–67. https://doi.org/10.1177/09526951231208992.

Garlen, J. C., & Sandlin, J. A. (2017). Happily (n)ever after: The cruel optimism of Disney's romantic ideal. *Feminist Media Studies, 17*(6), 957–971. https://doi.org/10.1080/14680777.2017.1338305.

Guo, M., & Liu, Z. (2025). Hysteria in empathy: Understanding virtual companionship and emotional connection between humans and AI. *Theory & Psychology, 35*(2), 163–184. https://doi.org/10.1177/09593543251319738.

Illouz, E. (1997). *Consuming the Romantic Utopia: Love and the cultural contradictions of capitalism*. Berkeley: University of California Press.

Sequeira, R. (2022). The sciences of love: Intimate 'democracy' and the eugenic development of the Marathi couple in colonial India. *History of the Human Sciences, 36(*5), 68–93. https://doi.org/10.1177/09526951221134469.

Sternberg, R. J., & Sternberg, K. (2024). A RELIC theory of love: The role of interpersonal, intrapersonal, and extrapersonal elements in love. *Theory & Psychology, 34*(5), 671–698. https://doi.org/10.1177/09593543241270922.

Thorne, S. R., Hegarty, P., & Hepper, E. G. (2019). Equality in theory: From a heteronormative to an inclusive psychology of romantic love. *Theory & Psychology, 29*(2), 240–257. https://doi.org/10.1177/0959354319826725.

Wolkomir, M. (2018). *Researching Romantic Love and Multiple Partner Intimacies: Developing a qualitative research design and tools*. Thousand Oaks, CA: Sage.

Key Terms

Attachment Theory A psychological model originating with John Bowlby and Mary Ainsworth that explains how early relationships with caregivers shape expectations and behaviours in adult romantic relationships.

Ghosting The act of suddenly and without explanation withdrawing from all communication in a romantic or dating context, leaving the other party without closure.

Liquid Love A term derived from Zygmunt Bauman's 'liquid modernity' to describe contemporary romantic relationships marked by fluidity, impermanence, and a retreat from long-term commitment.

Prolix Lexicon A term used in this chapter to describe the sprawling and ever-expanding vocabulary generated by users of digital dating platforms to name and make sense of fleeting or painful romantic experiences.

Romantic Ideal A cultural and historical notion of love grounded in courtship, exclusivity, and emotional transcendence, often symbolised by medieval or Victorian concepts of honour and devotion.

Situationship A modern, undefined romantic or sexual relationship that lacks the formal status or clear boundaries of traditional relationships, often used to describe the liminal space between casual and committed connection.

Solid Love A term used in contrast to 'liquid love' to describe romantic relationships rooted in long-term commitment, stability, and institutional norms such as marriage and monogamy.

Westermarck Effect A theory proposed by Edward Westermarck suggesting that individuals raised closely together during early childhood develop a natural aversion to sexual attraction towards one another, supporting incest avoidance.

Zombied A contemporary dating term referring to someone who reappears in a romantic context after having previously ghosted their partner, as if rising from the dead.

32

Tell Me Where It Hurts

Feminist Psychology's Critique of Hegemonic Masculinity

Chapter Overview

This chapter explores the emergence of feminist psychology as a radical critique of mainstream psychology's complicity with patriarchal power. Beginning with Phyllis Chesler's exposé of sexual abuse by male therapists in the 1970s, the chapter uncovers how feminist psychologists revealed the gendered assumptions underpinning both theory and clinical practice. These pioneers did not merely seek inclusion in psychology; they demanded its transformation. Drawing on personal narratives, standpoint epistemology, and survey data, feminist psychologists challenged the neutrality of 'objective' knowledge and exposed the normative violence of universalising male perspectives. Through the work of key figures such as Naomi Weisstein, Sandra Bem, Carol Gilligan, and Gail Lewis, the chapter explores how feminist critiques reshaped concepts of identity, morality, care, and justice. Using the critical thinking tool of hegemony, it demonstrates how dominant assumptions become naturalised until made visible by critique. Ontologically, feminist psychology questioned binary sex categories and the pathologisation of femininity; epistemologically, it redefined what counted as valid knowledge; politically, it fought to change institutional structures and ethical norms. By the end of the twentieth century, feminist psychology had begun to reimagine the psychology as a platform for collective empowerment and change.

Tell Me Where It Hurts

In June 1972, the psychologist Phyllis Chesler wrote a shocking exposé for *New York* magazine. Below the title 'The Sensuous Psychiatrists', the magazine's cover photograph was of a therapist in a suit cuddling a younger female patient on a leather couch. The caption suggestively read: 'Lie down and tell me where it hurts.' Chesler had found it disturbingly easy to recruit interviewees: she simply asked acquaintances if they had ever slept with their therapist. The therapists themselves proved surprisingly easy to track down. Asked whether they should sleep with their patients, one Greenwich Village psychotherapist replied: 'Very rarely. If they do, they should send them to another doctor. You lose your objectivity. I know I do.' 'Sometimes it's catastrophic,' another conceded, adding, 'but sometimes therapy proceeds pretty well.' These were respected professionals, not quirky caricatures from a Woody Allen movie. And they were not outliers. In 1966, writing in an academic journal, one psychoanalyst had described sex with patients as 'overt transference', a legitimate therapeutic

DOI: 10.4324/9781003565482-32

tool. 'A sexual involvement can indeed be a useful part of the psychotherapeutic process', Dr Martin Richards concluded in his *The Love Treatment: Sexual intimacy between patients and psychotherapists* (1971). Sexual exploitation wasn't merely ethical failure; it was hegemonic masculinity in action. The abuse persisted precisely because ethical violations had become normalised, embedded in a culture where male exploitation disguised itself as care. The systematic abuse of patients galvanised the feminist psychology movement. By giving authority to women's voices in the male-dominated profession of psychotherapy, feminist psychologists appropriated a strategy that the women's liberation movement had already deployed: they insisted that lived experience was a valid form of data that could be used to guide reform. Their campaign to outlaw sexual exploitation in therapy was successful. By 1977, every major psychological association had finally banned sexual contact between therapists and clients.

Chapter Contents

- The abuse of therapeutic power and the feminist exposure of institutional misogyny.
- Key feminist psychologists and their challenge to mainstream psychological norms.
- The critical thinking tool of hegemony: how feminist psychology made the invisible visible.

Chapter Objectives

- To explore how feminist psychology emerged as a challenge to patriarchal assumptions within psychological theory and practice.
- To understand the epistemological, ontological, and ethical contributions of key feminist psychologists.
- To apply the critical thinking tool of hegemony in analysing how dominant norms become naturalised in psychology.

CRITICAL THINKING TOOL
HEGEMONY

Hegemony refers to a form of power that is not maintained through force alone but through consent, through the shaping of culture, social norms, and everyday assumptions. Originally developed by Italian Marxist theorist Antonio Gramsci, the concept accounts for how dominant groups maintain control by persuading people that existing social arrangements are natural, inevitable, and desirable.

Hegemony works by embedding certain values and ideas so deeply within institutions, such as education, law, the media, and science, that they become invisible because they are 'common sense'. It is power over meanings and beliefs that structures social life. This is what makes hegemony so resilient: it operates through norms, narratives, and taken-for-granted unquestionable truths.

The concept of hegemony has been used in feminist psychology to expose how traditional psychology has often served patriarchal interests. Theories of development, emotion, intelligence, and sexuality often appeared neutral but were grounded in male experience, reflecting masculine assumptions as if they were universal. Feminist psychologists argued that this apparent neutrality was hegemonic: it made the male norm seem objective and scientific while obscuring women's experiences.

By identifying hegemonic assumptions within psychological theory and practice, feminist psychology reveals whose voices have been excluded, whose perspectives have been positioned as normative, and how power structures have shaped the discipline's knowledge base. Understanding hegemony allows us to recognise psychology as a cultural institution whose practices must be questioned, reimagined, and made more inclusive.

Introduction

Until the 1970s, mainstream psychology was presented as if representative of the entire human species. Female experience was marginalised, pathologised, or simply ignored. When women were studied, they were frequently portrayed as less rational, more emotional, and more dependent compared to men, a deviation from the implicit male norm.

It was in this context that feminist psychology emerged as both a critique and a reconstruction. Its earliest pioneers, such as Naomi Weisstein, challenged the presumed objectivity of psychology by revealing its androcentric foundations. They exposed how knowledge claims were shaped by hegemonic assumptions about gender, and how the language of science had often been structured in ways that silenced, distorted, or excluded women's voices.

Feminist psychology began with the shared recognition that something was wrong with common sense. That the experiences, lives, and perspectives of women, and of marginalised people more broadly, had been excluded or misrepresented within the psychological sciences. The project of feminist psychology, then, was to confront this cultural hegemony, to unmask the gendered power woven into apparently neutral theories, and to propose alternatives grounded in justice, reflexivity, and inclusion. This chapter explores how feminist psychologists achieved that. It traces their historical struggle to reshape institutions, their conceptual breakthroughs, and their ongoing efforts to confront patriarchal and disciplinary power.

Historical Issues

In the early 1970s, feminist psychologists began to organise, critique the discipline, and to build new spaces within it. In the United States, members of the American Psychological Association (APA) founded Division 35, the Society for the Psychology of Women, in 1973. In the UK, the Psychology of Women Section (POWES) was established within the British Psychological Society (BPS) in 1987. Across Europe, a patchwork of national and transnational feminist networks began to form, including the European Feminist Research Conference and later the European Association of Critical and Community Psychology, both of which were forums for feminist scholarship.

At the same time, feminist psychology began to reshape what was taught. In the 1980s and 1990s, feminist critiques entered undergraduate curricula. Courses on gender, power, and the psychology of women proliferated. But more importantly, these courses demanded a shift in *how* psychology was taught. Students were encouraged to ask whose voices were present in the research, whose were absent, and why. Concepts such as reflexivity, intersectionality, and situated knowledge were introduced as fundamental challenges to the presumed neutrality of psychological science.

This curricular transformation also disrupted the hegemonic canon of 'great men' and universal laws. Instead, feminist psychology highlighted the socio-historical embeddedness of knowledge, revealing how what counted as 'normal development' or 'healthy adjustment' often reflected white, middle-class, Western male values.

Key Individuals

Marie Langer (1910–1987) was an Austrian psychoanalyst who fled fascism and later worked in Argentina and Nicaragua, Langer fused Marxist, feminist, and psychoanalytic insights. She advocated for socially engaged, liberationist approaches to mental health. Her work connected feminist psychology to global struggles against authoritarianism and biopower. Langer co-founded the Internationalist Mental Health Network and was active in revolutionary solidarity movements. Her clinical practice became a space for imagining alternatives to capitalist and patriarchal structures. She believed that therapy could be a political act, especially in contexts of state violence, poverty, and displacement.

Carol Gilligan (b.1936) revolutionised moral psychology by challenging Kohlberg's male-centric model of ethical development. Her book *In a Different Voice* (1982) introduced a relational, care-based ethic as equally valid, but previously dismissed, moral reasoning. Gilligan's work exposed the hegemonic assumption that autonomy and justice were the highest moral ideals, placing connection at the centre instead. Her feminist ethic of care became influential in psychology, education, and political theory, offering a new way of valuing voice and difference in psychological development.

Naomi Weisstein (1939–2015) was a cognitive neuroscientist and activist. Weisstein's 1968 essay 'Psychology constructs the female' delivered a searing indictment of psychology's patriarchal assumptions. She argued that psychology had ignored women's real social conditions in favour of essentialist myths. A founding voice of feminist psychology, she fused science, satire, and political critique, insisting that 'what passes for scientific truth is often simply the voice of power'. Her work bridged cognitive science and feminism, proving that scientific rigour and political resistance need not be opposites.

Phyllis Chesler (b.1940) is a psychologist, writer, and activist. Chesler's *Women and Madness* (1972) revealed the psychiatric system's complicity in controlling women. By exposing how mental health diagnoses pathologised female emotion, sexuality, and defiance, Chesler disrupted hegemonic assumptions of normalcy and exposed how 'care' could become coercion. Her critique was grounded in interviews and lived accounts, which illuminated how therapists, often male, used diagnosis and treatment to reinforce patriarchal control. Chesler's early work laid the groundwork for reforms in therapeutic ethics and helped catalyse the feminist campaign against therapist–patient sexual abuse, which reshaped codes of practice across the profession.

Sandra Bem (1944–2014) was a leading critic of gender essentialism. Bem developed gender schema theory, showing how societal expectations shape individuals' cognitive processing of gender. Bem's Sex-Role Inventory challenged binary thinking by allowing for psychological androgyny. Her work dismantled the ontological rigidity of 'male' and 'female' categories and helped deconstruct hegemonic gender norms. She also warned of the psychological harm of rigid sex-role stereotyping, calling for a future in which individuals could live beyond the constraints of prescribed masculinity and femininity.

Gail Lewis (b.1951) is a British Black feminist scholar and psychoanalytic psychotherapist. Her work crucially explores the psychic and social dimensions of racialised subjectivity, powerfully critiquing Eurocentric psychology. Lewis foregrounds the legacies of colonialism and racism in shaping the psychic lives of Black and brown individuals in postcolonial Britain. She argues that psychology must be fundamentally rethought through Black feminist and decolonial lenses rather than simply by incorporating race into existing frameworks. Her analyses of 'misrecognition' and racialised melancholia offer unique psychoanalytic insights into the pain of marginalisation in dominant cultures.

Epistemological Issues

Feminist psychologists revolutionised the epistemology of the discipline by insisting that lived experience, particularly women's first-person narratives, was politically potent. Drawing on a tradition shared with feminist sociologists such as Diana Russell (*The Politics of Rape*, 1975) and Del Martin (*Battered Wives*, 1976), they used personal testimony to make visible the gendered violence and exploitation often hidden within therapeutic settings. This use of experience as authoritative evidence gave feminist psychology a unique epistemic legitimacy: it was rooted in the lives of women themselves, granting political authenticity and emotional resonance to calls for reform.

These same psychologists were astute strategists. Recognising that the language of scientific objectivity held sway within psychology, they began to translate experience into data. Through questionnaires and surveys, such as those developed by the Task Force on Sex Bias and Sex Role Stereotyping, they produced quantifiable, generalisable evidence of abuse and sexism in therapy. This tactic allowed them to speak truth to power in its own idiom. Such surveys transformed feminist counter-knowledge into evidence legible to mainstream science, even as this process subtly shifted the function of experience itself, from embodied resistance to statistical artefact.

One of feminist psychology's most profound interventions was epistemological. It challenged the assumption that knowledge could ever be neutral, value-free, or 'from nowhere'. Mainstream psychological research had long claimed objectivity, but feminist critics argued that this objectivity was in fact deeply hegemonic, centred on male, Western, middle-class norms disguised as universal truths. Instead, feminist philosophers such as Sandra Harding and Donna Haraway proposed *standpoint theory* and *situated knowledges* respectively. According to this approach, all knowledge is produced from a specific location, shaped by the social, cultural, and political position of the knower.

Linked to this is the feminist emphasis on reflexivity. Rather than claiming to be neutral observers, feminist psychologists adopted a doubled hermeneutic: making sense of data while acknowledging their embeddedness in the research process. They foregrounded the politics of interpretation and called for self-awareness about how power, privilege, and identity shape one's methods and conclusions. In the UK, Celia Kitzinger and Sue Wilkinson, for example, championed reflexive discourse analysis, a method that made power relations visible in both text and research practice.

Feminist epistemology extended into cultural critique, especially through the work of Rosalind Gill (b.1963). Gill's analysis of postfeminist media culture, particularly advertising, revealed how visual representations of women perpetuate hegemonic ideals under the guise of choice and empowerment. Gill's exploration of the 'midriff' figure—young, slim, desiring yet desiring to be desired—unpacked how commercial imagery codes femininity as a set of performative, self-policing ideals.

The Venezuelan psychologist Maritza Montero (b.1939) is a foundational figure in Latin American community and liberation psychology. Her work constitutes a seismic epistemological shift away from detached, positivist models of knowing towards participatory, dialogical, and emancipatory approaches. Montero argues that knowledge must emerge from lived experience, especially among marginalised populations. She actively rejects the imposition of Euro-American frameworks, critiquing their hegemonic tendencies and cultural irrelevance. Montero advocates for epistemic justice, where knowledge empowers communities to understand and transform their own social realities. Her commitment to participatory action research (PAR) positions knowledge as co-created, valuing reflexivity and critical consciousness.

Ontological Issues

Where mainstream psychology once treated categories like 'man' and 'woman' as natural and self-evident, feminist psychology insisted that these were social constructions, products of culture, language, and power. The field's ontological challenge was thus twofold: to dismantle existing categories that sustained hegemonic norms, and to develop alternative ways of understanding human identity.

The first ontological target was the gender binary itself. Feminist psychologists argued that 'male' and 'female' were socially constructed positions. Sandra Bem's gender schema theory demonstrated how early socialisation programmes individuals into rigid gender roles, shaping what they see, feel, and remember. Bem challenged the binary by developing the Bem Sex-Role Inventory, which validated androgyny as a psychologically healthy state. In doing so, she pushed against the ontological hegemony that equated difference with deviance and conformity with health.

Later feminist thought extended this critique further. Influenced by Judith Butler's theory of gender performativity, feminist psychologists began to treat gender as something enacted, something done rather than something *one is*. This marked a decisive break with essentialism and opened up new space for queer, trans, gender fluid, and non-binary voices within psychology.

The second ontological intervention came in the field of mental health and therapy. Feminist clinician psychologists such as Carol Gilligan and Jean Baker Miller argued that dominant psychological models valued autonomy, control, and individualism, values rooted in a masculine ideal. Their relational-cultural model reframed psychological well-being as the capacity to maintain mutual, empathic relationships. This model challenged the hegemonic assumption that independence is the highest developmental achievement, instead valuing *connection* as both a human need and a form of resistance to isolation, domination, and control.

Catriona I. Macleod (b.1964) powerfully challenged mainstream ontological assumptions, especially around constructs such as adolescence, agency, and reproductive choice. She demonstrated how these categories are inflected by colonial and apartheid histories, and by Western norms of development. In her book *Adolescence, Pregnancy and Abortion: Constructing a threat of degeneration* (2011), she argues that universalist categories often misrepresent youth in postcolonial contexts and perpetuate moral judgement and social control. Instead, Macleod advocates for contextual, relational, and politically reflexive ontologies which situate the self within specific histories and communities. Macleod's work exemplifies a radical feminist challenge that refuses to separate the psychological from the social, showing that categories of personhood are always constituted through relations of power and historical specificity.

Power

Feminist psychology has always been animated by a simple but radical insight: that psychology is not merely a body of knowledge but a *regime of power*. It categorises, diagnoses, prescribes, and pathologises. It teaches individuals how to think, feel, behave, and how to be 'normal'. From this perspective, feminist psychology is a struggle over the politics of life itself.

Drawing on Michel Foucault's concept of *biopower*, feminist psychologists revealed how psychology had become a tool for regulating the female body, mind, and sexuality. The DSM, with its gendered diagnoses from hysteria to Borderline Personality Disorder, served as a hegemonic script, shaping how women's pain, protest, or trauma could be spoken and heard. The work of Phyllis Chesler, for instance, laid bare how the psychiatric system infantilised women, sexualised their distress, and punished their resistance.

But feminist psychology also turned outward, to confront intersectional and global forms of power. Inspired by Kimberlé Crenshaw's articulation of intersectionality, feminist psychologists began to insist that gender could not be understood in isolation from race, class, disability, and sexuality. A white, Western, middle-class liberal feminism was not enough. Psychology had to be accountable to the multiplicity of lived experiences, and to the overlapping systems of domination that shaped them.

This paved the way for a transnational and decolonial feminist psychology, in which scholars from the Global South and communities of colour began to reimagine psychology from their own standpoints. Thinkers such as Linda James Myers (Afrocentric psychology) and Lélia Gonzalez (Afro-Brazilian feminist thought) challenged the field to decentre Euro-American norms and recognise the pluriversality of psychological life.

The South African psychologist Kopano Ratele (b.1969) is a leading figure in the study of masculinities, race, and decolonial theory. His work critically intervenes in the hegemonic norms of psychology, especially its treatment of men and masculinity in post-apartheid Africa. Ratele calls for a nuanced understanding of how colonialism, racism, and poverty shape African masculinities, viewing men as both agents and subjects of vulnerability. His research questions the implicit whiteness, Western-centrism, and individualism of mainstream models, advocating for a politicised, relational, and situated approach to male subjectivity. In *Why Men Hurt Women and Other Reflections on Love, Violence and Masculinity* (2022), Ratele imagines the possibility of a more loving masculinity in a society where structural violence, failures of government, and economic inequality underpin much of the violent behaviour that men display.

Such work demands a rethinking of power itself, as something exercised, contested, and refused. Feminist psychology reveals how power operates through silence, absence, and assumed neutrality. And by refusing these forms of epistemic and institutional hegemony, it offers something critique and transformation.

In this light, feminist psychology is a revolutionary project, one that insists that psychology must serve the oppressed. One that makes the couch not a site of control but of liberation. And one that reminds us that every act of knowledge is also an act of power.

Chapter Summary

Feminist psychology has never meekly asked for a seat at the table. It has stormed the halls of the discipline, demanding that psychology be rebuilt from its empirical assumptions to its moral core. This chapter has traced how feminist thinkers exposed the deep masculinist bias of mainstream psychological science, dismantled its exclusionary logic, and built, in its place, radical new frameworks for understanding identity, knowledge, mental health, and power. Whether through reflexive methodology, the deconstruction of gender binaries, or the global resistance to epistemic colonialism, feminist psychology has refused to separate theory from justice.

At its heart, this movement has fought back against the hegemonic forces that dictate what is normal, what is sane, and who gets to decide. It has rejected the false universalism of the 'objective' subject and insisted, again and again, that the lived experiences of women and marginalised people are not anecdotal, they are epistemological. From standpoint theory to care ethics, from Afrocentric healing to discourse analysis, feminist psychology has redefined what it means to know, to heal, and to be. And it has paid a price for its honesty. These gains had to be seized from a resistant discipline. They were fought for in committee rooms and classrooms, journals and protests, patient files and conference halls.

In 1972, Phyllis Chesler shattered the profession's genteel silence with her exposé on male therapists who sexually exploited their female clients. She revealed widespread, institutionalised abuse, where predation was cloaked in clinical jargon and consent was gaslit into therapeutic growth. The American Psychological Association held open debates on whether sex with patients might be 'beneficial'. Dr Martin Shepard published a book arguing that it could be part of the healing process. This was hegemony, not fringe ideas: when the abuse of power passes for care, and no one inside the system sees the harm.

Feminist psychologists saw it. And they would not let it stand. Their campaign to outlaw sexual contact in therapy was a revolutionary reimagining of what therapy could be: safe, accountable, just. By 1977, every major psychological association had rewritten its rules. The couch, once a site of exploitation, had been transformed into a site of resistance. Feminist psychology had spoken, and the discipline, at last, had to listen.

Reflective Questions

1. How did feminist psychologists expose the ethical failures of mainstream therapeutic practice in the 1970s?
2. What role does experience play in feminist psychology as a form of evidence?
3. How did key feminist thinkers such as Carol Gilligan and Sandra Bem challenge psychological assumptions about gender and development?
4. What is 'hegemony', and why is it a useful critical tool for analysing psychological knowledge and institutions?
5. In what ways did feminist psychology reimagine the purpose of psychological science itself?

Suggested Reading

Bookwala, J., & Newton, N. J. (2022). *Reflections from Pioneering Women in Psychology*. Cambridge: Cambridge University Press.

Burman, E. (2016). Fanon, Foucault, feminisms: Psychoeducation, theoretical psychology, and political change. *Theory & Psychology, 26*(6), 706–730. https://doi.org/10.1177/0959354316653484.

Dennis, P. M. (2020). Bishop Fulton J. Sheen: America's public critic of psychoanalysis, 1947–1957. *Journal of the History of the Behavioural Sciences, 56*(1), 36–51. https://doi.org/10.1002/jhbs.22000.

Dhar, A. (2020). Psychology: A discipline in trouble and trouble in the discipline. *Theory & Psychology, 31*(2), 310–312. https://doi.org/10.1177/0959354320945795.

Hare-Mustin, R. T., & Marecek, J. (1988). The meaning of difference: Gender theory, postmodernism, and psychology. *American Psychologist, 43*(6), 455–464. https://doi.org/10.1037/0003-066X.43.6.455.

Hubbard, K., & Hegarty, P. (2024). *A Feminist Companion to Conceptual and Historical Issues in Psychology*. Buckingham: Open University Press.

Kim, S., & Rutherford, A. (2015). From seduction to sexism: Feminists challenge the ethics of therapist–client sexual relations in 1970s America. *History of Psychology, 18*(3), 283–296. https://doi.org/10.1037/a0039524.

Maass, V. S. (2023). *Feminist Psychology: History, practice, research, and the future*. Westport, CT: Praeger.

Meijer, M. (2022). Making therapy more transparent: On Kevin R. Smith's therapeutic ethics. *Theory & Psychology, 33*(3), 424–432. https://doi.org/10.1177/09593543221131271.

Rutherford, A. (2021). *Psychology at the Intersections of Gender, Feminism, History, and Culture*. Cambridge: Cambridge University Press.

Rutherford, A., Vaughn-Blount, K., & Ball, L. C. (2010). Responsible opposition, disruptive voices: Science, social change, and the history of feminist psychology. *Psychology of Women Quarterly, 34*(4), 460–473.

Spandler, H., & Carr, S. (2022). Lesbian and bisexual women's experiences of aversion therapy in England. *History of the Human Sciences, 35*(3–4), 218–236. https://doi.org/10.1177/09526951211059422.

Stupak, R., & Dyga, K. (2018). Postpsychiatry and postmodern psychotherapy: Theoretical and ethical issues in mental health care in a Polish context. *Theory & Psychology, 28*(6), 780–799. https://doi.org/10.1177/0959354318802973.

Key Terms

Care Ethics A moral framework associated with Carol Gilligan that emphasises relationality, empathy, and the ethics of care over abstract principles of justice.

Epistemic Authority The power to define what counts as knowledge or valid evidence within a given discipline or context.

Feminist Psychology A critical movement within psychology that challenges gender bias, incorporates women's lived experiences, and seeks to transform both the theory and practice of psychological science.

Gender Schema Theory A framework proposed by Sandra Bem explaining how individuals internalise societal expectations about gender, shaping their perceptions, behaviour, and self-concept.

Hegemony A form of power in which dominant social groups maintain control, not through force but by making their worldview appear natural, normal, and inevitable.

Liberation Psychology A form of psychology, aligned with feminist goals that foregrounds social justice, historical context, and the lived experience of oppression in its theories and interventions.

Pathologisation The process by which normal behaviours or experiences are defined and treated as mental illness, often reinforcing social norms and hierarchies.

Psychopolitics A term capturing how psychological categories, diagnoses, and practices are bound up with broader systems of social and political control.

Quantified Experience The strategic use of surveys and numerical data to render women's lived experiences legible and credible within scientific discourse, often used to challenge institutional denial.

Sexual Politics of Therapy A feminist critique of the way power, gender, and desire intersect within therapeutic relationships, especially when male therapists exploit female clients under the guise of treatment.

Standpoint Epistemology The idea that knowledge is shaped by the social position of the knower, and that marginalised perspectives can offer more accurate or complete insights into power relations.

FREE
INSTRUCTOR & STUDENT RESOURCES

ONLINE RESOURCES

Visit the Instructor & Student Resources website at routledgelearning.com/bpscoretextbooks for free digital resources, including:

- Interactive quizzes and flashcards to test your knowledge
- Links to useful websites and videos
- Instructor manual, lecture slides, and course guide to enhance teaching and save instructors time

3 Acts of Resistance

Psychology and LGBTQIA+ Activism

Chapter Overview

This chapter explores the intersection between psychology and LGBTQIA+ activism, tracing the contested terrain of sexual and gender diversity through a critical historical and conceptual lens. Beginning with the legacy of psychological pathologisation and the erasure of queer lives, it examines how activists, scholars, and community movements resisted normative frameworks and challenged the authority of psychology to define 'normal' sexuality and gender. Key moments such as the removal of homosexuality from the DSM, the emergence of trans and intersex activism, and the impact of queer theory are examined alongside pivotal figures such as Evelyn Hooker and Celia Kitzinger. The chapter introduces 'activism' and 'queer theory' as its critical thinking tools, foregrounding the ways in which both political resistance and conceptual disruption have reshaped psychological knowledge. Ontologically, it explores how categories such as 'homosexual' have been historically constructed and contested, while epistemologically it challenges assumptions about objectivity, neutrality, and scientific authority. The chapter closes by reflecting on how contemporary psychology can learn from activist strategies and decolonial perspectives to build more inclusive, pluralistic, and reflexive frameworks. It invites students to see psychology as a site of struggle, ethics, social justice, and possibility.

Acts of Resistance

In 1973, aged 17, Celia Kitzinger was expelled from her school in rural Oxfordshire, not for violence, truancy, or poor performance but for 'suspected lesbianism'. In the early 1970s, in a quiet English village with no visible gay community, this indictment was both bewildering and devastating. 'I barely understood what, exactly, I was being accused of', she later wrote. Her search for answers led her to the psychology section of the local library. There, she discovered neither guidance nor empathy but condemnation. Psychology textbooks of the time treated lesbianism as a 'perversion'. Some endorsed conversion therapies. Others confidently diagnosed the 'causes of homosexuality': domineering mothers, absent fathers, broken families. One textbook described same-sex relationships as an 'adaptive dead end'. Even those who took a more tolerant view still portrayed homosexuality as something to be detected, managed, or prevented. The cumulative effect of this pathologising discourse contributed to a spiral of isolation and depression that culminated in a suicide attempt and a four-month stay in a psychiatric hospital. The very discipline that claimed to understand the mind had nearly destroyed hers. But rather than turn away from psychology, Kitzinger decided to challenge it from

DOI: 10.4324/9781003565482-33

within. She studied Experimental Psychology at the University of Oxford ('where I learned nothing about lesbians but a great deal about rats'), volunteered on lesbian and gay helplines, and began a PhD which became *The Social Construction of Lesbianism* (1987), a pioneering, uncompromising critique of how psychology misunderstands and misrepresents gay lives. Rejecting the idea that lesbians should be accepted because they were 'just like' heterosexuals, she wanted more than assimilation; she wanted transformation. Kitzinger's entry into psychology was an act of resistance. It reminds us that while psychology has often failed those it sought to study, its tools can be reclaimed, repurposed, and used to imagine something better.

Chapter Contents

- The historical entanglement between psychology and LGBTQIA+ pathologisation, including resistance to diagnostic authority and medicalised models of sexuality and gender.
- Key figures and movements that challenged dominant frameworks, alongside the emergence of queer theory.
- The critical thinking tools of activism and queer theory are used to explore how knowledge, power, and identity are produced, resisted, and reimagined.

Chapter Objectives

- To introduce students to the shifting relationship between psychology and LGBTQIA+ populations, from pathologisation to resistance and reparation.
- To identify and analyse the epistemological and ontological assumptions embedded in psychological approaches to sexuality and gender.
- To explore activism and queer theory as critical tools for rethinking the categories, practices, and political implications of psychological knowledge.

CRITICAL THINKING TOOL
ACTIVISM

Activism has played a pivotal role in transforming psychology's understanding of gender and sexual diversity. For much of the twentieth century, psychology did not simply reflect social prejudices; it formalised, legitimised and perpetuated them. Homosexuality was categorised as a mental disorder, psychological treatments were designed to 'correct' it, and queer lives were routinely framed in terms of pathology and deficit.

Activism disrupted this narrative. From outside the discipline, lesbian, gay, bisexual, trans, queer, intersex, asexual, and allies (LGBTQIA+) campaigned for depathologisation, protested at psychiatric conferences, and founded alternative support structures such as helplines, newsletters, and community clinics. In Britain, groups such as the Gay Liberation Front and the Minorities Research Group directly challenged psychological authority, calling out its role in

marginalising queer people. Activism exposed the moral assumptions that psychology had disguised as objectivity.

Activism also came from within the discipline. Celia Kitzinger, Sue Wilkinson, Adrian Coyle, and others brought personal and political urgency to their scholarship, insisting that lived experience could be a legitimate form of expertise and object of knowledge. This work reimagined psychology as a site of cultural negotiation and political struggle. Activism reminds us that knowledge does not float free of power, and that real change often begins when those excluded from psychology insist on their right to be heard, studied, and understood on their own terms.

Introduction

LGBTQIA+ psychology is both a subfield and a story. It is a story of marginalisation, resistance, and the uneasy relationship between psychology and sexual and gender diversity. From its earliest interventions, psychology has sought to define, classify, and often 'treat' non-normative sexualities and gender expressions. Yet this same discipline has also been reshaped, sometimes radically, by the people it once pathologised.

This chapter explores the history of LGBTQIA+ psychology in the UK and the United States, tracing its evolution from the mid-twentieth century to the present. It begins with the classification of homosexuality as a mental illness and charts a path through decriminalisation, the rise of activism, the AIDS crisis, and the eventual institutional recognition of LGBTQIA+ psychology within professional bodies such as the British Psychological Society and the American Psychological Association.

Central to this history is the idea that knowledge and identity are never neutral. The chapter examines how activism, both outside and within psychology, challenged dominant models, exposed the power relations embedded in diagnosis, and demanded new frameworks for understanding human diversity. The chapter also introduces *queer theory* as a companion to activism: a conceptual lens that questions how the very categories of gender and sexuality are created.

Historical Issues

The early relationship between psychology and LGBTQIA+ individuals was shaped by surveillance, suspicion, and control. In both the UK and the United States, homosexuality was initially framed as a disorder and a crime. Through the twentieth century, psychology played an active role in diagnosing, classifying, and attempting to 'treat' what it called sexual inversion, perversion, or deviance.

In the United States, the inclusion of homosexuality in the *Diagnostic and Statistical Manual of Mental Disorders* (DSM) in 1952 codified it as a mental illness. Clinical psychologists and psychiatrists applied treatments ranging from psychoanalysis to electroshock and conversion therapy. In the UK, parallel logics of pathologisation were in operation. The *Wolfenden Report* (1957) recommended decriminalising private consensual sex between men because homosexuality was seen as a condition best managed medically, not punished legally. Partial decriminalisation in 1967 through the Sexual Offences Act followed this rationale, reinforcing psychology's authority to define 'normal' sexual behaviour.

The 1970s saw growing resistance. Influenced by feminist thought, the civil rights movement, and the emerging gay liberation movement, activists began challenging the authority of the psy sciences. Public protests, including those staged at psychology conferences, demanded the removal of homosexuality from the DSM, which occurred in 1973. Similar critiques were voiced in the UK, though formal declassification came later. Activists pointed not only to clinical harm perpetuated but to the epistemological arrogance of a discipline that presumed the right to define others' identities.

The HIV/AIDS crisis of the 1980s brought further contradictions. Gay men were re-stigmatised as vectors of disease. Psychology began to engage more seriously with issues of grief, community resilience, and social stress. In the UK, the passage of Section 28 of the Local Government Act (1988), which prohibited the 'promotion' of homosexuality by local authorities, depleted public support services. Psychologists were both complicit in this environment and, increasingly, reacting against it.

By the 1990s, psychologists such as Celia Kitzinger and Adrian Coyle pushed for institutional recognition, culminating (after three attempts in nine years) in the British Psychological Society's Lesbian & Gay Psychology Section in 1998. This marked a paradigm shift, from gay people being subjects of research to becoming researchers and theorists.

Key Individuals

Magnus Hirschfeld (1868–1935) was a gay Jewish physician and arguably the most important early figure in the history of LGBTQIA+ psychology. He founded the Institute for Sexual Science in Berlin in 1919, which offered not only research and education but also medical care and legal advocacy for queer and trans individuals. Hirschfeld's activism was as important as his science: he was a pioneer in arguing that homosexuality was a natural variation, not a pathology. He promoted the term 'third sex' and worked on some of the earliest understandings of transgender identities. His work was violently suppressed by the Nazi regime, who looted and burned the Institute's extensive library and archives in 1933, forcing Hirschfeld into exile, where he died two years later.

Charlotte Wolff (1897–1986) was a Jewish-German physician, bisexual exile, and pioneering psychologist whose research integrated science with personal narrative. Born in Riesenburg, West Prussia, her early medical training in Berlin and experiences as an exile deeply informed her later work on human sexuality and identity. Her early career in Berlin involved work in family planning and health clinics, reflecting a commitment to social welfare that foreshadowed her later advocacy for marginalised sexual identities. In Britain, she wrote *Love Between Women* (1971) and *Bisexuality* (1977), offering compassionate and empirically grounded studies of marginalised identities. Wolff's refusal to separate her scientific voice from her personal experience made her a forerunner of feminist and queer methodologies.

Evelyn Hooker's (1907–1996) research, published in 1957, was a milestone in dismantling the medical model of homosexuality. By showing that gay and heterosexual men could not be distinguished on psychological tests, she disproved the assumption that homosexuality was inherently pathological. Her anonymous, community-based, and ethical methodology prefigured many of the values later championed by LGBTQIA+ researchers and activists. Her groundbreaking paper,

'The adjustment of the male overt homosexual', was first presented in 1956 at the American Psychological Association convention.

Ken Plummer (1946–2022) was a sociologist whose influence on LGBTQIA+ psychology stemmed from his work on narrative, identity, and the sociology of intimacy. His book *Telling Sexual Stories* (1995) explored how people construct sexual identities through storytelling. Plummer's work challenged essentialist models of sexual identity and inspired psychologists to adopt narrative and interpretative approaches that honoured subjective experience. Plummer's concept of 'intimate citizenship', introduced in his book *Intimate Citizenship: Private Decisions and Public Dialogues* (2003), is particularly relevant to LGBTQIA+ psychology. It explored how personal decisions about sexuality and relationships increasingly become matters of public debate and policy, thereby shaping individual rights and recognition.

Eve Kosofsky Sedgwick (1950–2009), though trained in literature, her impact on psychology, particularly through her book *Epistemology of the Closet* (1990), has been profound. She questioned rigid identity categories and emphasised secrecy, performativity, and affect in the formation of sexuality. Her ideas challenged psychologists to look beyond classification towards cultural context, narrative, and ambiguity. Sedgwick attracted international media attention in 1991 for her article 'Jane Austen and the masturbating girl'. Her ideas underpin much of queer-affirmative and post-structuralist psychology today.

Sue Wilkinson (b.1954) was a founding figure in institutionalising LGBTQIA+ psychology in the UK. Her contributions span feminist psychology and discourse analysis, studying how language structures knowledge and power in psychology. Her empirical research is characterised by a strong commitment to qualitative methodologies, particularly focus groups and conversation analysis, which she has utilised to explore diverse topics within feminist and health psychology. Her work includes studies on women's experiences of breast cancer and other health issues, the dynamics of coming-out conversations, and how language is used to construct and resist gendered and sexual norms in everyday talk.

Celia Kitzinger's (b.1956) career exemplifies the entanglement of the personal and the activist in psychological scholarship. Her early experience with exclusion shaped her opposition to heteronormativity from within the discipline. Her work centres voice, discourse, and lived experience as sources of psychological insight, employing qualitative methodologies, particularly discourse analysis and conversation analysis, to examine how heteronormativity is enacted and challenged in everyday interactions and institutional settings. She has written about how normative heterosexuality is accomplished in talk, the complexities of sexual refusal, and how people come out as lesbian, gay, or bisexual.

Adrian Coyle (b.1964) is best known for advancing qualitative psychological research that affirms LGBTQIA+ experiences. His studies of identity, religion, bereavement, and stigma have foregrounded how sexuality is understood and negotiated socially and personally. Coyle was central in developing inclusive guidelines within the British Psychological Society and helped legitimise LGBTQIA+ psychology as a field of serious scholarly and ethical inquiry. His research extensively utilises qualitative methodologies such as thematic analysis and discourse analysis to explore the nuanced lived experiences of LGBTQIA+ individuals. For example, he has conducted studies on how gay men negotiate their religious and sexual identities and the experiences of 'sense of presence' in bereavement among diverse populations.

Peter Hegarty (b.1969) is a psychologist and historian of psychology. Hegarty examines how psychology constructs its objects of study. His book *A Recent History of Lesbian and Gay Psychology* (2018) demonstrates how research practices have often reinforced racialised, gendered, and heteronormative biases. Beyond his work in LGBTQIA+ psychology, Hegarty's diverse research portfolio extends to intersex studies, where he critically examines the medicalisation of intersex variations and the public understanding of these experiences. He also conducts experimental social psychology research on how markers of social status, such as gender and 'race', bias scientific thinking about group differences, including studies on 'auditory gaydar' and how essentialist beliefs about sexual orientation influence prejudice and discrimination. His blend of archival analysis, experimental social psychology, and queer theory makes him one of the field's most important critical voices.

Epistemological Issues

The epistemology of LGBTQIA+ psychology has undergone a radical transformation, from a tradition that sought to uncover what was *wrong* with non-normative identities to one that increasingly asks how knowledge itself is structured by normativity, power, and voice. This shift in 'ways of knowing' has been driven by academic critique and the epistemic pressure of activism.

In its early years, psychology approached homosexuality and gender variance through a positivist lens. Researchers treated LGBTQIA+ individuals as pathological cases, typically studied in prisons, clinics, or psychiatric hospitals. Such work presumed objectivity but was often infused with cultural prejudice and heteronormative assumptions. The instruments used—projective tests, behaviourist protocols, and later diagnostic classifications—tended to frame non-heterosexuality and gender nonconformity as deficits, disorders, or developmental failures.

Activist resistance in the 1960s and 1970s demanded an epistemological reckoning. Rather than asking 'what causes homosexuality?' scholars began asking 'why is homosexuality being studied this way?' Evelyn Hooker's work was a harbinger of this shift, making it possible for feminist, lesbian, and queer scholars to advance into new methodological terrain.

Qualitative methodologies, especially discourse analysis, narrative methods, and interpretative phenomenological analysis, became methodological tools for reclaiming voice and complexity. Scholars such as Celia Kitzinger, Ken Plummer, and Adrian Coyle emphasised the importance of studying people *as subjects* rather than as objects, centring meaning-making, lived experience, and agency. These methods allowed psychologists to examine how identities are performed, narrated, and constrained by social discourses.

Activism also highlighted the need for participatory and ethical research practices. LGBTQIA+ communities have historically been misrepresented, leading to calls for more inclusive, collaborative, and transparent forms of inquiry. The rise of insider research, co-produced studies, action research, and reflective practice challenged the researcher–researched hierarchy and foregrounded accountability.

Crucially, queer theory added a final layer of epistemological disruption by questioning the categories themselves. If 'homosexuality', 'bisexuality', and 'gender identity disorder' are not timeless truths but historically contingent constructs, then psychological research must be reflexive about its own role in producing knowledge, and, by extension, identities.

Ontological Issues

LGBTQIA+ psychology has never simply been about representation or visibility; it has also challenged the ontological assumptions underpinning mainstream psychology, such as the claims that sexuality and gender are fixed and self-evident categories. The history of LGBTQIA+ psychology traces a shift from essentialist models of identity towards more fluid, performative, and socially constructed understanding of gender and sexuality. In doing so, it demonstrates how psychology has been both a site of constraint and a space for radical redefinition.

Early psychological approaches presumed that sexual orientation and gender identity were fixed, internal traits, stable, measurable, and biologically rooted. Homosexuality was treated as a deviance or inversion, and gender nonconformity was interpreted as developmental failure or psychosexual confusion. These frameworks were underpinned by a binary ontology: male/female, heterosexual/homosexual, normal/deviant. They did not merely describe the world; they *produced* subjects through the looping effects of clinical and diagnostic technologies acting on human kinds.

Activism and theory disrupted the essentialist paradigm. Feminist and queer scholars argued that categories such as 'lesbian' or 'transsexual' were not discovered but constructed, socially, historically, and linguistically. Judith Butler's theory of gender performativity challenged the notion that gender is an inner truth, proposing instead that it is enacted through repeated social performances. LGBTQIA+ psychologists applied this metaphor to reveal how psychological discourse reifies identities while claiming to observe them.

Intersex scholarship, notably the work of Georgiann Davis, pushed the ontological critique further. In *Contesting Intersex: The dubious diagnosis* (2015), Davis examined how medical and psychological institutions construct 'sex' itself through diagnostic categories such as Disorders of Sex Development (DSD), a term adopted in 2006 to replace 'intersex'. These classifications impose binary sex frameworks, pathologising bodily diversity and often justifying medically unnecessary and harmful interventions aimed at 'normalising' intersex bodies. Davis argued that intersex people are ontologically erased by discourses incapable of recognising variation as valid.

Through these critiques, LGBTQIA+ psychology has moved psychology itself away from understanding identities as natural kinds and towards viewing them as human kinds; malleable, culturally embedded, and responsive to social context. This ontological shift reflexively challenges psychology to rethink its assumptions not just about LGBTQIA+ lives but about all human variation.

Power

Power is not merely one theme among many in LGBTQIA+ psychology; it is the terrain upon which the entire field has been built. From its earliest engagements, psychology exercised power by naming, categorising, and treating LGBTQIA+ people according to heteronormative standards. Diagnoses of homosexuality as illness, 'gender identity disorder', or 'sexual deviation' were acts of epistemic authority. They shaped legal decisions, school policies, and therapeutic practices, often to the detriment of those they claimed to help.

Activism challenged this authority by exposing its human costs. The removal of homosexuality from the DSM in 1973 did not occur because of new data, but because activists such as Dr John Fryer disrupted conferences, demanded recognition, and revealed the institutional complicity of the psy sciences in enforcing social conformity. Similar interventions in the UK, such as resistance to Section 28, illustrated how psychological knowledge was part of broader political struggles over visibility, rights, and dignity.

Queer theory deepens this analysis by refusing to stop at inclusion. Where activism often asks, 'who has been left out?', queer theory asks, 'how did the categories themselves come to be seen as real?' Drawing on Foucault, Butler, and Sedgwick, queer theory critiques the very logics of identity and normality that psychology has historically upheld. It sees power not just in the repression of LGBTQIA+ lives but in the very production of identity categories—gay, lesbian, bisexual, trans—as knowable, fixed, and governable.

From this perspective, power is *productive*. Diagnostic categories do not merely reflect identities; they help create them through the looping effect. Queer theory reveals how even affirming labels can constrain lives, how the promise of visibility can also invite surveillance, and how 'acceptance' can become a subtle form of regulation. This does not mean abandoning political or therapeutic progress. Rather, queer theory urges constant vigilance: to question how knowledge is made, to ask whose lives are being represented, and to analyse what forms of difference are still rendered unthinkable. LGBTQIA+ psychology, then, must not only challenge injustice but must also continually reflexively interrogate its own assumptions, categories, and ambitions.

Chapter Summary

This chapter has traced the evolving history of LGBTQIA+ psychology, from its early pathologisation of gay lives to its transformation through activism, resistance, and critical rethinking. For much of the twentieth century, LGBTQIA+ individuals were classified by psychologists as mentally ill, deviant, or criminal, labels that legitimised broader systems of heteronormative control. But LGBTQIA+ psychologists, activists, and allies gradually challenged these frameworks, exposing their scientific flaws and human costs.

A central theme throughout has been the role of activism in reshaping how psychology understands and engages with sexual and gender diversity. Activist pressure shifted the field from deficit-based, positivist models to interpretative, qualitative, and community-informed approaches. Lived experience, once marginalised, gained status as a vital form of knowledge, reshaping both research and clinical practice.

In 2003, Celia Kitzinger and Sue Wilkinson married in Vancouver shortly after same-sex marriage became legal in British Columbia. Upon returning to the UK they discovered that their marriage had no legal standing, and with the introduction of the Civil Partnership Act two years later it was automatically downgraded to a civil partnership, something they fiercely resisted. Viewing this as a symbolic and legal injustice, they mounted a legal campaign for full recognition of their Canadian marriage, arguing that civil partnerships were a 'second-best' substitute and a violation of their human rights under the European Convention. In 2006, the High Court ruled against them, insisting that marriage in English law remained a union between a man and a woman. Disillusioned, they abandoned their appeal and removed their wedding rings in protest. But in 2014, following the enactment of the Marriage (Same Sex Couples) Act, their marriage was finally recognised by the UK government. At midnight on 13 March, in a quiet act of joyful reclamation, they marked the occasion with champagne and slipped their wedding rings back on.

Reflective Questions

1. How did psychology contribute to the pathologisation of LGBTQIA+ identities in the twentieth century?
2. What was the significance of Evelyn Hooker's research, and how did it challenge mainstream assumptions in psychology?
3. In what ways has queer theory redefined the way psychologists think about sexuality and gender?
4. Why is activism considered a critical thinking tool in the context of LGBTQIA+ psychology?
5. What does the story of intersex advocacy reveal about the relationship between medical power, psychological authority, and lived experience?

Suggested Reading

Beccalossi, C. (2020). Types, norms, and normalisation: Hormone research and treatments in Italy, Argentina, and Brazil, c. 1900–50. *History of the Human Sciences, 34*(2), 113–137. https://doi.org/10.1177/0952695120941193.

Drescher, J. (2015). Out of DSM: Depathologizing homosexuality. *Behavioral Sciences, 5*(4), 565–575. https://doi.org/10.3390/bs5040565.

Ellis, S. J. (2025). *Lesbian, Gay, Bisexual, Trans, Intersex, and Queer Psychology: An introduction* (Third ed.). Cambridge: Cambridge University Press.

Hegarty, P. (2018). *A Recent History of Lesbian and Gay Psychology: From homophobia to LGBT*. Abingdon, Oxon: Routledge, Taylor & Francis Group.

Hubbard, K. A., & Griffiths, D. A. (2019). Sexual offence, diagnosis, and activism: A British history of LGBTQIA+ psychology. *American Psychologist, 74*(8), 940–953. https://doi.org/10.1037/amp0000544.

Jones, R. M. (2023). Defeating the 'social danger' of homosexuality while 'forging the fatherland': Sexual science and biotypology in Mexico's national development, 1927–57. *History of the Human Sciences, 36*(5), 122–151. https://doi.org/10.1177/09526951231199581.

Minton, H. L. (1997). Queer theory: Historical roots and implications for psychology. *Theory & Psychology, 7*(3), 337–353. https://doi.org/10.1177/0959354397073003.

Rivers, I., & Ward, R. (2012). *Out of the Ordinary: Representations of LGBT lives*. Cambridge: Cambridge Scholars Publishers.

Russell, G. M., & Bohan, J. S. (2006). The case of internalized homophobia: Theory and/as practice. *Theory & Psychology, 16*(3), 343–366. https://doi.org/10.1177/0959354306064283.

Sutton, K. (2020). Kinsey and the psychoanalysts: Cross-disciplinary knowledge production in post-war US sex research. *History of the Human Sciences, 34*(1), 120–147. https://doi.org/10.1177/0952695120911597.

Taavetti, R. (2024). Low on the Kinsey scale: Homosexuality in Swedish and Finnish sex research, 1960s–1990s. *History of the Human Sciences, 37*(5), 21–44. https://doi.org/10.1177/09526951241245040.

Vasilovsky, A. T. (2018). Aesthetic as genetic: The epistemological violence of gaydar research. *Theory & Psychology, 28*(3), 298–318. https://doi.org/10.1177/0959354318764826.

Weinstein, D. (2018). Sexuality, therapeutic culture, and family ties in the United States after 1973. *History of Psychology, 21*(3), 273–289. https://doi.org/10.1037/hop0000043.

Woodman, D. (2023). *LGBT+ Communities: Creating spaces of identity*. London: IntechOpen.

Key Terms

Activist Psychology A form of psychological practice or scholarship that directly engages with social justice movements and seeks systemic change.

Conversion Therapy Discredited psychological and religious practices aimed at changing an individual's sexual orientation or gender identity.

Essentialism The belief that certain traits, behaviours, or identities are innate and fixed, often used in contrast with social constructionism.

Interpellation A concept from Louis Althusser referring to the way individuals are 'hailed' or called into social roles by ideology, often without awareness.

LGBTQIA+ An inclusive acronym referring to lesbian, gay, bisexual, transgender, queer/questioning, intersex, asexual people, and others with diverse sexualities and gender identities.

Minority Stress The chronic stress faced by members of stigmatised groups, including LGBTQIA+ individuals, due to discrimination and social exclusion.

Performative A concept popularised by Judith Butler to describe how gender is constituted through repeated actions rather than a stable identity.

Queer Theory An approach that questions fixed categories of gender and sexuality, emphasising fluidity, performativity, and the political nature of identity.

Section 28 A clause of the UK's Local Government Act 1988 that prohibited the 'promotion' of homosexuality by local authorities, including schools.

Social Constructionism The view that categories such as gender and sexuality are not fixed biological realities but constructed through culture, language, and social practices.

FREE INSTRUCTOR & STUDENT RESOURCES

ONLINE RESOURCES

Visit the Instructor & Student Resources website at routledgelearning.com/bpscoretextbooks for free digital resources, including:

- Interactive quizzes and flashcards to test your knowledge
- Links to useful websites and videos
- Instructor manual, lecture slides, and course guide to enhance teaching and save instructors time

34 'This Is Who I Am'

Black Psychology and Critical Race Theory's Unfinished Revolution

Chapter Overview

This chapter explores the critical intersection between Black psychology and Critical Race Theory (CRT), tracing how both have challenged psychology's complicity in systems of racial oppression. Starting with the pseudo-diagnosis of 'excited delirium', the chapter illustrates how psychology has not only reflected but helped construct racial hierarchies. It shows how the diagnostic language of the discipline has too often pathologised Black lives while claiming neutrality. Black psychology emerges as a revolutionary field, redefining the foundations of psychological thought. It offers alternative ways of knowing grounded in community, culture, resistance, and spirituality. The chapter introduces key figures, including Frantz Fanon, Na'im Akbar, Beverly Greene, and Tommy Curry, whose work exemplifies the ongoing struggle for epistemic and ontological justice. CRT provides the critical lens to examine structural racism, interest convergence, and the power of counter-storytelling in psychology. Ultimately, this chapter positions Black psychology as a moral, political, and intellectual revolution in the discipline. It invites students to engage with psychology as a practice shaped by power, history, and the demand for justice.

'This is Who I Am'

In the early hours of 23 March 2020, Daniel Prude, a 41-year-old Black man, was walking the streets of Rochester, New York, naked, distressed, and experiencing a severe mental health crisis. Fearful for Daniel's safety, his brother called 911 to seek help. What followed was a disastrous encounter. Responding officers placed a hood over Daniel's head and restrained him face-down on the pavement. One officer pressed a knee into his back; another forced his head into the concrete. Confused and frightened, he began to vomit. His voice grew weaker. Minutes later, he lost consciousness. Daniel died in hospital a week later. The medical examiner ruled his death a homicide, caused by complications of asphyxia in the setting of physical restraint. But the report also included a disputed phrase: 'excited delirium', a term with no formally recognised diagnostic status. Frequently invoked in fatal police restraint cases, and specifically applied to Black men in custody in the United States, it has been criticised for obscuring state violence behind a façade of medical neutrality. At a press conference to address Daniel Prude's death, Rochester Mayor Lovely Warren, herself a Black woman, reported that seven police officers involved

DOI:10.4324/9781003565482-34

in his arrest had been suspended. 'This is who I am', she said, aligning herself with the history of police brutality in her city. 'This is where I come from. And this is very personal to me.' Daniel Prude's death was a tragedy, and a case study in how psychological concepts, even when lacking scientific consensus, can be used to misdirect focus away from structural harms and collective responsibility towards individual pathology. A 2017 investigative report by Reuters found that 'excited delirium' had been listed as a factor in US autopsy reports, court records or other sources in at least 276 deaths that followed taser use since 2000. Black psychology arose to confront precisely these structural dynamics of injustice. It offers a vision for how the discipline can be reimagined, grounded in justice, truth, and the lived experiences of those too long abused by both official and unofficial, visible and invisible, modes of violence.

Chapter Contents

- The death of Daniel Prude and the racialised misuse of the 'excited delirium' psychological diagnosis.
- The emergence of Black psychology and its critique of mainstream psychological assumptions.
- Critical Race Theory as a lens for understanding epistemological power and resistance in psychology.

Chapter Objectives

- To explore the historical development of Black psychology as a response to racism and erasure within the discipline.
- To examine the key individuals, ideas, and cultural traditions that have shaped Black psychological thought.
- To apply the critical thinking tool of Critical Race Theory to understand how power operates through psychological categories and knowledge production.

CRITICAL THINKING TOOL
CRITICAL RACE THEORY

This chapter uses *Critical Race Theory* (CRT) to explore how racism is embedded in the very frameworks of psychological knowledge. CRT began in US legal scholarship in the 1970s, through the work of scholars such as Derrick Bell, Kimberlé Crenshaw, and Richard Delgado. It challenged the idea that racism is simply an aberration or a product of individual prejudice. Instead, CRT argues that racism is systemic, structural, and deeply woven into the everyday operations of law, education, medicine, and science.

For psychology, the implications of Critical Race Theory are deeply unsettling. CRT invites us to consider whether some of the discipline's most established methods and categories, those often presented as neutral or objective, may have played a role in sustaining racial inequality. From early intelligence testing to diagnostic frameworks in clinical psychology, the

field has at times participated in constructing and legitimising racial hierarchies, often without recognising its own complicity.

This chapter draws on several core ideas from CRT. *Structural racism* is the understanding that racism is a system of advantage that is embedded in institutions and maintained over time. *Interest convergence* is the insight that racial progress tends to occur only when it aligns with the interests of dominant groups. *Counter-storytelling* emphasises the importance of narrative and lived experience as a way of challenging official accounts. The *social construction of race* asserts that race is not a biological fact, a natural kind but is rather a human kind, a social actor with real consequences.

Introduction

This chapter explores how identity has been shaped, misrepresented, and ultimately reclaimed within psychology. Throughout the twentieth century, psychology often actively participated in their pathologisation. Psychological theories and testing regimes were used to define Blackness as deviant, deficient, or underdeveloped. Intelligence tests served to rank races, diagnostic labels disproportionately targeted Black men, and behavioural norms reflected white, middle-class values presented as universal truths.

Even approaches that aimed to be inclusive often reinforced inequality by failing to question the underlying frameworks they relied on. In response, Black psychologists began to develop a tradition of critique, resistance, and reimagination. This movement, known as Black psychology, emerged in the United States in the late 1960s to contest the very ways psychology understands race, identity, and mental health.

Using Critical Race Theory as our guide, this chapter explores how Black psychology has challenged the discipline's racial foundations and how it offers an alternative vision of psychological knowledge grounded in history, justice, and the lived experience of the marginalised.

Historical Issues

Even after the abolition of slavery in 1865, Black Americans faced systemic discrimination through segregationist laws, economic exclusion, and racist violence. This history of oppression and forced labour shaped the demographics, social structures, and cultural identities of African American communities. Despite the immense hardships of enslavement and subsequent discrimination, Black communities developed a unique African American identity that blended African cultural roots with the American experience. Black Americans contributed immensely to American culture, politics, science, literature, music, and social movements.

Based on Eurocentric assumptions and shaped by scientific racism, early psychology participated in the legitimation of white supremacy. IQ testing was used to argue for the intellectual inferiority of Black people. Racial difference was pathologised. Black voices were largely not heard. Psychology presented itself as universal, even as it served the interests of a racially stratified society.

In 1903, W. E. B. Du Bois offered a profound critique of this ideology in *The Souls of Black Folk*. His concept of 'double consciousness', the internal conflict of seeing oneself through the eyes of a racist society, was a declaration that Black interiority and experience must be central to understanding the human condition. Du Bois's work anticipated a psychology grounded in counter-storytelling, a principle that would later inform Critical Race Theory.

By the 1940s, Black psychologists such as Kenneth and Mamie Clark were making significant contributions to the discipline. Their groundbreaking Doll Studies, conducted in the 1940s, vividly demonstrated the profound psychological harm inflicted by racial segregation on Black children's self-perception. Their compelling findings were directly cited in the U.S. Supreme Court's landmark *Brown v. Board of Education* decision on 17 May 1954. The evidence from the Doll Studies was instrumental in disproving the core argument for segregation based on the 'separate but equal' doctrine, which had been established by the Plessy v. Ferguson ruling in 1896, by showing that separate facilities were inherently unequal due to their damaging psychological effects.

The Association of Black Psychologists was founded in 1968. The goal was not assimilation into a broken system but transformation: to create a psychology rooted in African values, community survival, and cultural pride. Robert V. Guthrie's *Even the Rat Was White* (1970) laid bare the exclusionary history of American psychology, giving rise to a generation of scholars committed to rewriting its foundations.

The turn of the twenty-first century brought new urgency. The Black Lives Matter movement reawakened critical debates about systemic injustice, police violence, and racial trauma, issues long central to Black psychology but only recently acknowledged by mainstream psychology. The call to decolonise the curriculum emerged as a challenge to psychology's complicity in racial harm.

Key Individuals

W. E. B. Du Bois (1868–1963), a sociologist and intellectual giant, laid the early foundations for Black psychology through his theory of 'double consciousness': the inner conflict experienced by Black Americans forced to see themselves through the lens of a racist society. His 1903 book *The Souls of Black Folk* framed the Black experience as psychologically complex, structurally conditioned, and politically urgent.

Francis Cecil Sumner (1895–1954) was the first African American to earn a PhD in psychology, in 1920. He faced significant discrimination in his career but became instrumental in developing psychology departments at historically Black colleges. His work included critiques of racial bias in psychological testing and education.

Inez Beverly Prosser (1895–1934) was the first African American woman to earn a PhD in psychology, in 1933. She conducted research on the effects of segregation versus integration on the mental health of Black children. Her findings suggested that segregated schools, while under-resourced, often provided safer emotional environments due to less exposure to racism.

Mamie Phipps Clark (1917–1983) and Kenneth Clark (1914–2005) conducted the famous Doll Studies, revealing internalised racism in Black children and its associated psychological harms. Their research was crucial to the U.S. Supreme Court's Brown v. Board of Education ruling, which ended school segregation. The Clarks demonstrated how empirical psychology could expose the deep psychological toll of structural racism and make scientific knowledge politically actionable.

Frantz Fanon (1925–1961) was a psychiatrist and anti-colonial theorist, best known for *Black Skin, White Masks* (1952) and *The Wretched of the Earth* (1961).

He explored how colonialism distorted Black subjectivity, creating alienation, self-hatred, and mental distress. Fanon diagnosed racism as a form of systemic psychopathology, treating decolonisation as both a political and psychological imperative.

William E. Cross Jr. (1940–2024) developed the Nigrescence model, which describes the process of Black racial identity development across several transformative stages. This framework offered a dynamic alternative to static, deficit-based accounts of racial identity. Cross's work has been foundational in education, counselling, and social psychology, highlighting how identity formation is shaped by social context, racialisation, and personal resistance.

Na'im Akbar (b.1944) advanced African-centred models of psychology that prioritised community, spirituality, and cultural continuity over pathology. He criticised mainstream psychology for defining Black behaviour in terms of deviation from white norms. Akbar's work asserted that liberation requires cultural reconnection, a vision of mental health rooted in Afrocentric cosmologies and values rather than in Eurocentric deficits.

Beverly Greene (b.1950) is a clinical psychologist whose work on intersectionality and marginalisation within therapeutic contexts foregrounds the complex interplay of race, gender, and sexual orientation. She has been a leading voice in queer Black feminist psychology, arguing that identity cannot be compartmentalised. Her work models how CRT principles can inform ethical, inclusive clinical practices that resist erasure.

Tommy J. Curry (b.1979) is a philosopher and public intellectual whose work has been instrumental in deepening the intellectual and political framework of Black psychology, especially through the lens of Critical Race Theory and Black male studies. Author of *The Man-Not: Race, class, genre, and the dilemmas of Black manhood* (2017), Curry critiques mainstream liberal and feminist accounts that, he argues, have often erased or misrepresented the specific historical and existential experiences of Black men. He insists on the importance of theorising Black masculinity through a lens of structural violence, colonial history, and empirical reality. Curry's work emphasises the ontological vulnerability of Black men in a white supremacist world and challenges psychology to confront the categories it uses to describe, diagnose, and intervene in Black lives.

Epistemological Issues

Black psychology is a radical proposal for doing knowledge differently. Informed by Critical Race Theory, Black psychology argues that knowledge is never neutral. It is shaped by cultural assumptions, institutional power, and racial hierarchies. Black psychologists have responded not only with critique but with a distinct set of epistemological strategies, methods, perspectives, and commitments that centre lived experience, cultural context, and structural critique.

Racism as Ordinary and Systemic

CRT begins with the insight that racism is a structural feature of institutions, including psychology. Black psychologists have shown how research frameworks often reproduce this structural racism. For instance, intelligence testing has historically pathologised Black children, assuming cultural inferiority based on biased metrics.

Social Construction of Race

Black psychologists have long contested the idea that race is a biological essence, a natural kind. Instead, they treat race as a social and historical construct, a human kind with material consequences. This understanding informs studies of racial identity development based on lived experience and social positioning. These models refuse to treat race as a control variable and instead make it central to psychological meaning-making.

Counter-Storytelling

One of the most distinctive techniques in Black psychology is counter-storytelling: the use of narrative, autobiography, oral history, and community testimony as valid sources of knowledge. Linda James Myers, for example, has drawn on African cosmologies and oral traditions to frame psychological insight in collective experience.

Critique of Meritocracy and Colourblindness

Psychology often presents itself as a meritocratic science, in which anyone can progress based on ability and objectivity. But CRT reminds us that 'objectivity' is often aligned with dominant white norms, while Black ways of knowing are seen as 'biased'. Scholars such as Robert V. Guthrie and Joseph White rejected colourblind science and built knowledge through community-engaged methods: focus groups, ethnographies, and participatory action research.

Ontological Issues

Historically, psychology has made implicit assumptions about what it means to be human, often based on white, Western, male norms. These assumptions shape who is studied, how mental health is defined, and what kinds of lives are deemed valuable, healthy, or pathological.

Pathologised Being

Classical psychology frequently positioned Black individuals as lacking intellect, morality, and emotion. Early eugenicist research and IQ testing classified Black people as genetically inferior, while twentieth-century diagnostic tools such as the DSM disproportionately pathologised Black distress. For example, rates of schizophrenia diagnoses rose sharply for Black men during the civil rights era because political resistance was reframed as psychiatric deviance. The very ontology of the 'Black mind' was misrepresented as disorderly, dangerous, or deficient.

Intersectionality

One of the most significant ontological interventions in Black psychology is Kimberlé Crenshaw's theory of *intersectionality*. Originally constructed to capture the unique experience of Black women who face both racial and gendered oppression, intersectionality has broadened to explore the entangled ways in which race interacts with class, gender, sexuality, and other identities. For psychology, intersectionality challenges the idea of the person as a stable, universal category. Instead, it proposes a dynamic and context-sensitive model of subjectivity. This has inspired new research approaches that examine the interplay between social position and psychological experience, for example, exploring how working-class Black girls interpret classroom authority, or how queer Black youth navigate healthcare systems.

Dehumanisation

The case of Daniel Prude provides a chilling example of dehumanising ontological violence. When Prude experienced a mental health crisis in Rochester, New York in 2020, the police restrained him face-down, placed a mesh hood over his head, and pressed his body into the pavement until he lost consciousness. Although the medical examiner ruled his death a homicide by asphyxia, the report also referenced *excited delirium*, a pseudo-diagnosis with no standing in mainstream psychology or psychiatry. Used overwhelmingly in cases involving the deaths of Black men in police custody, this term transforms human suffering into a clinical abstraction. It removes responsibility from institutions and blames the victim for their own subjugation. This is dehumanisation as ontological annihilation: it renders the Black subject as a threat to be subdued, rather than a person in need of care.

Black Subjectivity

In response to centuries of ontological erasure, contemporary Black psychologists are reclaiming subjectivity. Rather than allowing Blackness to be defined by lack, they foreground emotional depth, cultural creativity, and epistemic authority. Researchers explore the role of joy, resistance, and spiritual expression in Black communities. Studies on Black parenting styles, religious healing, or intergenerational trauma challenge deficit-based models and assert complex, situated humanity. These shifts reflect a deeper aim shared with Critical Race Theory: to move beyond merely documenting harm, and instead affirm the full, multifaceted being of those historically cast as 'less than'.

Ontological Repair

Afrocentric and Communal Models. Finally, Black psychology points to what can be recovered and reimagined. Afrocentric theorists such as Na'im Akbar and Linda James Myers propose models of selfhood rooted in African philosophical traditions. These frameworks challenge the Western ideal of the bounded, self-interested individual and instead define the person as deeply embedded in a spiritual, ancestral, and communal web. Mental health, in this view, is not the adjustment to social norms but the alignment with cultural purpose, relational ethics, and historical consciousness.

Power

Psychology does not exist outside systems of power; it has helped structure them. From its inception, the discipline of psychology has been used to name, measure, and manage difference. In the context of race, it has frequently operated as an instrument of control, classifying Black people as deviant, deficient, or dangerous. Black psychology emerged to challenge precisely this power, to expose how psychological knowledge has been used to legitimise inequality, and to propose alternatives.

The Racial Politics of Knowledge

Mainstream psychology has often served the interests of dominant groups by presenting their values as universal. Theories of intelligence, personality, and development have been built on studies of white, middle-class participants but applied across populations as if culturally neutral. This epistemological violence has real effects. For example, early twentieth-century psychologists such as G. Stanley Hall and Lewis Terman used IQ testing to argue for the biological inferiority of Black people, reinforcing segregation and exclusion under the guise of science. Even later, Arthur Jensen's 1969 claim that genetic differences accounted for racial disparities in IQ scores reasserted racial hierarchies in psychological terms.

Institutional Exclusion

The exclusion of Black psychologists from academic and professional spaces has been both overt and structural. Few Black psychologists held academic posts before the 1970s, and their work was frequently dismissed or marginalised. Journals, funding agencies, and conference programmes routinely rejected research that foregrounded racial or cultural variables as unscientific or 'too political'. In 1968, in response to this exclusion, a group of psychologists founded the Association of Black Psychologists (ABPsi). Among its founders was Joseph White, often credited as the father of Black psychology.

Policing and Surveillance

Psychological constructs have been weaponised in schools, courts, and police stations, where Black behaviour is often interpreted through a lens of suspicion. Black children are more likely to be diagnosed with 'behavioural disorders' and more likely to be punished for minor infractions. In the legal system, psychological profiling has been used to legitimise over-policing, and to paint Black defendants as inherently more violent or less remorseful.

Resistance and Reclamation

Black psychologists have forged new tools, practices, and institutions that affirm Black life rather than pathologise it. Scholars such as Na'im Akbar, Kobi Kambon, and Linda James Myers have developed Afrocentric frameworks that centre spirituality, community, and cultural identity. Akbar argued that many problems labelled as psychopathology in Black communities are, in fact, logical responses to systemic oppression.

Interdisciplinary Struggles

The struggle for justice cannot be contained within disciplinary borders. Frantz Fanon, a psychiatrist and anti-colonial theorist, wrote of the 'epidermalisation' of inferiority, the internalisation of racism as ontological wound. His work showed that psychology must grapple with colonialism, militarism, and capitalism if it is to understand the psychic life of the oppressed.

Chapter Summary

Black psychology is a rebuke, a reimagining, and a beginning. It exposes how psychology has too often mirrored the values of the dominant rather than listening to the suffering of the silenced. And it asks us to feel the weight of history and the urgency of justice. By centring the lived experience of Black communities, Black psychology refuses the idea that liberation is a luxury. It insists that psychology must reckon with the lives it has misunderstood, misrepresented, and harmed.

It is about confronting the foundational violence hidden in the discipline's categories, its tests, and its so-called diagnoses. 'Excited delirium' was never a real thing. Similar to the way the early nineteenth-century disorder of 'drapetomania' functioned, excited delirium was a fiction used to misdirect attention away from state violence and to turn victims into agents of their own oppression. It began with the deaths of over 30 Black women, wrongly attributed to spontaneous collapse, and was later used to excuse the deaths of countless Black men in custody.

But knowledge can be resisted. Words can be reclaimed. Thanks to the refusal of families, communities, and Black psychologists to accept erasure, terms like 'excited delirium' are finally being dismantled. This is not just about forensic reports or policy documents. It is about life and death. It is about the right to be named, to be mourned, to be human.

The struggle continues. Black psychology teaches us that justice is a political ideal and psychological imperative. The future of the discipline depends on who is heard, who is believed, and who is remembered. What comes next is not inevitable. It is a choice. And that choice begins now, with all of us.

Reflective Questions

1. What does Black psychology reveal about the relationship between science and power?
2. In what ways does Critical Race Theory challenge the idea of objectivity in psychological research?
3. How have key figures in Black psychology used cultural traditions, spirituality, and community as forms of resistance?
4. What does the case of Daniel Prude illustrate about the stakes of psychological diagnosis?
5. How can psychology be reimagined to centre justice, lived experience, and liberation?

Suggested Reading

Chakrabarty, N., Roberts, L., & Preston, J. (2014). *Critical Race Theory in England.* Abingdon, Oxon: Routledge.

Delgado, R., Harris, A., & Stefancic, J. (2023). *Critical Race Theory: An introduction* (Fourth ed.). New York: New York University Press.
Fielder, T. (2021). Psychoanalysis and anti-racism in mid-20th-century America: An alternative angle of vision. *History of the Human Sciences, 35*(3–4), 193–217. https://doi.org/10.1177/09526951211042784.
Flack, C. E., Whipple, C. R., & Robinson, W. L. (2025). A social-contextual analysis of African American adolescents' coping self-efficacy. *School Psychology.* Advance online publication. https://doi.org/10.1037/spq0000709.
Hochman, A. (2025). *The Race Illusion: On the reality of racialization and the myth of race.* Oxford: Oxford University Press.
Jones, R. L. (2004). *Black Psychology* (Fourth ed.). Hampton, VA: Cobb & Henry Publishers.
Nobles, W. W. (2006). *Seeking the Sakhu: Foundational writings for an African psychology* (First ed.). Chicago, IL: Third World Press.
Nwoye, A. (2017). African psychology and the emergence of the Madiban tradition. *Theory & Psychology, 28*(1), 38–64. https://doi.org/10.1177/0959354317742204.
Oppong, S. (2022). Indigenous psychology in Africa: Centrality of culture, misunderstandings, and global positioning. *Theory & Psychology, 32*(6), 953–973. https://doi.org/10.1177/09593543221097334.
Pettit, M. (2022). 'Angela's psych squad': Black psychology against the American carceral state in the 1970s. *Journal of the History of the Behavioural Sciences*, 58, 365–382. https://doi.org/10.1002/jhbs.22216.
Pettit, M. (2024). The racial economy of psychological care: Professionalism, social justice, and political action during American psychology's communitarian moment. *History of Psychology, 27*(3), 203–226. https://doi.org/10.1037/hop0000259.
Richards, G. (1997). *'Race', Racism, and Psychology: Towards a reflexive history*. London: Routledge.
Sawyer, T. F. (2000). Francis Cecil Sumner: His views and influence on African American higher education. *History of Psychology, 3*(2), 122–141. https://doi.org/10.1037/1093-4510.3.2.122.
Wynter, R., Campbell, N., Chaney, S., & Marks, S. (2025). The persistence of history: Racism, anti-Blackness, and the causes of mental ill health, c.1800–2020. *History of the Human Sciences*. https://doi.org/10.1177/09526951251331378.

Key Terms

Africentric Worldview A psychological and philosophical orientation that emphasises community, spirituality, collective identity, and interdependence, grounded in African cultural traditions.

Black Psychology A field developed by Black scholars to critique mainstream psychology's Eurocentric assumptions and to develop theories, methods, and practices rooted in Black experience, culture, and liberation.

Counter-Storytelling A method used in CRT and Black psychology that centres the narratives of marginalised people to expose the limitations and biases of dominant psychological and societal discourses.

Critical Race Theory (CRT) An intellectual and political framework that examines how racism is embedded in laws, institutions, and knowledge systems, and challenges claims to neutrality, objectivity, and colourblindness.

Dehumanisation The process of denying people's humanity, often through diagnostic or institutional language that masks violence, as seen in the use of terms such as 'excited delirium'.

Epistemic Violence The harm done when dominant knowledge systems erase or distort the experiences, histories, and worldviews of oppressed groups.

Excited Delirium A pseudo-medical label historically used to explain the deaths of Black people in custody, lacking scientific validity and widely discredited by medical organisations.

Liberation Psychology A branch of psychology that foregrounds social justice, structural critique, and the empowerment of oppressed communities, influenced by figures like Ignacio Martín-Baró and adopted by many Black psychologists.

Ontological Resistance A refusal to accept dominant definitions of what it means to be human, especially in the face of psychological and social systems that marginalise or pathologise Black identity.

Optimal Psychology A theory developed by Linda James Myers that centres African spiritual and communal values, proposing a model of mental health rooted in harmony, connectedness, and self-knowledge.

Standpoint Theory The idea that knowledge is shaped by social position and lived experience, often used in Black psychology to validate the perspectives of those historically excluded from psychological research.

Structural Racism A form of racism maintained through systemic inequalities in institutions, laws, and cultural norms rather than individual prejudice alone.

FREE INSTRUCTOR & STUDENT RESOURCES

ONLINE RESOURCES

Visit the Instructor & Student Resources website at routledgelearning.com/bpscoretextbooks for free digital resources, including:

- Interactive quizzes and flashcards to test your knowledge
- Links to useful websites and videos
- Instructor manual, lecture slides, and course guide to enhance teaching and save instructors time

35

The One with Rachel In It

Cognitive Neuropsychology and the Technological Sublime

Chapter Overview

This chapter explores the recent history of cognitive neuropsychology through the lens of the technological sublime, a concept that captures how awe, spectacle, and ideology shape our responses to brain science. The chapter asks why certain scientific discoveries feel emotionally and philosophically powerful. It argues that this power lies not only in what is discovered but in how such discoveries are presented, framed, and understood. Cognitive neuropsychology, with its vivid imaging tools and dramatic claims, generates not just data but meaning. This meaning is often saturated with cultural assumptions about identity, agency, and control.

Seven dimensions of the technological sublime are distributed across the chapter's main sections. Each dimension is anchored to key figures, theories, or controversies in contemporary cognitive neuropsychology. The chapter balances excitement with critique, showing how even the most stunning findings carry assumptions about what it means to be human. Ultimately, students are encouraged to reflect on the emotional and political appeal of brain-based explanations, and to consider what gets illuminated, and what remains obscured, when we gaze into the glowing image of the mind.

The One with Rachel In It

In 2005, deep in the medial temporal lobe of a man undergoing treatment for epilepsy, neuroscientists found something extraordinary. Using electrodes implanted directly into his brain, researchers from UCLA and Caltech presented the patient with a series of images. Most of them passed unnoticed at the neural level. But then came a photograph of Jennifer Aniston, famous for playing Rachel Green in the TV sitcom *Friends*. A single neuron began to fire, not wildly but reliably, like a devoted fan rising from the audience. The same happened when he was shown her name, and even when presented with a picture of her alongside her *Friends* co-star Courteney Cox. But not when he was shown other actresses. The researchers called it a 'concept cell'. The media inevitably dubbed it 'the Jennifer Aniston neuron'. What did this mean? Had they located the neurological seat of celebrity? The neuron was part of a much more complex, distributed network of associations. But

DOI: 10.4324/9781003565482-35

the idea of a single cell devoted to Jennifer Aniston was too perfect, too poetic, too *televisual* to ignore. This is the allure, and the danger, of cognitive neuropsychology's technological sublime. Technologies such as the EEG and the fMRI promise to make the invisible visible: to turn thought into light, and mind into image. The Jennifer Aniston neuron dazzled because of how it felt; awe-inspiring, uncanny, oddly intimate. In this chapter, we will explore how cognitive neuropsychology became one of the most spectacular branches of modern psychology: a field where truth is often framed as imagery, where data flirts with destiny, and where we are invited not just to study the brain but to fall in love with what it shows us.

Chapter Contents

- The 'Jennifer Aniston neuron' and the allure of brain-based explanations.
- Seven dimensions of the technological sublime in cognitive neuropsychology.
- Key individuals, methods, and debates in epistemology, ontology, and power.

Chapter Objectives

- To introduce students to cognitive neuropsychology as a field that studies both healthy and damaged brains.
- To examine how cognitive neuropsychological findings have contributed to public understanding of memory, emotion, and decision-making.
- To explore the technological sublime as a critical thinking tool, helping students understand why certain discoveries provoke awe and shape cultural narratives.

CRITICAL THINKING TOOL
THE TECHNOLOGICAL SUBLIME

Some aspects of cognitive neuropsychology sometimes feel more profound than others. Brain scans, glowing, vivid, and precise, often seem more convincing than diaries, observations, or interviews. Certain scientists come to be regarded as cultural prophets, their ideas received with something close to reverence. These reactions are symptoms of what critical theorists call the *technological sublime*. The term *sublime* originally described the emotional impact of vast natural landscapes, storms, mountains, and deserts, that made viewers feel overwhelmed and insignificant. But in the modern age, as historian David Nye has shown, this experience has migrated from nature to technology. Today, we experience the sublime not in front of cascading waterfalls but when confronted with MRI scans, neural networks, and brain–machine interfaces. These technologies produce more than data: they produce *wonder*. Cognitive neuropsychology is particularly susceptible to the technological sublime. It deals with the brain, an organ we associate with identity, agency, memory, morality, and love. When technologies claim to visualise or manipulate the brain, we are drawn in emotionally as well as intellectually. What we feel is not just insight. It is awe.

To help us think critically about this phenomenon, this chapter will return throughout to the seven elements of the technological sublime:

1. *Spectacular Authority*. The use of technologies, especially brain imaging, to convert abstract mental processes into vivid, colourful images that seem self-evidently true. The authority of these images rests less on what they prove and more on how they look: orderly, precise, and irrefutably scientific. This aesthetic spectacle can silence critique and elevate perception into fact.
2. *Miniaturisation of Selfhood*. A reductionist logic that suggests rich, multi-dimensional aspects of the human mind can be located in a single brain region or neuron. This fallacy reinforces the seductive idea that the essence of a person is 'in there somewhere', shrunken down to a pinpoint of grey matter.
3. *Epistemic Awe*. The reverence one feels when neuroscience appears to reveal the 'truth' behind the curtain, when data aligns with intuition and emotional significance. The sense that, finally, we can see what was once hidden: memory, desire, guilt, even love.
4. *Prediction and Control*. The promise that brain science can forecast behaviour, detect hidden intentions, or explain decisions before they happen. This fantasy of determinism appeals to our desire for certainty and mastery, and often underpins legal, medical, or marketing applications of neuroscience.
5. *Mythical Heroism*. The elevation of individual scientists, inventors, or entrepreneurs into mythical figures who bring light into darkness, those who name a neuronal process, decode emotion, or fuse mind with machine. Their discoveries are framed as revelations.
6. *Ideological Overreach*. The capacity of cognitive neuropsychology to shape ideologies beyond the laboratory, affecting how we understand gender, race, morality, education, even parenting. These ideas are not just scientific; they are world-making.
7. *Transcendence*. The evocation of something beyond the empirical, when neuroscience touches on the mystical, the ineffable, or the divine. Whether locating the 'God spot', romanticising consciousness, or imagining human–machine fusion, this dimension moves science into the realm of wonder, reverence, and esoteric belief.

Introduction

Cognitive neuropsychology investigates the relationship between brain and mind by studying both damaged and healthy brains. It explores how specific cognitive functions, such as memory, language, perception, or decision-making, map onto neural structures. Some of its most influential insights have come from studying patients with brain lesions or disconnection syndromes. Others have emerged from high-resolution brain imaging of typical adults performing mental tasks in the scanner. Together, these approaches aim to uncover how the brain gives rise to consciousness.

This chapter examines not only what cognitive neuropsychology has discovered but how those discoveries are framed in the popular imagination. It introduces the idea of the technological sublime, the sense of awe and authority that arises when brain science is made visible, heroic, or transcendent. From glowing scans to dramatic patient stories, from predictive algorithms to speculative futures, cognitive neuropsychology often transcends data by producing wonder.

Cognitive neuropsychology is one of the most compelling and captivating areas of psychology. To understand it, we will trace seven dimensions of the technological sublime, each one helping us critically unpack its emotional, aesthetic, and ideological power.

Historical Issues

In 1957, a young neuropsychologist named Brenda Milner began working with a patient who would change the history of psychology. Known as HM, the man had undergone radical brain surgery to remove large sections of his medial temporal lobes, including both hippocampi. The surgery stopped his epileptic seizures but it also produced a devastating side effect: an inability to form new memories. Milner's careful, longitudinal study of HM revealed that memory functioned not as a single system but as a set of distinct processes, dependent on specific brain structures. Her work laid the foundation for modern cognitive neuropsychology.

Milner's innovation was more than methodological. It embodied an early moment of mythical heroism in the field. In the story of HM, psychology gained its first great epic: a damaged mind, a brilliant researcher, and a scientific revelation. The Milner–HM narrative is still told in classrooms today because it is informative and dramatic. Milner becomes a quiet hero: a woman in a male-dominated discipline, uncovering the architecture of memory through patient, humane investigation.

Key Individuals

Benjamin Libet (1916–2007) conducted one of the most famous, and controversial, experiments in cognitive neuroscience. In the 1980s, he used an EEG to demonstrate that the brain's readiness potential preceded the conscious intention to act by several hundred milliseconds. This was interpreted by many as a direct challenge to free will. Libet's findings are often invoked in debates about volition, responsibility, and determinism, despite his own caution in interpreting the results. His work exemplifies the dimension of *prediction and control*: the idea that brain signals can foretell action before consciousness catches up.

Brenda Milner (b.1918) is a pioneer of modern cognitive neuropsychology. While working at the Montreal Neurological Institute under Wilder Penfield, she famously studied Henry Molaison (HM), a patient whose inability to form new long-term memories following surgical removal of his medial temporal lobes offered revolutionary insight into the brain's memory systems. Milner's work helped inaugurate the idea that cognition is modular, and that different memory systems could be dissociated by lesion.

Michael S. Gazzaniga (b.1939) is known for his groundbreaking studies of split-brain patients, conducted first with Roger Sperry in the 1960s. His concept of the 'left-hemisphere interpreter' profoundly shaped the public understanding of consciousness. He has written books that explore free will, neuroethics, and the limits of determinism. His work is an exemplar of the technological sublime in the mode of *epistemic awe*: split-brain studies exposing the bare mechanics of consciousness itself.

Oliver Sacks (1933–2015) played a defining role in popularising neuropsychology. His bestselling book *The Man Who Mistook His Wife for a Hat* (1985) brought rare neurological disorders into public awareness through elegant, compassionate storytelling. His patients were not data sources but persons with biographies. Sacks helped humanise cognitive dysfunction by illustrating how people construct meaning through and despite their neurological conditions. His work exemplifies the sublime through *mythical heroism*, though in Sacks's case the hero was the resilient, uncanny, and dignified patient.

Vilayanur S. Ramachandran (b.1951) is renowned for combining experimental creativity with a gift for public communication. His research on phantom limbs, mirror neurons, and synaesthesia has yielded both clinical tools and sweeping philosophical claims. Ramachandran's theories often extend into the symbolic and metaphysical. He has described the brain as 'the most complex thing in the known universe', and he frequently frames his own role as that of a scientific detective or explorer. His work illustrates the *miniaturisation of selfhood*, the idea that vast human experiences can be traced to a few cubic millimetres of cortex.

Antonio Damasio (b.1944) is best known for the somatic marker hypothesis, which posits that emotion plays a vital role in rational decision-making. His studies of patients with ventromedial prefrontal damage challenged the dualism between reason and feeling, showing that disconnection from bodily emotion leads to impaired judgement. Damasio's work contributed to a reconceptualisation of embodied cognition. His books evoke a form of the sublime grounded in *transcendence*, suggesting that by understanding how the brain feels we get closer to understanding the soul.

Elisabeth A. Phelps (b.1965) has played a central role in modern emotion neuroscience, particularly in exploring the amygdala's role in fear learning, memory modulation, and emotional regulation. She has demonstrated how neural circuits for fear intersect with culture, memory, and social context. Her use of fMRI to visualise the neural dynamics of emotion reflects the *spectacular authority* of brain imaging. Her work also intersects with *prediction and control*: the idea that if we understand the neural basis of fear, we might one day mitigate anxiety or trauma through direct neural intervention.

Alva Noë (b.1961) is a philosopher and cognitive scientist who advocates enactive and embodied approaches to consciousness. He challenges the idea that the brain alone explains mind, arguing instead that perception is an active, bodily process embedded in the social world. Noë's work is a critical counterpoint to the *technological sublime* directly confronting the dangers of *miniaturising selfhood*.

Epistemological Issues

In 2009, a team of researchers scanned the brain of a dead Atlantic salmon acquired from a fishmonger. The salmon was shown photographs of human faces expressing emotion, while its brain was monitored using functional magnetic resonance imaging (fMRI). After analysis, the researchers found apparent brain activity in the salmon. This was not a bizarre piscine neuropsychological séance; it was an epistemological warning. Without rigorous statistical correction, fMRI data can produce false positives so convincing that they could raise the dead. The point was sharp: fMRI results are powerful but also fragile. Since the 1990s, fMRI has become one of the most iconic technologies in psychology.

This is the essence of *spectacular authority*, one of the core dynamics of the technological sublime. fMRI scans lend a visual certainty to complex mental processes. Their colour gradients and anatomical precision give the impression of direct access to the mind. But this is an illusion. These images are not photographs; they are statistical algorithmic constructions, layered with assumptions, choices, and inferences. Yet they convince, precisely because they appear truthful. Cognitive neuropsychology did not invent this kind of authority but it perfected its form. Today, a brain scan can appear more persuasive than a personal account, more objective than behaviour, more real than experience.

In an era dominated by scans, algorithms, and localisation, Oliver Sacks practised a different kind of psychology. A neurologist by training and a storyteller by instinct, Sacks published a series of deeply human case studies that explored the subjective experience of neurological disruption. His patients, such as 'Witty Ticcy Ray', were treated as full persons, living through strange and often moving neurological transformations. Sacks offered insight grounded in narrative. The stories provoked their own form of *epistemic awe* grounded in pathos: a sense of wonder at what could be *felt, remembered, or experienced.*

Ontological Issues

In 2000, researchers at University College London discovered that the brains of London taxi drivers, who had memorised the intricate map of the city's streets to pass a gruelling test known as 'The Knowledge', showed increased volume in the posterior hippocampus, a region associated with spatial memory, compared to controls. The conclusion was powerful and intuitive: the brain adapts to experience. Structural change could be traced to cognitive training.

The implications were irresistible. If the hippocampus could grow through street navigation, then other aspects of the brain could also be shaped by experience. Environments could be designed to enhance memory. Training programmes could be developed to build better brains. These are the promises of the technological sublime in its prediction-and-control mode. The brain is no longer merely a site of explanation; it has become a target for engineering. It is a compelling vision offering a hopeful narrative: if the brain is plastic, the self is improvable.

In the early 2000s, mirror neurons were hailed as one of the most exciting discoveries in neuroscience. First identified in macaque monkeys, these neurons fired both when an action was performed and when it was merely observed. The implication was profound: perhaps the brain simulates other people's experiences internally, allowing us to empathise with them. This mimetic insight sparked an explosion of interest. Mirror neurons were credited with explaining everything from language acquisition to autism, dance, compassion, and even the origins of culture. Popular science articles called them the 'empathy neurons'. This is a clear expression of the technological sublime as *miniaturisation of selfhood*. Rich, multidimensional phenomena such as communication, affect, and identity were condensed into one tidy explanation, often located in a small patch of the premotor cortex. The self, in all its fluidity and variation, was reimagined as a function of a few firing cells.

In the wake of surgical procedures to treat epilepsy, split-brain patients, those whose corpus callosum had been severed, revealed something extraordinary: the brain could function without unified consciousness. When information was presented to just one hemisphere, patients behaved normally but could not always explain their actions. The left hemisphere, in particular, seemed to invent plausible stories for decisions it had not actually made. This finding led Michael Gazzaniga to propose the existence of a left-hemisphere 'interpreter', a mechanism for generating narrative coherence from incomplete information. The self, he suggested, might be not a single agent but a storytelling system.

Gazzaniga's work was scientifically rigorous, but it quickly escaped the confines of the lab. The idea of a divided brain found its way into popular psychology, philosophy, neuroscience education, marketing, and cultural theory. Today, the 'left brain' and 'right brain' are household terms, often deployed far beyond their original meanings. This is the technological sublime operating through *ideological overreach*. Neuroscientific ideas become cultural currency. They are used to explain everything from consumer choice to political orientation.

When Antonio Damasio proposed the somatic marker hypothesis, he did more than offer a model of decision-making. He reframed the relationship between emotion, embodiment, and consciousness, suggesting that rational thought depends on bodily feelings, internal signals that shape choices before conscious reasoning begins. This insight emerged from patients with damage to the ventromedial prefrontal cortex. These individuals retained intellectual competence but lost their capacity for sound decision-making. Damasio argued that they were not irrational but disconnected from the emotional cues that guide judgement.

Emotion, once dismissed as irrational, was reinstalled at the centre of selfhood, morality, and humanity. This is the technological sublime in its *transcendence* mode. Damasio's work gestures towards something larger than mapping brain function: the mystery of being, the unity of body and mind, the biological roots of ethics. It edges into neurotheology without invoking religion. The self possesses a kind of secular soul.

Power

In courtrooms around the world, the brain has acted as a witness. A scan showing reduced activity in the prefrontal cortex can be used to argue for diminished responsibility. A glowing amygdala may suggest impulsivity or trauma. Legal teams present these images as evidence, and jurors, unfamiliar with the methods behind them, often find them irresistibly persuasive. The rise of neuroscience in legal settings exemplifies the *spectacular authority* of the technological sublime. The same aesthetic force that lends credibility to fMRI in the lab, its clarity, colour, and apparent objectivity, is now mobilised in the pursuit of justice.

The same spectacular logic appears in education, marketing, and mental health policy. The appearance of insight often becomes more powerful than the insight itself. Psychology gains cultural capital not just by being right but by looking right. In this way, the brain scan becomes a tool of explanation and persuasion. And when persuasion enters the courtroom, the stakes become ethical.

Elon Musk founded Neuralink in 2016, a company with an ambition that bordered on science fiction: to connect the human brain directly to a machine. The goal was not just medical, treating paralysis or neurodegenerative disorders, but metaphysical. Musk spoke openly about using brain–computer interfaces to merge humanity with artificial intelligence, to augment cognition, and to protect consciousness from obsolescence. Musk himself was the story's central figure: the engineer-saviour, promising transcendence through technology. This is the technological sublime as *mythical heroism*. The scientist is a visionary, often cast in heroic or prophetic terms. Discovery becomes spectacle. Neuroscience becomes destiny. And the entrepreneur becomes a symbolic figure who condenses the hope, fear, and ambition of a culture dreaming of mastery over mind.

Chapter Summary

Cognitive neuropsychology is a discipline of extraordinary ambition. It seeks to understand the most intimate features of human life, memory, emotion, agency, attention, even selfhood, by tracing them to their neural roots. Its tools are powerful. Its findings are often astonishing. But as this chapter has shown, the authority of cognitive neuropsychology is never only scientific. It is also aesthetic, emotional, and cultural. That is the lesson of the technological sublime.

We have traced seven dimensions of this sublime across the field's most iconic studies, from Milner's discovery of memory systems to Damasio's theory of feeling, from courtroom scans to Neuralink's brain–machine interface. Along the way, we have seen how cognitive neuropsychology operates not only as a method of inquiry but as a producer of wonder, a generator of myth, and an instrument of persuasion.

This brings us back to that one neuron, flickering just once in the shadows, stimulated by a photograph of Jennifer Aniston. For a moment, we believed we had seen it: the essence of a person, the soul distilled into a single cell, the mind illuminated by the machinery of science. But what we found was a haunting quiet trace of our longing to make the self knowable, to tame memory, to pin meaning down like a butterfly in a glass case. It was beautiful but it was never enough. The technological sublime of neuroscience does not lie, it mourns. It offers us images of intimacy while quietly erasing the body. In that scan, we thought we saw a future of understanding. But what we must learn to see is everything the image excludes: the blur, the breath, the context, the life. That single neuron did not reveal the self. It reminded us how easily it can disappear.

Reflective Questions

1. Why did the 'Jennifer Aniston neuron' generate such excitement both inside and outside psychology?
2. What is meant by the 'technological sublime' in the context of cognitive neuropsychology?
3. How does the work of Oliver Sacks contrast with the use of fMRI and other forms of brain imaging?
4. In what ways can the promise of cognitive enhancement be both empowering and ethically troubling?
5. Why is it important to recognise the cultural and ideological dimensions of neuroscientific authority?

Suggested Reading

Beaulieu, A. (2002). Images are not the (only) truth: Brain mapping, visual knowledge, and iconoclasm. *Science, Technology, & Human Values*, *27*(1), 53–86. https://doi.org/10.1177/016224390202700103.

Beaulieu, A. (2003). Brains, maps and the new territory of psychology. *Theory & Psychology*, *13*(4), 561–568. https://doi.org/10.1177/09593543030134006.

Choudhury, S., & Slaby, J. (2012). *Critical Neuroscience: A handbook of the social and cultural contexts of neuroscience*. Oxford: Wiley-Blackwell.

De Vos, J., & Pluth, E., Eds. (2016). *Neuroscience and Critique: Exploring the limits of the neurological turn*. Abingdon, Oxon: Taylor & Francis.

Fisher, H. (2003). Categories and embodied objects: The subjective self and the psychologist within natural psychology. *Theory & Psychology*, *13*(2), 239–262. https://doi.org/10.1177/0959354303013002004.

Hayles, N. K., & Pulizzi, J. J. (2010). Narrating consciousness: Language, media and embodiment. *History of the Human Sciences*, *23*(3), 131–148. https://doi.org/10.1177/0952695110363646.

Hennig, B. (2010). Science, conscience, consciousness. *History of the Human Sciences*, *23*(3), 15–28. https://doi.org/10.1177/0952695110363353.

Kügler, P. (2012). The ever-shifting problem of consciousness. *Theory & Psychology*, *23*(1), 46–59. https://doi.org/10.1177/0959354312457112.

Liu, J., & Huo, Y. (2020). Recent advances in research on the association between consciousness and unconsciousness in China. *Theory & Psychology*, *30*(1), 99–120. https://doi.org/10.1177/0959354319895807.

Mills, J. (2019). The myth of the collective unconscious. *Journal of the History of the Behavioural Sciences*, *55*(1), 40–53. https://doi.org/10.1002/jhbs.21945.

Noë, A. (2010). *Out of Our Heads: Why you are not your brain, and other lessons from the biology of consciousness*. New York: Hill & Wang.

Nye, D. E. (2007). *American Technological Sublime*. Cambridge, MA: MIT Press.

Tallis, R. (2016). *Aping Mankind: Neuromania, Darwinitis and the misrepresentation of humanity*. Abingdon, Oxon: Routledge.

Žižek, S. (2023). *Hegel in a Wired Brain*. London: Bloomsbury Academic.

Key Terms

Cognitive Neuropsychology The scientific study of how cognitive functions are mapped onto brain structures, using both healthy individuals and those with brain damage to understand processes such as memory, language, and perception.

Functional Magnetic Resonance Imaging (fMRI) A neuroimaging technique that measures brain activity by detecting changes in blood flow, often used to create visually compelling maps of the 'active' brain during cognitive tasks.

Homunculus Fallacy The mistaken belief that there is a 'little person' or central executive inside the brain controlling thoughts or actions, often invoked critically when a specific brain region is said to 'do' something complex.

Jennifer Aniston Neuron A single neuron discovered in a patient's medial temporal lobe that consistently responded to images of Jennifer Aniston, symbolising both the wonder and the reductionism of brain localisation.

Mirror Neurons Neurons that fire both when an individual performs an action and when they observe that same action performed by others, often invoked to explain empathy, imitation, and social cognition.

Narrative Epistemology An approach to knowledge that values stories, case histories, and lived experiences as valid ways of understanding psychological phenomena—exemplified in the work of Oliver Sacks.

Neurotheology An emerging field that explores the relationship between brain activity and spiritual or religious experiences, often associated with claims about a 'God spot' or the neurological basis of transcendence.

Somatic Marker Hypothesis Proposed by Antonio Damasio, this theory suggests that emotions play a critical role in decision-making by marking certain options with bodily signals or 'gut feelings'.

Split-Brain A condition resulting from surgical severing of the corpus callosum, famously studied by Michael Gazzaniga, which reveals how each brain hemisphere can process information independently—often leading to surprising behavioural and perceptual dissociations.

Technological Sublime A critical concept that captures the awe, authority, and cultural power evoked by advanced technologies—such as brain scans—which seem to reveal hidden truths about the mind.

FREE INSTRUCTOR & STUDENT RESOURCES

ONLINE RESOURCES

Visit the Instructor & Student Resources website at routledgelearning.com/bpscoretextbooks for free digital resources, including:

- Interactive quizzes and flashcards to test your knowledge
- Links to useful websites and videos
- Instructor manual, lecture slides, and course guide to enhance teaching and save instructors time

36 Train Wreck Looming

Conceptual and Historical Issues and the Crisis in Psychology

Chapter Overview

This chapter examines five interlinked crises confronting psychology: the replication crisis, the ethical crisis, the W.E.I.R.D. crisis, the ecological crisis, and the legacy crisis. Each represents a challenge to the discipline's assumptions about how knowledge is produced, whose knowledge counts, and how psychology engages with power, history, and the planet. Far from being isolated problems, these crises reveal a discipline grappling with the consequences of its own epistemologies, ontologies, and entanglements with power. Drawing on key themes from throughout this textbook, each crisis is paired with a critical thinking tool: epistemic resilience, reflexivity, situated knowledge, the looping effect, and critical historiography. Together, these offer not just a diagnosis of psychology's predicament but a toolkit for renewal. The chapter concludes that psychology does not study timeless natural laws but human kinds, reflexive, historically contingent, and shaped by culture, language, and power. This is not psychology's weakness but its defining power. Psychology's categories do not merely describe the world; they help create it. The chapter concludes on an optimistic note.

Train Wreck Looming

At 9:32 a.m. on Wednesday, 26 September 2012, Emeritus Professor Daniel Kahneman, Nobel laureate and one of psychology's most esteemed figures, sent an email that would circulate around the world. The email specifically addressed a group of social psychologists specialising in 'priming effects', research that claimed that subtle cues in the environment can unconsciously influence a person's thoughts, feelings, or behaviours, without their awareness. In the email, Kahneman expressed deep concern over the growing scepticism surrounding priming effects, the 'poster child for doubts about the integrity of psychological research'. He warned of a 'train wreck looming' if the field did not take proactive steps to address these doubts. Classic studies had found that when people held a pencil between their teeth to mimic a smile, they found cartoons funnier. Unscrambling words associated with ageing, such as 'Florida' or 'wrinkle', made people pace more slowly down a corridor. These simple, surprising findings captured the imagination of both psychologists and the public. But by the early 2010s, replication attempts had begun to fail. Large-scale projects found no reliable evidence for the pencil-in-teeth effect and multiple teams failed to reproduce

DOI: 10.4324/9781003565482-36

the 'elderly priming' effect. All this raised the uncomfortable prospect that these famous results might have been experimental artefacts all along.

Kahneman's proposed solution was to set up 'a daisy chain of labs A-B-C-D-E-A, where each lab will replicate the study selected by its neighbor: B replicates A, C replicates B etc. . . . Have the replicating lab send someone to see how subjects are run . . . so that additional subjects can be run with confidence that the same procedure is followed.' While well intentioned, Kahneman's suggestion inadvertently highlighted an alarming issue: if replicating an experiment requires the original researchers' involvement to convey tacit knowledge not captured in published reports, then the foundational principle of the experiment as an independent and objective tool is deeply compromised. Kahneman's awkward proposal to rely on unarticulated, context-dependent expertise suggested that some psychological phenomena might not, in fact, be replicable. Psychology's 'replication crisis' revealed not just methodological shortcomings but a deeper epistemological fracture, one that unsettled the very nature of the psychological experiment itself. If a phenomenon appears only when the right people are present, under the right conditions, with the right tacit knowledge, then is an experiment a universal tool for discovering truth? Or is it just a fragile performance that works only when the stars align?

Chapter Contents

- Understanding the five crises shaping the discipline today.
- How epistemology, ontology, power, inclusivity, and history frame psychology's critical challenges.
- The role of conceptual and historical analysis in responding to the crisis.

Chapter Objectives

- To explain how the replication crisis, ethical crisis, W.E.I.R.D. crisis, ecological crisis, and legacy crisis expose structural problems within psychology.
- To analyse how psychology's knowledge production is shaped by epistemology, ontology, power, inclusivity, and history.
- To apply five critical thinking tools to address the five crises in psychology.

Introduction

Daniel Kahneman's 'train wreck' email was more than a desperate call for collegial cooperation. It was a moment of existential doubt for an entire discipline. Psychology had long aspired to the status of an empirical science, one where universal laws of mind and behaviour could be discovered through carefully controlled experiments. But Kahneman's 'daisy chain of labs' proposal implied that if significant results appear only when the original researchers are present to guide the ritual, then the experiment is no longer an unbiased window into nature. Instead, it is a social event, a fragile performance contingent on context, culture, expectation, and implicit knowledge.

This was the moment when the replication crisis exploded into public view. But it was only the first tremor of a more destructive earthquake. In recent years, psychology has faced at least five interlinked crises, each challenging the discipline in profound ways. The *replication crisis* exposed deep problems in how psychology produces knowledge and validates its findings. The *ethical crisis* revealed how psychological expertise can be co-opted by institutions of power, sometimes with devastating consequences. The *W.E.I.R.D. crisis* forced psychology to confront the colonial legacies embedded in its assumptions about what kinds of people it studies and whose knowledge counts. The *ecological crisis* signalled the limitations of psychology's traditional model of the individual, which remains disconnected from planetary ecological systems. The *legacy crisis* confronted psychology with its own contested history, challenging the discipline to reckon with the ways it has been shaped by racism, sexism, colonialism, and exclusion.

Together, these five crises demonstrate that psychology is not a stable, finished science but a discipline whose identity, methods, and assumptions are perpetually being shaped by history, culture, power, and context. To make sense of this, this chapter explores the five contemporary crises in psychology, each paired with a critical thinking tool drawn from the CHIP toolkit. Together, they form a set of instruments for diagnosing psychology's current predicaments, and, perhaps, its future possibilities.

1. THE REPLICATION CRISIS

An Epistemological Issue

The replication crisis is, fundamentally, an epistemological crisis. From the early 2010s, psychologists were forced to confront the uncomfortable reality that many of the field's most celebrated findings, including ego depletion, social priming, the marshmallow test, and power poses, could not be reproduced when tested independently. Long regarded as the gold standard of scientific validity, the principle of replication was failing. What emerged was not a pattern of isolated errors but a structural problem embedded in the discipline's epistemology, its very system of knowledge production. Over-reliance on small, homogeneous samples, the misuse of statistical significance testing, and publication bias towards flashy, positive results that suited the narrative of the sponsors created an epistemic culture where illusion could masquerade as fact.

As we discovered in Chapter 6, psychology's commitment to measurement was never purely empirical but was rooted in metaphysical assumptions including that mental phenomena were quantifiable, an illusion of objectivity that still haunts psychological research today. Chapter 7 showed that psychological knowledge has always been a situated phenomenon, shaped by the needs of specific clients and institutional contexts, undermining the belief that any single method or finding can achieve universal validity. Chapter 27 traced how the emergence of discursive psychology directly challenged experimental psychology's reductive epistemology, arguing that meaning is constructed through context, language, and social interaction.

Epistemic Resilience

Together, these histories make it clear that the replication crisis is about misplaced epistemological certainty. One response to the replication crisis could be the cultivation of *epistemic resilience*. Epistemic resilience requires recognising that all methods are partial, context-bound, and theory-laden. It calls for a mature, reflexive science, one that embraces methodological diversity and is comfortable with complexity, contestation, and uncertainty.

This means replacing psychology's brittle reliance on statistical rituals and narrow methods with practices that are transparent, pluralistic, and self-correcting. Open Science movements now champion practices such as preregistration, data-sharing, and replication as core scientific virtues rather than as peripheral chores. But epistemic resilience also demands methodological pluralism, an understanding that no single method can exclusively capture the complexity of human behaviour. Experimental methods remain important, but they must be complemented by longitudinal designs, qualitative research, participatory methods, and theoretical work that can contextualise and stabilise findings. This is not a sign of psychology's failure but of its maturation: a necessary shift away from simplistic models of certainty towards an epistemology that embraces the provisional, contested, and evolving nature of psychological knowledge.

2. THE ETHICAL CRISIS

A Power Issue

The ethical crisis in psychology is not simply about individual misconduct; it is a structural crisis of power. The revelation that psychologists were involved in designing torture programmes for the CIA after 9/11 exposed a discipline willing to compromise its ethical codes when aligned with state and military power. But this was no anomaly. Psychology's history is filled with examples where it served institutional agendas over individual welfare. Psychology has repeatedly transformed human suffering into data while sidestepping deeper questions about complicity and harm. As we saw with the case of shell shock (Chapter 13), psychology was used not just to treat traumatised soldiers but to manage their return to combat, serving military needs over psychological healing, an agonising dilemma for many psychologists at the time. Across the history of psychology, the problem has not been merely ethical lapses but a failure to reflexively interrogate who the discipline serves and how power flows through its practices.

Psychology's ethical crisis was made visible in multiple stories from the discipline's history. Chapter 22 revealed how psychological diagnoses were never neutral descriptions but acts of interpellation, calling people into being as particular kinds of subjects while simultaneously empowering and constraining them within systems of surveillance, normativity, and exclusion. Chapter 23 demonstrated that some of psychology's most celebrated experiments, such as those by Milgram and Zimbardo, were not just ethically problematic but functioned as dramaturgies of power, reinforcing parables of obedience, conformity, and authority aligned with Cold War ideologies. Chapter 30 showed how contemporary positive psychology operates as a tool of neoliberal governance, shifting responsibility for distress and inequality onto the individual, masking the structural roots of suffering under the language of happiness and self-optimisation.

Reflexivity

Taken together, these histories demonstrated that the ethical crisis was a structural problem rooted in psychology's entanglement with power. One solution to the ethical crisis could be embracing *reflexivity*, an ongoing, critical examination of psychology's own entanglement with power. Reflexivity demands both ethical vigilance and a critical interrogation of how psychology produces categories, narratives, and interventions that either sustain or challenge systems of inequality and control.

Reflexivity insists that psychologists move beyond technical compliance with ethical codes and instead confront the political, institutional, and economic forces that shape their work. This is the driving force behind movements such as community psychology and liberation psychology, which reject the illusion of neutrality and explicitly align psychological practice with social justice. Whether designing behavioural interventions, conducting therapy, or running experiments, reflexive psychology considers not only whether something is effective but also for whom it is effective and what ends it serves. Embedding reflexivity at the heart of psychology means recognising that all knowledge production is situated, value-laden, and carries individual and social consequences.

3. THE W.E.I.R.D. CRISIS

An Inclusivity Issue

The W.E.I.R.D. crisis refers to psychology's over-reliance on participants from Western, Educated, Industrialised, Rich, and Democratic societies, whose experiences were wrongly treated as representative of universal human nature. The crisis formally erupted in 2010 with a landmark essay by Joseph Henrich, Steven Heine, and Ara Norenzayan entitled 'The weirdest people in the world?' This research demonstrated that W.E.I.R.D. populations are psychological outliers in areas such as perception, reasoning, morality, and self-concept. The crisis revealed that much of what psychology claimed as general knowledge was, in fact, a narrow reflection of specific cultural, economic, and historical contexts. It exposed not just a sampling error but an epistemological failure rooted in the discipline's colonial and Eurocentric foundations.

Concerns about cultural bias in psychology have been raised for decades, as we have seen vividly illustrated in this book. Chapter 9 exposed how intelligence testing was never a culturally neutral endeavour but a technology of social ordering designed around the assumptions of W.E.I.R.D. societies, embedding white norms into what were presented as universal measures of innate ability. Chapter 28 extended this critique to the domain of emotion, revealing how feelings such as sadness, anger, and shame, often treated as biologically universal, are culturally constructed performances, shaped by language, norms, and historical context. Chapter 34 demonstrated how Black psychology emerged in the United States as a radical response to mainstream psychology's Eurocentric assumptions, centring the lived experiences, knowledge systems, and cultural epistemologies of Black communities.

Situated Knowledge

These histories made clear that the W.E.I.R.D. crisis was not simply a matter of unrepresentative samples but a profound error of exclusion, the assumption that psychological truths could ever be universal when they were built on culturally narrow foundations. The lesson was unmistakable: the path forward requires the wholehearted embrace of *situated knowledge*, recognising that all psychological knowledge is produced from specific locations, and that a genuinely inclusive psychology must be open to fundamentally different ways of understanding minds, selves, and societies.

Adopting the principle of situated knowledge means abandoning the myth of psychology as a culturally neutral science and embracing epistemic pluralism. Rather than pursuing claims of universal truth, psychology must focus on understanding for whom a claim is true, under what conditions, and within which cultural and historical contexts it holds. Situated knowledge compels the discipline to centre the voices, experiences, and epistemologies of those historically excluded from psychological research: Indigenous communities, the Global South, and marginalised groups within the West. It is not enough to simply add diverse participants to existing models; psychology must open itself to fundamentally different ways of knowing, theorising, and understanding what it means to be human.

4. THE ECOLOGICAL CRISIS

An Ontological Issue

The ecological crisis forces psychology to confront a profound ontological failure: its enduring assumption that the human mind is an isolated, self-contained entity, separate from ecological systems. This narrow ontology mirrors the logics of industrial capitalism, in which individuals are imagined as autonomous, rational consumers, bounded units of agency disconnected from the material and ecological systems that sustain life. This view reduces people to abstract psychological objects, defined by internal traits, cognitive processes, or behavioural outputs, while ignoring their entanglement with environments, communities, and planetary systems. As climate breakdown accelerates, this ontological blind spot becomes untenable. A psychology that continues to model the person as separate from nature cannot meaningfully address the psychological dimensions of ecological collapse, nor can it offer credible responses to the mental health crisis, existential anxieties, and collective traumas now emerging in the context of planetary instability.

This looming crisis was made visible across many episodes from psychology's history. Chapter 10 showed how experimental psychology erased questions of consciousness, sentience, and relationality by treating animals as mechanistic models, an ontological error that severed minds from ecological and multispecies contexts. Chapter 14 demonstrated how industrial psychology compounded this error by framing humans as machine-like inputs within economic systems, producing models of productivity and efficiency that intensified alienation from meaningful work. Chapter 29 traced how cognitive psychology, shaped by military and computational metaphors, reproduced an estranged ontology of the mind as a bounded, information-processing machine, disconnected from material, grounded reality.

The Looping Effect

One response to this ontological crisis would be to embrace Ian Hacking's concept of the looping effect, the recognition that psychological categories are active forces that reshape the people to whom they are applied. The looping effect has spiralled throughout this book. The more the world demanded isolated, mechanistic, and extractive subjectivities, the more psychology was reorganised to reflect and enact those demands. Together, this book has shown that the ecological crisis was not merely external to psychology but a direct consequence of its dominant ontologies. The path forward demands a radical ontological shift, towards viewing minds, identities, and well-being as inherently relational, embodied, and entangled within an ecosystem.

Psychology has helped nurture and validate the very forms of hyper-individualism, consumerism, and disconnection that now drive environmental destruction. An ontology that treats people as isolated atomistic units is no longer tenable. Psychology must instead adopt a relational, ecological ontology, one that understands the self as interdependent with others, with communities, and with the more-than-human world. This shift is a precondition for any meaningful psychological response to the climate crisis. It means redefining well-being not as individual achievement or resilience but as the health of entire social and ecological systems.

5. THE LEGACY CRISIS

A Historical Issue

The legacy crisis confronts psychology with its own uncomfortable history, one marked not only by innovative research but by exclusions, harms, and complicity. Far from being a neutral science, psychology has been deeply entangled with projects of colonialism, racism, sexism, eugenics, and social control. The crisis is not that this history exists but that the discipline has failed to reckon with how profoundly it continues to shape psychology today.

Numerous stories from the history of psychology contributed to the legacy crisis. Chapter 12 confronted psychology's central role in the eugenics movement, showing how research on intelligence, mental deficiency, and deviance provided the scientific rationale for forced sterilisation, institutionalisation, and racialised exclusion of the disabled. Far from being an aberration, eugenics was embedded in psychology's mainstream development. Chapter 16 revealed how early psychoanalysis, despite its radical ambitions, was structurally shaped by patriarchal and Eurocentric assumptions, marginalising maternal voices and non-Western subjectivities in favour of a male-centred developmental narrative. Chapter 32 examined how mainstream psychology historically pathologised femininity while rendering masculinity invisible as a social and psychological construct. It traced how hegemonic models of masculinity, centred on emotional poverty, libidinous autonomy, and permissive therapeutics, were embedded in psychological theories that framed these traits as normative, healthy, and rational. The chapter demonstrated how feminist psychologists challenged this gendered epistemology, exposing how the discipline both reflected and reinforced patriarchal values.

Critical Historiography

The pattern was unremitting: psychology's categories were produced within systems of power, whether patriarchal, biopolitical, disciplinary, or empowerment-inflected. One response could be the promotion of *critical historiography*, an active, reflective process of re-examining psychology's past, not as a neutral record of progress but as a contested history of power, exclusion, and resistance. Critical historiography demands that we regard these histories as central to the discipline's formation. Only by reckoning with this legacy can psychology remake itself as a discipline that is more scientifically honest and ethically just.

This means acknowledging both the harms psychology has enacted and the alternative traditions it has marginalised, such as Black psychology, Indigenous psychologies, feminist psychology, and community-based practice. Critical historiography rejects comforting myths of inevitable progress and instead treats history as a site of struggle over what psychology has been, and what it might still become. Only by confronting this history honestly can psychology begin the work of intellectual repair, building a discipline that is both more accurate and more just.

Epilogue

One of the reasons Daniel Kahneman was so alarmed by the collapse of social priming research was because it directly undermined key arguments in his 2011 book, *Thinking, Fast and Slow*. Entire sections of his bestseller relied on the idea that subtle, unconscious priming effects provided powerful evidence for the 'thinking fast', intuitive 'System 1' processes. When replication efforts failed, the empirical foundation for 'System 1' fast thinking was compromised. It was profoundly ironic. Kahneman's Nobel Prize-winning work had revealed how easily humans fall prey to cognitive biases, particularly the tendency to overgeneralise from small samples. He had himself been misled by the very heuristics he had spent his career diagnosing in others.

Kahneman's Nobel Prize, awarded in 2002, was not for psychology but for economic sciences. In fact, there is no Nobel Prize for psychology, and nor is there ever likely to be one. The reason is not historical oversight but something more fundamental. Unlike the natural sciences, psychology does not discover natural laws written into the fabric of the universe. It does not study natural kinds, stable, timeless entities. Psychology studies human kinds: reflexive, historically contingent, and shaped by language, culture, and power. This is a discipline where the act of observing, naming, and categorising the world actively participates in constructing it.

Throughout this book, we have seen that psychology is not merely a body of knowledge but a cultural, historical, and political project. Its categories do not simply describe reality; they help create it. The psyche is a moving target, shaped by the very theories, labels, and practices that psychology itself produces.

This is not psychology's weakness. It is its defining challenge, and its defining power. Because psychological knowledge loops back into lives, communities, and futures, psychology can never be neutral. Every theory is a story about what it means to be human. Every diagnosis, every test score, every category, is an intervention in the world.

In this book we have unearthed forgotten figures, buried histories, contested ideas, and glimpsed alternative futures. We have seen how psychology has been shaped, sometimes warped, by colonialism, capitalism, war, racism, and patriarchy. But we have also seen how psychologists have resisted, reimagined, and rebuilt, crafting psychologies of liberation, of care, of community, and of decolonisation.

The deepest lesson of this journey is that psychology must hold two truths at once. It is always contingent, situated, and shaped by history. But in that very contingency lies its greatest freedom: the freedom to change. Psychology's categories are not natural facts. They are cultural artefacts. And what has been made can be remade. The story of psychology is not finished. It is ours yet to write.

Reflective Questions

1. How did the replication crisis reveal deeper epistemological flaws in psychology, beyond just methodological errors?
2. In what ways does the ethical crisis show that psychology has been complicit with systems of power, rather than independent of them?
3. What does the W.E.I.R.D. crisis tell us about the limitations of psychology's claim to universality?
4. Why is the ecological crisis described as an ontological crisis, and how does the looping effect help explain psychology's role in it?
5. How does the legacy crisis demand a shift towards critical historiography, and what does this mean for how psychology understands itself?

Suggested Reading

Boynton, D. M., & Smith, L. D. (2006). Bringing history to life: Simulating landmark experiments in psychology. *History of Psychology, 9*(2), 113–143. https://doi.org/10.1037/1093-4510.9.2.113.

Broere, S. (2019). Picturing ethnopsychology: A colonial psychiatrist's struggles to examine Javanese minds, 1910–1925. *History of Psychology, 22*(3), 266–286. https://doi.org/10.1037/hop0000094.

De Vos, J. (2011). Depsychologizing torture. *Critical Inquiry, 37*(2), 286–314. https://doi.org/10.1086/657294.

Di Castri, T. (2023). The settler colonial roots and neoliberal afterlife of Problem Behaviour Theory. *Journal of the History of the Behavioural Sciences*, 59(2), 107–128. https://doi.org/10.1002/jhbs.22218.

Drumm, P. (2018). Australian fantasy revisited. *History of Psychology, 21*(3), 295–296. https://doi.org/10.1037/hop0000099.

Fisher, A., & Abram, D. (2013). Radical ecopsychology: Psychology in the service of life (Second ed.). New York: SUNY Press.

Henrich, J. P. (2020). *The WEIRDest people in the world: How the West became psychologically peculiar and particularly prosperous*. New York: Picador (Farrar, Straus & Giroux).

Lazard, L., & McAvoy, J. (2020). Doing reflexivity in psychological research: What's the point? What's the practice? *Qualitative Research in Psychology, 17*(2), 159–177. https://doi.org/10.1080/14780887.2017.1400144.

Leys, R. (2024). *Anatomy of a Train Wreck: The rise and fall of priming research*. Chicago, IL: University of Chicago Press.

Moghaddam, F. M. (2023). *How Psychologists Failed: We neglected the poor and minorities, favored the rich and privileged, and got science wrong*. Cambridge: Cambridge University Press. https://doi.org/10.1017/9781009071598.

Morawski, J. (2020). Psychologists' psychologies of psychologists in a time of crisis. *History of Psychology, 23*(2), 176–198. https://doi.org/10.1037/hop0000140.

Pickren, G. W., & Pickren, W. E. (2021). Signposts to decolonial futures in understanding and addressing our present crises. *Journal of the History of the Behavioural Sciences, 57*(4), 315–318. https://doi.org/10.1002/jhbs.22147.

Pols, H. (2007). Psychological knowledge in a colonial context: Theories on the nature of the 'native mind' in the former Dutch East Indies. *History of Psychology, 10*(2), 111–131. https://doi.org/10.1037/1093-4510.10.2.111.

Sturm, T., & Mülberger, A. (2012). Crisis discussions in psychology: New historical and philosophical perspectives. *Studies in History and Philosophy of Biological and Biomedical Sciences, 43*(2), 425–433. https://doi.org/10.1016/j.shpsc.2011.11.001.

Key Terms

Critical Historiography An approach to history that recognises it is always selective, contested, and shaped by power, and that recovering forgotten voices is part of reconstructing a more honest and just discipline.

Ecological Crisis A crisis that challenges psychology's assumption that the person is a self-contained, autonomous individual, separate from ecosystems and the material world.

Epistemic Resilience The ability of a knowledge system to withstand error, uncertainty, and bias by using transparent, pluralistic, and self-correcting methods.

Ethical Crisis A crisis that exposed how psychology has been complicit with systems of power, including its involvement in unethical practices such as torture, showing that psychological knowledge is never neutral.

Human Kinds Categories of people that are not fixed by nature but are shaped by history, culture, language, and social practices—and which in turn shape the people they describe.

Legacy Crisis A crisis where psychology is forced to confront its own history of harm, exclusion, and complicity in systems of racism, colonialism, sexism, and oppression.

Looping Effect A concept from philosopher Ian Hacking that describes how psychological categories shape the people to whom they are applied, creating feedback loops between knowledge and identity.

Natural Kinds Categories in the natural sciences that refer to stable, mind-independent phenomena such as chemical elements or biological species, unlike the reflexive categories studied in psychology.

Reflexivity A critical thinking tool that asks psychologists to examine how their own assumptions, values, and social positions shape the research they do and the knowledge they produce.

Replication Crisis A crisis in psychology that revealed how many famous studies could not be successfully repeated, exposing serious flaws in how the discipline produces and validates knowledge.

Situated Knowledge The idea that all knowledge is produced from particular cultural, historical, and social standpoints, meaning that no knowledge is completely neutral or universal.

W.E.I.R.D. Crisis A crisis that revealed how most psychological research is based on populations that are Western, Educated, Industrialised, Rich, and Democratic, raising questions about whose minds psychology actually studies.

FREE
INSTRUCTOR & STUDENT RESOURCES

ONLINE RESOURCES

Visit the Instructor & Student Resources website at routledgelearning.com/bpscoretextbooks for free digital resources, including:

- Interactive quizzes and flashcards to test your knowledge
- Links to useful websites and videos
- Instructor manual, lecture slides, and course guide to enhance teaching and save instructors time

Appendix: From Introspection to Big Data

A Conceptual and Historical Overview of Methodological Pluralism in Psychology

Introduction

Psychology is unusual among the sciences in the sheer range of methods it employs. From case studies to brain imaging, from ethnography to big data analysis, the field has never converged on a single approach. This diversity reflects psychology's complex relationship with its subject matter, its values, its history, and its politics. Human beings are at once biological, cognitive, social, and cultural, and no single method, whether experiment, survey, or interview, can capture that multidimensionality.

Different visions of human nature also shape methodological choices. Researchers who see people as information processors often turn to reaction-time experiments, while those who regard humans as cultural beings are drawn to ethnographic methods. Disputes about method are rarely neutral: they are often disguised conflicts over values.

Methods also emerge in response to wider contexts. War produced cognitive task analysis, social movements encouraged feminist and reflexive methods, and the digital revolution gave rise to big data psychology. Social institutions favour their own approaches: armies prefer tests, corporations rely on surveys, and communities advocate for participatory research. Some approaches serve reactionary ends such as sorting and excluding, while others aim to empower and liberate.

Pluralism is also tied to psychology's foundations. With no agreed-upon unit of analysis, whether neuron, individual, group, or culture, psychologists have turned to different methods to study different aspects of human reality. Paradigm shifts have reinforced this diversity: behaviourism, cognitivism, psychoanalysis, and humanism each pioneered their own methods.

Practical and ethical limits further drive pluralism. Some questions cannot be studied experimentally, leading psychologists to rely on longitudinal research, archival analysis, or naturalistic observation. Many phenomena cannot ethically be studied in the laboratory. Observational methods, natural experiments, and narrative approaches must be performed instead. Psychology has also borrowed from neighbouring disciplines: statistics from mathematics, ethnography from anthropology, neuroimaging from medicine, and discourse analysis from linguistics. These imports have further multiplied the range of methodological possibilities.

Psychology is both a science and a profession. Its dual identity requires multiple toolkits to serve researchers, clinicians, educators, and policymakers. Global diversity adds yet another dimension of complexity: non-Western and Indigenous traditions have introduced community-based and oral methods, broadening psychology beyond its Western core. For all these reasons, methodological pluralism is not a luxury but a necessity in psychology. It is how the discipline survives, adapts, and debates its future.

The history of methodological innovation in psychology can be divided into eight eras.

1. Early Observational and Descriptive Methods (Nineteenth Century)

Before psychology became a professionalised science, its methods were a patchwork of idiosyncratic curiosity. Charles Darwin (1809–1882) kept diaries of his children's development, practising naturalistic observation to link their behaviours with his evolutionary theory. William James (1842–1910) pioneered the use of introspection, systematically observing his own conscious experiences and describing his 'stream of consciousness' in poetic detail. Sigmund Freud (1856–1939) relied on detailed case studies, such as 'Anna O.' and 'Little Hans', blending clinical work with narrative description. Later, Jean Piaget (1896–1980) developed the clinical interview method, combining observation and dialogue to study how children's reasoning evolved.

These early descriptive and narrative methods struggled with reliability and generalisability. Freud's psychoanalytic interviews and James's self-observations lacked the reproducibility and control demanded by the natural sciences. Yet they offered rich, textured accounts of human experience that would later inspire qualitative traditions such as narrative analysis and life-history interviews. Here we see the first enduring tension in psychology: between *depth* (the thick description of unique cases) and *rigour* (the replicability of standardised procedures).

These methods also assumed that inner experiences, such as thoughts, feelings, and consciousness itself, was a legitimate object of study. Unlike later behaviourists, early psychologists believed that first-person accounts could directly access subjective states. But observation during this period was not neutral. The observer was almost always a European male intellectual, while the observed were often children, patients, women, or colonised peoples. The authority of the clinician-observer went largely unchallenged, while the voices of subjects rarely shaped the final narrative. Freud's patients' experiences were projected through his theoretical lens, and Darwin's children's behaviour served as evidence for his evolutionary argument. These practices reveal how power shaped whose experiences were recorded and how they were interpreted.

These observational and anecdotal approaches emerged in a pre-professional era. Psychology was not yet an academic discipline but was rather the pursuit of philosophers, physicians, and naturalists. Methods were eclectic and curiosity-driven, reflecting the social status of the 'gentleman scientist' who could afford to dabble across fields. Without laboratories or standardised protocols, early psychologists relied on anecdotal evidence, personal reflection, and narrative description. Far from naïve, these practices reflected a period when science itself was less specialised and when psychology was still struggling to define its place.

2. Experimental Methods (Late Nineteenth to Early Twentieth Century)

By the end of the nineteenth century, psychology was anxious to establish itself as a science equal in status to physics, chemistry, and physiology. Wilhelm Wundt (1832–1920) set up the first dedicated psychology laboratory in Leipzig in 1879, using reaction time methods and psychophysical measurement to study sensation and attention. Hermann Ebbinghaus (1850–1909) conducted painstaking memory experiments with nonsense syllables, attempting to quantify forgetting through his now-famous 'forgetting curve'. In Russia, Ivan Pavlov (1849–1936) carried out classical conditioning experiments with dogs, showing how behaviour could be shaped through controlled stimuli. In social psychology, Norman Triplett (1861–1934) investigated the effect of competition in his 1898 cycling experiments, while Max Ringelmann (1861–1931) studied group effort in what became known as the Ringelmann effect. Around 1910, W. H. Winch (1864–1935), an English school inspector, compared the relative effectiveness of various classroom conditions on fatigue and training. Such innovations signalled psychology's embrace of the experimental control group as its defining methodological principle.

The experimental method promised something radical: causal inference. Unlike introspection or case studies, experiments claimed to show not just what had happened but *why* they had happened. By systematically manipulating an independent variable and measuring its effect on a dependent variable, psychologists sought to mimic the explanatory power of the natural sciences. The cost was simplification: behaviour was reduced to tasks such as pulling levers, memorising syllables, or salivating at the sound of a bell. What was gained in rigour and internal validity was often lost in ecological validity, the extent to which findings could generalise to real life.

Experiments also carried a distinctive ontology. Human behaviour was treated as reducible to variables that could be isolated, manipulated, and measured. The richness of lived experience was translated into numbers, reaction times, and error rates. This reductionist approach embodied a growing scientism: the conviction that only knowledge produced through natural science methods counted as truly valid.

The experimental laboratory was not just a place of discovery but also of authority. The experimenter controlled the environment, the technical procedures, and the form of data, while the 'subject' was merely expected to obey. This hierarchy was dramatically illustrated in Francis Galton's (1822–1911) Anthropometric Laboratory of the 1880s, where members of the public paid to be measured and classified. Such practices gave psychology credibility as a science but entrenched a model where the subject's autonomy was subordinated to the experimenter's agenda. Much later, the term 'participant' replaced 'subject', signalling a more collaborative and ethical relationship.

3. Psychometrics and Diagnostic Methods (1900 to 1950s)

As psychology entered the twentieth century, the focus shifted towards measurement and standardisation. In France, Alfred Binet (1857–1911) and Théodore Simon

(1873–1961) developed the first intelligence test (1905) to identify children needing educational support. In the United States, Lewis Terman (1877–1956) adapted this into the Stanford–Binet, extending its reach. Charles Spearman (1863–1945) introduced factor analysis, a statistical technique used to argue for a single general intelligence (g) underlying all abilities. During the First World War, Robert Woodworth (1869–1962) created the Personal Data Sheet, an early personality inventory for screening recruits, paving the way for the Minnesota Multiphasic Personality Inventory (MMPI), developed in the 1940s by Starke Hathaway (1903–1984) and J. C. McKinley (1891–1950). Meanwhile, Hermann Rorschach (1884–1922) designed the Inkblot Test (1921), and Henry Murray (1893–1988) with Christiana Morgan (1897–1967) introduced the Thematic Apperception Test (TAT) in the 1930s, both projective tests designed to uncover unconscious motives. Together, these innovations signalled psychology's fascination with testing, classifying, and diagnosing individuals.

The dream of psychometrics was objectivity. Standardised tests appeared to yield numerical scores that could be compared across individuals, schools, or even nations, with reliability (consistency) and validity (accuracy) as central criteria. Yet profound questions remained: did IQ tests measure innate intelligence, or culturally specific skills? Were projective techniques scientific assessments, or elaborate forms of storytelling disguised as diagnosis? Psychometrics embodied psychology's ambition to make the intangible measurable, but also revealed the dangers of reification by treating abstractions such as 'intelligence' or 'personality' as if they were tangible things, such as gold coins or goldfish.

These methods reshaped the understanding of the human subject. People became bundles of traits, abilities, and pathologies, rendered as profiles of scores, scales, and categories. The 'psychological individual' was not merely discovered but actively constructed through testing.

The rise of testing was inseparable from institutions of power. Schools used IQ tests to stream children, armies used personality inventories to screen recruits, and clinics used diagnostic interviews to decide a course of treatment. Psychologists became gatekeepers of normality, controlling who was judged gifted, disordered, or deficient. The aura of scientific precision masked the real-world consequences: exclusion from education, justification of eugenic policies, or limited employment prospects.

The explosion of psychometric methods was driven by modernity's administrative needs. Expanding schools, industrial armies, and bureaucratic states required efficient means to classify and allocate people. The World Wars accelerated this trend: testing promised to identify leaders, soldiers, and 'unfit' individuals quickly and cheaply. In an era obsessed with productivity and efficiency, psychometrics flourished, laying the groundwork for today's data-driven systems of sorting and classification.

4. Correlational and Survey Methods (1920s to 1960s)

During the interwar years, psychology increasingly studied people in the aggregate. Rensis Likert (1903–1981) invented the Likert scale (1932), making it possible to systematically measure attitudes through surveys and questionnaires. Gordon Allport (1897–1967) promoted correlational methods to explore how personality traits clustered, helping to establish trait psychology. Lewis Terman (1877–1956) launched a landmark longitudinal study of gifted children in the 1920s, following participants across their lifespan, while Arnold Gesell (1880–1961) pioneered large-scale developmental assessments of infants and children. Social psychologists developed cross-sectional studies to compare groups at single points in time, and George Gallup (1901–1984) popularised the opinion poll as a tool of political forecasting. These innovations marked a decisive shift from the study of the individual to the study of populations, offering claims about human nature that were statistically generalisable.

The epistemological promise of correlational research was to reveal hidden patterns without experimental manipulation. By analysing statistical associations, psychologists claimed insight into real-world relationships. Yet the warning that 'correlation does not imply causation' remained central. (A link between ice cream sales and crime rates, for example, reflects a third variable—hot weather—rather than direct causality.) Survey methods raised additional concerns: were people's self-reports accurate, consistent, or merely reflections of social desirability? Nevertheless, statistical tools such as Pearson's correlation, Spearman's rank-order correlation, and Louis Thurstone's (1887–1955) factor analysis reinforced the legitimacy of quantitative approaches to complex social behaviour.

Ontologically, these methods redefined the individual as a data point within a distribution. Identity and behaviour gained meaning only through comparison with others. Longitudinal designs suggested that development followed predictable trajectories, while cross-sectional comparisons treated age, class, or culture as analysable variables. The focus shifted from singular lived experiences to populations and averages.

The rise of survey research reflected the needs of modern institutions. Governments, advertisers, and propagandists all relied on knowledge of public attitudes to shape policy, sell products, or mobilise citizens. Psychologists became gatekeepers of public opinion, their polling methods feeding into electoral strategy and commercial marketing. At the same time, large-scale studies helped define 'normality' across the life course, influencing education and welfare policies. Data collection thus functioned as both knowledge and control.

Psychology was not simply borrowing from statistics; it was reshaped by political and commercial demands for numbers about 'the masses'. The expansion of correlational and survey methods mirrored the transformations of the twentieth century. Mass democracy, consumer capitalism, and the growth of mass media demanded knowledge about populations on an unprecedented scale. The interwar fascination with propaganda and public opinion entrenched the value of surveys, as demonstrated by the Mass Observation 'anthropology at home' studies pioneered by Tom Harrisson (1911–1976), Charles Madge (1912–1996), and Humphrey Jennings (1907–1950).

5. Ethnographic and Alternative Methods (1930s to 1970s)

As the Great Depression and the Second World War disrupted societies, psychologists looked for insights beyond the laboratory. Kurt Lewin (1890–1947) developed action research, combining experimentation with social change in communities, schools, and workplaces. Marie Jahoda (1907–2001) and colleagues produced the

Marienthal ethnography (1933), using participant observation, interviews, and archival analysis to study the impact of unemployment in an Austrian village. Anthropologists such as Margaret Mead (1901–1978) and Ruth Benedict (1887–1948) imported ethnographic fieldwork into psychology, highlighting how culture shaped personality. William Foote Whyte (1914–2000) published *Street Corner Society* (1943), a classic of urban ethnography. Clinicians such as Carl Rogers (1902–1987) and Melanie Klein (1882–1960) developed the therapeutic interview into a rich source of data about lived experience. Together, these approaches widened psychology's gaze to culture, community, and meaning.

The appeal of qualitative and ethnographic methods lay in their capacity for thick description, detailed accounts that captured context and meaning rather than abstract variables. This provoked epistemological dilemmas: could participant observation or life-history interviews ever be objective? Were they science or storytelling? Advocates argued that immersion yielded insights inaccessible to experiments or tests, opening up an epistemological divide between positivist and interpretative approaches.

These methods reimagined the human subject as fundamentally cultural and social. Ethnographic fieldwork treated identity, emotion, and behaviour as products of meaning systems. Action research located people within communities as agents of change. Ontologically, psychology shifted from seeking universal laws to attending to situated practices; lived, local, embodied, and relational.

Power dynamics remained. Western researchers often exoticised non-Western cultures, framing them as 'other'. Margaret Mead's work, for instance, was criticised for cultural bias. Therapeutic interviews placed clients under the clinician's interpretative authority. Even action research, intended to empower, often left the researcher as the ultimate author. Yet these methods disrupted psychology's Eurocentrism, introducing marginalised voices, contexts, and problems into the discipline.

The turn to ethnographic and alternative methods was shaped by crisis. Economic collapse, war, and displacement made laboratory puzzle-solving seem trivial. Anthropological methods arrived amid colonial encounters and global war, when questions of culture became urgent. Postwar welfare states, too, needed tools to understand impoverished communities and struggling families. Psychology's methodological expansion was thus less elective than necessary.

6. Cognitive and Neuropsychological Methods (1950s to 1980s)

During the postwar period, psychology reinvented itself through the cognitive revolution. Laboratory memory experiments, such as the Stroop test by John Ridley Stroop (1897–1973), first published in 1935 but revived in the 1950s, along with serial recall tasks and problem-solving experiments, framed the mind as an information processor. Case studies such as patient 'HM' (Henry Molaison, 1926–2008, who lost the ability to form new memories after brain surgery) became landmarks in neuropsychology. Michael Gazzaniga (1939–2024) pioneered split-brain experiments in the 1960s, exploring hemispheric specialisation. Psychologists also turned to computer modelling, most famously Allen Newell (1927–1992) and Herbert Simon (1916–2001), whose programmes simulated aspects of human thought. These innovations were deeply entwined with wartime and Cold War technologies, radar, code-breaking, and the digital computer, which provided both metaphors and methods for understanding the mind.

The cognitive paradigm promised to explain unseen processes through controlled experimental tasks. Reaction times, error rates, and memory spans stood in for mental operations, making thought tractable by inference. Neuropsychological case studies attempted to link specific brain structures with cognitive functions. Computer simulation reinforced the belief that mental processes could be modelled algorithmically, raising questions about whether thinking was simply computation or something irreducibly mentalistic.

Ontologically, the mind was reframed as an information-processing machine. Cognition became circuitry, memory became storage, attention became a filter, and decision-making became computation. Lesion studies and split-brain experiments suggested that identity and consciousness could be localised in neural hardware. This mechanistic view offered powerful new ways of conceptualising human life, but it risked obscuring lived experience.

The prestige of cognitive and neuropsychological methods was fuelled by military and technological patronage. Cold War governments invested heavily in research to improve pilot vigilance, human–machine interfaces, and artificial intelligence. Psychology gained new status as a partner in medicine, defence, and technology. The discipline's priorities were increasingly shaped by war and surveillance, often sidelining social or ethical concerns.

The rise of these methods was thus inseparable from war and technology. The Second World War saw psychologists studying radar operators, pilot fatigue, and code-breaking. The Cold War extended this agenda, with the computer becoming both a metaphor and a method for mind and brain. Psychology's shift from behaviourism to cognition was not only a theoretical victory but also a redirection towards problems defined by military and technological imperatives.

7. Critical, Qualitative, and Reflexive Methods (1970s to 1990s)

By the 1970s, psychology had expanded rapidly, and with it came dissent. Feminist scholars such as Carol Gilligan (b.1936) pioneered feminist interviewing methods, emphasising empathy and reciprocity rather than detached questioning. Ann Oakley (b.1944) argued for reflexive qualitative interviews, in which the researcher's own position and influence had to be acknowledged rather than hidden. Jonathan Potter (b.1956) and Margaret Wetherell (b.1954) introduced discourse analysis, while Harvey Sacks (1935–1975), Emanuel Schegloff (b.1937), and Gail Jefferson (1938–2008) formalised conversation analysis as a rigorous way to study talk-in-interaction. Barney Glaser (1930–2022) and Anselm Strauss (1916–1996) developed grounded theory, a systematic approach to building theory inductively from qualitative data. Later, Virginia Braun (b.1972) and Victoria Clarke (b.1965) articulated thematic analysis as an accessible but flexible method. This period also saw the rise of autoethnography, where researchers analysed their own lived experience as data, and psychogeography, which explored the psychological dimensions of place and space. Collectively, these innovations challenged psychology's mainstream commitment to objectivity and positivism.

The epistemological foundation of these methods was the reflexive claim that knowledge is socially constructed. Discourse analysis treated language not as a window onto inner thought but as the medium through which social reality is created. Conversation analysis made its appeal to rigour by focusing on micro-level transcripts of verbal interactions, while grounded theory sought to build concepts and models directly from empirical data. Feminist researchers questioned whether the 'view from nowhere' was ever possible, arguing instead for knowledge situated in time and place. The result was not just a new set of tools but a fundamental challenge to psychology's positivist core. Qualitative and quantitative traditions often coexisted uneasily, with little integration.

Ontologically, the human subject was reimagined as discursive, relational, and narrative. Life-history interviews presented identity as a story told in context. Autoethnography blurred the distinction between subject and researcher, collapsing the boundary between self and other. The emphasis shifted from stable traits to fluid, co-constructed identities.

These methods were also explicitly political. Feminist methodologies highlighted power imbalances in the research encounter, rejecting one-way data extraction. Participatory approaches blurred the line between researcher and community, aiming to democratise knowledge. Yet power never disappeared entirely: researchers still decided what counted as data and how it would be represented. The methods themselves became sites of debate about knowledge, social justice, and authority.

The rise of critical, qualitative, and reflexive methods was inseparable from the wider social context. The expansion of higher education after the 1960s brought more women, working-class students, and scholars from previously excluded groups into the academy. The feminist movement, civil rights struggles, and postcolonial critique demanded new ways of knowing that could account for gender, race, and power. Psychology's positivist orthodoxy came under attack, not only theoretically but socially: new voices insisted that the discipline acknowledge the politics of knowledge itself.

8. Digital, Participatory, and Contemporary Methods (2000s to Present)

In the twenty-first century, psychology entered the digital age. Smartphones enabled experience sampling and ecological momentary assessment (EMA), where participants reported moods and behaviours in real time. The internet brought online surveys, virtual ethnography, and social media data analysis, offering access to unprecedented amounts of behavioural data. Neuroscience flourished through fMRI, EEG, PET scans, and transcranial magnetic stimulation (TMS), transforming the brain into an imageable object. At the same time, psychologists embraced participatory action research (PAR), associated with Orlando Fals Borda (1925–2008), and other community-based methods that co-produced research with participants. Mixed-methods designs, promoted by scholars such as John W. Creswell (1941–2023), became popular for integrating quantitative and qualitative approaches. These innovations revealed both the promise and the perils of psychology in the digital era.

The epistemology of digital methods revolves around data abundance. Big data psychology treats digital traces, such as likes, clicks, and retweets, as raw material for analysis. Algorithms, machine learning, and computational models offer new forms of prediction but raise questions of validity: do online behaviours really represent psychological states? Meanwhile, neuroscientific imaging embodies the allure of the 'brain scan' as truth, despite problems of overinterpretation and reproducibility. This tendency, known as neurorealism, reflects the cultural authority of colourful brain images. In contrast, participatory methods shift epistemology by valuing lived experience and collective knowledge, blurring the line between researcher and researched.

Contemporary methods also fragment the human subject into multiple ontologies. Neuroimaging portrays the person as a brain network; big data analysis renders them as a node in a digital system; EMA depicts them as a stream of self-reports across time. By contrast, participatory action research reasserts people as community agents and change-makers. This multiplicity reflects psychology's pluralism but also its disunity.

The power dynamics of contemporary methods are stark. Big data psychology often depends on corporate-owned platforms, raising concerns about surveillance, consent, and algorithmic bias. Brain imaging is frequently criticised for granting excessive authority to visual evidence. In contrast, participatory approaches explicitly redistribute power by involving communities in framing, conducting, and interpreting research. The current landscape thus spans the most top-down (algorithmic surveillance) and the most bottom-up (community co-production) models of psychological knowledge.

The rise of digital and participatory methods is inseparable from wider social and technological change. The internet revolution, social media, and smartphones created vast new data streams, while global movements for social justice demanded research that empowered rather than exploited participants. Psychology's methods reflect this paradox: the same technologies that enable surveillance and control also allow for new forms of collaboration and resistance.

The twenty-first century also brought about a reckoning. The replication crisis revealed that many landmark findings could not be reproduced, often due to small sample sizes, questionable statistical practices, and publication bias. This crisis forced psychology to confront the fragility of its own methods. It also sparked reforms: preregistration, open data, and larger samples have become central to a new culture of open science. The lesson is clear: methodological pluralism remains vital, but it must be balanced with transparency and reproducibility.

Suggested Reading

Ash, M. G. (1995). *Gestalt Psychology in German Culture, 1890–1967: Holism and the quest for objectivity*. Cambridge: Cambridge University Press.

Carson, J. (2006). *The Measure of Merit: Talents, intelligence, and inequality in the French and American republics, 1750–1940*. Princeton, NJ: Princeton University Press.

Converse, J. M. (1987). *Survey Research in the United States: Roots and emergence, 1890–1960*. Berkeley: University of California Press.

Danziger, K. (1985). The origins of the psychological experiment as a social institution. *American Psychologist, 40*(2), 133–140. https://doi.org/10.1037/0003-066X.40.2.133.

Danziger, K. (1990). *Constructing the Subject: Historical origins of psychological research*. Cambridge: Cambridge University Press.

Danziger, K. (1997). *Naming the Mind: How psychology found its language*. Thousand Oaks, CA: Sage.

Denzin, N. K., & Lincoln, Y. S. (Eds.). (2018). *The SAGE Handbook of Qualitative Research* (Fifth ed.). Thousand Oaks, CA: Sage.

Feest, U. (2005). Operationism in psychology: What the debate is about, what the debate should be about. *Journal of the History of the Behavioral Sciences, 41*(2), 131–149. https://doi.org/10.1002/jhbs.20079.

Gardner, H. (1985). *The Mind's New Science: A history of the cognitive revolution*. New York: Basic Books.

Gigerenzer, G., Swijtink, Z., Porter, T., Daston, L., Beatty, J., & Krüger, L. (1989). *The Empire of Chance: How probability changed science and everyday life*. Cambridge: Cambridge University Press.

Green, C. D. (1992). Of immortal mythological beasts: Operationism in psychology. *Theory & Psychology, 2*(3), 291–320. https://doi.org/10.1177/0959354392023003.

Hacking, I. (1990). *The Taming of Chance*. Cambridge: Cambridge University Press.

Leys, R. (2024). *Anatomy of a Train Wreck: The rise and fall of priming research*. Chicago, IL: University of Chicago Press.

Michell, J. (1999). *Measurement in Psychology: A critical history of a methodological concept*. Cambridge: Cambridge University Press.

Miller, G. A. (2003). The cognitive revolution: A historical perspective. *Trends in Cognitive Sciences, 7*(3), 141–144. https://doi.org/10.1016/S1364-6613(03)00029-9.

Morawski, J. G. (Ed.). (1988). *The Rise of Experimentation in American Psychology*. New Haven, CT: Yale University Press.

Poldrack, R. A. (2018). *The New Mind Readers: What neuroimaging can and cannot reveal about our thoughts*. Princeton, NJ: Princeton University Press.

Porter, T. M. (1995). *Trust in Numbers: The pursuit of objectivity in science and public life*. Princeton, NJ: Princeton University Press.

Potter, J., & Wetherell, M. (1987). *Discourse and Social Psychology: Beyond attitudes and behaviour*. Thousand Oaks, CA: Sage.

Smith, R. (1997). *The Norton History of the Human Sciences*. New York: W. W. Norton.

Stigler, S. M. (1999). *Statistics on the Table: The history of statistical concepts and methods*. Cambridge, MA: Harvard University Press.

Winston, A. S. (2003). *Defining Difference: Race and racism in the history of psychology*. American Psychological Association.

Zenderland, L. (1998). *Measuring Minds: Henry Herbert Goddard and the origins of American intelligence testing*. Cambridge: Cambridge University Press.

Index

For Product Safety Concerns and Information please contact our EU representative GPSR@taylorandfrancis.com Taylor & Francis Verlag GmbH, Kaufingerstraße 24, 80331 München, Germany